Principles of Environmental Law

Third Edition

Cavendish
Publishing
Limited

London • Sydney

Principles of Environmental Law

Third Edition

Susan Wolf, BA (Econ) (Hons), LLB (Hons)
Senior Lecturer in Law
University of Northumbria

Anna White, LLB (Hons)
Formerly Lecturer in Law
University of Northumbria

Neil Stanley, LLB (Hons)
Lecturer in Law and Solicitor
University of Leeds

Cavendish
Publishing
Limited

London • Sydney

Third edition first published in Great Britain 2002 by Cavendish Publishing Limited, The Glass House, Wharton Street, London WC1X 9PX, United Kingdom

Telephone: +44 (0)20 7278 8000   Facsimile: +44 (0)20 7278 8080

Email: info@cavendishpublishing.com

Website: www.cavendishpublishing.com

This title was previously published under the Lecture Notes series.

© Wolf, S, White, A and Stanley, N   2002

First edition   1995

Second edition   1997

Third edition   2002

British Library Cataloguing in Publication Data

Wolf, Susan, 1959–
Principles of environmental law – 3rd ed
1. Environmental law – Great Britain
I Title II White, Anna
1 Title III Stanley, Neil
344.4'1'046

ISBN 1 85941 581 4

Printed and bound in Great Britain

PREFACE

The authors of the first two editions of this text, Susan Wolf and Anna White, welcome the contribution of Neil Stanley to this, the third edition of *Principles of Environmental Law*. Neil brings with him the benefit of his experience in teaching mixed classes of both law and non-law students at undergraduate and postgraduate levels.

We are delighted that our publishers are able to offer this edition of the text in 'e book' format. Environmental law students now have the option of purchasing only those chapters of the text which correspond to their course requirements.

This edition has substantially revised and updated the previous edition which was published four years ago. In this edition, and bearing in mind the needs of the intended readership of this text, we have included a new introductory chapter which creates a framework to divide the 'meat' of the text into logical, comprehensible, if somewhat uneven, sections. After the introductory chapter, we outline the crucial role of environmental regulators, such as the Environment Agency, in the public control of private pollution. We then move on to a consideration of the main 'Command and Control' regulatory regimes: water pollution, waste management, IPC and IPPC, air pollution, contaminated land, statutory nuisance, and noise. This is followed by consideration of the role of private individuals, and groups, in the use of environmental law to achieve their private, as opposed to the regulator's public interest, objectives. Finally we consider the main forces which are driving the rapid change and development of environmental law.

We have endeavoured to strike the right balance between broad structure and detailed analysis. If we have disappointed the reader in any way then we would urge him or her to make us aware of his or her views and suggestions for improvement by emailing us at the following address: N.K.Stanley@leeds.ac.uk We are committed to continuous improvement and value all constructive comments.

We include coverage of several important recent developments in environmental law:

(i) The Pollution Prevention and Control Act 1999, implementing the IPPC Directive.

(ii) The Contaminated Land Regulations.

(iii) Causing water pollution and the 1999 House of Lords decision in *Empress Cars (Arbertillery) Ltd v National Rivers Authority*.

(iv) Environment Agency enforcement and prosecution policy.

(v) The Landfill Directive.

(vi) The Human rights Act 1998.

(vii) The increasing significance of public concern in environmental decision-making and policy processes.

At the end of the book we have included an extensive list of 'further readings' to assist students who wish to explore the issues we have addressed in greater detail, or, who may desire a reading list to 'kick start' research for coursework assessments.

Neil would like to thank the Study Leave Committee of the Law Department at the University of Leeds for enabling him to contribute to this text. He would also like to express his thanks to his family, for their patience and understanding, whilst he 'absented' himself from family life to work on this and other projects.

Susan Wolf
Anna White
Neil Stanley
September 2001

TABLE OF CONTENTS

TABLE OF CASES

TABLE OF STATUTES

TABLE OF STATUTORY INSTRUMENTS

Pollution Prevention Guidance

Planning Policy Guidance

TABLE OF EUROPEAN LEGISLATION

Directives

Regulations

TABLE OF ABBREVIATIONS

AQMA	air quality management areas
BAT	best available techniques
BATNEEC	Best Available Technologies Not Entailing Excessive Costs
BREF	BAT reference publication
BNFL	British Nuclear Fuels Ltd
BOD	Biochemical Oxygen Demand
BPEO	Best Practicable Environmental Option
BPM	Best Practicable Means
BRE	Building Research Establishment
CAA	Clean Air Act 1956/1968/1993
CFCs	Chloroflourocarbons
COPA	Control of Pollution Act 1974
DEFRA	Department of the Environment, Food and Rural Affairs
DETR	Department of the Environment, Transport and the Regions
DoE	Department of the Environment
DVLC	Driver and Vehicle Licensing Centre
EA 1995	Environment Act 1995
EA	Environment Agency
EC	European Community
ECHR	European Convention on Human Rights
ECJ	European Court of Justice
EEA	European Environment Agency
EEC	European Economic Community
EHO	Environmental Health Officer
EIA	Environmental Impact Assessments
EMAS	EC eco-management and audit scheme
EN	Enforcement Notice
EPA	Environmental Protection Act 1990
EU	European Union
HMIP	Her Majesty's Inspectorate of Pollution
HSE	Health and Safety Executive
IPC	Integrated Pollution Control
IPPC	Integrated Pollution Prevention and Control
LAAPC	Local Authority Air Pollution Control
MACs	Maximum Allowable Concentrations
MAFF	Ministry of Agriculture, Fisheries and Food
NA	Noise Act 1996
NGO	Non Governmental Organisation
NRA	National Rivers Authority

NSA	Nitrate Sensitive Area
NSNA	Noise and Statutory Nuisance Act 1993
NVZ	Nitrate Vulnerable Zone
NWC	National Water Classification
PHA	Public Health Act 1875/1936
PN	Prohibition Notice
PPCA	Pollution Prevention and Control Act 1999
PPG	Planning Policy Guidance Note
PPG	Pollution Prevention Guidance Note
PRN	Packaging Recovery Note
RCEP	Royal Commission on Environmental Pollution
RN	Revocation Notice
SAC	Special areas of Conservation
SEA	Single European Act 1996
SN	Suspension Notice
SPA	Special Protection Area
SPL	Significant Pollution Linkage
SSSI	Site of Special Scientific Interest
SWQO	Statutory Water Quality Objective
TEU	Treaty on European Union 1993
UK	United Kingdom
VN	Variation Notice
WA	Water Act 1989
WAMITAB	Waste Management Industry Training Board
WCA	Waste Collection Authorities
WDA	Waste Disposal Authorities
WIA	Water Industry Act 1991
WMP	Waste Management Paper
WN	Works Notice
WPZ	Water Pollution Zone
WRA	Water Resources Act 1991
WRAs	Waste Regulation Authorities

CHAPTER 1

ELEMENTS OF ENVIRONMENTAL LAW

1.1 The aims and objectives of this textbook and its intended readership

The authors aim to provide a succinct and accessible account of the core features of environmental law in England and Wales. As this text is part of the Cavendish 'principles' series of textbooks, the authors have the daunting challenge of addressing the key issues in just 500 pages. With this task in mind we have concentrated upon the issues which we believe to be – based upon our own teaching experience and a survey of environmental law courses currently on offer in UK Higher Education institutions – of most relevance to students studying environmental law as part of their undergraduate or postgraduate degree programmes. This book is written for *both* law and non-law students by authors who teach environmental law and appreciate the need for an accessible and understandable account of the law.

We have paid particular attention to the way in which the information is structured so as to provide the reader with a fairly simple framework to guide him/her through the text. In Chapter 1 we introduce the reader to the basic legal framework which governs the regulation of polluting activities in England and Wales; in Chapter 2 we outline the administrative and enforcement roles of the regulators and the enforcement, supervisory, and interpretative roles of the courts; in Chapters 3–9 we describe the main regulatory pollution control regimes: water, waste, Integrated Pollution Control (IPC) and Integrated Pollution Prevention and Control (IPPC), contaminated land, air, statutory nuisance, and noise; in Chapters 10–11 we discuss the use of environmental law by individuals, groups, or companies to protect property interests, human health and the environment, to oversee the activities of the regulators and to mount private prosecutions; and in the final chapters, Chapters 12–13, we focus upon the factors which are responsible for the rapid development of environmental law: the UK's membership of the European Union, the influence of international environmental law on national environmental law, public perception of risk, human rights and the emergence of new techniques to regulate environmental pollution.

This textbook focuses on those laws in England and Wales which are concerned with the regulation of polluting substances emitted from industrial, commercial, agricultural and domestic premises into the environment. Whilst we concede that environmental law encompasses a burgeoning collection of issues, extending well beyond pollution regulation, including such issues as nature conservation and planning law, we have been guided in the selection of content by the needs of our primary student readership. We concentrate on an analysis of the main 'vehicle' which is used to regulate pollution in England and Wales: the series of 'Command and Control' regulatory laws which address specific environmental problems. Whilst we do refer to certain aspects of European environmental law and international environmental, law we discuss developments at these levels in the context of how they impact upon national regulation by 'driving' the development of our own law forward.

This text is designed to explain how pollution control law is structured and operates in England and Wales. This requires the authors to focus on the 'shape' and 'pattern' of the content of the law. In adopting this approach we recognise that we run the risk of generalising at the expense of accuracy in specific cases. Short of writing an encyclopaedia on pollution law this problem is unavoidable! With this proviso in mind we would recommend that any reader with a specific environmental legal problem to resolve should seek professional advice. For those readers who wish to explore the issues which we address in the book in greater detail we have included, at the end of the book, a selection of further reading references.

In order to provide the reader with a 'mindset' (orientation) which will help him/her to grasp much of what follows we suggest that the reader spends a few minutes considering the following questions before embarking upon Chapters 2–13:

(a) What is 'pollution' and what is the 'environment'?

(b) What is environmental law?

(c) What is environmental law for? (What is its function or functions?)

(d) What are the main features of environmental law?

(e) Who uses environmental law and for what purpose(s)?

(d) What are the main driving forces behind the changes in and development of environmental law?

1.2 Environmental law: an overview

In this introductory chapter we provide an outline of environmental law as it relates to the regulation of polluting activities in England and Wales. In section 1.3 we consider some preliminary issues, especially the difficulties associated with the concepts of 'pollution' and 'environment', before moving on to discuss the components or elements of environmental law. We then refer to the persons who frequently use environmental law and their respective objectives. We then 'flag up' the primary functions of environmental law before considering the forces which are driving its rapid development. In section 1.4 we map out the structure of the public regulation of private polluting activities. By this we mean to refer to the regulation of the polluting activities of private legal persons, such as companies and individuals, by public regulatory bodies (such as the Environment Agency and the local authorities). Finally, in section 1.5 we outline the use of environmental law by private persons to protect private interests, to prosecute and to oversee the fairness and legality of decisions made by the public regulators.

1.3 Preliminary issues

1.3.1 'Pollution' and the 'environment'

Most of us think of 'pollution' in terms of something which is contaminated, unclean, spoilt, or irreparably damaged. For example, we may be outraged by the damage to our health caused by atmospheric pollution from a nearby factory, or we may be saddened that the pristine beauty of a local beach has been marred by an oil spill. Implicit in the term 'pollution' is the existence of some element of risk, threat, danger, or hazard to ourselves, or some other object such as an important wildlife habitat, which is important to us. 'Pollution' is a relative term. The level of threat or damage to humans, or some part of the wider environment perceived as important to humans, must be significant enough to trigger a recognition that 'pollution' has occurred. However, what is perceived as pollution by one person (or group or society) may not be perceived as pollution by another. The assessment of what constitutes pollution, in any given set of circumstances, will therefore vary with the values and risk perception of the relevant individual, group, or society.

1.3.1.1 Pollution

In environmental law there is no single, accepted, definition of pollution, however, the Royal Commission on Environmental Pollution (RCEP) (see RCEP, *Pollution in Some British Estuaries and Coastal Waters*, Third Report, Cm 5054, 1972, London: HMSO) has provided the following helpful definition:

> The introduction by man into the environment of substances or energy liable to cause hazards to human health, harm to living resources and ecological systems, damage to structure or amenity or interference with the legitimate uses of the environment.

Pollution is associated with risks to human health and property, plants, animals, habitats and ecological systems. Pollution is not restricted to the impact of chemical substances upon man or the environment, but may extend to the introduction of energy into the environment, such as the 'hot' cooling water discharged from a power station into a river, or electro-magnetic fields emitted by electrical apparatus, such as power lines.

In an environmental law context chemical substances and/or energy may be introduced into the environment in any of the following ways:

(a) a legal person (for example, an individual or a company) discharges chemicals and/or energy into the environment in accordance with the conditions of a licence issued by a regulator;

(b) a legal person discharges chemicals and/or energy into the environment in breach of licence conditions;

(c) a legal person discharges chemicals and/or energy into the environment without the benefit of a licence issued by a regulator authorising the discharge.

In the first scenario, there is no pollution within the meaning of the relevant legislation under which the licence was issued. The licence holder will have a defence against regulatory criminal offences alleging pollution of the environment. In the second scenario, the licence holder has caused pollution to occur by exceeding the terms of its licence. A criminal offence has been committed: breach of licence conditions. Readers should note that it is not necessary for the prosecution to prove that environmental harm has occurred as a result of the breach of licence conditions. If the breach is minor the regulator is likely to exercise its discretion not to prosecute. In the final scenario, whether pollution has occurred will generally depend upon the environmental impact of the substance and/or energy discharged and whether the process emitting the substance and/or energy requires a licence. If the discharge is small and does not result in significant environmental damage, pollution is unlikely to have occurred. However, whether such a discharge amounts to pollution may also depend upon the nature of the process emitting the substance and the identity of the substance itself. Some regulatory regimes (for example, IPC/IPPC) insist that a licence is obtained prior to discharge of *any* substance from an IPC/IPPC regulated process. Discharges made without the benefit of a licence will automatically be unlawful. In contrast to IPC and IPPC licenses, application for a water pollution discharge consent licence need only be made to the regulator if the substance and/or energy discharged into controlled waters is 'poisonous, noxious, or polluting'.

In regard to licensed discharges, Keith Hawkins In *Environment and Enforcement* (1984, Oxford: Clarendon) observed that: 'Pollution is an administrative creation.' This is a reference to the fact that, because the regulator controls the licensing process, especially the conditions attached to licences, it has the power to determine which discharges will, or will not, amount to pollution.

1.3.1.2 Environment

In its most general sense 'the environment' refers to our surroundings. It is often understood to include not only land, air and water, but also the built environment and the condition of the local neighbourhood. The environment can, for others, mean something more specific and refer to the conservation of natural habitats and ecology.

In an environmental law context, s 1(2) of the Environmental Protection Act (EPA) 1990 contains the following definition of the environment which provides a useful guide for the issues canvassed in this book:

> The 'environment' consists of all, or any of the following media, namely, the air, water and land; and the medium of air includes the air within buildings and the air within other natural or man-made structures above or below ground.

1.3.2 What is environmental law, who is using it and for what purpose or purposes?

Environmental law is primarily a mix of primary legislation (Acts of Parliament), secondary legislation (regulations or statutory instruments), judicial decisions reported in law reports, common law principles, European Community (EC) legislation (mainly in the form of directives) which are transposed into national law (usually in the form of regulations), European treaties and international law (found in treaties, conventions and protocols).

The study of environmental law is not confined to a study of the law which is written down in legislation (so called 'black letter' law), but it is also concerned with how the law is used to achieve the objectives of the key environmental stakeholders: the regulators, the regulated (especially businesses), central government, local government, industry associations, pressure groups, local amenity societies and the public. The Government, and its agencies, issue policy documents to public officials, in the form of official guidance, in a never-ending stream of White Papers, Green Papers, consultation documents, guidance notes and circulars. Although this guidance is not law, it is nevertheless important because it guides how the regulators (such as the Environment Agency) will use the law to achieve the regulator's statutory objectives.

It may therefore be helpful to conceive of environmental law, not as a collection of separate pieces of legislation and policy documents, but as a 'toolbox' containing a range of legal and policy instruments. Only those legal and policy tools which will achieve the objectives of the specific user will be applied to the problem in hand. Thus, a regulator will use the powers available to it, and which are built into the specific regulatory regime it administers, to enforce the compliance of regulated businesses with the relevant regulatory law. An individual who has sustained pollution damage to his property may resort to the common law, for example, using the tort of nuisance, to obtain compensation or other means of redress. An amenity group or society, such as Greenpeace or the Anglers Co-operative, may mount a private prosecution against a polluter in circumstances where a regulator has exercised its discretion not to prosecute. Alternatively, an amenity group, such as Friends of the Earth, may challenge, by way of a judicial review application (and subject to 'standing' restrictions) a regulator's decision to grant a pollution licence to an applicant. In this way, an amenity society may seek to bring a regulator to account for an allegedly unlawful decision. Environmental law is therefore not a simple application of the contents of legislation to particular facts. To understand environmental law properly we need to be aware of, not only the contents of the relevant law and policy, but also how the law and policy will be applied by the regulator, the private litigator, or the courts to resolve an environmental problem.

1.3.3 The function of environmental law

Much of environmental law concerns the *regulation* of polluting emissions discharged into the three environmental media – air, water and land. The primary function of environmental law is not to eliminate pollution, except in the case of a relatively few highly toxic pollutants, but to balance the polluting emissions generated by economic activity against the demands of society for a tolerably healthy environment. Polluting emissions must therefore be set, in most cases, by government (or its regulators) at levels which are acceptable to its two major stakeholders: regulated businesses and the public. This balancing task is performed on behalf of government by regulatory agencies such as the Environment Agency and the local authorities. Environmental law also has subsidiary preventative, remedial (clean-up) and compensatory functions.

1.3.4 What is driving the development of environmental law?

The early history of environmental law in England and Wales was characterised by a parochial focus on localised pollution problems. Reliance on the common law, especially the law of torts, to resolve individual disputes over pollution related property damage was overtaken by the need for legislation to address the gross, and widespread, pollution problems caused by the industrial revolution. A series of legislative enactments followed addressing specific problems: atmospheric pollution from the chemical industry, water pollution controls to prevent rivers becoming effluent channels and the regulation of statutory nuisances.

In the last three decades of the 20th century the UK's membership of the EC, together with the recognition of global pollution problems, has marked a turning point in the pace of environmental legal change. Over 200 pieces of European legislation have been passed to date which relate in various ways to the environment. Recent developments in international environmental law, especially regarding 'sustainable development' have helped to influence EC pollution policy and the development of new controls which are then transposed into the legislative systems of the EC's Member States. In addition, the public is both better informed of and more sensitive to environmental risks. As we have seen, especially in regard to the genetically modified crop protests, the public may be a powerful influence upon the regulation of environmental risks. The pattern of environmental pollution control, with its reliance on Command and Control regulatory regimes, has begun to change. The almost total reliance on the Command and Control regulatory model is giving way to a mixed approach to pollution control incorporating Command and Control and other tools such as eco-taxes, market mechanisms, environmental management systems, and self-regulation.

1.4 The public regulation of private pollution

Pollution regulation is primarily concerned with the *public regulation of private pollution*. In other words the State is tasked with the job of setting limits on the polluting activities of private enterprise (companies, firms, and individuals). The chief method employed by the State to regulate polluting emissions is the creation of series of *Command and Control* regulatory frameworks. Command and Control pollution regulation involves 'the "command" of the law and the legal authority of the State' (Hutter, B, *A Reader in Environmental Law*, 1999, Oxford: OUP). It is an approach to regulation which is characterised by several distinguishing features which are summarised below.

1.4.1 Primary legislation

Command and Control regulatory regimes are dependent upon legislation. Parliament passes an Act of Parliament (also referred to as a statute, enactment, or piece of legislation) which creates a broad framework for the control of various types of polluting activity. Implementation of an Act of Parliament is often phased in over an extended period of time and it is the Secretary of State who controls how quickly the individual sections of each statute come into force. Acts of Parliament are scrutinised by both Houses of Parliament prior to their becoming law. The public is not directly consulted in the drafting of new legislation.

1.4.2 Separate regulation of air, water, and land pollution

Command and Control regulatory regimes are often environmentally media-specific responses to problems caused by polluting discharges. For example, the Water Resources Act (WRA) 1991 establishes a regulatory framework to control the discharge of polluting substances and energy into the aquatic environment only. In contrast, the Integrated Pollution Control (see Pt 1 of the EPA 1990) regime regulates all discharges, emitted from a limited number of highly polluting activities, into *all three* environmental media.

1.4.3 The administrative and 'policing' functions of the regulator

Each Command and Control regime has its own regulatory agency which has the day to day responsibility for administering the relevant controls and policing compliance of regulated businesses with the law. Following the creation of the Environment Agency in 1996 the number of regulatory agencies in the UK was reduced (in consequence of the Environment Agency taking over the functions of the National Rivers Authority, the Waste Regulation Authorities and Her Majesty's Inspectorate of Pollution). The Environment Agency, the local authorities and the water services companies are the main regulatory agencies which we encounter in this textbook.

1.4.4 Licences authorising the discharge of polluting substances into the environment

Many Command and Control pollution statutes compel legal persons, especially businesses, who wish to discharge polluting substances into the environment to obtain a licence authorising such emissions. Pollution licences may be divided into two groups: licences which authorise the discharge of waste products into the environment (for example, a water pollution discharge consent, licensing the discharge of wastes into the aquatic environment), or licences which authorise the operational activities of an applicant (for example, a waste management licence or an IPPC licence authorising both the relevant process and the emission of wastes generated by that process). Licences may also be categorised according to whether they are 'anticipatory' (for example, the grant of a planning permission permitting the construction of a waste incinerator), or 'operational' (for example, a waste management licence regulating the day to day operational activities of the waste incinerator once it is constructed).

1.4.5 Notice based and other Command and Control regulatory regimes

Not all Command and Control regulatory regimes require prior licence based authorisation of polluting activity. Legislation may, as in the case of statutory nuisance, noise and contaminated land controls, impose a dual duty on the regulator to identify pollution problems in its area and ensure the rectification of the pollution problems so identified. After a statutory nuisance, noise, or contaminated land problem has been identified the regulator serves the person responsible for the problem with a notice specifying the necessary remedial works. In the case of air pollution control under the Clean Air Act 1993, where regulatory control is neither licence based nor notice based, the 1993 Act lays down strict limits on smoke (and similar) emissions. If these limits are breached the local authority may prosecute.

1.4.6 Licence conditions

In the water, waste and IPC/IPPC control regimes, each licence issued by the regulator is subject to detailed conditions which apply at the level of the individual polluting plant. The regulator has a wide discretion as to the conditions which it can include in each licence in order to achieve the objectives of the particular Command and Control regime. In addition, the regulator has the power to vary licence conditions. This power ensures that pollution control keeps pace with developments in technology and any new EC or international obligations.

1.4.7 Licence conditions and environmental standards

Licence conditions are set by reference to standards. An increasing number of standards emanate from the EC in the form of directives which are then transposed into national legislation (as regulations). Standards may be set by reference to specific 'objects' which require protection from the adverse impacts of pollution. These object based or target based, standards are designed to maintain the quality of the three environmental media (air, water and land) upon which the relevant objects (humans, animals, birds, fish, plants, habitats, or ecosystems) depend for a tolerably healthy existence. The standards set limits for the presence of various chemical substances in the relevant environmental media – air, water, or soil (for example, the Air Quality (England) Regulations 2000, the Bathing Waters Regulations 1991, and the Water Supply (Water Quality) Regulations 1999). The required environmental quality to sustain life is taken into account when the regulator sets the conditions of individual pollution licences. Alternatively, and more commonly, standards are set by reference to the activity which is responsible for generating pollution. These activity or 'source' based standards can either be in the form of emission standards (limits on specific chemical substances discharged, via pipe or chimney, from an industrial process), or product standards (for example, installation of catalytic converters in all new vehicles or the requirement that vehicle engines be able to run on lead free petrol), or process standards (for example, the use of a particular pollution abatement technology, or simply specifying the height of plant chimney discharging pollutants to atmosphere).

1.4.8 Command and Control regulatory systems are underpinned by criminal law offences

In the case of the licence based regulatory regimes failure to apply for a licence, or failure to abide by the terms of a licence once granted, will result in breach of the criminal laws contained in the legislation establishing the regulatory regime. In the case of non-licence based Command and Control regimes, failure to comply with the relevant remedial notice, or exceeding the emission limits specified in the legislation, constitute criminal law offences. The regulator has a wide discretion as to the enforcement action it may take in these circumstances to bring the polluter back into compliance with the law. The regulator is not obliged to prosecute each and every breach of the law which comes to its attention. In fact, prosecution is the exception rather than the rule.

1.4.9 Licences and legal compliance

Compliance with the terms of a licence entitles the licence holder to discharge substances and energy into the environment in compliance with the law and without fear of prosecution. Possession of and compliance with a licence provides the holder with a defence to any criminal charge relating to the emissions authorised by the licence.

1.4.10 Discretion

Regulatory agencies, such as the Environment Agency, local authorities, and the water service companies, are given a wide discretion in regard to how each regulator ensures compliance with the law. For example, a regulator may choose whether or not to prosecute an offending person (usually a business) in order to bring that person's activities back into compliance with the law. Alternatively, a regulator may use its administrative powers (for example, an enforcement notice) to secure the compliance of a regulated business, without recourse to mounting a criminal prosecution.

1.4.11 Regulator's powers of investigation

Regulatory agencies are given wide powers to enable them to fulfil their functions. These powers are detailed in the relevant Command and Control framework legislation. In particular, the regulator has the following investigatory powers: entry onto premises, examination, investigation, inspection, measurement, testing, recording, photography, removal of items and/or evidence, sampling, installation and operation of monitoring equipment.

1.4.12 Administrative powers

Regulatory agencies are given a range of administrative powers to enable them to fulfil their statutory obligations. These powers are especially important in ensuring that licence holders continue to comply with the terms of their licences. To secure compliance with environmental law, the regulator relies heavily upon the use of a wide range of notices including: Enforcement Notice (EN); Variation Notice (VN); Suspension Notice (SN); Revocation Notice (RN); Works Notice (WN); and Prohibition Notice (PN).

1.4.13 Definition of key legislative terms

The primary legislation establishing the relevant Command and Control regulatory framework uses wide flexible terms, for example, 'pollution' in the WRA 1991 and 'contamination' in the Environment Act 1995 (EA 1995). The definitions of these terms are subsequently interpreted by the regulator, via guidance notes, and by the courts, in litigation.

1.4.14 Secondary legislation

Secondary legislation (in the form of regulations and Statutory Instruments) supplements the primary legislation by providing the more detailed and technical content of the relevant regulatory regime. Regulations are generally prepared by the Secretary of State under the authority delegated to him by Parliament. There is little parliamentary scrutiny of the content of secondary legislation as the regulation is merely placed before Parliament for a limited period. The public may comment upon secondary legislation proposals where these are issued as consultation papers by the Government. Secondary legislation is frequently used to provide greater detail in regard to the general definitions contained in primary legislation and to provide data on the regulatory standards which are crucial to the setting of individual licences. European environmental legislation is invariably transposed into national law via secondary legislation.

1.4.15 Official guidance

A large volume of policy, in the form of official guidance notes, is issued by Government departments and regulatory agencies for the guidance of public decision making bodies. This is used to fill out the details of each pollution regulatory regime. This guidance does not have legal force, in the way in which primary and secondary legislation is law, but is important in guiding regulatory decision making. For example, guidance notes set out the procedures concerning applications for licences (discharge consents and operating licences) and appeals against refusals to grant licences. Guidance issued by the Environment Agency details its enforcement and prosecution policy.

1.4.16 Judicial review

A regulator's use of discretion, for example, in regard to the decision to set licence conditions for an industrial plant, or in regard to a decision not to prosecute a polluter, is subject to the supervisory jurisdiction of the courts. The courts, upon a judicial review action by an 'aggrieved person', may strike down a decision arrived at in breach of established procedure, but the court cannot substitute its own decision for that of the regulator. The courts therefore have a 'supervisory' jurisdiction over the decision making activities of the regulators. Judicial review is used by persons with 'standing' (a sufficient interest in the decision challenged) to ensure the accountability of regulators for their decisions. The courts scrutinise decisions for errors in procedure or unreasonableness. Thus, the regulatory agency is responsible for arriving at a decision on the merits of the case taking care to observe the correct procedure.

1.4.17 Appeals

Command and Control regulation is characterised by the right of regulated persons (businesses) to appeal against a wide range of regulatory decisions, such as the refusal to grant a licence, the conditions attached to a licence, the service of an abatement notice and the service of an Enforcement Notice.

1.4.18 Public registers

Publicly accessible registers of information are a further facet of Command and Control regulation. Registers contain information on the operation of the relevant licensing regime including: applications for licences, the identity of licence holders, relevant licence conditions, notices served on licence holders, sampling, details of any notices applied for or served in regard to variation, revocation, enforcement, works, etc, appeals, convictions and directions given by the Secretary of State.

1.4.19 Continuous control

Command and Control regulation is the primary tool used by the Government to regulate environmental pollution. It provides regulators, in the case of licence based regimes, with a coherent set of continuous controls which are capable of being tailored to the circumstances of each licence holder. The licence is the main vehicle through which the Government attempts to deliver its environmental policy targets.

1.4.20 The main Command and Control regimes

The main pollution Command and Control statutes are: the EPA 1990 (Pt I of which contains the IPC regime, Pt II waste management, and Pt III statutory nuisance), the WRA 1991 (water pollution controls), the Water Industry Acts of 1991 and 1999 (the regulation of discharges to sewers), the Pollution Prevention and Control Act 1999 (containing the IPPC regime which is set to replace IPC by 2007), the EA 1995 (introducing the contaminated land regime which forms Pt IIA of the EPA 1990), and the Control of Pollution Act 1974 (noise). These Command and Control regimes are discussed in detail in Chapters 3–9.

1.4.21 Pollution control, planning control, nature conservation and the historic built environment

The licence based or 'permitting' approach to regulation, evident in water pollution, waste management and IPC/IPPC regulation, is similar in structure to the control of building development, the central feature of which is the issue of a planning permission. In contrast, the protection of animal species, habitat (for example, Sites of Special Scientific Interest), landscape (for example, Areas of Outstanding Natural Beauty) and the historic built environment (Listed Buildings, Conservation Areas and Ancient Monuments) are achieved through a 'listing' process. This form of regulation (listing the 'objects' of the legislation and requiring specific permission for works which may affect or damage their intrinsic importance) has some similarity with contaminated land control. Once the regulator has identified contaminated land the details of the contaminated site are placed on a public register. In this way contaminated land is, in effect, 'listed'.

1.5 Private law and the regulation of pollution

In contrast to Command and Control regulatory regimes, such as the PPCA 1999, which create bureaucracies to regulate whole industries in the public interest, legal persons, especially individuals and companies, also have a role to play in the regulation of pollution. Any person may find it necessary to utilise environmental law in any of the following ways:

(a) to protect property and property related interests from the threat of environmental damage;

(b) to protect humans from the threat of environmental injury;

(c) to obtain compensation for damage to property and property related interests;

(d) to obtain compensation for personal injury caused by pollution;

(e) to challenge the decisions of regulators via a judicial review action;

(f) to mount a private prosecution against a polluter.

The reference to 'private law' is intended to convey to the reader the distinction between the role of private persons and the role of 'public' regulators. In the main, private persons are only concerned to advance their own private interests. They do not engage in environmental litigation for the greater good of society. Thus, we note that private persons resort to the common law in order to resolve 'one on one' disputes concerning damage to person or property caused by the polluting activities of a neighbouring property owner. The law therefore attempts to balance the competing interests of individual persons. In contrast, Command and Control regulation focuses upon 'the bigger picture'.

The polluting emissions of entire industries are regulated in order to safeguard public health and the wider environment. Regulatory law therefore attempts to achieve a balance between the needs of industry to be competitive (and not over-regulated) and the need of society for a tolerably clean environment.

Private persons seeking redress, often in the form of financial compensation, for damage caused to property or person (personal injury) will often resort to litigation to achieve their objectives. Such actions will often be based upon common law principles, especially those contained in the law of torts. The outcome of an individual common law action, whilst resolving the dispute between the parties to the litigation, may also set important legal precedents which have widespread application. One such example is the case of *Cambridge Water Co Ltd v Eastern Counties Leather plc* (1994) which drew widespread industry attention to the increased risk of civil liability for damage caused by the escape of polluting substances from land and business premises.

Private persons who wish to challenge the lawfulness of regulatory decisions, such as a decision to issue a licence to an applicant, or a decision not to prosecute a polluter, may mount a judicial review challenge. The objective of such proceedings is to persuade the court to strike down an unlawful decision which has been arrived at in breach of established procedure or is otherwise unreasonable. The judicial review process is only open to applicants with a sufficient interest in the decision which is the subject of the complaint. Private persons may also mount a private prosecution against a polluter, provided the legislation specifying the relevant offence does not exclude the right to launch a private prosecution. The role of private persons in the regulation of pollution, via private prosecutions, common law claims in tort, or applications for judicial review are discussed in Chapters 10–11.

ELEMENTS OF ENVIRONMENTAL LAW

This textbook focuses on the law relating to pollution control in England and Wales.

The terms 'pollution' and 'environment' are difficult to define.

The main vehicle which successive Governments have used to deliver pollution control in the UK is the Command and Control regulatory regime.

The function of each Command and Control regime, in relation to the environment, is the *regulation*, rather than the elimination, of polluting discharges to the three environmental media: air, water and land.

Command and Control regimes create public bodies, for example, the Environment Agency, to regulate the pollution generated by human activity: they have a national remit and a public protection focus. They are the vehicle which delivers the *public regulation of private pollution*.

Most Command and Control regimes regulate pollution either through licence based or remedial notice based controls. Regulators issue licenses and remedial notices and 'police' compliance with the terms of the relevant licences and notices.

Command and Control regimes are underpinned by criminal law offences.

Some Command and Control regimes contain civil law 'clean-up' powers.

Regulators are granted extensive administrative powers which enable them to enforce compliance with the relevant Command and Control legal regime without recourse to prosecuting lawbreakers.

Pollution licences authorise and legitimise the discharge of substances and energy into the environment. Licences contain conditions which are tailored to the individual circumstances of each licence holder. Generally, licence conditions are set so as to maintain or improve the quality of the environmental media (air, water, or land) into which polluting substances are discharged.

Command and Control licence based regimes are discussed in detail in Chapters 3 (water pollution), 4 (waste management) and 5 (IPC and IPPC controls). Command and Control remedial notice based regimes are discussed in Chapters 6 (contaminated land), 8 (statutory nuisance) and 9 (noise). Air pollution is dealt with in Chapter 7.

This textbook also addresses the role of individuals, groups and other legal persons in the regulation of pollution. The 'private' regulation of pollution focuses on the use of the common law to resolve 'one on one' disputes, often between neighbouring property owners. In these cases the law is resolving private legal disputes which, in most cases, will have minimal environmental impact when compared to the industry-wide remit of Command and Control regulatory controls.

The *private regulation of pollution*, discussed in Chapters 10–11, concerns the use of the common law to resolve disputes between private persons through court adjudication, challenges to the decisions of public regulators through the mechanism of judicial review and the right of a private legal person to mount a private prosecution.

The rapid changes in and development of environmental law largely result from the UK's membership of the EC and the changing 'cultural climate' concerning the tolerability of environmental risks and the sustainability of resource usage. These, and other issues which 'drive' the development of environmental law, are discussed in Chapters 12–13.

CHAPTER 2

THE ADMINISTRATION AND ENFORCEMENT OF ENVIRONMENTAL LAW

2.1 Introduction

As we noted in the previous chapter the main vehicle which the Government uses to regulate pollution in the UK is the Command and Control regulatory model. To be effective Command and Control regimes require the creation of administrative organisations capable of fulfilling two essential tasks: (i) the bureaucratic task of processing paperwork relating to the issue of licences to pollute (applicable to water, waste, Integrated Pollution Control (IPC) and Integrated Pollution Prevention and Control (IPPC) regimes) and notices to take action regarding pollution problems identified by the regulator (applicable to statutory nuisance, noise and contaminated land controls); and (ii) 'policing' compliance with the relevant licences, notices and other comparable regulatory controls. This later role entails the regulator in monitoring and enforcement roles.

Because of the historically reactive nature of pollution regulation in the UK, where successive Governments responded to pollution issues with the creation of layer on layer of Command and Control regimes in the period 1863–1972, UK pollution control presented a picture of a fragmented, complex, and unwieldy patchwork of separate controls. The last three decades of the 20th century have witnessed concerted Government efforts to achieve a more integrated and coherent set of regulatory controls. It is against this backcloth that we now turn to consider the role of the Environment Agency, and its forerunners, in the administration and enforcement of environmental law. In addition, we shall outline the role of the courts in the adjudication of disputes arising out of the administration and enforcement of environmental law.

On 8 July 1991 the former Prime Minister John Major announced the Government's intention to create a new authority with overall responsibility for the protection of the environment. The principal aim of the Government was to create a unified body which would have responsibility for the protection of the environment as a whole, bringing together the key regulatory pollution control functions affecting air, land and water. In order to do this the Government enacted the Environment Act 1995 (EA 1995) which established the Environment Agency, which became fully operational in April 1996. Prior to the establishment of the Environment Agency responsibility for various aspects of environmental protection and pollution control was largely divided between Her Majesty's Inspectorate of Pollution (HMIP), the National Rivers Authority (NRA), the Waste Regulation Authorities (WRA) and the local authorities, each exercising control under different statutory provisions. (The functions of HMIP, the NRA and the WRAs were transferred to the Environment Agency in April 1996 and each of these regulatory bodies ceased to exist from that date.)

The fragmentary system of control, which existed prior to the creation of the Environment Agency, reflected the way in which environmental legislation had developed in this country, largely in a piecemeal fashion and often in response to pollution problems or incidents. The pre-Environment Agency system of control was often criticised because it did not respect the cross-media integrity and indivisibility of the environment and also because it was unnecessarily confusing to those subject to it. As a consequence the Government took the view that the time was right for the creation of a new unified body, which would effectively provide not only greater co-ordination of environmental protection but would also provide a 'one stop' approach to pollution control, thus simplifying the burdens on industry.

Despite the creation of the Environment Agency in 1996, regulatory control is not entirely unified and it is still the case that some controls are exercised by the local authorities and the large water and sewerage companies. Local authorities still play a key role in environmental protection, indirectly through the planning system and also more directly in relation to air pollution, hazardous substances, statutory nuisances and now contaminated land. Their role is considered more fully at 2.5, below.

Because of the relatively recent creation of the Environment Agency, this chapter is broken down into four parts. First, it considers the system of regulatory control that was in operation prior to the EA 1995. The next section considers the reasons behind the creation of the Environment Agency. The chapter will then consider in detail the structure, role and powers of the Environment Agency, the local authorities and other bodies which still play a role in environmental protection. Finally, the chapter will consider the role of the courts in the administration of environmental law.

2.2 The system of control prior to the EA 1995

Prior to the enactment of the EA 1995 and the creation of the Environment Agency the system of pollution control was exercised through the auspices of a number of regulatory bodies. These were:

(a) HMIP;

(b) the NRA;

(c) the WRAs;

(d) the local authorities;

(e) the water services companies responsible for the sewage system.

As stated above, the functions of HMIP, NRA and the WRAs were transferred to the Environment Agency in April 1996 and these authorities ceased to exist from that date. The local authorities continue to play a key role in regulating pollution and their current role is considered more fully at 2.5, below.

2.2.1 Her Majesty's Inspectorate of Pollution

In a sense HMIP was a forerunner of the Environment Agency in that it was established to provide a co-ordinated system of pollution control. Prior to its formation in 1987 control of pollution was the responsibility of a number of central Government inspectorates: the Alkali Inspectorate (which was formed in 1863 and which was later called the Industrial Air Pollution Inspectorate); the Radiochemical Inspectorate; the Hazardous Waste Inspectorate; and the Water Pollution Inspectorate. (The functions of the Water Pollution Inspectorate were transferred to the NRA by the Water Act (WA) 1989.) HMIP was seen as a body which would enable a more co-ordinated system of pollution control, particularly through its administration of the system of IPC established by Pt I of the Environmental Protection Act (EPA) 1990.

HMIP, unlike the NRA was part of the Department of the Environment (DoE). HMIP operated on a regional basis with seven regions although it had a central office based in the DoE in London. The Head of HMIP was the Chief Inspector. Regional responsibilities were handled through the regional offices which employed in total over 430 staff. In addition, HMIP also contained a Technical Guidance Branch and a Monitoring Branch. In outline, HMIP was responsible for the following:

(a) regulation of the most seriously polluting processes through the system of IPC introduced by Pt 1 of the EPA 1990;

(b) regulation of sites which use, store or dispose of radioactive material under the Radioactive Substances Act (RSA) 1993;

(c) responsibilities under the Health and Safety at Work Act (HSWA) 1974 in relation to the air emissions of IPC processes;

(d) duties under the Water Industry Act (WIA) 1991 to act on behalf of the Secretary of State with regard to special category effluents discharged into the sewers;

(e) research on pollution control and also on radioactive waste disposal;

(f) statutory consultee in environmental impact assessments;

(g) oversight of the work of local WRAs;

(h) maintenance of public register on IPC authorised processes.

In carrying out these functions it appeared that HMIP was meant to serve the Government, industry and also the citizen. In addition to these various roles, HMIP provided expert advice and support to Government departments on a wide range of environmental issues. HMIP officials were involved in European Community (EC) working groups and other international bodies.

HMIP drew its powers from a number of statutory provisions including:

(a) Alkali etc, Works Act 1906 (repealed);

(b) HSWA 1974;

(c) EPA 1990;

(d) Water Resources Act (WRA) 1991;

(e) RSA 1993.

HMIP's main activity was the administration and enforcement of the system of IPC established under Pt I of the EPA 1990. During its period of office, HMIP was responsible for regulating over 200 categories of industry, 5,000 major industrial plants and 8,000 premises storing radioactive material. Once an industrial process had been authorised by HMIP, the Inspectorate was responsible for ensuring compliance with the conditions and standards it had laid down in the authorisations. Usually any authorisation granted would require the holder to carry out routine monitoring and to report the results to HMIP on a regular basis. These monitoring results, plus any obtained directly by HMIP Inspectors were on the public register. In addition to this HMIP inspectors carried out their own site inspections, either on a regular or *ad hoc* basis or in response to any complaints received. In recognition of the significant role that monitoring played, a new monitoring branch of HMIP was established in August 1991.

In terms of enforcement, HMIP had the power to revoke authorisations granted and also to halt a process where there was an imminent risk of serious pollution. In addition it had the power to bring prosecutions against offenders, which, if upheld in the magistrates' court, could lead to a fine of up to £20,000 or, on indictment, to an unlimited fine and/or a period of up to two years' imprisonment. To assist HMIP in the process of enforcement, its inspectors enjoyed considerable powers of investigation, particularly under s 17 of the EPA 1990 to enter premises and take samples. However, HMIP was often criticised for its poor prosecution record, particularly in contrast with the NRA which appeared much more willing to prosecute offenders. The following statistics illustrate the number of HMIP prosecutions during the period 1987–92.

HMIP prosecutions:

1987–88	3
1988–89	2
1989–90	4
1990–91	1
1991–92	11

In its publicity material (*Protecting Britain's Environment – The Work of HMIP*), it was stated that 'breaches of authorisations are normally dealt with quickly and effectively with the co-operation of the operator. But where this does not produce the necessary results, HMIP uses its powers of enforcement and prosecution'. Most critics of HMIP's 'poor' prosecution record failed to take account of the extensive array of enforcement powers which were available to HMIP to ensure that regulated businesses complied with the terms of their pollution licences. These powers, such as Enforcement Notices, Prohibition Notices and Revocation Notices were potentially so draconian that the threat of their use was more effective in achieving compliance than the comparable threat of prosecution.

In order to assist both industrialists and the chief inspectors, HMIP published a considerable amount of guidance material. Following the introduction of IPC, HMIP also began the process of publishing a new series of guidance notes covering all IPC processes. These guidance notes give advice on matters such as the best available technology for the particular process, pollution abatement techniques, operating procedures and importantly the emission standards to be achieved. The guidance notes are still relevant, albeit that the system of IPC is no longer administered by HMIP.

One of the Government's stated ambitions for HMIP was that it should be self-financing, recovering its costs from charges made for authorisations, variations, etc, of IPC processes. This reflects the notion that the polluter should pay, not just for remedying pollution, but also for the costs of pollution control. A charging scheme was introduced in April 1990. HMIP was required, by the EPA 1990, to set fees and charges so that income and relevant costs balance 'so far as practicable'. However, HMIP never managed to become completely self-financing.

The Environment Agency is now responsible for administering the system of IPC and the system of IPPC (which will replace IPC by 2007). The system of control is largely the same although the powers of inspection are now to be found in s 108 of the EA 1995.

2.2.2 The National Rivers Authority

The NRA was the main regulatory body with responsibility for controlling pollution of water, although it shared responsibility with HMIP in relation to those industrial processes subject to the IPC Regime established under Pt I of the EPA 1990.

The NRA was set up by the WA 1989, at the same time as water privatisation, to provide integrated management of river basins and the water environment in England and Wales. It took over the functions previously exercised by the Water Authorities. Although the NRA was established by the WA 1989, its constitution, function and powers were later to be governed by the

WRA 1991 and all the following sections relate to the 1991 Act. The NRA exercised a range of functions beyond pollution control, for example, it was also responsible for flood protection. In the context of environmental protection the record shows that the NRA was regarded by many as a strong regulator, willing to prosecute if necessary.

The NRA was established as an independent public body and it did not enjoy Crown Immunity. However, it was nevertheless accountable to the Secretary of State for the Environment. The Secretary of State had the power to issue directions to the NRA, although only after consultation with the authority, unless the direction was issued in an emergency situation. Details of any directions issued by the Secretary of State were published in the authority's annual report. The NRA was identified by the DoE as the 'competent body' to implement the requirements of numerous EC Directives concerning water quality.

Unlike HMIP, the NRA was a non-departmental body. The NRA had its national headquarters in Bristol but was structured on a regional basis with the regions corresponding to the catchment boundaries of the former regional Water Authorities. In 1993, NRA Northumbria and NRA Yorkshire were amalgamated and NRA South West and NRA Wessex Regions were merged to form NRA South Western. The NRA was assisted by a number of regional advisory committees that were required to act in a consultative role to the Authority providing advice on those areas within their spheres of influence. These committees were established under s 7 of the WRA 1991. There were three main advisory committees that operated in each region:

(a) Regional Rivers Advisory Committees;

(b) Regional Flood Defence Committees;

(c) Regional Fisheries Advisory Committee.

In addition there was an Advisory Committee for Wales. The advisory committee structure still exists and supports the Environment Agency in its water pollution functions.

When the NRA was established in 1989 it inherited the functions of the Water Authorities relating to pollution control, water resource management, flood defence, fisheries, navigation and conservation and recreation. The functions of the NRA (which have now been transferred in full to the Environment Agency) were laid down in s 2 of the WRA 1991 and covered the following areas:

(a) maintaining and improving water quality in controlled waters;

(b) regulating discharges into controlled waters;

(c) monitoring the extent of water pollution;

(d) managing and safeguarding water resources (abstraction);

(e) conserving amenity and promoting recreation;

(f) flood defence and land drainage;

(g) regulating fisheries (under the Salmon and Freshwater Fisheries Act 1975).

NRA Inspectors, often referred to as the 'river police' enjoyed various powers by virtue of ss 169–73 of the WRA 1991. (As in relation to HMIP the EA's pollution control powers of inspection are now to be found in s 108 of the EA 1995 which repealed s 169 of the WRA 1991.)

The WRA 1991 placed the NRA under a number of statutory duties which it was required to have regard to when exercising its various functions. The NRA was required by s 16 of the WRA 1991 generally to promote (to the extent that it considered desirable) the conservation and enhancement of the natural beauty and amenity of inland and coastal waters and of land associated with such waters; the conservation of flora and fauna which are dependent on the aquatic environment; and the use of such waters and land for recreational purposes. The NRA also had a duty to consider water supply issues and by virtue of s 15 it had to have regard, when exercising any of its powers, to the duties that are imposed on any water undertakers or sewage undertakers by Pts II–IV of the WIA 1991. The Environment Agency has similar duties in respect of water and these are discussed more fully at 2.4.8, below.

The policy of the NRA was to provide strong effective regulation in order to secure real environmental improvements of controlled waters. However, it did not view regulation as the only means at its disposal. The NRA placed an emphasis on changing attitudes and, hopefully, behaviour. As part of its pollution prevention campaign the NRA produced a short promotional video entitled *Pollution Prevention Pays*. The video was made widely available to businesses promoting the benefits of compliance and good practice. Nevertheless, since its creation in 1989 the NRA showed itself to be more willing to prosecute offenders than HMIP. Although prosecution figures are not conclusive of a strong enforcement policy the statistics are telling. Between 1989 and the end of 1994 the NRA had made over 2,200 successful prosecutions. These resulted in over £5 m in fines.

2.2.3 The Waste Regulation Authorities

WRAs were created by Pt II of the EPA 1990 as part of the overall reform of the waste regulatory regime. The WRAs' functions were carried out by the county councils, or in metropolitan areas the district councils. Special waste regulation authorities were created in Greater London, Greater Manchester and Merseyside. The WRAs were responsible for administering and enforcing the provisions under Pt II of the EPA 1990 relating to waste management and in particular the waste licensing system. WRAs were responsible for:

(a) preparation of waste disposal plans;

(b) control over the waste management licensing system;

(c) supervision of licensed activities;

(d) inspection of licensed land and landfill sites;

(e) maintaining public registers;

(f) reporting to the Secretary of State.

The functions of the WRAs were transferred to the Environment Agency and the WRAs no longer exist.

2.3 Reasons for change

The Government identified several reasons for change. On the one hand it was argued that there was a need to create a unified regulatory agency which would facilitate a more coherent approach to environmental control. For example, in relation to water pollution two systems of control operated, regulated by two different bodies. The system of IPC established by Pt I of the EPA 1990 is concerned with controlling the emissions of waste to air, land and water in order that pollution is controlled in a manner which will achieve the best practicable environmental option.

Therefore, HMIP as the body responsible for regulating processes subject to IPC was responsible for authorising discharges made into controlled waters as well as air and land. However, the NRA was the body responsible generally for regulating water pollution and enforcing the water pollution control provisions under the WRA 1991. Consequently, HMIP was required to consult the NRA before it set any conditions pertaining to discharges to controlled water. This meant effectively that the NRA had the power indirectly to determine any conditions which should be attached. Clearly, bringing control of water pollution and IPC under the auspices of one unified agency negated the need for this consultation. The problem of overlap was not confined to water pollution. A further example relates to the WRAs which were required also to consult closely with the NRA before setting any waste management licence conditions (under Pt II of the EPA 1990) in order to prevent any contamination of groundwaters from any leachate from a landfill site.

A further and very cogent reason for change was to simplify the system of control for those subject to it, namely the polluting industries and activities regulated under the various statutory provisions. It was not only the Government that advocated the creation of a unified regulatory agency, the idea was supported by many quarters of industry. It is worth considering the way in which the system of regulation, pre-Environment Agency, operated in order to grasp what was perceived in some quarters as a regulatory maze.

2.3.1 The regulatory authority maze – pre-Environment Agency

(This section relates to the variety of Command and Control regulatory regimes which were in existence prior to 1 April 1996.)

For any new or expanding industrial development it is necessary to obtain planning permission from a local planning authority before the development can go ahead. However, the developer may also need to seek further authorisations from the local authority depending on the nature of the project. For example, it may be necessary for the developer to obtain a noise consent from the local authority for the noise generated during the construction period. An industrial development may need to obtain a waste management licence or register with the WRA, which would normally be the county council. It might need to obtain Local Authority Air Pollution Control (LAAPC) authorisation if the development is a Part B prescribed process (under Pt I of the EPA 1990). There may be a need to obtain chimney height approval from the local authority or possibly even a hazardous substances consent.

In addition, an industrialist or industrial developer may need to obtain a consent from the NRA to discharge into water. Alternatively, if the process is prescribed for central control (a Pt A Process) it would require IPC authorisation from HMIP. If there were a need to abstract water from a local river, NRA approval would, however, still be required. There might be a need to discharge trade effluent into the drains and in these circumstances the consent of the sewerage undertaker must also be obtained. In short, a business might have to deal with several environmental protection bodies.

It becomes clear from looking at a hypothetical scenario such as this that any industrial developer had to understand the statutory controls that regulated the development and also know which regulatory bodies were responsible for controlling the various aspects of the development. Failure to obtain the correct permissions could (and still can) result in a criminal prosecution. Fines may be unlimited and the Crown Court has the power to impose a custodial sentence of up to two years. Reported cases suggest that the courts are becoming more willing to impose large fines and exercise the option of imprisonment. Additionally, both the WRA 1991 (s 217) and the EPA 1990 (s 157) provide that prosecutions may also be brought against company directors, managers, secretaries or other such officials if the offence was committed with their consent, connivance or negligence.

In the light of the complexity of the regulatory system and the consequences of breaching the regulatory controls, it really came as no surprise that industry and business supported the Government's call for the creation of a unified regulatory agency which would reduce the amount of bodies that a business might have to deal with.

2.3.2 The desire to achieve the best practicable environmental option

It is not only from the point of view of the industrialist that the picture was confusing. With so many organisations involved in various aspects of environmental protection it was often difficult to establish an overview of what polluting activities were going on and where, or more importantly to be certain that each body was exercising its functions in a manner which would benefit the environment as a whole. This respect for the integrity and indivisibility of the environment is at the heart of the decision to create a unified Environment Agency. Although HMIP was established in 1987 with the aim of achieving a more coherent approach to pollution control through the system of IPC, there was clearly still the need for a more integrated approach to pollution control. Whilst the authorities themselves were very active in publicising their work and increasing public awareness of their respective roles, the picture was still not entirely free of confusion.

The Government therefore saw the new Environment Agency as a means to develop a consistent and uniform approach to environmental protection, which would at the same time provide a more transparent system of control, more understandable to those subject to it. This desire to have a more co-ordinated approach to environmental protection was also generally supported by the environmentalists and pressure groups, many of whom believed that this unified approach would assist the Government in integrating environmental concerns into other Government policies. However, the environmental lobby has been critical of certain aspects of the Environment Agency and these criticisms are considered below.

2.3.3 Options for change

The desire to establish a unified approach to environmental control is not entirely new and it is clear that the Government was considering such an option as early as 1990 when it considered the possibility of creating an 'umbrella' organisation for overseeing the work of HMIP and NRA in *This Common Inheritance*, 1990. In July 1991 the then Prime Minister, John Major, made the first announcement that it was his Government's intention to create an Environment Agency. The process of bringing together HMIP, NRA and the WRAs has been a long drawn out and complex one, subject to much debate and consultation. In October 1991 the Government issued a consultation paper, *Improving Environmental Quality: the Government Proposals for a New Independent Environment Agency*. This suggested four options and sought views from all interested parties. The options suggested were as follows:

(1) The creation of an environmental agency and the retention of the NRA. The EA would assume the responsibilities of the WRAs and HMIP, less HMIPs water functions. The NRA would exercise control over all aspects of water pollution including HMIP's water pollution functions. The main criticism

of this option was that it still did not provide an integrated approach to pollution control.

(2) The environmental agency would be simply an umbrella organisation overseeing and co-ordinating HMIP and the NRA. Although this might secure a greater degree of co-ordination it would still not provide a unified approach for industry.

(3) The environmental agency would take over the functions of HMIP, NRA and the WRAs (the option finally selected).

(4) The environmental agency would take over HMIP and the WRAs and would also assume the NRA's water pollution functions but the NRA would continue to exist and exercise its remaining controls over matters such as fishing, flood defence and drainage.

The Government invited consultation on all four options. Much of the debate centred on Options 3 and 4 and the real issue was whether to retain the NRA, given its very wide ranging functions. Interestingly, the NRA did not favour a separation of its functions and its preferred option was full integration into the environmental agency. As stated the process of consultation was lengthy, however by 1992 the Government had stated that it would move forward with the creation of a unified Environment Agency, which would take over HMIP, the NRA and the WRAs (Option 3).

2.4 The Environment Agency

In November 1994 the Environment Bill was introduced before Parliament, its principal purpose being the creation of a new Environment Agency for England and Wales and a Scottish Environment Agency for Scotland (in addition the EA 1995 introduced new provisions relating to contaminated land, abandoned mines and national parks). The Environment Agency was established in July 1995 and became operational on 1 April 1996.

2.4.1 The structure of the Environment Agency

Section 1(1) established the new Environment Agency as a body corporate. The agency consists of between 8 and 15 members, of whom three are appointed by the Minister and the remaining members by the Secretary of State. In appointing members, both the Minister and the Secretary of State must have regard to the desirability of appointing a person who has experience of, and has shown some capacity in some matter relevant to the functions of the Environment Agency.

Like the former NRA, the Environment Agency is an independent body. HMIP, on the other hand, was part of the DoE. Although it is an independent body, the Environment Agency is nevertheless accountable to Parliament through the Secretary of State. The Environment Agency does not have crown immunity. In terms of staffing, most of the employees of the Environment Agency have been drawn from HMIP, NRA and the WRAs, thus retaining the expertise which had developed in those bodies.

2.4.2 Regional structure and regional environmental protection advisory committees

The Environment Agency is based upon a regional structure and this is augmented by the regional advisory committees under s 12 of the EA 1995 and the Welsh Advisory Committee under s 11. The regional boundaries are complicated. In terms of water management purposes the regional boundaries correspond exactly with the eight regional boundaries of the NRA, which were drawn up on river catchment areas. As far as pollution control functions are concerned the regional boundaries are those eight regions, modified to fit the local authority boundary which is closest to the water management boundary.

The Welsh Advisory Committee, which must meet at least once a year, is made up of members appointed by the Secretary of State. Its function is to advise the Secretary of State on matters affecting or connected with the carrying out of the EA's functions in Wales (s 11(1)). During the passage of the Environment Bill there were calls for a separate Environment Agency for Wales similar to the Scottish Environmental Protection Agency for Scotland. These calls were, however, dismissed, largely on the grounds that this would be an inefficient and wasteful use of resources.

Section 12 provides for the establishment of regional environmental protection advisory committees in both England and Wales (therefore note that in Wales there is a Welsh Advisory Committee and a regional environmental protection committee). By virtue of s 12(2), the EA is required to consult the relevant advisory committee as to any proposals relating generally to the manner in which the EA carries out its functions in that region and also to consider any representations made to it by the advisory committee. The committee consists of a chairman appointed by the Secretary of State and other members appointed by the EA. In addition to the regional environmental protection advisory committees, s 13 of the EA 1995 provides for the establishment of regional and local fisheries advisory committees on a similar basis.

The Environment Agency is under a duty to consult the relevant committee on any proposals relating generally to the manner in which it carries out its functions in that region.

2.4.3 Transfer of functions

On 1 April 1996 the Environment Agency became fully operational. Section 2 of the Environment Act 1995 (EA 1995) provides specifically for the transfer of functions to the Environment Agency of the following:

(a) the functions exercised by the NRA under the WRA 1991 and the Land Drainage Act 1991 and various other statutory provisions such as the Salmon and Freshwater Fisheries Act 1975. As a consequence of which the NRA was abolished. Thus, the EA has inherited the NRA's water resource management functions, pollution control functions and also its operational functions relating to flood defence, land drainage, navigation and fisheries;

(b) the waste management functions exercised by the WRAs under Pt II of the EPA 1990 and the Control of Pollution (Amendment) Act 1989;

(c) HMIP's responsibilities under Pt I of the EPA 1990. It should be noted here that the LAAPC controls exercised by local authorities under Pt I of the EPA 1990 are retained by the local authorities;

(d) HMIP's functions relating to radioactive substances under the RSA 1993;

(e) certain enforcement functions under Pt I of the HSWA 1974;

(f) certain functions of the Secretary of State (these are listed in s 2(2) of the EA 1995).

As a consequence of this transfer of functions the EA 1995 (Sched 22) has made a large number of amendments to most of the environmental protection legislation discussed in this book, notably the EPA 1990 and WRA 1991, in order that the legislation now refers to the EA rather than NRA, HMIP or the WRAs. Section 3 of the EA 1995 makes provisions for the transfer of property rights and liabilities specifically of the NRA and the WRAs.

In addition to the transfer of functions, the EA 1995 conferred certain new functions on the EA arising out of new provisions introduced in the said Act. These are:

(a) functions relating to contaminated land under s 57 of the EA 1995. The EA has specific powers relating to certain contaminated sites which have been designated as 'special sites' by a local authority. In addition, the agency has the power to give guidance to local authorities in respect of the latter's role in relation to contaminated land. For a further discussion of the contaminated land provisions see Chapter 6;

(b) functions relating to air quality under Pt IV of the EA 1995. The agency acts as a statutory consultee in relation to the Secretary of State's proposals for a national air quality strategy and also in relation to any regulations which he issues relating to air quality. For further discussion, see Chapter 7.

2.4.4 Aims of the Environment Agency

The principal aims and objectives of the Environment Agency are laid down in s 4 of the EA 1995. Section 4(1) states that it shall be the 'principal aim of the EA (subject to and in accordance with the provisions of [the] Act or any other enactment and taking into account any likely costs) in discharging its functions so as to protect or enhance the environment, taken as a whole, as to make the contribution towards attaining the objective of achieving sustainable development'. It is clear from this therefore that the Government envisages that the Environment Agency shall be guided by the objective of achieving sustainability. However, it is also very clear that this is not an absolute objective in so far as the principal aim of the Environment Agency is qualified in two ways. First, the aim is subject to and in accordance with any other provisions of the EA 1995 or any other enactment. Therefore, in situations where the EA 1995 or any other enactment places the Environment Agency under a duty to have regard to particular considerations, or instructs the Environment Agency to fulfil actions, then these other provisions will overrule the principal aim. Second the Environment Agency is required to take into account any likely costs of discharging its functions in the attainment of this aim. This includes the likely costs to any person and to the environment (s 56(1)). This latter qualification is considered more fully at 2.4.11, below.

The Secretary of State can issue guidance to the Environment Agency on any further objectives which are considered to be appropriate for the Environment Agency to pursue (s 4(2) of the EA 1995) and in particular the guidance must include advice on how, having regard to the Environment Agency's responsibilities and resources, it is to attain the objective of sustainable development (s 4(3)). Once again the reference to resources appears in the guidance given to the Environment Agency. Before issuing this guidance the Secretary of State must consult with the Environment Agency and any other appropriate bodies or persons (s 4(5)).

2.4.5 Sustainable development

Given that the principal aim of the Environment Agency is to use its powers to attain the objective of sustainable development, it is worth considering how the Government defines this all important concept. A widely accepted definition of sustainable development is to be found in the 1987 *Bruntland Report* (*Report of the World Commission on Environment and Development 1987*):

> ... development that meets the needs of the present without compromising the ability of future generations to meet their own needs.

The EA 1995, however, fails to provide a definition and sustainable development remains to be defined in the guidance notes referred to above.

2.4.6 General functions of the Environment Agency with respect to pollution control

The general functions of the Environment Agency are defined in s 5. Section 5(1) states that the Environment Agency's pollution control functions shall be exercisable for the purpose of preventing or minimising, or remedying or mitigating, the effects of pollution of the environment. The EA 1995 does not, however, provide a definition of 'pollution of the environment' and it has been suggested that the definition as provided in the EPA 1990 (Pt I, s 1(3) and Pt II, s 29(3)) should be used. In order to carry out these functions, or to establish a general picture about the state of the environment, the Environment Agency must compile information which it has either gathered itself or which has been obtained from some other source. Section 5 goes on to list several other functions of the EA, including:

(a) carrying out assessments of the environmental effect or likely effect of existing levels of pollution of the environment;

(b) reporting to the Secretary of State on the ways in which the Environment Agency considers it can prevent, minimise, remedy or mitigate the effects of pollution and reporting on the costs and benefits of such options (s 5(3)(ii));

(c) following developments in technology and techniques for preventing, minimising, remedying or mitigating the effects of pollution of the environment. This clearly relates to the Environment Agency's functions in respect of IPC under Pt I of the EPA 1990 and IPPC under the PPCA 1999.

2.4.7 Duties of the new Environment Agency

The EA is placed under certain statutory duties which it must have regard to when exercising any of its functions. Section 6 deals specifically with those duties pertaining to water, s 7 deals with the EA's general environmental and recreational duties and s 8 deals with the its duties with respect to sites of special interest. Section 39 provides that the Environment Agency is under a general duty to have regard to the costs and benefits in exercising its powers. This has already been referred to in relation to the general aims of the Environment Agency and is considered more fully at 2.4.11, below.

2.4.8 Section 6 – duties in respect of water

In the same way that the NRA was under a similar duty under the WRA 1991, the EA has specific duties regarding water. The EA is obliged, to the extent that it considers desirable, generally to promote the:

(a) conservation and enhancement of the natural beauty and amenity of inland and coastal waters and land surrounding them;

(b) the conservation of flora and fauna which are dependent upon the aquatic environment;

(c) the use of such waters and land for recreational purposes taking into account the needs of the chronically sick or disabled.

In terms of water resources the Environment Agency is also obliged to take all such action as it may from time to time consider necessary, in accordance with any directions issued by the Secretary of State, to be necessary or expedient to conserve, redistribute or generally augment water resources in England and Wales and also to secure the proper use of water resources. These duties are described as being 'without prejudice' to the Environment Agency's other duties under s 7 of the EA 1995.

2.4.9 Section 7 – general environmental duties

Section 7 deals with the general environmental duties placed upon the Secretary of State and the Environment Agency and in doing so draws a distinction between the Environment Agency's pollution control functions and non-pollution control functions.

When formulating or considering any proposals relating to any non-pollution control functions, the Secretary of State and the Environment Agency are under a duty to 'exercise any power' in respect of such proposals so as to further the conservation and enhancement of natural beauty and the conservation of flora, fauna and geological or physiographical features of special interest (s 7(1)(a)). This duty applies to such proposals made by the EA so far as may be consistent:

(a) with the purpose of any enactment relating to the functions of the Environment Agency;

(b) with any guidance given under s 4.

In the case of the Secretary of State this duty applies to him so far as it is consistent with:

(a) the objective of sustainable development;

(b) with his general duties regarding the water industry under the provisions of s 2 of the WIA 1991.

Where the proposals relate to the Environment Agency's pollution control functions the duty is worded differently (s 7(1)(b)). Here the Secretary of State and the Environment Agency must 'have regard' to the desirability of conserving and enhancing natural beauty and of conserving flora, fauna and geological or physiographical features of special interest. Clearly, the duty to have regard to these matters is less onerous than in relation to s 7(1)(a) above where the duty is to exercise any powers to further these matters. This difference was the subject of a great deal or criticism during the passage of the Environment Bill.

In addition, s 7(1)(c) requires the Secretary of State and the Environment Agency, when formulating or considering any proposals relating to any functions of the Environment Agency:

(a) to have regard to the desirability of protecting and conserving buildings, sites and objects of archaeological, architectural, engineering or historic interest;

(b) to take into account any effect which the proposals would have on the beauty or amenity of any rural or urban area or any such flora, fauna, features, buildings, sites or objects; and

(c) to have regard to any effect which the proposal would have on the economic and social well being of local communities in rural areas.

In addition to the above duties laid down in s 7(1), s 7(2) requires the Secretary of State and the Environment Agency, in formulating or considering proposals relating to any functions of the Environment Agency to:

(a) have regard to the desirability of preserving for the public any freedom of access to areas of woodland, mountains, moors, heathlands, downs, cliffs, the foreshore and other places of natural beauty;

(b) have regard to the desirability of maintaining the availability to the public of any facility for visiting or inspecting any building, site or object of archaeological, engineering or historic interest; and

(c) take into account any effect which the proposals would have on any such freedom of access or on the availability of any such facility.

Section 7(3) applies s 7(1) and (2) in relation to the Environment Agency's duties to water and sewerage undertakers.

2.4.10 Section 8 – environmental duties with respect to sites of special interest

The provisions of s 8 of the EA 1995 are based on the provisions of s 17 of the WRA 1991 which were repealed by the EA 1995. Under s 8(1) the Nature Conservancy Council for England or the Countryside Council for Wales may designate land as being of 'special interest' and notify the Environment Agency accordingly if it is their opinion that any area of land:

(a) is of special interest by reason of its flora, fauna or geological or physiographical features; and

(b) may at any time be affected by schemes, works, operations or activities of the EA or by an authorisation given by the Environment Agency.

The consequence of designating a site as being of special interest is that the Environment Agency is required to consult with the notifying body before carrying out or authorising certain works which are likely to affect the land. The requirement to consult does not operate in relation to anything done in an emergency (s 8(4)).

2.4.11 Section 39 – duty to have regard to costs and benefits

One of the underlying features of the Environment Agency, and probably one of the most contentious issues surrounding it, is the obligation placed on the it to have regard to the costs and benefit of exercising any of its powers. Section 39 provides that both the Scottish Environmental Protection Agency and the Environment Agency shall, in considering whether or not to exercise any power conferred upon by any legislation, or even in deciding the manner in which to exercise *any* such power, take into account the likely costs and benefits of the exercise, non-exercise or manner of exercise in question. This duty does not apply if, or to the extent that it is unreasonable in view of:

(a) the nature or purpose of the power; or

(b) in the circumstances of the particular case.

In addition, s 39(2) provides that the duty does not affect the Environment Agency's obligation to discharge any duties, comply with any requirements or pursue any objectives imposed upon it or given to it otherwise than under s 39. Reference to costs and benefits also appears in relation to the principal aims of the Environment Agency. It should be noted that s 56(1) provides that the definition of costs includes both costs to any person and also cost to the environment. The essence of this duty was described by the Secretary of State during the second reading stage of the bill where he asserted that, 'we cannot deliver on environmental demands unless we take into account the costs and ensure that they are proportionate to the benefits that we gain'. Hence an evaluation of the costs and the benefits that accrue from taking a course of action must be assessed.

This is an entirely new duty which was not imposed on the Environment Agency's predecessors. As stated above this has been one of the most controversial provisions in the EA 1995 and has led to widespread criticism from environmentalists. In particular many have suggested, in opposition to this duty, that it will lead to judicial review challenges by either industrialists or environmental protection groups who believe that the Environment Agency has not properly considered either the costs or the benefits of taking (or failing to take) a particular course of action.

2.4.12 Codes of Practice with respect to environmental duties

Section 9 empowers the Secretary of State and the Minister of Agriculture, Fisheries and Food to approve Codes of Practice which have as their purpose the provision of practical guidance to the Environment Agency concerning any of their duties detailed in ss 6(1), 7 and 8 and also to promote other practices which the Minister considers desirable for the Environment Agency to carry out. The Codes of Practice will be made by Statutory Instrument and may be modified or withdrawn. In carrying out its duties under ss 6(1), 7 and 8, the Environment Agency must have regard to any code of practice issued. In drafting any Code the Minister or Secretary of State must, however, first consult the Environment Agency, the Countryside Commission, the Nature Conservancy Council for England or the Countryside Council for Wales, the Historic Buildings and Monuments Commission for England, the Sports Council and other such persons as he considers appropriate to consult.

2.4.13 Powers of inspectors

The powers of EA inspectors are wide and are now provided for in a lengthy s 108 of the EA 1995 (previously s 17 of the EPA 1990). The powers conferred on the Environment Agency are also conferred on local authorities exercising their LAAPC functions under Pt I of the EPA 1990. The purpose of s 108 of the EA 1995 is to streamline the powers of entry and inspection across the range of pollution control functions now exercised by the Environment Agency, and these powers apply equally to pollution control functions under Pt II of the EPA 1990 (waste management) and the WRA 1991 (water discharge consents). Section 108 combines powers previously exercised by HMIP, the NRA and the WRAs.

It is essential that inspectors have adequate powers of entry and inspection in order to ensure compliance with the licences granted and also to identify instances where processes are being carried on without the appropriate licence. The powers listed in s 108 of the EA 1995 may be exercised for one or more of the following purposes:

(a) determining whether any pollution control legislation is being or has been complied with;

(b) exercising or performing pollution control functions;

(c) determining whether and, if so, how such a function should be exercised or performed.

Section 108 refers to persons authorised in writing. In practice this will be the inspectors employed by the Environment Agency (or the relevant local authority officers). An inspector has the following powers of entry and inspection:

(a) to enter at any reasonable time premises which he has reason to believe it is necessary for him to enter. This should normally be at any reasonable time unless there is an emergency, in which case entry is permitted at any time, and if need be, by force;

(b) on entering premises to take with him any other person duly authorised by the Environment Agency, and a policeman. The latter may be needed in situations where the inspector has reasonable cause to apprehend any serious obstruction in carrying out his duties;

(c) the inspector may also take any equipment or materials required for any purpose for which the power of entry is being exercised;

(d) to make such examination and investigation as may in any circumstances be necessary;

(e) to instruct that the premises or any part of them, or anything in them, be left undisturbed. The inspector may require that the premises or the part of the premises under investigation are not disturbed for as long as is reasonably necessary to enable him to carry out any examination or investigation;

(f) to take such measurements and photographs and make recordings as he considers necessary;

(g) to take samples, or instruct samples be taken, of any articles or substances found in or on the premises and also from the air, water or land in, on, or in the vicinity of the premises. Specific provisions relate to the possession, safekeeping and use in evidence of such samples;

(h) in the case of any article or substance found in or on premises which appears to him to be an article or substance which has caused or is likely to cause pollution of the environment, or harm to human health, to cause it to be dismantled or subjected to any process or test (but not so as to damage or destroy it unless that is necessary);

(i) to require information from any person – the inspector can require any person whom he has reasonable cause to believe to be able to give any information relevant to any examination or investigation to answer such questions as the inspector thinks fit to ask. The person answering the questions will be required to sign a declaration of truth to the answers;

(j) to inspect any information and to take copies – the inspector can require the production of any information that he considers necessary, including information held on computer. He also has the right to inspect and take copies of such information or any entry in the records;

(k) to require facilities and assistance – here the inspector can require any person to afford him such facilities and assistance with respect to any matters or things within that person's control or in relation to which that person has responsibilities. So, for example, the inspector can require an engineer on the premises to show him how the monitoring and testing equipment is working (or not working as the case may be);

(l) any other powers conferred by regulation by the Secretary of State. Certain information can be withheld from the inspector if it is subject to legal professional privilege. This covers correspondence between clients and their solicitors or legal professional advisors.

It is an offence not to comply with the requirements of the inspector or to obstruct him in carrying out his duty.

2.4.14 Environmental criminal offences

Command and Control regulation uses the criminal law to help enforce compliance with the provisions of the relevant regulatory regime. A range of criminal offences is built into and forms an intrinsic part of the legislation which created the relevant Command and Control regulatory framework. These criminal law offences and the sanctions associated with them are designed to provide the regulator with the 'muscle' to secure compliance with the law.

Typically these offences fall into the following categories:

Causing or knowingly permitting pollution	(This is a widely drafted offence which is applicable to both licence holders and non-licensed dischargers.)
Breach of licence conditions	(Targetted at licence holders.)
Breach of statutory duty	(For example, breaching the duty of care with respect to waste.)
Non-compliance with administrative notices issued by the regulator	(Aimed at licence holders who are required to take action in response to an administrative notice served upon it by the regulator. Typically the regulator will serve an Enforcement Notice specifying the introduction of operational improvements to reduce or eliminate pollution. Alternatively this offence is relevant to offenders who fail to comply with the terms of an abatement or similar notice.)
Personal liability of senior company officers, such as directors and managers who consent to or connive	

in the commission of an offence by their employing company.

Liability also extends to offences committed by the company which are attributable to the neglect of a senior company officer.

Most of these offences are offences of 'strict liability'. This phrase refers to the fact that the regulator does not need to establish that the polluter knew that what he was doing was wrong and would lead to a pollution incident.

2.4.15 Enforcement and prosecution policy

Enforcement is the process by which the regulator ensures that the law, as set out in the relevant Command and Control regulatory regime, is complied with. Enforcement primarily entails the regulator 'policing' the activities regulated by the relevant regime, be they compliance with the terms of a pollution licence, or compliance with the terms of an abatement notice. Compliance activities also extend to controlling unlicensed polluting activities. Through regular monitoring and inspection visits the regulator assures itself that the terms of licenses and notices are being complied with. In contrast, unlicensed discharges are often identified as a result of information received from the public. These incidents are investigated and dealt with in ways appropriate to the particular circumstances (for example, by either warning, caution or prosecution).

The regulator has a discretion (or choice) as to how it will enforce compliance with the relevant Command and Control regulatory regime. It has a range of 'tools' available to it to achieve the objectives of the relevant pollution control regime. It may prosecute any person who breaches environmental law or it may use its extensive range of administrative powers to assure compliance with the law. It may not even have to resort to the use of criminal or administrative sanctions since the threat of prosecution and the attendant bad publicity, or the threat of the use of its administrative powers, may be sufficient of themselves to ensure the offender's future observance of the law.

The general public would undoubtedly find it surprising to learn that the regulator does not automatically prosecute each and every violation of environmental law it identifies. In fact prosecution is the exception rather than the rule. However, the regulator's marked reluctance to prosecute should not be equated with a failure to perform its statutory duties. The primary objective of the regulator is to ensure a tolerably clean environment and in pursuance of that objective it will choose the tool which it believes is best suited to achieving that end.

Any person who is aggrieved that the regulator has exercised its discretion not to prosecute a polluter will, in most instances, have the option to mount a private prosecution. It is a feature of most UK environmental law that enforcement of the law is not the exclusive province of the regulator, however, relatively few private prosecutions are launched because of a number of practical considerations. Litigation is expensive: in addition to the costs involved in hiring lawyers must be added the cost of gathering evidence to prove the commission of an offence. Expert witnesses are often expensive. The scientific evidence required to prove a case may be complex and contested. If the private prosecutor loses its case then the defendant's costs may be awarded against him/her. Even if the private prosecutor wins the case, the sanction imposed by the courts may be disappointing. In certain circumstances the threat of mounting a private prosecution may exert sufficient pressure upon the regulator to persuade it to prosecute. It has been suggested that Friends of the Earth's inclination to mount a private prosecution was instrumental in persuading the Environment Agency to prosecute those responsible for the Sea Empress oil pollution (see *Environment Agency v Milford Haven Port Authority and Andrews* [1999] 1 Lloyd's Rep 673).

The apparent reluctance of regulators to use the formal apparatus of the law to prosecute a polluter may be due to a number of operational constraints. Regulators have limited financial and human resources at their disposal. The regulator may perceive that its resources are better spent in preventative monitoring and the provision of advice and guidance to regulated businesses than in litigation. The regulator may be reluctant to hand over control of the outcome of the case to the courts. This will inevitably happen if a prosecution is launched. Until relatively recently the courts tended to be lenient in the sanctions which they meted out to polluters. Litigation may also damage the ongoing, co-operational, relationship which the regulator has built up, over time, with the licence holder. Finally regulators possess an increasingly powerful armoury of administrative powers which it is open to them to use to secure the resolution of cases in terms on which they, rather than the courts, deem appropriate. Administrative powers such as the service of a Suspension Notice or a Revocation Notice are draconian and have the effect of stopping a business dead in its tracks temporarily or permanently. The use of these powers provides the regulator with flexible tools to control the environmentally damaging impacts of polluters without recourse to the courts.

2.4.15.1 Enforcement styles

Regulators in the UK have traditionally adopted a 'compliance' enforcement policy. The seminal work on compliance enforcement was written by Keith Hawkins in the mid 1980s. In *Environment and Enforcement* (1984) Hawkins explored the foundations of the compliance style of enforcement. Compliance was based on negotiation, conciliation, co-operation, and compromise. The regulator, in recognition of the fact that enforcement is an ongoing process, bargained with the polluter to arrive at a solution which 'fixed' the problem which had caused the polluter to breach environmental law in the first place. The objective of the enforcement process was to prevent harm rather than punish wrongdoing. Compliance enforcement is therefore remedial in nature and is chiefly concerned with the attainment of a tolerably clean environment at least cost. Compliance is incremental and recognises that enforcement is not a once and for all response to breaches of environmental law. Over a period of time the regulator is able to persuade the licence holder to introduce operational improvements which are designed to bring it back into compliance with the conditions of its discharge or operating licence.

Compliance enforcement tends to work precisely because the regulator rarely resorts to prosecution. As Hawkins observed: 'The polluter has goodwill, co-operation and most important, conformity to offer. The enforcement agent may offer in return two important commodities: forbearance and advice.' Generally, only blameworthy breaches of the law result in prosecution. The relevant breach is set in its social context and the blameworthiness of the polluter's conduct is the key to understanding the likely outcome of the enforcement process. Hawkins asserts: 'Pollution control is done in a moral, not a technological world.'

Hawkins identified that a zealous reliance on prosecution could be counter-productive. The regulator was likely to make better progress if it was able to demonstrate an understanding of the polluter's problems and adopted a patient and reasonable stance. In direct contrast to the compliance style of enforcement is the sanctioning, deterrence, or penal style of enforcement. The focus here is on coercing the polluter to comply with its legal obligations under threat of prosecution. The law is used to prohibit unacceptable conduct and punish transgressors. Typically the regulator adopts a confrontational stance in its dealings with offenders. This style of enforcement is common in ordinary policing activities where the prosecutor and offender are unlikely to have an ongoing relationship. In Hawkins' account of compliance enforcement in the water industry he records a telling comment from a regulatory pollution inspector : 'You can get so much more done by not upsetting people.'

In recent years a 'third way' enforcement style has emerged which advocates the selection of enforcement tools from both the compliance and sanctioning schools. This enforcement style is captured in Ayres and Braithwaite's *Responsive Regulation*. This approach is based upon a compliance pyramid. At the base of the pyramid are the co-operational tools such as advice and verbal warnings. In the event that the regulator encounters a difficult polluter it will, over time, increase the pressure on the polluter to comply with its legal obligations by moving up the 'compliance pyramid'. At the apex of the pyramid are criminal prosecutions and the use of administrative notices, such as a Revocation Notice, which will shut the offender down and put him out of business.

2.4.15.2 Environment Agency enforcement and prosecution policy

In 1998 the Environment Agency became the first regulatory agency in the UK to publish a publicly accessible enforcement and prosecution policy (the document can be accessed on the web at www.environment-agency.gov.uk). The introduction of the policy will help to standardise the agency's approach to the enforcement of compliance with the law across all parts of England and Wales. Nevertheless, the existence of the policy will not inhibit the exercise of the agency's regulatory discretion to choose whether or not to prosecute. The agency will continue to be free to decide on the action which it believes to be an appropriate enforcement response to any breach of the law which it encounters.

The Environment Agency recognises the benefits of using a wide range of enforcement tools including both prosecution and the agency's administrative powers:

> The use of the criminal process to institute a prosecution is an important part of enforcement. It aims to punish wrongdoing, to avoid a recurrence and to act as a deterrent to others. It follows that it may be appropriate to use prosecution in conjunction with other available enforcement tools, for example, a Prohibition Notice requiring the operation to stop until certain requirements are met. Where the circumstances warrant it, prosecution without prior warning or recourse to alternative sanctions will be pursued (para 19, EA Enforcement and Prosecution Policy).

The Environment Agency attempts to achieve its mission 'to provide a better environment for England and Wales' by providing education and advice and by regulating activities (para 1).

The EA states in para 6 of its policy that the purpose of enforcement is to ensure that preventive or remedial action is taken to protect the environment or to secure compliance with a regulatory system.

In deciding the appropriate enforcement action the Environment Agency is guided by four principles: (i) action will be proportionate to the environmental risks and the seriousness of the breach; (ii) whilst like cases should be treated alike (in the interests of consistency) Environment Agency staff will continue to exercise discretion; (iii) enforcement action will be targeted at those activities which pose the greatest threat to the environment; and (iv) transparency in regard to how the Environment Agency operates and what it expects others to do.

In deciding whether to prosecute, the Environment Agency adopts a two stage test: (i) is the evidence sufficient; and (ii) is a prosecution in the public interest? In regard to the latter limb of the test the Environment Agency will have regard to the aggravating and mitigating circumstances surrounding the alleged breach. In particular, it will have regard to: the environmental impact of the incident; the foreseeability of the incident; the intent of the offender; the previous history of offending; the attitude of the offender; the deterrent effect of prosecution; and the personal circumstances of the offender.

In regard to offences committed by companies, Environment Agency practice, in most cases, is to prosecute the company. Where there is evidence that the offence was committed with the consent of a senior company officer, or the offence was due to a senior officer's neglect, or the senior officer connived at the commission of the offence then the Environment Agency may also prosecute the senior company officer.

There is a presumption that the Environment Agency will prosecute in any of the following circumstances: incidents or breaches of the law with serious environmental consequences; operating without a licence; excessive or persistent breaches; failure to comply with remedial measures; reckless disregard for management or quality standards; failure to supply information without reasonable excuse or supplying false information; obstructing Environment Agency staff; and impersonating Environment Agency staff.

2.4.15.3 Key considerations in enforcement practice

The enforcement style or stance adopted by the regulator in any given case will, to a large extent, depend upon the following factors:

(a) the circumstances surrounding the breach of the law. In particular the extent of environmental damage, its visibility, and the culpability of the polluter. Visible and serious pollution incidents will be picked up by the public and will be reported to the regulator and the media. As regulators function in a political environment they will be alive to the fact that they need to be perceived as doing their job (as this is perceived by the public – prosecuting polluters) and they will probably prosecute. The more culpable the offender the more likely it will be that the regulator may have to adopt a sanctioning style of enforcement to punish and deter the offender from future transgressions;

(b) the compliance 'history' of the polluter will be taken into account by the regulator in deciding which enforcement tool to use to bring the polluter back into compliance with the law. If the offender is a problem polluter who shows no inclination to respond to the regulator's previous attempts to help it the regulator is likely to move up the enforcement pyramid;

(c) the contents of the regulator's publicly available enforcement policy will shape its response to a polluting incident, however, the existence of such a policy can never fetter a regulator's discretion to choose which enforcement tool it prefers to use;

(d) the range and content of the criminal charges available to the regulator is also relevant. The greater the range of offences the more likely it will be that the regulator will be able to fit the offence to the pollution incident. In addition, as most environmental offences are 'strict liability' offences, the regulator will find it easier to establish liability. Once the regulator has decided to prosecute the polluter there will be little chance of the polluter successfully mounting a defence. Thus the threat of prosecution will be a credible threat;

(e) in considering what action to take, especially a prosecution, the regulator will pay attention to the probable consequences of passing the control over the outcome of the case to the courts. Will the sanctions and sentencing options open to the courts have the desired deterrent effect? Are the sanctions available a credible deterrent? Assuming that the regulator has the evidence to establish the offence it will consider what the outcome of a prosecution is likely to be. It will be unlikely to prosecute if, on conviction, the offender is likely to receive only a minimal fine. Compliance enforcement and the threat of prosecution works better when penalties are credible. Until relatively recently maximum fines in magistrates' courts (where most cases are processed) were limited to £2,000. These have been increased, for most offences, to £20,000 but the regulator will also bear in mind whether the courts tend to restrict themselves to imposing lower levels of the available maximum. The regulator's view of what would be an appropriate sanction might not reflect the court's view. In addition, the regulator will be influenced by its impressions of the 'environmental awareness' of the courts. Do the courts perceive environmental pollution as morally unacceptable and will they reflect that opprobrium in the sanctions they impose? Too often in the past the punishment has appeared to the regulator not to fit the crime;

(f) the regulator will have regard to other enforcement tools. The regulator will usually have an extensive range of administrative powers available to it. The impact of Enforcement Notices can be significant – forcing the polluter to acquire and install expensive pollution abatement technology. The financial impact of these notices upon the polluter may outstrip the financial impact of the financial sanctions/penalties imposed by the courts. The use of an Enforcement Notice has certain advantages: (i) the regulator is able to maintain control of the outcome of the case; (ii) the polluter avoids adverse publicity and is given time to phase in the required improvement. Use of these powers also extends to pro-active preventive measures such as Works Notice, and remedial powers – clean-up;

(g) there are constraints on the regulator's ability to adopt a sanctioning style of enforcement. Regulators have limited financial and staffing resources which restrict their ability to opt for litigation. Regulators are largely funded from Government grants and in the current funding climate large increases in budgets are likely to be minimal. Regulators who adopted a sanctioning enforcement style would soon feel the backlash of industry pressure on Government to reign them in;

(h) the extent to which the public, the media, and political parties perceive pollution as a pressing problem impacts upon the regulator's mission. The media report on what concerns the public. Increasingly, pollution is a matter of public concern. The more the media reports the adverse impacts of pollution the more the public becomes sensitised to the issue. This process impacts upon political and legislative processes. Accompanying increases in the public understanding of the causes of pollution are calls for tighter regulation, both at national and EC level. Pollution is no longer perceived as a morally neutral 'quasi-crime' committed by high status white collar criminals. These days pollution is a crime which attracts just as much opprobrium as street crime.

2.4.15.4 The elements of criminal offences and case law

In the event that the regulator decides to prosecute a polluter it must select the relevant offence carefully for it must establish that all the elements of the relevant offence are present before it may allegedly hope to secure a conviction. For example, the prosecution of a person for allegedly polluting a watercourse by puncturing a drum of chemicals and allowing the contents to flow down a bank of a stream and into the stream itself will fail if the prosecutor uses s 85(3) of the WRA 1991, rather than s 85(1). Under s 85(3) of the WRA 1991, it is an offence to discharge trade or sewage effluent into controlled waters. The contents of the drum do not satisfy the 'trade effluent' requirement (unless the contents are waste) and the polluting substance is, arguably, not 'discharged', via a pipe or similar channel, into the stream and therefore the prosecution must fail. Section 85(1) of the WRA 1991 is a more widely drafted offence the elements of which would be satisfied by the circumstances described in this example.

Each Command and Control regulatory regime generates a body of case law, some of which is concerned with the interpretation of words and phrases which appear in the primary and secondary legislation establishing the regulatory framework. Each Command and Control regime generates its own case law and great care should therefore be exercised in embarking upon any attempt to apply the judicial reasoning in regard to the meaning of a word or phrase, as it appears in the case law appertaining to one regime, to that of another. Similarly, any word or phrase appearing in a criminal case does not necessarily have the same meaning when the same word appears in a civil case.

2.4.16 Criticisms of the Environment Agency

Reaction to the Environment Agency has been mixed. Despite the fact that the creation of such an integrated Environment Agency has been long awaited (and long promised) there is already a feeling that the new Environment Agency is 'compromised even before it begins' (Council for Protection of Rural England). Environmental pressure groups such as Friends of the Earth have also reacted with similar comments. The principal concerns about the Environment Agency are as follows:

(a) lack of independence;

(b) constraints on the way in which the agency can operate.

2.4.17 Lack of independence?

The fact that the Environment Agency is made up of members nominated by the Secretary of State for the Environment and the Minister for Agriculture has generated concerns about the independence of the Environment Agency. Concern has been expressed about the degree of ministerial control and the extent to which ministers can give guidance to the Environment Agency with respect to its aims and objectives. This concern has not just come from environmentalists or environmental pressure groups, but was also voiced by Lord Crickhowell, a former Chairman of the NRA. In the second reading debate of the Environment Bill in the House of Lords (December 1994) Lord Crickhowell warned against the wide ranging powers which the Government was taking to intervene in the Environment Agency's work. In a telling criticism the Chairman of the NRA stated that: 'Almost everything that the agency does, its regulatory arrangements, charging schemes, corporate plan and financial arrangements, has to be approved by ministers.'

2.4.18 Constraints on the way in which the Environment Agency can operate

During the passage of the Environment Bill, pressure groups expressed their concern about the terms upon which the Environment Agency should exercise its functions. In particular, an issue that has caused considerable disquiet is the requirement that the Environment Agency, when it considers whether and in what manner it will exercise any of its powers, must take into account the costs which are likely to be incurred as a result of the exercise of that power. This requirement has led, not surprisingly, to the view that environmental quality will be sacrificed to commercial interests.

2.5 The local authorities

Despite the creation of the Environment Agency local authorities continue to play a key role in terms of environmental protection. The provisions of the EA 1995 have, however, transferred the WRAs' functions, previously carried out by the local authorities to the Environment Agency. Other than that significant transfer of responsibilities the EA 1995 has done little to effect the overall functions of the local authorities.

The local authority sector is involved in various aspects of environmental protection which are described more fully in other parts of this book. This section intends only to provide a brief overview of the main environmental protection functions carried out by local authorities:

(a) responsibility for the planning control system (under the Town and Country Planning legislation) which requires local planning authorities to take environmental considerations into account in the preparation of development plans and also in respect of planning applications;

(b) district councils are responsible for investigating and abating statutory nuisances under Pt III of the EPA 1990. For many the statutory nuisance provisions represent the very localised aspect of pollution control, where polluting incidents in their very widest sense (noise, smells, animals) are controlled by the local authorities responding to complaints;

(c) local authorities are responsible under the Clean Air Act (CAA) 1993 for controlling emissions of dark smoke and they also have the power to control smoke emissions through the creation of Smoke Control Areas;

(d) local authorities are responsible for authorising the atmospheric emissions of certain prescribed processes under Pt 1 of the EPA 1990 and the environmental impacts of Part A2 installations and atmospheric emissions of Part B installations under the Pollution Prevention and Control Act 1999;

(e) local authorities are responsible for identifying areas of contaminated land under the provisions of Pt IIA of the EPA 1990 (inserted into the EPA 1990 by s 57 of the EA 1995). Sites which are designated as contaminated under the provisions of the Act fall under the regulatory control of the local authority unless the authority determines that the site is a special site, in which case the Environment Agency is the relevant enforcing authority. Part IIA of the EPA 1990 empowers local authorities and the Environment Agency to serve Remediation Notices on appropriate persons in order to secure the clean-up of contaminated sites;

(f) county councils, or in the metropolitan areas the district councils or London borough councils, have responsibilities as Hazardous Substances Authorities under the provisions of the Planning (Hazardous Substances) Act 1990.

2.6 Other bodies concerned with environmental protection

In addition to the Environment Agency and the local authorities, a number of other governmental or statutory organisations play a role in relation to environmental protection either in terms of promoting new legislation, acting in an advisory capacity or dealing with environmental regulation more indirectly. We now consider the role of the following organisations that can be said to fall into these other categories:

(a) the DoE (formerly forming part of the DETR and now forming part of DEFRA).

(b) the Secretary of State for Environment (and SOSDETR and SOSDEFRA);

(c) other Government departments;

(d) Royal Commission on Environmental Pollution;

(e) Office of Water Services;

(f) sewerage undertakers;

(g) English Nature and the Welsh Countryside Council;

(h) Health and Safety Executive;

(i) European Environment Agency.

2.6.1 The DoE

The DoE has principle responsibility for environmental legislation and policy and also for promoting new environmental legislation. It is responsible for issuing many of the regulations which provide the detailed mechanisms for environmental control. The department also issues various Guidance Notes and Circulars which are intended to assist either the regulatory authorities or applicants seeking consents from the various bodies. However, despite its name, the DoE is not solely or exclusively concerned with environmental protection. On the one hand it is responsible for a number of other areas such as housing, energy, construction, local government and planning. Also, because the environment is not something that can be considered in isolation, other Government departments such as the Department of Transport play a role in terms of environmental protection.

Organisationally the DoE has a number of specialist divisions dealing with the various aspects of environmental law. These are:

(a) the Directorate of Environmental Policy and Analysis, which is responsible for environmental policy and also provides the main interface with the EC;

(b) the Directorate of Pollution Control and Wastes, which deals with all aspects relating to waste policy and law. The directorate in particular is responsible for overseeing the waste management licensing system and provides guidance to the agency and the waste industry;

(c) Directorate of Air, Climate and Toxic Substances, which is responsible for a wide range of activities, including air pollution (it supervises the activities of the local authorities in respect of their air pollution control activities) and chemical safety;

(d) Planning and Development Control Directorate, which is the directorate that controls the planning and development control system. It is responsible for developing planning policy and also for administering the role of the Secretary of State in the planning system;

(e) the Water Directorate is responsible for overseeing all aspects of water supply and water quality;

(f) the Rural Affairs Directorate deals with wildlife and habitat conservation, National Parks, access to the countryside, Sites of Special Scientific Interest.

The department's stated aims for environmental protection are to:

(a) promote sustainable development;

(b) ensure prudent use of natural resources and to minimise waste;

(c) prevent and minimise pollution of air, land and water in cost effective ways;

(d) increase informed public participation in environmental decision making and the involvement of all sectors, especially business;

(e) ensure environmental concerns are reflected in all the Government's work both at the national and international level;

(f) reduce the burden of regulation, and make markets work for the environment;

(g) protect the environment, and save money, by encouraging better management methods and by promoting the cost effective use of energy.

2.6.2 The Secretary of State for the Environment

A glance through most of the chapters of this book will show that the Secretary of State for the Environment plays a key role in regulating environmental protection. This involves *inter alia*:

(a) dealing with appeals against decisions of the enforcement agencies;

(b) issuing directions, for example, to the Environment Agency concerning applications or to meet various EC law obligations;

(c) exercising various discretionary powers, for example, in the designation of Special Protection Areas under the Habitats Directive;

(d) reviewing waste disposal plans and waste recycling plans. Following the re-election of New Labour in 2001, the Government re-structured a number of Government departments. The Department of Environment, Transport, and the Regions (DETR) was amalgamated with the Ministry of Agriculture, Fisheries and Food (MAFF) to form the Department of Environment, Food and Rural Affairs (DEFRA). This resulted in the separation of environmental protection and the planning system. Planning is now part of the Department of Transport, Local Government and the Regions (DTLR).

2.6.3 Other Government departments

Although the DoE is the lead department for environmental policy, other Government departments have a significant role to play. It is established Government policy that all Government departments are under a duty to ensure that environmental considerations are taken into account in the development of all policies and programmes. So, for example, MAFF is responsible for agriculture policy and has taken a number of steps to protect the environment as part of that policy. MAFF also has important responsibilities under the WRA 1991.

2.6.4 The Royal Commission on Environmental Pollution

The Royal Commission on Environmental Pollution was established in February 1970 as a standing body to 'advise on matters, both national and international, concerning the pollution of the environment; on the adequacy of research in this field; and the future possibilities of danger to the environment'. It is a permanent body made up of experts in environmental matters who are appointed on the advice of the Prime Minister.

The Royal Commission has played an extremely important role in the development of current environmental legislation, not least because of its expert advice and also because it has had the opportunity to give objective advice on different choices to be made/actions to be taken. The Royal Commission has published a number of reports, some of which are referred to in this book. The reports provide a valuable insight into a variety of environmental problems and invariably set the agenda for debate and consultation. The reports are intended to give advice to the Government but, in fact, they have been very influential on UK environmental policy.

2.6.5 Sewerage undertakers

The sewerage network is operated by private companies known as sewerage undertakers. Notwithstanding the fact that they operate as private companies, the sewerage undertakers are responsible for licensing discharges into public sewers through the system of trade effluent consents. The disposal of trade effluent into a sewer (through a drain or sewer) requires a consent under s 118 of the WIA 1991. A consent must be obtained by serving a notice on the sewerage undertaker.

2.6.6 Office of Water Services

The Office of Water Services (OFWAT) was established in 1989 following privatisation of the water supply industry. Its principle function is to regulate the water supply industry in 'the public interest'. Although OFWAT is not specifically an environmental body it is required to ensure that the water undertakers have regard to their general environmental duties as laid down in the WIA 1991.

2.6.7 The Health and Safety Executive

The Health and Safety Executive (HSE) is responsible for the administration of the HSWA 1974. However, the boundaries between health and safety of workers and protection of the environment are not always clear and the HSE in fact fulfils a number of functions related to environmental protection. In particular, the HSE is involved in the regulation of certain activities which if not carried out properly could have serious environmental consequences. These include the regulation of asbestos installations handling hazardous substances. In addition, the HSE acts as a statutory consultee in relation to applications for IPC authorisation and IPPC permits.

2.6.8 English Nature and the Countryside Council for Wales

Part VII of the EPA 1990 created the Nature Conservancy Council for England (known as English Nature) and the Countryside Council for Wales out of the former Nature Conservancy Council. English Nature operates in England and the Countryside Council operates in Wales. English Nature does not have any pollution control powers or means of enforcement. Instead, it acts as the Government's statutory body on nature conservation and is responsible for promoting nature conservation generally. The powers of English Nature are contained in the Wildlife and Countryside Act 1981 as amended.

2.6.9 The European Environmental Agency

The European Environment Agency (EEA) was set up in 1994 following the adoption by the Council of Ministers in May 1990 of Council Regulation (EEC) 1210/90. After considerable debate as to where it should be located it was eventually decided that it should be based in Copenhagen. The functions of the agency are as follows:

(a) to provide the Member States with objective, reliable and comparable information about the environment;

(b) to ensure that the public is properly informed about the state of the environment.

The Management Board of the EEA is made up of one representative from each Member State, two representatives from the European Commission and a further two designated by the European Parliament. However, membership of the EEA is not confined to Member States of the European Union (EU) and other non-EU countries may join.

The main criticism of the EEA, as it currently exists, is that it has no role to play in the enforcement of environmental law. Its role is limited essentially to that of gathering and disseminating information on the state of the environment. The EEA is assisted by the European Environment Information and Observation Network which was set up to assist in the collection of information throughout the Member States which effectively links the environmental networks of the Member States into a Community-wide network.

2.7 The role of the courts in the administration and enforcement of environmental law

2.7.1 The principal functions

The courts have three principal functions with regard to environmental litigation:

(a) an adjudicatory role;

(b) an interpretative role; and

(c) a supervisory role.

2.7.2 Adjudication

The chief function of the courts is to reach decisions on the merits of the cases which come before them. As we have endeavoured to explain in this book, much of environmental law is about the regulation of human activity and the principal vehicle which is used to regulate activities such as the discharge of polluting emissions and the use of resources (such as land for building purposes) is the Command and Control regulatory regime. Each regulatory regime is underpinned by criminal law offences, and to a lesser degree, civil powers to remediate environmental damage.

The courts are called upon to adjudicate on disputes involving the operation of regulatory regimes, be they prosecutions commenced by the regulators for criminal law offences or the use of civil powers by regulators to force those persons responsible for environmental damage to engage in 'clean-up' operations. The courts also adjudicate upon actions commenced by private persons. These actions may be civil actions, based on the common law, in order to compensate the claimant for damage to person or property, or they may comprise challenges to the decisions of regulators. In addition, private persons may take advantage of the criminal laws contained in the legislation establishing regulatory Command and Control regimes, to mount their own prosecutions of polluters.

Once the courts have adjudicated upon an environmental dispute, be it a criminal prosecution by the Environment Agency, or a civil action brought by a private individual, it will, on conviction in a criminal prosecution, impose a penalty, or, in the case of a civil action, make an award of compensation or other relief. The sentencing policy of the courts plays an important part in ensuring compliance with Command and Control regulation and it is to a consideration of this that we now turn.

2.7.3 Sentencing

Criticism has, for many years, been levelled at the minimal penalties imposed on defendants in criminal prosecutions arising out of breaches of environmental law. It is only relatively recently that significant financial penalties have been imposed on some defendants, nevertheless the perception persists that the courts, especially the magistrates' courts are too lenient.

In 1998, the Court of Appeal decision in *R v F Howe & Son (Engineers) Ltd* shed some light on sentencing policy. In *Howe*, the defendant appealed against a fine of £42,000 imposed upon it by the Crown Court on conviction of breaches of s 2(1) of the HSWA 1974 and reg 4(2) of the Electricity at Work Regulations 1989, which caused the death of a workman. The Court of Appeal observed that the level of fines imposed in health and safety cases was generally too low and it went on to set out a number of sentencing guidelines. In particular the court identified a number of factors which were relevant to fixing an appropriate penalty:

(a) although it is often a matter of chance, in a health and safety incident, whether death or injury results from breach of the law, where death is the consequence, courts should regard death as an aggravating feature of the offence and the penalty imposed on the defendant should reflect public concern at the unnecessary loss of life;

(b) a deliberate breach of health and safety legislation with a view to cutting costs or maximising profits will seriously aggravate the offence charged;

(c) a failure to heed warnings is a seriously aggravating feature of an offence;

(d) mitigating features include a prompt admission of responsibility and guilty plea, prompt action to remedy deficiencies after they are brought to the attention of the defendant, and a good safety record.

The court indicated that the same standards would be expected to be attained regardless of the size and resources of a defendant company. It would also be open to the defendant to make submissions to the court in regard to the level of the financial penalty to be imposed upon conviction and its ability to pay, provided it produced its accounts well before the hearing. Although the *Howe* case is a health and safety case it is likely to be an influential guideline in the sentencing of environmental crimes.

It is also significant that the Sentencing Advisory Panel have been actively investigating sentencing policy in regard to a number of pollution offences. These include: polluting controlled waters; treating, depositing, or disposing of waste without a waste management licence; carrying out a prescribed IPC process without a licence or in breach of licence conditions; and breach of the packaging recycling and recovery obligations. The Sentencing Advisory Panel recommend that a distinction in sentencing is made between individual defendants and companies. It proposes that the starting point for the sentencing of individuals should be the fine, in recognition of the fact that pollution offences are generally non-violent and often result from the failure to devote adequate resources to preventing a breach of the law. The panel recommends that the culpability of the defendant is assessed on the basis of how far the defendant's conduct fell below the requisite standard. In determining the culpability of the defendant it is recommended that the court has regard to: whether the offence was deliberate; whether the defendant broke the law in order to make a commercial profit; whether the relevant breach of the law is part of a pattern of offending; whether the defendant has ignored advice provided by the regulator; whether the defendant ignored concerns expressed by its employees; and, whether the defendant has special knowledge of the risks posed by its activities. The panel has proposed that the fine should reflect the ability of the defendant to pay: 'The fine should be substantial enough to have real economic impact which, together with the attendant bad publicity resulting from prosecution, will create sufficient pressure on management and shareholders to tighten regulatory compliance and change company policy.' In regard to smaller companies the panel noted that a large fine might have a crippling effect on the company, an adverse impact on the local economy, and interfere with the company's attempts to bring itself back into compliance with the law. In regard to companies who commit pollution offences, the courts are limited in regard to the sentences which they can impose. In virtually all cases, a fine is imposed. In the case of human offenders, in addition to the ubiquitous fine, the courts have a number of other sentencing options at their disposal, including the following: absolute discharge, conditional discharge, community service, probation, suspended sentence, disqualification under the Disqualification of Directors Act 1986 (in regard to company directors) and imprisonment. The use of disqualification is rare but was used in 2000 in regard to the conviction of the Managing Director of a pharmaceutical company who was disqualified for four years.

2.7.4 Interpretative role

The courts have an important role in the interpretation of words and phrases which appear in primary and secondary legislation. In addition they have a similar role in regard to the interpretation and application of common law principles in civil actions.

For example, the House of Lords has recently given the meaning of 'causing' in s 85 of the WRA 1991 a very strict interpretation in the context of a criminal offence whose purpose is to punish any person who causes pollution of controlled waters (see *Empress Cars (Arbertillery) Ltd v NRA* (1998)). Similarly, in *Cambridge Water Co Ltd v Eastern Counties Leather plc* (1994), the House of Lords gave detailed consideration to the application of a civil claim based on the common law torts of nuisance and the rule in *Rylands v Fletcher* (1868).

2.7.5 Supervisory role

The High Court, Court of Appeal and House of Lords exercise, in regard to public bodies such as regulators, a supervisory jurisdiction. This entails the consideration of judicial review challenges by persons who are aggrieved by the outcome of decisions made by public bodies. In a judicial review action the court reviews the process by which the decision was made in order to confirm that it was not made in an unlawful manner. In other words, the court supervises how the relevant administrative decision was arrived at. In an environmental context, judicial review challenges often relate to the granting of licenses, such as water pollution discharge consents, or decisions relating to the enforcement of the law (such as the Environment Agency choosing not to prosecute a polluter). Applications for judicial review are usually based on one or more of the following grounds.

2.7.5.1 Illegality
Under this heading it is alleged that a public body, such as the Environment Agency, has not acted in accordance with its legal powers, either because it misunderstood them, or because it has deliberately ignored them.

2.7.5.2 Procedural flaw
The public body fails to follow the correct procedure in reaching a decision.

2.7.5.3 Relevant and irrelevant considerations
The public body takes into account something which it should have disregarded or it fails to take into account something which it was required to take into account. This applies only where the matters considered or ignored are set out in or implied by statute.

2.7.5.4 Irrationality
This ground applies where no reasonable public body, which understood the relevant law and faced the same set of circumstances, could have acted in the way in which the public body in question has acted.

2.7.5.5 Procedural unfairness
Under this heading it is alleged that the process by which a decision has been reached by a public body is unfair. This could include failing to allow someone who has a 'legitimate expectation', arising either from an express promise by a

public authority or from the existence of a regular practice which the applicant can reasonably expect to continue, to participate in the decision making process, for example, by giving them an opportunity to make representations to the public body before it reaches its decision.

2.7.5.6 Improper delegation of powers

The public body has purported to delegate powers to someone which only it can exercise. For example, this might involve the attempted delegation of authority to make decisions relating to the grant or refusal of pollution licenses.

2.7.5.7 Who can bring a judicial review action?

In order to bring a judicial review action a person (individual, company, etc) must demonstrate that they have *locus standi*, or in other words, the right to bring the action. The test laid down for 'standing', as it is referred to, appears in Ord 53, r 3(7) of the Rules of the Supreme Court. The applicant must show 'sufficient interest in the matter to which the application relates'. An applicant whose direct personal interests have been affected by the decision of a public body will have standing to challenge the decision. In addition, the court may also allow a challenge by a person, group, or organisation acting in the public interest. Whether such a person, group, or organisation has standing depends upon a variety of factors including the importance of the legal issues at stake, the absence of any other responsible challenger, the nature of the alleged breach of duty against which the challenge is made, and the previous involvement and reputation of the applicant in regard to the issue which forms the basis of the challenge. Over the last few years the High Court has shown an increased willingness to grant standing to environmental organisations to enable them to challenge the decisions of regulators. In *R v HM Inspectorate of Pollution and Another ex p Greenpeace Ltd (No 2)* (1994) the court granted Greenpeace standing to challenge the decision of HMIP to grant a licence authorising the operational activities of a nuclear reprocessing plant because Greenpeace was 'an entirely responsible and respected body with a genuine concern for the environment … who, with its particular experience in environmental matters, its access to experts in the relevant realms of science and technology not to mention law, is able to mount a carefully selected, focused, relevant, and well argued challenge'.

2.7.5.8 Speed

Applications for judicial review must be made 'promptly'. This requirement means, in most cases, that the application must be lodged with the court within three months of the decision or activity which forms the basis of the complaint. The use of strict time limits enables developments with environmental impacts to proceed without the constant threat of challenge at a late stage in the projects' completion. In *R v Secretary of State for Trade and Industry ex p Greenpeace Ltd* (1998), leave to commence a judicial review action was refused because of undue delay. Laws J observed that 'the courts have very firmly stated that a judicial review applicant must proceed with particular urgency where third party interests are involved'.

2.7.5.9 Relief

Upon a successful challenge the court may make any of the following orders.

An Order of Certiorari cancels a decision of a public body which is invalid or has been made improperly. The court may order the matter be sent back to the body which made the original decision so that the matter may be reconsidered using the correct procedure. An Order of Mandamus compels a public body to carry out specified actions in accordance with the legal duties to which it is subject to. An Order of Prohibition restrains a public body from acting in a particular way.

The court may also make a declaration of the correct legal position and may award damages.

THE ADMINISTRATION AND ENFORCEMENT OF ENVIRONMENTAL LAW

The system of environmental regulatory control has gone through significant change as a result of the creation of the Environment Agency, which was established by the EA 1995 and which became operational in April 1996. The Environment Agency took over the following functions:

(a) the functions exercised by the NRA under the WRA 1991 and the Land Drainage Act 1991 and various other statutory provisions;

(b) the waste management functions exercised by the WRAs under Pt II of the EPA 1990 and the Control of Pollution (Amendment) Act 1989;

(c) HMIP's responsibilities under Pt I of the EPA 1990. It should be noted here that the LAAPC controls exercised by local authorities under Pt I of the EPA 1990 are retained by the local authorities;

(d) HMIP's functions relating to radioactive substances under the RSA 1993;

(e) certain enforcement functions under Pt I of the HSWA 1974;

(f) certain functions of the Secretary of State (these are listed in s 2(2) of the EA 1995).

In addition to the transfer of functions, the EA 1995 conferred certain new functions on the Environment Agency arising out of new provisions introduced in the said Act. These are:

(a) functions relating to contaminated land under s 57 of the EA 1995. The Environment Agency has specific powers relating to certain contaminated sites which have been designated as 'special sites' by a local authority;

(b) functions relating to air quality under Pt IV of the EA 1995.

Overall responsibility for the environment is vested within the DoE (now DEFRA) although other Government departments such as the Department of Transport also play a key role in environmental protection through the development of their policies.

The Secretary of State for the Environment plays a key role in regulating environmental protection. This involves, *inter alia:*

(a) dealing with appeals against decisions of the Environment Agency or the local authorities;

(b) issuing directions, for example, to the Environment Agency concerning applications or to meet various EC law obligations;

(c) preparing national strategies for air quality and waste management.

The local authority sector plays an important part in controlling pollution and environmental protection. Its main functions can be summarised as follows:

(a) responsibility for the planning control system which requires local planning authorities to take environmental considerations into account in the preparation of development plans and also in respect of planning applications. Planning authorities are also involved in Environmental Impact Assessments;

(b) district councils are responsible for investigating and abating statutory nuisances under Pt III of the EPA 1990. Local authorities may also decide to adopt the provisions of the Noise Act 1996 in which case they have responsibility for controlling night time noise nuisances;

(c) local authorities are responsible under the CAA 1993 for controlling emissions of dark smoke and can control smoke emissions through the creation of Smoke Control Areas;

(d) local authorities are responsible for authorising prescribed processes under Pt I of the EPA 1990 for LAAPC. This function is carried out by the district councils;

(e) responsibility as Hazardous Substances Authorities under the provisions of the Planning (Hazardous Substances) Act 1990.

A number of other agencies play an important role in the area of environmental protection. These include the:

(a) Royal Commission on Environmental Pollution;

(b) Office of Water Services;

(c) sewerage undertakers;

(d) the Nature Conservancy Council for England (English Nature) and the Welsh Countryside Council;

(e) HSE;

(f) European Environment Agency.

The courts have three principal functions or roles in regard to environmental criminal prosecutions and environmental civil actions which come before them. These roles comprise: (i) an adjudicatory role; (ii) an interpretative role; and (iii) a supervisory role.

CHAPTER 3

WATER POLLUTION

3.1 Introduction

This chapter is concerned with the regulation of water pollution and water quality. Without pollution controls water would become grossly polluted and unusable for a wide range of human and non-human needs. Humans require clean water for drinking and other uses such as food production and agriculture. Once water has been used it is returned to the aquatic environment as an effluent. These effluent discharges into surface waters and sewers must be regulated so as to maintain a sufficiently high quality of the receiving waters to meet our needs. These needs vary according to the use which is made of the available surface and ground waters. Thus, an industrial discharge of effluent into a river will be tightly controlled if there is a fishery downstream of the industrial plant, or water is abstracted from the river for human consumption.

The control of water pollution through Command and Control legislative regulation has a longer history than similar environmental controls over waste disposal or atmospheric pollution, nevertheless, it shares a basic and recognisable structure with other environmental media based controls. That structure is reflected in the arrangement of the material in this chapter, the majority of which concerns the *public regulation of pollution generated by businesses and individuals*.

3.2 Control over water pollution: an overview

The WRA 1991, as amended by the Environment Act (EA) 1995, provides the main regulatory control framework relating to the prevention and control of water pollution in England and Wales. The Environment Agency is responsible for controlling pollution of 'controlled waters' and for achieving the improvements in water quality required in order to meet statutory water quality objectives.

The control of water pollution is exercised by the Environment Agency through a system of authorised discharge consents (licence). Any discharge made into controlled waters must be authorised by the Environment Agency (with the exception of discharges made from Integrated Pollution Control (IPC) and Integrated Pollution Prevention and Control (IPPC) licenced processes). The system of consents enables the Environment Agency to control, by means of conditions, the nature and volume of contaminants discharged into surface and ground waters in order to achieve improvements in water quality. Discharges made without consent, provided they are poisonous, noxious or polluting, or in breach of the conditions attached to a discharge consent, constitute criminal offences but prosecution does not automatically follow. The Environment Agency employs inspectors who have wide ranging powers to secure compliance. In the event that there is a discharge into controlled waters without consent or in breach of consent conditions, the Environment Agency has the power to prosecute. Various statutory defences exist. The fines for water pollution offences may be unlimited if a case is dealt with by the Crown Court and, indeed, some of the fines have been very high. In addition, under s 161 of the WRA 1991, the Environment Agency has the power to take action to avoid pollution of controlled water or to 'clean up' after an incident. It can then recover its reasonable costs from those responsible for the pollution. The costs of clean-up may well far exceed any fine imposed by a court.

3.3 Polluting substances and polluting activities

In order to comprehend the development and 'shape' of regulatory water pollution controls we need to have some understanding of the activities which are chiefly responsible for water pollution and the substances which are discharged, by those activities, into the aquatic environment. There are four key questions: (i) which activities are the main polluters?; (ii) what substances do these activities discharge into the aquatic environment?; (iii) what properties do these substances possess which are problematic?; and (iv) what factors will affect the impact of such pollutants upon the waters into which they are discharged?

The main water polluters are industry and commerce. According to various estimates there are between 75,000–100,000 water pollution discharge consents granted to licence holders entitling them to discharge substances into the aquatic environment. In addition to these 'consented', legitimate, discharges, industrial activity is associated with a large number of accidental spillages of chemical substances, such as oils and fuels. Every individual is also partly responsible for the discharge of treated sewage, from the numerous sewage treatment works spread throughout the UK, into rivers and streams. Pollution from agriculture is also problematic, especially in regard to fertilisers, and pesticides, which 'run off' the land when it rains, and are carried into our river systems. In addition, chemicals used in sheep dipping operations may be allowed to pollute both surface and groundwaters. Run-off from mining waste tips (slag heaps), which are rich in metals, also cause pollution. Pollutants may leach out from the base of waste sites, especially old landfills, and cause contamination of groundwaters. Abandoned mines also cause pollution when old mine workings fill up with water, become contaminated and then discharge into surface waters.

The substances which, when discharged into the aquatic environment, cause pollution are those which have one or more of the following properties:

(a) they deoxygenate water, for example, agricultural slurry and milk;

(b) they cause eutrophication, for example, fertilisers which accelerate algal growth;

(c) they block out light which disrupts plant growth, for example, suspended solids, such as silty water pumped out of a construction site and discharged into a stream;

(d) they are toxic to humans, plants and animals, for example, pesticides and heavy metals;

(e) they cause diseases, for example, water borne infections such as cryptosporidium;

(f) they damage amenity, for example, dyes from the textile industry and detergents (causing foaming); and

(g) they have undergone change, due to the presence of energy, for example, water which is abstracted from a river in order to provide cooling water for a power station. The water is heated in the cooling (energy exchange) process and is then re-introduced into the river where it may have an adverse impact upon the ecology of the river system.

The impact of polluting substances and energy upon the waters into which they are discharged will vary with a variety of factors including:

(a) the rate of flow (to disperse and dilute the pollutant) of the receiving water system;

(b) the volume of the receiving water system;

(c) the geology and topography of the relevant area in which the river system is situated (for example, the impact of an agricultural spillage of slurry, which deoxygenates a river, will be mitigated by the presence of a downstream waterfall which re-oxygenates the river);

(d) upstream or downstream uses of a river system (for example, the presence of urban and industrial areas discharging pollutants into a river upstream of a polluter, or the presence of a sensitive area, such as a Site of Special Scientific Interest, downstream of a polluter).

Whilst the public regulatory apparatus of the WRA 1991 has the primary role to play in the control of water pollution, the private regulatory activities of individuals and environmental groups are also relevant. Such persons use private prosecution, judicial review of regulatory decision making, and common law tortious actions to achieve their objectives. In the context of the 'private' regulation of pollution it is important to bear in mind the differing aims of the criminal and civil law and the differing aims of the public regulators and ordinary individuals or regulated companies.

Private prosecutions, based on criminal law offences contained in the relevant primary and secondary legislation, are concerned with punishing the polluter and enforcing compliance with the law through the deterrent effect of prosecution. Civil actions are, in the context of environmental pollution, concerned with obtaining compensation for damage to property or person (personal injury) caused by pollution.

Regulatory agencies, such as the Environment Agency and local authorities, 'police' compliance with the law laid down in Command and Control legislation (for example, WRA 1991, Environmental Protection Act (EPA) 1990 and EA 1995). The objectives of individuals, environmental groups and companies in their use of environmental law vary. Environmental groups may mount a private prosecution against a polluter if it disagrees with the exercise of regulatory discretion not to prosecute. An individual may commence an action against a polluter, using the tort of nuisance, to compensate him for pollution damage to his property. A regulated business may wish to challenge, by way of a judicial review action, a decision by the regulator to refuse an appeal against service of an Enforcement Notice.

In a civil law context possession of and compliance with the conditions of a water pollution discharge consent will not provide a defence in a civil action brought by any person against the holder of a water pollution discharge consent (s 100(b) of the WRA 1991).

3.4 The historical development of the public regulation of water pollution

Legislative attempts to prevent and control water pollution date back to the 1860s. Since that time, various Government administrations have introduced new controls and have established new criminal offences. The following section is intended to provide a very brief overview of the history of those controls. The first Act of Parliament to attempt to control water pollution was the Rivers Pollution Prevention Act of 1876. Although there had been previous Acts which had dealt with water pollution, they were primarily aimed at improving public health (the Public Health Act 1875), or the productivity of salmon fishing (the Salmon Fisheries Act 1861). The Rivers Pollution Prevention Act 1876 created several offences in relation to the discharge or dumping of certain specified solid matter into any stream; discharges of solid or liquid sewerage matter into any stream; or discharging poisonous, noxious or polluting liquid from any factory or manufacturing process. The Rivers Pollution Prevention Act 1876 also introduced a number of defences, including the defence that the 'best practicable means' had been employed to render pollutants harmless. Despite the creation of these offences the Act was regarded as ineffective.

The Rivers Pollution Prevention Act 1876 was replaced by the Rivers (Prevention of Pollution) Act 1951. This Act created the offence of causing or knowingly permitting any poisonous, noxious or polluting matter to enter into a stream and it also introduced the first system of discharge consents. It required all new discharge outlets to have a licence. However, any existing discharge outlets were not required to have a licence unless they were altered, or the composition of the discharge itself was altered or increased. The Rivers (Prevention of Pollution) Act 1961 extended the consent procedure to cover certain types of discharges that were operational before the 1951 Act, thus extending the coverage of the new licensing procedure. The 1961 Act also provided a much stricter regime insofar as it removed certain defences that had been available under the 1951 Act. The Control of Pollution Act 1974 repealed both the 1951 and 1961 Acts.

3.4.1 The 1991 Water Acts

The starting point in considering the current legislative controls is the Water Act (WA) 1989 which, although superseded by consolidating legislation in 1991, was the Act which established the National Rivers Authority (NRA). It also led to the privatisation of water supplies and sewerage services. In 1991, Parliament passed five Acts which aimed to consolidate the various legislative provisions relating to all aspects of the water industry and control of water pollution. The main Acts were the Water Industry Act (WIA) 1991 and the Water Resources Act (WRA) 1991. The provisions of the WRA 1991 provide the main framework for control of water quality and quantity and are considered in detail below. The WIA 1991 (and WIA 1999) contain provisions relating to water supply and sewerage services; however, some provisions are related to environmental protection, particularly in relation to the controls over the quality of drinking water. The EA 1995 resulted in the transfer of the NRA's water pollution functions to the Environment Agency.

3.4.2 Other statutory controls

In addition to the controls within the main water legislation, various other statutes contain provisions which relate to the control and prevention of water pollution or the maintenance of water quality standards. These include:

(a) the EA 1995;

(b) the EPA 1990;

(c) the Salmon and Freshwater Fisheries Act (SFFA) 1975;

(d) the Land Drainage Act 1994.

3.5 The water industry and the WIA 1991

The water industry covers a wide range of diverse activities, all of which share a common involvement in the water cycle, ranging from the collection and treatment of water and its supply to the provision of sewers and sewage works. It also covers those bodies involved in the control of pollution, the regulation and control of fishing, navigation, flood defence, land drainage, conservation and recreational activities.

The water industry has undergone many changes since the 1940s, primarily as a result of reorganisation and privatisation. Before 1948, the responsibility for water supply and also sewage disposal fell to the local authorities. In 1948, the River Boards Act established 32 River Boards which were organised on a catchment area basis. The River Boards acquired responsibility for most of the activities in the water industry including water supply and sewage disposal. In 1963, the River Boards were taken over by 27 River Authorities as a consequence of the WRA 1963. The River Authorities had responsibility, among other things, for pollution control. However, it was not really until 1973 that there was any real attempt to achieve an integrated control of the industry. The WA 1973 established 10 Regional Water Authorities which took charge of managing the various water functions in the relevant river basin areas. The WA 1973, however, did permit the continued existence of a number of statutory private water companies.

Although the WA 1973 was intended to provide a more coherent framework for control, it did not tackle one of the main problems that had thus so far existed in the industry. The regional water authorities had responsibility for pollution control but were at the same time themselves major polluters in their capacity as operators of sewage disposal works. This 'gamekeeper and poacher' scenario gave rise to a great deal of criticism of the water industry. Consequently, the industry went through further reorganisation in 1989 with the WA 1989, which led to the privatisation of the water supply and sewerage services and the creation of the NRA. In 1991, the Government consolidated the legislation controlling the water industry and now the WIA 1991 provides for the regulation of water supply and sewerage.

The position today is that the supply of water and the provision of sewerage services rests with privatised water service companies (known as water undertakers and sewerage undertakers). In addition, there are also water companies which are only responsible for the supply of water and play no role in relation to sewerage services. The office of the Director General of Water Services was established to regulate the activities of the privatised water industry.

3.6 Controlled waters

The pollution controls which are contained in the WRA 1991 apply only in respect of waters defined as 'controlled waters' and the Environment Agency *can only exercise its controls over pollution in relation to those waters*. Section 104 of the WRA 1991 provides a definition of controlled waters which includes:

(a) inland fresh waters – including lakes, ponds, rivers or water courses above the fresh water limit;

(b) ground waters – that is waters contained in underground strata: wells, boreholes and aquifers;

(c) coastal waters – including all estuarine waters up to the fresh water limits of rivers and water courses;

(d) territorial waters – the seas within the three mile 'limit'.

These terms are defined much more fully in s 104 as follows:

> Inland fresh waters means the waters of any relevant lake or pond or of so much of any relevant river or watercourse as is above the fresh water limit. 'Relevant lake or pond' means any lake or pond, including reservoirs, which, whether it is natural, artificial, above or below ground, discharges into a relevant river or watercourse or into another lake or pond which is itself a relevant lake or pond. The Secretary of State is empowered to provide by order that any lake or pond which does not discharge into a relevant river or watercourse or into a relevant lake or pond is to be treated as a relevant lake or pond, or to be treated as if it were not a relevant lake or pond as the case may be.

> A 'watercourse' includes all rivers, streams, ditches, drains, cuts, culverts, dikes, sluices, sewers and passages through which water flows, except mains and other pipes which belong to the authority or a water undertaker or are used by a water undertaker or any other person for the purpose only of providing a supply of water to any premises.

> 'Relevant river or watercourse' means any river or watercourse, including an underground river and an artificial river or watercourse, which is neither a public sewer nor a sewer or drain which drains into a public sewer. The Secretary of State has the power to provide by order that a watercourse of a specified description is to be treated for these purposes as if it were not a relevant river or watercourse.

> The 'fresh water limit', in relation to any river or watercourse, means the place for the time being shown as the fresh water limit of that river or watercourse in the latest map deposited by the Secretary of State with the authority for that purpose.

> 'Ground waters' are defined as any waters which are contained in underground strata. An underground strata means strata subjacent to the surface of any land.

> 'Coastal waters' means waters which are within the area which extends landward from the baselines of the territorial sea as far as the limit of the

highest tide or, in the case of the waters of any relevant river or watercourse, as far as the fresh water limit of the river or watercourse, together with the waters of any enclosed dock which adjoins waters within that area. The relevant territorial waters are those waters which extend seaward for three miles from the baselines from which the breadth of the territorial sea adjacent to England and Wales is measured. This definition is subject to the power of the Secretary of State to provide by order that any particular area of territorial sea adjacent to England and Wales is to be treated as if it were an area of relevant territorial waters.

3.7 The regulators' statutory water pollution responsibilities

3.7.1 The NRA

Between 1989 and 1 April 1996, the NRA was the main regulatory body with responsibility for controlling water pollution, although it shared responsibility with Her Majesty's Inspectorate of Pollution (HMIP) in relation to those industrial processes that are governed by the IPC regime under Pt I of the EPA 1990. By virtue of s 2(1)(a)(i) of the EA 1995 the water related (including pollution control) functions of the NRA were transferred to the Environment Agency and the NRA ceased to exist, as did the IPC functions of HMIP which were also transferred to the Environment Agency. Consequently, the Environment Agency is now the primary regulatory body which is concerned with water pollution, nevertheless it is useful to consider at this juncture the role of the NRA during the period 1989 to 1996.

The NRA was set up in 1989 by the WA 1989 to provide integrated management of river basins and the water environment in England and Wales. The constitution, functions and powers of the NRA were prescribed by the WRA 1991. The NRA was a body corporate, unlike HMIP which was part of the Department of the Environment (DoE). When the NRA was established it inherited the functions of the water authorities relating to pollution control, water resource management, flood defence, fisheries, navigation and conservation and recreation. The responsibilities of the NRA as laid down in s 2 of the WRA 1991 were as follows:

(a) water resources (Pt II of the WRA 1991);

(b) water pollution (Pt III of the WRA 1991);

(c) flood defence and land drainage (by virtue of Pt IV of the WRA 1991 and other enactments);

(d) fisheries (by virtue of Pt V of the WRA 1991 and other enactments);

(e) navigation authority, harbour authority or conservancy authority which were transferred to the NRA by virtue of Chapter V of Pt III of the WA 1989 (and other provisions);

(f) functions assigned to the NRA by any other enactment.

The NRA was required by s 16 of the WRA 1991 to promote the conservation and enhancement of the natural beauty and amenity of inland and coastal waters and of land associated with such waters; the conservation of flora and fauna which are dependent on the aquatic environment; and the use of such waters and land for recreational purposes. The way in which the NRA was required to carry out this duty was described in the Code of Practice on Conservation, Access and Recreation which was issued pursuant to s 18(1) of the WRA 1991, and also in the Water and Sewerage (Conservation and Recreation) (Code of Practice) Order 1989 SI 1989/1152. The NRA also had a duty to consider water supply issues and by virtue of s 15 it had to have regard, when exercising its powers, to the duties that are imposed on any water undertakers or sewage undertakers by Pts II–IV of the WIA 1991. During its period of operation the NRA established itself as a strong regulator, willing to prosecute offenders where necessary.

3.7.2 The Environment Agency

By virtue of s 2 of the EA 1995 the functions of the NRA under the WRA 1991 and various other statutory provisions were transferred to the Environment Agency. In addition the water pollution control functions exercised by HMIP under the IPC regime (Pt I of the EPA 1990) were also transferred to the Environment Agency, giving the Environment Agency overall control over water resources and water pollution. For a further discussion of the details of the transfer of functions and the reasons for the establishment of the Environment Agency, see Chapter 2.

3.7.3 Environment Agency duties in respect of water

Section 6 of the EA 1995 obliges the Environment Agency, to the extent that it considers desirable, generally to promote the:

(a) conservation and enhancement of the natural beauty and amenity of inland and coastal waters and land surrounding them;

(b) the conservation of flora and fauna which are dependent upon the aquatic environment;

(c) the use of such waters and land for recreational purposes taking into account the needs of the chronically sick or disabled.

In terms of water resources the Environment Agency is also obliged to take all such action as it may from time to time consider (in accordance with any directions issued by the Secretary of State) to be either necessary or expedient to conserve, redistribute or generally augment water resources in England and Wales and also to secure the proper use of water resources. These duties are described as being 'without prejudice' to the Environment Agency's other environmental duties under s 7 of the EA 1995.

3.8 Discharge consent licences

The licence is the primary vehicle through which the quality of the aquatic environment is regulated. A licence, issued by the Environment Agency (and referred to as a 'discharge consent') is required to authorise the following activities:

(a) discharging trade or sewage effluent into 'controlled waters';

(b) discharging trade or sewage effluent through a pipe from land into the sea beyond the three mile territorial limit of coastal waters;

(c) discharging trade or sewage effluent into controlled waters which are subject to a s 86 of the WRA 1991 prohibition.

The licensing system is underpinned by the criminal law offences contained in s 85 of the WRA 1991.

The Environment Agency is empowered to issue consents in relation to any discharge of trade or sewage effluent into controlled waters. The practical reality of these provisions is that a discharger must obtain a consent for each discharge. Many discharge consents relate to sewage treatment works. The WRA 1991 provides that a person will not have committed an offence under s 85 if the discharge is carried out in accordance with the conditions included in the consent. The detailed provisions relating to the granting of discharge consents are contained in Sched 10 to the Act. (It should be noted that the EA 1995 amended Sched 10 entirely.)

3.8.1 Applying for a discharge consent licence

Section 88 of the WRA 1991 provides that applications for discharge consents are made in accord with Sched 10 to the Act and the Control of Pollution (Applications, Appeals and Registers) Regulations 1996 SI 1996/2971. The provisions of Sched 10 have been replaced with a completely new Sched 10 by virtue of the EA 1995.

An application for a discharge consent under the WRA 1991 has to be made to the Environment Agency on the prescribed form accompanied by any such information that the Environment Agency may reasonably require or any information prescribed by the Secretary of State. Supplying false information is a criminal offence (s 206 of the WRA 1991). If the Environment Agency requires any further information from the applicant it can serve a notice on the applicant to that effect. Section 1(3) of the schedule states that a failure to provide information requested will not invalidate the application, however, s 3(3) states that where a person has failed to comply with his obligation to provide further information the Environment Agency may refuse to proceed with the application. The Environment Agency has four months from the date on which the application was submitted to reach a decision unless a longer period is agreed with the applicant. If a decision is not reached within four months or the agreed period then the application is deemed to have been refused.

3.8.2 Consultation and publicity requirements

Schedule 10 of the WRA 1991 also deals with the consultation and publicity requirements. Previously details of applications were required to be published by the NRA in both the *London Gazette* and in a local newspaper. Schedule 10 as amended by the EA 1995 states that applications must be advertised by, or on behalf, of the applicant in such a manner as may be prescribed in Regulations made by the Secretary of State. The relevant regulations are the Control of Pollution (Applications, Appeals and Registers) Regulations 1996 SI 1996/2971.

The 1996 Regulations specify that the application must be advertised in a local newspaper and in the *London Gazette*. In addition, the applicant must notify relevant local authorities and water service companies. The Environment Agency has a discretion to dispense with publicity where it appears that the discharge will have 'no appreciable effect' on the controlled waters into which the substance or substances are discharged. DoE Circular 17/84 provides guidance on the circumstances in which a discharge will have no appreciable effect on the receiving waters.

The Environment Agency has to allow a period of six weeks for consultees to have the opportunity to submit their representations back to the Environment Agency and the Environment Agency is then required to consider any representations made, including any made by the public. The Secretary of State has the power to exempt any class of application from these consultation requirements.

3.8.3 Discharge consent conditions

On receipt of an application for a discharge consent the Environment Agency is under a duty to consider whether the application should be granted, either unconditionally or subject to conditions, or refused. As stated above, a decision should normally be given within four months. The Environment Agency may refuse to deal with an application if the applicant has not provided all the required information or if the application is not accompanied by the appropriate fee. As far as fees are concerned a charge is made in respect of each discharge (with the exception of minor discharges below certain thresholds). A further annual charge may also be payable by the consent holder. Consents may be granted subject to such conditions as the Environment Agency may think fit.

Conditions may relate to:

(a) the composition of the proposed discharge, especially in regard to Biochemical Oxygen demand (BOD), toxicity and suspended solids;

(b) volume;

(c) rate of flow;

(d) position of discharge pipe/outlet;

(e) provision of monitoring and metering equipment;

(f) sampling, recording, and provision of information to the Environment Agency.

The conditions contained in each discharge consent will reflect the quality of the waters into which the effluent is discharged. Therefore conditions will be strict if there is a fishery or drinking water abstraction point downstream of the discharge point.

Currently discharge consent conditions tend to fix maximum numerical limits on the substances which make up the effluent discharge, however, at some point in the future discharge consents may be based on the toxicity (that is, the toxic impact of the discharge on the receiving waters) of the discharge.

Any breach of the numerical limits detailed in the discharge consent conditions will be an offence (s 85(6) of the WRA 1991), but it is unlikely that the Environment Agency will prosecute isolated, 'technical' breaches of discharge consent conditions.

It is possible for the Environment Agency to specify, via a condition, the installation of abatement technology to pre-treat the effluent before it is discharged into controlled waters. The use of discharge consent conditions to compel pre-treatment of the discharge is rare, but note the biological pre-treatment required by the Urban Waste Water Treatment Directive, and the policy preference is for the discharger to have 'ownership' and control of the technology employed to meet consent conditions.

In reaching a decision upon whether or not to grant a discharge consent, and the conditions to be included in the consent, the Environment Agency must have regard to all relevant considerations. If the Environment Agency fails to do this its decision may be challenged by way of a judicial review application, although in practice, an appeal is more likely and is cheaper. The considerations which the Environment Agency must have regard to include:

(a) any relevant water quality standards and water quality objectives (see s 83 of the WRA 1991), in regard to the waters into which substances are discharged;

(b) the impact of the discharge on downstream users (for example, a water company abstraction point where water is abstracted for drinking use, agricultural uses such as irrigation, fisheries, and any sensitive ecological sites such as Sites of Special Scientific Interest);

(c) the 'cocktail' effect of the discharge when combined with current and future upstream and downstream discharges;

(d) the Environment Agency's general and specific (water pollution) environmental duties contained in the EA 1995;

(e) the responses received by the Environment Agency from consultees and members of the public in regard to the discharge consent application;

(f) any relevant European Community (EC) standards relating to both the nature of the proposed discharge and the quality of the receiving waters;

(g) any relevant EC directive, such as the Hazardous Substance Directive (76/464/EEC), concerning the elimination or minimisation of certain substances discharged into the aquatic environment.

Discharges which are made 'under and in accordance with' the relevant consent will be able to take advantage of the s 88 of the WRA 1991 defence, however, if any discharge contains substances not specified in the consent then this will constitute a breach of s 85(6) of the WRA 1991. Most consents include conditions excluding, and therefore outlawing, the discharge of any substance not referred to in the consent. Where such a condition applies to a sewerage consent (a consent relating to a sewage works) the condition will be ineffective except to the extent that it was 'reasonably practicable' for the sewerage undertaker to exclude non-consented substances. This reflects the special problems encountered by sewerage undertakers where the design of the sewerage system itself prevents the undertaker from controlling all substances which are present in, and discharged into, controlled waters. For example, a torrential downpour, may cause an overflow which results in untreated sewage entering controlled waters. If the presence of the unconsented substance is due to the illegal introduction or disposal of substances into the sewer which the undertaker cannot treat then the undertaker may take advantage of the special defence for sewerage undertakers provided by s 87(2) of the WRA 1991.

3.8.4 Appeals

Appeals against Environment Agency licensing decisions are made to the Secretary of State (s 91 of the WRA 1991). Appeals are heard by Planning Inspectors and the Secretary of State is only involved in important appeals. A person can appeal to the Secretary of State against: the Environment Agency's refusal to grant a consent; against the conditions in the consent; against a variation; or against revocation. The Secretary of State has four months within which to determine the appeal and failure to make a decision within that period will mean that the appeal is deemed to have been refused. Appeals are complete rehearings of the original Environment Agency decision. The relevant appeal procedures are detailed in the Control of Pollution (Applications, Appeals and Registers) Regulations 1996 SI 1996/2971.

3.8.5 Reviewing discharging consents

Schedule 10, para 7 of the WRA 1991 states that the Environment Agency *may* from time to time review a discharge consent. Where the Environment Agency has reviewed a consent, it has, if necessary, the power to vary the conditions of the consent, revoke the consent, or impose conditions on consents which have been granted unconditionally.

3.8.6 Revocation and variation of discharge consents

The original consent will state a period, which must not be less than four years, within which the Environment Agency cannot vary or revoke the consent. Prior to the amendments contained in the EA 1995 a consent could not be varied within a two year period. Variation or revocation within that stated period can only occur with the agreement of the consent holder. However, after that period, the Environment Agency can exercise its powers to vary or revoke a consent. The Secretary of State also has the power to direct the Environment Agency to vary or revoke a consent (see Sched 10, para 9).

Generally no compensation is paid upon variation or revocation of a discharge consent, but compensation is payable if the Secretary of State makes a direction requiring a variation because of human health or nature conservation considerations.

The power to vary discharge consents is necessary for the following (non-exhaustive list of) reasons: to take account of changes in scientific knowledge which reveal new risks; to take account of the presence of new businesses discharging pollutants into controlled waters; and, to take account of changes in the law, such as the introduction of a new EC directive.

3.8.7 Weaknesses in the discharge consent licensing system

One of the main weaknesses of the discharge consent scheme under the WRA 1991 is that it only applies to specific identifiable discharges from a known spot, that is, through a pipe. Other more diffuse sources of pollution such as agricultural run-off and accidental spillages cannot easily be controlled by the discharge consent system, although criminal liability may occur in such circumstances.

3.8.8 Section 86 Prohibition Notices

The Environment Agency can serve notice (under s 86 of the WRA 1991) on a person who is discharging into controlled waters but who does not require a licence to authorise the discharge, prohibiting the discharge or prohibiting the continuation of the discharge. Alternatively, the notice may prohibit the discharge unless certain conditions are observed. It is an offence to discharge in contravention of the terms of a Prohibition Notice. This device is used to regulate selected discharges which do not require, in most cases, to be controlled by the licensing process. Prohibition Notices may be used to control the following discharges: soakaways from trade premises, discharges from storm drains and substances prescribed by regulations.

3.8.9 Water quality and discharge consent licences

The ability to assess and classify (categorise) the quality of controlled waters is an important aspect of the WRA 1991 regulatory regime since it provides the Environment Agency with a benchmark which will enable it to plan any necessary changes in discharge licence conditions.

The quality of the waters into which a polluting substance is discharged will form a key consideration in regard to the exact conditions incorporated into an individual water pollution discharge consent. If the quality of the receiving waters is high and downstream users require that quality standard to be maintained, for example, because they own fishing rights, then the conditions attached to the consent will be strict.

In the late 1970s the National Water Council (NWC) developed a non-statutory water classification scheme as a guide to the setting of river quality objectives (see below). This scheme has been superseded by a statutory scheme (see ss 82–84 of the WRA 1991) but provides a useful insight into the link between water quality and water usage.

3.8.9.1 The NWC water classification system

The NWC water classification system reflected potential uses of water and provided for the following broad classes:

(a) Good Quality – class 1a – water of high quality suitable for potable supply abstractions; game or other high class fisheries; high amenity value.

(b) Good Quality – class 1b – water of less high quality than class 1a but usable for substantially the same purposes.

(c) Fair Quality – class 2 – waters suitable for potable supply after advanced treatment; supporting reasonably good course fisheries; moderate amenity value.

(d) Poor Quality – class 3 – waters which are polluted to an extent that fish are absent or only sporadically present; may be used for low grade industrial abstraction purposes; considerable potential for further use if cleaned up.

(e) Bad Quality – class 4 – waters which are grossly polluted and are likely to cause nuisance.

3.8.9.2 Statutory water quality standards

It was in fact the WA 1989 which introduced a system for setting statutory water quality standards and objectives but the relevant provisions are now to be found in ss 82–84 of the WRA 1991.

Section 82 of the WRA 1991 enables the Secretary of State to make regulations which classify controlled waters into categories which reflect the standard of quality and the uses to which the water can be put, for example, drinking, bathing and fishing. The regulations specify the standard the waters must attain in order to fall within each classification. In accordance with this power, and also to implement EC directives in this area, a number of regulations have already been made but the system is by no means complete. The classification of water is necessary before water quality objectives (under s 83) can be established. The criteria specified in regulations made under s 82 in relation to any classification of water must consist of one or more of the following requirements:

(a) general requirements as to the purpose for which the waters to which the classification is applied are to be suitable (in other words water may be classified according to the use to which it will be put);

(b) specific requirements as to the substances that are to be present in or absent from the water and as to the concentrations of substances which are or can be present in the water;

(d) specific requirements as to the other characteristics of those waters.

The following regulations have been introduced under s 82:

(a) Surface Water Classification Regulations 1989 SI 1989/1148 and the Surface Waters (Abstraction for Drinking Water) (Clarification) Regulations 1996 SI 1996/3001. These regulations give effect to the EC Abstraction Directive (75/440/EEC) and prescribe a system for classifying waters according to their suitability for abstraction as drinking water;

(b) Surface Water (Dangerous Substances) (Classification) Regulations 1989, 1992, 1997 and 1998 SI 1989/2286, SI 1992/337, SI 1997/2560 and SI 1998/389, which give effect to the EC Dangerous Substances Directive

(76/464/EEC) and its daughter directives by prescribing a system for classifying inland, estuarine and coastal waters according to the presence in them of concentrations of certain dangerous substances. The regulations list a number of dangerous substances and state the concentration of each which should not be exceeded in fresh or marine waters;

(c) Bathing Waters (Classification) Regulations 1991 SI 1991/1597, which give effect to the Bathing Waters Directive (76/160/EEC) and which prescribe a system for classifying relevant territorial waters, coastal water and inland waters which are bathing waters;

(d) Surface Waters (River Ecosystem) (Classification) Regulations 1994 SI 1994/1057. Unlike the aforementioned regulations, the River Ecosystem Regulations do not implement the provisions of an EC directive. The Regulations lay down a system of classifying inland freshwaters which are relevant rivers or water courses.

(e) The Surface Waters (Fishlife) (Classification) Regulations 1997 SI 1997/1331 and the Surface Waters (Shellfish) (Classification) Regulations 1997 SI 1997/1332 which prescribe systems for classifying freshwater fish waters and shellfish waters.

3.8.9.3 Statutory water quality objectives

Once a range of classifications has been established under s 82, the Secretary of State will set a Statutory Water Quality Objective (SWQO) for each stretch of controlled waters. The SWQO established for each body of controlled waters will incorporate a water classification (and the water quality standards referred to in the classification regulations) as a target to be attained by the Environment Agency. In turn the Environment Agency is under a duty (s 84 of the WRA 1991) to exercise its functions, especially in regard to discharge consents, to achieve and maintain SWQOs. The Environment Agency risks a judicial review challenge if it does not exercise its powers (for example, in regard to the grant and variation of discharge consents) in ways which will achieve the SWQOs as far as practicable.

3.8.9.4 River quality improvements

Studies carried out in 1999 reveal continuing improvements in the quality of surface waters in the UK. 95% of Britain's rivers are rated good or fair. These statistics represent a 3% improvement on 1990 studies.

3.8.10 Powers of inspection

The powers of inspection and entry are now contained within s 108 of the EA 1995. These powers have been dealt with more fully in Chapter 2. The powers listed in s 108 are exercisable in respect of the Environment Agency's water pollution functions and can be used for one or more of the following purposes:

(a) determining whether any pollution control legislation has been complied with;

(b) for exercising or performing its pollution control functions;

(c) determining whether, and if so, how such a function should be exercised.

The powers include the following:

(a) enter at any reasonable time (or in an emergency at any time) any premises which the inspector believes it is necessary for him to enter;

(b) make such examination and investigation as may be necessary in the circumstances;

(c) carry out inspections, measurements, tests;

(d) take photographs and make recordings as necessary;

(e) remove samples of water, effluent, land or articles;

(f) carry out experimental borings;

(g) install and operate monitoring equipment.

3.9 Water pollution offences

3.9.1 Criminal liability underpins the WRA 1991

The WRA 1991 discharge consent licensing system is underpinned by a number of offences, the majority of which are contained in s 85 of the WRA 1991. The offences are targeted at two types of polluting activity – (i) discharging polluting matter into controlled waters in circumstances in which the discharger has no licence authorising its discharge and (ii) discharges which are in breach of the conditions of the dischargers' licence.

Strictly speaking the WRA 1991 regulatory regime *does not require* all persons who discharge substances into the aquatic environment to obtain a discharge consent prior to making the discharge. The regulatory system uses the criminal law, especially the threat of prosecution, as a tool to encourage dischargers to obtain licences authorising their discharges into controlled waters. Thus, if you have obtained a discharge consent licence from the Environment Agency and are complying with its terms, you will have a complete defence to a s 85 of the WRA 1991 prosecution. If you have not obtained a licence, then your only hope is likely to be that your discharge was not 'poisonous, noxious or polluting'. The main offences underpinning the WRA 1991 are to be found in s 85 of the WRA 1991.

3.9.2 Section 85 of the WRA 1991

A person contravenes s 85 of the WRA 1991 if he causes or knowingly permits:

(a) any poisonous, noxious or polluting matter or any solid waste matter to enter controlled waters;

(b) any matter, other than trade effluent or sewage effluent, to enter controlled waters by being discharged from a drain or sewer in contravention of a prohibition imposed under s 86 of the WRA 1991;

(c) any trade effluent or sewage effluent to be discharged into any controlled waters or from land (in England and Wales) through a pipe, into the sea outside the seaward limits of controlled waters;

(d) any trade effluent or sewage effluent to be discharged in contravention of any prohibition imposed under s 86 of the WRA 1991, from a building or from any fixed plant either onto or into any land or into any waters of a lake or a pond that are not inland fresh waters;

(e) any matter whatever to enter any inland fresh waters so as to tend to impede the proper flow of the waters in a manner leading, or likely to lead to substantial aggravation of pollution due to other causes or the consequences of such pollution.

Paragraphs (a)–(e) correspond to sub-ss (1)–(5) of s 85 of the WRA 1991. Breach of the conditions of a discharge consent is also an offence under s 85 of the WRA 1991.

The majority of these offences (the ones referring to 'causing' and also s 85(6) of the WRA 1991) are offences of strict liability. This means that it is irrelevant whether the defendant intended to cause the offence. The defendant's state of mind is not one of the elements of the offence which the prosecution must establish. As long as the defendant did the act which caused the pollution incident he will be guilty. In contrast the 'knowingly permitting' offences require the prosecution to prove that the defendant was aware that a pollution incident had taken place but took no action to bring the incident to an end. Each of the sub-sections containing the words 'causing or knowingly permitting' in effect contain two separate offences – 'causing' the pollution and 'knowingly permitting' the pollution. The main offences (those most frequently used by the Environment Agency in mounting a prosecution) are s 85(1), (3) and (6) of the WRA 1991 and s 4 of the Salmon and Freshwater Fisheries Act (SFFA) 1975.

Section 85(1) of the WRA 1991 is a widely drafted general offence covering an array of circumstances in which polluting substances may enter controlled waters. The term 'entry' covers situations in which polluting matter enters controlled waters from both point (for example, a pipe) and non-point or diffuse (for example, field 'run-off') sources. Section 85(3) of the WRA 1991 is limited to trade and sewage effluents which are discharged into controlled waters usually via a pipe or channel.

It is not uncommon for the Environment Agency to prosecute a polluter for both s 85(1) and (3) of the WRA 1991 offences, provided the elements of each offence can be established. More than one person may have caused a single pollution incident and the Environment Agency has a discretion to prosecute any of those persons.

Section 85(6) of the WRA 1991 is limited to discharge consent licence holders. As the offence is an offence of strict liability the discharge does not have to be poisonous, noxious or polluting. All that the Environment Agency is required to prove is that the licence holder exceeded the conditions of its licence.

3.9.3 Elements of the s 85 of the WRA 1991 offences

If the Environment Agency decides to prosecute it must be able to establish that each element of the relevant offence is present before it can prove its case to the satisfaction of the court. A number of the key words or phrases used in each of the s 85 of the WRA 1991 offences are not defined in the WRA 1991 (or the earlier incarnations of this legislation) and so we must consider the judicial interpretations of these terms which appear in case law.

3.9.3.1 Causing

The leading cases on the meaning of 'causing' water pollution are the House of Lords' decisions in *Alphacell Ltd v Woodward (1972) and Empress Car Co (Arbertillery) Ltd v NRA* (1998). In the *Alphacell* case the defendant paper manufacturer was charged with an offence, under s 2 of the Rivers (Prevention of Pollution) Act 1951, with causing polluting matter to enter a river. This offence is similar to s 85(1) of the WRA 1991. Settling tanks in the paper factory overflowed, when vegetation clogged up the pumps which maintained the level of effluent in the tanks. The tanks filled up and overflowed causing polluting matter to enter a river. An overflow channel led directly from the tanks to the river. Although the factory had a discharge consent (licence), this could not save the defendant company from prosecution because the conditions attached to the licence were breached when the settling tank effluent entered the river. Alphacell argued unsuccessfully that it had not caused the polluting matter to enter the river, rather, the presence of vegetation in its settling tanks was the real cause of the incident. Rejecting Alphacell's submission the court held that the act of constructing and operating the effluent tanks was a positive and deliberate act which led to the overflow which caused the pollution of the river. Lord Wilberforce stated:

> In my opinion, 'causing' here must be given a common sense meaning and I
> deprecate the introduction of refinements such as *causa*, effective cause or *novus
> actus*. There may be difficulties where acts of third parties or natural forces are

concerned but I find the present case comparatively simple. The appellants abstract water, pass it through their works where it becomes polluted, conduct it to a settling tank communicating directly with the stream, into which the polluted will inevitably flow if the level rises over the overflow point.

The test set out in the *Alphacell* decision relating to the meaning of 'causing' water pollution simply requires the defendant to carry on an activity which gives rise to a pollution incident. Provided the defendant's activities could be said to be intentional all that was necessary to prove liability was to establish a link between the defendant's activities and the pollution of controlled waters.

The decision in *Empress Cars* concerned the prosecution of a car sales company for causing red diesel fuel oil to enter controlled waters contrary to s 85(1) of the WRA 1991. The defendants maintained an oil storage tank on their site. The tank was protected by a bund wall. Standing outside the bund was a much smaller oil drum which was connected to the oil tank by a rubber hose. From time to time the defendants would take oil from the drum. The open/close valve on the tank was not lockable and site security was poor. A trespasser entered the site and opened the valve on the oil tank. Oil flowed from the tank to the drum which rapidly filled up and overflowed. The escaped oil found its way into the surface water drains and from there entered controlled waters. The defendant argued that it had not caused the oil pollution but had merely created the circumstances whereby a trespasser could enter the site, turn on the oil storage tank valve and cause the pollution. The defendant submitted that the act of the trespasser broke the chain of causation linking the defendant to the pollution and absolved it of liability. The House of Lords rejected this argument and found the defendant guilty.

Lord Hoffman gave the leading judgment of the court in which he laid down five key guides for judges and magistrates who might be faced with determining the question who or what had caused a pollution. First the relevant court should require the prosecution to identify what it was that the defendant had done to cause pollution. If the defendant had not done anything at all then the prosecution for 'causing' must fail. The prosecution need not prove that what the defendant did was the *immediate* cause of the pollution. Maintaining the storage tank was doing something even if the immediate cause of the pollution was lack of maintenance, a natural event, or the act of a third party, such as a trespasser. Once it had been established that the defendant had done something the court must then decide whether what the defendant had done was a cause of the pollution. It was quite conceivable that a single pollution incident would have several causes. If the defendant had done something which had produced a situation in which a polluting substance could escape into controlled waters, but a necessary precondition of that escape was the act of a third party or a natural event, then the court had to consider whether that act or event *was a normal fact of life or was something extraordinary*. If it was a matter of ordinary occurrence (something normal), it would not break the chain of causation and the defendant would be liable for causing the pollution. Only extraordinary or abnormal events act to break the chain of causation.

The *Empress Cars* case has important ramifications for defendants charged with causing water pollution. Liability has been extended to situations in which the defendant fails to take appropriate steps to guard against the actions of trespassers and other third parties, equipment failure, or natural events. The Hoffman test for events which operate to break or interrupt the causal chain has created a situation in which s 85(1) of the WRA 1991 creates almost absolute liability for escapes of pollutants into controlled waters. The prospect that a defendant will be able to establish that an extraordinary event has occurred is very slim indeed. It is also clear from the judgment of Lord Clyde that a failure to take precautions in relation to the risk of an escape of polluting substances will amount to 'doing something' for the purposes of establishing liability.

The very strict judicial approach to liability will be tempered by Environment Agency enforcement and prosecution policy. However, a very strict rule of liability may act as a disincentive to businesses who take their environmental management responsibilities seriously. They may be disinclined to invest in pollution prevention if the courts will hold them strictly liable for causing water pollution irrespective of the efforts they have made to control polluting emissions.

The Hoffman test may be difficult to apply in practice. A terrorist bomb which damages storage tanks and causes a pollution incident may well be an extraordinary event if it occurs in rural North Yorkshire but may not be extraordinary in Northern Ireland. The test is a 'fact and degree' test (that is, it depends on the particular circumstances). The *Empress* decision has been applied in at least two decided cases. In *Environment Agency v Brock plc* [1998] Env LR 607, the failure of a pump valve caused leachate, from a landfill site, to spray out and enter controlled waters. The defendant was convicted of the s 85(1) of the WRA 1991 offence, irrespective of the fact that the immediate cause of the pollution was defective equipment. There was no evidence that the defendant had been in any way negligent. The escape of polluting substances had occurred due to a latent defect in a seal on the valve which failed (see the similar case of *CPC (UK) Ltd v NRA* [1995] Env LR 131). It is submitted that the defendant was rightly convicted because the design of the landfill leachate collection system was something which was under the defendant's control. The failure of the valve seal, although a rare occurrence, was not an extraordinary event. In *Environment Agency v British Steel plc* (unreported, 30 November 1999) the defendant was charged with causing polluting matter (mill coolant) to enter controlled waters contrary to s 85(1) of the WRA 1991. The defendant submitted that the combined failure of a hose, which had been poorly installed by one of its employees, and the failure of a sub-contractor's employee (a security guard in the employ of RCO, a security company), to act appropriately in response to an alarm (audible and visual alarms were ignored) warning of an impending pollution, was an extraordinary event absolving the defendant of liability. The Stipendiary Magistrate who heard the case applied the Hoffman test and convicted the defendant. It is clear from this decision that the court was not diverted by the fact that the immediate cause of the pollution incident was the failure of the defendant's agent to respond to an alarm.

3.9.3.2 Knowingly permitting

Price v Cromack (1975) provides a useful illustration of the difference between the 'causing' offence and the offence of 'knowingly permitting'. A farmer was charged with 'causing' pollution when a lagoon on his land failed and waste animal products were released into a river. The farmer had a contract with an animal products firm which allowed the firm to discharge animal waste products into the lagoons on the farmer's land. The farmer was acquitted of the 'causing' charge on the basis that he had not caused the pollution. Whilst he had permitted the build up of the waste on his land, he could not be said to have caused the pollution. Had he been charged with knowingly permitting pollution, then the verdict would probably have been different.

3.9.3.3 Entry

The term 'entry' in s 85(1) of the WRA 1991 refers to a wide range of scenarios in which polluting matter may enter controlled waters. The term covers situations in which polluting matter is deliberately introduced into controlled waters, such as the deliberate pouring of the contents of a drum of pesticides into a stream, accidental spillages of polluting matter into surface drains, leaky pipes and tanks which cause polluting matter to escape into groundwaters, and 'run-off' from farmers fields entering a river over a wide area. 'Entry' covers the introduction of polluting substances into controlled waters from point (pipe) and diffuse (run-off) sources.

3.9.3.4 Discharge

The term 'discharge' in s 85(3) of the WRA 1991 has a more restricted meaning than 'entry' and refers to discharges from pipes, channels, or similar features into controlled waters. It is possible that polluting matter from a single incident could both enter and be discharged into controlled waters. If an unprotected (for example, a tank with no protective surrounding barrier or bund) oil storage tank were to rupture on an industrial site situated adjacent to a river or canal, some of the escaping oil could flow into the surface drains and be discharged into controlled waters, whilst a further quantity of oil could flow down the river or canal bank and enter controlled waters.

3.9.3.5 Poisonous, noxious or polluting

This term has a wide meaning. Poisonous matter entering or discharged into controlled waters is often associated with large fish kills and is therefore largely unproblematic. 'Polluting' may cover the discharge of dyes or detergents into controlled waters in quantities which do little damage to the ecology of the receiving waters but are polluting in the sense that they damage the amenity of controlled waters. Streams will be discoloured by the presence of dyes and banks of foam, caused by the presence of detergents, are unsightly. In *NRA v Egger (UK) Ltd* (1992), the court held that the term 'polluting' requires the substance which has entered controlled waters to have the likelihood or capability of causing harm to humans, animals and plants. In *R v Dovermoss Ltd* (1995), the defendant argued that slurry which had contaminated a spring could only be 'polluting matter' if actual harm had resulted from its introduction into controlled waters. The Court of Appeal held that the definition of 'polluting' should be based on the *Oxford English Dictionary*'s definition – 'to make physically impure, foul or filthy; to dirty, stain, taint, befoul'. Polluting material was the 'sort of material which, if introduced into the water reduces the quality of the water'. On this basis, the court held that there was no need to prove harm. The question was whether the matter was capable of causing or likely to cause harm to receiving waters. Whether or not a substance polluted water is a question of fact.

3.9.3.6 Controlled waters

Although the term 'controlled waters' is defined in s 104 of the WRA 1991 this definition is not comprehensive and the courts have been active in expanding our understanding of this term.

In *R v Dovermoss Ltd* (1995), the Court of Appeal was asked to interpret the term 'controlled waters'. In this case Welsh Water had received a number of taste complaints from consumers whose drinking water had been supplied from a spring. It was discovered, following investigations, that the water contained excessive amounts of ammonia which were traced back to two fields adjacent to a stream. The fields were owned by Dovermoss Ltd. Slurry had been spread on these fields. As a result of a heavy rainfall the stream had deviated from its normal course and ran over the slurry covered fields into the spring, thus contaminating the spring. Dovermoss were charged and convicted with causing polluting matter to enter controlled water contrary to s 85 of the WRA 1991. Dovermoss appealed on a number of grounds. One of their arguments was that the water, which had been diverted from its normal course was no longer controlled waters within the meaning of s 104 of the WRA 1991. The Court of Appeal held that the term controlled waters included 'waters of any watercourse', not, as it was argued, water in any watercourse. The court went further and stated that the term watercourse refers to the channel rather than the water itself. Consequently, waters from a watercourse (such as the stream) remain controlled waters even where the water has departed from its normal course

In *Environment Agency v Brock plc* [1998] Env LR 607, the court held that a man-made ditch could fall within the definition of controlled waters provided the ditch connected to and drained into controlled waters.

3.9.3.7 Effluent, substance, sewage effluent and trade effluent (see s 221 of the WRA 1991)

(a) 'Effluent' means any liquid, including particles of matter and other substances in suspension in the liquid.

(b) 'Substance' includes micro-organisms and any natural or artificial substance or other matter, whether it is in solid or liquid form or in the form of a gas or vapour.

(c) 'Sewage effluent' includes any effluent from the sewage disposal or sewerage works of a sewerage undertaker but does not include surface water.

(d) 'Trade effluent' includes any effluent which is discharged from premises used for carrying on any trade or industry, other than surface water and domestic sewage. For the purposes of this definition, any premises wholly or mainly used (whether for profit or not) for agricultural purposes, fish farming, scientific research or experiment, are to be deemed to be premises used for carrying on a trade.

3.9.4 Criminal liabilities of directors and other third parties

Section 217 of the WRA 1991 extends liability for water pollution offences to senior company officials. Section 217 states that, where a body corporate is guilty of an offence under the Act, then any director, manager, secretary or other similar officer may also be personally liable and be guilty of that offence. However, in order to secure a conviction under s 217, it is necessary to prove that the offence was committed with the consent or connivance of, or is attributable to any neglect on the part of, that person. In practice, the regulatory authorities have rarely prosecuted company officials under s 217 of the WRA 1991 (or s 157 of the EPA 1990), although the fact that individuals cannot hide behind the company veil should provide some deterrent against negligent environmental management. A successful s 217 prosecution is more likely in small companies where the senior officers are intimately concerned with the day to day running of the business. Unlike larger companies, they are not shielded by several layers of middle management.

3.10 Statutory and other defences

3.10.1 Authorised discharges

Section 88 of the WRA 1991 provides that a person will not be guilty of an offence under s 85, in respect of the entry or discharge of matter into controlled waters, if the entry or discharge is made under and in accordance with a consent provided by the Environment Agency under the WRA 1991. In addition to consents under the WRA 1991, it will also be a defence if the entry or discharge is made under and in accordance with:

(a) an IPC authorisation for a prescribed process designated for central control under Pt I of the EPA 1990;

(b) an IPPC permit granted to pursuant to the Pollution Prevention and Control Act (PPCA) 1999;

(c) a waste management licence or a waste disposal licence granted under Pt II of the EPA 1990 (there is an exception where the offence is of discharging trade or sewage effluent or where a prohibition is in force);

(d) a licence granted by the Ministry of Agriculture, Fisheries and Food under Pt II of the Food and Environment Protection Act 1985 (authorising the deposit of waste at sea);

(e) s 163 of the WRA 1991 or s 165 of the WIA 1991 (concerned with discharges for works purposes);

(f) any local statutory provision or statutory order (for example, a drought order) which expressly confers power to discharge effluent into water; or

(g) any prescribed enactment (that is, legislation).

Therefore, any discharges made into controlled waters which are authorised by any of the above will not be in breach of s 85. The WRA 1991 in general, and s 88 in particular, does not include what is commonly referred to as a 'due diligence' defence. An example of such a defence is to be found in s 33(7)(a) of the EPA 1990. A defendant may avail itself of this defence in regard to prosecution for the waste offences detailed in s 33 of the EPA 1990 if the defendant can establish that it has taken all reasonable precautions and exercised all due diligence to avoid the commission of an offence. The absence of such a defence in the WRA 1991 has attracted criticism (McFarlane, 'The *Empress* decision: a plea for common sense'). One commentator has suggested that the basis of s 85 of the WRA 1991 liability could be changed to give effect to this criticism (Stanley, 1999).

3.10.2 Other defences

In addition to the defence that a discharge is authorised under the provisions listed above, the WRA 1991 also provides a number of other defences in s 89.

A person will not be guilty of an offence under s 85 in respect of an entry of any matter into any waters or any discharge if:

(a) the entry is caused or permitted, or the discharge is made, in an emergency in order to avoid danger to life or health; and

(b) that person takes all such steps as are reasonably practicable in the circumstances for minimising the extent of the entry or discharge and of its polluting effects; and

(c) particulars of the entry or discharge are furnished to the EA as soon as reasonably practicable after it occurs (s 89(1)(c) of the WRA 1991). Section 89(a) implicitly refers to danger to man rather than danger to flora and fauna.

In addition to the above defences a number of discharges made in a number of specific situations are exempted from the provisions of the Act. A person will not be guilty of an offence under s 85 by reason:

(a) of causing or permitting any discharge of trade or sewage effluent from a vessel (s 89(2)) (these discharges are regulated by bylaws);

(b) of his depositing the solid refuse of a mine or quarry on any land so that it falls or is carried into inland freshwater if the deposit is authorised by the Environment Agency, no other site for the deposit is reasonably practicable, and he takes all reasonable steps to prevent the refuse from entering those inland freshwaters. (This defence does not apply except in respect of the entry of any poisonous, noxious or polluting matter into any controlled waters (s 89(4)));

(c) a Highway Authority or other person entitled to keep open a drain by virtue of s 100 of the Highways Act 1980 will not be guilty of an offence under s 85 by reason of his causing or permitting any discharge to be made from a drain kept open by virtue of that section unless the discharge is made in contravention of a prohibition imposed under s 86 (s 89(5)).

Section 87 of the WRA 1991 contains defences relating to the privatised water companies (referred to as sewerage undertakers) which run the sewerage treatment and disposal systems. It is the responsibility of sewerage undertakers to ensure, through the WIA 1991 licensing system relating to sewers, that it can effectively treat the trade and sewage effluent it has licensed to receive and treat in its sewage works. This is given legal effect to by s 87(1) of the WRA 1991. This provision deems sewerage undertakers to have caused pollution of controlled waters in circumstances where it cannot treat the effluent it has itself licensed to accept and, in consequence, it breaches its own discharge consent granted by the Environment Agency. The position is different, however, in circumstances where the sewerage undertaker receives unlicensed effluent to treat. In this case the sewerage undertaker may avail itself of the benefit of the s 87(2) of the WRA 1991 defence and escape liability for causing water pollution.

Farmers who act in accordance with best agricultural practice may escape liability if a water pollution incident occurs. Although farmers have no due diligence defence, their adherence to best agricultural practice will be taken into account when the Environment Agency exercises its discretion whether to prosecute.

3.11 Proving water pollution

In carrying out their investigations, EA inspectors have the power to take samples of water or effluent, which may later be used as evidence in court to substantiate a criminal case (s 108 of the EA 1995).

3.12 Enforcement

3.12.1 Environment Agency enforcement powers

The Environment Agency has various powers at its disposal which enable it to ensure that authorised dischargers comply with consent conditions, to investigate any breaches of consents and also to detect and investigate pollution incidents. The Environment Agency can exercise control through the consent system, using its power to prohibit certain discharges or by varying or revoking a consent. The Environment Agency may also decide to bring criminal proceedings against a person who contravenes the provisions of the Act.

3.12.2 Enforcement policy

Whether the Environment Agency will choose to enforce compliance with the law by means of a prosecution will, to a large extent, depend upon the Environment Agency's 1998 enforcement and prosecution policy (see 2.4.15). Essentially, the Environment Agency bases its decision whether or not to prosecute upon the aggravating and mitigating circumstances surrounding the commission of the relevant offence. Of particular significance will be the severity of environmental damage resulting from the pollution incident.

The Environment Agency's water pollution statistics for 1998 (*Water Pollution Incidents in England and Wales – 1998*, 1999, Environment Agency) reveal the following picture. The Environment Agency responded to 28,670 reports of water pollution incidents in 1998, of which in 17,863 cases (referred to as 'substantiated' pollution incidents) there was evidence of pollution. These figures represented a 9% decrease on the previous years' tally of substantiated incidents. This was the fourth successive year in which the number of substantiated incidents had declined. Of the total number of substantiated incidents in 1998, 24% related to the sewage and water industries, 20% to industry, 11% to agriculture, 10% to transport, 7% to domestic and residential and 28% to other sources. The main categories of polluting substances were: oil – 30%; sewage – 24%; organic wastes – 11%; chemicals – 8%; silt – 7%; and other pollutants – 20%. Unfortunately, the statistics provide no information on the total number of recorded breaches of discharge consents and therefore we have no data on the magnitude of the water pollution problem caused by persistent, minor, breaches of discharge consents.

The Environment Agency's enforcement policy (para 28) confirms that the Environment Agency will normally prosecute in the case of 'incidents or breaches which have significant consequences for the environment' and therefore there is a presumption of prosecution in the case of Category 1 (that is, major) incidents.

In 1998 the Environment Agency successfully prosecuted 262 cases (of which 185 incidents actually occurred in 1998) representing about 1% of the total number of substantiated water pollution incidents occurring in 1998. The strict liability nature of many water pollution offences ensures that there is little prospect of the defendant being able to mount a successful defence. In the vast majority of cases, some 93%, the Environment Agency secures a conviction.

3.12.3 Penalties for water pollution offences

A person who contravenes the provisions of Pt III of the WRA 1991, or the conditions of any consent given under the Act, will be guilty of a criminal offence and liable:

(a) on summary conviction, to imprisonment for a term not exceeding three months, or to a fine not exceeding £20,000 or to both;

(b) on conviction on indictment, to imprisonment for a term not exceeding two years or to a fine (of unlimited amount) or to both (s 85(6)).

The average fine imposed by the courts in respect of water pollution convictions in 1998 (excluding the Welsh Region of the Environment Agency whose statistics were distorted by the £4 m fine, reduced to £750,000 on appeal, imposed on the defendant in the *Sea Empress* prosecution) was £3,335. This is in line with the gradual upward trend in the level of fines for water pollution offences but is some way short of the £20,000 maximum financial penalty which may be imposed in the magistrates' court. Interestingly, there is some evidence of an increased willingness, on the part of the Environment Agency, to make greater use of the Crown Court's ability to impose higher penalties than the magistrates' court. The imposition of a financial penalty by the courts to deter water polluters appears to be the rule in the criminal courts. Only rarely will a custodial penalty be imposed.

3.13 Preventative approaches to water pollution control

3.13.1 Introduction

The WRA 1991 contains provisions which enable the Environment Agency to take a more preventive approach to water pollution, whereby harm is prevented by means of anticipatory action. Section 161 of the WRA 1991 in particular empowers the Environment Agency to take action to avoid pollution of controlled waters. This section also equips the Environment Agency with extensive clean-up powers. In addition to s 161, ss 92–95 of the WRA 1991 contain provisions relating to the prevention of pollution. These provisions are particularly useful in relation to more diffuse sources of pollution such as run-off arising from agricultural activities. However, we begin our examination of the preventive role of the Environment Agency by reference to the advisory documents which it has produced.

3.13.2 Pollution advice and information

The Environment Agency produces a range of documents and other media to educate and guide licence holders and others as to best environmental management practice to minimise the risk of substances escaping containment to pollute controlled waters.

Prior to the creation of the Environment Agency the NRA produced, and issued on request, a free pack of information, comprising leaflet and video, entitled *Pollution Prevention Pays*. This initiative formed part of the regulatory campaign to highlight common errors in operational practice which were often the real causes of pollution incidents. The key features of the Pollution Prevention Pays initiative are summarised below:

(a) site drains – distinguish between surface drains (draining into controlled waters) and foul drains (draining to sewer); colour code drainage systems; drainage plans should be accessible;

(b) deliveries – label maximum content of storage tanks; gauges should be installed to give a visual display of tank levels; build bund walls; isolate delivery areas from drains; pipes should be above ground or placed in 'sleeves'; install automatic cut-off valves to prevent overfilling; install high level alarms in storage tanks; and ensure the supervision of unloading and loading operations;

(c) storage – check bund walls in good repair with no valves in bund wall to drain rain water; drum storage areas should be bunded and roofed; use sturdy drums and label appropriately; install oil interceptor pits on surface drains to minimise the risk of pollution of controlled waters;

(d) security – ensure adequate perimeter security through proper fencing; CCTV surveillance, and install locks on open/close tank valves;

(e) training and emergency planning – ensure adequate staff training and prepare contingency plans.

This initiative demonstrates the link between poor environmental management practice and the increased probability that the Environment Agency will exercise its discretion to prosecute should a pollution incident occur on a poorly managed site.

The Environment Agency has also produced a range of 20 Pollution Prevention Guidance notes (PPGs) which are provided free on request to enquirers. Environment Agency staff will draw the attention of businesses to relevant PPGs as part of their rolling programme of routine site inspection visits. The PPGs cover the following topics:

PPG 1 – general guide to the prevention of pollution of controlled waters;

PPG 2 – above ground oil storage tanks;

PPG 3 – the use and design of oil separators in surface water drainage systems;

PPG 4 – disposal of sewage where no main drainage is available;

PPG 5 – works in, near or liable to affect water courses;

PPG 6 – working at demolition and construction sites;

PPG 7 – fuelling stations: construction and operation;

PPG 8 – safe storage and disposal of used oils;

PPG 9 – pesticides;

PPG 10 – highway depots;

PPG 11 – industrial sites;

PPG 12 – sheep dip;

PPG 13 – the use of high pressure water and steam cleaners;

PPG 14 – boats and marinas;

PPG 15 – retail premises;

PPG 16 – schools and other educational establishments;

PPG 17 – dairies and other milk handling operations;

PPG 18 – control of spillages and fire fighting run-off;

PPG 19 – garages and vehicle service centres;

PPG 20 – dewatering underground ducts and chambers.

Adherence by farmers to agricultural best practice in regard to the water pollution risks identified in *The Water Code Revised* (1998) will be an important factor which the Environment Agency takes into account when deciding whether to pollute a farmer for causing a water pollution incident.

3.13.3 Section 92 of the WRA 1991

Under s 92, the Secretary of State has the power to make provisions (by means of regulations) for:

(a) prohibiting a person from having custody or control of any poisonous, noxious or polluting matter unless prescribed works and prescribed precautions and other steps have been taken for the purpose of preventing or controlling the entry of the matter into any controlled waters;

(b) for requiring a person who already has custody or control of, or makes use of, poisonous, noxious or polluting matter to carry out such works for that purpose and to take precautions and other steps for the same purpose as may be prescribed.

Using these powers, the Control of Pollution (Silage, Slurry and Agricultural Fuel Oil) Regulations were introduced in 1991. These regulations require persons with custody of silage, livestock slurry or fuel oil to carry out works and take precautions, and other steps, for preventing pollution of controlled waters.

Essentially s 92 and the regulations made under it are designed to minimise the risk of highly polluting substances escaping containment and causing water pollution. The regulations may specify, as a condition of being allowed to store and handle such substances, that farmers adhere to a range of controls and standards relating to the design, construction, and operation of manufacturing and storage facilities, especially relating to silage making, slurry lagoons and agricultural fuel and oil stores. Regulations on industrial oil storage are pending and proposals are awaited on chemical storage. Regulations made pursuant to s 92 may create criminal offences and administrative remedies which will be similar to the discharge consent system.

Draft regulations have been issued under s 92 of the WRA 1991 in regard to design standards for above ground oil storage tanks over 200 litres capacity. The regulations will, when passed, apply at once to all new oil storage tanks whilst existing tanks must comply within five years (existing 'at risk' tanks must comply within two years).

The draft regulations do not apply to below ground tanks in view of the powers available to the EA in the Groundwater Regulations 1998 and the Anti-Pollution Works Notices Regulations 1999.

3.13.4 Water Protection Zones: general zoning control

A further mechanism for preventing water pollution is contained in s 93 of the WRA 1991 and allows for the designation of Water Protection Zones (WPZs). Where the Secretary of State, after consultation with the Minister of Agriculture, Fisheries and Food considers that it is appropriate to prohibit or restrict the carrying on in a particular area of activities which he considers are likely to result in the pollution of any controlled waters, he may by order make provision:

(a) designating an area as a WPZ; and

(b) prohibiting or restricting the carrying on in the designated area of such activities specified or described in the order.

Section 93 orders may themselves prohibit or restrict specific activities or alternatively they can establish a system under which the Environment Agency is empowered to decide which activities are prohibited or restricted. They are especially useful in controlling diffuse pollution such as agricultural run-off which falls outside the ambit of the discharge consent pollution controls. Similar to the discharge consent licensing system, s 93 orders can establish procedures for obtaining consent to engage in restricted activities and provide for criminal offences for breach of the relevant provisions. The detailed procedure for making a s 93 order is contained in Sched 11 to the WRA 1991. An example of a designated WPZ is located on the River Dee. The special regulatory regime on the Dee controls the use and storage of a number of polluting substances. It is mainly applicable to industrial sites (IPC/IPPC sites, farms, retail premises, and construction sites are exempt) and the content of each consent is dependent upon the outcome of a risk assessment. Carrying out the activities specified in the relevant order without a consent or in breach of consent conditions is an offence. A due diligence defence is available as well as a defence based upon the defendant's ability to prove that he/she/it was not aware of the regulated activity itself or was not aware of the extent of the storage or use of regulated substances.

3.13.5 Nitrate Sensitive Areas: specific control

In addition to the designation of WPZs, areas may also be designated as Nitrate Sensitive Areas under s 94 of the WRA 1991. (Nitrate pollution cannot be controlled under the mechanisms of the WPZs.) The Secretary of State for Environment and the Minister for Agriculture (or National Assembly for Wales) acting together have the power to designate areas as Nitrate Sensitive Areas (NSAs), where they consider that it is appropriate, in order to prevent or control the entry of nitrate into controlled waters as a result of the use of any land for agricultural purposes. Designation of an area is made by Order and the Order may:

(a) require, prohibit or restrict the carrying on, either on or in relation to any agricultural land in the area, of specified activities; and

(b) provide for specified or determined amounts to be paid in compensation in respect of the obligations imposed as a result of the designation.

Where an area has been designated as an NSA and the relevant Minister considers it appropriate, he may enter into an agreement to allow for payments to be made to the owner of the freehold interest in any agricultural land in the area (or with the permission of the freehold owner, or with any other person having another interest in the land) where that person accepts obligations with respect to the management of the land or other obligations imposed under the agreement. Management agreements run with the land and bind successors in title.

NSA orders can only be made, following designation, at the request of the Environment Agency, rather than at the request of other interested parties such as an environmental organisation, and can only be applied for if the

Environment Agency is of the opinion that its other regulatory powers are inadequate. An order is required to identify both the agricultural land from which the nitrate is likely to emanate and the controlled waters which will be affected. The consent of the Treasury is required.

An order may either impose mandatory or voluntary controls on the relevant NSA. Voluntary control orders are available to be applied in any designated NSA. Mandatory orders are made pursuant to Sched 12 to the WRA 1991. They can include positive obligations (for example, the construction of bund walls) as well as restrictions and prohibitions. Approximately 32 NSAs have been designated (under the Nitrate Sensitive Areas (Designation) Order 1990 and Nitrate Sensitive Areas Regulations 1994) so far. Farmers in the affected areas receive compensation payments in return for undertakings of five years' duration in regard to farming practices.

3.13.6 Nitrate Vulnerable Zones

Nitrate Vulnerable Zones (NVZs) were created by the Protection of Water Against Agricultural and Nitrate Pollution (England and Wales) Regulations 1996 to give effect to the Nitrates Directive (91/676/EEC). The regulations provide for the designation of NVZs in areas which have nitrate pollution problems arising from agricultural land use. NVZs are designated zones in which nitrate levels in surface waters exceed levels recommended by the Drinking Water Directive (80/778/EEC) or nitrate levels in groundwaters exceed 50mg/litre. Sixty-eight NVZs have been designated to date. The Environment Agency monitors nitrate levels in other areas, as well as NVZs, to review the national picture.

Once a NVZ has been designated the Secretary of State for the Environment produces an action plan for each NVZ to reduce and/or prevent nitrate water pollution (Action Programme for Nitrate Vulnerable Zones (England and Wales) Regulations 1998). In contrast to NSAs, NVZs are mandatory, as provided by the directive, and compensation is not payable.

3.14 The clean-up of polluted water

3.14.1 Anti-Pollution Works Notices and clean-up operations

Section 161 of the WRA 1991 provides the Environment Agency with an important set of powers which enable the Environment Agency to take preventive action where it identifies a pollution risk, and post-incident remedial action following a pollution.

Under s 161(1), where it appears to the Environment Agency that any poisonous, noxious or polluting matter or any solid waste matter is likely to enter or has entered any controlled water, the Environment Agency will be entitled to carry out remedial works to clean-up the pollution. The section provides that the following works and operations may be carried out:

(a) preventing any matter entering controlled waters;

(b) removing or disposing of polluting matter;

(c) remedying or mitigating any pollution caused by its presence in the waters; or

(d) so far as it is reasonably practicable to do so, of restoring the waters, including any flora and fauna dependent on the aquatic environment of the waters, to their state immediately before the matter became present in the waters.

The Environment Agency is entitled to carry out and recover the costs of any investigations in order to establish the source of the matter and also the identity of the person who caused or knowingly permitted it to be present in controlled waters or at a place from which it is likely to enter controlled waters.

The EA 1995 (Sched 22) inserted a new provision (s 161(1A)) which provides that the power to carry out works (not the power to carry out investigations) is only exercisable in cases where:

(a) the Environment Agency considers it necessary to carry out the works forthwith; or

(b) it appears to the Environment Agency, after carrying out reasonable enquiry, that no person can be found on whom to serve a Works Notice (WN) under s 161A.

However, s 161(3) provides that where the Environment Agency carries out any such works or operations as are mentioned in s 161 it will be entitled to recover the expenses reasonably incurred in doing so. Expenses may be recovered from any person who, caused or knowingly permitted the matter in question to be present at the place from which it was likely to enter any controlled waters or who caused or knowingly permitted the matter in question to be present in any controlled waters. The Environment Agency can exercise these powers independently of any criminal proceedings which they might initiate.

The Environment Agency has issued guidance on the circumstances in which it will use its s 161 power: *Environment Agency Policy and Guidance on the Use of Anti-Pollution Works Notices*. Section 161 may not be used by the Environment Agency to override the authority of a discharge consent authorising the discharge of substances into controlled waters. In such circumstances, the Environment Agency must apply for a variation of the discharge consent.

3.14.2 Works Notices

The Anti-Pollution Works Notice is likely to be a powerful compliance enforcement tool in view of the fact that the cost of clean up is likely to far exceed any penalty imposed by the courts in regard to any linked prosecution. The Environment Agency now has the power to compel polluters to take (and bear the cost of) preventive or remedial action themselves, rather than relying upon the Environment Agency's power to undertake the clean-up works and then attempt to recover the relevant costs from the person responsible. Under s 161A–D, the Environment Agency may serve an Anti-Pollution Works Notice on the polluter, or potential polluter, requiring it either to remedy the pollution or take specified preventive action to stop pollution occurring. The Works Notice procedure is not applicable in those circumstances where immediate action is required or where the polluter cannot be found.

Section 161A, inserted into the WRA 1991 by the EA 1995, provides a new procedure for the serving of Works Notices. The Environment Agency may serve a Works Notice on any person who caused or knowingly permitted the poisonous, noxious or polluting matter, or solid waste matter in question to be present either in any controlled waters or at the place from which it is likely to enter any controlled waters. The Works Notice is a legal notice which requires the person on whom it is served to carry out the works or operations specified in the notice. A Works Notice must specify the time periods within which the person must comply. Section 161A(4) provides that before serving a WN the Environment Agency should endeavour to consult the person concerning the works that are to be specified in the notice. The Anti-Pollution Works Regulations 1999 SI 1999/1006 detail the form and content of WNs and the requirements for consultation.

A WN may include conditions which require the person served with the notice to carry out works or operations in relation to land or waters even where he has no legal right to do so, for example, where the land is outside his ownership or control. Section 161B provides that any person whose consent is required before any works or operations are carried out *shall* grant, or join in granting the necessary rights in relation to any land or waters, thus enabling the person served with the Works Notice to carry out the required works. For example, a Works Notice might require A to go onto B's land in order to carry out necessary clean-up works and B must grant A the right to go onto his land and carry out those specified works. Section 161B(5) provides that a person who grants such rights is entitled to compensation from the person on whom the Works Notice is served. The details of the compensation arrangements are detailed in the 1999 Regulations.

Section 161C provides for the right of appeal to the Secretary of State against a WN within 21 days of the notice being served. As with the compensation arrangements, the detailed provisions relating to the appeals procedure are to be determined by the Secretary of State in regulations.

The provisions of s 161 are important. They allow for the costs of clean-up to be met by the polluter rather than the taxpayer, and to that extent are illustrative of the 'polluter pays' principle in action. Of course, difficulties will arise where the polluter cannot be identified, in which case the Environment Agency will bear the cost of clean-up. During its period of regulatory control the NRA used the powers under s 161 successfully on a number of occasions. For example, in 1993 the NRA used its powers in respect of an incident in the Anglian Region where the NRA recovered £99,000 from a polluter for the costs of restocking a polluted watercourse with fish. However, according to statistics produced by the National Audit Office in 1995 the NRA recovered less than 40% of its costs. In practice, clean-up costs may be very high and often greater than any fine imposed by the courts and as such the provisions of s 161 are seen by many as an equal if not greater deterrent than a court-imposed fine. In *Bruton and NRA v Clarke* (1994), the county court limited the NRA's recovery costs under s 161 to those costs necessarily incurred as a result of the pollution. In that particular case, the NRA was not entitled to recover the costs of improving a fishery damaged in a pollution incident.

3.15 Access to information

The Environment Agency is required to maintain a publicly accessible register of data relating to the regulation of controlled waters (s 190 of the WRA 1991). The register contains details of: applications for discharge consents, consents and consent conditions, water quality objective (WQO) notices, IPC authorisations and IPPC permits, samples (taken by any person) and any analysis thereof. Inspection of the register is free but a reasonable charge is made for copying. The contents of the register have, on occasion, been used as both evidence in criminal prosecutions and civil actions.

3.16 The private regulation of water pollution

Individuals with 'riparian rights' (that is, property owners whose land adjoins a watercourse and who therefore own the bed and banks of the relevant river or stream, but not the waters flowing in them) are often well placed to take action against polluters who damage their property related interests. They have the right to receive water in its natural state, subject only to reasonable use by upstream users (*Chasemore v Richards* (1859)). Any interference with the quantity and quality of the water the riparian owner receives is actionable, based on the tort of nuisance.

3.16.1 The common law and water pollution

According to the courts, the law relating to the rights of riparian owners is well settled. A riparian owner is entitled to:

... have the water of the stream, on the banks of which his property lies, flow down as it has been accustomed to flow down to his property, subject to the ordinary use of flowing water by upper proprietors, and to such further use, if any, on their part in connection with their property as may be reasonable under the circumstances. Every riparian proprietor is thus entitled to the water of his stream, in its natural flow, without sensible diminution or increase and without sensible alteration in its character or quality. (*John Young & Co v Bankier Distillery Co* (1893), *per* Lord McNaughton.)

In the *John Young* case a whisky distillery obtained an injunction, in an action based on private nuisance, because the activities of an upstream mine owner had changed the chemistry of the water and so had unreasonably interfered with the whisky manufacturer's riparian right to receive the water in its natural state. A riparian owner can bring an action for damages or can seek an injunction. Interference with fishing rights can also give rise to an action in nuisance. In *Cook v South West Water plc* (1992), the plaintiff, Cook, owned three-quarters of a mile of riparian salmon and trout fishing rights. During 1990, South West Water, which operated three sewage works upstream from the plaintiff's stretch of river, discharged detergent and phosphates into the river which damaged the river's ecosystem and also seriously interfered with fishing. The plaintiff brought an action in nuisance against South West Water seeking both damages and an injunction.

In addition to a claim in nuisance, it may be possible for a riparian owner to make a claim in trespass. The tort of trespass on land has many functions and its application for environmental purposes has only been a more recent and limited development. Trespass involves the unjustifiable physical interference with land, arising from intentional or negligent entry onto the land. The key issues which must be present in order for an action in trespass to be brought are that the trespass was direct, that the act was intentional or negligent and that there is a causal link between the directness of the act and the inevitability of the consequences. An example of a successful claim in trespass in relation to water pollution can be found in the case of *Jones v Llanrwst UDC* (1911) in which it was held that sewage, which had been released into a river which had passed downstream and settled on the plaintiff's land, was a direct interference and amounted to trespass.

The tort of negligence may also have application in water pollution cases. In *Scott-Whitehead v National Coal Board* (1987), the defendant, a regional water authority, was found to be negligent for failing to advise a farmer that the water he was abstracting from a stream (in accordance with an abstraction licence granted by the water authority) to irrigate his crops contained a strong chlorinated solution. The farmer's potato crop was damaged as a consequence of using the chlorinated water and the court held that the water authority was liable in negligence.

3.16.2 Private prosecutions

The WRA 1991 allows individuals as well as the Environment Agency to commence legal proceedings for offences under the Act. One such private prosecution was brought by Greenpeace in *Greenpeace v Albright and Wilson* (1991). More recently Greenpeace brought an unsuccessful action against ICI in *Greenpeace v ICI* (1994). Greenpeace brought this latter private prosecution under s 85(1) of the WRA 1991 and the case illustrates one of the dangers faced by private prosecutors. Greenpeace was required to pay over £28,000 towards ICI's legal costs. Clearly, only large environmental pressure groups such as Friends of the Earth or Greenpeace can afford to run the financial risks of losing legal actions. However, in addition to traditional environmental pressure groups, the Anglers Associations have availed themselves of these rights as well as resorting to common law actions to secure injunctions or obtain damages.

3.17 Disposal into sewers

The disposal of effluent into sewers is inextricably linked to pollution of controlled waters. Industrial processes generate enormous quantities of waste which is either discharged on land as solid waste, emitted into the atmosphere or, in the case of liquid wastes, it may either be discharged into controlled waters or released into the sewers. The discharge of trade effluent into sewers is controlled directly by the sewerage undertakers, exercising their powers under the WIA 1991, but also indirectly by the Environment Agency. Sewerage undertakers grant consents for the disposal of trade effluent into the sewers but they are then required to obtain consent from the Environment Agency to release the final treated effluent into controlled waters. The WIA 1991 regulates the discharge of trade effluents into sewers and s 87 of the WRA 1991 deals with the discharge of sewage effluent into controlled waters.

3.17.1 Discharges of sewage into controlled waters

The 10 privatised water companies which operate as both water and sewerage undertakers are responsible for discharging large quantities of effluent from treatment plants, into controlled waters. The sewerage undertakers receive trade effluent through the sewers which they then treat and finally dispose of, after treatment, into controlled waters. The sewerage undertakers are therefore effectively responsible for all discharges made from their sewers or treatment plants into controlled waters. The sewerage undertakers control the trade effluent disposed of into the sewers by means of trade effluent consents which they grant under s 118 of the WIA 1991.

Although the sewerage undertakers treat waste from other sources, they are, like other industrial polluters, subject to the provisions of the WRA 1991. Since s 85 of the WRA 1991 makes it an offence to discharge sewage effluent into controlled waters, sewerage undertakers are themselves required to obtain a water discharge consent from the Environment Agency in order to legally discharge treated sewage from each of their sewage treatment plants.

Although it has been stated that the sewerage undertakers are subject to the same provisions as other licensed dischargers under the WRA, they do nevertheless benefit from an additional defence under s 87 of the WRA 1991, that is not available to other persons. Section 87 of the WRA 1991 deals specifically with discharges into and from public sewers. Under s 87, a sewerage undertaker will not be guilty of an offence under s 85 if the discharge is in breach of consent conditions where:

(a) the breach is attributable to a discharge which another person caused or permitted to be made into the sewer (that is, an illegal discharge);

(b) the sewerage undertaker was not bound to receive the discharge into the sewer (that is, the discharge was not authorised by a licence); and

(c) the undertaker could not reasonably have been expected to prevent the discharge into the sewer (this may be due to the design of the sewage treatment process).

This defence recognises that sewerage undertakers deal with effluent from a variety of sources which are treated and then discharged from the sewer or works under the terms of a discharge consent. If the final discharge from the sewerage undertaker is in breach of consent conditions the undertaker will not be guilty of an offence if the reason for the breach was due to the unauthorised discharge of effluent into the sewer, providing it can be shown that the undertaker could not reasonably have expected the unauthorised discharge into the sewer. The availability of this defence was considered in the case of *NRA v Yorkshire Water Services Ltd* (1995). In this case an unidentified person discharged iso-octonal, an industrial solvent into a sewer. The water company had not granted any consent to any person to discharge this substance into the sewers and therefore the initial discharge by the unknown person was unlawful. The iso-octonal travelled by means of gravity through the sewers into a sewage treatment plant, which it disabled, and was discharged in an almost undiluted state into controlled waters. Yorkshire Water Services were charged with causing poisonous, noxious or polluting water (that is, the discharge of the sewerage) into controlled waters contrary to s 85 of the WRA 1991. The House of Lords held that there was sufficient evidence for a court to find that the water company had caused the discharge from the sewerage works (reaffirming the strict test of causing laid down in *Alphacell v Woodward* (1972)). However, on the facts the House of Lords held that the water company could rely on the special defence available in s 87(2) of the WRA 1991. The water company could not reasonably have been expected to prevent the discharge of the iso-octonal into the sewer.

3.17.2 Discharges of trade effluent into the sewers

Given that sewerage undertakers are subject to the same controls as any other discharger (subject to the availability of the additional defence, discussed in 3.17.1 above), they are required to maintain a tight control on the effluent they are prepared to accept into the sewers and, for this reason, the disposal of trade effluent into a sewer requires a separate consent from the sewerage undertaker under s 118 of the WIA 1991.

3.17.3 Trade effluent consents: s 118 of the WIA 1991

The disposal of trade effluent into a sewer requires a trade effluent consent under s 118 of the WIA 1991 and it is an offence to discharge any trade effluent from trade premises otherwise than in accordance with the conditions of a consent obtained from the sewage undertaker. The definitions of 'trade effluent' and 'trade premises' are provided in s 141 of the WIA 1991. Trade effluent means any liquid, which is partly or wholly produced in the course of any trade or business, but does not include domestic sewerage. Trade premises include premises used for industry or any trade, research and agriculture.

The application for a consent is made by means of serving a trade affluent notice on the sewerage undertaker. At least two months' notice must be given of an intention to discharge and the notice has to provide details of the proposed discharge, including information about the proposed quantity and composition of the trade effluent and the maximum daily volume of the discharge. Following the service of a notice the sewerage undertaker has to decide whether or not to grant the consent and the relevant conditions to attach. Failure to determine the notice within two months constitutes a deemed refusal enabling the applicant to appeal.

Section 121 of the WIA 1991 gives the sewerage undertaker wide discretion as to the conditions that can be imposed. Conditions may relate to the time of day during which effluent may be discharged into sewers, temperature, acidity or alkalinity, inspection of sewers, testing and monitoring of effluent and the keeping of records. When framing conditions of WIA 1991 licences, the sewerage undertaker must have regard to the conditions in its own water discharge consent, issued by the EA, under the WRA 1991. In addition, a condition will be imposed which sets out the amount payable to the undertaker for receiving the trade effluent. In setting trade effluent consent conditions sewerage undertakers have regard to the criteria in *Trade Effluent Discharged to the Sewer* (1986) which specify the key objectives or purposes of trade effluent control. These include:

(a) the protection of the integrity of the sewage system (that is, the conducting pipes);

(b) the protection of personnel;

(c) the protection of sewage treatment works (from substances and objects which will cause damage);

(d) the protection of the environment from the impact of treated sewage; and

(e) to ensure that dischargers pay a reasonable charge for sewage treatment.

Consent conditions are set by reference to the ability of the sewer system to treat the proposed discharge. Substances, such as metals or solvents, which the sewage treatment works cannot cope with will be excluded from the terms of the discharge consent. In such circumstances the discharger must pre-treat its effluent to remove the banned substances.

The sewerage undertaker has various powers in respect of trade effluent consents. The consent may be varied on two months' notice, although the undertaker can only do so after two years from the grant of the consent. This power is essential so that the sewerage undertaker can respond to the tightening by the Environment Agency, of the terms of the discharge consent licenses of its sewage treatment works. A variation of the consent is possible within the two year period but compensation will be payable unless the need for the variation has resulted from circumstances which were not foreseen when the consent was last varied. In contrast to the WRA 1991, there is no provision in the WIA 1991 relating to the revocation of trade effluent discharge consents. A person aggrieved by a consent condition or variation has the right of appeal to the Director General of Water Services under s 122 of the WIA 1991. The discharger and sewerage undertaker may enter into an agreement under s 129 of the WIA 1991 as an alternative to the trade effluent discharge consent licensing process. The terms of such an agreement enable the discharger to pay the capital costs involved in constructing a new sewage treatment plant where the existing works already are at maximum capacity.

3.17.4 Special consents

Certain types of effluent, known as 'special category effluents', require a special consent because they are potentially harmful and are difficult to treat. The Trade Effluents (Prescribed Processes and Substances) Regulations 1989, as amended (by SI 1992/339), prescribe the particular substances that fall into this category.

In cases where the trade effluent is special category effluent the sewerage undertaker must consult the Environment Agency and ask whether the discharges should be prohibited, or if not, whether the agency requires any specific conditions to be imposed (s 120(1) of the WIA 1991). The sewerage undertaker commits a criminal offence if it fails to comply with this duty.

3.18 Water abstraction

The quality of water is not simply determined by what is discharged into it. Water quality is inextricably linked to water quantity. If water levels are low, there is less water available to dilute waste and effluents and this may cause a reduction in water quality. Therefore, it is appropriate in a chapter on water pollution to consider the legal controls that exist in relation to the abstraction of water. The Environment Agency is under a statutory duty to secure the proper use of water resources. Under s 19 of the WRA 1991, the Environment Agency is under a duty to conserve and increase the available water resources. The agency therefore has to assess the need for new developments and ensure that the most appropriate schemes are licensed, taking into account the environmental impact of new developments on existing users.

Before legislation was enacted to control the use of water, the common law had developed various rules which determined the rights of riparian owners to abstract water. These have largely been superseded by the legislation but need to be considered.

3.18.1 Riparian rights

Owners of property adjoining a river, known as riparian owners or occupiers, have the right to what the courts called the 'ordinary use of water flowing past their land'. In *Miner v Gilmore* (1859), Lord Kingsdown stated that:

> By the general law applicable to running streams, every riparian proprietor has a right to what may be called the ordinary use of water flowing past his land; for instance to the reasonable use of the water for his domestic purposes and for his cattle, and this without regard to the effect which such use may have, in case of a deficiency on a proprietor lower down the stream.

Not only does this view have potentially detrimental consequences for riparian owners further downstream, it clearly takes no account of any environmental consequences of such actions. However, the position is qualified to the extent that uses which may be regarded as extraordinary can only be carried out if they do not cause harm to lower riparian occupiers. Therefore, if one riparian owner wished to use water for what would be described as an extraordinary use, they could only do so if it would not harm the rights of others. This was the view taken in the case of *Rugby Joint Water Board v Walters* (1967), where the court stated that the water removed must either have no effect on the river or it must be returned to it substantially undiminished in quantity or quality. This more recent decision appears to reflect the changing attitude to the environment in so far as the decision is couched in terms of the quality of the river in its own right.

3.18.2 Statutory controls over water abstraction

As stated above, the common law rules have now been replaced by legislative controls over water abstraction. Growing concern about the problems of over-abstraction, water shortages, rivers drying out and the consequent loss of natural habitat led to legislative controls aimed at controlling the abstraction of water. The first attempts to provide a means of control were contained in the WA 1945, which provided some limited controls over water abstraction. However, it was the WRA 1963 which aimed to provide the first comprehensive control over water abstraction, as it prohibited the abstraction of water without an abstraction licence.

When the requirement for an abstraction licence was first introduced, many industrial companies had already been abstracting water for use in their industrial processes for many years. Section 33 of the WRA 1963 provided a special entitlement for such users, automatically granting a Licence of Right to any person who was entitled to abstract water from a source or supply in a river authority area at the date that s 33 came into force, or to a person who had a record of five years' continuous abstraction. These Licences of Right are presumed by the WRA 1991; however, such licence holders are now required to pay for their abstraction rights.

3.18.3 Abstraction licences under the WRA 1991

Abstraction licences are now granted by the Environment Agency. In order to apply for an abstraction licence, it is usually necessary to be either:

(a) an occupier of the land adjacent to the inland water; or

(b) an occupier of land above the underground strata from which the water is drawn.

The licence is issued to the occupier of land. Once his occupation ceases, the licence will lapse and the new occupier will need to notify the Environment Agency if he or she wishes to take over the licence. Water undertakers are required to apply for a licence for the water that they abstract from water courses. Sections 27 and 29 of the WRA 1991 provide various exceptions to the need to obtain an abstraction licence. Owners of the land through which water flows may use for domestic or agricultural purposes a maximum of 20 cubic metres each day without the need for a licence.

An application for an abstraction licence is made to the Environment Agency in accordance with the Water Resources (Licences) Regulations 1965 (as amended). The application must be accompanied by a fee. Notice of the application is publicised by the applicant in the *London Gazette* and a local newspaper. The EA is required when considering an application for an abstraction licence to consider:

(a) representations made in response to publicity;

(b) representations made arising from consultation with bodies such as English Nature;

(c) the effect of the proposed abstraction on other existing licence holders;

(d) the effect on other users of the supply.

3.18.4 Water abstraction licence conditions

The Environment Agency can attach conditions to licences which may require the abstractor to return the water to the watercourse after use. Monitoring of the amounts of water abstracted will usually be required as a condition of the licence. When considering whether to grant a licence or the conditions to be attached to it, the Environment Agency must consider whether the grant of licence will prevent another current licence holder, or someone extracting water for domestic or agricultural purposes, from abstracting their full entitlement. If the proposed abstraction will affect existing abstractors in this manner, then the Environment Agency must refuse to grant a licence unless the person affected agrees to the grant of the new licence.

An abstraction licence may be varied either by the Environment Agency acting on its own initiative or at the request of the licence holder. If the Environment Agency decides that it intends to vary a licence, then a licence holder has a right of appeal to the Secretary of State. If the holder suffers damage as a result of the Secretary of State's decision, he or she may recover compensation from the Environment Agency. Once a licence is granted, the EA is not liable to derogate from the grant of the licence.

The Water Bill contains provisions relating to the reform of the water abstraction licensing system and provisions which will align water pollution and contaminated land controls.

In regard to water abstraction licences, the Water Bill will take out of licensing controls approximately 40% of existing licence holders, most of whom are farmers, who abstract less than 20 cubic metres of water in a 24 hour period. The Bill provides the EA with the power to require licence holders to enter into water resource management agreements with the agency. The Bill requires the large water service companies to prepare and publish drought plans in regard to the maintenance of water supplies. The compensation provisions contained in the WRA 1991 are restricted or abolished. Compensation will only now be paid if the EA varies an abstraction licence within four years of the date of issue. The right of existing licence holders to compensation is abolished from 2012 provided the revocation or variation of licence is made to protect waters or wildlife from serious damage.

3.19 Controls relating to drinking water

The water service companies and water companies are responsible for the supply of drinking water. The legal controls which regulate their activities can be found in the WIA 1991. Although many of the provisions in this Act are outside the scope of this book, it is clear that the duty to provide wholesome drinking water is inextricably linked to the quality of water abstracted for such purposes. Section 67 of the WIA 1991 requires that water supplied for drinking purposes must be 'wholesome' at the time of supply. Section 70 makes it an offence to supply water unfit for human consumption which, if tried on indictment, can lead to an unlimited fine. Wholesome water is defined in the Water Quality Regulations 1989 which implements a number of EC directives. The EC has played a key role in determining the standards of water used for drinking water. Member States are required to comply with the standards laid down in Directive (75/440/EEC) on Surface Water for Drinking which requires that surface waters that are used for drinking water are fit for that purpose. The Member States are also required to comply with the Drinking Water Directive (80/778/EEC).

3.20 The interface of the WRA 1991 and WIA 1991 with other statutory water pollution controls

3.20.1 Part I of the EPA 1990

In addition to the controls under the WRA 1991 and the WIA 1991 discussed above, Pt I of the EPA 1990 also provides controls which relate to water pollution. Part 1 of the EPA introduced IPC as a system for controlling pollution from the most seriously polluting processes which are prescribed by the Act. Processes which are subject to IPC are controlled also by the Environment Agency, which seeks, under the IPC system, to control pollution discharged into all environmental mediums, including water, in order to achieve the best practicable environmental option. In other words for the most seriously polluting processes subject to IPC, the controls over water pollution, are not seen in isolation but are dealt with by considering the impact of the prescribed activity on the environment as a whole.

3.20.2 The PPCA 1999

The PPCA 1999 has introduced IPPC which will replace IPC controls completely by 2007. The licences issued under the PPCA 1999 control all environmental impacts of licenced installations including discharges to controlled waters.

3.20.3 Part II of the EPA 1990

Additionally, Pt II of the EPA 1990 which is concerned with waste management is also relevant. Before granting a waste management licence under Pt II of the EPA 1990, the EA must consider the likely effect of a waste deposit on groundwater.

3.20.4 Part IIA of the EPA 1990

Part IIA of the EPA 1990 establishes the contaminated land regime. The pollution pathways regulated under Pt IIA of the EPA 1990 include contamination of groundwaters.

As regards the overlap between water pollution controls and contaminated land, the Bill will alter the test for determining when land is contaminated so that less property is stigmatised for what is, in effect, minor pollution. Currently, land is contaminated in Pt IIA of the EPA 1990 if it is in such a state that 'pollution of controlled waters is being, or is likely to be caused'. The change proposed in the Water Bill will only trigger contaminated land remediation where 'significant pollution of controlled waters is being caused or there is a significant possibility of such pollution being caused'.

3.20.5 The SFFA 1975

In addition to the offences established by the WRA 1991, s 4(1) of the SFFA 1975 provides that it is an offence where a person 'causes or knowingly permits to flow, or puts, or knowingly permits to be put, into waters containing fish or into any tributaries of waters containing fish, any liquid or solid matter to such an extent as to cause the waters to be poisonous or injurious to fish or the spawning grounds, spawn or food of fish'. Although the WRA 1991 provides the main provisions relating to water pollution, charges may be brought under s 4 where fish or their spawning grounds are actually injured.

3.21 Water pollution: the pace of regulatory change

The UK's membership of the EC has had important consequences for the UK in regard to improvements in water quality and the regulation of water pollution. The European Commission has been very active in drawing up a series of water related directives, which when passed by the European Parliament, must then be transposed into national law. These directives have sought to set standards for the regulation of a wide range of activities including:

(a) discharges of dangerous substances into the aquatic environment;

(b) bathing water quality;

(c) regulation of nitrate levels;

(d) sewage effluent treatment processes;

(e) drinking water quality;

(f) water quality for freshwater fish and shellfish.

These directives establish clear parameters and objectives and their effects are channelled through to individual dischargers, via the discharge consent licensing system. Most water directives fall into two types:

(a) those, such as the Dangerous Substances Directive which set emission limits (emission standards); and

(b) those, such as the Bathing Water Directive, which set quality objectives linked to actual or intended use of the relevant waters (quality objectives).

One weakness of the emission standard approach to regulation is illustrated by the structure of the Dangerous Substances Directive. The purpose of the directive is to reduce and/or eliminate the presence of specified dangerous substances (that is, substances with toxic, persistent, carcinogenic, and bio-accumulative properties). The substances to be regulated are split into two categories: List I Black List substances which should be eliminated and List II Grey List substances which should be reduced.

Black list substances are regulated via the discharge consent licencing system. Licence conditions either relate to the maximum emission limit values detailed in the directive, or by reference to the environmental quality of the receiving waters (as reflected in the SWQO set for the relevant waters).

The regulation of grey list substances is controlled by Member States rather than the EC. Member States are required to develop their own environmental quality standards with the aim of reducing the presence of grey list substances in each stretch of water through the discharge consent licensing system.

The directive establishes a regulatory framework to control dangerous substances but is dependent upon individual 'daughter directives' to set specific standards for each substance. In 1982 the EC Commission identified 129 black list substances but almost two decades later less than 20% are the subject of daughter directives. When one compares the progress made to date with the approximate number of chemical substances known to exist (5 m) one begins to realise the chief shortcoming of the emission standard approach.

In 1997 the Commission issued a proposal for a Water Framework Directive (COM(97) 49) (as amended) with the intention of providing a greater degree of coherence of water pollution regulation and water resource management. In 2000, the EC Parliament passed a new Water Framework Directive (2000/60/EC) which is to be transposed into Member State's legal systems by the end of 2003. Whilst many of the existing statutory controls in the WRA 1991, WIA 1991, EPA 1990 and EA 1995 (and associated regulations) meet the majority of the requirements of the directive, it is understood that some legislative change will be necessary to fully implement the directive. The directive aims to achieve 'good status' for all surface and groundwaters by the end of 2015. The directive aims to: (a) arrest the deterioration of aquatic ecosystems; (b) protect and enhance aquatic ecosystems; and (c) promote sustainable water use and supply (quality and quantity). Interestingly the directive: (i) adopts a river basin approach to regulation; (ii) requires all Member States to achieve a minimum 'good' quality target for all waters by 2010; and (iii) combines the regulation of surface waters and groundwaters.

WATER POLLUTION

Water, like air, is vital for human existence. The pollution of water poses serious environmental challenges which need to be addressed to secure the continuing availability of a sufficient quantity of water which is fit for human consumption.

Although the WRA 1991 provides the main statutory provisions for controlling water pollution and prosecuting offenders, the common law still provides a means of redress for people who suffer damage from water pollution.

The Environment Agency is responsible for controlling pollution of 'controlled waters' and for achieving the improvements in water quality required in order to meet statutory water quality objectives (the functions of the NRA were transferred in full to the Environment Agency and the NRA ceased to exist in 1996).

Controlled waters are defined in s 104

Sections 82–83 of the WRA 1991 enable the Secretary of State to classify controlled waters and set water quality standards and water quality objectives. By s 84 the Environment Agency and the Secretary of State are under a general duty to exercise their powers as far as practicable to meet the specified water quality objectives.

Section 85 of the WRA 1991 creates a range of offences which involve causing or knowingly permitting various types of water pollution. The meaning of causing has been considered in *Alphacell Ltd v Woodward* (1972) and *Empress Cars*. 'Causing' involves doing something. 'Knowingly permitting' is a separate offence.

Section 88 of the WRA 1991 provides that a person will not be guilty of an offence under s 85 in respect of the entry or discharge of matter into controlled waters if the entry or discharge is made under and in accordance with a water discharge granted by the agency under the WRA 1991.

In addition to consents under the WRA 1991 it will also be a defence if the entry or discharge is made under and in accordance with:

(a) a licence granted under Pt I of the EPA 1990 or the PPCA 1999;

(b) a Waste Management Licence granted under Pt II of the EPA 1990 (there is an exception where the offence is of discharging trade or sewage effluent or where a prohibition is in force);

(c) a licence granted under Pt II of the Food and Environment Protection Act 1985 (authorising the deposit of waste at sea);

(d) s 163 of the WRA 1991 or s 165 of the WIA 1991 (concerned with discharges for works purposes);

(e) any local statutory provision or statutory order which expressly confers power to discharge effluent into water; or

(f) any prescribed enactment.

Section 89 provides further defences.

The WRA 1991 also enables preventative action to be taken to avoid water pollution by virtue of ss 92–95 of the WRA 1991.

Section 161 enables the Environment Agency to undertake works to either prevent pollution or to clean up where pollution has taken place. Sections 161A–D enable the agency to serve a Works Notice on any person causing water pollution.

Section 190 of the WRA 1991 requires the EA to maintain a publicly accessible register of information relating to the regulation of controlled waters.

Persons whose 'riparian rights' are damaged by the activities of polluters may claim compensation using the common law principles in the law of torts (nuisance, negligence, trespass, and the rule in *Rylands v Fletcher*).

The WRA 1991 does not restrict the right of any person to commence a private prosecution in regard to breaches of the WRA 1991.

Discharges of trade and sewage effluent to the sewer system are regulated by the Water Industry Act 1991. The large privatised water service companies (which are responsible for both water supply and sewage treatment) regulate such discharges by means of a discharge licensing system (s 118 of the WIA 1991). Discharges into the sewers without the benefit of a licence or in breach of licence conditions are unlawful.

The abstraction of water from surface and groundwaters (controlled waters) is regulated by the EA under the WRA 1991 using a licensing system.

The large water service companies and the smaller water companies supply drinking water to consumers. Section 67 of the WIA 1991 requires that this water is 'wholesome'. Under s 70 of the WIA 1991, it is an offence to supply water that is unfit for human consumption.

A new Water Bill is currently in the 'system' and is likely to lead, when it becomes law, to a major overhaul of the water abstraction licensing system.

Current water pollution control regimes in all EC Member States will be amended to give effect to the new European Water Framework Directive (2000/60/EC) which must be transposed into UK law by December 2003. Under the new directive, all surface and groundwaters must achieve 'good status' by 2015.

CHAPTER 4

WASTE MANAGEMENT

4.1 Introduction

Part II of the Environmental Protection Act (EPA) 1990, as amended by the Environment Act (EA) 1995, and supplemented by the Waste Management Regulations 1994, the Special Waste Regulations 1996, and the Controlled Waste (Registration of Carriers and Seizure of Vehicles) Regulations 1991 (as amended) comprise the main elements of the regulatory regime relating to the management of solid waste arisings in England and Wales. The EPA 1990 has introduced a stricter and more extensive regulatory framework than had previously existed under the Control of Pollution Act (COPA) 1974. In particular the EPA 1990 has introduced a statutory duty of care which creates 'cradle to grave' responsibility for all persons in the waste chain who handle waste from the time it is created to the time it is finally disposed of. The definition of 'waste' has been amended, as a result of European Community (EC) legislation, so that a greater range of solid wastes are now subject to regulatory control. In addition, special controls apply to wastes which are particularly dangerous or difficult to handle.

Waste management licensing controls have been transferred to the Environment Agency which is equipped with a wide range of administrative powers and criminal law offences to enable it to enforce compliance with the terms of waste management licences.

Progressive waste policy, largely driven by EC policy developments, has brought about a planned and pro-active approach to solid waste regulation with an emphasis on waste reduction and recycling. In contrast to COPA 1974 the EPA 1990 focuses upon the management of waste throughout its lifecycle rather than concentrating simply upon its disposal.

The EPA 1990 is an example of a Command and Control regulatory regime which requires those persons (usually companies) who engage in waste management operations to obtain a waste management licence authorising and legitimising those activities. There are, however, a significant number of activities which are exempt from the legal obligation (in s 35 of the EPA 1990) to obtain a waste management licence. These controls represent a coherent and integrated response to the problems associated with the high level of waste production in an industrialised society.

4.2 The problem of waste

Since the industrial revolution, pollution of the landscape has been associated with the accumulation of unwanted solid waste materials. The UK is estimated to generate around 400 m tonnes of waste divided as follows: 35% industry and commerce; 25% mining; 18% agricultural; and 5% household. Today the constant increase in wastes has become a cause for major concern. The UK, Germany, France and Italy produce 85% of the total volume of wastes in the European Union and 78% of the dangerous substances. In addition to the increased volume of waste, there has been a significant change, since the 1950s, in the nature of waste generated. Although the volume of domestic waste has increased, the weight and density has decreased. Domestic waste is no longer largely cinders and ash, but contains more packaging materials, particularly plastics. This has resulted in the need for bigger dustbins and more frequent collections. Some evidence suggests that the use of larger dustbins results in the generation of more waste! About 90% of all household rubbish is tipped as landfill.

4.2.1 Methods of disposal

In the UK, waste is largely disposed of by means of landfill (approximately 70–85% of regulated waste is disposed of in landfill). Other means of disposal include incineration and chemical treatment. Only a small percentage of waste is incinerated. All means of disposing of waste raise objections, either from environmental protection groups or from residents who object to the disposal of waste in their locality. The NIMBY (not in my back yard) philosophy is one which causes problems especially for the development of new waste incinerators and landfills. Inevitably, the disposal of waste will become more and more problematic as the amount of waste increases and the land available for landfill decreases.

4.2.2 Landfill and co-disposal

One of the particular problems faced in the UK arises out of the practice of co-disposal of waste. The UK now has a large number of abandoned landfill sites which historically, when operational, accepted a wide range of differing types of waste including inert solids, chemical and organic wastes. Often the exact composition of landfill sites is unknown. Surface and ground water contamination by leachate discharges is a particular problem. Equally, the effect that these sites have on the environment is not known. In a study of 100 UK landfill sites, 54% performed no monitoring of ground water and 50% had no gas monitoring boreholes. Where monitoring had taken place, over 50% had found surface or ground water contamination and a further 50% had found gas migration.

The current predominance of landfill as the preferred waste disposal option reflects the fact that, in most parts of the UK, it is by far the cheapest method of disposal. Landfilling does, however, have a number of disadvantages:

(a) even in well engineered sites contaminants may leach into the ground to cause pollution of groundwaters;

(b) it adversely impacts upon the amenity of people living nearby because of the smell, noise, traffic, vermin, flies and litter associated with the operation of a landfill;

(c) there is a risk of methane build-up and explosion;

(d) methane is a greenhouse gas which contributes to global warming;

(e) landfilling generates public concern in regard to its impact upon man and the environment.

The volume of waste currently landfilled is set to be considerably reduced as a result of the waste reduction targets contained in the Landfill Directive and the introduction of the landfill tax.

4.2.3 Incineration and other methods of disposal

Incineration as a means of waste disposal is not widely practised in the UK as compared to other European countries. According to the 17th report of the Royal Commission on Environmental Pollution, UK incinerators only accounted for the disposal of 7% of waste arising. In 1991 there were over 200 incineration plants in the UK licensed by Waste Regulatory Authorities. Thirty of these were municipal incinerators; most of the remaining incinerators were for clinical waste or were privately owned. Clinical waste incinerators had been exempt from pollution controls and waste licensing because they benefited from Crown Immunity. This was removed in 1991 following recommendations of the Royal Commission on Environmental Pollution in its 11th report.

There are considerable differences of opinion about the desirability of incineration as a means of waste disposal. Incineration has a number of advantages over landfill. Unlike landfill, it does not produce leachate and methane, and it is able to cope with the disposal of some hazardous wastes which are unsuitable for landfilling. Incineration greatly reduces the volume of solid waste requiring final disposal. The new breed of Energy from Waste incinerators produce electricity as a by-product of the incineration process.

Conversely, incineration is more expensive than landfill. Incinerators have high capital costs and their construction may be considerably delayed by opposition to such developments encountered in the town and country planning process. Whilst incinerators do reduce the volume of material which requires disposal on or in land, they produce residues, such as bottom ashes and liquid effluent from the gas scrubbers (which clean the gases discharged to air) which will require careful disposal.

Air pollution is, however, the most significant problem associated with incineration of waste. Incineration may produce dioxins and other hazardous atmospheric pollutants which cause high levels of public concern.

Although there are concerns about the polluting effects of incinerators, there are rigorous controls over their operation. Incinerators are controlled under the following regimes:

(a) Town and Country Planning Regime (see *Gateshead MBC v Secretary of State for the Environment* (1993));

(b) waste management licensing system;

(c) Integrated Pollution Control (IPC) and Integrated Pollution Prevention and Control (IPPC).

Incinerators must meet the standards laid down in Directives (89/369/EEC), (89/429/EEC) and (94/67/EEC) which relate to the incineration of hazardous waste. In addition to landfilling and incineration, waste may be disposed of by the following methods which fall outside the ambit of the EPA 1990:

(a) landraise – this form of solid waste disposal (for example, the construction of slag heaps) is usually associated with the disposal of mine or quarry wastes;

(b) discharge of waste to sewers;

(c) discharge of waste to controlled waters;

(d) landspreading of wastes to 'condition' agricultural land.

4.3 The historical development of statutory waste controls

4.3.1 Public health protection

The system of waste regulation in this country has its roots in public health controls. Before 1972, there was no legislation primarily concerned with waste production and disposal. There were some basic provisions in the Public Health Acts of 1848 and 1936 which enabled local authorities to remove house and trade refuse and to require removal of any 'accumulation of noxious matter'. The Public Health Act 1936 placed the local authorities under a statutory duty to inspect their areas to detect 'statutory nuisances' including 'any accumulation or deposit which is prejudicial to health'. (These provisions are now enacted by ss 79–82 of the EPA 1990.) However, the aim of this early legislation was to protect public health from the problems of disease and vermin associated with the industrial revolution rather than dealing with the environmental problems associated with waste creation.

4.3.2 Town and country planning controls

The Town and Country Planning Act (TCPA) 1947 provided the first preventive legislation requiring new developments, including waste disposal sites, to obtain planning permission (that is, a planning permit or licence). The deposit of waste on land is 'development' within the terms of the town and country planning regime and requires planning permission. Certain waste facilities may now require an environmental assessment to be carried out as part of the planning process. Current planning controls relating to waste are now to be found in the TCPA 1990.

4.3.3 The COPA 1974

Growing concern in the early 1970s about the detrimental environmental effects of waste led the Government to set up two working groups on refuse disposal and toxic waste. The reports of these two groups provided the impetus for the COPA 1974. However, prior to that legislation, the Government introduced the Deposit of Poisonous Wastes Act 1972 in response to a series of incidents concerning indiscriminate dumping of toxic wastes. The 1972 Act is now repealed but it was the first attempt at statutory control of industrial waste disposal in the UK.

The COPA 1974 was the first attempt at achieving a degree of comprehensive pollution control in the UK. It introduced the requirement for local authorities to make plans regarding the waste generated in their areas and also introduced a system of licensing to control sites where waste was deposited. The Act required all Waste Disposal Authorities (WDA) (which were the county councils in England and the district councils in Wales and Scotland) to draw up a plan for the disposal of all household, commercial and industrial waste generated in its area. These plans were to be reviewed and modified by the WDA where appropriate. The authorities were placed under a statutory duty to publicise the draft plans, giving the public an opportunity to make representations. In addition, there was a requirement that the WDAs consult with the water authorities, other levels of local government and other relevant bodies. Waste plans had to include information on the types and quantities of waste which would arise in the area, or be brought into it during the period of the plan, the methods of disposal and the provision of waste sites. The WDAs were also under a statutory duty to consider what arrangements could reasonably be made for reclaiming waste materials.

4.3.4 COPA 1974 – site licensing

The COPA 1974 introduced a comprehensive licensing system for the disposal of waste on land, over and above the existing planning controls. It made it an offence to deposit household, commercial or industrial waste on land, unless the land in question was licensed by a WDA. In May 1994, the site licence provisions of COPA 1974 were superseded by the waste management licence system under Pt II of the EPA 1990. Existing COPA 1974 licences were automatically transferred into EPA 1990 waste management licences. As many existing licence holders obtained their licences under the COPA 1974 regime, it is necessary to compare the two systems of waste regulation.

4.3.5 Defects in the COPA 1974

The COPA 1974 was the first comprehensive piece of legislation to tackle environmental pollution in an integrated way, and regulated air pollution, noise nuisance and waste on land. In fact, the COPA 1974 was used as a model for the EC Directive on Waste Framework (75/442/EEC). However, the COPA 1974, despite its worthy aims, was defective in the following ways:

(a) the regulatory bodies were responsible for both waste regulation and waste disposal operations and this gave rise to a conflict of interest (that is, the poacher and gamekeeper issue);

(b) the regulatory bodies had very limited powers to refuse a licence application or control the transfer of licences;

(c) only those licence conditions which related specifically to the licensed activity, that is, the deposit of waste, could be enforced. Conditions relating to the management of sites and monitoring, for example, were unenforceable;

(d) licences could be surrendered at will. Disreputable licence holders could surrender licences to avoid obligations and liabilities arising from the licensed site.

4.4 Part II of the the EPA 1990

Waste management regulation in this country has undergone substantial reorganisation in recent years. Part II of the EPA was enacted to provide a more comprehensive regime for dealing with waste on land, and also to address some of the defects in the COPA 1974 system. The EPA 1990, as amended by the EA 1995, created a regulatory framework which has been supplemented by detailed secondary legislation. In May 1994, the Waste Management Licencing Regulations were finally introduced, bringing into force the provisions relating to the licensing system. With a few notable exceptions (s 61 in particular), most of the provisions of Pt II of the EPA 1990 are now in force.

The EPA 1990 did far more than re-enact the provisions of the COPA 1974. It introduced a number of very significant changes in the whole of the waste chain. In particular, the EPA 1990 shifted the focus from the concept of waste disposal under the provisions of the COPA 1974 to the concept of waste management. The imperative behind the Act was that the legislative controls should relate to waste at all points in the waste chain creating a 'cradle to grave' system of control. The main changes introduced by the EPA 1990 are summarised below. The EPA 1990:

(a) introduced a much stricter licensing system, particularly in relation to qualifications of licence holders, licence conditions and surrender of licences;

(b) established a statutory duty of care applicable to anyone who imports, produces, carries, keeps, treats or disposes of controlled waste;

(c) reorganised the functions of the regulatory authorities to avoid the poacher and gamekeeper scenario that existed under the COPA 1974.

4.4.1 The EA 1995

In relation to waste management the Environment Act (EA) 1995 introduced a new definition of 'directive waste' to accord with the EC Waste Framework Directive (75/442/EEC), as amended. The principal change brought about by the EA 1995 was the transfer of the waste regulatory functions of the Waste Regulation Authorities (WRAs) to the newly established Environment Agency. The EA 1995 also made a number of amendments to the waste management licensing system, for example, the Environment Agency's enforcement powers were strengthened. The EA 1995 repealed s 61 of the EPA 1990 (concerned with closed landfills). On a more strategic level s 92 of the EA 1995 inserted s 44A into the EPA 1990 which empowered the Secretary of State with responsibility for producing a national waste strategy and ss 93–95 of the EA 1995 introduced new provisions concerning producer responsibility for waste.

4.5 What is waste?

The statutory definition of waste, contained in Pt II of the EPA 1990 as amended by the EA 1995, is crucial to understanding the remit of waste management controls in the UK. The definition distinguishes those substances, materials, and articles which fall within the statutory definition and are therefore regulated by the Command and Control regulatory regime contained in Pt II of the EPA 1990, and those which fall outside the regime and are therefore not subject to the EPA 1990 controls.

The original definition of waste contained in the EPA 1990 has been amended to take account of EC Directives (75/442/EEC) and (91/156/EEC). Before we turn to examine the rather complex statutory definition the following introductory remarks are called for.

It is helpful to think of a waste substance, material, or article from the perspective of the person who wishes to dispose of it. A substance, material, or article will, as a general rule, be waste if the intention of the person who produced it, or who is currently in possession of it, is to rid (that is, dispose) himself of it. The substance, material, or article is 'waste' regardless of any commercial value it has. For example, a sawmill will produce large quantities of sawdust as a by-product of its timber cutting operations. This material may be of no further use to the sawmill and the owner of the sawmill will desire to rid himself of it. The sawdust is 'waste' and continues to be so despite the fact that it may be sold, as a raw material feedstock, to a fibreboard manufacturer. This aspect of the definition of waste is reflected in Government policy guidance. Department of the Environment (DoE) Circular 11/94 draws attention to the critical issue: 'Has the substance or object been discarded so that it is no longer part of the normal commercial cycle or chain of utility?'

4.6 The legal definition of waste

4.6.1 Directive waste

Section 75(2) and (3) of the EPA 1990 provides the original statutory definition of waste, referred to in the statute as 'controlled waste', which determined which substances and objects were subject to the waste management controls in Pt II of the EPA 1990. These provisions have been amended by Sched 2B to the EPA 1990, regs 1(3) and 24(8), and Sched 4, para 9 of the Waste Management Licensing Regulations 1994, to provide us with a new definition of waste: 'directive waste'. Directive waste is defined in Art 1(a) of the Waste Framework Directive (75/442/EEC), as amended by Directive (91/156/EEC) as 'any substance or object in the categories set out in Annex 1 (of the Directive) which the holder discards, or intends to discard, or is required to discard'.

The definition of 'directive waste' comprises a two stage test. Directive waste is:

(a) a substance or object falling within the 16 categories in Annex 1 of the directive. (The 16 categories are reproduced in Sched 4 of Pt II of the Waste Management Regulations 1994);

WHICH

(b) the holder discards, intends to discard, or is required to discard.

The 16 categories of substances or objects referred to in the Waste Management Regulations 1994 are summarised below:

(1) production or consumption residues not otherwise specified below;

(2) off specification products (for example, rejects);

(3) products whose 'sell by' date has expired;

(4) materials which have been spilled, lost, or have undergone other mishap (for example, materials contaminated by accident);

(5) materials contaminated or soiled as a result of planned actions (for example, residues from cleaning operations, packing waste materials, waste containers, etc);

(6) unusable parts (for example, reject batteries, exhausted catalysts, etc);

(7) substances which no longer perform satisfactorily (for example, contaminated acids and solvents);

(8) residues from industrial processes (for example, metal smelting slags and still bottom residues);

(9) residues from pollution abatement processes (for example, scrubber sludges, baghouse dusts and spent filters);

(10) machining or finishing residues (for example, lathe turnings and mill scales);

(11) residues from raw materials extraction and processing operations (for example, mining residues and oil field slops);

(12) adulterated materials (for example, oils contaminated with PCBs);

(13) any materials, substances, or products whose use has been banned by law;

(14) products for which the holder has no further use (for example, agricultural, household, office, commercial and shop discards);

(15) contaminated materials, substances, or products resulting from land remediation (for example, contaminated soils);

(16) any materials, substances, or products which are not contained in the above categories (a miscellaneous 'catch-all' provision).

This list is an illustrative guide to the type of substances or objects which will fall within the definition of directive waste provided they are discarded. They are not the final word on what will, or will not, fall within the definition of directive waste.

4.6.2 What is meant by 'discarded'?

The Department of the Environment (DoE) Circular 11/94 suggests a number of questions that should be answered in order to determine whether something is waste or not. These are:

(a) Has the item been discarded so that it is no longer part of the normal commercial cycle or chain of utility?

    ○ If the answer is no the matter is not waste.

(b) Has the item been consigned to a disposal operation?

    ○ If the answer is yes it is almost certainly waste.

(c) Has the item been abandoned or dumped?

    ○ If the answer is yes it is waste.

(d) Has the item been consigned to a specialised recovery operation?

    ○ If the answer is yes it is waste.

(e) Can the item be used in its present form without being subjected to a specialised recovery operation?

    ○ If the answer is yes then the item may well not be waste.

(f) Does the owner have to pay for the item to be taken away?

    ○ If the answer is yes this would usually suggest the matter is waste, however there are exceptions.

(g) Will the person who receives the item regard it as something to be disposed of rather than a useful product?

    ○ If the answer is that the item is a useful product it may be waste.

(h) Has the item been reprocessed such that it can now re-enter the commercial cycle?

    ○ If the answer is yes it is no longer waste.

Therefore, it can be seen from the list of suggested questions that an object in one of the 16 waste categories in Sched 2B will not be waste, if, for instance, it is sent to a recovery operation or is sold to a specialist recovery operation. On the other hand, it will be regarded as waste, according to the DoE circular, if it is sent to a disposal operation, is discarded, abandoned, dumped or otherwise dealt with as if it were waste. Schedule 4 to the Waste Management Licensing Regulations 1994 provides definitions of disposal and recovery operations.

4.6.3 What constitutes a disposal operation and what constitutes a recovery operation?

Disposal operations (listed in Sched 4, Pt III of the Waste Management Licensing Regulations 1994) include:

(a) landfill or land raising;

(b) land treatment of waste such as biodegradation of sludge in soil;

(c) deep injection;

(d) surface impoundment;

(e) incineration;

(f) permanent storage.

Recovery operations (listed in Sched 4, Pt IV of the Waste Management Licensing Regulations 1994) include:

(a) solvent recovery;

(b) recycling/recovery of organic substances which are not used as solvents;

(c) recycling/reclamation of metals and their compounds;

(d) recovery of waste oil;

(e) spreading waste on land for agricultural purposes.

Substances consigned to a recovery operation will not automatically be waste. There is a distinction, however, between recovery operations and specialist recovery operations. Waste consigned to a specialist recovery operation will always be waste. Unfortunately, no definition of specialist recovery operations is provided. However, it is apparent that a specialist recovery operation is one in which waste materials are recovered or recycled for reuse in a way which removes or reduces the threat posed by the original waste and which results in a new raw material.

The DoE Circular 11/94 gives various practical examples of when something is waste, however as stated earlier, the circular is neither definitive nor legally binding.

Whether a substance or object is discarded by the waste holder depends upon whether the substance or object has been consigned to a waste recovery operation or a waste disposal operation. If it has then the material is directive waste (see *Mayer Parry Recycling Ltd v Environment Agency* [1999] Env LR 489; *Inter-Environnement Wallonie v Regione Wallonie* [1998] Env LR 625; and the combined *Tombesi* litigation in *Tombesi* [1998] Env LR 59).

'Directive disposal operations' are the activities listed in Sched 4 of Pt III of the Waste Management Regulations 1994 and include disposal by landfilling and incineration. Schedule 4 contains an illustrative, as opposed to a definitive, list of disposal operations.

'Directive recovery operations' are listed, for illustrative purposes, in Pt IV of the Waste Management Regulations 1994. These activities include operations where the recovery process is part of a larger industrial process (sometimes referred to as being within the 'normal industrial cycle'). Distinguishing between normal industrial processes and specialised recovery operations is partly dependent upon the official guidance contained in Circular 11/94. This guidance describes specialised recovery operations as those which (i) reuse substances or objects which are no longer part of the normal industrial cycle of use, or (ii) recycle substances or objects in ways which reduce the threat originally posed by them.

In *Mayer Parry Recycling Ltd v Environment Agency* (see above) the High Court considered the factors which could be taken into account in deciding whether an operation was a normal industrial process or a recovery operation. Of considerable significance was whether the business, which was the relevant waste producer or waste holder, was listed in the Waste Framework Directive as a recovery operation (such as a metals recycling business). There is a rebuttable presumption that the activities carried out by a recovery business constitute recovery operations.

4.6.4 Controlled waste

Most of the provisions in Pt II of the EPA 1990 refer to 'controlled waste'. Sections 75(4) to (7) of the EPA 1990 define the wastes which are 'controlled' by Pt II of the EPA 1990. The definition of controlled waste in s 75(4) of the EPA 1990 stated controlled waste as 'household, industrial or commercial waste or any such waste'. This definition has been amended by the Waste Management Licensing Regulations 1994 which amend the provisions of the Controlled Waste Regulations 1992 SI 1992/588 so that anything which is not directive waste shall not be treated as controlled waste. Although controlled waste is broken down into three categories (see below), it is nevertheless directive waste. The classification of controlled wastes into three broad heads is largely important in terms of the provisions relating to collection. For example, household waste is collected free of charge (with a few exceptions) whereas charges are made for the collection of commercial and industrial waste.

* *Household waste* includes waste from domestic properties, caravans, residential homes, educational establishments, hospitals, nursing homes (subject to Regulations).

* *Industrial waste* means waste from any of the following premises: factories (see Factories Act 1961); public transport premises; premises used to supply gas, water, electricity, sewerage, postal or telecoms services. Waste from construction or demolition operations is also termed industrial waste as is

waste from contaminated land. Industrial waste is sometimes referred to as trade waste.

- *Commercial waste* includes waste from premises used wholly or mainly for the purposes of a trade or business or for the purposes of sport, recreation or entertainment, except household, industrial, mining, quarrying and agricultural waste, or any other waste specified in Regulations.

Not all types of waste are 'controlled'. For example, waste from agricultural premises, waste from mines and quarries, explosive or most radioactive waste fall outside the ambit of the Pt II, EPA 1990 regulatory controls.

4.6.5 Special waste

4.6.5.1 Introduction

Special waste, like other directive waste, is subject to waste management regulation under Pt II of the EPA 1990, however, because special waste is dangerous and/or difficult to dispose of it is subject to additional controls. Special wastes include acids, alkalis, asbestos, pesticides and flammable solvents. Special wastes are 'special' because of their harmful properties. For example, they may be flammable, irritant, corrosive, toxic or carcinogenic.

4.6.5.2 The Control of Pollution (Special Waste) Regulations 1980

The original definition of special waste was contained in the Control of Pollution (Special Waste) Regulations 1980 SI 1980/1709. The regulations were commonly known as s 17 regulations because they were enacted under the provisions of s 17 of the COPA 1974. The 1980 regulations provided a definition of special waste and also established a detailed system of written documentation which would accompany the transfer of special waste, known as the consignment note system. The purpose of the regulations was to control the movements of those special wastes which by definition were dangerous or difficult to dispose of. The definition of special waste under the 1980 regulations was by means of an inclusive list and set of criteria. The term 'special waste' applied to all prescription only medicinal products (as defined by s 130 of the Medicines Act 1968) and any controlled waste which consisted of or contained any substances listed in Sched 1 of the regulations, if it was also dangerous to life, or had a flash point of 21°C or less. This definition was subject to some criticism on the basis that the criteria laid down defined special waste not by reference to possible environmental damage, but by reference to the possible effect on human health.

4.6.5.3 The Special Waste Regulations 1996 and the definition of special waste

The 1980 regulations were replaced in 1996 by new regulations introduced under the auspices of s 62 of the EPA 1990. The Special Waste Regulations 1996 SI 1996/972 came into force on 1 September 1996. The regulations give effect to the provisions of the EC Hazardous Waste Directive (91/689/EEC). The 1996 regulations provide a new definition of special waste and in doing so extend the controls over wastes which were not previously defined as special. In addition, the 1996 regulations modified the system of consignment notes established in the 1980 regulations.

The provisions of the EPA 1990 dealing with the waste offences, licensing system and duty of care apply equally to special waste. However, since special waste is by definition dangerous and difficult to dispose, any offences involving special waste will tend to attract higher sanctions.

The definition of waste as provided in the 1996 Special Waste Regulations, essentially has two component parts. Effectively, the definition covers waste on the hazardous waste list (reg 2(1)), as required by the EC directive, but also includes a further catch-all provision (reg 2(2)) to ensure that wastes which were previously defined as special under the 1980 regulations continue to be defined as special waste under the 1996 regulations. The definitions provided are complex and reference should be made to Sched 2 to the regulations.

4.6.5.4 Official guidance

The 1996 Special Waste Regulations are supported by official guidance: *Special Wastes: A Technical Guidance Note on their Definition and Classification* (DETR, 1999).

Of particular significance in the regulations are the provisions which relate to:

(a) the requirement for special waste holders to give a minimum of three days' notice to the Environment Agency before moving a consignment of special waste. There are limited exceptions to the requirement to pre-notify the Environment Agency of special waste movements (for example, lead acid batteries, movements of waste for storage purposes between companies in the same company group, and defective products which are returned to manufacturers or suppliers). Notification is effected by a consignment note system which obviates the need to complete a waste transfer note (see Duty of Care provisions below). A fee of £15 is currently payable per consignment;

(b) a ban on waste carriers and consignees (i) mixing special waste with normal directive waste, unless mixing is necessary to ensure the safe disposal of special waste, and (ii) mixing certain classes of special waste;

(c) consignment notes which provide improved descriptions of special waste, especially its hazardous properties;

(d) improvements in record keeping. In addition to the special waste consignment note system any person who deposits special waste is required to keep details of the location of each deposit. Generally this information will be recorded on a map of the relevant site. Records must be maintained throughout the lifetime of the site (for example, a landfill site) and must be passed on to the Environment Agency at the time the site licence is surrendered or revoked;

(e) simplification of procedures in regard to regular special waste movements;

(f) periodic regulatory inspections of the premises of special waste producers;

(g) the introduction of 14 hazard criteria (see Sched 2, Pt II, Special Waste Regulations 1996) to determine when directive waste is also 'special waste'.

4.6.5.5 Waste on the Hazardous Waste List

Regulation 2(1) of the 1996 Special Waste Regulations states that (subject to provisions in reg 2(5) and (6) – see below), special waste is any controlled waste (that is, directive waste): (a) to which a six digit code is assigned in the list set out in Pt I of Sched 2 to the Regulations. The list is far too long to reproduce in a text of this nature; however, the following extract gives an example of what the list looks like.

Waste Code	Description
05	wastes from petroleum refining
	natural gas purification and
	pyrolitic treatment of coal
0501	oily sludges and solid wastes
050103	tank bottom sludges
050104	acid alkyl sludges
050105	oil spills
050107	acid tars
050108	other tars

Inclusion in the list does not necessarily mean the waste is special waste. Regulation 2(1) states that the waste must also demonstrate any of the properties specified in Pt II of the schedule (subject to the provisions in reg 2(3)). Part II of the schedule provides a list of hazardous properties as follows:

H1	Explosive
H2	Oxiding
H3-A	Highly flammable
H3-B	Flammable
H4	Irritant

H5   Harmful

H6   Toxic

H7   Carcinogenic

H8   Corrosive

H9   Infectious

H10   Teratogenic

H11   Mutagenic

H12   Substances or preparations which release toxic or very toxic gases in contact with air, water or land

H13   Substances or preparations capable by any means, after disposal, of yielding another substance, eg, a leachate, which possesses any of the characteristics listed above.

H14   Ecotoxic

Each of these properties is defined. For example, in relation to H1, 'Explosives' are substances and preparations which may explode under the effect of flame or which are more sensitive to shocks or friction than dinitrobenzene.

Regulation 2(3) deals with the determination of whether or not a waste displays certain of the properties (toxic, very toxic, harmful, corrosive, irritant or carcinogenic) mentioned in Pt II.

4.6.5.6 Other wastes which are special waste

In addition special waste is (subject to provisions in reg 2(6) – see below) any controlled waste (that is, directive waste) which:

(a) displays any one of the following properties:

- o H3 – a 'highly flammable' (liquid substances and preparations having a flash point below 21ºC);
- o H4 – 'irritant': non corrosive substances and preparations which, through immediate, prolonged or repeated contact with the skin or mucous membrane, can cause inflammation;
- o H5 – 'harmful': substances and preparations which, if they are inhaled or ingested or if they penetrate the skin, may involve limited health risks;
- o H6 – 'toxic': substances and preparations (including very toxic substances and preparations), which if they are inhaled or ingested or if they

penetrate the skin, may involve serious, acute or chronic health risks and even death;

- o H7 – 'carcinogenic': substances and preparations which, if they are inhaled or ingested or if they penetrate the skin, may induce cancer or increase its incidence;
- o H8 – 'corrosive': substances and preparations which may destroy living tissue on contact;

(b) in addition, special waste is any controlled waste which is a medicinal product as defined in s 130 of the Medicines Act 1968 of a description, or falling within a class, specified in an order under s 58 of that Act (medicinal products on prescription only).

4.6.5.7 Exceptions

Certain wastes which fall within the definition of special waste are excepted, by virtue of reg 2(5) and (6). Household waste is excepted unless it comprises clinical waste, asbestos, synthetic oils and greases, and minerals (reg 2(6)). Also there are exceptions where a quantity of waste comprises less than 3% special waste (reg 2(5)).

4.6.6 Radioactive wastes

The Waste Management Regulations 1996 apply to radioactive wastes which fall outside the ambit of s 78 of the EPA 1990. Section 62 of the EPA 1990 empowers the SOSE to make regulations which provide for the control of radioactive wastes under the special waste control regime. Such controls will only apply to radioactive wastes which have harmful properties characteristic of special wastes.

4.7 The system of waste regulation

By virtue of the EA 1995 the Environment Agency was tasked with the responsibility for the waste management licensing system under Pt II of the EPA 1990. The Environment Agency, not only has responsibility for waste management licensing, but is also responsible for waste carrier licensing, special waste licensing, and 'policing' the duty of care. Prior to the establishment of the Environment Agency the system of waste regulation was administered by WRAs. The WRAs ceased to exist on 1 April 1996 when the Environment Agency took over their functions. Since the system of waste regulation has undergone significant change in recent years it is useful at this point to briefly consider some of those changes and to comment on the role fulfilled by the WRAs during their period of operation between 1990 and 1996.

4.7.1 Part II of the EPA 1990 prior to the EA 1995 amendments and the creation of the Environment Agency

Part II of the EPA 1990 was introduced in part to address some of the deficiencies of the COPA 1974 and to introduce a much stronger licensing system and system of waste regulation. Under the regulatory system established by the COPA 1974, local authorities were placed in the position of being both waste regulators, issuing waste disposal licences, and operating their own waste disposal sites. This type of situation is often referred to as a 'gamekeeper/poacher' scenario and often gives rise to conflicts of interest. The reasoning behind the administrative changes in the EPA 1990 was that local authorities should no longer be able to act as both regulators and operators of waste facilities and the EPA 1990 sought to provide for a division of responsibilities. Another principle reason for change was to ensure that waste disposal operations were no longer subsidised but run on a proper economic basis with charges reflecting the full economic cost of running the operation. In other words the intention was to make waste disposal operations more competitive and subject them to market forces.

The EPA 1990 therefore created three different levels of waste authority each with a different role in relation to waste management. These were defined in s 30 of the EPA 1990 as:

(a) Waste Regulation Authorities (WRAs);

(b) Waste Disposal Authorities (WDAs);

(c) Waste Collection Authorities (WCAs).

WDAs and WCAs continue to operate but the functions of the WRAs have been transferred in full to the Environment Agency.

4.7.2 WRAs (now repealed)

In non-metropolitan local authorities the WRAs were the county councils. In metropolitan areas the WRAs were the district councils, with special authorities established for Greater London, Greater Manchester and Merseyside. WRAs were intended to 'regulate' the waste industry and had no operational responsibilities. Where a local authority was both a WRA and WDA then provisions in the EPA 1990 required the local authorities' WDA functions to be carried out 'at arm's length'. Section 30(7) made it the duty of each authority which was both a WRA and a WDA to make administrative arrangements for keeping these functions separate. This meant that the actual operational functions of the WDA were not carried out by the authority itself but by a 'waste disposal contractor'. Section 30(5) defines a 'waste disposal contractor' as a person who in the course of business collects, keeps, treats or disposes of waste, being either:

(a) a company formed for all or any of these purposes by a waste disposal authority; or

(b) a company, partnership or individual (sole trader).

4.7.3 WDAs

The WDA is normally the county council in non-metropolitan areas and the district council in metropolitan areas. Special arrangements exist in London, Manchester and Merseyside The functions of the WDA are:

(a) making arrangements for the disposal of controlled waste collected in the area by WCAs;

(b) formation of waste disposal companies;

(c) provision of municipal waste sites for household waste to be deposited by residents;

(d) provision of transfer stations;

(e) waste recycling.

Section 51 of the EPA 1900 places WDAs under a duty to provide places where residents can deposit household waste and to arrange for the disposal of that waste and the waste collected by the WCAs.

4.7.4 WCAs

WCAs are the district councils or London boroughs. Their functions are:

(a) to arrange for the collection of household waste in their area;

(b) to arrange for the collection of commercial or industrial waste on request;

(c) to provide bins/receptacles;

(d) to collect waste and to deliver for disposal as directed by the waste disposal authority;

(e) to investigate, draft plans and make arrangements for recycling.

4.7.5 Waste collection

WCAs are placed under a statutory duty to collect household waste free of charge (except where the waste is not reasonably accessible and other arrangements can be made). In certain circumstances, WCAs can charge for household waste collection. (See Sched 2 to the Controlled Waste Regulations 1992.) They include large items, garden waste and other difficult wastes or waste produced from commercially run residential premises.

The WCAs also have a duty, if requested by the occupier of premises in its area, to collect commercial waste, and may charge a reasonable sum for the collection and disposal of the waste unless the authority considers it inappropriate to do so.

The WCAs are required by s 48 of the EPA 1990 to deliver the waste collected to such places as directed by the WDAs unless the WCAs intend to recycle the waste. If the WCAs keep the waste for recycling purposes they will still need to secure the consent of the WDAs, since WDAs have the power to buy and sell waste for recycling purposes.

4.8 The waste management licensing system

The requirement for a waste management licence to legitimise directive waste disposal operations and directive waste recovery operations lies at the heart of the waste regulatory regime established by the EPA 1990. The acquisition of a waste management licence and compliance with its conditions will shield the licence holder from liability for s 33(1)(a) and (b) of the EPA 1990 offences. Nevertheless activities which are carried out in accordance with the terms of a waste management licence may still constitute a criminal offence under s 33(1)(c) of the EPA 1990.

The Environment Agency is responsible for regulating the waste management licensing regime and is equipped with a range of enforcement powers to ensure that licence holders comply with their licences. The current regime is a considerable improvement on the former waste management licensing system contained in the COPA 1974.

The system of waste management licences came into force in May 1994 by virtue of the Waste Management Licensing Regulations 1994 SI 1994/1056 (as amended). The regulations were enacted some four years after the EPA 1990, although this should be seen as an improvement on the COPA 1974, where some of the provisions took over 10 years to come into effect (and others never came into effect!). COPA 1974 licensed sites automatically became EPA 1990 licensed sites on 1 May 1994. The new system is complex and all waste producers need to determine, by reference to the Waste Management Licensing Regulations, whether or not they need to obtain a waste management licence or whether they are exempt. In the latter case they may still need to register with the WRA.

The main changes in the licensing system introduced by Pt II of the EPA 1990 as amended are as follows:

(a) applicants for licences must satisfy the 'fit and proper person test';

(b) all aspects of the licence are enforceable at all times, that is, not only when the disposal operations are in progress;

(c) the Environment Agency must agree any proposed licence transfer;

(d) new arrangements in respect of surrender of licences.

The effectiveness of the waste management licensing regime is also improved by:

(a) a range of widely drafted criminal offences to underpin the EPA 1990;

(b) a range of administrative enforcement powers which provide the Environment Agency with an alternative mechanism, to prosecution, to enforce compliance with the terms of licences;

(c) a duty of care, breach of which constitutes a criminal offence, applying to everyone in the 'waste chain', and which ensures that directive waste is properly handled from 'cradle to grave'.

4.8.1 Definition of a waste management licence

Section 35 of the EPA 1990 defines a waste management licence as a:

> ... licence granted by a waste regulation authority authorising the treatment, keeping or disposal of any specified description of controlled waste in or on specified land or the treatment or disposal of any specified description of controlled waste by means of a specified mobile plant.

(Section 35 must now be interpreted by reference to the fact that licensing relates to both directive disposal and directive recovery operations and that the EA is the relevant waste authority.)

Where the Environment Agency grants a licence, it will include any conditions that it thinks are appropriate. There are two different types of waste management licence: the site licence and the mobile plant licence. The site licence is granted to the person in occupation of the land. Occupation is not defined but will be someone who has some degree of control associated with or arising from the presence on or use of land. The mobile plant licence is granted in respect of mobile plant which is defined under s 29(9) (subject to a power to further definition by regulation) as 'plant which is designed to move or to be moved, whether on roads or other land'.

4.8.2 Exemptions

The combined effect of reg 17 and Sched 3 of the Waste Management Regulations 1994 is to exempt a range of activities from waste licensing control. Sites operating exempt activities are nevertheless required to register with the Environment Agency, and supply details of the activity, the place it is being carried on, and the exemption relied upon. Under reg 18(1), it is an offence to carry on an exempt activity without registration, save that this requirement does not apply to private individuals. Except in very limited circumstances, detailed in Sched 3, there is no exemption from licensing in the case of special waste.

The main exempt activities referred to in reg 17 and Sched 3 of the Waste Management Regulations 1994 are:

(a) temporary storage (for example, in a skip) of directive waste at the place of production pending disposal or recovery. 'Temporary' is not defined and will depend upon the particular circumstances;

(b) temporary storage of special waste by the waste producer at the place of production, subject to limitations, including, quantity and security arrangements;

(c) activities related to recovery and reuse such as bailing, compacting, and shredding;

(d) the storage or deposit of demolition and construction waste for construction related use at the place of demolition/construction;

(e) the deposit of organic materials to 'condition' land;

(f) a wide range of recycling activities including the collection of paper, cardboard, plastics, glass, textiles, and drink cans.

Also exempt is the disposal of waste within the curtilage (that is, the small area of land around a building) of a dwellinghouse (s 33(2)).

Exempt activities, except for the household waste exemption, are still subject to the prohibition contained in s 33(1)(c) of the EPA 1990 but are free of the requirements of s 33(1)(a) and (b). Further guidance on exemptions is given in Annex 5 of Circular 11/95.

The power to exclude certain activities from the licensing regime is given to the SOSE by s 33(3) and (4) of the EPA 1990. The SOSE can make regulations, excluding certain activities involving the deposit, keeping, treatment or disposal of waste, from the need to have a licence. Council Directive (91/156/EEC) permits exemptions from the licensing system providing there are other adequate controls. This is reflected in s 33(4) which states that the SOSE when exercising his powers in respect of exemptions should have regard to the expediency of excluding from the controls imposed by the waste management licensing system:

(a) any deposits which are small enough or of such a temporary nature that they may be so excluded;

(b) any means of treatment or disposal which are innocuous enough to be excluded;

(c) cases for which adequate controls are provided by other legislation.

There is some evidence that exempt sites are being used to dispose of directive waste which would ordinarily have been consigned to a landfill site, for example, by diverting inert materials for landscaping use. In view of this, the

EA is likely to press for changes in waste management law. In particular, the EA would benefit from powers to inspect exempt disposal operations, to charge for inspections and to require annual exemption registrations. It is understood that the EA would also like to see greater specifity in regard to the types of waste which benefit from exemption and changes in planning law to ensure that some exempt sites acquire planning permission authorising development.

4.8.3 The applications procedure

Applications for a waste management licence must be made in writing to the appropriate regional office of the Environment Agency accompanied by the fee payable under s 41 of the EPA 1990. There is now a standard application form which must be completed by all applicants. Where the applicant fails to provide the Environment Agency with any information required, the Environment Agency has the right to refuse to proceed with the application (s 36(1)(a) of the EPA 1990). Section 36 deals with the applications procedure and determines the considerations that the Environment Agency must take into account.

The making of false statements in any waste management licensing application (and in any applications for licence modification, transfer, or surrender) is an offence (s 44 of the EPA 1990). The maximum penalty on summary conviction in a magistrates' court is a £5,000, however, on conviction in the Crown Court the maximum penalty is an unlimited fine and/or gaol term of up to two years. There is, in such cases, a presumption of prosecution.

By virtue of s 36(3), the Environment Agency may not reject an application that has been properly made unless:

(a) the applicant is not a fit and proper person;

(b) the rejection is necessary to prevent pollution to the environment, harm to human health or serious detriment to the amenities of the locality.

Therefore, there are only two grounds for refusal; these are considered more fully below. The Environment Agency must either grant a licence or give notice of rejection within four months of receiving the application, unless an extension is agreed in writing with the applicant. Failure to deal with the application in the prescribed time is deemed a rejection (except where the delay is due to the applicant's failure to supply information requested by the Environment Agency to process that application).

4.8.3.1 Charges

As in other pollution control regimes discussed in this book, 'polluters' are required to pay for the system that controls them. The application of the 'polluter pays' principle in this instance means that charges are levied by the Environment Agency for the following:

(a) applications for waste management licences;

(b) applications for modification of the licences;

(c) transfers;

(d) surrender;

(e) subsistence, to cover the costs of the Environment Agency's supervision of the licence.

Charges for waste management licences are provided for by s 41 of the EA 1995.

4.8.3.2 Consultation and publicising the application

If the Environment Agency is minded to grant a waste management licence, it must consult with a variety of public bodies and consider any objections or representations it receives. The agency must consult the Health and Safety Executive (s 36(4)) and the appropriate planning authority. In certain protected areas (for example, a Site of Special Scientific Interest) the application must be referred to the Nature Conservancy Council for England (English Nature) or the Countryside Council for Wales. The period for consultation is 28 days. If there is any disagreement arising out of the consultation then the matter must be referred to the SOSE for decision. In reaching its decision on a waste management licensing application the Environment Agency must have regard to official guidance (s 35(8)). The relevant advice is largely contained in Waste Management Paper Number 4, 'Licensing of waste facilities', and Circular 11/94.

Arguably one significant weakness in the licensing process is the lack of effective public participation, although the Environment Agency is trialing a new procedure for the licensing of contentious sites. Waste management licensing applications are not required to be advertised in the local press. Currently central government views public participation in the waste management licensing process as superfluous on the basis that the public was provided with the opportunity to make representations and objections at the planning stage.

The Environment Agency is also required by the Waste Management Licensing Regulations to have regard to the protection of groundwater when determining a licence application. The regulations give effect to the Groundwater Directive (80/68/EEC). A new s 36A of the EPA 1990 was inserted by the EA 1995. Where the Environment Agency proposes to impose a licence condition which requires the licence holder to carry out works or do anything on land which he is not legally entitled to do (for instance requiring the licence holder to take soils samples on neighbouring land), then the Environment Agency must serve a notice on the person who owns or occupies the land (s 36A(3)). The notice will set out the relevant conditions, indicate the nature of the works that are to be carried out and specify a date by which representations are to be made to the Environment Agency. The Environment Agency must consider any representations made. Similarly, if the Environment Agency proposes to vary a waste management licence and impose such conditions they must also consult the owner occupier of the relevant land.

4.8.3.3 The fit and proper person test

The Environment Agency has a discretion whether or not to grant a waste management licence in circumstances where the applicant is not a fit and proper person. This is an entirely new requirement introduced by the EPA 1990 and specifically addresses one of the principal defects in the COPA 1974 system, namely that almost any person could obtain a waste disposal licence irrespective of their 'track record' in waste management.

Section 74(3) of the EPA 1990 provides that a person shall be treated as not being a fit and proper person if it appears to the Environment Agency:

(a) that he or another relevant person has been convicted of a relevant offence;

(b) that the management of the activities which are to be authorised by the licence are not or will not be in the hands of a technically competent person; or

(c) that the person to hold the licence has not made and has no intention of making or is no position to make financial provision adequate to discharge the obligations arising from the licence.

There are three elements to the test: the first relates to previous convictions for relevant offences; the second to the technical competence of the applicant; and the third to the applicant's financial position:

(1) *The relevant offences* – These are set down in the 1994 Waste Management Licensing Regulations, and include a range of pollution related offences. However, s 74(4) of the EPA 1990 provides that, if the Environment Agency considers it proper to do so in any particular case, it may treat a person as a fit and proper person notwithstanding that he has been convicted of a relevant offence. The Environment Agency will clearly have to take into account matters such as the gravity of any previous offences and whether or not it was a one-off offence, possibly with mitigating circumstances. The fit and proper person test in this particular regard does not simply concern the applicant but also relates to other 'relevant persons' which includes (s 74(7)):

(a) any employee of the applicant who has been convicted of a relevant offence; or

(b) a company of which the applicant was a director, manager, secretary or similar officer and which has been convicted of a relevant offence;

(c) or where the applicant is a company, any current director, manager, secretary or similar officer of the company who has been convicted of a relevant offence, or was an officer of another company when that company was convicted of a relevant offence. (See *R v Boal* [1992] QB 591 and *Woodhouse v Walsall Metropolitan BC* [1994] Env LR 30 as to who is a 'manager' for the purposes of the Act and proper person test.)

(2) *Technical competence* – The management of the licensed facility must be in the hands of technically competent persons (see reg 4 of the Waste Management Licensing Regulations 1994). A person is technically competent if he holds one of the certificates awarded by the Waste Management Industry Training and Advisory Board (WAMITAB) or a Certificate of Technical Competence. The precise qualification is determined by reference to the type of waste facility and waste that it takes. Transitional provisions concern 'existing managers'. These are persons who registered with WAMITAB before 10 August 1994, and were employed as managers in the year prior to registration. Managers of sites licensed under previous legislation, such as the COPA 1974, are presumed to be competent.

(3) *Financial resources* – The Environment Agency will need to be certain that the licence holder is in a position financially to be able to discharge the obligations arising from the licence. This means that the licence holder will need to show that he has adequate financial resources to comply with the conditions of the licence and to meet any liabilities or remedial action if a pollution event occurs, for example, through insurance, bank guarantee or contingency fund. Waste Management Paper No 4 (WMP) 'Licensing of waste management facilities' provides useful guidance on all these aspects of the fit and proper person test. In particular the guidance in WMP 4 refers to specific stages in the life of a waste management site where adequate financial provision is critical: acquisition, preparation, operation, restoration, landscaping and aftercare (especially monitoring). These stages in the lifecycle of a site should be reflected in the applicant's business plan for the site.

If the fit and proper test is satisfied the Environment Agency is under a duty to grant a waste management licence to the applicant (s 36(3)).

4.8.3.4 Rejection necessary to prevent pollution

Even if an applicant is deemed to be a fit and proper person, the Environment Agency must not grant a licence if it is satisfied that rejection is necessary to prevent pollution of the environment (pollution of the environment is defined in s 29 of the EPA 1990) or harm to human health. In most cases, this will not be an issue and the Environment Agency should be able to impose sufficiently rigorous conditions to ensure that the activity does not harm the environment or human health.

The Environment Agency can refuse an application if the activity would cause serious detriment to amenities of the locality, but they cannot have regard to this particular aspect if the activity in question has planning permission. The justification for this is that questions of amenity will already have been taken into account by the planning authority.

Section 36(3) is particularly relevant to the risk of groundwater contamination posed by waste management sites. The Waste Management Licensing Regulations 1994 provide guidance on the conditions which the regulator should include in a waste management licence to prevent or minimise the risk of escape of dangerous substances into controlled waters. One key condition will be the installation of an impermeable membrane or liner to reduce the risk of substances leaching out of the base of the site (for example, a landfill) into groundwater.

4.8.3.5 Planning and waste

The Environment Agency must refuse an application for a waste management licence if planning permission, or a certificate of lawful use or development, or an established use certificate, is required for the activity which the applicant proposes to carry on (s 36(2)) and the site does not have the benefit of such permission.

4.9 Licence conditions

The objective of the licensing system is to regulate the day to day operation of waste facilities. This should be achieved by unambiguous conditions which leave the operator in no doubt as to what the required standards are and how they are to be met. Each condition should be necessary, comprehensive, unambiguous and enforceable otherwise it will be unreasonable and challengable. In *AG's Ref (No 2 of 1988)* [1990] QB 77, the Court of Appeal struck out a site licence condition requiring a waste site to be operated so as not to cause a nuisance to adjacent property owners. The condition did not relate to the purposes of COPA 1974 (the forerunner of Pt II of the EPA 1990) and was therefore unlawful. Guidance issued by the SOSE in Waste Management Papers (see WMP 4) assists the Environment Agency in regard to the choice of appropriate conditions. Conditions attached to a waste management licence should not duplicate planning conditions relating to the use of the site for waste management purposes. The SOSE also has the power to prescribe in regulations the conditions to be attached to a licence, by virtue of s 35(6) of the EPA 1990. For example, reg 12 of the Waste Management Regulations 1994 prohibits the imposition of conditions designed purely to secure health and safety at work objectives. Regulation 14 prescribes conditions to be included in a waste management licence to comply with the Waste Oils Directive (75/439/EEC).

Section 35(3) of the EPA 1990 provides that a waste management licence will be granted on such terms and subject to such conditions as appear to the Environment Agency to be appropriate, and these conditions may relate to the activities authorised, the precautions to be taken and the works to be carried out. In practice, conditions will be set which cover fundamental issues such as the site infrastructure and site operation. They will also stipulate monitoring and record-keeping requirements, security and methods of avoiding nuisances. In practice, many of the conditions set in the licence will be the outcome of negotiation between the Environment Agency and the applicant.

The conditions that can be included in a licence can cover matters before the site becomes operational (that is, site preparation and insurance), during operation and, importantly, can include conditions after the waste operation has ceased (such as the monitoring of methane emissions and leachate production). The conditions may also extend to waste other than controlled (directive) waste (s 35(5)). The conditions will detail the types and quantities of waste which can be treated, kept or disposed of. They will also specify detailed operational matters such as methods of receiving waste, security arrangements, monitoring arrangements and after care of the site.

One condition which may be attached is particularly important: s 35(4) enables a condition to be set on a new application and also on a modification or suspension of an existing licence, requiring the holder to carry out works or do other things even though he is not generally entitled to do them. For example, a licence holder may be required to carry out sampling or monitoring on neighbouring land owned by another person. Section 35(4) further provides that any person whose consent would be required should grant or join in granting the holder of the licence such rights in relation to land as will enable the holder to comply with such a condition. (Although as noted above a person has the right to be consulted and make representations under s 36A.) WMP4 suggests that this power will be used sparingly and only when absolutely necessary. Provisions exist for compensation to be payable where conditions of this sort are imposed. Finally, it should be noted that the SOSE has the power to make regulations specifying conditions to be attached to licences.

4.9.1 Compensation to third parties

In the light of the provisions of s 35(4) of the EPA 1990 discussed above, s 35A of the EPA 1990 (inserted by Sched 22 of the EA 1995) provides that any person whose consent would be required under ss 35(4) and 38(9A) and who has granted the licence holder any rights in relation to land is entitled to be paid compensation by the licence holder. By s 36A(4) of the EPA 1990, the SOSE has the power to issue regulations prescribing a scheme of compensation (see Waste Management Licences (Consultation and Compensation) Regulations 1999 SI 1999/481).

The Environment Agency has been granted significant administrative powers to 'police' licence holders' compliance with the terms of their waste management licences. These powers are important because they enable the Environment Agency to retain control of the outcome of the enforcement process without resorting to prosecution and thereby handing control over the outcome of the case to the courts. As we shall see these powers are potentially draconian, for they enable the Environment Agency to put persistently poor operators out of business, either temporarily or permanently. Licence holders are not entitled to compensation when their operating licences are varied, suspended, or revoked (unless the relevant notice is successfully appealed).

4.10 Administration and enforcement powers

4.10.1 Variation of licences

Waste management licences can be varied by means of a Variation Notice (VN) either by the Environment Agency or at the request of the licence holder (s 37 of the EPA 1990). The Environment Agency is under a duty to vary the conditions of the licence where it is necessary to ensure licenced activities 'do not cause pollution of the environment or harm to human health or become seriously detrimental to the amenities of the locality affected by the activities' (s 37(2)) or to comply with regulations made under s 35(6)). Alternatively, the Environment Agency may choose to serve a Revocation Notice (RN).)Where the Environment Agency wishes to vary the licence because it considers a variation is desirable then it may only vary the conditions if a variation is 'unlikely to require unreasonable expense on the part of the holder' (s 37(1)(a)). Consultation is required if the Environment Agency serves a VN. Where the variation requires the licence holder to carry out works on someone else's land, then the Environment Agency is required to consult with the relevant landowner, and as noted above, compensation may be payable. The SOSE also has the right to direct the Environment Agency to modify conditions. Any variation of a licence must be effected by a notice served on the licence holder. Section 37A provides for consultation before variation in similar terms to s 36A where the variation will require the grant of rights by a third party. Although, by virtue of s 37A(9), consultation may be postponed in the event of an emergency.

Alternatively, the licence holder may want to seek a variation of the licence, for example, to accommodate different types of wastes or to extend operations. A licence holder must apply to the Environment Agency for a variation and pay the appropriate fee. Failure to determine an application to vary a licence within a period of two months, unless the period has been extended by agreement in writing, will result in the Environment Agency being deemed to have rejected the application. A licence holder can appeal to the SOSE against the decision of the Environment Agency regarding variation.

4.10.2 Transfer of licence

Waste operations are businesses run on commercial lines. Many are very profitable. Like all businesses, the ownership and control of the business can change hands. It is therefore necessary in such circumstances for there to be a transfer of the licence to the new owner/operator. Section 40 of the EPA 1990 deals with the rights of transfer. A licence may be transferred on the joint application of present holder and transferee using the prescribed form and on payment of the prescribed fee. However, the Environment Agency can only agree to the transfer if it is satisfied that the transferee is a fit and proper person. As in the other provisions relating to licences, a right of appeal exists to the SOSE. If the Environment Agency fails to determine an Environment Agency application for transfer within a period of two months (unless applicants agree in writing) the application will be deemed to have been rejected by the Environment Agency.

4.10.3 Revocation and suspension of licences

The powers of revocation and suspension (provided in s 38 of the EPA 1990) available to the Environment Agency are dependent upon certain circumstances. A licence may be revoked in whole or in part, although it can only be partially revoked if the reason is the lack of technical competence of the management. The partial revocation of the licence allows for continuing obligations to be imposed on the licence holder even if operation of the site is no longer permitted. Partial revocation may occur where the Environment Agency revokes only that part of a licence which authorised the reception and management of special waste. Complete revocation is unlikely, in most cases, because the Environment Agency will require aftercare licence conditions to remain in force.

The Environment Agency has a discretion whether to serve a Revocation Notice (RN). The notice will specify when the revocation is to take effect and which activities the notice applies to. Revocation can take place if:

(a) the licence holder ceases to be a fit and proper person as a result of a relevant offence (s 38(1) of the EPA 1990) or the management is no longer in the hands of a technically competent person (s 38(2));

(b) continuation of the licensed activities will cause pollution of the environment or harm to human health or serious detriment to amenities in the locality (s 38(1)) and these cannot be avoided by modifying conditions;

(c) the licence holder fails to comply with a s 42 notice requiring compliance with a condition of the waste management licence (s 42(6)); or

(d) the licence holder fails to pay the annual subsistence charge (s 41(7)).

The Environment Agency may suspend the licence in the following circumstances (s 38(6)):

(a) the licence holder is no longer a fit and proper person on the grounds of technical competence;

(b) the licensed activities have caused or are about to cause serious pollution of the environment or serious harm to human health;

(c) continuation of the licensed activities will continue to cause serious pollution of the environment or serious harm to human health;

(d) the licence holder fails to comply with the terms of a condition of the waste management licence (s 42(6)).

The Environment Agency has a discretion whether to serve a Suspension Notice (SN). If it chooses to serve an SN the notice will specify the dates when the suspension will commence and cease. SNs will only suspend site activities and will not affect precautionary measures designed to prevent contaminants escaping from the site.

Compensation may be payable by the Environment Agency to the site operator if, on appeal against the service of an SN, the SOSE rules that the Environment Agency acted unreasonably in suspending the waste management licence (s 43(7)).

Whilst a suspension is in effect the licence has no effect and therefore does not authorise the activities specified in the licence. However, notwithstanding suspension the Environment Agency may require the licence holder to carry out works to deal with or avert pollution or harm (s 38(9)). The measures which the licence holder is required to take under s 38(9) may extend beyond the ambit of the pre-suspension licence conditions. Again, like s 35(4), the Environment Agency may require the licence holder to do works on land which he is not otherwise entitled to do. For example, the Environment Agency may require the licence holder whose license has been suspended to carry out clean-up operations on neighbouring land. Any person whose consent would be required must grant the licence holder such rights as will enable him to fulfil the Environment Agency's requirements. A person should normally be consulted under s 36A, however the Environment Agency may postpone the service of a notice or consideration of any representations in emergency situations. A licence holder who fails without reasonable excuse to comply with any requirements under s 38(9) commits a criminal offence. The maximum penalty on summary conviction in the magistrates' court is a fine of £5,000. On conviction in the Crown Court, the maximum penalty is an unlimited fine and/or a gaol sentence of two years. In the case of special waste offences, a maximum six month term of imprisonment may be imposed in the magistrates court and a five year gaol sentence in the Crown Court. Section 38(13) allows the Environment Agency to take enforcement proceedings in the High Court in order to obtain an injunction forcing the person whose license has been suspended to carry out the required works. This is a new provision which effectively strengthens the enforcement powers of the Environment Agency.

4.11 Surrender of licences (s 39 of the EPA 1990)

It is in relation to the surrender of licences that the EPA 1990 makes some very significant changes to the COPA 1974. A fundamental flaw of the COPA 1974 waste regime was that licence holders could surrender their licences and walk away leaving the local authority with the problem of cleaning up a poorly run site. In point of fact, this is precisely what happened to many licensed sites in the months and weeks before the EPA 1990 came into force in May 1994. Many COPA licence holders surrendered their licences to avoid an automatic transfer to an EPA waste management licence and the more stringent responsibilities that that entailed. In particular, operators taking this rather radical course of action were aware of the difficulties they would face in surrendering a waste management licence. In short, the EPA 1990 provisions, concerning the surrender of licences, are much stricter than the COPA counterparts and it is no longer possible for licence holders to give up their licence at will (except in the case of mobile plant licences).

A waste management mobile plant licence may be surrendered at any time by its holder, but in the case of a site licence, the licence can only be surrendered with the agreement of the Environment Agency. If the Environment Agency accepts the application for surrender, it will issue the licence holder with a 'certificate of completion'. However, the Environment Agency can only accept the surrender if it is satisfied that the condition of the relevant land is unlikely to cause pollution of the environment or harm to human health. In order to come to a decision about surrender, the Environment Agency must first inspect the land and consider any information provided by the licence holder about the state of the land. The information which the licence holder will be asked to supply includes: site location, details of all activities carried out on site and their respective locations, the times during which various activities were being carried out on site, the quantity of waste handled, hydrogeology, methane production and leachate production. The Environment Agency has three months to determine the application or a longer period if it is agreed in writing with the applicant. The Environment Agency may, however, determine within that period that they cannot accept the surrender until certain information is supplied about the site or until it has undergone remedial works. For this reason, the licence holder should always keep accurate and detailed records about the wastes that have been deposited in order to facilitate and speed up the process of surrender.

4.12 Rights of appeal

In all of the various provisions discussed above, it has been noted that the applicant or licence holder has a right of appeal. Section 43 of the EPA 1990 provides a right of appeal to the SOSE against a determination by the Environment Agency in the following instances:

(a) an application for a licence or a variation of the conditions of a licence is rejected;

(b) a licence is granted subject to conditions;

(c) the conditions of the licence are varied;

(d) a licence is suspended;

(e) a licence is revoked;

(f) an application to surrender a licence is rejected; or

(g) an application to surrender a licence is not decided upon within three months; or

(h) an application for the transfer of a licence is rejected.

An appeal must be made within six months of the relevant decision. Details of appeal procedures are to be found in the Waste Management Licensing Regulations 1994 as amended by the 1995 Regulations (SI 1995/288).

The appellant and the Environment Agency may choose whether an appeal proceeds by way of a full hearing or by written representations (a paper based appeal). Appeals are generally heard by inspectors appointed by the SOSE.

Appeals normally suspend the effect of modification and revocation applications (s 43(4) of the EPA 1990) pending the outcome of the appeal unless the Environment Agency indicates, by notice, that the effect of a modification or revocation should not be suspended because of the overriding need to prevent pollution of the environment or harm to human health(s 43(6)). Suspension Notices are unaffected by appeals (s 43(5)). Any waste management licence holder who is aggrieved by the Environment Agency's use of its s 43(6) power or its suspension power (s 38) may request the SOSE to rule on whether the Environment Agency has acted unreasonably. If the SOSE rules in favour of the licence holder the Environment Agency may be ordered to pay compensation (s 43(7)).

4.13 Supervision and monitoring

The Environment Agency has a general duty to monitor and supervise all licensed activities (s 42). It must take the necessary steps to ensure that the licensed activities in their area do not cause pollution of the environment, harm to human health or serious detriment to the amenities of the locality. The

Environment Agency must also take steps to ensure that licence holders comply with licence conditions.

In addition, the Environment Agency will also carry out inspections of its area to ensure that there are no unlicensed activities such as fly-tipping. Unlicensed waste disposal will constitute a breach of s 33 of the EPA 1990.

4.13.1 Powers of Environment Agency officials

In order to carry out its enforcement functions the Environment Agency employs inspectors whose function it is to inspect and monitor sites, to ensure compliance with the legislation. The powers of inspection and entry, contained in ss 108–10 of the EA 1995 enable the Environment Agency inspectors:

(a) to enter at any reasonable time premises which he has reason to believe it is necessary for him to enter. This should normally be at any reasonable time unless there is an emergency, in which case entry is permitted at any time, and if need be, by force;

(b) on entering premises to take with him any other person duly authorised by the Environment Agency, and a policeman. The latter may be needed in situations where the inspector has reasonable cause to apprehend any serious obstruction in carrying out his duties;

(c) the inspector may also take any equipment or materials required for any purpose for which the power of entry is being exercised;

(d) to make such examination and investigation as may in any circumstances be necessary;

(e) to instruct that the premises or any part of them, or anything in them, be left undisturbed. The inspector may require that the premises or the part of the premises under investigation are not disturbed for as long as is reasonably necessary to enable him to carry out any examination or investigation;

(f) to take such measurements and photographs and make recordings as he considers necessary;

(g) to take samples, or instruct samples be taken, of any articles or substances found in or on the premises and also from the air, water or land in, on, or in the vicinity of the premises. Specific provisions relate to the possession, safekeeping and use in evidence of such samples;

(h) in the case of any article or substance found in or on premises which appears to him to be an article or substance which has caused or is likely cause pollution of the environment, or harm to human health, to cause it to be dismantled or subjected to any process or test (but not so as to damage or destroy it unless that is necessary);

(i) to require information from any person – the inspector can require any person whom he has reasonable cause to believe to be able to give any information relevant to any examination or investigation to answer such questions as the inspector thinks fit to ask. The person answering the questions will be required to sign a declaration of truth to the answers;

(j) to inspect any information and to take copies – the inspector can require the production of any information that he considers necessary, including information held on computer. He also has the right to inspect and take copies of such information or any entry in the records;

(k) to require facilities and assistance – here the inspector can require any person to afford him such facilities and assistance with respect to any matters or things within that person's control or in relation to which that person has responsibilities. So, for example, the inspector can require an engineer on the premises to show him how the monitoring and testing equipment is working (or not working as the case may be);

(l) any other powers conferred by regulation by the SOSE. Certain information can be withheld from the inspector if it is subject to legal professional privilege. This covers correspondence between clients and their solicitors or legal professional advisors.

4.13.2 Section 71 of the EPA 1990

Section 71 empowers the Environment Agency to serve a request for information on any person in order to obtain information relevant to the performance of the Environment Agency's statutory responsibilities. Failure to provide such information or knowingly providing false information is a criminal offence. There is a defence of 'reasonable excuse' but this does not apply to a refusal based on a violation of the rule against self-incrimination (see *R v Hertfordshire CC ex p Green Environmental Industries Ltd* [2000] 1 All ER 773 and [2000] 2 WLR 373). The s 71 power may only be used by the Environment Agency if it already has sufficient information which will form the basis of the s 71 request (see *JB and M Motor Haulage v London Waste Regulation Authority* [1993] Env LR 243). The maximum penalty on summary conviction in the magistrates' courts for breach of s 71 is a £5,000 fine. If the matter is committed to the Crown Court the maximum penalty is an unlimited fine and/or a gaol sentence of two years.

4.13.3 Seizure of vehicles

Section 6 of the EPA 1990 empowers the Environment Agency to seize any vehicle which has been used for specified illegal activities. If the Environment Agency has been unable, through its informational powers, to obtain details of the ownership of vehicles suspected of being involved in illegal waste disposal operations the Environment Agency may make an application to a magistrate for seizure of the relevant vehicle.

4.14 Clean-up powers

Section 59 of the EPA 1990 gives the Environment Agency and the WCAs power to require the removal of controlled (directive) waste where the waste has been deposited in contravention of the conditions of a waste management licence or in breach of s 33(1)(c) of the EPA 1990. The relevant authority may serve a notice on the occupier, requiring the waste to be removed, or specifying the steps to be taken to mitigate the consequences of the deposit. At least 21 days must be allowed to comply with the notice, during which time the recipient has a right to appeal to the magistrates' court. Such an appeal must be allowed if the court is satisfied that the appellant neither deposited nor knowingly caused or knowingly permitted the deposit, or if there is a material defect in the notice (s 59(3)).

If the occupier fails to take necessary action, then the authority can do so and recover its costs from the occupier (s 59(6)) or, in appropriate cases, from the person who deposited or knowingly caused or knowingly permitted the deposit of waste.

In the event of an emergency at a waste management site the Environment Agency has the power (s 42(3)) to carry out works and recover its costs from the licence holder.

The Environment Agency may, in circumstances in which immediate action is necessary to prevent pollution of the environment or harm to man, remove illegally deposited waste, or take other steps if the occupier of the land was not responsible for the deposit, or if the occupier cannot be traced (s 59(7)). The Environment Agency may only recover costs which were necessarily incurred from the person who deposited, or knowingly caused, or knowingly permitted, the illegal waste deposit (s 59(8)).

The s 59 remedial power may be used in conjunction with a s 33 prosecution, or it may be employed independently of any prosecution.

Lodging an appeal will suspend the operation of the s 59 notice until the appeal is determined (s 59(4)). Failure to comply with a s 59 notice constitutes a criminal offence but any prosecution may only be heard in the magistrates' court (s 59(5)). The maximum penalty, on conviction of the offence, is a £5,000 fine. The offence is a 'continuing' offence which attracts a further penalty of a maximum fine of £1,000 for every day the offence continues after conviction.

4.14.1 Statutory civil liability for the deposit of waste

In addition to s 59, which empowers the Environment Agency to require the removal of waste deposited in contravention of the conditions of a waste management licence, s 73(6) imposes civil liability on the person or persons responsible for damage caused by the deposit of directive waste in contravention of s 33(1) or s 63(2). Damages may be claimed by any person sustaining property damage or personal injury. Section 73(6) liability is strict and an action may be commenced by any person. In addition, such persons have the option of commencing a common law tortious action against the person responsible for the damage.

Section 63(2) of the EPA 1990 provides that it is an offence for any person to deposit or knowingly cause or knowingly permit the deposit of non-controlled waste (that is, waste which is not regulated because, for example, it is exempt) if the relevant waste has special waste characteristics (that is, it is dangerous or difficult to dispose of) and is deposited without a licence, in breach of licence conditions, or without some other form of permission.

The circumstances giving rise to an unlawful deposit of waste include:

(a) deposit of wastes which are not in accordance with the conditions of a waste management licence;

(b) waste deposited in a manner likely to cause pollution of the environment or harm to human health;

(c) deposit of exempt wastes which constitute an unlawful disposal.

The person who deposited the waste which caused the damage will be liable, save in those circumstances in which the injured party was totally at fault or chose to run the risk of incurring damage. In those cases where the defendant was not totally to blame contributory negligence issues arise.

In addition to the person who deposited the relevant waste, liability may extend to any person or persons who knowingly caused or knowingly permitted the waste deposit.

4.15 Waste offences

The regulation of waste is identical to other Command and Control pollution control regimes in that it is underpinned by a range of criminal offences. The main offences are contained in s 33(1); however, these offences must take account of the changes to the definition of waste, contained in the Waste Management Regulations 1994 and implementing the EC Waste Framework Directive (91/156/EEC). Section 33(1) of the EPA 1990, as amended by the Waste Management Regulations 1994, contains the key waste offences.

4.15.1 Section 33 offences

Section 33 of the EPA 1990 provides that it is an offence to:

(a) deposit controlled (directive) waste, or knowingly cause or knowingly permit controlled (directive) waste to be deposited in or on any land, unless a waste management licence authorising the deposit is in force and the deposit is in accordance with the licence (s 33(1)(a) of the EPA 1990); this offence applies to all deposits, whether temporary or permanent. The deposit of waste is not limited to directive disposal or directive recovery operations;

(b) treat, keep or dispose of controlled (directive) waste, or knowingly cause or knowingly permit controlled (directive) waste to be treated, kept or disposed of:

- in or on any land; or

- by means of any mobile plant;

- except under and in accordance with a waste management licence (s 33(1)(b) of the EPA 1990). This offence is restricted to directive disposal operations and directive recovery operations;

(c) treat, keep or dispose of controlled (directive) waste in a manner likely to cause pollution of the environment or harm to human health. (s 33(1)(c) of the EPA 1990). This offence applies to any person whether or not they hold a waste management licence.

Section 33(1)(a) and s 33(1)(b) each comprise a combination of alternative ways of committing the relevant offence. For example, the offence in s 33(1)(a) may be committed by someone who deposits directive waste (an offence of strict liability), or it may be committed by someone who knowingly causes or permits a deposit of waste (see *R v Leighton and Town and Country Refuse Collections Ltd* [1997] Env LR 411).

The offences of 'knowingly causing' or 'knowingly permitting' contained in s 33(1)(a) and s 33(1)(b) are strict even though they require some degree of knowledge on the defendant's part. In *Shanks and McEwan (Teeside) Ltd v Environment Agency* [1997] Env LR 305, a waste company was prosecuted by the Environment Agency for knowingly permitting the deposit of controlled waste (that is, directive waste) in contravention of a condition of its waste management licence. The defendant argued, unsuccessfully, that although it knew that a deposit of waste had occurred, it was not aware that the deposit had breached a condition of its operating licence. The court held that the defendant's knowledge of the deposit was sufficient to establish liability and it was unnecessary for the prosecution to prove that the defendant knew that the deposit would breach the conditions of its operating licence. Knowledge of a deposit may be inferred from the facts (see *Kent CC v Beaney* [1993] Env LR 225).

The very act of operating a landfill site will be interpreted by the courts as constructive knowledge, on the part of the site operator, that deposits are taking place and it is not necessary for the prosecution to demonstrate knowledge of individual breaches of licence conditions (see *Shanks* case above).

This interpretation of 'knowingly cause' or 'knowingly permit' in effect imposes strict liability for breaches of waste management licence conditions.

The inclusion of 'knowingly cause' appears to have been inserted into s 33(1)(a) and s 33(1)(b) to cover the situation where one person orders another to deposit waste (for example, a waste producer contracts a carrier to transport waste to the nearest suitable landfill site, but the carrier fly-tips the waste on waste ground), and the waste consignor is unaware that the consignee deposits the waste illegally.

Section 33(1)(c) makes it an offence to treat, keep or dispose of controlled (directive) waste in a manner likely to cause pollution of the environment or harm to human health. It makes no reference to knowingly causing or knowingly permitting, nor does it make it a defence to be operating in accordance with a waste management licence. It is possible for a person to be operating in accordance with a waste management licence and yet still be committing an offence under s 33(1)(c). All that is required is that treatment, keeping or disposal, is likely to cause pollution of the environment or harm to human health. 'Pollution of the environment' refers to harm to flora and fauna, whilst 'harm' refers to both harm to living organisms and ecological systems. Section 33 is especially useful in combating the problem of fly-tipping. In effect s 33 imposes a minimum 'standard' in regard to the handling, storage, or disposal of directive waste.

4.15.2 Meaning of 'deposit'

The word 'deposit' has an extended meaning primarily to counter arguments by waste producers and waste handlers that the presence of waste on site does not constitute a 'deposit' because the waste has not reached its final destination. This argument has been raised, unsuccessfully, in order to evade liability for s 33 offences. In *R v Metropolitan Stipendiary Magistrate ex p London Waste Regulation Authority* [1993] 3 All ER 113, the High Court held that 'deposit' covered both temporary and permanent deposits of waste. Furthermore 'deposit' includes the continuing activities on a waste management site. In *Thames Waste Management Ltd v Surrey CC* [1997] Env LR 148, the defendant waste management company was convicted of breaching the terms of its waste management licence and therefore committing an unlawful deposit of waste. One of the licence conditions required waste, which had been deposited on the site, to be covered over on the day of deposit. The defendant argued, unsuccessfully, that the failure to cover the waste occurred after the waste had already been deposited. The court held that the word 'deposit' could cover continuing activities specified in the waste management licence. Thus, the 'deposit' continued until it was covered over.

4.15.3 Other waste offences

In addition to the main offences created by s 33(1), the EPA 1990 also creates a number of other specific offences such as:

(a) s 33(6) – a person who contravenes any condition of a waste management licence commits an offence (this is an offence of strict liability);

(b) s 33(5) – where controlled (directive) waste is carried in and deposited from a motor vehicle, the person who controls or is in a position to control the use of the vehicle shall be treated as knowingly causing the waste to be deposited, whether or not he gave any instructions for this to be done; This provision is designed to address the problem of the illegal fly-tipping of waste. Section 33(5) should be read in the light of the Environment Agency's s 6 power relating to the seizure of vehicles used for unlawful waste related activities. If the Environment Agency is unable to obtain information, through its s 7 and s 71 powers, in regard to any vehicle suspected of being used for fly-tipping, it can apply to a magistrates' court for a warrant to seize the vehicle. After seizure the Environment Agency may publicise the seizure and, if no one comes forward to claim the vehicle, it may dispose of it (reg 23);

(c) s 44 – making false statements when applying for a waste management licence is an offence;

(d) s 60 – creates the offence of interfering with a waste site and receptacle for waste unless that person has the consent of the relevant authority, contractor or other person;

(e) s 63(2) – makes it an offence to deposit waste other than controlled (directive) waste in certain circumstances.

4.15.4 The household waste exemption

The main exemption from the waste offences is in relation to household waste. The offences contained in Pt II of the EPA 1990 do not apply in relation to household waste from a domestic property which is treated, kept or disposed of within the curtilage of the dwelling by or with the permission of the occupier of the dwelling (s 33(2)). It should be noted that the following will not be treated as household waste for the purpose of this exception; any mineral or synthetic oil or grease; asbestos; clinical waste. In addition the Waste Management Licensing Regulations 1994 exempt certain activities from the s 33(1)(a) and (b) offences.

4.15.5 Defences

It is clear from the wording of s 33(1)(a) and s 33(1)(b) of the EPA 1990 that an offence will not be committed if the deposit, treatment, keeping or disposal of controlled (directive) waste is in accordance with a waste management licence and the conditions attached to the licence. Therefore, compliance with a waste management licence and all its conditions will provide a defence to these two offences. Compliance with the terms of a waste management licence, however, affords no defence in relation to a s 33(1)(c) offence, although in practice it may help to establish one of the other defences available.

Section 33(7) also provides a number of additional defences. To succeed in defending a s 33 prosecution, a person charged must prove:

(a) he took all reasonable precautions and exercised all due diligence to avoid the commission of the offence. This defence is often associated with the defendant proving that it has set up an adequate system to avoid the commission of an offence. For example, in *Durham CC v Peter Connors Industrial Services Ltd* [1993] Env LR 197, a waste carrier who was contracted to make regular visits to a waste producers premises to collect waste in an awaiting skip was not allowed to take advantage of the s 33(7)(a) defence. The waste carrier had not checked the contents of the skip on every occasion it had collected a skip from the waste producers premises and the court held that the waste carrier had not done enough to inform itself of the nature of the waste which was being collected. To avail itself of the defence a specific enquiry had to be made of any person who knew what the waste was and whether a deposit of the waste would be unlawful; or

(b) he acted under instructions from his employer and neither knew, nor had reason to suppose, that the acts done by him constituted a contravention of s 33(1); or

(c) the acts alleged to constitute the contravention were done in an emergency to avoid danger to human health. However, to rely on this defence it is necessary to fulfil two further criteria, namely that the person seeking to rely on the defence took all such steps as were reasonably practicable in the circumstances for minimising pollution of the environment and harm to health and that as soon as reasonably practicable after they were done, particulars of the incident were given to the Environment Agency. Section 33(7)(c) restricts this defence to circumstances in which emergency action was taken to avoid danger to the public but not danger to the environment. The onus is on the defendant to prove that the circumstances constituted an emergency and the court will employ an objective test in deciding whether the circumstances constituted an emergency (see *Waste Incineration Services Ltd v Dudley Metropolitan BC* [1993] Env LR 29).

The courts will determine as a question of fact whether a person can rely on any of these defences.

4.15.6 Penalties

A person committing an offence could be liable to an unlimited fine or even imprisonment for a period of up to two years. Section 33(9) of the EPA 1990 details the penalties as follows:

(a) on summary conviction, to imprisonment for a term not exceeding six months or a fine not exceeding £20,000 or both; and

(b) on conviction on indictment, to imprisonment for a term not exceeding two years or an unlimited fine or both.

The penalties are more serious if special waste is involved. Prison sentences are rare for environmental crimes; however, the courts have imposed terms of imprisonment on convicted waste offenders in several instances.

In most cases, the penalty for a waste offence will be a fine. Although the fine may not always be that great in relation to the company's resources, the poor publicity arising from a prosecution may be more damaging.

4.15.7 Personal liability

Section 157 of the EPA 1990 opens up the possibility of making company directors and managers personally liable for waste offences. Where a waste offence has been committed by a company, the senior management may also be personally liable for the offence. However, it has to be proved that the offence was committed with their consent or connivance or be attributable to their neglect.

There has been considerable debate in regard to who is a 'manager' for the purposes of s 157 of the EPA 1990 and similar offences (for example, s 217 of the WRA 1991, s 210 of the WIA 1991 and s 37 of the Health and Safety at Work etc Act 1974). The courts have developed and applied a 'controlling officer' test to determine who is a 'manager' for the purposes of s 157 of the EPA 1990 and similar offences. In *R v Boal* [1992] QB 591 and [1992] 3 All ER 177, the defendant was the assistant general manager of a large bookshop. The defendant took charge of the bookshop whilst the general manager was on holiday. During the time he was in charge serious breaches of the Fire Precautions Act 1971 came to light. The defendant was prosecuted and acquitted. The court held that although the defendant was fourth in the seniority in the company he was not a manager within the 1971 Act. In *Woodhouse v Walsall Metropolitan BC* [1994] Env LR 30, the defendant was the general manager of a waste management company. He was prosecuted, under the COPA 1974, for breaches of the company's waste management site licence. The court held that Woodhouse was not a manager for the purposes of COPA 1974. Although he was a site manager he was not in a position of real authority regarding the overall running of the company and was not in a position to guide or control company policy. In the Scottish case of *Armour v Skeen* 1976

SLT 71, the Director of Roads of Strathclyde Regional Council was convicted of health and safety offences which led to the death of an employee. In reaching its verdict the court referred to the fact that the defendant had responsibility for implementing the local authority's health and safety policy and as such was of sufficient seniority to be a 'director, manager, secretary or similar officer'. This case will be of interest to any senior company manager who has responsibility for devising and implementing a company's environmental policy.

Offences, such as s 157 of the EPA 1990, are not offences of strict liability and the prosecution must prove that:

(a) the defendant consented to the commission of the offence; or

(b) the defendant connived at the commission of the offence; or

(c) that the offences was attributable to the defendant's neglect.

Consent requires some affirmative act or approval (see *Huckerby v Elliott* [1970] 1 All ER 194). The defendant must be aware that an environmental offence is being committed and acts in a way which indicates that he is giving positive approval to the breach (for example, a company's plant malfunctions resulting in a breach of the terms of the company's pollution or operating licences, and a director orders production to continue). Connivance suggests acquiesence in conduct which is likely to lead to the commission of an offence (for example, a director is aware of some illegality and, whilst he does not actively encourage the breach, he allows it to continue, says nothing about it and chooses not to make any enquiry). Neglect has been defined as 'a failure to perform a duty which the person knows or ought to know' (see *Re Hughes* [1943] 2 All ER 269). Whether any particular director has been guilty of neglect will depend upon the nature and extent of the directors' duties.

4.16 Special waste offences

Regulation 16 of the Special Waste Regulations 1996 requires any person who makes a deposit of special waste in or on any land to record the location of the deposit. Records must be kept until the person surrenders his waste management licence. The site records will comprise either of a site plan marked with a grid or a site plan with overlays on which deposits are shown in relation to the contours of the site. Regulation 17 prohibits any establishment or undertaking which carries out the disposal or recovery of special waste, or which collects special waste, from mixing different categories of special waste, or from mixing special waste with waste which is not special waste.

4.16.1 Offences – reg 18

It is a criminal offence for any person (other than a member, officer or employee of the Environment Agency) to breach any of the provisions in regs 1–17. In addition, it is also an offence to furnish any false information or to make a false entry in any record or register. A person who commits an offence under the Special Waste Regulations is liable to a fine not exceeding level 5 on the standard scale if the case is dealt with by the magistrates. On indictment the penalty may be an unlimited fine or imprisonment of up to five years, or both. The regulation also makes special provision for the personal liability of a director, manager, secretary or other similar officer of a company, if the offence was committed with their consent, connivance or negligence. Regulation 18, however, does provide a defence. Regulation 18(3) states that it shall be a defence for a person charged with an offence if he can prove that he was not reasonably able to comply with the provision in question by reason of an emergency or grave danger and that he took all reasonable steps as were reasonably practicable in the circumstances for:

(a) minimising any threat to the public or the environment;

(b) ensuring that the provision in question was complied with as soon as reasonably practicable after the event.

4.16.2 Proposed changes to special waste controls

New regulations are proposed and are expected to come into force in 2002. It is proposed that the phrase 'special waste' be replaced with the phrase 'hazardous waste' to bring the current special waste provisions in line with the Hazardous Waste Directive (91/689/EEC). In effect, this would introduce a new definition of 'hazardous waste' and such waste would comprise: (i) any waste listed as hazardous in the European Waste Catalogue (published in the Official Journal of the EC on 16 January 2001); (ii) any waste which is not listed but which displays the hazardous properties listed in Annex II of the directive; and (iii) all prescription medicines.

Other changes which are likely to be implemented relate to:

(1) a duty on the EA to inspect hazardous waste producers and hazardous waste facilities on a regular basis;

(2) compulsory registration of special waste producers. Such persons would be required to identify the types and amounts of hazardous waste they intend to consign during the year, an estimate of the number of consignments and the intended treatments or disposal sites for waste streams produced;

(3) the end of the requirement to pre-notify the EA of hazardous waste movements;

(4) a requirement that hazardous waste producers supply the EA with quarterly information relating to hazardous waste consignments;

(5) a requirement on hazardous waste management sites to provide quarterly information on hazardous wastes received;

(6) changes in the consignment note system relating to multiple consignments;

(7) changes to the fee structure to reflect the need to recycle more waste;

(8) an obligation to separate wastes where this is technically and economically viable;

(9) a reduction in the household waste exemption to bring the controls in line with the Hazardous Waste Directive.

4.17 Waste strategy for England and Wales

4.17.1 National waste policy

Until the dawn of the 1990s there was no coherent national waste policy in the UK. Waste policy tended to be largely a local authority concern. However, amendments made to the EC Waste Framework Directive in 1991 (91/156/EC) coincided with central government recognition of the need for a more coherent and planned strategy to deal with the ever increasing quantity of waste produced in the UK.

During the period 1990–2000, the Government produced four key policy documents: *This Common Inheritance* (Cm1200, 1990), *Making Waste Work* (Cm 3040, 1995, DoE), *A Way With Waste* (1999, DETR) and the *Waste Strategy for England and Wales* (Cm 4693, 2000, DETR). These policy documents revealed the Government's key waste objectives:

(a) to reduce the amount of waste generated;

(b) to make the best use of waste;

(c) to give preference to waste management options which minimise the immediate and future risk of pollution of the environment and harm to human health.

Together these objectives represent a sustainable waste strategy for the 21st century. As part of its national strategy the Government has set national waste reduction, waste recovery, and waste recycling targets. The Government intends to achieve these targets by a combination of regulatory licence based controls, eco-taxes, planning controls and information and education initiatives.

Whilst *This Common Inheritance* introduced the concept of the 'waste hierarchy' in 1990, ranking the waste management options in descending order of preference (minimisation, recycling, recover, and disposal), practical progress, at local level, in achieving the Government's waste policy vision was slow. The use of s 50 of the EPA 1990 to achieve national coverage of waste management plans, as required by the Waste Framework Directive, was not particularly successful and the WRAs had made rather 'steady' progress in the preparation of waste disposal plans in an attempt to comply with the requirements of the directive.

In 1994 the objectives contained in the Waste Framework Directive, as amended, were transposed into national law by the Waste Management Regulations 1994 (see Sched 4 to the 1994 regulations). Section 50 of the EPA 1990 was repealed and replaced by ss 44A and 44B requiring the SOSE to prepare a national waste strategy replacing the previous system of waste disposal plans.

Section 44A requires the SOSE to prepare a national waste strategy for England and Wales. The strategy is required to contain policies in relation to the recovery and disposal of waste in England and Wales. The strategy details the policies for attaining the objectives set out in Sched 2A to the EPA 1990. Schedule 2A sets out the objectives that the national waste strategy should aim to achieve. Its starting point is that waste should be recovered or disposed of without endangering human health and without using processes or methods which could harm the environment and in particular without:

(a) risk to water, air, soil, plants or animals;

(b) causing nuisances through noise or odours; or

(c) adversely affecting the countryside or places of special interest.

The other principal objective is to secure an integrated and adequate network of waste disposal installations taking account of the best available technology not entailing excessive costs. Other objectives include ensuring self-sufficiency in waste disposal, encouraging the prevention or reduction of waste production, and encouraging the recovery of waste by recycling, reuse or reclamation.

The strategy includes provisions relating to each of the following:

(a) the type, quantity and origin of waste to be recovered or disposed of;

(b) general technical requirements; and

(c) any special requirements for particular wastes.

In preparing the strategy the SOSE consults with the Environment Agency and other bodies or persons representative of local government and industry and any other bodies or persons that he considers appropriate.

The actual preparation of the national waste strategy for England and Wales (and similar plans for Scotland and Northern Ireland) has taken time to come to fruition largely due to informational uncertainties in waste arisings. The strategy was completed and published in May 2000. 'Waste Strategy 2000 for England and Wales' is the national plan for the purposes of the Waste

Framework Directive. The strategy sets the following waste reduction targets, which are reviewed at five-yearly intervals:

(i) to reduce the amount of waste (industrial and commercial) going to landfill by 85% of 1998 levels by 2005;

(ii) to recover 40% of municipal waste and 25% of household waste by 2005;

(iii) to recycle/compost 30% of household waste and 45% of municipal waste by 2010.

Since the waste management licensing system is not the ideal vehicle to address waste minimisation and waste recycling targets, the strategy incorporates the use of eco-taxes (such as the landfill tax) and producer responsibility obligations (such as the packaging directive). These non-licensing regulatory tools are designed to provide the necessary financial incentive to bring about greater waste minimisation and waste recovery efforts.

4.17.2 The Waste Framework Directive

The 1975 Waste Framework Directive (75/442/EEC) as amended in 1991 by Directive (91/156/EEC) have influenced the shape of UK waste law and policy in the following ways:

(a) the original definition of 'controlled waste' in the EPA 1990 has been amended to reflect the waste definition favoured by the EC – 'directive waste' (Directive (91/156/EEC));

(b) EC waste policy created the need for a centralised national waste strategy (Art 6);

(c) the EC goal of self sufficiency in the treatment and disposal of waste (Art 5) has influenced national waste strategy;

(d) the creation of a 'waste management hierarchy' of waste policy objectives drives EC and Member State national waste policy (Arts 3 and 4).

The relevant EC policy objectives are:

(a) the prevention of and/or reduction of waste (see Art 174(2) of the EC Treaty);

(b) the recovery of waste produced;

(c) the recovery or disposal of waste without endangering human health or the environment.

To a marked degree the framework directive reflects the regulatory structure created by Pt II of the EPA 1990. For example, the framework directive:

(a) imposes a duty of care (Art 8 and s 34 of the EPA 1990) on all persons in the waste chain;

(b) obliges all waste disposal and waste recovery operations to be licensed (Arts 9 and 10 and ss 35–42 of the EPA 1990);

(c) obliges waste producers, handlers, recoverers, and disposers to keep proper records (Art 14 and the EPA 1990 duty of care waste transfer note system).

The EC Waste Framework Directive objectives were transposed into UK law by the Waste Management Regulations 1994 (see Sched 4). Whilst the regulations form part of national law they do not create rights and obligations and cannot therefore be relied upon directly by individuals. These objectives are therefore not 'directly effective' in litigation before national courts.

In *R v Bolton Metropolitan BC ex p Kirkman* [1998] Env LR 719 the Court of Appeal held that the Waste Framework Directive expressed objectives rather than legal requirements. The court went on to hold that the effect of transposing the objectives into national law was to create a separate legal duty, applying to regulators, to ensure the attainment of the Sched 4 objectives. There is some debate as to how strict this duty will be in practice. For example, does the duty merely require the regulatory decision maker to have regard to the attainment of the objectives in determining questions which concern the Sched 4 objectives? Are the waste objectives just one of several issues which must be taken into account in regulatory decision making, but leaving the final weighting of the factors to the discretion of the regulator? Alternatively does the duty oblige the regulatory decision maker to achieve the Sched 4 objectives thereby restricting the extent of the decision makers discretion? In *R v Leicestershire CC, Hepworth Building Products and Onyx (UK) Ltd ex p Blackfordby and Boothcorpe Action Group* (unreported, 15 March 2000), the judge viewed the waste framework objectives as a factor which the decision maker must take into account but the weight which had to be accorded to the objectives was a matter entirely within the discretion of the decision maker.

4.17.3 The Landfill Directive

In July 1999 the EC issued legislation relating to the harmonisation of landfill standards (the Landfill Directive (99/31/EC)). The directive was required to be transposed into national law by July 2001 (this has not yet received official approval, but the draft regulations may be viewed on the DEFRA website). The directive's main objective is to bring about a reduction in the amount of methane producing, biodegradable household and municipal waste which is disposed of in landfill sites.

Article 5 of the directive has set the following reduction targets based on 1995 waste arisings:

(a) a 25% reduction by 2006;

(b) a 50% reduction by 2009;

(c) a 65% reduction by 2016.

The deadlines for achievement of these targets may be extended where more than 80% of household and municipal waste was landfilled in 1995. Since waste disposal in the UK falls into this category the UK has been granted an extra four years to achieve each target. The conditions of all waste management licences and some IPPC permits will require amendment to enable the national targets to be achieved.

The Landfill Directive will have additional impacts upon national landfilling practice. The more important of these impacts are:

(a) all waste is to be pre-treated (for example, sorting and compacting) before disposal;

(b) co-disposal of wastes (for example, the practice of landfilling hazardous wastes with non-hazardous wastes) is banned;

(c) waste sites are required to install technology to control landfill gas and leachate (for example, collecting methane and using it to produce electricity);

(d) proper financial provision is required to deal with site aftercare.

4.17.4 Other waste directives

In addition to the general waste controls set out in the Waste Framework Directive other directives have been created which regulate specific wastes. The Hazardous Waste Directive (78/319/EEC, as amended by 91/689/EEC), is a 'daughter' directive of the Waste Framework Directive and is concerned with the management of wastes which have properties which make the wastes dangerous or difficult to handle. These properties are specified in the annexes to the directive (for example, toxicity). Much of the directive has been implemented in UK law by the Special Waste Regulations 1996.

Directives (89/369/EEC) and (89/429/EEC) ('daughter' directives of the Air Framework Directive (84/360/EEC) on air pollution from industrial plant) regulate the operation of municipal waste incinerators, whilst hazardous waste incineration is dealt with by the Hazardous Waste Incineration Directive (94/67/EC). Other wastes which are the subject of EC directives include: the Titanium Dioxide Directive (78/176/EEC), the Waste Oils Directive (75/439/EEC), the Batteries and Accumulators Directive (91/157/EEC) and the Packaging Directive (94/62/EC).

4.17.5 Producer responsibility

Section 93 of the EA 1995 enables the SOSE to introduce regulations which oblige manufacturers to recycle, recover, or reuse products or materials. The intention is to impose waste reduction targets on business sectors to enable national targets to be met and EC legislation to be complied with. (See EC Directive on Packaging and Packaging Waste 94/62/EC.)

The 1994 Packaging Directive, transposed into national legislation by the Producer Responsibility Obligations (Packaging Waste) Regulations 1997 SI 1997/648 set a national target of 50% of waste packaging to be recycled and recovered by 2001. The 1997 regulations are based on the concept that the responsibility for meeting the national target will be shared amongst the producers of packaging materials and the retail users of their products. Businesses which fall within the ambit of the packaging regulations purchase packaging recovery notes (PRNs) from other businesses which recover and recycle packaging waste. In this way, each business is able to meet the recycling and recovery targets set for it by the EA. Businesses who engage in the following activities: the manufacture of cardboard, cardboard box manufacturing, the filling or packing of cardboard boxes, and the sale of cardboard packaged goods to retailers, are subject to the producer responsibility obligations provided each business produces, handles, or supplies more than 50 tonnes of packaging each year and has an annual turnover of £2 m. Businesses which satisfy these criteria must register with the Environment Agency and supply data upon which the Environment Agency bases its calculation of the volume of waste packaging which must be recycled. Alternatively any business may join a 'compliance scheme' where several businesses are aggregated together for administrative convenience. Each business certificates its own compliance with the targets set by the Environment Agency.

Packaging regulated by the directive includes boxes, jars, bottles, shrinkwrap, and pallets. The regulations require the recycling or recovery of packaging waste. Recycling includes reprocessing the materials so that they can be used again, either for its original purpose or an alternative purpose. Recovery refers to processes which recover some benefit from the waste such as burning the waste in an energy from waste incinerator to produce electricity.

The main packaging offences are failing to register with the Environment Agency and failing to take 'reasonable steps to achieve the recycling or recovery target set for the relevant business. The maximum fine in the magistrates' court on summary conviction is £5,000. Conviction on indictment in the Crown Court is punishable by an unlimited fine. The Packaging Directive is likely to be the first in a line of similar directives. Producer responsibility obligations are likely to encompass electrical goods in the near future.

4.17.6 Landfill tax

In 1996 the Government introduced a tax on waste going to landfill. See the Finance Act 1996, the Landfill Tax Regulations 1996, the Landfill Tax (Qualifying Materials) Order 1996 and the Landfill Tax (Contaminated Land) Order 1996. The landfill tax reflects the Government's principal aim; namely the reduction of waste by taxing waste going to landfill. Landfilled 'active' waste (for example, organic methane producing waste) currently attracts a tax of £12 a tonne, whilst 'inactive' waste (for example, construction waste) is £2 a tonne. Certain wastes are exempt. The tax is paid by landfill companies who pass on the tax, via landfill gate fees, charged to waste producers and carriers.

The impact of the tax on waste reduction is, so far, somewhat questionable. There is some evidence that the introduction of the tax has led to an increase in fly-tipping and diversion of inert or inactive wastes to activities which are exempt, such as landscaping.

The creation of a Landfill Tax Credit Scheme enables landfill operators to claim a tax credit for any payments they make to approved environmental organisations. Environmental projects which have been approved under the scheme include amenity improvement schemes, sustainable management education projects, and reclamation and restoration of contaminated land.

4.18 Waste planning

4.18.1 The waste disposal plan

Section 99 of the EA 1995 places specific responsibility upon the SOSE to produce a national waste strategy. The Waste Framework Directive (75/442/EEC) imposes an obligation on Member States to produce a waste plan. Prior to the introduction of the EA 1995 it was originally planned that this would be done through the auspices of waste disposal plans under s 50 of the EPA 1990. Section 50 of the EPA 1990 required each WRA to prepare a waste disposal plan. In order to do this the WRAs were required to carry out an investigation to decide what arrangements were needed for treating or disposing of controlled waste within their area so as to prevent or minimise pollution to the environment or harm to human health. Waste disposal plans had to specify the kinds and quantities of controlled waste the WRA expected to find in its area, or to be transported in or out of the area; methods of disposal; licensing policy; the sites and disposal methods in use and expected to come into use; and the expected costs, for the period of the plan. The WRA was also under a duty to have regard to the desirability, where reasonably practicable, of giving priority to recycling waste. Section 50 was repealed by the EA 1995 and replaced by the national waste strategy under s 44A of the EPA 1990.

In addition to the national waste strategy, waste local plans and waste recycling plans are still of relevance.

4.18.2 Development control, development plans and the waste local plan

The town and country planning system controls the geographical siting of all waste management sites. A planning permission (licence) must be obtained to authorise the use of land for waste management activities (s 36(2) of the EPA 1990).

Local authorities are responsible for much of the administration of the planning system. The decision (often referred to as 'development control') to grant planning permission for a waste management site is the responsibility of the County Planning Authority (or metropolitan or unitary authority) (see Sched 1 to the TCPA 1990). Planning permission is required to 'develop' land. 'Development' is defined in s 55(2) of the TCPA 1990 and includes both 'operational' development (for example, building a waste incinerator) and a 'material change of use' of land (for example, using a redundant quarry as a landfill site). Section 55(3)(b) provides that 'development' includes the deposit of refuse or waste materials on land. Such activities constitute a material change of use.

The decision whether to grant or refuse a planning application for a new waste incinerator will be taken by the County Planning Authority (or metropolitan or unitary authority) on the basis of the policies contained in the relevant development plan and any material considerations (which include Government policy guidance). The content of policies contained in the development plan will, in the light of s 54A of the TCPA 1990, have an important effect on the outcome of the application. Development plans will include policies concerning waste related developments.

The waste policies which are relevant to a planning application for a landfill or other waste site may be scattered amongst a range of documents. In those parts of the country where the main local authority administrative unit is the county, the relevant waste policies will be found in the County Structure Plan, the Waste Local Plan (prepared by local authority district councils) or a combined minerals and waste plan. In metropolitan areas the structure plan and local plan are combined into a unitary plan.

Any conditions attached to a waste related planning permission should only be imposed for a planning purpose such as access to the site, restoration of the site after closure, the extent of tipping, and the phasing of operations. Conditions should not be imposed which duplicate the operational conditions the Environment Agency may choose to impose when determining a waste management licensing application for the same site. Typically such conditions, relating to operational matters, include the duration of the waste management activities on the site, the types of wastes which are to be tipped, and record keeping.

County planning authorities are required by the Planning and Compensation Act 1991 to prepare a waste local plan or, at least, to combine a waste local plan with a minerals local plan. The waste local plan addresses the land use implications of the authority's waste policies. Therefore, it deals with issues such as the need for sites and waste facilities and where these should be located, having regard to geological and hydrological considerations. The waste local plan should not be confused with the waste disposal plan which is a WRA responsibility.

4.18.3 Waste recycling policy and waste recycling plans

In 1990, the UK Government set targets for the recycling of household waste (25% of household waste) to be met by the year 2000. However, according to Government statistics, the current average recycling rate for household waste is just under 6%. Although s 49 of the EPA 1990 requires WCAs to prepare recycling plans to ensure that the targets are met, very few have made any real efforts to achieve the targets.

Waste recycling is largely the responsibility of the WCA, although the WDAs have certain powers and duties in this regard. The main provisions relating to recycling are contained in the following sections of the EPA 1990:

(a) s 49 – WCAs are under a duty to investigate what arrangements can practicably be made for recycling household and commercial waste. They must prepare a waste recycling plan and keep it under review;

(b) s 46(2) – the WCAs can require household waste to be placed in separate receptacles if certain wastes are going to be recycled;

(c) s 52 – has introduced a system of recycling credits to encourage recycling.

The WCA is required by s 49 to prepare a waste recycling plan. The WCA in preparing the plan has to consider the effect that recycling proposals will have on the amenities in the locality and also the likely cost or saving to the authority. A copy of the plan should be made available for the public to inspect.

4.19 The interface between the waste management regime and other regulatory pollution controls

4.19.1 IPC

The recovery or disposal of directive waste, providing it forms an integral part of an IPC licensed process is exempt from the need to obtain a waste management licence (reg 16(1)(a) of the Waste Management Regulations 1994). Section 28(1) of the EPA 1990 provides that it is not possible to include a condition in an IPC authorisation regulating the final disposal of directive waste in or on land.

4.19.2 IPPC

The IPPC Directive introduces integrated controls over waste disposal sites, such as landfill sites. Approximately 900 large landfill sites (that is, those capable of accepting over 710 tonnes of waste per day and with a total capacity of over 25,000 tonnes) fall within the IPPC regime. The smaller landfills continue to be controlled under the waste management licensing provisions of Pt II of the EPA 1990. All waste management installations which are subject to IPPC will also be subject to the requirements of the EC Waste Framework Directive and therefore operators of IPPC licensed waste management installations must be fit and proper persons in order to be granted an IPPC permit.

4.19.3 Water pollution

Liquid effluent is not waste which falls to be regulated by the waste management licensing regime in Pt II of the EPA 1990 and the Waste Management Licensing Regulations 1994. Waste in liquid form is controlled by a combination of the Water Resources Act 1991, the Urban Waste Water Treatment Directive (91/271/EEC) and the Urban Waste Water Treatment (England and Wales) Regulations 1994.

In regard to the threat of groundwater pollution from waste disposed (but not waste recovery activities) of to landfill reg 15 of the Waste Management Licensing Regulations 1994 provides that a waste management licence will only be granted if the Environment Agency is satisfied that adequate measures exist to prevent pollution of groundwaters by the substances listed in List I and II of the Groundwater Directive (80/68/EEC). In such circumstances the landfill site will be exempt from the Groundwater Regulations 1998.

4.19.4 Contaminated land

The contaminated land remediation notice procedure does not apply (see s 78YB(3) of the EPA 1990) where contamination results from an illegal deposit of waste (for example, an illegal deposit of waste in an unlicensed landfill rather than contamination caused by pollutants escaping from an underground storage tank) and the power to require the removal of the waste is available to the Environment Agency under s 59 of the EPA 1990.

4.19.5 Town and country planning

Before the Environment Agency can issue a waste management licence, it must be satisfied that the waste management operation has planning permission by virtue of s 36(2) of the EPA 1990. The applicant will need to demonstrate that he has a planning permission certificate of lawful use or development or an established use certificate.

4.19.6 Statutory nuisance

Statutory nuisances may arise in relation to waste in two instances. The deposit of controlled (directive) waste could amount to an accumulation, prejudicial to health or a nuisance under s 79(1)(e) of the EPA 1990. Alternatively, the resultant smell from the waste could, if prejudicial to health or a nuisance, constitute a statutory nuisance under s 79(1)(d).

4.19.7 The Planning (Hazardous Substances) Act 1990

Additional controls are available under the Planning (Hazardous Substances) Act 1990. Prior to this, the control of developments under the town and country planning regime could exert little control over the use of hazardous substances in developments. It was possible for factories and manufacturers to introduce new hazardous products and uses without requiring the need for further planning consent.

The Planning (Hazardous Substances) Act 1990, which was brought into force on 1 June 1992, requires that the keeping of any hazardous substance on, over or under land, beyond small quantities, will require the consent of the Hazardous Substances Authority (usually the London boroughs, the district councils in metropolitan counties and the district planning authorities elsewhere). Before a 'hazardous substances consent' is granted, the Hazardous Substances Authorities consider whether the proposed storage or use of a hazardous substance is appropriate in a given location.

4.20 The duty of care

One of the most significant features of the EPA 1990 was the introduction of a statutory duty of care (on 1 April 1992) in relation to the handling of waste. The Royal Commission for Environmental Pollution recommended the introduction of such a statutory duty of care in relation to waste. In its 11th report, *Managing Waste: The Duty of Care* (1985), the Royal Commission recommended that a duty of care be placed on everybody involved in the waste chain:

> The producer [of waste] incurs a duty of care which is owed to society, and we would like to see this duty reflected in public attitudes and enshrined in legislation and codes of practice.

The objective of s 34 of the EPA 1990 is to ensure that all persons in the waste chain who produce, handle, treat, or dispose of directive waste take reasonable steps to:

(a) store the waste properly;

(b) package the waste in adequate packaging or containers;

(c) describe the contents of packaged or containerised waste properly so that the next person in the waste chain can handle it safely;

(d) hand the waste over only to an authorised person;

(e) complete a waste transfer note recording details of the consignment of the waste to the next person in the waste chain;

(f) check that the waste is properly disposed of.

Thus, every person in the waste chain, from waste producer to waste disposer, is obliged to act responsibly in regard to waste, especially at the point when the waste is handed over (consigned) to the next person in the waste chain. The s 34 duty of care creates statutory 'cradle to grave' responsibility for waste.

Failure to observe the s 34 duty is a criminal offence (s 34(6)). This offence is a 'relevant offence' for the purpose of ascertaining who is a fit and proper person to operate a waste management facility and hold a waste management licence.

The duty of care is set out in s 34 of the EPA 1990 and is supplemented by regulations made under s 34(5), the Environmental Protection (Duty of Care) Regulations 1991 SI 1991/2839, as amended, and official guidance in the form of a Code of Practice. The Code of Practice, initially issued in 1991 was revised in 1996 to take account of the revised statutory definition of waste and the extension of the duty of care to scrap metal facilities. Any person who fails to comply with the duty imposed by s 34 or with the regulations commits a criminal offence (s 34(6)). It is not necessary for any environmental damage to have been caused or for there to be a breach of s 34. All that is required is that there has been a breach of the duty of care. There is no statutory provision allowing for a civil action where damages have been caused as a result of a breach of s 34. On summary conviction in a magistrates' court a breach of the duty of care can lead to a maximum fine of £5,000 or on indictment an unlimited fine.

According to the Code of Practice the duty of care is designed 'to be an essentially self-regulating system which is based on good business practice'. For example, the Code states that if a waste holder is certain that waste he or she handles is being wrongly managed by another person then he or she should, at first instance, refuse to deal with that other person (for example, refuse to transfer waste to that person). The Code goes on to say, that it may not always be possible to take such a course of action, and that if appropriate a person should bring the matter to the attention of the Environment Agency.

Section 34 creates a form of self-regulation underpinned by the criminal law sanction of s 34(6). Any waste producer or waste holder who transfers waste to a 'dodgy' waste carrier who undercuts the going rate charged by legitimate carriers for waste carriage may not only face prosecution for breach of the duty of care (s 34(6)), but also prosecution for knowingly causing the deposit of waste (s 33) provided the waste carrier illegally deposits (fly-tips) the waste in or on an unlicensed site. Furthermore civil liability may also be incurred in regard to damage caused by the illegal deposit of waste (s 73(6)).

4.20.1 The duty applies to waste holders

Section 34(1) applies to any person who imports, produces, carries, keeps, treats or disposes of controlled (directive) waste or, as a broker, has control of such waste. Essentially, this means any person in the waste chain from producer to disposer. (DoE Circular 19/91 uses the shorthand term 'waste holder' to refer to all persons who are subject to the duty.) Section 34(2) provides the only exception to the duty: occupiers of domestic premises who produce household waste on their property.

A waste broker is a person who may exercise control over waste, but may not necessarily hold it. For the purposes of the duty, they can be considered as sharing responsibility for any transfer of waste that they arrange with the actual parties who effect the transfer.

Regulation 20 of the Waste Management Regulations 1994 brings waste brokers and waste dealers within the waste management regulatory regime. Waste brokers and waste dealers must register with the Environment Agency and failure to do so constitutes a criminal offence (reg 20). The Environment Agency has a discretion to refuse registration based on the applicant`s previous record of relevant offences.

Holders of waste management licenses, discharge consent licenses, WCAs, WDAs, registered charitable and voluntary waste carriers are exempt.

4.20.2 What does the duty of care involve?

Any person bound by the duty must:

> ... take all such measures applicable to him in that capacity as are reasonable in the circumstances:
>
> (a) to prevent any other person committing the offences in s 33;
>
> (b) to prevent the escape of the waste from his control or that of any other person;
>
> (c) to ensure that if the waste is transferred, it is transferred only to an 'authorised person' or to a person 'for authorised transport purposes'; and
>
> (d) when waste is transferred, to make sure that it is accompanied by a written description of the waste which will enable other persons to avoid a contravention of s 33 of the Act and to comply with the duty under s 34(1)(b) to prevent the escape of waste.

4.20.3 Elements of the duty of care

4.20.3.1 To take all such measures applicable to him in that capacity as are reasonable in the circumstances

Section 34(1) requires anyone bound by the duty of care to take 'all such measures as are applicable to him in that capacity as are reasonable in the circumstances' to avoid a breach of the statutory duty.

This requirement limits the duty of care in two respects. First, waste holders are only required to take all measures that are applicable to them in their respective capacities. Second, such measures need to be reasonable in the circumstances. The responsibility of the individual waste holder is limited and the duty is a subjective one and depends in part upon the holder's relationship to the waste.

The extent of the waste holders responsibility under s 34(1) will vary with the capacity of the waste holder and extent of control the waste holder has over the waste. The waste holder will therefore be expected to take different measures to comply with the duty of care varying with his capacity as a waste: producer, importer, carrier, keeper, treater, disposer, dealer, or broker. For example, the waste producer will bear primary responsibility for ensuring that the waste is accurately described.

Secondly, a waste holder is only expected to take measures that are reasonable in the circumstances. It is here that the Code of Practice is of importance since it provides guidance for waste holders on the measures that are reasonable in different circumstances. The circumstances which affect what is reasonable will include:

(a) what the waste is;

(b) the dangers it presents in handling and treatment;

(c) how it is dealt with;

(d) what the holder might reasonably be expected to know or foresee.

4.20.3.2 To prevent any other person committing offences under s 33

The first element of s 34 comprises a duty to prevent any other person committing offences under s 33. A waste holder must not only take steps to ensure that he does not breach s 33, but he must take reasonable steps to ensure that any other person who has control of his waste does not breach s 33. For example, a waste producer's s 34 responsibilities do not end with the transfer of the waste to a waste carrier. Not only must the waste producer check the waste carriers credentials (carriers registration certificate), but it is also the waste producer's responsibility to ensure that the waste arrives at a waste management site licensed to accept the relevant waste.

The Code of Practice advises waste transferors (consignors) to halt any waste transfer if the waste holder suspects that the waste will not be dealt with properly if handed over to the consignee. Such a situation might arise if a waste carrier arrives at the consignor's premises, very soon after carrying away an initial load of waste, to load up for a second time and arousing the consignor's suspicions that the first consignment of waste has been illegally disposed of (fly-tipped). The waste holder must act responsibly, as judged by an objective (reasonable man) standard, having regard to the waste holder's resources and knowledge. In the circumstances outlined above, the waste holder should first check the position with the waste carrier and, if the explanation given is unsatisfactory, inform the EA. Higher standards will be expected of the big waste operators in view of their greater resources. Clearly, it is for the waste holder to draw up a contract with a carrier/waste manager which incorporates provisions that enable the waste producer periodically to check the site (for example, a waste transfer station site), check that records and transfer notes are being kept and to allow for termination of the contract in the event of the waste manager losing his licence. The contract should require the waste disposal contractor to comply with all of the relevant laws and licence requirements and should ideally cover matters of liability, ownership of the waste, insurance and indemnities against liability. In practice, many arrangements are made without any written contract or are made by means of a standard contract which does not adequately cover all of the important issues.

The Code of Practice provides good practical advice on complying with this element of the duty. However, it should be emphasised that compliance with the Code of Practice does not ensure that the duty of care is being adequately met.

4.20.3.3 *To prevent the escape of waste from his or her control or that of any other person*

In order to prevent the escape of waste, producers of waste should label it properly and package it in such a way as to prevent escape and leakage whilst on site, in transit, or in storage. Consideration should also be given to preventing any escape in subsequent transfer or transfers and up to the final treatment or disposal. Since escape can occur in a variety of circumstances, care will need to be taken to address all possibilities. For example, escape may occur where there is a spillage or where containers have been overfilled; it can occur when adverse weather conditions result in waste being blown away or washed down storm drains. Vandals may cause waste to escape, hence the need for security as well as containerisation. The waste producer, in particular, should take into account the time it will take for the waste to reach its final destination and the mode in which it will be carried or stored at a transfer station. Containerisation should be adequate for all of these different situations. For example, black bin bags will almost certainly be inadequate. The suitability of packaging is particularly important where the wastes include flammable or corrosive substances.

4.20.3.4 *To transfer the waste only to authorised persons and for authorised transport purposes*

To comply with the duty of care, it is also essential to ensure that waste is only transferred to authorised persons or to a person for authorised transport purposes. These are defined respectively in s 34(3) and (4) of the EPA 1990.

Section 34(3) states that the following are authorised persons:

(a) a Waste Collection Authority;

(b) a holder of a waste management licence;

(c) persons exempted by regulations made by the SOSE under s 33(3);

(d) a registered carrier under s 2 of the Control of Pollution (Amendment) Act 1989;

(e) any person not required to be registered under the Control of Pollution (Amendment) Act 1989.

Transferors of waste should make sure that they are only transferring their waste to an authorised person. If waste is being transferred to a carrier, then the carrier must be registered under the Control of Pollution (Amendment) Act 1989. Subject to limited exceptions (prescribed in the Controlled Waste (Registration of Carriers and Seizure of Vehicles) Regulations 1991 SI 1991/1624 and SI 1998/605), any person carrying waste in the course of a waste transport business, or in any other way for profit, must be registered with the Environment Agency. It is an offence under s 1(1) of the 1989 Act to carry (directive) waste without registering with the Environment Agency as a waste carrier. The offence may only be dealt with summarily in the magistrates' court and the maximum penalty is a £5,000 fine. Anyone intending to transfer waste to a carrier should check that the person is registered (or exempt from the need to register) with the Environment Agency. The Environment Agency maintains a register of waste carriers which is open to public inspection. It is necessary for the person handing over the waste to a carrier to check the actual certificate of registration since photocopies are not proof of registration (official duplicates of the original certificate are available from the Environment Agency). Moreover, the transferor should also carry out regular checks to ensure that the registration has not lapsed (for example, due to revocation).

4.20.3.5 Exemptions

Under reg 2 of the 1991 Regulations exemptions are granted to a variety of waste carriers including:

(a) a waste producer who uses its own vehicles to transport waste (except demolition and construction waste);

(b) local authorities, charities, and voluntary groups.

The 1989 Act and 1991 regulations are targeted at carriers who transport waste as a commercial venture. Therefore the incidental carriage of waste, on a non-profit basis, by private individuals falls outside the ambit of the legislation.

4.20.3.6 Rejection of registration applications

The Environment Agency may refuse to register any applicant who it believes not to be a desirable carrier. A carrier will not be desirable if:

(a) the carrier, or a person closely connected with the carrier, has been convicted of a relevant offence (listed in Sched 1 of the 1991 Regulations); and

(b) the Environment Agency considers it undesirable that the carrier be authorised to carry (directive) waste (reg 5).

The provisions of the Rehabilitation of Offenders Act 1974 apply to any 'spent' relevant offence.

4.20.3.7 Revocation

The Environment Agency may revoke a carrier's registration certificate where the carrier ceases to be a desirable carrier (reg 10). For example, a carrier who is convicted of a 'relevant offence' such as illegally fly-tipping waste contrary to s 33(5).

4.20.3.8 Appeals

There is a right of appeal to the SOSE against a refusal to grant a carriers registration certificate (licence) or regarding the Environment Agency`s decision to revoke an existing registration certificate.

4.20.3.9 Renewal and surrender

Waste carriers licenses (certificate of registration) are of three years' duration and must be renewed if the carrier wishes to operate lawfully. A carrier may surrender its registration certificate at any time.

4.20.3.10 Stop and search

Section 5(1) empowers both the Environment Agency and the police to stop and search vehicles which are reasonably believed to be transporting waste but which are not covered by a waste carrier's registration certificate.

4.20.3.11 Authorised transport purposes

Section 34(4) lists the following as authorised transport purposes:

(a) the transport of controlled (directive) waste within the same premises and between different places in those premises;

(b) the transport to a place in Great Britain of controlled (directive) waste which has been brought from a country or territory outside Great Britain not having been landed in Great Britain until it arrives at that place;

(c) the transport by air or sea of controlled (directive) waste from a place inside Great Britain to a place outside Great Britain.

4.20.3.12 The written description

Waste producers are responsible for ensuring that, when they transfer waste, the waste is accompanied by an adequate written description. This description should provide sufficient information to enable all persons who might foreseeably come into contact with the waste to ensure that they can handle the waste safely. The description must be sufficient to ensure that other waste holders in the waste chain can avoid committing offences under s 33. The level of detail necessary in the transfer note will vary with the properties of the waste.

The Environmental Protection (Duty of Care) Regulations 1991 (made under s 34(5)) which came into force on 1 April 1992 established a system of transfer notes and record keeping of waste transfers to help waste holders to comply with this element of the duty of care. However, the transfer note does not necessarily provide the full written description. Neither does the transfer note have to accompany the waste, although it is safer if it does so. The regulations place responsibilities on the transferor and transferee of waste to keep detailed records of all waste transfers. On completion of the transfer of waste both the transferor and transferee must complete and sign a transfer note. The transfer note provisions contained in these regulations do not apply, by virtue of reg 2(3) to transfers of special waste where a consignment note system operates. (The consignment note system is described in more detail below.) Under the Environmental Protection (Duty of Care) Regulations a transfer note must include details of the following:

(a) identification of the waste;

(b) quantity;

(c) whether it is loose or in a container at time of transfer;

(d) place and time of transfer;

(e) name and address of both the transferor and transferee;

(f) whether the transferor is the producer or importer;

(g) if the transferee is authorised for transport purposes.

All parties involved in the transfer must keep a copy of the transfer note and the written description for at least two years. The Environment Agency may serve a notice demanding copies of transfer notes and these must be supplied within seven days. While all transfers of waste must be documented, the regulations do not require each individual transfer to be separately documented. It is possible for a single transfer to cover multiple consignments transferred at the same time or over a period not exceeding a year. However, this can only apply where the description is provided before the first consignment and all the other consignments covered by the note are the same.

4.20.4 The consignment note system for special waste

The Control of Pollution (Special Waste) Regulations 1980 introduced a detailed consignment note system in relation to special waste. This system remains but it has been slightly simplified by the 1996 regulations. The purpose of the consignment note system is to enable the Environment Agency to control and monitor the movements of special waste, through a system of pre-notification and transfer documentation, enabling control of special waste at every stage, from production to final disposal. The consignment note system also fulfils the requirements of the duty of care in respect of special waste. Therefore only one set of documentation is required.

4.20.4.1 Pre-notification

The Special Waste Regulations provide for a mandatory system of consignment notes which must be prepared by the producer of special waste, before the waste may be removed from the premises at which it is produced. Producers of special waste are under a statutory duty to comply with the consignment note procedure.

The regulations provide for three different procedures:

(a) the standard procedure;

(b) the procedure for repeat shipments of the same waste;

(c) the procedure for a carrier's round.

Regulation 4 of the 1996 regulations introduces a system of coding of consignment notes. The Environment Agency is required to supply, to any person who requests, or to a carrier, a code which will be used in relation to the consignment of waste. The code may consist of letters, numbers, or symbols or even a bar code which would enable the consignment or carriers to be identified electronically. When the Environment Agency assigns a code there is a fee of £15, unless the consignment consists entirely of lead acid motor vehicle batteries, in which case the fee is £10.

4.20.4.2 The standard procedure

The regulations require five copies of a standard form, known as the consignment note to be prepared by the special waste producer:

(a) The producer must complete Pts A and B on each of the copies. The producer will give full details of the nature of the waste and the consignment. The producer will also use the code provided by the Environment Agency.

(b) The producer must send one copy to the Environment Agency in whose area the waste is to be disposed of. The note must be sent not more than one month and not less than three working days before the waste is moved.

(c) The waste carrier completes Pt C on each of the remaining four copies. The carrier has to certify that the waste has been collected and also that the details provided by the producer in Pts A and B are correct.

(d) The waste producer must then fill in Pt D on each of the remaining four copies. The producer certifies that the waste carrier is either a registered carrier or is exempt from registration.

(e) The waste producer then has to keep one of the four copies on a register. The producer is required to keep records of consignment notes for at least three years.

(f) The waste carrier takes the remaining three copies and these travel with the consignment of special waste.

(g) When the waste is delivered the waste carrier gives the operator of the disposal site (known as the consignee) the three copies. The consignee then has to complete Pt E on each of the three copies, certifying that the consignee is licenced to receive the waste. The consignee retains one copy on a register. The register is maintained until the licence is surrendered.

(h) The consignee returns one copy to the waste carrier who must also retain this copy on a register for a period of at least three years.

(i) The remaining copy is sent to the Environment Agency.

Thus, it can be seen from these requirements that a record of all the waste transfers are retained and that the Environment Agency can keep track of all special waste movements. A simplified procedure operates in instances where several identical consignments of waste are sent from the same waste producer to the same disposal site over a period of 12 months.

4.20.4.3 Procedure for carrier's rounds

In addition there is an alternative procedure where the same waste carrier regularly collects similar consignments of waste from a series of different waste producers over a period of 12 months. This only operates where the waste carrier takes the waste to the same disposal or recycling facility. The intention of this alternative procedure is clearly to reduce the amount of paperwork that the carrier has to complete.

4.20.5 The Code of Practice

In 1991, the SOSE issued a Code of Practice which provided practical guidance on how to discharge the duty of care (*Waste Management, The Duty of Care, A Code of Practice*). The 1991 Code was replaced with a new Code in 1996. The Code recommends a series of steps which would normally be enough to satisfy the requirements of the duty. Its importance, however, is reflected in the fact that, by virtue of s 34(10), the Code of Practice shall be admissible in evidence and, if any provision of the Code appears to the court to be relevant to any question arising in the proceedings, it shall be taken into account in determining that question. It is therefore important that all those who are subject to the duty of care are familiar with the Code. The Code is not law but ranks as important administrative guidance.

4.20.6 Breach of the duty of care

Any person who fails to comply with the duty of care, or the documentation requirements laid down in the Environment Protection (Duty of Care) Regulations 1991, commits a criminal offence and will be liable, on summary conviction, to a fine not exceeding £5,000. On indictment, the Crown Court can impose an unlimited fine. Once again, directors and senior management may be personally liable for a breach of s 34. It is, therefore, in the interests of management to ensure that adequate training programmes and systems are in place to ensure that all relevant staff understand the requirements of the duty of care at all times.

Finally, breach of the duty of care could result in a person being deemed not to be a fit and proper person for the purposes of obtaining, maintaining or revoking a waste management licence.

4.20.7 Civil liability

It has already been noted that the EPA 1990 (under s 73(6)) provides a statutory civil remedy for any person who has suffered damages as a consequence of another person's breach of s 33. However, no such statutory remedy exists in relation to a breach of the duty of care. Damages may be available through common law actions such as nuisance.

4.20.7.1 EC directive on civil liability for waste

Although the duty of care as currently defined does not apply strict liability to waste producers, it may be amended in the future, should the proposed Directive on Civil Liability for Damage Caused by Waste be adopted. This directive will radically alter the current liability of waste producers and waste controllers (that is, anyone who handles waste). The directive, if adopted in its current form, will make a producer or controller of waste liable under civil law for damage or injury caused by the waste, irrespective of fault on their part. In addition, the draft directive also contains proposals concerning liabilities arising out of co-disposal (see COM (89) 282, COM (91) 219: Civil Liability for Damage Caused by Waste).

WASTE MANAGEMENT

The SOSE is responsible for producing a national waste strategy.

The definition of waste is contained in s 75(2) of the EPA 1990 has been amended to implement the definition of directive waste contained in the EC Waste Framework Directive (75/442/EEC) (as amended).

There are two elements to the definition of waste:

(a) the material or object must come within any of the categories listed in Sched 2B to the EPA 1990; and

(b) the material or object must have been discarded by its holder and there must be an intention to discard.

DoE Circular 11/94 provides guidance on the definition of waste.

Special waste is defined in the Special Waste Regulations 1996.

The Environment Agency is responsible for regulating the waste management provisions contained in Pt II of the EPA 1990 as amended by the EA 1995.

Section 33 of the EPA establishes the main waste offences. An offence will not be committed under s 33(1)(a) or (b) if the deposit, treatment, keeping or disposal of controlled (directive) waste is in accordance with a waste management licence granted by the Environment Agency.

Applications for a waste management licence are made in writing, accompanied by a fee, to the Environment Agency. Before granting a waste management licence the agency must consider whether:

(a) a planning permission is in force;

(b) the applicant is a fit and proper person;

(c) rejection of the application is necessary to prevent pollution.

Conditions will be attached to the licence which regulate the types and quantities of waste and the day to day operation of the waste facility.

Waste management licences can be:

(a) varied;

(b) revoked;

(c) suspended.

Surrender of a waste management licence is subject to the provisions of s 39 of the EPA 1990. A waste management licence can only be surrendered if the Environment Agency issues a Certificate of Completion.

The EPA 1990 provides a right of appeal to the Secretary of State against determinations by the Environment Agency.

The duty of care

One of the most significant features of the EPA 1990 was the introduction of a statutory duty of care.

The duty of care is set out in s 34 of the EPA 1990 and is supplemented by the Environmental Protection (Duty of Care) Regulations 1991 and a Code of Practice.

Breach of the duty of care

Any person who fails to comply with the duty imposed by s 34 or with the regulations commits a criminal offence. It is not necessary for any environmental damage to have been caused or for there to be a breach of s 33. All that is required is that there has been a breach of the duty of care.

Section 34(1) provides that the duty of care applies to any person who imports, produces, carries, keeps, treats or disposes of controlled (directive) waste or, as a broker, has control of such waste.

Section 34(2) provides the only exception to the duty for occupiers of domestic premises who produce household waste on their property.

Any person bound by the duty must: '... take all such measures applicable to him in that capacity as are reasonable in the circumstances':

(a) to prevent any other person committing the offences in s 33;

(b) to prevent the escape of the waste from his or her control or that of any other person;

(c) to ensure that if the waste is transferred, it is transferred only to an 'authorised person' or to a person 'for authorised transport purposes'; and

(d) when waste is transferred, to make sure that it is accompanied by a written description of the waste which will enable other persons to avoid a contravention of s 33 of the Act and to comply with the duty under s 34(1)(b) to prevent the escape of waste.

CHAPTER 5

INTEGRATED POLLUTION CONTROL AND INTEGRATED POLLUTION PREVENTION AND CONTROL

5.1 Introduction

Integrated Pollution Control (IPC) and Integrated Pollution Prevention and Control (IPPC) are typical Command and Control regulatory regimes in that they use 'licensing' as the primary pollution control mechanism. They differ from other regulatory regimes in that they are designed to control polluting discharges from a relatively narrow range of highly polluting industries. In contrast to the single environmental media focus of the water pollution controls contained in the Water Resources Act (WRA) 1991 and the waste management controls contained in Pt II of the Environmental Protection Act (EPA) 1990, the IPC and IPPC regimes are designed to regulate polluting emissions, discharged by industrial processes, into *all three environmental media* (air, water and land). Thus, industrial sites subject to IPC or IPPC generally require only one licence authorising all polluting discharges from that site. IPC and IPPC are 'one stop shops' and it is not necessary for the site operator to obtain separate licenses in respect of polluting discharges to water, air and land from the regulators who police each of those statutory regimes. IPC and IPPC adopt an *holistic* perspective, paying attention to the polluting impacts of the emissions discharged by industries into the environment as a whole. Any licence issued under the IPC regime will only authorise discharges into the environmental media (air, water, or land) which cause the least damage to the environment. This is the Best Practicable Environmental Option (BPEO) principle which guides IPC regulatory decision making in respect of sites which are discharging pollutants into more than one environmental medium. The BPEO principle is not specifically referred to in the IPPC controls but its influence has helped shape the contours of the IPPC controls.

IPC regulates a range of polluting processes (fuel and power, chemicals, minerals, metals, waste disposal and miscellaneous industries such as paper mills) and polluting substances (such as sulphur dioxide and carbon dioxide emissions into air, DDT and mercury discharges to controlled waters, and solvents discharged onto land). Several processes which require authorisation under the IPC regime may be carried on from the same premises. Whilst IPC focuses on the control of polluting emissions into the three environmental media, IPPC is concerned with a wider range of environmental impacts caused by the operation of predominantly industrial installations. The focus of IPPC extends beyond polluting emissions and includes energy use and efficiency, raw material usage, waste minimisation, noise, vibration, heat effects and accident prevention measures.

The IPC regime had only been existence for some six years when, as a result of European Community (EC) legislation, it began to be superseded by the new IPPC regime in the late 1990s. The IPPC regime, introduced in the UK by the Pollution Prevention and Control Act (PPCA) 1999 to implement the Integrated Pollution and Control Directive (96/61/EC), is intended to replace IPC controls by 2007. Consequently, it is necessary to understand how both regulatory regimes function. Many businesses will continue to be regulated by the IPC regime for some time to come but new businesses, and substantial changes to existing businesses, will, in many cases, be immediately subject to IPPC controls.

5.2 The development of an integrated approach to pollution control

The historical development of IPC has its roots in the industrial revolution. The creation of the Alkali Inspectorate, by the Alkali Act 1863, was the first attempt to regulate the toxic by-products of the emergent chemical industry. This regime addressed, somewhat ineffectively, only one aspect of the pollution problems associated with industrial production. Meanwhile smoke and other pollutants were being pumped into the atmosphere at an alarming and unregulated rate.

From the 19th century to well into the 20th century the standard UK response to pollution problems was to create separate regulatory regimes to deal with problems reactively, as and when they arose. This created a complicated and fragmented jigsaw of overlapping regulatory regimes. Regulated industries experienced difficulties in keeping abreast of the different investigatory and enforcement powers available to the various regulatory authorities. One of the most significant drawbacks of this reactive and piecemeal approach to pollution control was the failure to focus on the environment as a whole. A more sanction orientated enforcement policy by one regulator might have the undesired effect of encouraging businesses to divert their wastes into less tightly regulated environmental media. This situation was not helped by the absence of environmental quality standards which could provide benchmarks in regard to which the terms of Command and Control licences could be set. Regulatory regimes had an 'end of pipe' focus which took a very narrow view of the impact of environmental pollution on the environment. The 'environment' was essentially the environmental media (air, water and land) into which pollutants were discharged and regulated by the particular regulatory regime. The general public had difficulty identifying the correct regulatory authority to complain to and this reduced the accountability of some regulators.

In 1976 the Royal Commission on Environmental Pollution referred to some of the shortcomings of UK pollution control in its fifth report on air pollution (Cmnd 6731). In particular it recognised the need for a comprehensive regulatory body which could integrate the existing disparate and fragmented legal controls policed by a multitude of regulatory bodies.

The Royal Commission on Environmental Pollution asserted the need for an integrated approach to pollution control to replace the single environmental medium approach that had developed in the UK. The report stated that:

> The reduction of emissions to the atmosphere can lead to an increase in wastes to be disposed of on land or discharged to water. If the optimum environmental solutions are to be found, the controlling authority must be able to look comprehensively to all forms of pollution arising from industrial processes where different control problems exist.

In practical terms, this means that where a manufacturer selects a manufacturing process which reduces or eliminates the need to discharge into water, this may have a knock-on effect in terms of the emissions he makes into the atmosphere or the amount of solid waste that needs to be disposed of. The single medium approach, which had developed in a largely piecemeal fashion in this country, could not take account of this interrelationship between different environmental media.

The Royal Commission report also referred to the 'transferability of pollution':

> The three principal forms of pollution – of air, water and land – are often very closely linked. In order to reduce atmospheric pollution, gases or dusts may be trapped in a spray of water or washed out of filters. This leaves polluted water, if not discharged to a sewer or direct to a river or the sea, can be piped into a lagoon to settle and dry out, leaving a solid waste disposal problem. The pollutant may even go full circle by blowing off the lagoon as dust.

The report identified other examples of the transferability of pollution, such as water seeping through refuse tips and smoke from the incineration of rubbish or sludge. The absence of a co-ordinated view, and the fragmented approach to pollution control that had developed in the UK, meant that this interrelationship was largely ignored. Decisions on water discharges taken by the water authorities were largely taken in isolation of decisions made by the waste disposal authorities, the local authorities exercising their clean air functions or the Alkali Inspectorate. The Royal Commission could find little evidence of co-ordination between the various agencies. This lack of co-ordination meant that, in practice, industries that had been prevented from releasing hazardous substances into a particular medium could choose another means of disposal – for example burning or burying – and effectively divert the wastes into another medium where the regulatory regime and rules were less stringent. The Royal Commission, therefore, recommended the need for a more co-ordinated approach or a cross-media approach so that pollutants were not simply transferred from one medium to another. There was clear evidence of the need for a new regulatory authority which could control the whole process and achieve the 'best practicable environmental option'. Her Majesty's Inspectorate of Pollution (HMIP) was established in 1987 to provide a more co-ordinated and integrated system of pollution control and was given specific responsibility under Pt I of the EPA 1990 to administer the new system of IPC created under that Act. The functions of HMIP were transferred to the Environment Agency in April 1996 by s 1 of the Environment Act (EA) 1995, demonstrating the continued desire to provide a more co-ordinated system of pollution control.

5.3 IPC: achieving the best practical environmental option

The EPA 1990 established a system of pollution control which aimed to fulfil the recommendations of the Royal Commission. The system is known as Integrated Pollution Control or IPC and was initially controlled by HMIP but is now regulated by the Environment Agency. To implement the Royal Commission's recommendations, the system of IPC was established to prevent or minimise pollution of the environment due to the release of substances into any environmental medium (and thus takes a cross-media approach). IPC does not cover all industrial processes but concentrates only on the most seriously polluting processes. These seriously polluting processes are regulated by a means of prior approval in which the process obtains an authorisation (that is, a licence) from the Environment Agency. In deciding whether to grant approval, the Environment Agency must consider the impact of the process on all three environmental media and determine the means of operation that would result in the BPEO.

In its 12th report in 1988, the Royal Commission dealt with the issue of the best practical environmental option and defined it in the following way:

> The selection of BPEO requires a systematic approach to decision-taking in which the practicability of all reasonable options is examined and in which environmental impact is a major factor in the final choice.

There is therefore a requirement that the Environment Agency considers the process as a whole and authorises the option that provides the most benefit or the least damage to the environment as a whole, at acceptable cost.

5.4 Overview of IPC

Part I of the EPA 1990 establishes two systems of pollution control:

(a) IPC for the most seriously polluting processes which were originally regulated by HMIP but which are now regulated by the Environment Agency; and

(b) Local Authority Air Pollution Control (LAAPC) for those processes which should not be allowed to operate without an authorisation, but are not so seriously polluting as to fall within the central control of the Environment Agency. Local authorities regulate these less seriously polluting processes in regard solely to their atmospheric emissions.

Section 6 of the EPA 1990 requires that certain *prescribed processes* must not be carried on, or certain *prescribed substances* must not be released into any environmental medium, without prior authorisation from either the Environment Agency or the relevant local authority. To carry on a prescribed process or discharge a prescribed substance without an authorisation is a criminal offence (s 23(1)(a)). Regulations prescribe two lists of processes, those in the 'A' list to be controlled by the Environment Agency and those in the 'B' list to be controlled by the local authority in whose area the process takes place.

Where a process is prescribed for central control by the Environment Agency, then it regulates, by means of an authorisation (licence), releases into all environmental media. The Environment Agency must take into account the process as a whole in terms of the releases into air, water and land. In reaching its conclusions about the levels of discharges and emissions, it is required to have regard to achieving the 'best practicable environmental option', known simply as BPEO. Where the process is designated for control by a local authority, the local authority can only regulate any emissions that such a process makes into air. That does not mean, of course, that processes designated for LAAPC only discharge into air. It means that such processes must seek an authorisation from the relevant local authority (which will be the district council or London borough council) for the atmospheric emissions and if they discharge into controlled waters they will be required to seek a separate consent from the Environment Agency (formerly the National Rivers Authority (NRA)) under the WRA 1991. Therefore, for these 'less seriously polluting' processes there is no 'IPC'.

For the purposes of Pt I of the EPA 1990, the definition of environment is 'all, or any, of the following media, namely the air, water and land; and the medium of air includes the air within buildings and the air within other natural or man-made structures above or below ground' (s 1(2)).

The Secretary of State (SOSE) for the Environment has issued regulations prescribing those processes and substances which should be subject to control under Pt I of the Act and which should be subject to either IPC or LAAPC (see the Environmental Protection (Prescribed Processes and Substances) Regulations 1991 SI 1991/472). If a process falls into one of the categories listed in the regulations, then it must obtain an authorisation as specified in the regulations, that is, from either the Environment Agency or the local authority, depending on whether the process is an 'A' list process or a 'B' list process. The regulations do provide for a small category of exemptions. Authorisations from the Environment Agency or the local authority may either be refused or granted subject to conditions and it is a criminal offence to operate a process in contravention of any specific condition or general conditions attached to such authorisations such as the Best Available Techniques Not Entailing Excessive Cost (BATNEEC) condition.

One of the features of Pt I of the EPA 1990 is the degree to which it is supplemented by further regulations which lay down the detailed provisions relating to applications, the operation of authorisations, public consultation, public registers, powers of inspectors, enforcement powers and appeals (see the Environmental Protection (Applications, Appeals and Registers) Regulations 1991 SI 1991/507). It is estimated that some 2,000 processes are subject to IPC control and 12,500 processes subject to LAAPC.

The provisions in Pt I relate to both the Environment Agency and local authorities, the Act refers to them as the 'enforcing authorities'. However, reference will usually be made in this chapter to the Environment Agency only. Where there are differences between the IPC and LAAPC procedures then specific mention will be made.

5.5 Prescribed processes and substances

5.5.1 What is a process?

The definition provided in s 1, Pt I of the EPA 1990 is that a process means any activities carried on in Great Britain, whether on premises or by means of mobile plant, which are capable of causing pollution of the environment. 'Activities' are further defined as industrial or commercial activities or activities of any other nature whatsoever (including, with or without other activities, the keeping of a substance). There may be several processes carried on in a plant at the same time. The term 'process', therefore, has been given a very wide meaning and it is clear from the definition that even storage (keeping a substance) may constitute a process if it is capable of causing pollution. The definition of 'process' was considered in the case of *HMIP v Safety Kleen UK Ltd* (1994). Safety Kleen were prosecuted by HMIP in respect of an incident in which some 13,000 litres of 'cemfuel' (a fuel produced from waste solvents) escaped from a tanker which was parked overnight at the company's premises. Large quantities of the fuel ended up in controlled waters. Safety Kleen had an IPC authorisation in respect of its solvent recovery plant and this expressly excluded the release of substances into controlled waters. At first instance the defendant company argued that they were not guilty of breaching conditions since the parked tanker was not a prescribed process and was therefore not subject to any conditions. However, the magistrates' court held that the description of the prescribed process in the authorisation included any other process carried on at the same location by the same person as part of that process. The court accepted therefore that the definition of process included the keeping of a substance in a tanker and found the defendant guilty. The company was fined £7,500 after they put forward mitigating arguments concerning their speedy response to the incident and the subsequent implementation of measures to avoid future similar incidents.

5.5.2 Pollution of the environment

Pollution of the environment is central to the definition of a 'process'. It is defined in s 1(3) of the EPA 1990 in terms of the release into any environmental medium from any process of substances which are capable of causing harm to man or any other living organism. Harm is defined in s 1(4) as harm to the health of living organisms or other interference with the ecological systems of which they form a part. In the case of man this includes offence to any of his senses or harm to his property.

Since it is an offence to 'carry on' a prescribed process without an authorisation, there may be a question as to what constitutes carrying on. Cases which have considered this question (albeit not within the context of the EPA 1990), suggest that there must be an element of repetition or series of acts and that the person carrying on the process must have control and direction of it.

5.5.3 The Prescribed Processes and Substances Regulations 1991

Using his powers under s 2 of the EPA 1990 the SOSE has enacted regulations which prescribe the processes and substances which should be controlled under Pt I of the EPA 1990. The following regulations have been enacted:

(a) The Environmental Protection (Prescribed Processes and Substances) Regulations 1991 SI 1991/472, which has been amended and further amended by the following regulations;

(b) SI 1991/836;

(c) SI 1992/614;

(d) SI 1993/1749;

(e) SI 1993/2405;

(f) SI 1994/1271;

(g) SI 1994/1329;

(h) SI 1995/3247;

(i) SI 1996/2678.

Schedule 1 to the regulations contains the descriptions of *processes* prescribed for control, and Scheds 4–6 prescribe the *substances* subject to control. Schedule 1 of the regulations is broken down into chapters, each dealing with a broad industrial sector. Within each of these broad sector headings, there is a more detailed list of industrial processes. These are further sub-divided into Pt A processes and Pt B processes. Part A processes are subject to IPC and Pt B processes are subject to LAAPC.

5.5.4 Industrial sectors

Schedule 1 is sub-divided into chapters which relate to the following broad industrial sectors:

Chapter 1 –   Fuel Production Processes, Combustion Processes (including power generation);

Chapter 2 –   Metal Production and Processing;

Chapter 3 –   Mineral Industries;

Chapter 4 –   The Chemical Industry;

Chapter 5 –   Waste Disposal and Recycling;

Chapter 6 –   Other industries.

Within each of these chapters there is a further sub-division into more detailed industrial processes, so, for example, within Chapter 4 on the Chemical Industry the following processes are included:

(a) petrochemical processes;

(b) the manufacture and use of organic chemicals;

(c) acid processes;

(d) inorganic chemical processes;

(e) chemical fertiliser production;

(f) pesticide production;

(g) pharmaceutical production;

(h) the storage of chemicals in bulk.

For each of these processes there is more detailed description and also a breakdown between those activities which are classified as a Pt A process (IPC) or a Pt B process (LAAPC). The following example best demonstrates this:

Chemical fertiliser production:

• Pt A:

(a) the manufacture of chemical fertilisers;

(b) the conversion of chemical fertilisers into granules.

• Pt B:

Nil.

5.5.5 How to find out whether a process is prescribed for IPC or LAAPC

In order to determine whether a process falls under Pt A or Pt B, it is necessary to find the description of the relevant process in the regulations. So, for example, if you are trying to determine whether a factory that manufactures ink is subject to IPC or LAAPC, you would first of all need to determine which broad industrial sector it falls into. Since it is not obvious which broad industrial grouping it falls into, the best starting point is the chapter on Other Industries (Chapter 6). From there, one can find s 6.6 'the manufacture of dyestuffs, printing ink and coating materials'. Under this sub-section, the manufacture and formulation of printing ink is determined to be a Pt B process. However, the process will only need an authorisation from the relevant local authority where the carrying on of the process is likely to involve the use of 100 tonnes or more of organic solvents in any 12 month period at the location in question.

5.5.6 What happens when a plant operates more than one process?

Many companies operate large industrial plants where a number of different industrial processes are carried out at the same location. In these circumstances the company may have applied for one or more authorisations in respect of the different processes. In the event that there is a dispute, or it is not clear which category (or indeed categories) a particular plant should fall into, Sched 2 of the regulations assists with a number of rules of interpretation. The issue of which category a plant falls into is more than academic and has practical implications for the plant concerned. An application for an authorisation from the Environment Agency is considerably more expensive than one from the local authority. The rules of interpretation provide for situations where a process appears to fall into two categories or where a plant undertakes a number of different processes falling into several categories. The rules are lengthy, but the most important one covers situations where a particular plant operates a process which overlaps Pt A and Pt B. In such circumstances, the whole process will be controlled centrally as an IPC process by the Environment Agency.

5.5.7 Prescribed substances

By virtue of s 2(5) of the EPA 1990, the SOSE can also prescribe certain substances for control and, accordingly, the release of the prescribed substances requires authorisation under s 6. The list of prescribed substances can be found in Scheds 4, 5 and 6 to the Prescribed Processes and Prescribed Substances Regulations 1991 (as amended). Substances are prescribed in relation to the environmental medium in which they are released:

(a) *Schedule 4: Substances released into the air*:

Oxides of sulphur and other sulphur compounds;

Oxides of nitrogen and other nitrogen compounds;

Oxides of carbon;

Organic compounds and partial oxidation products;

Metals, metalloids and their compounds;

Asbestos (suspended particulate matter and fibres), glass fibres and mineral fibres;

Halogens and their compounds;

Phosphorous and its compounds;

Particulate matter.

(b) *Schedule 5: Substances released into water*:

Mercury and its compounds;

Cadmium and its compounds;

All isomers of hexachlorocyclohexane;

All isomers of DDT;

Pentachlorophenol and its compounds;

Hexachlorobenzene;

Hexachlorobutadiene;

Aldrin;

Dieldrin;

Endrin;

Polychlorinated Biphenyls;

Dichlorvos;

1,2–Dichloroethane;

All isomers of trichlorobenzene;

Atrazine;

Simazine;

Tributyltin compounds;

Triphenyltin compounds;

Trifluralin;

Fenitrothion;

Azinphos-methyl;

Malathion;

Endosulfan.

(c) *Schedule 6: Substances released on to land*:

Organic solvents;

Azides;

Halogens and their covalent compounds;

Metal carbonyls;

Organo-metallic compounds;

Oxidising agents;

Polychlorinated dibenzofuran and any congener thereof;

Polychlorinated dibenzo-p-dioxin and any congener thereof;

Polyhalogenated biphenyls, terphenyls and naphthalenes;

Phosphorous;

Pesticides;

Alkali metals and their oxides and alkaline earth and their oxides.

5.5.8 Exemptions

The 1991 regulations as amended provide for a number of situations where a process is exempt from the need to obtain an authorisation. These exemptions apply to those processes where the amount of any prescribed substance released is trivial. In particular by virtue of reg 4, a process cannot be taken to be a Pt A process if the process cannot result in:

(a) the release to air of prescribed substances, or there is no likelihood that it will result in the release to air of any such substance except in a quantity which is so trivial that it is incapable of causing harm, or its capacity to cause harm is insignificant; and

(b) the release of prescribed substances into water except in a concentration which is no greater than the background concentration, or in a quantity which does not, in any 12 month period, exceed the background quantity by more than the amount specified in Sched 5 to the regulations;

(c) the release on to land of any prescribed substances or there is no likelihood that it will result in the releases on to land of any such substance, except in a quantity which is so trivial that it is incapable of causing harm or its capacity to cause harm is insignificant.

A process cannot be a Pt B process unless it will, or there is a likelihood that it will, result in the release into the air of one or more of the prescribed substances, unless the quantity which is released is so trivial that it is incapable of causing harm or its capacity to cause harm is so insignificant.

In *Tandridge DC v P&S Civil Engineering Ltd* (1995), the district council prosecuted the defendant company on the ground that the company was operating a prescribed process, a tarmac production plant, without authorisation. The defendant contended that the district council had not proved that the exceptions under reg 4 did not apply. The question of where the burden of proof lies in respect of these exceptions was considered by the Divisional Court by way of case stated. The Divisional Court held that the burden of proving exceptions was clearly on the defendant and that this is clearly stated in s 101 of the Magistrates' Court Act 1980. On the facts, the defendant had not produced any evidence regarding the discharge levels and it was not able to benefit from the exceptions. Thus it is clear that any one wishing to benefit from these exceptions must clearly establish that they fall within the exceptions. There are a number of additional specified exceptions. These include processes carried on in working museums which are intended to demonstrate matters of historical interest, processes carried on in schools for educational purposes and domestic processes which are incidental to the use of a private dwelling. The running of aircraft, hovercraft, cars, trains and ships are also excluded. The list of exceptions is contained in s 4 of the regulations.

5.6 Licensing: the need for an authorisation

Section 6 of the EPA 1990 provides that:

> No person shall carry on a prescribed process after the date prescribed or determined for that description of process by or under Regulations under s 2(1) ... except under an authorisation granted by the enforcing authority and in accordance to the conditions to which it is subject.

Once it has been determined whether a process is a prescribed process or is a process which is discharging a prescribed substance, an application for an authorisation for that process must be made to the appropriate enforcement agency. It is only an offence for a person to carry on the prescribed process without an authorisation after the date prescribed or determined. Such dates have been prescribed by regulations issued under s 2(1) and these regulations prescribed a timetable for applications to be made to avoid an enormous influx of applications once the provisions came into force (see section below – 'Phasing in IPC').

An IPC authorisation is required to operate:

(a) any process subject to IPC;

(b) any proposed new process in any IPC category;

(c) any existing process in any IPC category where a 'substantial change' in the process is proposed.

The s 6 obligation to obtain an IPC authorisation should now be interpreted in the light of the provisions of the PPCA 1999.

An application for IPC authorisation is made to the relevant regional office of the Environment Agency. It should be noted here that, where the process is prescribed for LAAPC, the application for authorisation is made to the local authority in whose area the prescribed processes are (or are to be) carried on. LAAPC applications may also be made for prescribed processes carried on by means of mobile plant, in which case the application is made to the local authority in whose area the person carrying on the business has his principal place of business.

5.6.1 Phasing in IPC

Pt I of the EPA 1990 was implemented in April 1991. At the time of the EPA 1990 came into force, many plants were operating under authorisations from previous legislation but they were still required to obtain an IPC authorisation from HMIP. However, given the large number of plants concerned, and the time it would take to process all of the applications, the government recognised that they needed to include provisions for a phased programme of applications. Consequently, a rolling programme of applications was established, which required applications to be made on a sectoral basis by specified deadlines.

Applications for authorisations had to be submitted by the date prescribed in Sched 3 to the Environmental Protection (Prescribed Processes and Substances) Regulations 1991. As noted above, these regulations have since been amended by further regulations to take account of delays in the system. The Regulations specified a time period within which applications had to be submitted, for example, not earlier than 1 November 1995 and not later than 31 January 1996 for those processes covered in Chapter 6 'Other Industries'. HMIP actively took steps to ensure that all companies were aware of the deadlines well in advance. This was usually done in association with relevant trade associations and business organisations.

The first sector to be covered under this phased in programme were the combustion processes. This was necessary in order to meet the deadline of an EC Directive (88/609/EEC) concerned with large combustion plants (that is, power stations). The phased in programme was completed in 1996.

5.6.2 New processes

As far as new plants were concerned, the phased-in programme was not applicable. An authorisation had to be obtained before operation began. This usually occurred at the same time as planning permission was sought for the development. The Environment Agency could agree to a staged application for new developments, enabling it and the operator to discuss the proposal at the design stage and moving on later to the detailed application.

5.6.3 Processes undergoing substantial change

There were also specific provisions for existing plants which had undergone a substantial change. An existing plant was defined as one which has operated for the previous 12 months. Where modifications or alterations to the plant were proposed, which were deemed to amount to a substantial change, then the operator was required to obtain an immediate authorisation, irrespective of the deadlines stated in the programme of applications. Substantial changes to existing IPC licensed processes will now trigger IPPC controls.

5.6.4 What amounts to substantial change?

Substantial change is defined in s 10(7) of the EPA 1990 as 'substantial change in the substances released from the process or in the amount or any other characteristic of any substance so released'. If a Process Guidance Note (that is, official guidance issued by HMIP/Environment Agency) is available for the prescribed process, this will provide examples of changes which are either substantial or not. Changes which are not substantial may still require a variation of the conditions of the authorisation. Once again, it is advisable to seek the advice of the Environment Agency.

5.7 IPC applications

Schedule 1 to the EPA 1990 provides details about the form of the licence application and the information that it must contain. It also deals with publicity requirements. In addition, the form and content of applications is specified in the Environmental Protection (Application, Appeals and Registers) Regulations 1991, as amended.

Applications to the Environment Agency for authorisations to operate IPC processes require a substantial input from the applicants. A search through the IPC registers held by the Environment Agency will reveal that some of the applications are supported by many hundreds of pages of documentation. It is estimated that most applications take between 100–500 man hours to prepare and, indeed, many are prepared on behalf of companies by specialist consultants.

Applications must be made on the appropriate form, together with relevant supporting information. The following information is required:

(a) the name and address of the applicant;

(b) if the applicant is a company, the registered number and office;

(c) the address of the premises where the prescribed process is being (or will be) carried on;

(d) a map or location plan;

(e) a description of the prescribed process;

(f) a list of prescribed substances used in connection with or resulting from the prescribed processes;

(g) a list of any other substances used in connection with or resulting from the prescribed processes and which might cause harm if released into any environmental medium;

(h) a description of the techniques to be used for preventing the releases into any environmental medium of such substances, for reducing the releases of such substances to a minimum and for rendering harmless any such substances which are released;

(i) details of any proposed releases of such a substance into any environmental medium and an assessment of the environmental consequences;

(j) proposals for monitoring the release of substances and the environmental consequences of such releases;

(k) details of how the process will comply with 'any specific conditions' and how the process will operate using the best available techniques not entailing excessive cost;

(l) any other additional information that the applicant wants the enforcing authority to take into account when considering the application.

The information provided in the application must be clear, comprehensive and, of course, accurate. The Environment Agency can serve a notice on the applicant requiring further information to be supplied by a specified date. The application procedure for IPC licences has now been repealed by the PPCA 1999 and the following sections (5.7.1–5.7.4) are therefore of historical interest.

5.7.1 Fees and charges

One of the Government's intentions when HMIP was created in 1987 was that it should eventually become self-financing. One justification for this cost recovery scheme was that it would be an application of the 'polluter pays' principle, with those processes polluting the environment paying for the system of regulation that controls their activities. However, the charging scheme was controversial and HMIP were never able to generate sufficient income from fees and charges to become self-financing.

This desire for self-financing is continued in relation to the Environment Agency. Section 8 of the EPA 1990 which covered fees and charges in respect of IPC and LAAPC processes now only concerns LAAPC. Section 41 of the EA 1995 details the Environment Agency's charging scheme. An application to the enforcing authority must be accompanied by the requisite fee. The charging scheme for IPC is detailed in a document produced by the Environment Agency *Charging Scheme for Integrated Pollution Control* which is produced annually. The 1996–97 document states the charging scheme operates on the basis of the following categories of charges:

(a) an application fee to cover the costs of considering each application;

(b) a subsistence charge payable annually for the holding of each IPC authorisation to cover:

- the ongoing costs of inspection, monitoring and enforcement by enforcing authority staff,

- a contribution to recouping previous years' under-recovery,

- the costs of independent monitoring;

(c) a supplementary charge where applicable;

(d) a substantial variation fee, to cover the costs of considering an application for subsequent variation of an authorisation.

Charges are not made in respect of processes. In order to relate the size of IPC fees and charges to the amount of regulatory effort involved, payments due on particular processes are linked to the number of defined 'components' which the process contains. The definitions of components for each category of process are set out in the Appendix to the charging scheme. The charging scheme gives examples of how the component system operates. For example, a large combustion process which comprised three boilers of 100MWth, three gas turbines of more than 50MWth, and one waste gas treatment plant would comprise 3+3+1=7 components.

The fees and charges for LAAPC authorisations are lower. The penalties for not paying the annual subsistence charge are serious. If the authorisation holder fails to pay the relevant annual subsistence fee, the enforcing authority can serve a written notice on the holder of the authorisation revoking the authorisation or can take other enforcement action (s 8(8) of the EPA 1990).

5.7.2 Processing the application

When the application is received, the enforcing authority must either grant the authorisation, subject to any conditions required, or it must refuse the application. The enforcing authority cannot grant an authorisation if it considers that the applicant will not be able to carry on the process in compliance with the conditions attached to the authorisation. There is no requirement within Pt I of the EPA 1990 that the applicant be a fit and proper person in the same way that there is in relation to waste management licences contained within Pt II of the Act. The SOSE has the right, if he thinks fit, to intervene in the processing of an application and issue directions to the enforcing authority as to whether or not they should grant the authorisation.

Once an application was received, it would normally be decided upon within a period of four months. However, the period could be extended with the agreement of the applicant. In an attempt to speed up the process, and also to ensure greater consistency between applications, the Environment Agency could issue 'template' authorisations which were described as generic authorisations which could be applied to many industrial processes with the minimum of modification.

5.7.3 Consultation

Consultation is an important part of the process of dealing with IPC applications. Before reaching a decision on an application, the Environment Agency is required to carry out a consultation exercise and seek the views of a number of bodies. In all cases, the views of the Health and Safety Executive must be sought. In addition, the following organisations are consulted:

(a) the Ministry of Agriculture Fisheries and Food (where the process is in Wales, then the Secretary of State for Wales will be consulted instead);

(b) the sewerage undertaker, where the prescribed process involves or may involve the releases of any substance into a sewer;

(c) the Nature Conservancy Council for England (English Nature) or the Countryside Council for Wales, where the process may involve releases of any substance which affects a site of special scientific interest;

(d) the harbour authority, where the process involves a release of any substance into a harbour;

(e) the district council in whose area the process will be carried on;

(f) the local fisheries committee, where the process involves a release of any substance into relevant territorial waters or coastal waters.

5.7.4 Advertising

In addition to the consultation exercise, there are also provisions for the advertising of applications in order to ensure that other interested parties, such as local residents, have the opportunity to comment on the application. An advert must be placed in a local newspaper providing details about applications (for authorisation or variation), and also in the *London Gazette* if the process is subject to IPC. Details relating to consultation and advertising are contained in the Environmental Protection (Applications, Appeals and Registers) Regulations 1991 SI 1991/507, as amended.

5.8 Conditions

Authorisations can either be granted subject to conditions or refused. The conditions imposed in an authorisation are the principal mechanism by which the enforcing authorities can control or prevent the releases of substances into the environment and by which the UK cannot only abate pollution but fulfil its obligations under community law and other international treaties.

In deciding upon conditions, the Environment Agency and the local authorities are guided by s 7 of the EPA 1990 which deals specifically with conditions. As such, s 7 is of vital importance since it spells out what considerations the Environment Agency and the local authorities must take into account and, importantly, what the objectives of the conditions are. It also introduces the concepts of BATNEEC and BPEO. Section 7 provides that both the Environment Agency and the local authorities must include conditions which they consider appropriate for achieving certain stated objectives. In particular, conditions must be included which:

(a) the enforcing authority considers appropriate for achieving the objectives laid down in s 7(2) – BATNEEC;

(b) comply with any directions given by the SOSE for the implementation of obligations under EC or international law;

(c) comply with any limits or requirements, and achieve any quality standards or quality objectives, prescribed by the SOSE;

(d) comply with any requirements applicable to the grant of authorisations specified by or under a plan made by the SOSE under s 3(5) of the EPA 1990 (see below);

(d) comply with any other directions given by the SOSE in relation to all authorisations, certain types of authorisation or an individual authorisation;

(e) appear to the enforcing authority to be appropriate.

Whatever conditions are included in the authorisation, it is important to note that they are all subject to administrative law principles – they must be necessary, they should be clear and of course they must be lawful. In addition, no conditions can be imposed for the purposes only of securing the health of the people who work at the plant where the process is being carried on.

In setting conditions, not only must the enforcing authority take into account directions given by the SOSE, they must also set conditions which meet the objectives laid down in s 7(2) known as the BATNEEC conditions.

Before considering the BATNEEC provisions in detail, it is important to consider the role that the SOSE plays in giving directions and making plans.

5.8.1 The role of the SOSE

Section 7 refers to directions issued by the SOSE, to quality standards and objectives prescribed by him and also to plans. The SOSE is empowered to make such plans, directions and regulations by virtue of s 3.

Section 3 empowers the SOSE to make regulations which establish standards, objectives or particular requirements in relation to particular prescribed processes, or particular substances, and also to develop strategic plans aimed at reducing pollution. This power is significant in that it enables the SOSE to comply with obligations laid down in EC Directives.

Using s 3, the SOSE can make regulations which lay down quality objectives or quality standards in relation to any substance which may be released in any medium. Regulations may also prescribe standard limits for the concentration of substances, the amount, or the amount in any period, which may be released, or even any other characteristic of that substance in any circumstance in which it may be released.

5.8.2 Plans

The SOSE can also, under s 3, make plans for:

(a) establishing limits for the total amount, or the total amount in any period, of any substance which may be released into the environment in the UK or any area within it;

(b) allocating quotas, as regards the release of substances, to persons carrying on processes in respect of which any such limit value is established;

(c) establishing limits so as progressively to reduce pollution of the environment;

(d) the progressive improvement in the quality objectives and quality standards established by the above mentioned regulations issued under s 3.

The system of IPC enables the Environment Agency to ensure that the UK complies with its obligations under EC law. In particular, the Environment Agency is required to ensure that, in drawing up conditions of authorisations, the UK satisfies any quality standards or quality objectives laid down in EC directives. Certain directives are particularly relevant in this context, such as Directive (88/609/EEC) on the limitation of emissions of certain pollutants into the air from large combustion plants and Directive (84/360/EEC) on the combating of air pollution from industrial plants.

5.8.3 Specific conditions

In the light of what has been said above, specific conditions will be imposed which state expressly the quantities and compositions of substances that can be released, when and where they can be released, and the duration of the releases.

5.9 The implied BATNEEC condition

In setting conditions, both the Environment Agency and the local authorities are required by virtue of s 7 of the EPA 1990 to comply with the directions issued by the SOSE, discussed above, and also to meet the objectives laid down in s 7(2).

These objectives are:

(a) to ensure that, in carrying on a prescribed process, the best available techniques not entailing excessive cost will be used for;

(b) preventing the release of substances prescribed for any environmental medium into that medium or, where that is not practicable, by such means for reducing the release of such substances to a minimum and for rendering harmless any such substances which are so released; and

(c) for rendering harmless any other substances which might cause harm if released into any other environmental medium.

This section is of the utmost importance. It introduces the concept of BATNEEC and requires that, in setting the specific conditions, the 'best available techniques not entailing excessive cost' are employed to prevent releases or to render them harmless. The BATNEEC requirement applies to the specific conditions laid down by the Environment Agency. However, in addition to those aspects which are specifically covered by a condition in the authorisation, s 7(4) states that there is also an *implied general condition in every authorisation* that, in carrying on the process, the person carrying it on must use BATNEEC to achieve the same purposes. The specific and implied general conditions relating to the BATNEEC are considered in detail below.

5.9.1 What are the 'best available techniques not entailing excessive cost'?

The concept of BATNEEC is of vital importance. BATNEEC is to be used both in relation to expressly stated conditions and also as a general implied condition.

The purpose of using BATNEEC is to prevent the release of substances into the environment or, where that is not practicable, to reduce the release to a minimum and render any releases harmless. In the context of IPC and LAAPC, the types of conditions that fulfil the requirements of BATNEEC can relate to such things as:

(a) the actual technology and machinery used;

(b) the qualifications, training and supervision of the workforce;

(c) the design, layout and maintenance of the factory;

(d) the amounts, compositions, etc, of the substances used in the process.

BATNEEC is not a fixed standard, it will alter over a period of time. For existing processes, in particular those that pre-date the introduction of the IPC system, the requirement to use BATNEEC is a gradual process. Authorisations will generally require a timetabled upgrade programme, allowing the operator to achieve the prescribed BATNEEC conditions over a period of time and importantly allowing the operator to spread the costs of achieving this. Where a process is a new one a different view will be taken of what constitutes excessive cost and an applicant will be expected to meet BATNEEC immediately. This is made clear in the Department of the Environment Guidance on the interpretation of BATNEEC. It should be noted that the local authorities and the Environment Agency are under a statutory duty (s 4(9)) to follow developments in technology and techniques for preventing or reducing pollution of the environment in relation to relevant processes.

5.9.2 BATNEEC: The implied condition

Any aspect of a process that is not regulated by a specific condition is nevertheless subject to an implied BATNEEC condition (see s 7(7) of the EPA 1990). It is clear that HMIP endeavoured as far as possible to make the conditions as clear and as specific as possible in order to minimise any reliance on the implied general condition.

In order to achieve some degree of consistency between regions with regard to the interpretation of BATNEEC across a particular industry, sector or process, a number of guidance notes have been issued.

5.9.3 Guidance notes

The local authorities and the Environment Agency inspectors are assisted in their IPC and LAAPC work by a number of published guidance notes issued by the SOSE. They are under a duty to have regard to the guidance provided. For IPC processes, industry guidance notes have been published covering the fuel and power sector, metal industry, mineral industry, chemical industry and the waste disposal industry. These provide general guidance for the industry sector. They contain information on the processes that fall within that sector, relevant EC directives and information about available abatement technologies and techniques, sampling and monitoring. In practice, the content of the guidance notes indicates the approach that the Environment Agency or local authority is likely to take in the authorisation.

In addition to these general guidance notes, detailed process guidance notes are also published covering individual processes.

Local Authority Air Pollution Guidance Notes have also been issued providing guidance on Pt B processes. General guidance notes are available, and provide very useful information on general matters such as the applications procedure, public registers and the appeals procedure. These are supported by specific process guidance notes which give advice in particular on the techniques appropriate for the control of air pollution for individual processes. In addition, the SOSE has issued a further guidance note for local authorities on upgrading of existing processes and this adds to the information already given in the process guidance notes.

5.9.4 Failure to comply with conditions

Failure to comply with the conditions attached to an authorisation is an offence (s 6 of the EPA 1990). This includes failure to comply with any of the specific conditions and also failure to comply with the implied BATNEEC condition. In the event that legal proceedings are brought concerning a failure to satisfy the BATNEEC condition, the burden of proof falls squarely on the operator. He must prove that there was no better available technique that could be used without entailing excessive cost.

5.10 Best Practical Environmental Option – BPEO

The important feature of IPC is that it replaces the single medium approach to pollution control with an approach that takes into account the environment as a whole. When the Environment Agency is considering a process prescribed for central control, it must have regard, when drawing up the conditions of the authorisation, to all of the environmental media involved. Where the process involves the release of substances into more than one medium, the objective includes ensuring that the best available techniques not entailing excessive cost are used for minimising the pollution which will be caused to the environment as a whole by the releases, having regard to the Best Practicable Environmental Option, known as the BPEO. In other words, the aim is to minimise pollution by the application of BATNEEC having regard to the BPEO.

Unfortunately, the EPA 1990 does not provide a definition of what is meant by the BPEO. It is clear that it will involve a balancing exercise, taking into account ways in which, for example, a slight increase in air emissions might radically reduce discharges to water, and weighing up what is 'best' for the environment as a whole. Using this example, although emissions to air might be greater than if there were a single medium approach, the small increase in atmospheric emissions is more than offset by the reduction in water pollution. The Royal Commission definition serves as useful guide into what is intended:

> A BPEO is the outcome of a systematic consultative and decision–making procedure which emphasises the protection and conservation of the environment across land, air and water. The BPEO procedure establishes, for a given set of objectives, the option that provides the most benefit or least damage to the environment as a whole, at acceptable cost, in the long term as well as the short term.

5.11 Public registers

As in other parts of the EPA 1990, and other environmental legislation, there is a requirement that information pertaining to IPC and LAAPC processes are maintained on public registers. Section 20 of the EPA 1990 requires the Environment Agency and the local authorities to maintain public registers which contain information on:

(a) LAAPC/IPC applications;

(b) LAAPC/IPC authorisations;

(c) Variation, Enforcement and Prohibition Notices issued;

(d) revocations of authorisations;

(e) emission monitoring results provided to the enforcing authority;

(f) details of any enforcement action taken by the enforcing authority against operators;

(g) details of any convictions for offences under s 23(1);

(h) details of any appeals;

(i) details of any directions from the SOSE.

5.11.1 Exemptions from publicity requirements

There are only two exceptions to the requirement for information to be publicly available. By s 21, information may be excluded if it affects national security and, by s 22, a more widely used provision, information may be excluded on the grounds of commercial confidentiality.

5.11.2 Exclusion on the grounds of national security

Under s 21, the SOSE may issue directions requiring information to be left off the register:

... if, and so long as, in the opinion of the Secretary of State, the inclusion in the register of that information, or information of that description, would be contrary to the interests of national security.

Where the Environment Agency excludes information on this ground, then it must inform the SOSE that it has done so. It is possible that an applicant may wish information to be excluded on the grounds that they believe its inclusion would be contrary to the interests of national security. If this is the case, the person seeking to rely on s 21 should give notice to the SOSE specifying the information and indicating its apparent nature. The person must notify the Environment Agency that he or she has done this and, as a consequence, the information cannot be included on the register until the SOSE has determined that it should be included.

5.11.3 Exclusion on the grounds of commercial confidentiality

It is much more likely, and indeed more common, that a company will want to exclude information from the public registers because they do not want the public generally, or competitors specifically, to have access to such information. For example, a company may have pioneered a new process or product or may not want to reveal what raw materials are used. Provision is made for information to be excluded on the basis that the information is 'commercially confidential'. Section 22(11) defines commercially confidential information as information which, if it were contained in the register, would 'prejudice to an unreasonable degree the commercial interests of that individual or person'.

If a company wishes information to be excluded on this ground, then it must apply to the Environment Agency for a determination. The Environment Agency must reach a decision within a period of 14 days beginning with the date of the application for exclusion. Failure to make a determination within 14 days will result in the information being deemed to be commercially confidential.

5.12 Transfer of an authorisation

Once an authorisation has been granted, it is possible to transfer the authorisation to another person. In the event that a company or business is sold, or is taken over, it will be necessary for the new owner to obtain an authorisation if they wish to carry on the process. Before entering into a contract for the sale of the business, the prospective owner would be well advised to establish that the business has the relevant authorisation, otherwise they might enter into a situation where they are themselves 'carrying on the process' and, consequently, acting in breach of s 6 by operating a prescribed process without authorisation.

Section 9 makes specific provision for the transfer of authorisations, and allows the holder of an authorisation to transfer the authorisation to another person who intends to carry on the process. The new holder must notify the Environment Agency within 21 days of the transfer taking place. There is no requirement that the agency is consulted before the transfer takes place. This contrasts with the situation in relation to waste management licences, where the agency would need to be satisfied that the new licensee was a fit and proper person. However, it would clearly be extremely prudent for the transferee to check the position with the agency beforehand, since the Environment Agency has the power to revoke a licence if it considers the holder cannot comply with the conditions.

5.13 Monitoring of an IPC authorisation

The Environment Agency ensures compliance with the standards laid down by a number of means including:

(a) regular site visits;

(b) analysis of monitoring data;

(c) investigation of problems and complaints;

(d) specifying on-line monitoring by the process operator.

All IPC authorisations will include conditions which require the process operator to monitor discharges and emissions from the prescribed process in order to ensure compliance with conditions. Moreover, the authorisation will usually contain a condition that where there is a breach of condition the process operator informs the agency. Failing to tell the Environment Agency that there has been a breach of condition constitutes a further breach. As stated above, the Environment Agency, through its inspectors, will respond to complaints from the public and it operates a 24 hour telephone line for the public to call if they become aware of any polluting incident.

The Environment Agency is guided by an enforcement and prosecution policy, which was discussed more fully in Chapter 2. The policy clearly makes reference to monitoring as this is an integral part of overall enforcement. For instance, the policy states that inspection should be targeted primarily towards those whose activities give rise to the most serious environmental damage or pollution, or where the hazards are less well controlled.

5.13.1 Reviewing authorisations

The Environment Agency is under a duty to review the conditions of the authorisations that it has granted. The EPA 1990 requires that this happens 'from time to time' but in any event at least every four years. The Secretary of State has the right to alter this period (see reg 3).

5.14 Powers of enforcement

The EPA 1990 arms the Environment Agency and the local authorities with a wide range of investigatory, administrative enforcement, criminal prosecution and remedial powers to enable them to enforce compliance with the conditions of the authorisations that they have granted, and also to take action against processes that are operating without authorisation. The powers of enforcement include the following actions:

(a) variation and revocation of authorisations;

(b) Enforcement Notices (ENs) and Prohibition Notices (PNs);

(c) powers to secure compliance with the above notices;

(d) power to enter property;

(e) power to carry out examinations and investigations;

(f) powers of seizure;

(g) power to take steps to remedy harm.

5.14.1 Variation of authorisations

It has already been noted that the Environment Agency is under a statutory duty to review all authorisations at least every four years. As a consequence of that review, the Environment Agency may decide that it is necessary to alter or vary the conditions of the authorisation. A variation of an authorisation may be necessary to comply with new quality objectives or standards, or directions issued by the SOSE. Alternatively, the person carrying out the process may wish to make changes to the authorised process. For example, it might be the case that changes are made to the actual process or the substances handled or discharged, in which case it may be necessary for the authorisation holder to seek a variation of the authorisation. Sections 10–11 make provision for variation of authorisations by the Environment Agency (s 10) or at the instigation of the authorisation holder (s 11).

5.14.2 Variation by the Environment Agency

Section 10 enables the Environment Agency (or the local authority) to vary an authorisation at any time in order to incorporate new conditions in order to comply with the requirements of s 7. To vary the notice, the Environment Agency must serve a written Variation Notice on the holder of the authorisation, specifying the variations which it has decided to make and the date or dates from which the new conditions will have effect. Variation takes effect from the date specified in the notice. The authorisation holder will be required by the Variation Notice to inform the Environment Agency, within a specified period, of what action it proposes to take to comply with the varied conditions. The authorisation holder will also be required to pay a variation fee. Sometimes, a variation will result in a substantial change to the process that is authorised. Where the Environment Agency is of the opinion that, as a result of requiring variations there will be a substantial change, they must notify the authorisation holder of that opinion. Section 10(3) of the EPA 1990 inserted by the EA 1995, provides that the Environment Agency may serve a further notice which varies a Variation Notice. Substantial changes to IPC licenced processes will now trigger IPPC controls.

5.14.3 Variation by licence holder

Section 11 deals with situations where the authorisation holder applies for a variation in the authorisation. The procedure is described in Pt II of Sched I to the EPA 1990. An application may be made at any time by an authorisation holder requesting that the authorisation be varied. The application for the variation must be made on the prescribed form and must be supported by information prescribed in regulations and any other information that the Environment Agency requires. When the Environment Agency receives a request to alter or change a process it must consider the following:

(a) whether the proposed change would involve a breach in any of the conditions of the existing authorisation;

(b) if it would not involve such a breach, whether they would be likely to vary the conditions of the authorisation as a result of the change;

(c) if the variation does involve a breach of the authorisation, whether or not it would consider varying the authorisation so that the change may be made; and

(d) whether the change would involve a substantial change in the manner in which the process is being carried on.

The Environment Agency must, after taking these considerations into account, notify the applicant of its decision and the variations that it would consider making. The position then depends on whether the proposed changes amount to a substantial change or not. If they do not, then the applicant may apply for the relevant variations. If, on the other hand, the Environment Agency determines that the proposed change would amount to a 'substantial change' and notifies the applicant accordingly, then the applicant must apply for a variation if he wishes to proceed with the changes. This differs from the former situation where the applicant has a choice of whether or not to apply for a variation. However, in practice, if the Environment Agency has determined that a variation is required for a proposed change and the authorisation holder proceeds with the change without seeking the appropriate variation, they lay themselves open to the possibility of enforcement action by the Environment Agency. The SOSE has the power, by virtue of the EA 1995 (Sched 22) to call in applications for variations, in the same way that he can call in applications for authorisations.

5.14.4 Revocation of authorisations

The Environment Agency can serve a written notice of revocation on the holder of an authorisation where the holder fails to pay the necessary charges associated with the authorisation. In addition, the Environment Agency is also empowered to revoke an authorisation at any time, by virtue of s 12, and can revoke an authorisation where it has reason to believe that the prescribed process has not been carried on at all or for a period of 12 months. The SOSE may also issue a direction to the Environment Agency as to whether the Environment Agency should revoke an authorisation.

Revocation of an authorisation is clearly an important enforcement tool, since it means that, once the revocation becomes effective, the prescribed process cannot continue to be carried on without an offence being committed under s 6. Therefore, it is important that the authorisation holder has adequate notice of revocation and the right of appeal. Section 12(1) provides that notice of revocation must be served in writing on the person holding the authorisation, and s 12(3) provides that it shall have effect from the date specified in the notice. The authorisation holder must have at least 28 days' notice from the date the notice is served and the date specified in the notice. The Environment Agency can withdraw the Revocation Notice (RN), or vary the date specified in it, at any time up until the date that the revocation takes effect.

An appeal against a decision of the Environment Agency to revoke an authorisation must be made to the SOSE. Where an appeal is made, the revocation will not take effect until the final determination of the appeal or the withdrawal of the appeal (s 15(8)).

5.14.5 Enforcement Notices

Section 13 provides the Environment Agency with the power to serve an 'Enforcement Notice' (EN) in two circumstances:

(a) if, in the opinion of the Environment Agency, the person carrying out the prescribed process under an authorisation is contravening any condition of the authorisation; or

(b) is likely to contravene any such condition.

Therefore, the Environment Agency is equipped to deal with situations where there has been a breach of the authorisation or it can take anticipatory action where it is of the opinion that a breach is likely to occur.

Procedurally, the notice must state that the Environment Agency is of this opinion, it must specify the matters which constitute the contravention or which make a contravention likely, and it must also specify the steps that must be taken to remedy the situation and the date by which such steps must be taken. Once again, the SOSE has the power to issue a direction to the Environment Agency as to whether it should exercise its powers under s 13. Failure to comply with an EN is an offence (s 23). A new s 13(4) of the EPA 1990, incorporated by the EA 1995, enables the agency to withdraw an EN.

5.14.6 Prohibition Notices

Prohibition Notices (PNs) are different to ENs in that they are not aimed at dealing with situations where there has been, or is likely to be, a breach of an authorisation. The aim of the PN is to enable the Environment Agency to take action in situations where the carrying on of the process involves an imminent risk of serious pollution.

Section 14 provides:

> If the enforcing authority is of the opinion, as respects the carrying on of a prescribed process under an authorisation, that the continuing to carry it on, or the continuing to carry it on in a particular manner, involves an imminent risk of serious pollution of the environment the authority shall serve a notice (a 'prohibition notice') on the person carrying on the process.

There is no requirement for there to be a contravention of the authorisation. Section 14(2) specifically states that the PN be served whether or not the manner of carrying on the process in question contravenes a condition of the authorisation. As with ENs, the PN must state the Environment Agency's opinion, specify the risks involved, specify what steps are to be taken to remove the risk and the period of time in which such steps should be taken. Where the notice applies only to a part of the prescribed process then it may also apply conditions to that part of the process. The SOSE can issue direction to the Environment Agency as to whether a notice should be served and what matters it should specify in it.

5.14.7 Power to secure compliance with Enforcement Notices and Prohibition Notices

Failure to comply with an EN or PN is an offence triable either way in the magistrates' court or the Crown Court (s 23(1)(b)). Under s 24 of the EPA 1990 the Environment Agency can also seek an injunctive remedy from the High

Court to secure compliance with a notice if it feels that a criminal prosecution will not provide an effective remedy.

5.14.8 Powers of Environment Agency inspectors

The powers of inspectors are wide and are now provided for in a lengthy s 108 of the Environment Act 1995 (previously s 17 of the EPA 1990). The powers conferred on the Environment Agency are also conferred on local authorities exercising their LAAPC functions under Pt I of the EPA 1990. The purpose of s 108 was to streamline the powers of entry and inspection across the range of pollution control functions now exercised by the Environment Agency, and these powers apply equally to control functions under Pt II of the EPA 1990 (Waste Management) and the WRA 1991 (water discharge consents). Section 108 combines the powers previously exercised by HMIP, the NRA and the Waste Regulation Authorities (WRAs).

It is essential that inspectors have these powers of entry and inspection in order to ensure compliance with the authorisations granted and also to identify instances where processes are being carried on without the appropriate authorisation. The powers listed in s 108 of the EA 1995 may be exercised for one or more of the following purposes:

(a) determining whether any pollution control legislation is being or has been complied with;

(b) exercising or performing pollution control functions;

(c) determining whether and, if so, how such a function should be exercised or performed.

Section 108 refers to persons authorised in writing. In practice this will be the inspectors employed by the Environment Agency (or the relevant local authority officers). An inspector has the following powers of entry and inspection:

(a) to enter at any reasonable time premises which he has reason to believe it is necessary for him to enter. This should normally be at any reasonable time unless there is an emergency, in which case entry is permitted at any time, and if need be, by force;

(b) on entering premises to take with him any other person duly authorised by the Environment Agency, and a policeman. The latter may be needed in situations where the inspector has reasonable cause to apprehend any serious obstruction in carrying out his duties;

(c) the inspector may also take any equipment or materials required for any purpose for which the power of entry is being exercised;

(d) to make such examination and investigation as may in any circumstances be necessary;

(e) to instruct that the premises or any part of them, or anything in them, be left undisturbed. The inspector may require that the premises or the part of the premises under investigation are not disturbed for as long as is reasonably necessary to enable him to carry out any examination or investigation;

(f) to take such measurements and photographs and make recordings as he considers necessary;

(g) to take samples, or instruct samples be taken, of any articles or substances found in or on the premises and also from the air, water or land in, on, or in the vicinity of the premises. Specific provisions relate to the possession, safekeeping and use in evidence of such samples;

(h) in the case of any article or substance found in or on premises which appears to him to be an article or substance which has caused or is likely cause pollution of the environment, or harm to human health, to cause it to be dismantled or subjected to any process or test (but not so as to damage or destroy it unless that is necessary);

(i) to require information from any person – the inspector can require any person whom he has reasonable cause to believe to be able to give any information relevant to any examination or investigation to answer such questions as the inspector thinks fit to ask. The person answering the questions will be required to sign a declaration of truth to the answers;

(j) to inspect any information and to take copies – the inspector can require the production of any information that he considers necessary, including information held on computer. He also has the right to inspect and take copies of such information or any entry in the records;

(k) to require facilities and assistance – here the inspector can require any person to afford him such facilities and assistance with respect to any matters or things within that persons control or in relation to which that person has responsibilities. So, for example, the inspector can require an engineer on the premises to show him how the monitoring and testing equipment is working (or not working as the case may be);

(l) any other powers conferred by regulation by the SOSE. Certain information can be withheld from the inspector if it is subject to legal professional privilege. This covers correspondence between clients and their solicitors or legal professional advisors.

Section 23 of the EPA 1990 makes it an offence not to comply with the requirements of the inspector or to obstruct him in carrying out his duty.

5.14.9 Powers to remedy harm

Where a process has been operating without authorisation, in breach of conditions or in breach of a EN or PN, then the Environment Agency has the power (s 27) to remedy any harm that may have occurred. In this respect, remediation work can be carried out by the Environment Agency and any costs incurred by it can be recovered from the offender. In addition, s 26 makes provision for the court to make an order for a person convicted of these particular offences to remedy the matter. The court can choose to do this in addition to, or instead of, imposing a fine.

5.15 Offences

Section 23 sets out the offences in relation to IPC and LAAPC processes. These include:

(a) operating a process without authorisation;

(b) failure to comply with an authorisation condition;

(c) failure to comply with an EN or PN;

(d) obstructing an inspector;

(e) failure to comply with the requirements of an inspector;

(f) providing false information on any records that are required to be maintained as a condition of the authorisation.

Through its monitoring and as a result of inspections the Environment Agency inspectors are usually able to detect breaches of authorisations, either as result of public complaints, or because there has been a pollution incident. The Environment Agency, relies on the information received from complainants and, to this extent, pressure groups and citizens can play a role in securing the enforcement of environmental law.

Section 157 of the EPA 1990 states that where an offence is committed by a company it is possible that any director, manager, secretary or other similar officer (or a person who was purporting to act in such a capacity) of the company may also be guilty. However, in order to establish this personal criminal liability it has to be proved that the offence was committed with that person's consent or connivance or to have been attributable to any neglect on their part. Section 158 also provides that where an offence has been committed by any person due to the act or default of some other person, that other person may be charged with and convicted of the offence. The effect of this provision is that it could expose senior company officials to the risk of prosecution.

5.15.1 Enforcement policy

The Environment Agency's enforcement and prosecution policy is considered in detail in Chapter 2. The Environment Agency's policy does not apply to the local authorities which also have responsibility in terms of enforcing the provisions of Pt I of the EPA 1990 in respect of Pt B prescribed processes (LAAPC).

In general terms it is clear that the intention is that breaches of authorisation standards and other problems should be dealt with quickly and effectively with the co-operation of the operator. However, it is also very clear that the Environment Agency will strive to avoid problems occurring in the first instance by providing advice and assistance to those subject to the system of IPC control.

Notwithstanding this, the Environment Agency does have a number of enforcement tools at its disposal, notably ENs and PNs which have already been discussed, warning, caution and, ultimately, prosecution. However, it is also worth noting that before taking any of these steps an inspector may often write a letter to an alleged offender which sets out any remedial action which the Environment Agency expects to be taken. Where an inspector sends out such a letter it must set out in clear terms what needs to be done, why, within what period, and what relevant law applies. It should also explain to the recipient that he, she or it has 10 working days to make any representations to the Environment Agency if it is thought that the action required is not justified. The Environment Agency should not take formal enforcement action during the 10 working days period, unless immediate action is justified by the risk. Thus, it can be seen from this that the Environment Agency can seek to resolve problems or deal with breaches of the law in an informal manner which gives the 'polluter' the opportunity to sort things out before any formal action is taken.

As far as prosecution is concerned the EA's enforcement policy makes it clear that this is an issue for the discretion of the Environment Agency. Clearly a breach of IPC authorisation does not result in automatic prosecution and the Environment Agency will consider the circumstances of each case and what would be gained by a prosecution.

5.15.2 Penalties

Section 23 of the EPA 1990 lays down the various penalties for the offences created in the same section. The offence of carrying on a prescribed process without an authorisation, failing to comply with an EN or PN can result in a maximum fine of up to £20,000 in the magistrates' court or six months' imprisonment or both. On conviction on indictment in the Crown Court, the penalty can increase to an unlimited fine or to between two and five years' imprisonment.

Evidence suggests that the magistrates are willing to impose sizeable fines for offences committed under IPC. For example, in a case brought by HMIP against Southern Refining Services (SRS) in 1994 (*HMIP v Southern Refining Services Ltd* (1994)), Newbury magistrates imposed a fine of £12,000 for an air pollution incident caused by SRS's procedures for dealing with residues from a distillation process. In addition, the magistrates made an award of costs against SRS of over £6,000. The case concerned an air pollution incident which occurred as a result of an operator mistakenly adding quantities of the biocide sodium dichloroisocyanurate to a process, instead of sodium carbonate. This resulted in the release of noxious fumes, including chlorine gas. The release lasted for 10–15 minutes. As a result of the incident, more than 20 of the company's workforce had to be treated for eye irritation. The company showed themselves willing to co-operate with HMIP during the subsequent investigation. The company was charged with, and pleaded guilty to, a breach of an IPC authorisation under s 23(1) of the EPA 1990. Three breaches were identified by HMIP: failure to take all practicable means to prevent fugitive emissions; failure to provide staff with appropriate written operating instructions; and failure to label drums correctly. The case is interesting because the magistrates, unusually, took the turnover and the profitability of the company into account when determining the level of fine. The turnover of the company was reported to be £500,000 and its profit between £80,000 to £100,000.

5.16 Rights of appeal

Section 15 of the EPA 1990 provides various rights of appeal in relation to all parts of Pt I and, as such, it should be remembered is equally applicable to LAAPC. In addition to s 15, the Environmental Protection (Application, Appeals and Registers) Regulations 1991 SI 1991/507 provide detailed information about the appeals procedure. An appeal must be brought within two months of the relevant decision or determination.

A right of appeal lies with the person seeking the authorisation or the authorisation holder against the following:

(a) refusal to grant an authorisation;

(b) the conditions attached to an authorisation;

(c) refusal to grant a variation of an authorisation sought by the authorisation holder (under s 11);

(d) revocation of an authorisation;

(e) a Variation Notice, EN or PN.

No appeal may be brought against a decision which implements a direction made by the SOSE.

In addition, s 22 allows a right of appeal concerning exclusion of commercially confidential information from the register.

The SOSE can take the following actions in appeal cases:

(a) affirm the decision taken by the Environment Agency or local authority;

(b) where the decision was a refusal to grant an authorisation or a variation of an authorisation, the SOSE may direct the Environment Agency or local authority to grant the authorisation or vary it accordingly;

(c) quash all or any of the conditions of an authorisation;

(d) quash a decision to revoke an authorisation;

(e) give directions as to the conditions to be attached to authorisations;

(f) quash, affirm or modify a variation, EN or PN.

5.16.1 The form of appeal

Although the appeal is to the SOSE, the SOSE has the power by virtue of s 114 of the EA 1995, to delegate the hearing of appeals to chief inspectors. Alternatively, the SOSE may direct that the hearing takes the form of a local inquiry. As stated above, the details of the appeals procedure are laid down in SI 1991/507.

5.17 The interface between IPC and other pollution controls

One of the principal reasons for establishing the Environment Agency was to achieve a degree of uniformity across the environmental protection regimes thus far regulated by different bodies. The creation of the Environment Agency has removed the need for HMIP, the NRA and the WRAs to consult each other on areas of shared concern and therefore a number of statutory provisions requiring that consultation have been repealed. For example, HMIP was required by s 28, Pt I of the EPA 1990 to consult the NRA regarding any discharges to controlled water from IPC processes before granting an IPC authorisation. Nevertheless, the system of IPC described in this chapter does not provide a completely integrated system of controlling all polluting activities. The system sits alongside other control mechanisms and so it is worth considering the relationship between IPC and other legislative controls.

5.17.1 Waste

Processes that operate under an IPC authorisation are exempted from the waste management licensing system. However, the Environment Agency cannot attach any conditions to an IPC authorisation concerning the final disposal by deposit in or on land of directive waste. Where a process involves the final disposal of controlled (directive) waste deposited in or on land then it is subject to the licensing controls under Pt II of the EPA 1990. A person or business carrying on the process may then need to obtain a waste management licence in addition to the IPC authorisation.

5.17.2 Statutory nuisance

Section 79 in Pt III of the EPA 1990 deals with the relationship between the controls under Pt I of the Act and the statutory nuisance provisions under Pt III. A local authority cannot institute summary proceedings without the consent of the SOSE in respect of a nuisance falling under s 79 if proceedings could be instituted under Pt I of the EPA 1990. However, this provision does not prevent a citizen commencing their own action under s 82, or a local authority from serving an abatement notice under s 80.

5.17.3 Discharges into sewers

Many IPC processes will involve the discharge of trade effluent into the sewers. Although the IPC authorisation will attach conditions concerning the discharge the process operator will still require a trade effluent consent from the sewage undertaker by virtue of s 118 of the Water Industry Act 1991. Where it is proposed that special category effluent is discharged into the sewer the sewerage undertaker is duty bound to consult the Environment Agency before granting a trade effluent consent. In fact, it is a criminal offence if the undertaker fails to consult the Environment Agency.

5.18 IPC and IPPC

5.18.1 Introduction

In late 1996 the EC passed the IPPC Directive (96/61/EC) which required all Member States to set up a Command and Control licensing system of regulation in regard to the activities listed in Annex 1 of the directive. The IPPC control regime as detailed in the directive is similar, in many respects, to IPC except that the primary objective of IPPC is to regulate environmental impacts of highly polluting industrial activities, rather than the IPC focus on the regulation of all environmental emissions from highly polluting industrial processes.

The IPPC Directive was transposed into national legislation by the Pollution Prevention and Control Act (PPCA) 1999. The legislative framework contained in the 1999 Act is supplemented by the Pollution Prevention and

Control (England and Wales) Regulations 2000 (PPC Regulations 2000). IPPC controls are to be phased in over the period 1999–2007. Activities commenced after 31 October 1999 are immediately subject to IPPC, as are substantial changes to existing processes which are currently subject to IPC control.

The IPPC Directive obliges Member States to prevent or, where prevention is not possible, reduce pollution *and* environmental impacts from the range of installations listed in Annex 1 of the directive. A licensing system is used to regulate the activities of the listed installations.

Each IPPC licence (referred to as a 'permit') is designed, not only to regulate environmental emissions discharged to all three environmental media (air, water, and land) but also the environmental impacts of the following: energy use and efficiency, raw material consumption, noise, vibration, accident prevention measures, and heat (thermal effects). Regulatory control, as specified in permit conditions, extends beyond day to day operational controls to include aftercare and site remediation. In contrast to a number of other EC directives the IPPC Directive requires permits to be set by reference to local conditions and any applicable environmental quality standards. The UK has taken advantage of the terms of the directive to extend the scope of IPPC control to include activities which are currently regulated under IPC controls as Pt B processes (that is, local authority air pollution control). It has been necessary to extend IPPC control to Pt B processes since the entire IPC regime will be phased out by 2007 and processes subject to local authority air pollution control would be left unregulated.

IPPC replaces the dual system of IPC controls (regulating the highly polluting emissions from Pt A processes, regulated by the Environment Agency, and less polluting emissions to the atmosphere, regulated by the local authorities) by a 'single' system of control applying to the *installations* listed in Annex 1 of the IPPC Directive. Under the IPPC regulatory regime the Environment Agency regulates the highly polluting installations (Pt A(1) installations). However, in contrast to their previous IPC responsibilities, local authorities now have a greater regulatory role under IPPC: they are responsible for regulating Pt A(2) installations in regard to *all environmental impacts*, and Pt B installations regarding atmospheric emissions only (rather than atmospheric impacts).

IPPC controls, like their IPC counterparts, use process standards to determine licence conditions. In particular, 'best available techniques' (BAT) must be employed by installation operators to prevent and/or reduce the environmental impacts of regulated installations.

5.18.2 IPPC distinguished from IPC

Not only does IPPC have a wider focus than IPC, regulating environmental impacts rather than environmental emissions, but its ambit is also significantly wider. There are approximately 7,000 'listed' installations subject to IPPC control as opposed to the 2,000–2,500 Pt A and 12,500 Pt B processes subject to IPC control. In particular, IPPC has extended control to large landfill sites, intensive agricultural production units, and food and drink factories.

IPPC regulates 'installations' rather than 'prescribed processes'. IPPC regulation is therefore a site, or plant based, method of regulation. This avoids the potential complexity of IPC regulation where several individually licensed processes are all undertaken on the same site.

IPPC provides a greater role for local authorities who have assumed responsibility for the regulation of the environmental impacts of Pt A(2) installations to all three environmental media, in addition to their existing Pt B regulatory role. Thus, for the first time, local authorities extend their remit beyond 'policing' atmospheric emissions from Pt B processes. In contrast to IPC, IPPC provides no exemptions from the need to obtain an IPPC permit.

IPPC's adoption of a BAT standard for all installations contrasts with the BATNEEC condition incorporated in IPC authorisations, however, in reality the two standards are similar since, when determining IPPC permits the regulator must have regard to the 'proportionality principle' requiring it to take the economic viability of the BAT standard into account.

Under IPC, the Environment Agency and the local authorities are required to review authorisations at least once every four years. IPPC does not specify a mandatory timetable for reviewing permits although official guidance may recommend timetables for each industry sector.

5.18.3 IPPC Licensing

IPPC permits are required to authorise the activities undertaken at each installation. In deciding whether or not to grant a permit the Environment Agency or local authority must take into account the statutory objectives of IPPC: to prevent, or reduce, pollution and environmental impacts of regulated installations.

'Pollution' (see reg 2 of the PPC Regulations 2000) has a wider meaning under IPPC, than its equivalent IPC definition (s 1(3) of the EPA 1990) and includes emissions which may be harmful to humans or environmental quality. The term also extends to activities which cause offence to human senses, damage to property, or impair or interfere with amenities and other uses of the environment. The largely anthropocentric (human centred) definition of pollution is clearly intended to focus attention upon the wide range of environmental impacts caused by human activity. These impacts are commonly referred to as 'externalities'. The definition reflects the wider IPPC focus on impacts rather than a narrower range of polluting emissions. Readers should note that the emission focused BPEO concept is not relevant to IPPC regulation.

5.18.4 'Listed' activities which are subject to IPPC

Schedule 1 to the PPC Regulations 2000 lists and divides 'activities' into six chapters:

(a) energy industry,

(b) chemical industry,

(c) metal production and processing industries,

(d) minerals industry,

(e) waste management industry,

(f) other activities.

Each of the six industry chapters is subdivided into a further set of groupings. Finally, each industry grouping is split into two smaller groups reflecting the regulatory body responsible for 'policing' the relevant installation. Part A(1) activities are regulated by the Environment Agency and Pt A(2) and B installations are regulated by the local authorities.

The six industry chapters include activities which were not previously subject to IPC. Of particular note is the inclusion of large waste management facilities, food and drink manufacturing and intensive agricultural production units. Annex 1 of the IPPC Directive contains details of thresholds. Activities falling below the thresholds are excluded, for example, small landfill sites.

5.18.5 Installations

The term 'installation' (see reg 2) refers to any stationary technical unit where a prescribed activity is carried out and any other directly associated activities carried out on the same site which have a technical connection with the prescribed activities and which could have an effect on pollution. This widely drafted definition appears to exclude mobile plant but is otherwise comprehensive. Official guidance will be necessary to clarify this somewhat opaque definition.

5.18.6 Listed substances and permit conditions

Schedule 5 to the PPC Regulations 2000 lists substances which might be discharged by installations into air or water. Where significant amounts of these substances are to be discharged from an installation the IPPC permit must include conditions which set either limit values or environmental quality standards for the relevant substances.

5.18.7 Exemptions

There is no exemption from the necessity of obtaining a permit if the relevant installation falls within the parameters of IPPC. Installations which have only 'trivial' ('trivial' is a term which has no statutory definition and, as yet, no official guidance) environmental impacts will require a permit but the permitting process will be simpler.

5.18.8 Applying for a permit

The application process is detailed in regs 7 and 10 and Sched 4 of the PPC Regulations 2000.

An application (accompanied by the relevant fee) must contain the following essential information:

(a) condition of the site – (information is required regarding any pollution risks posed by the site. The applicant may use any Environmental Impact Assessment (EIA), prepared in regard to a linked planning application for the site, to help satisfy this requirement. Details relating to site condition will be used, at the time of site closure, for the purpose of comparing the relative condition of the site before and after the cessation of activities);

(b) raw materials and energy usage relevant to the proposed activity;

(c) waste minimisation and waste prevention measures;

(d) emissions and environmental impacts;

(e) technology and techniques to reduce emissions and impacts which are currently incapable of elimination;

(f) accident prevention;

(g) monitoring proposals;

(h) a non-technical summary of the foregoing information.

5.18.9 Advertising the permit application

Any applicant who requires a permit or who operates an existing permitted facility but is planning a substantial change to the relevant installation must advertise details of the application in a local newspaper, and in the case of Pt A(1) and Pt A(2) installations, in the *London Gazette* (see Sched 4 to the PPC Regulations 2000). The relevant press notice must contain the following information:

(a) applicant's name and address;

(b) a brief description of the proposed activities;

(c) a reference to any public register containing relevant information relating to the applicant;

(d) an invitation to make representations to the relevant regulator (Environment Agency or local authority) within 28 days of the appearance of the press notice.

This procedure is similar to planning applications since it provides an opportunity for the general public to participate in the licensing process.

5.18.10 Consultation and participation

As in the case of IPC, IPPC permit applications are subject to consultation with a number of statutory bodies including:

(a) the Health and Safety Executive;

(b) the relevant health authority;

(c) the Nature Conservancy Council (if emissions could affect a Site of Special Scientific Interest);

(d) the relevant water service company;

(e) the relevant sewerage undertaker;

(f) the relevant planning authority (regarding proposed waste management sites);

(g) an EC Member State (where the SOSE is 'aware' that the application, if granted, is likely to have significant affects on the relevant Member State).

In addition to the statutory consultees the Environment Agency and local authorities consult one another regarding Pt A(1) and Pt A(2) applications.

The consultation process is administered by the regulator responsible for the relevant installation. Within 14 days of receipt of the permit application or variation application the regulator is required to notify the consultees (with the exception of affected Member States) of the application and provide a minimum 28 day period (which may be extended) within which the consultee can make representations. Responses received from consultees are material considerations which the regulator must have regard to in reaching a decision on the application. Normally, the application should be decided within four months of the date it was lodged with the regulator but this period may be extended by agreement.

5.18.11 The considerations which are material to the permit decision

The decision to grant an application for a permit (with conditions) or refuse it will be taken by the regulator (Environment Agency or local authority) on the basis of the information submitted by the applicant, the representations made by consultees and the public, matters specified in the PPC Regulations 2000, and any other material considerations, such as official guidance relating to what constitutes BAT for the relevant installation.

In most cases it is anticipated that, like planning applications,the decision will be made on the merits of each individual application. However, the option exists to decide applications on the basis of 'general binding rules'. This is a decision process which will probably apply to simple installations, such as intensive agricultural installations, and would set standard permit conditions in accordance with the relevant set of general binding rules.

The regulator (Environment Agency or local authority) is under a duty to refuse the application if it considers that the applicant will not be able to comply with the permit conditions which would be included were the application to be approved (reg 10(3)). It is quite likely that this IPPC duty will enable the regulator to take into account whether the applicant is fit to carry on the activities detailed in the application, bearing in mind the applicant's compliance history. Where the application relates to a waste management site the regulator will be compelled to reject the application if (i) the applicant is not a fit and proper person (reg 4) or (ii) no planning permission authorising waste management usage for the site exists.

5.18.12 Best available techniques

Also material to the permit decision are the IPPC objectives which require all applicants to operate their installations in ways which use best available techniques (BAT) to prevent pollution of the environment. In regard to Pts A(1) and (2) installations applicants must operate their installations so as to avoid the production of waste, recover and/or recycle any wastes produced, avoid or reduce the environmental impact of wastes produced which require disposal, use energy efficiently, and prevent accidents (see regs 7–11).

The requirement for IPPC permit holders to employ BAT is detailed in regs 12–14. The BAT obligation is applicable, not only to the technology employed in operating the installation, but also encompasses the design, construction, maintenance, and decommissioning of the installation. Official guidance, in the form of 'BREF' (BAT reference) notes and other guidance will provide supplementary information on what is considered to be BAT in each industry sector subject to IPPC.

Bearing in mind that IPPC is applicable to all EC Member States, in contrast to IPC which has a UK remit, guidance as to what will constitute BAT is now an EC matter. Under Art 16(2) of the IPPC directive the EC Commission has established a pan-European forum for the exchange of information on BAT. The IPPC Information Exchange Forum will publish its findings tri-annually. The forum will have an important input into the final form of BREF guidance notes, especially concerning what BAT can achieve in regard to reductions in emissions, energy consumption, and raw material usage. BREF notes will be material to both individual permit applications and what is considered to be BAT in each of the six industry sectors subject to IPPC.

In contrast to the equivalent IPC BATNEEC requirement, BAT does not itself include any reference to cost/benefit considerations in determining the techniques which fulfil the BAT test. Nevertheless, cost/benefit considerations are relevant because of the applicability of the EC proportionality principle. Under the BATNEEC test, not only were the costs and benefits of a particular technique taken into account, but also the capacity of each industry sector to buy in the relevant technique. BAT differs from BATNEEC in regard to the materiality of the economic viability of an industry sector as a relevant consideration.

5.18.13 The meaning of BAT

The PPC Regulations 2000 provide much of the detail on what constitutes BAT. A summary of the key points is provided here.

Best

This term refers to the effectiveness of any technique to be employed by an applicant to achieve a high level of environmental protection. There may be several techniques which could be employed to achieve the requisite level of environmental protection and in such circumstances they will all satisfy the 'best' criterion.

Available

This term refers to the availability of techniques. Techniques are available if they have been developed on a sufficiently large enough scale which enables the applicant to acquire and install/implement them. This is a stricter criteria than the equivalent term in the BATNEEC test. Techniques will not be treated as available in any of the six industrial sectors subject to IPPC control if economic or technical conditions in the relevant industry prevent the technique being viable. Material to the question of whether a specific technique is available will be its costs and benefits, and its current manufacture and/or use in the UK.

Techniques

This term is wider than 'technology' and includes considerations such as the design, construction, maintenance, and decommissioning of the relevant technique.

5.18.14 'Call in' power

The SOSE has the power to 'call in' an IPPC permit application for his own decision (Sched 4, para 14 of the PPC Regulations 2000). Where an application is called in, the SOSE cannot make the decision himself on the application but he directs the regulator as to whether it should grant or refuse the application. In the event that he directs that the application should be granted he has the power to direct the conditions which are to be included in the permit. Before directing the regulator as to the outcome of the permit application the SOSE will either hold a public inquiry or an informal hearing into the application.

5.18.15 The transfer and surrender of IPPC permits

Regulation 18 of the PPC Regulations 2000 details the procedure to apply for a transfer of all or part of the activities authorised by the installation permit to another person (usually the company which is in the process of acquiring the permit holders' business). A joint application by the existing and proposed permit holder is necessary specifying the date on which the transfer is required to take effect. The regulator may only reject the application if it considers that the proposed permit holder would not be able to comply with the permit conditions, or, in the case of the proposed transfer of a waste management installation permit, that the proposed permit holder is not a fit and proper person.

The regulator has two months to determine the application but this period may be extended by agreement. Somewhat unusually, a failure by the regulator to deal with the application within the relevant timescale will lead to a deemed transfer rather than a deemed refusal.

Under reg 19 of the PPC Regulations 2000 the regulator is not permitted to accept a surrender of an existing permit unless it is satisfied that any necessary clean up works have been satisfactorily completed. Part A(1) and A(2) installation permit holders must make a specific application to the regulator regarding a proposed surrender of its permit. The application can relate to all or part of the authorised activities at the relevant installation. The application must include the following information:

(a) the name and address of the permit holder;

(b) a plan of the installation indicating whether the whole or part of the installation is subject to the application;

(c) a site report specifying the present condition of the site and any changes which have occurred since the permit was originally granted;

(d) details of the precautionary steps taken to avoid pollution and any remedial action taken to return the installation to a satisfactory state.

The regulator must be satisfied that the installation does not pose any pollution risk before it can accept the surrender. The onus falls squarely on the permit holder to provide the regulator with sufficient information which will convince the regulator that the installation is in a satisfactory condition, poses no risk of pollution and therefore the regulator can safely accept the surrender. The permit holder is presumed to be responsible for any material difference in the condition of the installation as revealed in the pre-permit report and the present condition of the installation.

The regulator has three months to reach a decision on the surrender application, although this period may be extended by agreement. Failure to determine the application within the relevant timescale results in a deemed refusal.

5.18.16 Powers of regulatory officials

5.18.16.1 Administrative enforcement powers

IPPC regulators (Environment Agency and local authorities) have an extensive array of enforcement powers at their disposal to ensure that the permit holder complies with the terms of its permit (PPC regs 23–25). These powers enable the regulators to retain tight control over authorised activities without having to resort to prosecution as a control mechanism.

The regulator is subject to a duty (PPC reg 23) to supervise authorised activities. Regulators are required to take any steps which are necessary to ensure that the permit holder complies with the conditions attached to its permit. How the regulator chooses to secure compliance with permit conditions is a matter for regulatory discretion. The following administrative powers are the most significant.

5.18.16.2 Enforcement Notice (EN)

The regulator may serve an EN on a permit holder if the regulator believes that the permit holder has breached, or is likely to breach, any permit condition (PPC reg 24). An EN will specify the breach, the remedial action required, and the timescale during which the remedial action must be completed. Failure to comply with an EN is a criminal offence (PPC reg 32).

5.18.16.3 Revocation Notice (RN)

The regulator may revoke all or part of the activities authorised by the permit via service of a RN (PPC reg 21). In regard to waste management installations a RN may be served where the permit holder ceases to be a fit and proper person. As the service of a RN is a rather heavy weight enforcement option it is only likely to be used in the face of persistent non-compliance. An appeal against a RN suspends the operation of the notice pending the outcome of the appeal hearing.

5.18.16.4 Suspension Notice (SN)

The regulator has a duty to serve a Suspension Notice (SN) if it considers that the operation of an installation involves an imminent risk of serious injury (PPC reg 25). If such a risk exists a SN must be served irrespective of whether permit conditions have been observed. The duty to serve a SN does not apply in circumstances in which the regulator intended to take action in any event. A SN may be used to suspend all or part of the permitted activities.

5.18.16.5 Variation Notice (VN)

The regulator has a discretion to review permits at any time (PPC reg 17) subject to official guidance relating to the permit review process. The Variation Notice (VN) power enables the regulator to tighten permit conditions in response to changes in circumstances, such as changes in industry sector BAT, or the emergence of new environmental risks. IPPC permit holders are obliged to inform the regulator of changes made to the installation which may have environmental impacts. The receipt of such information may act as a trigger and prompt the regulator to review and vary the current permit conditions. VNs may also be served in two further instances: (i) where the permit holder wishes to vary the terms of the permit; and (ii) the Environment Agency specifies new conditions applicable to Pt A(2) installations which the local authorities must implement.

A VN application must include the following information:

(a) the name, address, and telephone number of the permit holder;

(b) the address of the installation;

(c) the proposed changes and their environmental impacts.

The regulator has the power to require the permit holder to provide further information to enable the regulator to process the VN application.

5.18.17 Appeals

IPPC permit holders have a right of appeal to the SOSE against the following:

(a) the service of a RN, VN, EN and SN;

(b) a refusal to grant or a refusal to vary a permit (refusals include deemed refusals);

(c) the imposition of unreasonable permit conditions;

(d) the regulator's decision that information relating to the permit is not commercially confidential and should be included on the public register.

Appeals must be lodged within six months of the regulatory decision appealed against except in the case of appeals against ENs, SNs and VNs (where the time limit is two months from the date of the relevant notice), RNs (where the appeal must be lodged before the notice takes effect) and appeals against commercial confidentiality (where the time limit is 21 days from the relevant decision). Only in the case of RN appeals is the operation of the notice suspended provided the appeal is lodged in time. Appeals may be heard by way of a full hearing or written representations (that is, a paper based appeal) and the SOSE has the power to order that an appeal proceed by way of a full hearing, in public, irrespective of the wishes of the applicant.

5.18.18 Public registers

The IPPC regime makes provision for a public register of information in much the same way as the current IPC regime.

5.18.19 Criminal law enforcement

In common with other Command and Control license based regulatory regimes, IPPC is underpinned by a number of criminal offences (PPC reg 32). These offences are not expected to be used frequently given the extensive range of administrative enforcement powers available to regulators. It is a criminal offence to:

(a) operate an IPPC installation without a permit;

(b) breach permit conditions;

(c) fail to give notice of a permit transfer;

(d) fail to comply with an EN or SN;

(e) intentionally make false entries in official records.

5.18.20 Sentencing

All offences may be summarily tried in the magistrates' court or on indictment in the Crown Court. The maximum penalty in the magistrates' court is a fine of up to £20,000. The maximum penalty in the Crown Court is an unlimited fine and/or a gaol sentence of up to two years.

5.18.21 Injunction

Where a permit holder has failed to comply with an EN or SN the regulator may apply for an injunction provided that it can establish that enforcement of the relevant criminal law has failed to secure adequate compliance with the EN or SN.

5.18.22 Remedial powers

Both the magistrates' and Crown courts may, in the case of failure to comply with ENs and SNs, make an order that any environmental damage resulting from the relevant offence be remedied by the defendant. The regulator, subject to the prior written approval of the SOSE, also has a further remedial power available. Where an installation has been operated without a permit, or in breach of permit conditions, the regulator can take reasonable steps to remedy any harm resulting from the commission of the offence and recover its costs from the defendant.

5.18.23 The interface of IPPC with other regulatory controls

There are a number of regulatory regimes whose remits overlap with IPPC. The more important of these regulatory controls are referred to below.

5.18.23.1 Waste management

IPPC will take approximately 900 landfill sites out of the waste management licensing regime in Pt II of the EPA 1990. Small landfill sites will continue to be licenced and regulated under the EPA 1990.

The application of IPPC regulation to large landfill sites is expected to be phased in by 2003. What constitutes BAT for these installations is detailed in the Landfill Directive. Certain waste disposal and waste recovery operations, subject to the thresholds referred to in the regulations fall within IPPC control.

5.18.23.2 Contaminated land

Strictly speaking there should be no overlap between the IPPC regime and the contaminated land controls in Pt IIA of the EPA 1990. Any IPPC installation which is contaminated by the permit holder will be remediated, at the latest, at the time of the application to surrender the IPPC permit utilising the powers in the PPCA 1999 and the PPC regulations 2000.

Site contamination which precedes IPPC control may be dealt with either under the contaminated land controls or under s 27 of the EPA 1990 relating to IPC controls and breach of an IPC authorisation.

The standard of clean-up required under the IPPC regime (to accord with the condition of the site before commencement of the activities authorised in an IPPC permit) is higher than the standard required under the contaminated land regime ('suitable for use'). This has ramifications for an applicant who wishes to apply for an IPPC permit. An applicant who fails to identify any pre-existing site contamination before commencement of IPPC regulated activities will almost certainly be required to clean up all contamination discovered irrespective of whether the contamination relates to the permit holders' IPPC activities or not.

5.18.23.3 Water pollution

Since local authorities have no experience of issuing water pollution discharge consents it was recognised that the regulation of A(2) installations might be problematic for local authorities in regard to aquatic discharges. To address this potential problem the Environment Agency has been tasked to supervise the imposition of water related permit conditions for A(2) installations. The Environment Agency has power to notify local authorities of the minimum conditions, relating to aquatic discharges, which the Environment Agency requires to be included in any A(2) permit. The Environment Agency also has a discretion to require the imposition of stricter conditions to take account of local circumstances. Compliance with an IPPC permit will provide a statutory defence to any s 85 of the WRA 1991 prosecution.

5.18.23.4 Sewer discharges

There is an overlap of regulatory controls in regard to discharges from IPPC installations to sewers. All discharges to sewers must be licensed by the relevant sewerage undertaker under the WIA 1991. Since such discharges have environmental impacts they may be the subject of IPPC permit conditions.

5.18.23.5 The town and country planning system

In contrast to waste management facilities regulated under Pt II of the EPA 1990 IPPC permit applicants are not obliged to obtain planning permission as a prerequisite of obtaining an IPPC permit. In practice, planning and IPPC controls may overlap in regard to the type of conditions which are appropriate to impose in both planning permissions and IPPC permits. Decision makers in the planning system (local planning authorities and planning appeal inspectors) are required to focus on the land use implications of a proposed development and should avoid imposing conditions which would be replicated in the IPPC permitting process. How far 'land use' considerations extend into and overlap with both the IPC and IPPC regimes will depend upon the circumstances of each case and it is therefore difficult to indicate with any degree of certainty where planning regulation ends and IPC and IPPC begin. What is clear, however, is the fact that a decision maker in the planning system cannot refuse to have regard to the polluting impacts of a proposed development when determining a planning application.

Readers should note that the IPPC Directive and the EIA Directive make provision for the interchange of information. Thus the Environmental Statement, produced for the purposes of a planning application, may be used to provide information on site condition and environmental impacts of the installation as part of the IPPC permit process.

5.18.23.6 Statutory nuisances

Since IPPC regulation focuses upon environmental impacts, IPPC permits will include, if relevant, conditions relating to noise, vibration and similar environmental impacts. Local authorities are barred from using their statutory nuisance powers in Pt III of the EPA 1990 to deal with noise and other problems which the IPPC regulator can address, using the relevant IPPC enforcement powers. Local authorities may nevertheless use their statutory nuisance powers on an IPPC installation in circumstances where the relevant nuisance falls outside the remit of IPPC controls.

Irrespective of the limitations on local authority power to take statutory nuisance action against an IPPC permit holder, an individual may use s 82 of the EPA 1990 to lodge a complaint against an IPPC permit holder in respect of an alleged nuisance.

INTEGRATED POLLUTION CONTROL AND INTEGRATED POLLUTION PREVENTION AND CONTROL

IPC

Part I of the Environmental Protection Act (EPA) 1990 establishes two systems of pollution control:

- Integrated Pollution Control for the most serious polluting processes which are regulated by the EA; and

- Local Authority and Pollution Control. Local authorities regulate only the atmospheric emissions of other prescribed processors.

- Section 6 of the EPA 1990 requires that certain *prescribed processes* must not be carried on or certain *prescribed substances* must not be released into any environmental medium without prior authorisation from either the Agency or the relevant local authority.

- Section 2 of the EPA 1990 enables the Secretary of State to issue regulations prescribing processes and substances for control. See the Environmental Protection (Prescribed Processes and Substances) Regulations 1991 SI 1991/472, as amended.

- Section 7 of the EPA 1990 – the conditions imposed in the authorisation (licence) is the principal mechanism for controlling the release of polluting substances into the environment.

BATNEEC and BPEO

In particular, s 7 of the EPA 1990 introduces the concept of BATNEEC.

Processes subject to IPC will be required to use the 'best available techniques not entailing excessive cost' to minimise pollution to the environment as a whole; to achieve the Best Practicable Environmental Option (BPEO).

Processes subject to LAAPC will be required to use BATNEEC to minimise pollution of the air.

Information about all IPC and LAAPC authorisations is maintained on a public register, subject to exceptions under ss 21 and 22 of the EPA 1990.

Enforcement

Enforcement is secured through the following:

(a) variation of revocation;

(b) Enforcement Notices (ENs) and Prohibition Notices (PNs);

(c) power to enter property;

(d) power to examine, investigate and seize;

(e) power to prosecute;

(f) power to take steps and remedy harm.

Rights of appeal

Appeal against the Environment Agency decisions are made to the SOSE for the Environment.

IPPC

The chief objective of the IPPC regulatory regime is to control the environmental *impacts* of a number of highly polluting industries. By contrast, the objective of IPC is to regulate environmental *emissions* from a similar range of polluting industries.

The PPCA 1999 and the PPC Regulations 2000 implement the IPPC Directive (96/61/EEC).

The IPPC regulatory regime is licence based and applies to operators of 'installations' engaged in 'activities' listed in Annex 1 of the IPPC directive. It has been estimated that 7,000 installations will be subject to IPPC regulation.

Licence conditions include installation, aftercare and remediation provisions.

Operators of IPPC installations must employ 'best available techniques' (BAT) to prevent or reduce the environmental impacts of their installations. Official guidance in the form of BREF notes will provide advice on what is considered to be BAT in each regulated industry sector (energy, chemicals, metals, minerals, waste, and 'other activities').

Local authorities have a greater regulatory role in regard to IPPC than they currently have under IPC.

The IPPC regime will completely replace IPC controls by 2007.

CHAPTER 6

CONTAMINATED LAND

6.1 The contaminated land legacy

6.1.1 Introduction

The industrial revolution and subsequent manufacturing activity in the 20th century has left the UK with a significant contaminated land legacy. However, the problem of Britain's 'Badlands', although recognised for many years, has only recently begun to be addressed with the introduction of the Contaminated Land regulatory regime in Pt IIA of the Environmental Protection Act (EPA) 1990. The delay in tackling contaminated land may be due to the low visibility of the issue. Contamination of the land is literally out of sight and out of mind. In addition, the introduction of licence based controls over many aspects of present day industrial pollution, for example, Integrated Pollution Control (IPC), has deflected attention away from historic contamination of the land.

6.1.2 Activities typically associated with land contamination

Many old industries which existed in the 19th and early 20th centuries have either been swept away or have adapted to modern production methods. Whilst the land upon which these old industries stood has been redeveloped, and old buildings replaced with modern ones, it is probable that, in some circumstances, historic contamination of the soil and sub-soil remains as a ghostly legacy. This is especially true of contaminants which are not biodegradable.

The following activities are typically linked to historic land contamination: gas and coking works which produced tars and other residues; closed landfill sites with leachate and methane emission problems; tanning works which used solvents to degrease animal skins; metal works smelting toxic metals such as lead; plating works; heavy engineering works; chemical works using powerful acids and alkalis; petro-chemical works; asbestos production; premises which handled and stored hazardous substances, for example, docks, railways, and Ministry of Defence property; and factories which manufactured pesticides.

6.1.3 Specific incidents

The evacuation of an entire community, whose homes had been built on a former hazardous waste site, at Love Canal in North America in the late 1970s, and a similar incident in Lekkerkerk in Holland, helped to focus international attention upon the health implications of the redevelopment of contaminated land. In 1976 methane which had migrated from a closed landfill at Loscoe in Derbyshire caused an explosion which destroyed a bungalow. These are just a brief sample of the incidents which helped to draw attention to the problem of historic land pollution.

6.1.4 The risks associated with contaminated land

Contaminated land, containing toxic chemicals, poses a threat to the health of humans, plants and animals. Harmful chemicals can enter the food chain via crops grown in contaminated soil. These crops, or the animals which feed upon them, are then eaten by humans and toxic substances are ingested. Alternatively chemicals, such as solvents or pesticides, may leach out of closed landfills and enter groundwaters. Groundwaters (that is, aquifers) are commonly used to supply water for human consumption. The dust from buildings insulated with asbestos may be inhaled with serious consequences to health.

Many chemical substances, which are present in and contaminate land, are either not biodegradable or take many years to break down into less harmful chemicals. The *Cambridge Water* case, which is discussed in detail in Chapter 10, illustrates the persistence and longevity of solvents and their ability to migrate, through underground strata, over significant distances.

The chemicals which are present in contaminated land may cause damage to crops and livestock. They may even, if they are corrosive, damage building foundations and service pipes and cables.

Contaminated land may also result in property blight and property stigma. Residential developments erected on closed landfills may be blighted if methane enters sub-floor areas. If a risk of explosion exists the property will either become unsaleable or the price must be reduced to reflect that risk. Property stigma occurs in cases where contamination has been remediated but the fact that the land on which the property stands was contaminated causes the market price of the property to be depressed. The stigma associated with nuclear waste contamination is apparent in the case of *Blue Circle v Ministry of Defence* [1999] Env LR 22.

6.1.5 The extent of the contaminated land problem

Currently there are no reliable data on the extent of the problem in the UK. A House of Commons Select Committee Report suggests that:

(a) 5,000–10,000 contaminated sites exist, covering

(b) 27,000–100,000 hectares.

6.1.6 The Government's initial response

The EPA 1990, as originally drafted, contained a provision (s 143 of the EPA 1990) which, if brought into force, would have created a register of potentially contaminated parcels of land. The Government carried out extensive consultations in regard to the proposed contaminated land register (see *Let the Buyer be Better Informed*) but, in view of the strength of objections, it decided not to implement the s 143 register. The main flaw in the register was that it identified *potentially* contaminated sites. There was no mechanism whereby the presence of contaminating substances could be identified and remediated. There were fears that the register would only serve to blight property.

6.2 The contaminated land regime

6.2.1 Introduction

In contrast to the majority of the 'Command and Control' regulatory controls discussed in this book the regulation of contaminated land is not licence based. The damage, in the main, has already been done and the law responds reactively by: (i) identifying the relevant parcels of land which are 'contaminated'; (ii) identifying the person or persons responsible for the contamination; and (iii) allocating the cost of clean up between the responsible person or persons.

The main function of the contaminated land regime is to address the problem of historic pollution, however, the relevant controls do recognise and take account of the fact that current industrial and other activities may cause contamination. Thus, the regime is both retrospective and prospective.

6.2.2 Defining contaminated land

Of great significance to the ambit of the contaminated land regime is the method by which 'contaminated' land is distinguished from uncontaminated land. Section 78A(2) of the EPA 1990 defines contaminated land as:

> ... any land which appears to the local authority in whose area it is situated to be in such a condition, by reason of substances in, on or under land, that:
>
> (a) significant harm is being caused or there is a significant possibility of such harm being caused; or
>
> (b) pollution of controlled waters is being or is likely to be, caused.

It is important to note that the definition refers to the central role of 'harm' in identifying contaminated land. Land may be polluted but if the presence of the pollutants does not, or is not likely to, cause harm to humans or the environment then no remedial action is necessary and the land will not be 'contaminated' so as to fall within the ambit of s 78A(2) of the EPA 1990.

Section 78(4) defines 'harm' as:

... harm to the health of living organisms or other interference with the ecological systems of which they form part and, in the case of man, includes harm to his property.

The combined effect of ss 78A(2) and 78(4) is to clarify that it is only unacceptable (that is, harmful) risks to man or the environment which converts polluted land into 'contaminated land'. In assessing whether the risk of harm is unacceptable the regulator must have regard to which substance(s) present in land are harmful (for example, are they toxic or explosive?), the means or 'pathways' by which the contaminants may come into contact with man or the environment, and the costs and benefits of engaging in remedial (clean-up) works. Section 78A(2) also highlights the risk to man and the environment posed by a key pathway: the threat that contaminants will leach through the ground and cause groundwater pollution.

The regulator (referred to as the 'enforcing authority') must 'act in accordance' with the official guidance relating to the meaning of 'contaminated land' when exercising its statutory functions (see DETR Circular 2/2000, 'Contaminated Land: Implementation of Pt IIA of the EPA 1990'). The fact that the regulator is obliged to act in accordance with the guidance, to the extent that it addresses the meaning of 'contaminated', will curtail the regulator's discretion as to the identification of which parcels of land fall within the contaminated land control regime.

Circular 2/2000 must be consulted to gain a fuller understanding of the criteria which are employed to determine whether land is contaminated. Section 78A(2) refers to the phrases 'significant harm' and 'significant possibility'. These phrases can only be understood by reference to the concept of 'pollutant linkage' which appears in the circular. A pollutant linkage is the link between:

(a) the presence of a substance in the ground;

(b) a 'receptor', such as a human or a Site of Special Scientific Interest; and

(c) a 'pathway' via which the substance comes into contact with and harms the receptor.

Whether any given set of circumstances constitutes 'a significant pollution linkage' will depend upon the vulnerability of the receptor, the magnitude of the threat posed by the contaminating substance(s), the timescale during which there is exposure to harm and the probability that the contaminant will escape along the envisaged pathway. When combined, these criteria, comprise the components of a risk assessment.

The circular adopts a restricted interpretation of 'receptor': man, nature conservation sites subject to protective legislation, buildings and other property (for example, crops and livestock). In regard to the type of harm envisaged, triggering the relevant controls, the circular details these on a receptor by receptor basis. As regards damage to crops and buildings the circular requires a substantial reduction in crop value or substantial building damage. In regard to nature conservation sites the circular specifies the requirement of irreversible or substantial adverse changes in ecosystem functioning affecting a substantial part of the nature conservation site. In the case of harm to humans the circular refers to serious injury, birth defects, and reproductive impairment.

In circumstances where harm has not yet occurred but the regulator is required to assess whether a 'significant possibility' of harm exists, the circular draws the regulator's attention to the primary importance of the magnitude of the relevant threat. A 'significant possibility' of harm to humans will exist if the relevant risk is medically unacceptable. In contrast, in the case of non-human receptors a significant possibility of harm will arise if the risk assessment reveals that it is more likely than not that there will be a significant possibility of harm.

A 'balance of probabilities' risk assessment also applies to contaminants which pose a threat to controlled waters. The harm envisaged is the damage caused by the entry of contaminants which have a poisonous, noxious, or polluting impact upon controlled waters. (see s 78(9)).

The regulator is entitled to take into account the combined impact, or 'cocktail effect', of more than one parcel of land in assessing whether land is contaminated. The combined effect of two or more parcels of land may satisfy the definition of contaminated land where treated separately each parcel on its own would not (see s 78X(2)).

6.3 The statutory framework of the contaminated land regime

6.3.1 Overview of the contaminated land regulatory framework

Part IIA of the EPA 1990 (introduced by the Environment Act (EA) 1995) and supplemented by the Contaminated Land (England) Regulations 2000 SI 2000/227, the Contaminated Land (Wales) Regulations 2000 and Circular 2/2000 ('Contaminated Land: Implementation of Pt IIA of the EPA 1990'), together comprise the current contaminated land regulatory regime controls.

Local authorities (borough councils, district councils and unitary authorities) have been allocated the major responsibility for the identification and remediation of contaminated land. The Environment Agency is responsible for the clean-up of the most severely contaminated sites, the provision of technical guidance, and the preparation (with local authority input) of a periodic report on contaminated land in England and Wales (s 78U).

The contaminated land regime shares some similarities with statutory nuisance controls: each regime is largely a reactive form of control; each regulator has a statutory duty to inspect its area; regulation is not licence based but revolves around the service of a notice specifying the remedial works which are required to be completed within a set timescale; non-compliance with the remedial notice is a criminal offence; the local authority has responsibility for the administration of the regulatory regime (although the Environment Agency regulates the more severely contaminated sites); extensive rights of appeal are available; and, details of the remedial notice, and other information, is placed by the regulator on a publicly accessible register of information.

6.3.2 The duty to identify and 'list'

Section 78B(1) obliges local authorities to inspect, from time to time, their areas to identify contaminated land. In regard to the more severely contaminated sites (known as 'special sites') the Environment Agency is the enforcing authority. Each local authority is tasked with the complex job of assessing whether any land in its area satisfies the relevant contaminated land criteria. Once it is satisfied that a parcel of land is contaminated land the authority must serve a Remediation Notice on the owner or occupier of the relevant land. Since details of the Remediation Notice are entered on a public register the authority, in effect, 'lists' contaminated land. Once listed there is no mechanism to 'de-list' or remove details of the land from the public register.

In the course of investigating whether land is contaminated the local authority has identical investigatory powers to those of the Environment Agency contained in s 108 of the EPA 1990. The more important of these powers include: entry, inspection, experimental boring and sampling. These powers will be available to the regulator if other avenues of information have not been sufficient to establish whether the land is contaminated. To avail itself of these powers there must be a 'reasonable possibility' of establishing a link between the presence of contaminating substances in the ground and contamination causing significant harm, contamination causing a significant possibility of significant harm, or pollution of controlled waters.

In regard to potentially contaminated land which could cause actual or threatened harm to nature conservation sites the local authority must consult with and take into account any comments made by English Nature or the Environment Agency. These comments should assist the local authority in deciding whether the land is contaminated.

6.3.3 Special sites

Having satisfied itself (and formally recorded its decision) that the land it has investigated is contaminated land, the authority must then decide whether the land qualifies as a special site. The definition of 'special site' is contained in the Contaminated Land (England) Regulations 2000 and in regard to which the Environment Agency is the relevant enforcing authority. Special sites are: (i) contaminated sites where the actual or threatened contamination is serious; or (ii) the site is one whose remediation would benefit from the Environment Agency's expertise in regard to the nature and extent of remediation works. It is envisaged that the following sites would fall into this category: IPC/IPPC sites, nuclear industry sites, Ministry of Defence sites and land causing pollution of controlled waters or breaches of drinking water quality standards.

The local authority consults the Environment Agency before designating the site as a special site. Details of the fact that the site is a special site are entered on the public register. The local authority has a duty (s 78C) to notify the Environment Agency, the owner and/or occupier and any other person who might be responsible for the cost of remediation that the site has been designated as a special site. The Environment Agency retains its s 108 investigation powers in regard to special sites (s 78Q). Interestingly, the Environment Agency has the power to de-list special sites but the site will nevertheless remain listed as contaminated land. Where a special site is de-listed the local authority resumes its role as the enforcing authority.

6.3.4 Duty to notify and consult

Immediately the local authority has decided that a parcel of land fulfils the statutory land criteria it has a legal obligation (see s 78B) to notify the following persons that the land has been formally designated or listed as contaminated land:

(a) the owner;

(b) the occupier;

(c) any other person who appears to the local authority to be liable for all or part of the remediation costs;

(d) the Environment Agency. Notification to the Environment Agency triggers consultation on whether the site qualifies as a special site.

Except in those cases where the contaminated land poses an imminent danger of serious harm or pollution of controlled waters (ss 78G and 78H), mandatory provision is made for a minimum three month period of consultation between the local authority and the person or persons who are thought to be responsible for the cost of clean-up. These provisions are designed to provide the opportunity to reach a negotiated agreement on the extent of and responsibility for remedial works. Even if agreement cannot be reached it is envisaged that the consultation device will help narrow down areas of dispute between the enforcing authority and the persons responsible for remediation of the contamination. If agreement is reached the person or persons responsible for remedial works sign an undertaking, referred to as a remediation statement, detailing the necessary works and the relevant timescale. These details are then entered onto the public register (s 78H(7)). Provision may be made for the phased completion of the remedial works. Where, on a cost/benefit basis, the enforcing authority concludes that remedial works are not justified the authority is required to note this on the public register in the form of a remediation declaration (s 78H(6)). Despite the existence of a remediation declaration the land remains listed as contaminated land.

6.3.5 Remediation Notice

Where the consultation period has elapsed without the successful conclusion of of a remediation statement the enforcing authority must, by virtue of s 78E, serve a Remediation Notice on the 'appropriate person or persons' who is/are responsible for bearing the cost of clean up. The Remediation Notice is similar in format to a statutory nuisance abatement notice. It will specify the works and the relevant timescale to complete them (s 78E(1)). In determining the works required the enforcing authority is obliged (s 78E(4)) to undertake a cost/benefit assessment and must take into account the environmental benefits of remediation (see Circular 2/2000).

The enforcing authority may not serve a Remediation Notice in the following circumstances:

(a) where it appears to the enforcing authority that imminent danger of serious harm or water pollution exists;

(b) where remediation may be effected under other regulatory controls;

(c) where remediation would be unreasonable (s 78H(5) and (6));

(d) where the remedial works are undertaken voluntarily pursuant to a remedial statement (s 78H(5)(b));

(e) where the enforcing authority is the owner of contaminated land or has caused contamination (s 78H(5)(c));

(f) where one of the persons who have been served with a Remediation Notice would suffer hardship (s 78N(3)(e)). In these circumstances any other responsible person will also escape liability (s 78H(5)(d));

(g) where reasonable efforts have been made to locate the appropriate person but these efforts have failed (s 78N(3)(f));

(h) where, in the case of pollution of controlled waters, the appropriate persons are owners or occupiers.

Despite the fact that the enforcing authority is precluded from serving a Remediation Notice in the circumstances detailed above the authority has a discretion to undertake the works itself and then endeavour to recover its costs from the responsible person.

6.3.6 The appropriate person

The selection of the person or persons responsible for the remediation of contaminated land and the just application of the relevant cost of clean up between two or more responsible persons is one of the more contentious aspects of the contaminated land regime. The division of liability for remedial costs depends upon the concept of 'the appropriate person'. Section 78F(2) defines the appropriate person as 'the person, or any of the persons, who caused or knowingly permitted the substances, or any of the substances, which have been the cause of the contamination to be in or under the land'. Section 78K makes it clear that the appropriate person may also be the person from whose land substances have escaped which has caused the contamination of someone else's land.

6.3.7 Causing or knowingly permitting contamination

Liability for causing or knowingly permitting contamination is strict, however, in regard to the allocation of the cost of remediation between the appropriate persons the contaminated land regime does provide mechanisms to mitigate the potential financial impact of liability. Significantly there is no defence to causing contamination based on the use of 'best practice' (otherwise referred to as 'a state of the art' defence). It seems likely that 'causing contamination' will be interpreted in much the same way as causing water pollution. The 'appropriate person' in s 78F(2) will be someone who has engaged in, or is engaging in, an active operation which has caused, or is causing, contamination. Maintaining tanks, pipes, and cables from which contaminants have escaped will therefore all be active operations attracting liability. More than one person can cause contaminants to be present in or under land (for example, a contractor who negligently installs an underground storage tank resulting in contamination of the site). Once contaminated land has been identified by an enforcing authority it is presumed that the owner or occupier of the site, at the date the contamination occurred, caused the contamination. If this presumption does not accord with the facts the onus is on the owner or occupier to establish that someone else caused the contamination

It seems probable that the phrase 'knowingly permitted' in s 78F(2) refers to the dual requirement that the owner or occupier knew that contamination existed and had the power to prevent contamination (for example, by removing the contaminating substances from the site). Thus, the owner and occupier must not only be aware that the substance is present on site but also that the substance has the capacity to cause contamination if it escapes containment. In view of the purpose of the legislation and the extent of contamination, in a national context, it seems likely that the owner or occupier will not be able to escape liability because of any subjective ignorance of the risks which would have been obvious to a reasonable site owner or occupier. Thus, the presence of storage tanks on site should alert a potential purchaser or leaseholder (that is, owner or occupier) to the risk of contamination. A purchaser acquiring contaminated land, in such circumstances, effectively permits the presence of contaminants and is therefore liable. A prudent purchaser would have recognised the risk of contamination and addressed this in the terms of the property acquisition deal (through warranties and indemnities). Whether someone caused or knowingly permitted contamination will be decided on the balance of probabilities (that is, more likely than not).

6.3.8 Site owners and occupiers

6.3.8.1 Who pays?

The contaminated land regime contains fairly complex arrangements for identifying which past or present owners and/or occupiers of contaminated land are liable for all or part of the remediation costs. Primary responsibility, according to Circular 2/2000, rests with 'Class A persons'. Class A persons are the person or persons who have caused or knowingly permitted the presence of contaminating substances in or under land. In the event that the current owner or occupier is not a Class A person, they will only be liable, as a Class B person, if, after reasonable inquiry, no Class A persons can be found (s 78F(4)).

The term 'owner' is defined in s 78A as the person who is entitled to receive the market rent for the property, however, mortgagees not in possession and insolvency practitioners are not owners (s 78X(3)). 'Occupier' is not defined.

Where land is contaminated with several substances it will be necessary to establish whether the current owner or occupier is responsible for all or only part of the contamination. If the owner or occupier is only responsible for the presence of some of the substances which are present then the owner or occupier will be liable as a Class A person in regard to the contamination he or she caused. In regard to other contaminating substances on site the owner or occupier may also be liable as a Class B person if the relevant Class A person or persons cannot be found.

6.3.8.2 Government objectives and standard of remediation required

In the 1994 consultation paper, *Paying for our Past*, the Government set out the principles and objectives on which the contaminated land regime was intended to operate:

(a) the Government recognised that it was necessary to bring large tracts of contaminated land back into beneficial use;

(b) the standard of clean-up of contaminated land would be based on a 'suitable for use' concept. Clean-up works to remediate the land would only be necessary if the contamination, present in the land, posed actual or potential risks to man or the environment which were considered to be unacceptable. In assessing what, if any, remediation works were required it was necessary to have regard to the actual (that is, current) or intended use of the contaminated land. Thus, if planning permission was sought to redevelop a site for housing, the extent of clean-up works would reflect that intended use and its attendant risks, especially to humans. The 'suitable for use' concept is therefore distinguishable from the 'polished earth' approach of the 'Superfund' legislation in the USA (Comprehensive Environmental Response Compensation and Liability Act 1980) or the similar, and now discontinued, 'multifunctional' approach in Holland which required contaminated land to be cleaned up so that it was fit for any use;

(c) the contaminated land regime would target, prioritise and address the most serious cases of contamination first;

(d) the financial impact of the contaminated land regime on the economy and specific industries and landowners would be taken into account;

(e) the creation of a contaminated land regime would clarify responsibility for the clean-up of contaminated land and enable contaminated land to be bought and sold under proper market conditions.

6.3.9 Allocating the cost of remediation

Having identified the responsible 'appropriate person or persons' the enforcing authority must then determine the extent of each person's liability for clean-up. The enforcing authority's discretion in the allocation of liability is tightly constrained by the Circular 2/2000 guidance.

The enforcing authority allocates liability by undertaking the following sequential tasks:

(a) it identifies the number of pollutants present which could cause significant harm. In effect it identifies significant pollution linkages;

(b) it identifies the Class A persons for each pollutant. In other words the Class A liability groups for each significant pollution linkage;

(c) it identifies, in the absence of Class A persons, the Class B liability group for the relevant significant pollution linkage;

(d) it applies the Class A and Class B exclusion tests;

(e) it apportions the remediation costs between the remaining (non-excluded) liable persons.

Exclusion tests are applicable where a Class A or B liability group has more than one person in the relevant liability group. The function of the test is to exclude from liability those persons who are not especially blameworthy and therefore should not, in fairness, be burdened with liability.

There are six Class A person exclusion tests which are applied sequentially:

1 this test excludes liability for mortgage lenders (and other providers of finance), insurance underwriters, persons who have provided technical, legal, or scientific advice and landlords whose tenants caused the contamination;

2 this test excludes those persons, who, realising that contaminants are present, have transferred (sold) the land to a purchaser at a reduced price;

3 this test excludes persons who have sold contaminated land with information regarding the contamination so that it is reasonable to expect the purchaser to bear the cost of remediation;

4 this test excludes persons whose liability is based upon an unforeseeable change of circumstances, such as the introduction of new substances which combine with existing substances to produce a contamination problem;

5 this test excludes new activities which unforeseeably have resulted in the escape of substances already present;

6 this test excludes new development which gives rise to new significant pollution linkages.

Class B persons are excluded from liability if they are occupiers or tenants paying a market rent but have no long term financial interest in the land which would benefit from clean up works.

The exclusion tests may not be used to exclude the liability of all persons in a liability group. In the event that a liability group reaches agreement on the allocation of their respective liabilities and informs the enforcing authority of the voluntary agreement the terms of the agreement prevail over any other allocation favoured by the enforcing authority except to the extent that the agreement is a sham device intended to avoid liability. This situation could arise if the terms of the agreement purported to transfer liability to a group member, who would in consequence, suffer hardship, thus preventing the enforcing authority serving a Remediation Notice on that person.

In liability groups whose members include two or more related companies those companies will be treated as one person for the purpose of applying the exclusion tests.

In the interests of justice the financial standing of each member of a liability group is irrelevant for the purpose of applying the exclusion tests.

6.3.10 Allocating costs between appropriate persons

The enforcing authority will apportion remediation costs in accordance with the relative responsibility of each appropriate person. The enforcing authority will, in arriving at its allocation, have regard to the duration of the period during which each responsible person was in occupation of the land and was using contaminating substances. An accurate assessment will, in most cases, largely depend upon the availability of reliable information. In default of receiving a reasonable amount of information upon which to base an assessment, the enforcing authority may apportion the remediation costs equally between the non-excluded members of the relevant Class A or B liability group.

6.3.11 Duty to serve a Remediation Notice

Once the allocation and apportionment processes are concluded the enforcing authority is subject to a legal duty to serve a Remediation Notice on the appropriate person or persons (s 78E(1) of the EPA 1990 and reg 4 of the Contaminated Land (England) Regulations 2000).

Remediation Notices must contain sufficient information including:

(a) a description of the work which is required to be undertaken;

(b) the identity of the person required to do the work;

(c) the proportion of the costs each person must bear;

(d) the timescale within which the work must be completed;

(e) the identity of each appropriate person;

(f) the reason(s) for serving the notice; and

(g) rights of appeal.

A further Remediation Notice may be served, even if the original notice has been complied with, if it transpires (as a result of the original remediation work) that further works or different works are necessary.

Upon successful completion of the remedial works the enforcing authority is obliged to enter details of the remediation work on the public register. In appropriate circumstances it may indicate on the register that no further remedial work is anticipated.

6.3.12 Failure to comply with a Remediation Notice

Non-compliance with a Remediation Notice without reasonable excuse is an offence (s 78M). The offence is a 'summary' offence and therefore may only be heard in a magistrates' court. Penalties reflect the distinction between the contamination of industrial and other land. In the case of industrial, trade, or business premises the maximum financial penalty is a £20,000 and a further daily penalty of up to £2,000 for every day the Remediation Notice is not complied with. In the case of other land the maximum fine and daily penalty are £5,000 and £500 respectively (s 78M(3) and (4)).

6.3.13 Completion of remediation works

The enforcing authority has the power to complete the remediation, specified in the notice, where the notice has not been complied with (s 78N), and the authority is entitled to recover its reasonable costs (s 78P), unless this will cause hardship.

The enforcing authority's costs may be secured by means of a legal charge on the legal title of the contaminated land. A person served with a charging order notice has a right to lodge an appeal in the county court within 21 days of receipt of the notice (s 78P(8)).

6.3.14 Appeals

A right of appeal against the service of a Remediation Notice is contained in s 78L(1). The appeal must be lodged within 21 days of receipt of the notice and will suspend the operation of the notice. Appeals relating to special sites are dealt with by the Secretary of State, otherwise appeals are dealt with by magistrates courts.

In regard to special site appeals the Secretary of State may hold a public inquiry into the appeal (which will allow third parties to participate in the appeal process), but in most cases he is likely to transfer the appeal to the Planning Inspectorate. Interestingly, planning inspectors may be assisted by assessors who have relevant expertise. In contrast, appeals to the magistrates court will be dealt with by a stipendiary magistrate, who, whilst legally qualified, is unlikely to have any expertise in contaminated land issues.

The grounds of appeal are detailed in reg 7 of the Contaminated Land (England) Regulations 2000, and include:

(a) appeals based on submissions that the land is not contaminated;

(b) that the recipient of the Remediation Notice is not an appropriate person;

(c) that the appellant should have been excluded from liability;

(d) the notice is unreasonable; and

(e) the enforcing authority failed to act in accordance with the guidance contained in Circular 2/2000.

In a magistrates' appeal the winner will be entitled to reasonable costs. Costs are generally not available in appeals heard by planning inspectors.

6.3.15 The public register

The contaminated land register, maintained by each enforcing authority, contains details of: Remediation Notices, remediation statements, declarations, notices, appeals, convictions, remediation work (see s 78R and Sched 3 to the Contaminated Land (England) Regulations 2000).

6.3.16 Tax incentives

The Finance Act 2001 has introduced a valuable tax incentive which is designed to encourage the remediation of contaminated land. The Act is targeted at companies which have purchased land which was in a 'contaminated state' at the time of purchase and which incur 'qualifying land remediation expenditure' after 10 May 2001. The amount of tax relief is 150% of the qualifying expenditure which is offset against Corporation Tax.

6.4 Interface with other controls

6.4.1 The subsidiary role of contaminated land controls

The interface between contaminated land controls and other regulatory regimes is particularly important in that the contaminated land regime is designed to 'kick in' only when other statutory controls are unable to tackle contamination effectively.

The clean-up powers built into other regulatory regimes, for example water pollution, waste management and IPC/IPPC, have several significant advantages over contaminated land controls. These powers are quicker, less complex (no complicated liability rules to apply), and more accessible than their contaminated land counterparts. Clean-up powers in the licence based regimes have the key advantage of 'joint and several liability' application. In other words the regulator can choose which one of several polluters is pursued to bear the cost of remediation. If land contamination occurs on a site subject to licence based regulatory controls, the clean-up powers contained in the relevant statute may be used to completely remedy the damage caused by the contamination, without the restriction, as in the case of contaminated land, of limiting the extent of the remedial works to the current use of the land.

6.4.2 Water pollution

One of the key pollution concerns of the contaminated land regime is the risk of contaminated land causing pollution of groundwaters. An overlap exists between s 161 of the WRA 1991 (Works Notice powers) and the remediation procedure in the contaminated land controls. The s 161 of the WRA 1991 clean-up power applies to situations where pollution has occurred or is likely to occur. It may be used proactively and reactively.

The Environment Agency has published guidance addressing the potential conflict between the two regimes (see 'Environment Agency policy on the use of Anti-Pollution Works Notices'). The guidance advises that where land has been formally 'listed' as contaminated land the contaminated land controls will apply because the enforcing authority is legally obliged to serve a Remediation Notice. Where land has not been formally listed as contaminated, the s 161 of the WRA 1991 powers will apply.

6.4.3 Waste management

In the case of contamination of waste management sites caused by breach of licensed activities, priority is given to the use of the clean-up powers contained within the waste management regime. Section 78YB(2) precludes the enforcing authority from serving a Remediation Notice in such circumstances. In addition the waste management regime has priority where contamination arises as a result of the unlawful deposit of directive waste (s 78YB(3)). In such circumstances the regulator will use its s 59 clean-up powers.

6.4.4 IPC and IPPC

The contaminated land Remediation Notice procedure may not be used to address contamination which has arisen as a result of the licensed activities of IPC and IPPC processes (s 78YB(1)). If contamination occurs the regulator will use its s 27 powers to deal with the problem. Land upon which an IPC or IPPC process is being carried on may be listed as contaminated land if it fulfils the relevant contaminated land definition. In this regard the baseline assessment prepared for the purposes of obtaining an IPPC permit will provide valuable information to the enforcing authority on the question of whether the land is contaminated.

6.4.5 Statutory nuisance

Statutory nuisance abatement controls do not apply where land is in a 'contaminated state' (Sched 2, para 89 of the EA 1995). Statutory nuisance controls do not apply even where the relevant land in a contaminated state does not pose significant harm to man or the environment (s 78A(2)). Thus, land which is in a contaminated state, but is not posing a risk of significant harm to man or the environment, falls outside the remit of statutory nuisance controls and contaminated land controls.

6.4.6 Town and country planning

There is some degree of overlap of planning controls with contaminated land regulation at the strategic planning and individual planning decision levels. The content of development plans provide an important mechanism enabling planning authorities (the local authorities) to plan the appropriate re-development of 'brownfield' sites which may also be contaminated. The Government has set a target of 60% of new housing to be constructed on brownfield sites and 100% of contaminated land to be brought back into beneficial use by 2030.

Contamination is a 'material consideration' in individual planning applications and must be taken into account in reaching a decision upon the application. The local planning authority, if it grants planning permission for development on contaminated land, may impose planning conditions to address risks to man and the environment posed by the presence of contaminants on site. For example, a condition requiring the venting of methane from sub-floor areas if residential development on a closed landfill is contemplated.

Government planning advice relating to contaminated land appears in Circular 1/95 and Planning Policy Guidance Note 23.

CONTAMINATED LAND

The Contaminated Land regime is found in Pt IIA of the EPA 1990 and the Contaminated Land (England) Regulations 2000.

It is estimated that there are between 5,000–10,000 contaminated sites in the UK.

'Contaminated land' is defined in s 78(2) of the EPA 1990.

Only unacceptable risks posed by land to man or the environment will trigger the contaminated land controls.

The local authorities bear the major regulatory burden for the identification and remediation of contaminated land but the Environment Agency has responsibility for the more seriously polluted 'special sites'.

Local authorities have a duty (s 78B(1)) to inspect their areas in order to identify the presence of contaminated land.

Details of all contaminated sites are entered onto a public register.

Following identification of a contaminated site consultation takes place, especially between the regulator and the owner and occupier of the relevant land.

Agreement may be reached voluntarily between the persons responsible for the cost of clean-up.

The contaminated land regime does not take a 'polished earth' approach to remediation (clean-up). The regime employs the 'suitable for use' concept to determine the extent of clean-up.

Where it is not possible to reach a voluntary agreement in regard to who is responsible for clean-up costs the regulator is under a duty to serve a Remediation Notice (s 78E) on the 'appropriate person or persons' (s 78F(2)) who is/are responsible for remediation costs. Failure to comply with the notice, without reasonable excuse, is an offence (s 78M).

Liability for causing or knowingly permitting contamination is strict.

The regime contains complex rules to identify (i) the past and present land owners and occupiers who are responsible for remediation, and (ii) the allocation of the clean-up costs between the 'appropriate persons'. There are exclusion tests to mitigate the financial impact of the controls.

The regulator has power to undertake remedial (clean-up) works and recover its costs from the appropriate person or persons.

There are extensive rights of appeal.

The contaminated land controls are designed to 'kick in' only in those circumstances where remedial powers in other statutory pollution controls are unable to resolve the relevant contamination problem.

CHAPTER 7

ATMOSPHERIC POLLUTION

7.1 Introduction

Atmospheric pollution in England and Wales is regulated by legislative controls which reflect the historic development of the law as it has moved away from a localised, reactive, response to pollution problems to a more integrated and planned response to pan-European and global threats associated with airborne pollutants.

The three main air pollution controls comprise:

(a) the Integrated Pollution Control (IPC) and Integrated Pollution and Control (IPPC) licence based controls relating to a range of highly polluting industries detailed in Pt I of the Environmental Protection Act (EPA) 1990 and the Pollution Prevention and Control Act (PPCA) 1999;

(b) the criminal sanction based controls over the emission of smoke and other particulate matter from chimneys and furnaces detailed in the Clean Air Act (CAA) 1993; and

(c) controls relating to vehicle emissions. These controls encompass engine efficiency standards, the chemical composition of fuels, the mandatory use of catalytic converters, eco-taxes, price differentials between different types of fuel and the use of traffic management powers.

These controls are supplemented by the Environment Act 1995 (EA 1995), which has enabled the Secretary of State to create a national air quality strategy. Due to the inherent mobility of atmospheric pollution and its transboundary impacts the development of the law is largely driven by a combination of international and European Community (EC) responses to the global threat of climate change.

7.2 Problems caused by air pollution

Atmospheric pollution poses three major threats:

(a) the threat to human health, particularly respiratory illnesses such as asthma, and skin cancer linked to ozone layer depletion in the upper atmosphere – Jonathan Porritt, in his book *Where On Earth Are We Going?*, makes the claim that 'one day's breathing in Bombay is equivalent to smoking 10 cigarettes'. Most people are aware of the health risks associated with smoking and have the choice as to whether or not they smoke. Unfortunately, we cannot exercise that choice about the air we breathe;

(b) the threat to ecosystems, particularly the damage caused by acid rain – acid rain is created by the release of the following gases into the atmosphere: sulphur dioxide, nitric oxide, nitrogen dioxide, ammonia, ozone and hydrocarbons. Chris Rose in his book, *The Dirty Man of Europe*, states: 'Britain, too, has been quietly ravaged by acid rain. In the UK, lakes in Snowdonia National Park, most of mid-Wales, the Lake District, Cairngorms, Pennines and even the Surrey Heaths, are dead or dying from acidity.'; and

(c) the threat of severe climatic disruption caused by global warming of the atmosphere with excessive levels of greenhouse gases – global warming has not only been linked to the increasing incidence of storms, droughts, forest fires, floods, and attendant crop and property damage, but there has also been research which suggests that global warming may lead to the disruption of the ocean current systems upon which the world's climatic patterns depend for their stability. Ironically, in the long term, the main consequence of heating the atmosphere may be the onset of a new ice age. It is therefore imperative that effective and timely steps are taken to control the production of greenhouse gases. The problem undoubtedly exists but the political will to take the issue seriously is lacking in some countries.

7.3 Historic controls

The problems associated with air pollution are not new. Legislation aimed at controlling acidic emissions from alkali works dates back to 1863 (see the Alkali Act 1863). The 1863 Act, like so many that followed it, was reactive; it was introduced following the recommendations of a Royal Commission to address pollution from alkali works, especially the very damaging emissions of hydrochloric acid gas. The 1863 Act was extended in scope in the Alkali Act of 1874, and both were consolidated in 1906 with the Alkali Works Regulation Act 1906. The provisions of the 1906 Act were repealed by the EA 1995.

Legislation aimed at controlling smoke and similar atmospheric emissions was later introduced by the Public Health Acts of 1875 and 1936 and the Public Health (Smoke Abatement) Act 1926. These Acts were not successful in dealing with the problems of smoke pollution, and it was not until the Clean Air Act (CAA) 1956 that there was a comprehensive attempt to control all smoke emissions from domestic fires and commercial and industrial premises.

The CAA 1956, like the earlier legislation, was introduced to combat an existing air pollution problem. In London in 1952, some 4,000 people lost their lives as a result of the 'great smog'. Smogs, which occur more frequently now in places like India, occur when fog combines with smoke particles. The result is that the fog is very dense (smog is a very apt description: it is really a smoke-filled fog), visibility is reduced and breathing impaired. The CAA 1956 was extended in scope by the CAA 1968 and the provisions have now largely been consolidated in the CAA 1993, which is considered in more detail below.

7.4 Government policy and proposals for the future

The Government's early policy in relation to air pollution was set out in *This Common Inheritance* in 1990. This expression of Government policy was, in part, concerned with the protection of public health. In the second year report on the Government's programme outlined in the 1990 report, there was a commitment to further action to reduce air pollution. In particular, it was suggested that, in addition to traditional legal controls, the Government would also explore the use of economic instruments. For example, measures to ensure that charges incurred by transport users reflect the full costs of their journeys. The landfill tax in relation to waste is a further example of how economic and fiscal measures can be employed to reduce pollution or encourage recycling.

7.4.1 Air quality: meeting the challenge

In March 1994 the Department of the Environment (DoE) published a discussion paper, *Improving Air Quality*, which was followed in January 1995 by *Air Quality: Meeting the Challenge – the Government's Strategic Policies for Air* which set out the Government's policies for air quality management. The 1994 discussion paper recognised that the existing approach to air quality was somewhat fragmented and also that there should be a move to what was described as a more effects based approach, with revised air quality standards based principally on human health effects. *Meeting the Challenge* put forward the following policies and proposals:

(a) a new framework of national air quality standards and targets. Two main levels of air quality were proposed:

- the first is a long term target in which nine key pollutants will be rendered harmless to health and the environment. The following were the nine pollutants seen as posing the greatest concern:

    Ozone, Benzene, 1.3-Butadiene, Sulphur Dioxide (SO_2), Carbon Monoxide (CO), Nitrogen Dioxide (NO_2), particles, Polycyclic Aromatic Hydrocarbons (PAHs) and lead.

    This target will be achieved through measures such as the introduction of less polluting production processes and products;

- the second level is essentially a trigger or an alert threshold which indicates when air quality is so poor that an immediate response would be justified to prevent serious damage to health. Such measures might include banning cars from city centres. Local authorities already have the legal powers to impose traffic restrictions, but as yet they have not used these powers to protect air quality by imposing traffic bans.

(b) The establishment of a framework for local air quality management and, in particular, concentrating action on those local areas where progress is slow. Local authorities will be responsible for reviewing air quality and they will be under a duty to designate Air Quality Management Areas (AQMAs) if they are not attaining air quality targets. The AQMAs are to be controlled in a similar fashion to the smoke control areas (see below).

Local authorities will be required to draw up air quality management plans which set out their proposals for meeting air quality targets.

(c) Vehicle emissions are seen as a major contributor to air pollution and the strategy suggests an action plan to reduce the contribution of road transport to air pollution, particularly in urban areas. In AQMAs, local authorities will be required to appraise their development and transport policies against an air quality assessment. Planning Policy Guidance Note 23 on Planning and Pollution Control will be revised to reflect these changes. Planning Policy Guidance Note 13 on Planning and Transport already recognises the relationship between planning transport uses and air quality; however, it is not clear to what extent its recommendations are currently being delivered through the system of development plans.

7.5 The Environment Act 1995

Part IV of the EA 1995 contains provisions which are intended to implement the policies set out in *Meeting the Challenge*. Part IV includes provisions aimed at securing a national air quality strategy and also provisions concerned with local air quality management. In particular, Pt IV provides a framework for ensuring that the UK meets a number of objectives in reducing and controlling the pollutants listed above.

7.5.1 National air quality strategy

By virtue of s 80 of the EA 1995, the SOSE is under a duty to publish a national air quality strategy. The strategy may also contain policies for implementing any obligations under EC law or international agreements. It is clear that the EC has played a key role in regard to the regulation of air pollution and a number of directives exist which deal with specific pollutants, such as ozone and sulphur dioxide. In addition the SOSE is under a duty to review his policies (s 80(4)) from time to time. The national air quality strategy must include statements with respect to the following:

(a) standards relating to the quality of air;

(b) objectives for the restriction of levels at which particular substances are present in air; and

(c) measures which are to be taken by local authorities and other persons for the purpose of achieving those objectives.

The strategy, which can consist of more than one report, has to cover the whole of Great Britain (with the exception of Northern Ireland, which is not covered by the EA 1995). The Environment Agency is required by s 81 of the EA 1995 to have regard to the national strategy when exercising its functions.

7.5.2 Local Air Quality Management Areas (AQMAs)

Part IV of the EA 1995 places particular responsibilities on the local authority sector to achieve, at a local level, the national air quality strategy. Although the provisions that are about to be discussed place additional burdens on local authorities, they have generally been welcomed by the local authority associations, such as the Association of Metropolitan Authorities. However, it remains to be seen how quickly local authorities will be able to respond to the new demands placed upon them and whether they have sufficient resources to fulfil their obligations.

Section 83 of the EA 1995 places each local authority under a duty to carry out a review from time to time of the present and likely future air quality within its area. Where a local authority carries out such a review it must also assess whether air quality standards or objectives are being achieved, or are likely to be achieved within the relevant period. If it appears that any air quality standards or objectives are not being achieved, or are not likely to be achieved, the local authority must identify the parts of their area where this is the case.

Section 38 makes provision for the establishment of the local air quality management areas suggested in *Meeting the Challenge*. Where it appears that any air quality standards or objectives are not being achieved, or are not likely to be achieved the local authority must then designate, by order, the relevant area as an AQMA (referred to in the Act as a designated area). Following a subsequent air quality review the order may be varied or revoked, in the latter case only if it appears that the air quality standards and objectives are being achieved, or are likely to be achieved within the relevant period.

Once an order has been made to designate an area as an AQMA, the local authority is under a duty to exercise its powers in order to reduce pollutants. Section 84 deals with the duties of local authorities in relation to designated areas. These are as follows:

(a) the local authority must carry out a further assessment in order to supplement the initial information;

(b) the local authority must prepare a report of the more detailed second assessment referred to above within 12 months of the order becoming operational; and

(c) it must prepare a written action plan which details how and when the local authority intends to exercise its powers to achieve the air quality standards and objectives. If the plan is made by a district council then the relevant county council can make recommendations. These recommendations must be taken into account (s 86). In the event of disagreement the matter can be referred to the SOSE. In fact, by virtue of s 85 the SOSE enjoys reserve power to carry out the review and assessment stages, either directly or through a third party.

7.5.3 Powers of the SOSE (ss 87 and 88 of the EA 1995)

In addition to the power to resolve disputes, the SOSE is given considerable power under s 87 to make regulations for:

(a) implementing the national air quality strategy;

(b) implementing EC or international law obligations;

(c) prescribing air quality standards;

(d) prescribing objectives for the restriction of levels at which particular substances are present in air;

(e) conferring or transferring powers to local authorities;

(f) controlling the details of reviews;

(g) regarding procedural steps.

Before issuing such regulations the SOSE is required to consult with the Environment Agency, local authorities, industry and other appropriate bodies or persons. In addition, by virtue of s 88, the SOSE can issue guidance to local authorities on any relevant matter.

7.6 Other legislative controls

The local authorities (the district councils, London borough councils, the metropolitan districts and unitary authorities), through their environmental health departments and officers, play a key role in controlling air pollution. They are involved in four areas of air pollution control:

(a) providing authorisation for industrial processes governed by the Local Authority Air Pollution Control (LAAPC) contained in Pt I of the EPA 1990 and equivalent IPPC regulatory controls contained in the PPCA 1999;

(b) enforcing the provisions of the Clean Air Act (CAA) 1993;

(c) enforcing the provisions of Pt III of the EPA in relation to those statutory nuisances which have an impact on the quality of air (see Chapter 8);

(d) AQMAs under Pt IV of the EA 1995 (as described above).

Emissions into the air are also controlled by the Environment Agency through the system of IPC and IPPC described in Chapter 5. The Environment Agency regulates the most seriously polluting industrial processes and, in doing so, controls not only emissions into air but also discharges into water or on land in order to secure the best practical environmental option.

Other controls exist under:

(a) the Health and Safety at Work Act 1974;

(b) EC legislation;

(c) international conventions and protocols.

7.7 Local authority air pollution control

Local authorities are responsible for controlling the atmospheric emissions of certain prescribed industrial processes. Usually, it will be the district council or the London borough council that exercise these powers. Part I of the EPA 1990 establishes a two tier system of control over certain prescribed industrial processes. Processes are prescribed for control under either system by the SOSE by means of regulation. The Environmental Protection (Prescribed Processes and Substances) Regulations 1991 SI 1991/472 (as amended) identify those processes which fall under the central control of the Environment Agency or the control of the relevant local authority. Part B processes in the regulations fall under the latter.

Where a process falls into Pt B of the regulations, it must be authorised by the local authority in whose area the process is based. Local authorities are required to regulate the process so as to prevent or minimise the pollution of the environment due to the release of prescribed substances into the air. The system of LAAPC only permits the local authority to control atmospheric emissions, whereas the central system of IPC enables the control of substances into all environmental media to secure the Best Practical Environmental Option (BPEO).

In regulating these prescribed processes, local authorities have the power to set down conditions in authorisations which secure the objectives laid down in s 7 of the EPA 1990. In particular, processes should use the Best Available Techniques Not Entailing Excessive Costs (BATNEEC) to prevent the release of substances into the air or, where that is not practicable by such means, to reduce the release to a minimum and to render harmless any substances that are released.

The IPC and LAAPC responsibilities of the local authorities are currently being phased out and replaced by equivalent responsibilities under the PPCA 1999. Chapter 5 examines the transition from IPC and LAAPC to IPPC in detail. Under the IPPC regime local authorities are responsible for regulating Pt A(2) installations in regard to all environmental impacts and Pt B installations in regard to atmospheric emissions only.

7.8 The Clean Air Act (CAA) 1993

It has already been stated that the first legislative controls over atmospheric emissions date back to the Alkali Act 1863. This early legislation did not, however, control the emissions of smoke from industrial processes. The use of coal and the consequent emissions of smoke and grit particles resulted in serious pollution and health problems. However, it was not until the CAAs of 1956 and 1968 that there was any comprehensive attempt to control emissions of smoke, dust and grit from industrial premises. The CAA 1956 was introduced to prohibit the emission of dark smoke from any domestic or industrial chimney. A chimney was defined as any structure or opening through which smoke is emitted. Its scope was extended by the CAA 1968 which prohibited emissions of dark smoke from any industrial or trade premises, even though the emission was not made from a chimney. The provisions of these Acts have now been consolidated into the CAA 1993. Enforcement of the CAA 1993 is by the local authorities, who may act in respect of smoke arising within their areas or affecting their areas.

7.8.1 Relationship between the CAA 1993, Pt I of the EPA 1990 and the PPCA 1999

Before considering the details of the CAA 1993, it is important to note the relationship between these controls and the controls over atmospheric emissions under Pt I of the EPA 1990 (IPC and LAAPC) and the equivalent IPPC regulatory controls in the PPCA 1999. The provisions of Pts I–III of the CAA 1993 do not apply to any process regulated under Pt I of the EPA 1990. Section 41 of the CAA 1993 excludes IPC and LAAPC processes from the date of authorisation. Similarly, the CAA 1993 does not apply to installations regulated by the PPCA 1999.

7.8.2 Offences under the CAA 1993

The CAA 1993 controls emissions of smoke, dust and grit by means of criminal offences. The following are the main offences:

(a) emission of dark smoke – from a chimney or from industrial premises other than from a chimney;

(b) emission of dust and grit from non-domestic furnaces;

(c) emission of smoke from a chimney in a Smoke Control Area;

(d) various offences relating to the installation of furnaces.

Prosecutions under most provisions of the CAA 1993 are dealt with in the magistrates' court.

7.8.3 The 'dark smoke' offences (ss 1 and 2)

The CAA 1993 creates numerous criminal offences, including the so called dark smoke offences. Sections 1 and 2 of the 1993 Act prohibit the emission of dark smoke from different categories of premises; s 1 requires the emission of dark smoke to be through a chimney whereas s 2 does not. The offences are strict liability offences, although various activities are exempted from the provisions.

Section 1 prohibits:

(a) the emission of 'dark smoke' from the chimney of any building (s 1(1)); or

(b) from a chimney which serves the furnace of any fixed boiler or industrial plant (s 1(2)).

The provisions cover dark smoke emissions from the chimneys of domestic premises as well as industrial or commercial premises. Where an offence has been committed under s 1(1), liability will rest with the occupier of the building from which the dark smoke is emitted. In the case of dark smoke emissions from a chimney serving a fixed boiler or industrial plant (s 1(2)), the person having possession of the boiler or plant will be liable if an offence is committed.

A person guilty of an offence under s 1(1) as respects a chimney of a private dwelling is liable to a fine not exceeding level 3 on the standard scale (£3,000), whereas in any other case the fine should not exceed level 5 (£5,000) on the standard scale.

Section 2 prohibits the emission of dark smoke from industrial trade premises. Unlike s 1, the s 2 emission need not be through a chimney. Trade or industrial premises are premises which are used for an industrial or trade purpose or premises on which matter is burnt in connection with any industrial or trade purpose. A s 2 offence may be committed either by the occupier of the premises or any other person causing or permitting the emission. In the case of *Sheffield CC v ADH Demolition Ltd* (1984), it was held that premises could include a demolition site and that there was no requirement for the land to be covered by a building. The burning of rubbish on a demolition site may also amount to an industrial or trade process. A person guilty of an offence under s 2 shall be liable on summary conviction to a fine of up to £20,000.

7.8.4 What is dark smoke?

Smoke includes soot, ash, grit and gritty particles emitted in smoke. Dark smoke is defined by reference to a device known as the Ringlemann Chart. Smoke which is determined to be as dark or darker than shade 2 on the Ringlemann Chart is 'dark smoke' for the purposes of the Act. The Ringlemann Chart indicates differing shades of darkness. The chart consists of a piece of card with cross-hatching in black on a white background so that a known percentage of white is obscured. The chart needs to be placed at some distance from the observer who will then be able to see that the lines merge into different greyish/black shades. The different shades are numerically categorised; 0 equals white and 5 equals dense black. Shades 2–4 increase by degrees so that shade 1 indicates a 20% obscuration of the white, shade 2 equals 40%, and so on. In order to compare the shades with the smoke, it is necessary to place the card between the observer and the smoke (the chart is usually mounted on a wooden or metal frame). The observer usually stands about 50 ft from the chart in order to match the smoke colour with the chart. The matching should normally take place in good daylight conditions.

By virtue of s 3 of the CAA 1993, a court must be satisfied in any legal proceedings for breach of s 1 or s 2 that the smoke is as dark as defined. However, there is no requirement for an actual comparison of the smoke with the chart. It is sufficient that the court is certain that the method was properly applied and that the smoke was thereby determined to be dark.

There is no requirement in the CAA 1993 for the defendant to have caused or knowingly permitted the discharge of dark smoke. The offence is a strict liability one. There are, however, a number of defences and exemptions which are considered below. Breach of s 1 is a criminal offence and a person may be liable on summary conviction to a fine of up to £3,000 (level 3) for emissions from private dwellings otherwise £5,000 (level 5). Breach of s 2 may result in a fine not exceeding £20,000.

7.8.5 Notification that an offence has been committed

The occupier of the premises must be notified of the offence by the local authority environmental officer 'as soon as may be'. This will usually mean that an environmental health officer or officer from the local authority advises the occupier verbally. However, the local authority is required to confirm this notification in writing within a period of four days. Failure to give notice will provide the defendant with a defence to any charges made under ss 1, 2 and 20. Unlike other pollution offences discussed in this book, the offence can only be tried by the magistrates' court.

7.8.6 Strict liability and burden of proof

The CAA 1993 presumes that there will have been an emission of dark smoke from industrial or trade premises in any case where material is burned on those premises and the circumstances are such that the burning would be likely to give rise to the emission of dark smoke. The burden of proof falls squarely on the occupier (or any other person causing or permitting the burning) to show that no dark smoke was actually emitted.

7.8.7 Exemptions

Section 1(3) of the CAA 1993 provides certain exemptions from the above offences. These are contained in the Dark Smoke (Permitted Periods) Regulations 1958 SI 1958/498, which establish the following exceptions whereby no offence is committed if the emissions of dark smoke are made within certain periods:

(a) the emission of dark smoke is permitted for a defined number of minutes (between 10–40) during an eight hour period. The precise number of minutes depends on the number of furnaces which feed into the chimney and whether or not the emission involves the blowing of soot;

(b) in any event, the continuous emission of dark smoke cannot at any time exceed four minutes and the continuous emission of black smoke must not at any time exceed two minutes in any half hour period.

The Clean Air (Emissions of Dark Smoke) (Exemptions) Regulations 1969 SI 1969/1263 also provide exceptions relating to the burning of certain materials in the open. The following are exempt from the s 2 of the CAA 1993 offence:

(a) burning timber and other waste material which results either from the demolition of a building or from the clearance of a site upon which there is building operation or engineering construction;

(b) burning explosive which has become waste and any material which has become contaminated by such explosive;

(c) burning tar, pitch or asphalt and other matter in connection with any resurfacing;

(d) burning animal and poultry carcasses where the animals have died or have been slaughtered due to a disease;

(e) burning containers which have been contaminated by any pesticide or toxic substance used for veterinary or agricultural purposes.

However, for these exceptions to apply, the person seeking to rely on the exceptions would need to satisfy certain conditions. Among other things, there is the requirement that there is no other reasonably safe and practicable method of disposing of the matter. Other conditions relate to the manner in which the burning takes place and that steps are taken to minimise the emission of dark smoke. The fire must be carried out under the supervision of the occupier of the premises concerned.

7.8.8 Defences

Section 1(4) of the CAA 1993 provides that where a breach of the dark smoke provisions occur then a number of defences may be raised in any proceedings. These defences exist when a number of circumstances arise:

(a) when lighting the furnace from cold; or

(b) when there has been some unforeseeable and unavoidable failure of the furnace or apparatus connected with the furnace; or

(c) when unsuitable fuel has been used when suitable fuel is unobtainable and that the least unsuitable fuel was used.

Garner's *Encyclopaedia of Environmental Law* suggests that the defence of lighting a furnace from cold might only be available in relation to the initial ignition of the furnace and not each time the furnace is restoked after a period (that is, overnight) of being damped down.

These defences are all subject to the important *caveat* that all practicable steps were taken to prevent or minimise the emissions of dark smoke.

As far as the s 2 offence is concerned, s 2(4) provides a defence if it can be proved that the emission was inadvertent and that all practicable steps had been taken to prevent or minimise it. It appears from the statute that both these elements will be required before a defendant can rely on the defence. 'Practicable' is defined here in a similar way to 'practicable' in the context of 'best practicable means'. Therefore, regard must be had to factors such as local conditions and circumstances; financial implications; and the current state of technical knowledge.

Finally, if the person charged with an offence under either of these sections has not been served with a written notification of the offence from the environmental health department of the local authority within the prescribed four day period, this will provide him with an additional defence by virtue of s 51.

7.8.9 Grit, dust and fumes

Section 5 establishes similar offences to the dark smoke offences in relation to grit, dust and fumes emitted from furnaces. Grit is defined by the Clean Air (Emission of Grit and Dust from Furnaces) Regulations 1971 SI 1971/162, which also prescribes the limits of grit and dust emissions from certain specifications of furnaces. Dust does not include dust emitted from a chimney as an ingredient of smoke and fumes means any airborne matter smaller than dust.

It is an offence if, on any day, the grit or dust emitted from a chimney serving a specified furnace is over the prescribed emission limits laid down in the regulations. Monitoring equipment is required to measure emissions accurately and the Ringlemann Chart procedure is not applicable. The occupier will be guilty of the offence unless he can successfully raise the defence that the best practicable means had been used to minimise or prevent the emission. It should be noted here that the defence requires the best practicable means to be employed rather than any practicable means. However, in circumstances where the regulations do not specify a prescribed limit (that is, certain furnaces are not covered by the regulations) it will still be an offence for the occupier if he fails to use any practicable means to minimise the emission of grit or dust from the chimney.

7.8.10 Control over the installation of non-domestic furnaces

Section 4 of the CAA 1993 provides that, before installing a furnace over a certain size (basically a non-domestic boiler), the person seeking to make the installation must obtain the approval of the local authority. The section also stipulates that all new non-domestic boilers should, so far as practicable, be smokeless. Any one who installs a furnace in contravention of this requirement is committing an offence, but if the local authority has approved the installation, it is deemed to comply with the requirements of the section.

Additionally, all non-domestic furnaces over a certain energy value must comply with the provisions contained in ss 6–8. Furnaces falling under these sections must be fitted with local authority approved grit and dust arrestment equipment. The arrestors must be properly maintained and used, if used for the following purposes:

(a) to burn pulverised fuel; or

(b) to burn, at a rate of 45.4 kg or more an hour, any other solid matter; or

(c) to burn, at a rate equivalent to 366.4 kilowatts or more, any liquid or gaseous matter.

There are certain exemptions from these provisions and these are specified in s 7. In particular, the SOSE has used his powers under s 7 to prescribe by regulation that furnaces of a certain class (for example, mobile furnaces) may be exempted (see the Clean Air (Arrestment Plant) (Exemption) Regulations 1969). Alternatively, it is possible to apply to the local authority for an exemption under s 7. The local authority can only grant an exemption if it is satisfied that the emissions of grit or dust will not amount to a statutory nuisance.

The local authority may also require the occupier of these furnaces to comply with certain monitoring requirements in relation to the measurement of grit, dust and fumes. In turn, the occupier has the right to request that the local authority make and record such measurements and the local authority will be required to do so from time to time. A right of appeal to the SOSE is available if the local authority refuses to approve the proposed equipment.

7.8.11 Control over chimney height

Section 14 empowers the local authorities to control the height of chimneys for the purposes of regulating air pollution. The thinking behind these controls is based on the principle of dilute and disperse. Tall chimney stacks are supposed to enable the more effective dispersion of pollution in order to dilute it to harmless levels. The control under s 14 exists in addition to the normal planning controls which the planning authority can exert.

If any one is seeking to:

(a) erect a new chimney to serve a furnace;

(b) enlarge an existing chimney to serve a furnace;

(c) replace a chimney with an increased combustion space;

then they must make an application to the local authority for chimney height approval. The local authority will determine the application by reference to the 'Third memorandum on chimney heights' which assists with the calculation on chimney heights. The local authority must take into account various factors and, in particular, must not grant approval for a chimney unless it is satisfied that its height will be sufficient to prevent, as far as practicable, the chimney emissions becoming prejudicial to health or a nuisance.

The local authority can either approve the chimney height with or without conditions. Once again, there is a right of appeal against the decision of the local authority to the SOSE.

7.8.12 Smoke Control Areas

The ability to establish Smoke Control Areas is one of the principal features of the CAA 1993 and provides a means by which local authorities can control, in particular, smoke from domestic properties. A local authority has the power (see s 18 of the CAA 1993) to declare all or part of its area as a Smoke Control Area and does so by a Smoke Control Order. In addition, the SOSE has the power, by virtue of s 19, to order a local authority to designate a Smoke Control Area. Two or more local authorities may combine to declare a larger Smoke Control Area (see s 61(3)).

The Smoke Control Order may designate certain classes of building; it may exempt specific buildings or classes of buildings or fireplaces. It has been suggested that the widespread adoption of Smoke Control Areas has been an important factor in achieving compliance with the Sulphur Dioxide Directive (80/779/EEC).

Once an area has been designated as a Smoke Control Area, then an occupier of a building in the area is guilty of an offence if smoke (note, this includes any shade of smoke) is emitted from a chimney of that building. However defences are available if:

(a) the emission resulted from the use of an authorised fuel; or

(b) the emission resulted from the use of a fireplace exempted by regulations.

Authorised fuels are defined by the Smoke Control Areas (Authorised Fuel) Regulations 1991 SI 1991/1282. Various regulations exempt certain classes of fireplace (the Smoke Control (Exempted Fireplaces) Orders).

It is also an offence to buy solid non-authorised fuel for use in a smoke control area (unless of course it is for an exempt fireplace) and it is also an offence to retail unauthorised fuel for unauthorised use in a Smoke Control Area.

7.9 Statutory nuisances relating to air quality

The provisions relating to statutory nuisance are considered in Chapter 8. However, in the context of controls over air pollution, it should be noted that the following matters may constitute a statutory nuisance if they are either prejudicial to health or a nuisance:

(a) any premises in such a state so as to be prejudicial to health or a nuisance (this could cover odour emissions from such premises even though smell is specifically mentioned in (c) below);

(b) smoke, fumes or gas emitted from premises so as to be prejudicial to health or a nuisance;

(c) any dust, steam, smell or other effluvia arising on industrial, trade or business premises.

However, it should be noted that, in relation to (b) above, where the emission of smoke can be controlled under the CAA 1993 the statutory nuisance provisions do not apply. Therefore, this statutory nuisance is largely concerned with smoke which is less than 'dark' from non-domestic premises.

7.10 Pollution from motor vehicles

There is no doubt that the emissions from motor vehicles are a major source of atmospheric pollution. Ninety-eight per cent of the UK's benzene emissions arise from vehicle emissions. Eighty-seven per cent of the UK's carbon monoxide emissions come from petrol engined vehicles. Linked to these statistics is the further fact that vehicle emissions have increased by 50% since

1970, although there is some evidence of a downward trend since the introduction of cars fitted with catalytic converters. Pollution emission 'gains' linked to improvements in motor vehicle engine efficiency and the development of less polluting fuels have been offset by increases in the number of motor vehicle journeys made. Vehicle emissions are also largely responsible for emissions of other pollutants such as 1,3-butadiene which has been shown to be linked to increased risks of lymphoma or leukaemia.

The problem of vehicle emissions was one of the main themes in *Meeting the Challenge* which put forward five proposals. These were:

(a) new standards for technology, emissions and flues;

(b) planning policies and local transport strategies aimed at reducing the need to travel and encouraging more environmentally friendly modes of transport;

(c) new environmental responsibilities in partnership with public service and fleet operators;

(d) stricter enforcement of emissions regulations, and in particular targeting those vehicles doing the most damage to the environment;

(e) voluntary action and guidance.

It is clear that for many local authorities with heavy traffic flows that vehicle emissions are going to pose the biggest single problem in terms of meeting air quality standards and objectives. Better traffic management and local transport strategies are seen as important in reducing the use of vehicles. In areas which designate AQMAs, the action plan may need to embrace traffic management issues. For example, restricting access to a particular area or roads, regulating traffic flows and speed, and encouraging other transport modes, such as park-and-ride. Local authorities have the power under the Road Traffic Regulation Act 1984 to prohibit, restrict or regulate vehicles, or particular types of vehicle.

7.11 EC legislation

The EC had a relatively slow start in terms of its programme of legislation aimed at controlling air pollution. The first directive establishing air quality standards was not adopted until 1980 (Directive 80/779/EEC). Since then, the EC has adopted various measures aimed at combating atmospheric pollution, particularly in response to acid rain. Generally speaking, EC air pollution measures can be categorised into the following broad types.

(a) Emissions from industrial plants

Of particular importance is the Large Combustion Plant Directive (88/609/EEC). This has been implemented in the UK through the system of IPC. In addition, Directive (84/360/EEC) established that new industrial plants must use the best available technologies not entailing excessive cost and Directive (89/369/EEC) deals with emissions from municipal waste incineration plants. In 1996 the EC introduced an Integrated Pollution Prevention and Control Directive (96/61/EC) which has been implemented into national law by the PPCA 1999. The IPPC directive is, in effect, an extension to the existing IPC and LAAPC licence based controls over a number of highly polluting industries.

(b) Air pollution affecting the ozone layer and global warming

EC regulations 3322/88 and 549/91 have now banned the use of CFCs (chlorofluorocarbons). Regulation 549/91 also controls the emission of HFCs (hydrofluorocarbons).

(c) Air quality standards

The EC passed the Air Quality Framework Directive (96/62/EC) in 1996. This directive is intended to be supplemented by a number of daughter directives to control 12 pollutants. The first of the daughter directives (99/30/EC) specifies binding limits for lead, sulphur dioxide, nitrogen dioxide, and small particulate matter (PM 10). The remaining pollutants are ozone, carbon monoxide, benzene, polyaromatic hydrocarbons (PAH) and the toxic metals – arsenic, mercury, cadmium, and nickel.

(d) Vehicle emission standards

The EC has enacted various directives which aim to control the emissions from vehicles. Initially the directives in this area were intended to harmonise standards in order to promote the free movement of goods (namely vehicles). In 1991 the EC adopted Directive (91/441/EC) which imposed strict standards on the emissions from passenger cars and a similar directive (93/59/EC) was adopted in relation to light commercial vehicles. However since then the emission limits have been made more stringent with a further directives relating to passenger cars (94/12/EEC). In addition to setting emission limits the EC has also adopted various Directives which seek to control the content of fuels in order to reduce emissions of lead and sulphur. These are dealt with below. However it is worth noting that the Commission recognises that the problem of vehicle emissions can not simply be addressed by legislative measures. The Commission has also proposed a variety of other measures concerned with traffic management. The Commission's green paper on impact of transport on the environment, 1992 COM (92) 46 Final (1992) considers the impact that vehicle emissions will have on the environment by the year 2010 and suggests a number of actions which need to be taken.

(e) Product quality standards

A variety of directives have been concerned with improving product quality standards particularly in relation to fuel products. Examples include Directive (76/716/EEC) and Directive (99/32/EC) on the sulphur content of liquid fuels and Directive (98/70/EC) on the chemical composition of fuels.

(f) Atmospheric pollution and waste reduction

The Landfill Directive (99/31/EEC) came into force in July 1999 and must be transposed into UK law by July 2001. One important aspect of the directive is that it will drastically reduce the amount of municipal waste currently being landfilled: 65% reduction of 1995 levels by 2016. This will result in an increase in the amount of municipal waste that is incinerated. Whilst the directive will deliver an important reduction in methane emissions from landfill sites it will increase atmospheric emissions from incinerators. (see Directives 89/369/EEC and 89/429/EEC relating to municipal waste incinerators).

Section 80 of the EA 1995 placed a duty on the SOSE to prepare and publish a national air quality strategy and in June and August 1996 the DoE published a draft UK national air strategy, for consultation. The main emphasis in the draft is on ambient air quality and the impact on human health, rather than on the environment. At the core of the strategy are the setting of air quality standards and air quality objectives. The draft proposes air quality standards for the concentration in air of eight pollutants, benzene, 1,3-butadiene, carbon monoxide, lead, nitrogen dioxide (Nox), ozone, particles and sulphur dioxide.

7.12 Acid rain, global warming and the international dimension

Air pollution is a global environmental issue and attracts international attention. The study of international environmental law falls outside the scope of this book, but the transboundary nature of atmospheric pollution in particular makes it necessary to include some commentary.

The UK has committed itself to a number of international conventions which require the Government to take steps to reduce the emission of certain pollutants.

(a) 1979 Convention on Long Range Transboundary Air Pollution

Agreed in Geneva in 1979, this convention was not ratified by the UK until 1980. Signatories agreed to endeavour to limit and, as far as possible, reduce and prevent air pollution, especially pollutants associated with the production of acid rain. The Convention resulted in three international protocols concerned with the reduction of sulphur dioxide (SO_2) emissions; emissions of oxides of nitrogen (NO_x); and emissions of volatile organic compounds (VOCs).

(b) The 1985 Vienna Convention for the Protection of the Ozone Layer

Parties to the Vienna Convention, including the UK which ratified it in 1987, have agreed the Montreal Protocol on Substances that Deplete the Ozone Layer. The protocol requires the signatories to freeze and reduce the production of various CFCs and halons.

(c) 1992 Convention on Climate Change

This Convention was agreed by over 150 parties at the United Nations Earth Summit in Rio de Janeiro. The Convention is aimed at reducing emissions of greenhouse gases. The 1997 Kyoto Protocol to the Convention establishes targets for six greenhouse gases: carbon dioxide, oxides of nitrogen, methane, HFCs (hydrofluorocarbons), PFCs (perfluorocarbons), and sulphur hexafluoride (SF 6). The combined target for the six gases represents a very modest 5% reduction of 1990 emission levels for these gases. The targets are to be achieved by 2012. Developing countries, in contrast to developed countries, are not bound by the reduction targets.

The convention and protocol have generated some interesting debates in regard to the factors which may be taken into account when assessing whether a state has attained the protocol targets. For example, to what extent should the presence of existing forests and the planting of new forests act as 'carbon sinks' locking up carbon dioxide generated by developed countries which are parties to the convention and protocol?

In order to meet the UK`s targets for the reduction of the main greenhouse gases specified in the Kyoto Protocol (a reduction of 12.5% of 1990 levels of the six gases between 2008 and 2012), the Government has, in the Finance Act 2000, introduced a new tax known as the 'climate change levy'. This tax will 'bite' as from April 2000. The tax is a levy on business energy usage and is intended to reduce energy consumption. By reducing energy consumption, the Government intends to lower the production of greenhouse gases in the UK.

The levy is payable by energy suppliers of both primary fuels (such as coal and natural gas) and secondary fuels used for lighting, heating, powering appliances and machinery. Energy suppliers will recover the levy from their customers. There are some important exemptions, including : domestic use of fuel and power, vehicle fuel, fuel products which are not energy-related (for example, raw material usage and lubricants), renewable energy production and energy from combined heat and power plants. The levy is based on the energy content of the relevant fuel rather than its carbon content. There are reductions in the levy for energy intensive industries such as steel, glass, paper, aluminium, metal foundries, food and drink production, and cement (this is not an exhaustive list). In these sectors, the tax is to be reduced by up to 80%. Each of these sectors has entered into an agreement with DEFRA (or its predecessor DETR) which specifies the periodic targets which must be met for each industry sector to qualify for the relevant tax reductions.

ATMOSPHERIC POLLUTION

Problems of air pollution

Pollution of the atmosphere results in both long term adverse environmental consequences but also causes health problems and can cause death.

Legal controls

The legal controls over air pollution are contained in:

(a) Pt I of the EPA 1990 – IPC and LAAPC – the system of LAAPC only permits the local authority to control atmospheric emissions, whereas the central system of IPC enables the control of substances into all environmental media to secure the BPEO;

(b) the PPCA 1999 implements the Integrated Pollution Prevention and Control Directive (96/61/EC). IPPC regulatory controls will replace IPC and LAAPC controls by 2007;

(c) the CAA 1993 – controls emissions of smoke, dust and grit by means of criminal offences.

The CAA 1993

The following are the main offences:

(a) emission of dark smoke

  – from a chimney; or

  – from industrial premises other than from a chimney;

(b) emission of dust and grit from non-domestic furnaces;

(c) emission of smoke from a chimney in a Smoke Control Area;

(d) various offences relating to the installation of furnaces.

Section 1 prohibits:

(a) the emission of 'dark smoke' from the chimney of any building (s 1(1)); or

(b) from a chimney which serves the furnace of any fixed boiler or industrial plant (s 1(2)).

Section 2 prohibits:

- the emission of dark smoke from industrial trade premises.

Although the offences are strict liability certain exemptions and defences are available.

Section 5 establishes similar offences to the dark smoke offences in relation to grit and dust and fumes.

Section 4 of the CAA 1993 provides that before installing a furnace over a certain size (basically a non-domestic boiler) the person seeking to make the installation must obtain the prior approval of the local authority.

Section 14 empowers the local authorities to control the height of chimneys for the purposes of regulating air pollution. The thinking behind these controls is based on the principle of dilute and local authorities can take preventive action to reduce air pollution from smoke by designating an area as a Smoke Control Area.

In the context of air pollution the following provisions of s 79 of the EPA 1990 may provide a means by which the pollution can be abated by a local authority exercising its powers under the EPA 1990 in relation to statutory nuisances:

(a) any premises in such a state so as to be prejudicial to health or a nuisance (this could cover odour emissions from such premises even though smell is specifically mentioned in (c) below);

(b) smoke, fumes or gas emitted from premises so as to be prejudicial to health or a nuisance;

(c) any dust, steam, smell or other effluvia arising on industrial, trade or business premises.

Air quality strategy and AQMAs

Part IV of the EA 1995 requires the SOSE to publish a national air quality strategy (s 80).

Section 82 of the EA 1995 places local authorities under a duty to review air quality.

Section 83 of the EA 1995 provides for the establishment of AQMAs.

CHAPTER 8

STATUTORY NUISANCE

8.1 Introduction

Chapter 10 considers the ways in which the common law can provide a means of protecting the environment and some of the inherent difficulties faced when bringing common law actions. Common law actions, especially the law of torts, are now supplemented by the provisions of ss 79–82 of the Environmental Protection Act (EPA) 1990, which provides that certain matters may constitute 'statutory nuisances' and as such may, if not abated, result in the commission of criminal offences incorporated into the EPA 1990 (see s 80(4) of the EPA 1990). The control of statutory nuisances rests largely with the environmental health departments of the local authorities. However, it is also possible for a 'person aggrieved' by a statutory nuisance to commence proceedings in the magistrates' court in order to secure the abatement of the nuisance (effectively by-passing the local authority statutory provisions). The purpose of putting certain nuisances on a statutory footing was to provide a quicker, cheaper and more effective means of dealing with nuisances than by means of a common law action.

The current statutory nuisance provisions can be found in ss 79–82 of the EPA 1990 as amended by the Noise and Statutory Nuisance Act (NSNA) 1993. However, the provisions are not new and, in fact, the EPA 1990 consolidates provisions from legislation dating back to the Public Health Act (PHA) 1875 and then the PHA 1936, which first placed certain nuisances on a statutory footing in recognition of the growing health problems associated with industrial development and some of the limitations of the common law in addressing these problems. The PHA 1936 has now been repealed and re-enacted by the EPA 1990. One of the problems with this straightforward re-enactment is that there has been no redefinition of the statutory nuisances which were introduced by the PHA 1936 to protect public health, but are now intended to protect the environment. Although statutory nuisances were intended to control pollution, the main objective of the legislation was to protect public health rather than protect the environment. In addition to the original list of statutory nuisances, noise nuisances are drawn from the Control of Pollution Act (COPA) 1974 and also the NSNA 1993. Many of the cases cited in this chapter concern the PHA 1936, but are still relevant in the context of the EPA 1990. Section 79(1) of the EPA 1990 placed a duty on local authorities to periodically inspect their areas for statutory nuisances; nevertheless, the regulation of statutory nuisances is a largely reactive regulatory tool.

Section 57 of the Environment Act (EA) 1995 has inserted a new Pt IIA into the EPA 1990 concerned specifically with contaminated land. The contaminated land provisions which are discussed at length in Chapter 6 are modelled on the statutory nuisance provisions in Pt III of the EPA 1990. As a consequence, s 79(1A) of the EPA 1990 states clearly that no matter shall constitute a statutory nuisance to the extent that it consists of, or is caused by, any land being in a contaminated state. This is clearly intended to avoid overlap of the provisions and where any land is deemed to be contaminated then it will not be dealt with under the statutory nuisance provisions discussed in this chapter.

8.2 What are the statutory nuisances?

The matters or activities that constitute statutory nuisances are listed in s 79 as follows:

(a) any premises in such a state as to be prejudicial to health or a nuisance;

(b) smoke emitted from premises so as to be prejudicial to health or a nuisance;

(c) fumes or gases emitted from premises so as to be prejudicial to health or a nuisance;

(d) any, dust, steam, smell or other effluvia arising on industrial, trade or business premises and being prejudicial to health or a nuisance;

(e) any accumulation or deposit which is prejudicial to health or a nuisance;

(f) any animal kept in such a place or manner as to be prejudicial to health or a nuisance;

(g) noise emitted from premises so as to be prejudicial to health or a nuisance;

(ga) noise that is prejudicial to health or a nuisance and is emitted from or caused by a vehicle, machinery or equipment in a street;

(h) any other matter declared by any enactment to be a statutory nuisance.

It should be noted that point (ga) was added by the NSNA 1993. Noise nuisances are considered in greater detail in Chapter 9.

8.3 Prejudicial to health or a nuisance

The list of matters that may potentially constitute statutory nuisances is wide and covers many different situations, ranging from noise as a result of a party to the accumulation of waste materials on land. In practice, many of the matters that are statutory nuisances are very localised incidents which may not generally be regarded as major or serious environmental problems. However, it is at the local level that most people are concerned about environmental problems. A vacant site used for dumping rubbish may not have serious or global environmental consequences but can cause considerable problems for people living and working near the site. It may attract vermin, it may give rise to noxious or offensive smells and it may result in a loss of local amenity. In that sense, the vacant site affects the environment of those affected by it and as such is no less of an environmental problem to the people concerned.

However, the matters listed in s 79 are not automatically statutory nuisances. They become so if they are either prejudicial to health or a nuisance. This phrase includes two separate and alternative limbs and it is not necessary to show that a matter is both a nuisance and prejudicial to health. This was affirmed in *Betts v Penge UDC* (1942).

8.3.1 Prejudicial to health

Section 79(7) defines 'prejudicial to health' as meaning 'injurious, or likely to cause injury'. This definition includes two limbs: 'injurious to health', that is, actual harm, and 'likely to cause injury', that is, anticipated harm. The definition is the same as that given in the PHA 1936. Its meaning was considered by the Divisional Court in the case of *Coventry CC v Cartwright* (1975). The case concerned a vacant site owned by the city council. The council took no steps to prevent people from depositing household refuse and building materials, such as brick, tarmacadam, earth, scrap iron and broken glass, on the site. A complaint was made by a local resident that the deposits constituted a statutory nuisance in that there was an accumulation or deposit which was prejudicial to health and a nuisance. The argument that it was a nuisance was based on the loss of amenity, an argument rejected by the court. However, the case is important because of its consideration of the meaning of the phrase 'prejudicial to health'. Initially, the magistrates found that the building materials on the site were prejudicial to health on the basis that anyone entering the site might injure themselves on the rubble and they consequently made an abatement order. However, on appeal, their decision was overturned by the Divisional Court. The Divisional Court concerned itself with the question of whether or not the inert materials on the site could be prejudicial to health and in doing so came to the conclusion that it could only be prejudicial to health if it was likely to cause a threat of disease or attract vermin. It was held that the definition of prejudicial to health did not encompass inert materials which could cause physical injury to people who walk on it. In reaching this decision, the court considered that the statute (in the instant, the PHA 1936) defined prejudicial to health as meaning 'injurious or likely to cause injury to health' and concluded that this did not extend to physical injury from cuts and the like. In his judgment, Widgery CJ stated that, in relation to the words prejudicial to health: '... the underlying conception of the section [s 92(1)(c) of the PHA 1936] is that that which is struck at is an accumulation of something which produces a threat to health in the sense of a threat of disease, vermin or the like.' The case of *Cunningham v Birmingham CC* [1998] Env LR 1 confirms that the test for whether something, such as the state of premises, is 'prejudicial to health' is an objective test. (see, also, *Southwark BC v Simpson* [1999] Env LR 553).

8.3.2 What is meant by nuisance?

The courts have equated nuisance in this context with common law nuisance, especially private nuisance involving interference with enjoyment of property. In *National Coal Board v Neath BC* (1976), it was held that the word 'nuisance' meant either a public or a private nuisance at common law. It therefore involved an act or omission materially affecting the comfort and quality of life of a class of the public or an interference for a substantial period with the use and enjoyment of neighbouring property. It should be noted that, like common law nuisance, the interference must emanate from a neighbouring property (*National Coal Board v Thorne* (1976)). This requirement was, however, relaxed in later cases.

The problem with using the common law notion of private nuisance is that there is no clearly applicable standard and whether a nuisance exists will depend (subjectively) on the particular circumstances. As will be illustrated in Chapter 10, one of the features of the common law of nuisance is the achievement of a balance between competing rights, with each case turning on its facts. Where there is no actual physical damage to person or property, but only a reduction in the enjoyment of a property (for instance, as a consequence of loud noise or offensive smells), then the courts have also indicated that much will depend upon the location where the nuisance is complained of. In the often quoted case of *Sturges v Bridgman* (1879), Thesiger LJ stated that 'what would be a nuisance in Belgrave Square would not necessarily be so in Bermondsey'. This narrow approach is problematic in the context of environmental protection. Environmental problems often transcend spatially defined areas and should not be seen in such narrow terms. Moreover, it is precisely in the industrial and run-down areas where there are more likely to be statutory nuisances occurring, and there is no justifiable reason why in these more vulnerable areas the protection of the law should be less than in those areas where the chances of statutory nuisances occurring are more remote.

8.3.3 Interference with personal comfort

The courts require evidence that the nuisance interferes with a person's personal comfort, as opposed to land or physical possessions, largely because the concept of statutory nuisance was based on the need to protect public health. This was aptly demonstrated in *Wivenhoe Port v Colchester BC* (1985), where the court held that nuisance, in the context of statutory nuisance, did not have its wide common law meaning but should be confined to personal discomfort. In the judgment, Butler J made the following statement:

> To be within the spirit of the Act [PHA 1936] a nuisance, to be a statutory nuisance, had to be one interfering materially with the personal comfort of the residents, in the sense that it materially affected their well-being although it might not be prejudicial to their health. Thus, dust falling on motor cars might cause inconvenience to their owners; it might even diminish the value of their motor car; but this would not be a statutory nuisance. In the same way, dust falling on gardens or trees, or on stock held in a shop would not be a statutory nuisance. But dust in eyes or hair, even if not shown to be prejudicial to health, would be so as an interference with personal comfort.

Here Butler J refers to the 'spirit of the Act', which was intended to protect public health. However, statutory nuisances are now contained in the EPA 1990 which has as its *raison d'être* the protection of the environment and thus quite different aims to public health legislation. The restrictive approach adopted by the courts would not serve such aims, indeed dust falling on grass and trees is precisely the type of activity which causes environmental problems.

8.3.4 Criticisms of the present approach

The restrictive approach adopted by the courts has been criticised by the House of Commons Environment Committee who, in their report on *Contaminated Land* (1990), recommended that the concept of nuisance should be capable of being used to protect the natural environment as well as public health. Unfortunately, the Government rejected this particular recommendation, claiming that it would result in local authorities being 'inundated with requests to take action from well-intentioned, but over-enthusiastic residents who had read a report in the *New Scientist* or had been influenced by a *Panorama* programme'. It therefore seems that the statutory nuisance provisions offer a means of protecting public health and interests in land but only a limited means of protecting the environment in its own right.

8.3.5 Identifying a statutory nuisance

In practice, the local authority environmental health officer will make an initial determination whether the matter complained of constitutes a statutory nuisance on the basis of it being prejudicial to health or a nuisance. The officer will therefore be required to take into account the nature of the neighbourhood and also whether the matter complained of amounts to a nuisance in common law or is just (as sometimes happens) a vexatious complaint. The environmental health officer (EHO) will pay particular attention to the following considerations: the nature of the activity alleged to constitute a nuisance; the locality; the relevant time; the duration of the alleged nuisance;

and, the utility of the activity creating the alleged nuisance. The EHO will only need to satisfy himself/herself on the balance of probabilities that a nuisance has occurred or is likely to occur before he/she is obliged to take abatement action. The local authority has no authority to act unless it is satisfied that a statutory nuisance exists or is likely to occur or recur (s 80(1) of the EPA 1990).

8.3.6 Burden of proof

The burden of proof which applies is the criminal one. In other words, it must be established beyond reasonable doubt that the matter complained of exists and that the defendant is responsible for it. This was clearly illustrated in the case of *London Borough of Lewisham v Fenner* (1995). Fenner commenced proceedings against the local authority, under s 82 of the EPA 1990 (see below for a discussion of the way in which individuals can commence statutory nuisance proceedings under s 82). His complaint was against the noise from the dehumidifying equipment at a local swimming pool operated by the local authority. The principal issue in the case was the nature of statutory nuisance proceedings and the burden of proof. Fenner complained that the noise caused him to lose sleep. The Crown Court judge held that loss of sleep can be injurious to health. The Crown Court judge took the unusual steps of visiting the pool during the day and the pool management agreed to voluntarily shut down the dehumidifier during the night. The noise itself was continuous and droning but fell below the recommended 30–40 decibels recommended in British Standard 8233. As a matter of fact it was found that the noise had affected Fenner's health and had caused annoyance to another person, but on the basis that the noise fell within advisory standards the court could not feel satisfied that the criminal burden of proof for a noise nuisance had been discharged.

8.4 Exemptions

Section 79(2)–(6) provides a number of specific exemptions from the list of statutory nuisances. These are dealt with below under each category of nuisance:

(a) Section 79(1)(a) – 'Any premises in such a state as to be prejudicial to health or a nuisance'. Premises does not simply mean buildings but is defined in s 79(7) as including land and any vessel other than one powered by steam reciprocating machinery. The definition clearly encompasses the garden of a dwelling house (see *Stevenage BC v Wilson* [1993] Env LR 214). This particular head of statutory nuisance has been used on occasion by council house tenants to force the local council to deal with defective council houses. The state of the premises will not be a statutory nuisance if it affects only the occupants. However, where the premises are in such a state that the occupants are disturbed from noise outside (for example, caused by inadequate sound insulation), this was thought to be a statutory nuisance (*Southwark London BC v Ince* (1989)). However, disturbance due to external, traffic generated noise is excluded from the ambit of statutory nuisance (see *London Borough of Haringey v Jowett* [1999] NPC 52). In the unreported case of *East Riding of Yorkshire Council v Yorkshire Water Services Ltd* (23 March 2000) it was held that sewers are not 'premises' within the meaning of the statutory nuisance regime contained in the EPA 1990. In addition, submissions based upon the potentially wider remit of statutory nuisance contained within an environmental statute (that is, the EPA 1990), as opposed to a public health statute, were rejected by the court.

(b) Section 79(1)(b) – 'Smoke emitted from premises so as to be prejudicial to health or a nuisance'. This particular statutory nuisance was not included in the PHAs but replaces provisions from the Clean Air Act (CAA) 1956. Premises occupied by the armed forces are exempt from this section, as are certain activities listed in s 79(3) such as smoke emitted from a chimney of a private dwelling within a smoke control area and dark smoke emitted from a chimney of a building serving a boiler or furnace. These latter exempt activities will not constitute a statutory nuisance under Part III of the EPA 1990 but are controlled under the provisions of the CAA 1993.

(c) Section 79(1)(c) – 'Fumes or gas emitted from premises so as to be prejudicial to health or a nuisance'. Section 79(1)(c) only applies to domestic premises. Fumes are defined as any airborne solid smaller than dust and gas is defined as vapour and moisture precipitated from vapour.

(d) Section 79(1)(d) – 'Any dust, steam, smell or other effluvia arising on industrial, trade or business premises so as to be prejudicial to health or a nuisance'. Steam emitted from a railway locomotive engine is exempted. This is the only statutory nuisance which is limited to industrial, trade or business premises. The terms 'industrial, trade or business' have been given a wide interpretation and include activities such as manufacturing and service activities such as banking. The term 'effluvia' refers to the flow of harmful or unpleasant substances, such as vapours or gases, onto the complainant's property (see *Malton Board of Health v Malton Manure Co* (1879) 4 Ex D 302).

(e) Section 79(1)(e) – 'Any accumulation or deposit which is prejudicial to health or a nuisance'. This has been held to mean 'an accumulation of something which produces a threat to health in the sense of a threat of disease, vermin or the like' (*Coventry CC v Cartwright* (1975)). In this particular case, the accumulation of building materials, scrap iron and broken glass was not an accumulation that was prejudicial to health, so as to be within the intent (or purpose) of the legislation. The fact that the materials could cause injury when walked on was not relevant. In *R v Carrick DC ex p Shelley* (1996), it was held that pollution from sewage outfalls, such as sanitary towels and condoms washed upon a beach, constituted a statutory nuisance under s 79(1)(e). However, a mere accumulation that does not create any physical interference with the legitimate activities of anyone else is not likely to be a statutory nuisance. The relevant deposit need not result from human action (see *Margate Pier v Town Council of Margate* (1869) 33 JP 437: a case involving the natural accumulation of seaweed).

(f) Section 79(1)(f) – 'Any animal kept in such a place or such a manner as to be prejudicial to health or a nuisance'. Both smells and noise from animals may constitute statutory nuisances although in *Morrisey v Galer* (1955), it was held that this particular statutory nuisance was intended to deal with nuisances arising from insanitary or defective premises where animals were kept and not noisy animals. Thus, in this case the court placed a strict interpretation on the statutory provision. Nevertheless, noise from animals is covered under s 79(1)(g) below.

(g) Section 79(1)(g) – 'Noise emitted from premises so as to be prejudicial to health or a nuisance'. Noise nuisance was previously contained in the COPA 1974 (ss 58 and 59). Noise is defined as including vibration. Aircraft noise (other than noise from a model aircraft) is exempt from this provision but controlled under other specific legislation. As in a smoke nuisance, premises occupied by the armed forces are exempt from this particular section.

(h) Section 79(1)(ga) – 'Noise that is prejudicial to health or a nuisance and is emitted from or caused by a vehicle machinery or equipment in a street'. This statutory nuisance will be considered in full in Chapter 9.

(i) Section 79(1)(h) – 'Any other matter declared by any enactment to be a statutory nuisance'. This catch-all provision enables other statutory nuisances created by any other act to be dealt with under the statutory nuisance procedures of the EPA 1990, for example, nuisances caused by mines and quarries (see Mines and Quarries Act 1954).

8.5 Responsibility of the local authorities

Section 79(1) places all district councils and London borough councils under a duty to inspect their area from time to time to detect any statutory nuisance actually occurring or likely to occur, which ought to be dealt with under ss 80 and 80A of the Act. They are also under a duty to take such steps as are reasonably practicable to investigate complaints made by people living in the area about statutory nuisances. The duty is therefore twofold. The local authority has to carry out its own checks and has to respond to complaints made. In practice, it is the environmental health departments and officers that are responsible for enforcing this legislation and they will carry out the inspections and deal with the complaints. In some areas, particularly the large cities, some local authorities have night patrols who are concerned primarily with noise control.

8.5.1 Duty to inspect

The duty to inspect and detect statutory nuisances is tempered by the requirement that these inspections only have to be carried out from time to time. One of the problems here is that the expression 'time to time' is not defined by the Act, thus making the obligation very imprecise.

8.5.2 Duty to respond to complaints

The duty to respond to complaints was established by the EPA 1990. Prior to its introduction, local authorities were not actually required to respond to complaints, although in practice complainants provided useful information about the occurrences of statutory nuisances within the local authority area. The duty to respond to complaints made by people living in the area is qualified by the fact that the authority only has to take such steps as are reasonably practicable to investigate the complaint. Again, this expression is not defined and could potentially cause problems.

However, if the complainant presents credible evidence of the existence of a nuisance to the local authority and the local authority declines to fulfil its statutory duty by inspecting the alleged nuisance then the complainant could judicially review the local authority's adopted course of action.

In *R v Carrick DC ex p Shelley* [1996] Env LR 273, the defendant local authority received a statutory nuisance complaint relating to the presence of sewerage debris (from a sewage outfall pipe) washed up on a beach in its area. The authority refused to utilise its statutory nuisance powers pending the outcome of other proceedings which were not directly related to its statutory nuisance functions. The complainant successfully challenged, on a judicial review application, the authority's decision to do nothing. Once it was clear that a statutory nuisance existed the authority was obliged by law to serve an Abatement Notice on the water and sewerage company responsible for the statutory nuisance. (See, also, *R v Falmouth and Truro Port Health Authority ex p South West Water Ltd* [2000] NPC 36.)

Local authorities are increasingly finding that they are facing severe financial problems. Whether the authority can take into account its own financial situation in determining what is reasonably practicable is not clear. However, if the Secretary of State finds that a local authority is in default of these duties, he can, by virtue of Sched 3, transfer the function to himself.

8.5.3 Local authorities' investigative powers

In order to carry out their functions of inspection and investigation, local authority environmental officers can enter any land with the people and equipment that they consider necessary. The officers can also carry out any inspections, measurements and tests and can also take away samples and articles. These powers are provided by Sched 3 to the EPA 1990. The purpose of the inspection and investigation is to establish whether or not there is a statutory nuisance (or whether one is likely to occur) and to gather any evidence which may be needed in subsequent court proceedings. Once a local authority environmental officer is satisfied that a statutory nuisance is occurring, or is likely to occur, then an Abatement Notice must be served.

8.6 Abatement Notices

Section 80 provides that an authority must serve an Abatement Notice when it is satisfied that a statutory nuisance:

(a) exists;

(b) is likely to occur; or

(c) is likely to recur in its area.

Therefore, the authority can take preventive action in order to stop a statutory nuisance happening. The requirement to serve the Abatement Notice is mandatory. The authority has no discretion once it is aware of the statutory nuisance. However, the section does not say anything about the need for the likely occurrence to be imminent. It is enough that it is likely to occur. Also, when one considers that the concept of 'prejudicial to health' also extends to 'likely to cause injury', the local authority must serve an Abatement Notice if it believes that circumstances exist which make injury likely.

8.6.1 The form of the notice

Although there is no prescribed form for an Abatement Notice, it must nevertheless state the following in a manner which is clear and understandable to the recipient:

(a) the nature of the statutory nuisance;

(b) the action or works required to abate it;

(c) time limits for compliance;

(d) the rights of appeal to the magistrates' court.

The Abatement Notice can impose conditions:

(a) requiring the abatement of the nuisance or prohibiting or restricting its occurrence or recurrence;

(b) requiring the execution of such works, and the taking of such other steps, as may be necessary for any of these purposes.

The Abatement Notice should be easily understood by the recipient of the notice and with the degree of particularity to make it clear what is required. In *Network Housing Association Ltd v Westminster CC* (1995), the city council served an Abatement Notice on the housing association which required them to carry out alterations in order to reduce the noise to a specified decibel level. Since the Abatement Notice was not sufficiently clear in defining what works were required it was quashed.

Disputes regarding the alleged lack of clarity of Abatement Notices has generated an extensive body of caselaw. In some circumstances it seems that the local authority must exercise great care in the drafting of Abatement Notices. In those cases where the notice requires the recipient to do something (that is, undertake works) the courts appear to require greater precision than in those cases where the recipient is required to refrain from doing something. In *Kirklees Metropolitan Council v Field and Others* [1998] Env LR 337, a rock face, in serious danger of collapse, was the statutory nuisance referred to in an Abatement Notice. The Court of Appeal held that the notice was invalid because it did not specify the works which were necessary to abate the nuisance. This decision was overruled by the subsequent decision of the Court of Appeal, in *R v Falmouth and Truro Port Health Authority ex p South West Water Ltd* [2000] NPC 36, on the basis that the authority should not be obliged to specify what works were necessary since this could interfere with the ability of the recipient of the notice to choose the works which would enable it to comply with the Abatement Notice. It seems that that the local authority's ability to specify the necessary works in the notice are confined to those cases where the recipient of the notice does not have the technical expertise to decide what works are necessary to comply with the notice.

8.6.2 Who must the notice be served on?

The provisions regarding the serving of Abatement Notices are contained in s 80 of the EPA 1990. Normally, the local authority is required to serve the notice on the person responsible for the nuisance. Where the nuisance arises from any defect in the structural character of a building then the notice should be served on the owner of the premises. In circumstances where the person responsible for the nuisance cannot be found, or the nuisance has not yet occurred, then the notice must be served on the owner or occupier of the premises. In relation to vehicles, machinery or equipment, the person responsible will be the driver or operator.

The person responsible for the nuisance is defined in s 79(7) as the person to whose:

(a) act;

(b) default; or

(c) sufferance,

the nuisance is attributable.

This is a wide definition and could include not only the person who created the nuisance, but also a third person/party who failed to take any appropriate preventive or corrective action where they had some legal requirement to do so. It can also include third persons who, on becoming aware of the problem, took no steps to remedy the situation. This was confirmed in the case of *Clayton v Sale UDC* (1926), where an owner was held liable for a statutory nuisance on his land consequent upon the activities or defaults of another (see s 80(2)(c)). It would also appear that a local authority could serve a notice on a previous owner of land, rather than the current owner, if it decides that the previous owner was the person who caused the nuisance rather than the present owner. The terms 'owner' and 'occupier' are not defined in the Act.

Where the statutory nuisance relates to a vehicle, the person responsible also includes the person whose name the vehicle is registered in and any other person who is the driver of the vehicle. Where the statutory nuisance relates to machinery or equipment the person responsible can also include any person who is for the time being the operator of the machinery or equipment.

8.6.3 What if more than one person is involved?

Section 81(1) deals with the situation where more than one person is responsible for the statutory nuisance. In these circumstances, s 80 still applies to each of the persons, irrespective of whether or not what any one of them is responsible for would, by itself, amount to a statutory nuisance. Therefore, if two persons are involved in an action which jointly amounts to a statutory nuisance, they will both be responsible for the statutory nuisance even if their individual actions do not by themselves amount to such a nuisance. Although the Abatement Notice should be served in the first instance on the person responsible for the nuisance, this should be read as meaning that the authority is obliged to serve separate notices on all the parties that may have contributed to the statutory nuisance.

8.7 Appeals against an Abatement Notice

By virtue of s 80(3) of the EPA 1990, a person upon whom an Abatement Notice is served is entitled to appeal against it by making a complaint to the magistrates' court. He must be informed of this right in the Abatement Notice. Where a person decides to lodge an appeal, he must do so within 21 days from the day on which the Abatement Notice was served. The grounds of appeal are laid down in the Statutory Nuisance (Appeals) Regulations 1995 SI 1995/2644. The grounds are as follows:

1   the Abatement Notice is not justified by s 80 of the EPA 1990 – the appellant would be arguing that the matter did not constitute a statutory nuisance;

2   the Abatement Notice is defective or contains an error;

3   the authority has unreasonably refused to accept compliance with alternative requirements, or that the requirements laid down in the Abatement Notice are unreasonable or unnecessary;

4   the period(s) for compliance in the notice is not reasonably sufficient for the purpose;

5   there has been an error in the service of the notice – for example, the notice has been served on the wrong person. An appeal may also be made if the appellant argues that it is 'equitable' for the notice to be served on some other person, either *instead of* the appellant or *as well as* him. Whether the wrong person has been served will be determined by reference to s 80(2);

6   the best practicable means were used to prevent or counteract the effect of a nuisance from trade or business premises or for a noise nuisance under s 79(1)(ga) that the best practicable means were used to prevent or counteract the noise from or caused by a vehicle, machinery or equipment being used for industrial or trade purposes;

7   in relation to a nuisance under s 79(1)(g), or (ga), the requirements imposed by the Abatement Notice are more onerous than the requirements which may have been determined by means of other noise controls under the COPA 1974;

8   in relation to a nuisance under s 89(1)(ga) (noise emitted from or caused by vehicles, machinery or equipment) the requirements imposed by the Abatement Notice are more onerous than the requirements of any condition of a consent given under the NSNA 1993 (provisions relating to loudspeakers in streets or on roads).

The magistrates' court has wide powers when dealing with appeals against Abatement Notices. It can:

(a) correct any procedural defect in the notice, quash the notice or vary the notice;

(b) dismiss the appeal;

(c) make such order as it thinks fit regarding:

  • any works which need to be carried out and the contribution to be made by any person to the cost of the work; or

- the proportion of expenses that a local authority may recover from the appellant and from any other person.

8.7.1 Effect of an appeal upon an Abatement Notice

In general, and provided the notice is appropriately worded by the relevant local authority, the lodging of an appeal will not suspend the Abatement Notice and the person served with the notice will still be required to comply with the conditions of the notice This is particularly so where the nuisance to which the Abatement Notice relates is either injurious to health or likely to be of such a limited duration that suspension of the notice would render it of no practical effect. However, this should be clearly stated in the notice. This general provision does not apply in the following circumstances:

(a) where compliance with the Abatement Notice would involve any person in expenditure or the carrying out of works before the hearing of the appeal and the works or cost would be out of proportion in relation to the expected public benefit;

(b) in the case of a nuisance under s 79(1)(g) or (ga) of the EPA 1990 the noise to which the Abatement Notice relates is noise necessarily caused in the course of the performance of some duty imposed by law on the appellant.

These provisions are to be found in the Statutory Nuisance (Appeals) Regulations 1995 SI 1995/2644.

8.7.2 Duration of an Abatement Notice

Unless it is otherwise stated, an Abatement Notice is of unlimited duration. In *Wellingborough DC v Gordon* (1991), the defendant, Mr Gordon was served an Abatement Notice in 1985 in respect of a noise nuisance. Three years later in 1988 the defendant held a birthday party to which the police intervened in the early hours of the morning requesting that the volume of the music was turned down. The district council prosecuted Mr Gordon for breach of the Abatement Notice served in 1985. The magistrates found the defendant not guilty, but on appeal the High Court held that the Abatement Notice was still valid. Interestingly, in this case there had been no complaints about the noise levels in 1988 and the High Court acknowledged that this was an isolated incident but in their view these factors did not constitute a reasonable excuse for breaching the original notice.

8.8 Non-compliance with an Abatement Notice

Section 80(4) establishes that it is a criminal offence for a person served with an Abatement Notice either to contravene or fail to comply with any requirement or prohibition imposed by the notice, without reasonable excuse.

If an Abatement Notice is not complied with, the authority that has issued the notice has three options:

(a) abate the nuisance;

(b) institute summary proceedings; or

(c) take proceedings for an injunction in the High Court.

8.8.1 The authority can abate the nuisance

The authority can abate the nuisance and do whatever may be necessary in execution of the notice (s 81(3)). A typical example of this is where audio-equipment is removed to abate a noise nuisance. The authority can take this course of action irrespective of whether they take proceedings for non-compliance. In the event that the authority does take action either to abate the nuisance or prevent it happening, then it can, by virtue of s 81(4), recover any expenses reasonably incurred. This would normally be from the person whose acts or omissions caused the nuisance. If that person is the owner of the premises, the expenses can be recovered from any person who is for the time being the owner of them. This would cover situations where, for instance, a previous owner caused a nuisance, but the present owner could be made responsible for the reasonable expenses incurred by the authority. Should the matter of cost recovery go before the court, the court has the power to apportion the expenses between persons whose acts (or omissions) caused the nuisance, in a manner that the court considers fair and reasonable.

The NSNA 1993 provides additional assistance to the local authorities in the form of a newly inserted s 81(a) of the EPA 1990, which enables the local authority serving a notice to recover costs, to make a charge on the premises owned by the person in default.

8.8.2 The authority can institute summary proceedings

If a person fails to comply with an Abatement Notice and commits an offence under s 80(4), the authority can only institute proceedings in the magistrates' court. The penalty for nuisance offences (see s 80(5) and s 80(6)) depends on whether the nuisance has occurred on industrial, trade or business premises. For nuisances arising on non-industrial, trade or business premises, the maximum penalty is £5,000 plus a further £500 for each day that the offence continues after the conviction. However, where the nuisance occurs on industrial, trade or business premises the maximum fine is £20,000 (but no additional daily fines can be made). The magistrates also have a discretion to make a compensation order of up to £5,000.

8.8.3 The authority can take proceedings in the High Court

The third option available to the authority against a person who fails to comply or contravenes with an Abatement Notice is to take proceedings in the High Court (s 81(5) of the EPA 1990). This option is available if the authority is of the view that proceedings in the magistrates' court (under s 80(4)) would afford an inadequate remedy. The aim would be to obtain an injunction to secure the abatement, prohibition or restriction of the statutory nuisance. The authority can take this course of action at any time after service of an Abatement Notice, even if summary proceedings have not been concluded (see *Hammersmith London BC v Magnum Automated Forecourts Ltd* [1978] 1 WLR 50). Failure to comply with an injunction may result in a prison sentence. In *Bristol CC v Huggins* (1995), Mr Huggins was jailed for three months for breaching an injunction which was obtained by Bristol City Council after two prosecutions under the EPA 1990 failed. The circumstances surrounding the application for an injunction must be sufficiently serious otherwise there is little prospect of the High Court exercising its discretion to grant the remedy.

8.9 Defences against non-compliance with an Abatement Notice

Any person who contravenes or fails to comply with the terms of an Abatement Notice, without reasonable excuse, is guilty of an offence (s 80(4)). However, s 80(7) provides a defence of best practicable means. Subject to certain exceptions, it will be a defence to prove that the best practicable means were used to prevent or counteract the effects of the nuisance. Section 80(4) provides that it will only be an offence to contravene or to fail to comply with the requirements of an Abatement Notice provided the defendant does not have a reasonable excuse.

8.9.1 What is meant by 'reasonable excuse'?

The EPA 1990 does not define 'reasonable excuse'. The test laid down by the courts appears to be an objective one. That is whether a reasonable person would consider the excuse consistent with a reasonable standard of conduct. Therefore what constitutes reasonable excuse will be a matter of fact. In the case of *Saddleworth Urban Development Corp v Aggregate and Sand* (1970) it was held that lack of finance could not constitute a reasonable excuse.

Similarly, in *Wellingborough BC v Gordon* [1993] Env LR 218, the court rejected a submission that there was a 'reasonable excuse' based on the length of time (three years) between service of the Abatement Notice and its breach. Neither is there a 'reasonable excuse' based on the argument that a common law action on identical facts would fail.

The alleged reasonable excuse must relate specifically to a problem encountered in attempting to comply with the Abatement Notice. The 'reasonable excuse' element of the offence under s 80(4) of the EPA 1990 cannot be used as the means to challenge the grounds upon which the Abatement Notice was served. Challenges to Abatement Notices are best addressed through the appeal process (see *AMEC Building Ltd v London Borough of Camden* [1997] Env LR 330).

If the defendant produces evidence to support its submission that the defendant had a reasonable excuse for carrying on the activity alleged to constitute a statutory nuisance the local authority must prove, beyond reasonable doubt, that the activity was not reasonable (see *Polychronakis v Richards and Jerrom Ltd* [1998] Env LR 346).

8.9.2 The 'best practicable means' defence

Section 80(7) provides the defence that the best practicable means were used to prevent or counteract the nuisance. The defendant must be able to establish the defence on the balance of probabilities (that is, more likely than not) rather than beyond reasonable doubt. The definition provided in s 79(9) of the EPA 1990 states that best practicable means is to be interpreted by reference to the following provisions:

(a) practicable means reasonably practicable having regard among other things to:
- local conditions and circumstances;
- the current state of technical knowledge; and
- the financial implications;

(b) the means to be employed include:
- the design, installation, maintenance and manner and periods of operation of plant and machinery; and
- the design, construction and maintenance of buildings and structures;

(c) the test is to apply only so far as compatible with any:
- duty imposed by law;
- safety and safe working conditions; and
- exigencies of any emergency or unforeseeable circumstances.

In circumstances where a Code of Practice under s 71 of the COPA 1974 (noise minimisation) is applicable, regard must be given to the guidance given in the code.

8.9.3 Limitations to the 'best practicable means' defence

The 'best practicable means' defence is, however, only available where the nuisance arises on industrial trade or business premises. Section 80(8) lists its availability as follows:

(a) in the case of nuisances (a), (d), (e), (f) or (g) the defence is only available if the nuisance occurs on industrial, trade or business premises;

(b) if the nuisance falls under category (ga) then the defence is generally not available unless the noise is emitted from or caused by a vehicle, machinery or equipment being used for industrial, trade or business purposes;

(c) in the case of smoke emitted from premises (79(1)(b)) the defence of best practicable means is not available except where the smoke is emitted from a chimney;

(d) the defence of best practicable means is not available at all in relation to the nuisances under s 79(1)(c) and (h).

8.9.4 What is best practical means in practice?

The onus is on the company or business seeking to rely on the defence to prove that the best practicable means were employed. The issue of the costs of employing best practical means and the effect on profitability was considered in *Wivenhoe Port v Colchester BC* (1985). The port authority argued that it had used the best practicable means but was not able to use certain dust arrestment equipment because of the cost and impact on profitability. The court accepted that the profitability of the defendant was a relevant factor to be taken into account, but went on to say that the company needed to show, on the balance of probabilities, that the operation would go from profit to loss, or become so uneconomical that the company could not profitably continue if the dust machinery was used.

In *Manley v New Forest DC* (unreported, 29 July 1999), it was established that the defendant dog breeder was already using best practicable means to minimise noise at the time an Abatement Notice was served on him. The High Court reversed the decision of the Crown Court that best practicable means could be established by the defendant agreeing to relocate his business to a non-residential area. The court held that relocation in such circumstances was going beyond the purpose of the statutory nuisance controls contained in Pt III of the EPA 1990.

8.9.5 Special defences

Special defences exist regarding noise and other nuisances in regard to (i) construction sites, and (ii) noise abatement zones (see Chapter 9 – Noise).

8.10 Action by citizens

Section 82 of the EPA 1990 provides that any person aggrieved by a statutory nuisance has the right to complain to the magistrates' court in order to obtain a court order to bring the nuisance to an end. Failure to comply with a court order under the section is an offence. Section 82 enables any person to bypass the local authority statutory nuisance process.

The provision enables any person who is aggrieved by the nuisance to commence proceedings which are likely to be cheaper and quicker than a common law private nuisance action. There is no requirement that the complainant is an occupier of premises or a neighbour of adjoining premises.

The phrase 'person aggrieved' has appeared in various other statutes and has been widely interpreted by the courts. In *AG (Gambia) v N'Jie* (1961), Lord Denning asserted that the words 'person aggrieved' should not be subjected to a restrictive interpretation. However, he went on to say that the words:

> ... do not include, of course, a mere busybody who is interfering in things which do not concern him; but they do include a person who has a genuine grievance because an order has been made which prejudicially affects his interests.

It seems, therefore, that a person must at least be in some way prejudicially affected by the alleged nuisance. More recently, in *Sandwell Metropolitan BC v Bujok* (1990), a council tenant alleged that the defective state of her council house gave rise to a statutory nuisance under the PHA 1936. Mrs Bujok was entitled to bring proceedings against the council as a person whose health, and that of her family, was prejudicially affected by the premises. Section 82 is of particular value when the person concerned is complaining about a statutory nuisance created by a local authority and has been useful in enabling people to bring actions against the local authority in respect of council houses and premises which are prejudicial to health or a nuisance. The number of these cases has been increasing in recent years. The fact that the local authorities act as the statutory bodies responsible for controlling statutory nuisances does not provide them with any immunity against actions against them, as can be seen in the *Sandwell* case.

Aggrieved persons can only commence proceedings to secure the abatement of an existing nuisance or its recurrence. They cannot, under these provisions, bring an action to prevent a statutory nuisance, such as a potentially noisy party, since the magistrates' court, unlike the local authority, does not have anticipatory powers.

8.10.1 Section 82 proceedings

When a person complains to the magistrates' court, then there is a requirement that the defendant is informed, in writing, of the matter complained of and that such action is going to be taken. For noise nuisances, the complainant must give three days' notice but the period of notice is 21 days in respect of the other nuisances. Before taking action in proceedings brought under s 82, the magistrates must be satisfied that one of the following conditions exists:

(a) the alleged nuisance exists; or

(b) an abated nuisance is likely to recur on the same premises, or in the same street.

The court can make the following orders:

(a) requiring the defendant to abate the nuisance within a specified time and to carry out any works necessary for that purpose;

(b) prohibiting a recurrence of the nuisance and requiring the defendant to carry out any necessary works to prevent the recurrence. A time period for carrying out such works will be specified in the order;

(c) impose a fine of up to £5,000;

(d) order the relevant local authority to do anything which the convicted person was required to do by the court order, after it has given the authority the opportunity to be heard.

Where the nuisance is such as to render premises unfit for human habitation, the court can prohibit the use of the premises for human habitation until the court is satisfied that the premises have been made fit for such a purpose.

Failure to comply with a nuisance order from the magistrates is an offence and can result in a fine of up to £5,000 (plus £500 for each day that the offence continues).

STATUTORY NUISANCE

Prejudicial to health or a nuisance

Certain matters contained in s 79 of the EPA 1990 may constitute statutory nuisances if they are prejudicial to health or a nuisance. Prejudicial to health is defined as 'injurious or likely to cause injury'. The nuisance limb is equated with common law nuisance, but the courts have tended to require demonstration that the nuisance materially affects personal comfort.

Responsibilities of the local authorities

Local authorities are under a duty to inspect their areas and also to respond to complaints concerning statutory nuisances. If a local authority is satisfied that a statutory nuisance exists or is likely to occur or recur, it must serve an Abatement Notice.

The Abatement Notice must clearly state requirements for abating the nuisance, works required and time for compliance. Failure to comply with an Abatement Notice is a criminal offence.

Right of appeal

A right of appeal against the Abatement Notice exists to the magistrates' court. The appeal must be brought within 21 days of service of the notice (s 80(3)) on the grounds stated in Statutory Nuisance (Appeals) Regulations 1995.

Non-compliance

Non-compliance with an Abatement Notice is an offence (s 80(4)).

A local authority can:

(a) abate the nuisance themselves and recover costs;

(b) commence summary proceedings in the magistrates' court for failure to comply with the notice;

(c) take proceedings in the High Court for an injunction on the belief that (a) and (b) will not provide a sufficient remedy.

Action by citizens

Section 82 provides that a person aggrieved by a statutory nuisance may complain directly to the magistrates' court.

CHAPTER 9

NOISE POLLUTION

9.1 The problem of noise pollution

9.1.1 Introduction

Noise is a natural consequence of everything that we do. It forms part of our everyday background and for the most part we just accept it or at least tolerate it. Nevertheless, noise has the capacity to cause conflict between those who are generating it and those who hear it but do not wish to. Indeed, the Wilson Committee (Wilson, 1963) recognised the subjective and conflictual nature of the problem when it defined noise as 'sound which is undesired by the recipient'.

Noise regulation poses its own distinctive problems:

(a) noise is transient and mostly it is a source of temporary irritation;

(b) noise is not inherently dangerous. It does not accumulate in our bodies or the wider environment. It is not toxic to man and the environment as many chemical substances are;

(c) the impact of noise on humans is highly subjective. Although it is possible to measure the level at which noise begins to damage hearing the impact of less damaging sound is problematic. The differential impact of noise upon humans varies with the time of day and the susceptibility of the individual. Unwanted noise at night which disturbs sleep is a serious issue;

(d) it may be difficult to disentangle offending 'noises' from background noises or the general noise level in the area;

(e) how should regulatory controls tackle the problem? Should controls 'bite' at (i) the immediate point of noise production (for example, motor vehicle exhaust systems and construction site noise), (ii) some point between the noise producer and the noise recipient (for example, construction of a noise barrier, either internally via sound insulation, or externally via a 'bund' to deflect noise away from the recipient), or the point at which the noise reaches the recipient's property (for example, installation of double glazing);

(f) what types of regulatory controls should be employed? The following list indicates some of the choices available: (i) product standards (noise emission limits applying to lawnmowers, car exhaust systems, etc), (ii) licence based controls (for example, Integrated Pollution Prevention and Control (IPPC) installations and Health and Safety at Work controls in factories), (iii) reactive controls (for example, statutory nuisance), (iv) public order controls (Crime and Disorder Act 1998), and (v) separation controls (for example, planning controls providing geographical separation between incompatible land uses);

(g) noise is regulated by a patchwork of fragmented controls.

In most circumstances unwanted noises will not cause people to complain, but there are clearly circumstances where either the volume, duration or repetition (or all three) will cause sufficient aggravation to cause the recipient of the unwanted noise intrusion to take legal action, or in some instances resort to more dramatic measures. Most people are familiar with complaints between neighbours concerning excessive noise from music systems, dogs barking or the constant drone of lawnmowers, but these complaints rarely lead to legal proceedings. However, people are increasingly more concerned about noise levels and neighbourhood noise in particular. They are also more aware of the effects that noise can have upon them and are consequently more likely to complain. This is clearly borne out by statistics, some of which are shown later.

Modern industrial society generates an enormous quantity of noise and it is bound to increase as more and more aeroplanes arrive and depart at airports and as more and more cars take to the roads. There are also more opportunities for creating noise in a society which relies heavily upon domestic appliances (the noisy washing machine and lawnmower). Stereo and audio equipment have become more sophisticated, more powerful, more affordable and more commonplace and people are able to play music at high volumes. The dawn of the ghettoblaster and the personal stereo means that loud music is something which frequently occurs in the street as well as in the home.

Although there is a general assumption that rural areas are quieter they are not without their own noise problems. Heavy machinery used in farming can also be a source of aggravation to local residents (see *Chapman v Gosberton Farm Produce* (1993), below). Many people who move out of the inner cities and urban areas to the country are surprised at the lack of peace and quiet that they had envisaged.

9.2 Neighbourhood noise

Neighbourhood noise, defined for the purposes of this text as the noise inside and outside homes is a growing area of concern. In a 1990 survey carried out by the Building Research Establishment (BRE) of 1,000 dwellings, it was found that 56% were exposed to daytime noise levels exceeding the World Health Organisation's then recommended day time level of 55dB (defining day as 7 am–12 pm . The recommended day time and night time levels have now been reduced to 45dB and 35dB respectively), above which noise levels cause annoyance. In a BRE survey in November 1991, it was also found that 30% of people had their home life spoilt to some extent by noise and that 1% had their home life totally spoilt.

Neighbourhood noise complaints constitute the greatest source of noise complaints in England and Wales. Research from the University of Salford's Department of Housing and Environmental Health indicates that some 25% of complaints to local authorities relate to general household noise. The diagram (Figure 1) shows that over 60% of noise complaints received by Local Authority Environmental health officers came from domestic sources.

Figure 1

Noise complaints received by environmental health officers by source of noise: 1989/90 (England and Wales)

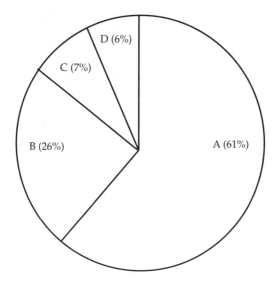

A	Domestic Premises
B	Industrial & Commercial Premises
C	Roadworks Construction & Demolition
D	Other

Note:
1 Percentages are based on numbers of complaints per million people
2 Road and air traffic and other sources of noise not covered by COPA 1974

Source: IEHO

The number of complaints about neighbourhood noise has increased in recent years (see Figure 2). The number of noise related complaints, excluding road traffic and aircraft noise, received by Local Authority environmental health departments has rocketed from approximately 55,000 in 1980 to 242,000 in 1997. However, not everybody suffering a noise nuisance will necessarily complain. According to research carried out by the BRE between 60% and 70% of people who endure noise from neighbours never complain and only about 16% contact an Environmental Health Officer.

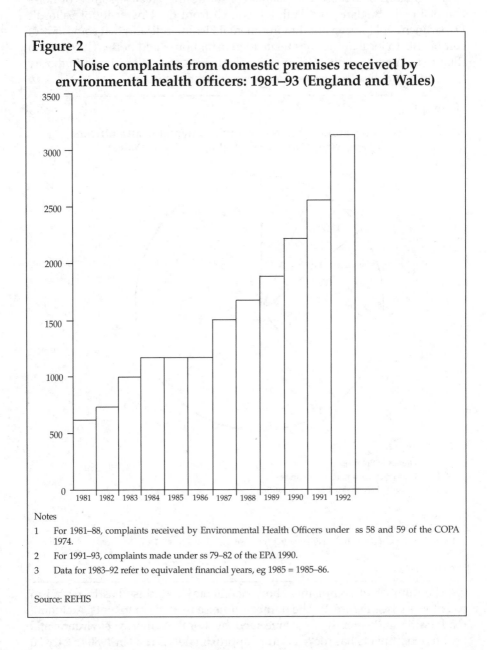

Figure 2

Noise complaints from domestic premises received by environmental health officers: 1981–93 (England and Wales)

Notes

1   For 1981–88, complaints received by Environmental Health Officers under ss 58 and 59 of the COPA 1974.

2   For 1991–93, complaints made under ss 79–82 of the EPA 1990.

3   Data for 1983–92 refer to equivalent financial years, eg 1985 = 1985–86.

Source: REHIS

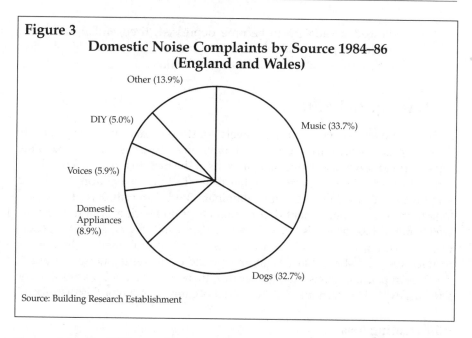

Figure 3

**Domestic Noise Complaints by Source 1984–86
(England and Wales)**

Other (13.9%)

DIY (5.0%)

Music (33.7%)

Voices (5.9%)

Domestic
Appliances
(8.9%)

Dogs (32.7%)

Source: Building Research Establishment

Research by the BRE reveals that over two-thirds of noise complaints concern loud music or dogs barking. Figure 3 shows the breakdown of domestic noise complaints by source over the period 1984–86 in England and Wales.

In 1993 the BRE carried out a research exercise, through a discussion group, to establish how people at home react to environmental noise, and to interpret what they mean when they describe their reaction to noise (BRE, *Effects of Environmental Noise on People at Home*, 1993).

The participants in the groups were exposed to a variety of noises. It was found that the reactions of people were different depending on factors such as age, sex, personality, lifestyle and occupational status. The BRE categorised three basic levels of reaction.

Level 1 – Where the noise began or was relatively quiet, typically people ignored the noise, became curious as to its source where this was not apparent, or some became mildly irritated.

Level 2 – Where the noise continued or became louder some of the participants, mostly men, displayed anger, bitterness and annoyance towards the creator of the noise. Other participants, mostly women, had a tendency to suppress their feelings and direct them inwards, causing them to feel tense, frustrated and anxious.

Level 3 – Where the noise continued for an even longer period of time or was very loud or emotive, the participants displayed the strongest reactions of all. Those who became angry at Level 2 tended to talk of hatred and hostility and some even spoke of murder or revenge. The second group that had directed their feelings inwards at Level 2 showed a capacity to become depressed, tired and upset. Some spoke of guilt and shame. A number also spoke of physical symptoms such as headaches and migraine.

9.3 Damage to health

Although unwanted noise or excessively loud noise may be aggravating to those who do not wish to hear it, does it have any harmful effect? Unlike other types of pollution, noise is transient, it exists at the time that it is generated and cannot be said to have a permanent harmful effect on the environment in the same way that toxic wastes can contaminate land. Nevertheless, it can have long term or even permanent detrimental effect on hearing, health or mental well being. CS Kerse in his book *The Law Relating to Noise* notes that exposure to excessive noise can result in a range of physiological effects. Quoting Dr Samuel Rosen he states that: 'At an unexpected or unwanted noise, the pupils dilate, skin pales, mucous membranes dry; there are intestinal spasms and the adrenals explode secretions. The biological organism, in a word, is disturbed.'

9.3.1 Hearing loss

Noise can cause both temporary and permanent hearing loss. Temporary loss of hearing is typified by either sounds being perceived as muffled or a ringing in the ears. Once the exposure to the noise has ended, hearing should return to normal after about forty-five minutes. Repeated exposure to noise might prevent the ear from recovering so readily and may cause permanent hearing loss.

Excessive levels of noise continued over a sustained period can cause serious damage to hearing and may, as stated above, even cause hearing loss (noise induced hearing loss). There are many occupations that expose workers to enough loud noise to cause this type of hearing loss. Equally, deafness may occur as a result of a very sudden and loud noise.

9.3.2 Loss of sleep

Loss of sleep and the associated health problems arising from loss of sleep is a more common complaint. Aeroplane noise in particular has a much more significant impact on sleep loss than do other noises. Residents living close to major airports, notably Heathrow, will testify to this particular problem. Loss of sleep can result in a person becoming irritable, they may find it difficult to concentrate and it may in turn result in a diminution of physical well being and health.

9.3.3 Discomfort

Unwanted noise is always likely to irritate after continued periods of time, however, it is also the case that it may cause actual physical discomfort. Apart from causing a headache, noise may result in feelings of severe discomfort such as nausea.

9.3.4 Psychological problems

Noise may also cause serious mental problems. In one particular case (*Middlesborough CC v Stevens* (1993)) the continuous playing of the song *I Will Always Love You* recorded by Whitney Houston was enough to cause the neighbour to suffer what was described as 'psychological torture'. Even if noise does not cause a particular physical problem, it can, if it continues over a long period of time or at anti-social hours, cause the listener to become aggravated, weary and aggressive. In short it can affect the quality of life.

9.4 Problems regarding the legal regulation of noise

Whilst excessive or continued levels of noise may be unacceptable, certain levels of noise must be accepted in order that modern society can function. Construction sites for instance generate a significant amount of noise from mobile plant, pneumatic drills, etc and cause many local residents to complain. Yet we, nevertheless, expect and, in most instances, welcome new developments, which can create jobs and which can enhance towns and cities. All activities and processes generate noise and we all expect to be able to continue those activities without interference from others. This raises certain problems regarding the legal regulation of noise, in that there will necessarily be a need to achieve a balance between the rights of individuals, groups or companies to make noise and the rights of others not to suffer at their expense. This weighing of considerations is familiar in the common law of nuisance where the courts have to consider whether what is complained of is unreasonable.

9.4.1 The subjectivity of noise problems

The other problematic feature of controlling noise is that it is a particularly subjective issue. What amounts to intolerable noise for one person may be disregarded or even considered desirable by others. Pop concerts, raves and parties are typical examples. Some people will be able to accept certain levels of noise, whereas others may suffer in terms of their mental or physical health as a consequence of that same noise. The sensitivity of hearing varies from person to person and other factors such as age can play a large part in determining responses. Noise may be problematic, not only in relation to its volume, but also in regard to its ability to irritate the recipient. Intermittent, disturbing, and repetitive noises whilst not inherently dangerous may cause significant annoyance and emotional disturbance.

In October 1994 the Department of Environment established a Noise Working Party to review the effectiveness of neighbour noise controls contained in Pt III of the Environmental Protection Act (EPA) 1990 (the statutory nuisance controls discussed below). The working party made the following recommendations, some of which have been incorporated into the Noise Act (NA) 1996:

(a) good practice guidance should be made available to local authorities on the management of noise services;

(b) local authorities should be encouraged to provide information to residents about their authority's noise complaints service. They should promote public awareness of neighbour noise issues;

(c) there should be general guidance on the sorts of noise problems that might constitute a statutory nuisance;

(d) local authorities should be able to respond to public complaints outside working hours;

(e) there should be more streamlined arrangements in relation to obtaining warrants to enter premises, to temporarily confiscate noise making equipment, or to silence intruder alarms;

(f) a Code of Practice should be issued to the police and to local authorities to encourage effective local arrangements for dealing with noise complaints;

(g) there should be specific power of temporary confiscation of noise making equipment and local authorities should be able to levy an administrative charge for its return. Additionally, local authorities should be able to seek permanent confiscation of noise making equipment following prosecution;

(h) there should be a separate criminal offence in relation to night time noise disturbances.

9.5 The nature of legal controls

Traditionally, noise problems have been addressed through the common law, principally by means of private nuisance actions. However, in more recent times legislation has been introduced which attempts to control noise levels. There are various different ways in which legislation seeks to control the level of noise. In general, measures seek to control the level of noise emissions, either through product specifications or preventative action by means of prior consents. Alternatively, adverse levels of noise can be controlled through mechanisms which enable regulatory authorities to take measures to abate noise nuisances.

In the first instance, legislation exists to set precise noise emission levels for particular classes of machinery and vehicles and, in addition, there are a number of Codes of Practice which set out recommended noise levels for the likes of intruder alarms and ice cream van chimes. Predicted noise from construction works can be regulated in advance by means of a noise consent issued by a local authority (under the provisions of the Control of Pollution Act (COPA) 1974 (see 9.12, below, on specific noise controls).

The other mechanism for dealing with noise pollution is through a system of sanctions. In some instances, noise can be controlled where it constitutes a statutory nuisance. Local authorities have various powers which enable them to abate noise nuisances and bring criminal proceedings if the person responsible for the noise nuisance ignores the Abatement Notice. Failure to comply with an Abatement Notice is a criminal offence. The enactment of the NA 1996 provides for immediate sanctions in the form of on the spot fines, designed to bring night time noise nuisances to an immediate end. The provisions of the NA 1996 and the statutory nuisance provisions under the EPA 1990 are considered below.

In addition to these legal measures, the levels of noise can to some extent be controlled in the first instance through good planning which takes account of the potential noise generation of developments at the planning stage. Planning authorities are in fact required to consider the problems of noise when taking planning decisions in order to avoid noise nuisances occurring. Planning Policy Guidance Note 24 gives guidance to local authorities on the use of their planning powers to minimise the adverse impact of noise.

9.6 Measuring noise

Despite the fact that responses to different noises vary widely it is possible to objectively measure sound. Sound can be measured either in Hertz (Hz) which measures the frequency of sound (the number of pressure variations per second). Sound can also be measured in decibels.

The decibel (dB(A)) measure is more widely used because it provides a better measure of the response of the human ear to loudness as the ear responds to changes in the noise level. The decibel is effectively a logarithmic scale with 0 dB corresponding to the quietest audible sound (the threshold of hearing) whilst 140 dB represents a sound at which pain would probably occur. As stated above the usual form of measurement is dB(A) where the 'A' refers to the frequency weighting used in sound meters, enabling them to effectively mimic human hearing.

The Control of Noise (Measurements and Registers) Regulations 1976 SI 1976/37 prescribes the decibel as the method for measuring noise in relation to the legal controls discussed in this chapter. In addition they also provide on how noise levels can be calculated when it is not possible to measurement.

...e courts are familiar with the use of decibels as measurements of noise although they will often seek a further description of the noise from the complainant. In *Halsey v Esso Petroleum Co Ltd* (1961) the use of decibels was affirmed by the court and an indication was given as to the effect of different levels of noise:

> Between 40 and 60 decibels the noise is moderate, and between 60 and 80 it is loud. Between 80 and 100 it is very loud and from 100 to 120 it is deafening.

9.7 Common law

9.7.1 Nuisance

It is well established that adverse noise can constitute an actionable nuisance at common law. Noise may give rise to either a public nuisance or a private nuisance. In some circumstances it may be both.

In *Halsey v Esso Petroleum Co Ltd* (1961), it was held that a noise nuisance from tanker lorries at night on the public highway was both a public and a private nuisance. However, private nuisance actions are the most common because the impact of a public nuisance must be widely felt if it is to form the basis of a common law action.

9.7.2 Private nuisance

A private nuisance is one which unlawfully interferes with a person's use or enjoyment of land or some right connected with it. In order to bring an action, damage must be suffered. In terms of noise nuisances the damage may be physical since vibrations may result in property damage or may damage hearing. However, it is more likely that a noise nuisance will interfere with a person's enjoyment of property through, for example, loss of sleep. There is no need to establish that the noise complained of is injurious to health to establish that it constitutes a nuisance (*Vanderpant v Mayfair Hotel Co Ltd* (1930)).

In a nuisance action the courts are required to balance the rights of the owner of land to do what he wants against the rights of the owners of neighbouring land to be free from unreasonable interference. This necessarily involves the court dealing with each case on its merits taking into account all the relevant circumstances. The courts have developed a number of general principles and will take into account a number of factors.

9.7.3 Temporary interferences

The nature of the interference will be a significant factor in determining whether an action succeeds. A minor interference may still amount to a nuisance where there is physical damage, either to property or person, whereas in other cases the interference must be *substantial*. In *Walter v Selfe* (1851), the test was said to be whether there was 'an inconvenience materially interfering with the ordinary comfort physically of human existence, not merely according to plain and sober and simple notions amongst the English people'.

With regard to noise nuisances it will clearly, like other nuisances, be a question of degree. It is here that noise can pose particular problems, because noise is often a temporary occurrence. As a general rule the courts have found that a temporary interference is less likely to constitute a nuisance than one which is permanent or occurs regularly. A classic example of this reasoning can be found in the case of *Leeman v Montagu* (1936). Here it was held that the noise from cockerels sounding their dawn chorus was not an actionable nuisance whereas, if the noise from the cockerels had taken place in a residential area for weeks, damages and an injunction may have been granted. However, it is clear that noise which results in loss of a single night's sleep can be a nuisance (*Andreae v Selfridge & Co Ltd* (1938)). In a more recent case brought under the statutory nuisance provisions of the EPA 1990, *East Northamptonshire DC v Fossett* (1994), the defendant F argued that 'nuisance' under the EPA 1990 has its common law meaning and therefore a single isolated instance of noise was not enough since there must be a 'course of action'. This argument was rejected by the Divisional Court which stated that no case had held that excessive noise continuing all night could not amount to a nuisance to neighbouring residences.

The time of day, however, may be a factor for consideration. Noise disturbances during the night are more likely to constitute a nuisance than a noise made during the day.

9.7.4 Locality

It is well known that the courts will take into account the character of an area when determining whether an action is unreasonable and constitutes a nuisance (*Sturges and Bridgman* (1879)). The logical conclusion of this in relation to noise is that in peaceful suburban areas the courts are more likely to regard noise as a nuisance than in built-up industrial areas. However, this does not exclude the possibility of bringing an action in private nuisance in industrial areas nor does the fact that an area is already noisy remove the possibility of success. In *Roskell v Whitworth* (1871) a congregation at a Roman Catholic Church succeeded in obtaining an injunction to restrain the use of a steam hammer in an iron and steel works because it interfered with their prayers and the comfortable enjoyment of the rectory house (see, also, *Rushmer v Polsue and Alfieri Ltd* (1906)).

Since it is a well established principle in the law of nuisance that locality will have a bearing on whether a nuisance action will succeed, to what extent will the grant of planning permission alter the characteristics of a neighbourhood and provide a defence against a nuisance action. In *Gillingham BC v Medway (Chatham) Dock Co* (1992), planning permission had been granted to the Medway port authority for the construction of a port facility on the site of the former Chatham Royal Naval Dockyard. The Royal Naval Dockyard when it was operational had not generated much traffic unlike the new port facility. Local residents complained to the local authority about the noise and other pollution from the round the clock heavy goods vehicle traffic to and from the port. In proceedings against the port authority the council sought to restrain the passage of the heavy goods vehicles through the neighbourhood at night on the grounds that it constituted a public nuisance.

The court held that the grant of planning permission could alter the character of the area and may have the effect of rendering 'innocent activities which prior to the change would have been an actionable nuisance'. It was held accordingly that the noise from the traffic was not an actionable nuisance.

However this ruling has since been considered by the Court of Appeal in *Wheeler v JJ Saunders Ltd* (1995). Here planning permission was granted for two pig-weaning houses. An action in private nuisance was brought because of the smell generated by the pigs. The defendants in the action sought to rely on the *Gillingham* case by arguing that the grant of planning permission for the pig houses meant there could not be an actionable nuisance. This argument was rejected by the Court of Appeal which held that the grant of planning permission was no defence to an action in nuisance. Staughton LJ was clear that:

> ... the court should be slow to acquiesce in the extinction of private rights without compensation as a result of administrative decisions which could not be appealed and were difficult to challenge.

9.7.5 Nature of the noise generating activity

The courts have also demonstrated some reluctance to interfere with noise arising from construction sites. This reflects the principle that the courts must have regard to the nature and desirability of the operation that is causing the alleged nuisance. In *Andreae v Selfridge* (1938) the defendant company was developing a site close to the plaintiff's hotel. It was held that if operations of this particular nature are reasonably carried out, and all proper steps are taken to ensure that no undue inconvenience is caused to neighbours then the neighbours must put up with the noise. However, in *De Keyser's Hotel Ltd v Spicer Bros Ltd* (1914) it was held that the defendant's building operations constituted a nuisance because they were not carried out in a reasonable and proper manner. The case was brought by the hotel on the grounds that the noise from the construction was so loud that the guests at the hotel and after-dinner speakers were unable to make themselves heard!

However, it appears that the courts have effectively recognised that building operations cannot happen without generating noise and that they are usually only short lived operations where the benefits outweigh the temporary discomforts. Legislation now exists to control the noise from construction sites (ss 60 and 61 of the COPA 1974), although it is still possible to bring a private action in nuisance.

9.7.6 Sensitivity of the claimant

It is well established that for an interference to be actionable it must be one which affects an ordinary person and not one who is abnormally sensitive. In *Robinson v Kilvert* (1889), in which the plaintiff claimed that heat from the defendant's property which was situated in the basement, was having an adverse effect on the brown paper stored in his premises. It was held that there was no actionable nuisance because:

> ... a man who carries on an exceptionally delicate trade cannot complain because it is injured by his neighbour doing something lawful on his property, if it is something which would not injure anything but an exceptionally delicate trade.

The rationale behind this principle is consistent with the law of nuisance. An example of abnormal sensitivity was given in *Heath v The Brighton Corp* (1908). In this case the vicar of a church sought an injunction to restrain the noise from the defendant's power station. The vicar failed because the noise was neither interrupting services nor had it affected attendance at church, it merely irritated the vicar. Therefore it appears to follow that there can no be regard to a claimant who has an acute sense of hearing.

9.7.7 Intent of the parties

Finally in relation to noise nuisances the courts have been willing to take into account the malicious intent of the parties. In *Hollywood Silver Fox Farm Ltd v Emmett* (1936), the court granted an injunction to the plaintiff which restrained his neighbour from firing his guns during breeding time. The guns were fired by the defendant in spite, following an argument between the defendant and the plaintiff. Therefore, if the defendant's noise is made with the intention of causing annoyance to his neighbour, then he may be liable even if the interference would not amount to a nuisance if done in the ordinary and reasonable use of property. A good example of this occurred in *Christie v Davey* (1893). The defendant's intentional banging of trays on a party wall in retaliation for the noise caused by the neighbour's musical sessions was held to constitute an nuisance.

9.7.8 Remedies

The main remedies available in private nuisance actions are:

(a) abatement;

(b) injunction;

(c) damages.

The advantage of common law actions, despite the problems noted, is that they enable claimants to seek damages. If the intention of the claimant is to bring an end to the noise problem a swifter and cheaper remedy is to ask a local authority to commence proceedings under the statutory nuisance provisions of the EPA 1990.

9.7.9 An interest in land

There are several problems in bringing an action in private nuisance and traditionally it has been necessary to demonstrate that the claimant has an interest in land.

The creator of the relevant nuisance is the person who is liable, and unlike the claimant does not need to have a proprietary interest in land where the nuisance arises. The occupier of the property from which the nuisance emanates will normally also be liable, although usually the creator of the nuisance and the occupier will be the same person (see *Sedleigh-Denfield v O'Callaghen* (1940)). A landlord will only be liable for any nuisance which emanates from premises where such a state of affairs is the ordinary and necessary consequences of granting the lease (see *Tetley v Chitty* (1986)).

9.7.10 Public nuisance

A public nuisance is defined as an unlawful act or omission which materially affects the reasonable comfort and convenience of a class of Her Majesty's subjects who come within the sphere or neighbourhood of its operation. Unlike private nuisance, there is no need to prove any interest in land.

In *AG v PYA Quarries Ltd* (1957), it was held that it is a question of fact whether a sufficiently large enough group of people have been affected for the nuisance to be called public.

A public nuisance is both a tort and a criminal offence and the case is brought by the Attorney General (or an individual with the consent of the Attorney General and in his name), who may seek an injunction to prevent a public nuisance.

For a private claimant to seek damages in a case of public nuisance, he must prove that he has suffered some special damage over and above that suffered by the general public. It is not necessary for the claimant to have an interest in land. Damages may be available to compensate for personal injury and for economic loss from the responsible party. As in private nuisance, an action may be brought against the creator of the nuisance, the occupier of premises and/or the landlord.

In relation to noise problems, public nuisance actions are rare.

9.7.11 The advantages and disadvantages of bringing an action in nuisance

Given the very nature of the law of nuisance and the weighing of considerations by the court it will not always be easy to predict the likely outcome of a case. In addition, proceedings often take a very long time (which in noise disputes may often mean that the noise nuisance continues unabated) and are often very expensive.

Despite the disadvantages and problems of bringing a successful action in nuisance there are a number of distinct advantages. On the one hand, the civil courts have the ability to award unlimited damages and the range of matters which can be complained of and which may constitute a nuisance is very wide.

9.8 Contract and licensing

An individual may also be able to secure a remedy through a contract. A good example would be a tenancy agreement whereby a claimant may bring an action based upon rights and covenants contained in a tenancy agreement. In any landlord and tenant relationship there is an implied (although it may also be expressly stated) covenant for the quiet enjoyment of the land, and this can be enforced by either of the parties to the agreement.

In addition it will also be possible for a tenant, or the landlord at a tenants request, to enforce a covenant, such as not to cause a nuisance, against another tenant.

9.8.1 Licensing

Licensing may in some circumstances provide a means of controlling noise. Under s 4 of the Licensing Act 1964, conditions aimed at reducing noise from licensed premises may be attached to the granting of an on-licence. The Local Government (Miscellaneous Provisions) Act 1982 (in London the provisions are contained in the London Government Act 1963) provide for the licensing of music and dancing in public. Breach of a licence condition or failing to obtain a licence may result in a fine of up to £20,000 or six months' imprisonment on summary conviction. Outside London the provisions only relate to indoor events. Whether an activity is public in this context depends upon whether any member of the public may participate, regardless of whether any payment is required.

The Private Places of Entertainment (Licensing) Act 1967 established similar controls in relation to private events promoted for private gain, however for the provisions of this Act to apply they must be adopted by the relevant local authority.

9.9 Statutory controls

The main statutory provisions which relate to noise are as follows:

(a) Land Compensation Act 1973;

(b) Health and Safety at Work Act 1974;

(c) COPA 1974;

(d) Civil Aviation Act 1982;

(e) EPA 1990;

(f) Noise and Statutory Nuisance Act 1993;

(g) Town and Country Planning Act 1990;

(h) NA 1996.

The Health and Safety at Work Act 1974 deals with noise in the workplace, the Land Compensation Act 1973 deals with a local authority's duty to insulate buildings against noise created by public works such as road building and the Civil Aviation Act 1982 deals with noise generated from civil aircraft. These are matters which fall outside the main environmental controls and are not considered in this book. (However, it should be noted that in relation to the Civil Aviation Act 1982 it is not possible to bring an action in either trespass or nuisance in relation to noise generated from the flight of civil aircraft. Noise from civil aircraft is controlled by a separate regime under regulations.)

This chapter will concentrate on the provisions contained in the COPA 1974, the EPA 1990, the Noise and Statutory Nuisance Act 1993 and the NA 1996.

9.9.1 Noise as a statutory nuisance

The provisions in the EPA 1990 relating to noise nuisances were amended by the NSNA 1993. The majority of the new provisions came into force in January 1994. In particular the 1993 Act incorporated a new statutory nuisance into the EPA 1990 at s 79(1)(ga).

9.9.2 Sections 79(1)(g) and (ga) of the EPA 1990

Section 79(1)(g) and (ga) of the EPA 1990 provide that noise can be a statutory nuisance in the following circumstances:

Section 79(1)(g): 'noise emitted from premises so as to be prejudicial to health or a nuisance'; and

Section 79(1)(ga): 'noise that is prejudicial to health or a nuisance and is emitted from or caused by a vehicle, machinery or equipment in a street'.

The EPA 1990 does not provide any particular definition of noise other than to say in s 79 that it includes 'vibration'.

9.9.3 Prejudicial to health or a nuisance?

Before considering the noise statutory nuisances in any detail it is necessary to consider the general provisions relating to statutory nuisance. Although s 79 of the EPA 1990 lists certain states of affairs that may constitute statutory nuisances, they will only be statutory nuisances if they are either prejudicial to health or a nuisance. The definition includes two separate and alternative limbs and it is not necessary to show that a matter is both a nuisance and prejudicial to health. This was affirmed in *Betts v Penge UDC* (1942) where it was held that it is not necessary to show that a matter complained of is prejudicial to health in order for it to constitute a statutory nuisance. The Divisional Court held that it was sufficient to show that the matter (in the case in point the matter concerned the state of premises) was such as to interfere with personal comfort for there to be a statutory nuisance.

(a) Prejudicial to health

Section 79(7) of the EPA 1990 defines prejudicial to health as meaning 'injurious, or likely to cause injury'. This definition includes two limbs, 'injurious to health', that is, actual harm, or 'likely to cause injury', that is, anticipated harm. The definition is the same as that given in the Public Health Act 1936. For a discussion of what is meant by the term 'prejudicial to health', see Chapter 8. However, in the context of noise nuisance it was held in *Southwark London BC v Ince* (1989) that a house which was inadequately insulated against noise, so that noise from a nearby railway adversely affected the occupants, was prejudicial to health.

(b) What is meant by nuisance?

The courts have equated nuisance in this context with common law nuisance, private or public, with the focus primarily on private nuisance therefore involving interference with enjoyment of property. In *National Coal Board v Neath BC* (1976) it was held that the word 'nuisance' meant either a public or a private nuisance at common law. It should also be noted that like the common law nuisance the interference must be with *neighbouring* property (*National Coal Board v Thorne* (1976)).

9.9.4 Noise from premises – s 79(1)(g)

Like all of the statutory nuisances in s 79 of the EPA 1990, noise from premises may only constitute a statutory nuisance if it is either:

(a) noise emitted from premises so as to be *prejudicial to health*; or

(b) noise emitted from premises so as to be a *nuisance*.

This particular statutory nuisance was not included in the Public Health Act 1936 but was drawn from ss 57–59 of the COPA 1974. Under the COPA legislation the term 'premises' was not defined. In *Tower Hamlets LBC v Manzoni* (1984), the court held that the term premises did not include a street and therefore noise from a street could not be controlled under the statutory nuisance provisions of COPA 1974. The EPA 1990 however provided a definition of 'premises' as including land. It remains unclear whether this definition encompasses a street.

In the context of this particular head of statutory nuisance the meaning of prejudicial to health was considered in *Southwark London BC v Ince* (1989). It was held that a house which was inadequately insulated against noise so that noise from a nearby railway adversely affected the occupants was a statutory nuisance because it was prejudicial to health.

Since noise is much more likely to interfere with enjoyment, rather than cause injury or be injurious to health, the nuisance limb needs some further definition. In general, the nuisance limb of statutory nuisance is based on the common law concept. This means that when the court is required to consider whether noise constitutes a nuisance it will take into account various matters including:

(a) the duration and time of the noise;

(b) the nature of the activity giving rise to the noise;

(c) the harm suffered by the person affected;

(d) the neighbourhood where the noise took place.

It also means that in practice the environmental health officer who is usually responsible for exercising the local authority's statutory nuisance functions will need to make a similar determination.

9.9.5 Noise in a street which is emitted from a vehicle, machinery or equipment – s 79(1)(ga)

This particular statutory nuisance was incorporated into s 79 of the EPA 1990 by the NSNA 1993. The amendment was made largely because the EPA 1990 did not provide sufficient protection from noise in streets (see above, *Tower Hamlets LBC v Manzoni and Walder* (1984)).

A street is defined as a 'highway and any other road, footway, square or court that is for the time being open to the public'. It is clear that a great deal of noise is generated in streets not only from vehicles but from ice cream vans, people playing loud music and of course the interminable sounds of car alarms going off. Not all street noises are covered. Certain exceptions are provided: it does not apply to noise created by traffic, the armed forces or by political demonstrations (or demonstrations supporting or opposing a campaign or cause). Traffic is understood to mean vehicles in motion.

Section 79(1)(ga) only refers to street noises emitted from vehicles, machinery or equipment. The question remains about the position of noise which emanates from the street but is not emitted from any of these particular sources.

9.9.6 Responsibility of the local authorities

Section 79(1) places all district councils and London borough councils under a duty to inspect their area from time to time to detect any statutory nuisance which ought to be dealt with under ss 80 and 80A of the EPA 1990. They are also under a duty to take such steps as are reasonably practicable to investigate complaints about statutory nuisances made by people living in the area. The duty is therefore twofold. The local authority has to carry out its own checks and has to respond to complaints. In practice it is the environmental health departments and officers that are responsible for enforcing this legislation and they will carry out the inspections and deal with the complaints. In some areas, particularly the large cities, some local authorities have night patrols who are concerned primarily with noise control. According to the National Society for Clean Air, in *Controlling Neighbourhood Noise,* complaints about neighbours 'may be fully investigated, receive minimal attention or may not be investigated at all'.

In determining which complaints to investigate many local authorities operate what is known as the 'three neighbour rule'. This effectively means that the local authority will not take action unless they have received complaints about noise from three separate sources. Some local authorities operate a policy of first sending a warning letter to the person they have received the complaint against.

(a) Duty to inspect

The duty to inspect and detect statutory nuisances is tempered by the requirement that these inspections only have to be carried out from time to time. One of the problems here is that the expression time to time is not defined by the Act thus making the obligation very imprecise.

(b) Duty to respond to complaints

This duty to respond to complaints was established by the EPA 1990. Prior to its introduction, local authorities were not actually required to respond to complaints made although, in practice, complainants provided useful information about the occurrences of statutory nuisances within the local authority area. The duty to respond to complaints made by people living in the area is qualified by the fact that the authority only has to take such steps as are reasonably practicable to investigate the complaint. Again this expression is not defined and could potentially cause problems. Local authorities are increasingly finding that they are facing severe financial problems. Whether the authority can take into account its own financial situation in determining what is reasonably practicable is not clear. However, if the Secretary of State for the Environment (SOSE) finds that a local authority is in default of these duties he can, by virtue of Schedule 3, transfer the function to himself.

A number of local authorities operate a 24 hour service. In 1991–92 only 25% offered such a service, but since then the numbers have increased to 32% in 1992–93 and 36% in 1994–95.

(c) Local authorities investigative powers

In order to carry out their functions of inspection and investigation local authority environmental officers can enter any land with the people and equipment that they consider necessary. The officers can also carry out any inspections, measurements and tests and can also take away samples and articles. These powers are provided by Sched 3 to the EPA 1990. The purpose of the inspection and investigation is to establish whether or not there is a statutory nuisance (or whether one is likely to occur) and to gather any evidence which may be needed in subsequent court proceedings. Once a local authority environmental officer is satisfied that a statutory nuisance is occurring or is likely to occur then an Abatement Notice must be served.

(d) Determining whether a statutory nuisance exists

In practice, the local authority environmental health officer will make an initial determination whether the matter complained of constitutes a statutory nuisance on the basis of it being prejudicial to health or a nuisance. He or she will therefore be required to take into account the nature of the neighbourhood and also whether the matter complained of amounts to a nuisance in common law or is just (as sometimes happens) a vexatious complaint. As with the common law this makes it very difficult to predict whether or not a noise will amount to an actionable statutory nuisance. An environmental health officer may have to make a number of visits to determine whether a nuisance exists, particularly in relation to noise nuisances which by their very nature are often sporadic. Complainants are well advised to keep a written record of the times and frequency that noise disturbances take place and also, where possible, to get third parties to witness the disturbances for evidential purposes.

In relation specifically to noise complaints, the environmental health officer may take noise measurements where this is possible.

Once an environmental health officer or local authority is satisfied that a statutory nuisance exists or is likely to occur then an Abatement Notice must be served on the person responsible.

9.9.7 Noise Abatement Notices

As stated above, once it has been determined that a statutory nuisance exists or is likely to occur then an Abatement Notice must be served on the person responsible.

Section 80 of the EPA 1990 provides that an authority must serve an Abatement Notice when it is satisfied that, in its area, a statutory nuisance:

(a) exists;

(b) is likely to occur; or

(c) is likely to recur.

Therefore the authority can take preventative action in order to stop a statutory nuisance happening. The requirement to serve the Abatement Notice is mandatory. However, s 80 does not say anything about the need for the likely occurrence to be imminent. It is enough that it is likely to occur. Also when one considers that the concept of prejudicial to health also extends to 'likely to cause injury', the local authority must serve an Abatement Notice if it believes that circumstances exist which make injury likely.

9.9.8 The form of the notice

Although there is no prescribed form for an Abatement Notice it must nevertheless state the following in a manner which is clear and understandable to the recipient:

(a) the nature of the statutory nuisance;

(b) the action or works required to abate it;

(c) time limits for compliance;

(d) the rights of appeal to the magistrates' court.

The Abatement Notice can impose a variety of conditions, including conditions:

(a) requiring the abatement of the nuisance or prohibiting or restricting its occurrence or recurrence;

(b) requiring the execution of such works, and the taking of such other steps, as may be necessary for any of these purposes.

There is no need to specify a time limit when prohibiting the recurrence of a nuisance. In *R v Birmingham City Justices ex p Guppy* (1988) the city council served an Abatement Notice on G who was having a noisy party. The notice imposed the three following requirements:

(a) to prohibit the noise amounting to a nuisance;

(b) immediately to cease permitting the use of the sound equipment to produce a noise so as to be a nuisance; and

(c) to take all other steps as may be necessary for that purpose.

Two months later the noise nuisance recurred on three successive nights and G was convicted of three offences of non-compliance with the notice. G sought judicial review of the convictions specifically on the grounds that the prohibition of recurrence in the notice was invalid since no time limit for compliance was specified. The High Court held that it is necessary for a notice to include a time limit for compliance where it requires the abatement of a nuisance or the execution of works, but not where it prohibits the recurrence of a nuisance.

9.9.9 Should the notice set a prescribed decibel level?

In *R v Fenny Stratford JJ ex p Watney Mann* (1976) three residents were disturbed by the noise from a juke box in a local public house. Proceedings were brought under s 99 of the Public Health Act 1936 against the company that owned the pub and the local magistrates' court issued a nuisance order which stated that the 'nuisance should be abated' and 'the level of noise in the premises should not exceed 70 decibels'. Watney Mann applied for judicial review arguing that the terms of the notice were not clear. The High Court quashed the notice on the grounds that it was void for reasons of uncertainty, in that it did not:

(a) state where the noise meter should be positioned; and

(b) the magistrates had failed to consider the likelihood and relevance of other sources of noise such as general conversation.

However, in two more recent cases the courts appear to take a more lenient attitude towards this issue. In *East Northamptonshire DC v Fossett* (1994), F was served with an Abatement Notice which required F to control all activities, including musical ones, so as not to cause a nuisance. The district council had served the notice because it was aware that an all night rave was to take place at F's club. The rave took place and the noise could be heard within one mile of the club. F was prosecuted for breach of the notice. The magistrates held that the noise levels amounted to a nuisance, but stated that the Abatement Notice was void on the grounds of imprecision and uncertainty. The district council appealed by way of case stated. In response F argued, following *Watney Mann* (see above), that a decibel level should have been set by the notice. The Divisional Court distinguished that case as one on a recurrence of a nuisance. In *Fossett*, the Divisional Court held that since the notice was served to prevent a likely nuisance the district council would have had to speculate unnecessarily if they had tried to set a decibel level and, on the facts, the district council had been forced to act quickly. F further argued that the notice was uncertain and he could not possibly know what an acceptable level of sound should be since the notice had failed to set one down. The Divisional Court rejected these arguments.

In a further case, *Myatt v Teignbridge DC* (1994), M kept 17 dogs. The district council served an Abatement Notice on her which required her to 'cease the keeping of dogs'. A further notice was served which stated that she had to 'reduce the number of dogs kept at the premises to no more than two and to take such steps as are necessary in the housing, welfare and management of the dogs to ensure they do not cause a nuisance'. M failed to comply with either notice and was prosecuted by the district council. She appealed by way of case stated. The Divisional Court held that the issue was whether or not the recipient of the notice knows what is wrong from the notice. On the facts the court held that M must have known what the cause of complaint was and although the notice could have been drawn up more carefully it was sufficient to make it clear to the recipient what was wrong.

These two later cases suggest a more lenient attitude towards the drafting of Abatement Notices and suggest that it is not necessary to prescribe a decibel level. However, it is clear that the courts will not be too prescriptive and that they will take into account the facts of the case.

9.9.10 On whom must the notice be served?

The provisions regarding the serving of Abatement Notices are contained in s 80 of the EPA 1990. Normally the local authority is required to serve the notice on the person responsible for the nuisance. Where the nuisance arises from any defect in the structural character of a building then the notice should be served on the owner of the premises. In circumstances where the person responsible for the nuisance cannot be found, or the nuisance has not yet occurred, then the notice must be served on the owner or occupier of the premises.

In relation to vehicles, machinery or equipment the person responsible will be the driver or operator. In circumstances where the noise nuisance has not occurred or arises from an unattended vehicle, machinery or equipment, the Abatement Notice should be served on the person responsible for the vehicle. If that person cannot be found the Abatement Notice can be affixed to the vehicle following a determination of the authority to that effect. This particular provision was introduced by the NSNA 1993 and is now contained in s 80(a) of the EPA 1990.

The Abatement Notice must specify the time for compliance. With noise nuisances, that may be immediately. Non-compliance with an Abatement Notice without reasonable excuse is a criminal offence.

9.9.11 The 'person responsible for the nuisance'

The person responsible for the nuisance is defined in s 79(7) of the EPA 1990 as the person to whose:

(a) act;

(b) default; or

(c) sufferance,

the nuisance is attributable. This is a wide definition and could include not only the person who created the noise nuisance, but also a third person/party who failed to take any appropriate preventative or corrective action where they had some legal requirement to do so. It can also include third persons who on becoming aware of the problem took no steps to remedy the situation. This was confirmed in the case of *Clayton v Sale* UDC (1926) where an owner was held liable for a statutory nuisance on his land consequent upon the activities or defaults of another.

In *Network Housing Association Ltd v Westminster CC* (1995), an Abatement Notice was served on a landlord in respect of noise under s 79(1)(e) of the EPA 1990 (noise emitted from premises) following a complaint from a tenant to the city council. The complainant claimed he was being disturbed by the ordinary residential use of the flat above. The Abatement Notice required the housing association to carry out alterations to the flat to reduce the noise levels to a prescribed decibel level. The court found that the noise in question was the noise of everyday living and it was the lack of sound insulation between his and a neighbour's flat that constituted it a nuisance. The housing association argued that there was no act on its part, nor indeed any default or sufferance, since it had no knowledge of the nuisance when it acquired the premises. However, the court rejected these arguments and held that the landlord was the person responsible. The housing association had allowed the nuisance to continue after it had come to its attention in 1991. However, on appeal to the Divisional Court, the Divisional Court held that the Abatement Notice did not specify the type of works to be carried out and was void because of lack of certainty.

9.9.12 What if more than one person is involved?

Section 81(1) of the EPA 1990 deals with the situation where more than one person is responsible for the statutory nuisance. If two persons are involved in an action which jointly amounts to a statutory nuisance they will both be responsible for the statutory nuisance even if their individual actions do not by themselves amount to such a nuisance. Although the Abatement Notice should be served in the first instance on the person responsible for the nuisance (s 80(2)) this should be read as meaning that the authority is obliged to serve separate notices on all the parties that may have contributed to the statutory nuisance.

9.9.13 Appeals against an Abatement Notice

A person who is served an Abatement Notice is entitled to appeal against it by making a complaint to the magistrates' court (s 80(3) of the EPA 1990). He or she must be informed of this right in the Abatement Notice. Where a person decides to lodge an appeal they must do say within 21 days from the day when the Abatement Notice was served. The grounds for appeal are not laid down in the EPA 1990 but are provided in the Statutory Nuisance (Appeals) Regulations 1995.

The grounds are:

(a) the Abatement Notice is not justified by s 80 of the EPA 1990. In other words, the appellant argues that the matter did not constitute a statutory nuisance;

(b) the Abatement Notice contains some informality, is defective or contains an error;

(c) the authority has unreasonably refused to accept compliance with alternative requirements, or that the requirements laid down in the Abatement Notice are unreasonable or unnecessary;

(d) the period for compliance in the notice is not reasonably sufficient;

(e) there has been an error in the service of the notice; for example the notice has been served on the wrong person. An appeal may also be made if the appellant argues that it is 'equitable' for the notice to be served on some other person either instead of the appellant or in addition to the appellant. Whether the wrong person has been served will be determined by reference to s 80(2). In relation to noise nuisances that the notice should have been served on the person responsible for the vehicle, machinery or equipment instead of the appellant;

(f) the best practicable means (BPM) were used to counteract the effect of a nuisance from trade or business premises;

(g) in relation to a nuisance under s 79(1)(g) of the EPA 1990 the requirements imposed by the Abatement Notice are more onerous than the requirements which may have been determined by means of other noise controls under the COPA 1974 or the NSNA 1993 (such as consents relating to loudspeakers).

The magistrates' courts have wide powers when dealing with appeals against Abatement Notices. They can:

(a) correct any procedural defect in the notice, quash the notice or vary the notice;

(b) dismiss the appeal;

(c) make such order as it thinks fit regarding:

  ○ any works which need to be carried out and the contribution to be made by any person to the cost of the work; or

  ○ the proportion of expenses that a local authority may recover from the appellant and from any other person.

9.9.14 Effect of an appeal upon an Abatement Notice

In general the lodging of an appeal will not suspend the operation of an Abatement Notice and therefore the person served with a notice will still be required to comply with the conditions of the notice. However, this general provision does not apply in circumstances where:

(a) the Abatement Notice requires expenditure on works and that the expenditure required would be out of proportion to the expected public benefit; or

(b) in the case of a nuisance under s 79(1)(g) or (ga) the noise to which the Abatement Notice relates is noise necessarily caused in the course of the performance of some duty imposed by law on the appellant.

These provisions are to be found in the Statutory Nuisance (Appeals) Regulations 1995 SI 1995/2644.

9.9.15 Failure to comply with an Abatement Notice

Section 80(4) of the EPA 1990 establishes that it is an offence for a person served with an Abatement Notice to either contravene or fail to comply with any requirement or prohibition imposed by the notice, without reasonable excuse. If an Abatement Notice is not complied with, the authority that has issued the notice has three options.

(a) The authority can abate the nuisance and recover its cost

The authority can abate the nuisance and do whatever may be necessary in execution of the notice (s 81(3)). A typical example of this is where audio equipment is removed to abate a noise nuisance. Police support is often required when environmental health officers try to seize equipment. According to the *Neighbour Noise Working Party*, in their 1995 report, there has been some uncertainty about the use of s 81(3) to temporarily confiscate noise making equipment and until amendments introduced by the NA 1996, there was no specific provision for the return of seized equipment to owners. Local authorities often used s 43 of the Powers of Criminal Courts

Act 1973 to obtain a court order to confiscate permanently equipment used to commit or facilitate the commission of an offence. The provisions relating to seizure of equipment have now been amended by the NA 1996 and are covered more fully at 9.10.7, below.

An authority can abate a nuisance irrespective of whether it takes proceedings for non-compliance. In the event that the authority does take action either to abate the nuisance or prevent it happening, then it can, by virtue of s 81(4) of the EPA 1990 recover *any* expenses reasonably incurred. This would normally be from the person whose acts or omissions caused the nuisance. If that person is the owner of the premises the expenses can be recovered from any person who is for the time being the owner of them. This would cover situations where, for instance, a previous owner caused a nuisance, but the present owner could be made responsible for the reasonable expenses incurred by the authority. Should the matter of cost recovery go before the court, the court has the power to apportion the expenses between persons whose acts (or omissions) caused the nuisance, in a manner that the court considers fair and reasonable.

The NSNA 1993 provides additional assistance to the local authorities in the form of a newly inserted s 81(A) which enables the local authority serving a notice to recover costs to make a charge on the premises owned by the person in default.

If the noise is from a car alarm the officer has the power to open the vehicle, if necessary by force, and immobilise the alarm. The expenses incurred by a local authority in abating a nuisance can be recovered with interest (s 81A of the EPA 1990). The local authority can also place a charge (that is, a debt secured on property and recouped when the relevant property is sold) on the premises. This new provision was inserted into the EPA 1990 by s 10 of the NSNA 1993.

(b) The authority can institute summary proceedings

If a person commits an offence under s 80(4) the authority can institute proceedings in the magistrates' court. The penalty for nuisance offences depends on whether the nuisance has occurred on industrial, trade or business premises or not. For nuisances arising on non-industrial, trade or business premises the maximum penalty is £5,000 plus a further £500 for each day that the offence continues after the conviction. However, where the nuisance occurs on industrial, trade or business premises the maximum fine is £20,000 (but no additional daily fines can be made).

(c) The authority can seek an injunction

The third option available to the authority against a person who fails to comply with or contravenes an Abatement Notice is to take proceedings in the High Court (s 81(5) of the EPA 1990). This option is available if the authority is of the view that proceedings in the magistrates' court (under s 80(4)) would afford an inadequate remedy. The aim would be to secure an injunction to secure the abatement, prohibition or restriction. The authority can take this course of action even if summary proceedings have not been exhausted and equally there is no requirement that the authority has suffered damage from the nuisance. Failure to comply with an injunction may result in a prison sentence. In *Bristol CC v Huggins* (1994), Mr Huggins was jailed for three months for breaching an injunction which was obtained by Bristol City Council after two prosecutions under the EPA 1990 failed.

This enables the local authority to obtain an interlocutory injunction to stop a nuisance, despite the availability of appeal proceedings in the magistrates' court.

9.9.16 Defences

The following defences are available in relation to noise nuisances:

(a) Reasonable excuse

It will be a defence if the defendant can prove that there was a reasonable excuse for not complying with the Abatement Notice. Unfortunately the EPA 1990 does not define reasonable excuse. The test is whether it is an excuse that a reasonable man would consider consistent with a reasonable standard of conduct. What constitutes a reasonable excuse will therefore be a matter of fact. Reasonable excuses have included non-receipt of the Abatement Notice (*A Lambert Flat Management Ltd v Lomas* (1981)). A birthday celebration or party will not constitute a reasonable excuse.

(b) The BPM defence

Where a noise nuisance has been alleged in relation to noise from a vehicle, machinery or equipment then it is a defence to show that the best practicable means (BPM) were used to prevent or counteract the nuisance. The defence is only available where the vehicle, machinery or equipment is used for industrial, trade or business premises (s 80(8)(aa) of the EPA 1990). The defence was considered in *Chapman v Gosberton Farm Produce Co Ltd* (1993) where a company in Boston, Lincolnshire received prepared packed horticultural produce from heavy goods vehicles during the night. Complaints were made to the district council about the noise from the lorries and also about the noise from the refrigeration equipment. In proceedings before the magistrates the company argued that the best practicable means had been used to counteract the effect of the noise. The company maintained that they had sought planning permission to erect a soil bank and screening (to provide a sound screen) as part of a wider application to extend their business and this fulfilled the BPM. The magistrates accepted this defence but their decision was overruled by the

Divisional Court. The upper court held that the burden of proof in establishing the BPM lies on the defendant (s 101 of the Magistrates' Court Act 1980) on a balance of probability, and it could not be said that a simple planning application was enough to discharge the burden of proof since the application for planning permission had not been determined.

Defendants have often found it relatively easy to take advantage of this defence on the basis that any work required would be too expensive in relation to their means (AJ Waite, 'Neighbourhood noise in the UK' (1994) 6(4) Environmental Law and Management 130–36).

In considering what constitutes BPM in this context, s 79 adds an additional factor not relevant in other statutory nuisances. In circumstances where a Code of Practice (issued under s 71 of the COPA 1974) is applicable, then regard must be had for the guidance given in the code.

(c) Codes of Practice

Section 71 of the COPA 1974 enables the SOSE to prepare and approve Codes of Practice for the purpose of giving guidance on the appropriate methods of minimising noise in relation to specified types of plant and machinery. Codes of Practice issued under s 71 include construction and open sites SI 1984/1992, SI 1987/1730; audible intruder alarms SI 1981/1829; ice cream van chimes SI 1981/1828; model aircraft SI 1981/1830.

(d) Additional defences

In addition, s 80(9) of the EPA 1990 contains a defence specific to a failure to abate a noise nuisance or act in accordance with a prohibition or restriction in a noise Abatement Notice. The basis of this defence is essentially that the local authority has given its consent to a particular level of noise under the provisions of ss 60–67 of the COPA 1974 and that the Abatement Notice attempts to impose a higher standard. The provisions of ss 60–67 are described more fully below.

9.9.17 Burden of proof in statutory nuisance proceedings

Within the context of proceedings involving statutory nuisances the burden of proof which applies is a criminal one. In other words it must be established beyond reasonable doubt that the matter complained of exists and that the defendant is responsible for it.

9.9.18 Problems with the statutory nuisance procedures

Although the statutory nuisance procedures offer the means for action to be taken by the local authority, on behalf of a complainant, they do not offer an immediate remedy. It is only after a person has failed to abate a nuisance that punitive action in the courts may be taken.

9.9.19 An aggrieved citizens action – s 82 of the EPA 1990

The right exists in relation to all of the statutory nuisances contained in the EPA 1990 for an aggrieved person to make a complaint in the magistrates' court (s 82 of the EPA 1990). Before a person can do this they must give notice. In relation to noise nuisances under s 79(1)(g) and (ga), three days' notice is required rather than the standard 21 days' notice.

One of the main limitations with the so called aggrieved citizens action is that the magistrates' court cannot make an order unless a statutory nuisance has occurred. In other words preventative action cannot be taken by an individual.

Before taking action in proceedings brought under s 82 the magistrates must be satisfied that one of the following conditions exists:

(a) the alleged nuisance exists;

(b) an abated nuisance is likely to recur on the same premises, or in the same street.

The court can make the following orders:

(a) requiring the defendant to abate the nuisance within a specified time and to carry out any works necessary for that purpose;

(b) prohibiting a recurrence of the nuisance and requiring the defendant to carry out any necessary works to prevent the recurrence. A time period for carrying out such works will be specified in the order;

(c) the magistrates can also impose a fine of up to £5,000, with a further fine of up to £500 for each day that the offence continues after conviction;

(d) the court can order the relevant local authority to do anything which the convicted person was required to do by the court order, after it has given the authority the opportunity to be heard. This is only likely to happen where the court makes a second nuisance order because the first has not been complied with.

Where the nuisance is such as to render premises unfit for human habitation, the court can prohibit the use of the premises for human habitation until the court is satisfied that the premises have been made fit for such a purpose.

Failure to comply with a nuisance order from the magistrates is an offence and can result in a fine of up to £5,000 (plus £500 for each day that the offence continues).

9.9.20 Compensation

Since statutory nuisance proceedings are criminal proceedings, the magistrates' court can make a compensation order in favour of persons aggrieved by the nuisance under s 35 of the Powers of Criminal Courts Act

1973. This is limited to a sum of up to £5,000. No such limit exists if a compensation order is granted by the Crown Court.

9.10 The NA 1996

The NA 1996 received royal assent on 18 July 1996. The provisions of the Act do not create a new noise nuisance but provide for a special summary procedure in relation to night time noise.

Section 1 of the NA 1996 enables local authorities to adopt, should they wish to do so, the provisions of the Act. Local authorities are free to determine whether they wish to adopt the provisions or not, and it is this discretionary element which has given rise to the greatest amount of criticism. A local authority, should it determine to adopt the provisions in its area, must give at least three months' notice in the local newspapers. By mid-1999 only nine local authorities had formally adopted the 1996 Act. Some commentators have suggested that the limited take up is, in part, due to the fact that the Act will increase demands on strained local authority budgets. Under the Act authorities are subject to a duty to investigate complaints immediately and therefore this may involve overtime payments.

9.10.1 Complaints

The NA 1996 provides that in an area where the provisions have been adopted the local authority is under a duty to respond to certain complaints. If a complaint is made by an individual present in a dwelling during night hours, that excessive noise is being emitted from another dwelling, the local authority must ensure that an officer of the local authority takes reasonable steps to investigate the complaint. Night hours are defined as being between 11 pm–7 am.

9.10.2 Investigation and service of Warning Notice

If, after carrying out an investigation, the local authority officer (usually the environmental health officer) is satisfied:

(a) that the noise is being emitted from a dwelling during night hours; and

(b) the noise, if it were measured from within the complainant's dwelling, would or might exceed the permitted level which is detailed in Circular 8/97. The relevant noise levels are 35db (if the underlying noise level does not exceed 25db) or 10db above the relevant background noise (if the underlying noise level is 25db or more). An increase of 10db over a background level of 25db will double the loudness of the noise.

The officer may serve a Warning Notice on any person at or near the offending dwelling who appears to be responsible for the noise. In the event that no such person can be found, the notice can be left at the dwelling.

It is clear that it is the local authority officer who is responsible for making the decision as to whether the noise does or is likely to exceed the permitted level. He also needs to decide whether it is necessary to assess the noise levels either within or outside the complainant's dwelling. It is also a matter of discretion whether or not the noise level needs to be measured using any noise measuring device.

In deciding whether a nuisance exists the local authority will primarily rely upon the results of their noise measuring instruments. Consequently there is no need to take into account factors, such as locality, which are material to the exercise of the local authority's functions.

9.10.3 Person responsible for the noise

A person is responsible for the noise emitting from a dwelling if he is the person to whose:

(a) act

(b) default; or

(c) sufferance,

the emission of the noise is wholly or partly attributable. This test is the same as that used under the statutory nuisance provisions discussed earlier.

9.10.4 The Warning Notice

The environmental health officer has discretion in relation to whether or not to serve a Warning Notice. The Warning Notice may start as little as 10 minutes after the service of the notice and must end at 07.00 am. The notice will state that the person responsible for any noise which exceeds the permitted levels has committed a criminal offence liable on summary conviction to a fine not exceeding Level 3 on the standard scale.

9.10.5 Defences

The NA 1996 provides the following defence:

• there was reasonable excuse for the act, default or sufferance.

9.10.6 Evidential issues

Section 7 of the NA 1996 lays down the evidence that may be admitted to a court in summary proceedings for an offence under s 4. It includes:

(a) documentary evidence of an offence without the attendance in court of the local authority officer (unless by virtue of s 7(6) attendance is required by the defendant); and

(b) evidence from noise measuring devices.

9.10.7 Powers of entry and seizure and disposal of equipment

Section 10 of the NA 1996 provides a power of entry by force under a magistrate's warrant. The NA 1996 makes specific provision for the seizure and disposal of equipment, such as audio and stereo equipment. The relevant provisions are s 10 and Sched 1 to the Act. The provisions of the NA 1996 in this regard also extend to the statutory nuisance provisions under the EPA 1990 and make it clear that the power of a local authority to abate a nuisance under s 81(3) of the EPA 1990 includes the power to seize and remove equipment which it appears to the local authority is being or has been used in the emission of a noise nuisance under s 79(1)(g) of the Act.

9.10.8 Fixed penalty notices

The NA 1996 was introduced to provide a speedy resolution of noise problems. In addition to a maximum penalty of £1,000, the 1996 Act introduced a fixed penalty procedure.

Where a local authority officer has reason to believe that a person:

(a) is committing an offence; or

(b) has just committed an offence under the Act,

the officer *may* issue a fixed penalty notice. This essentially gives the person in receipt of the penalty notice the opportunity of discharging any liability under the act upon payment of a fixed penalty. The fixed penalty is currently set at £100.

9.11 Bylaws

The first legislation in the UK expressly dealing with noise was in the form of bylaws. Section 235(1) of the Local Government Act 1972 allows district councils to make bylaws for the 'good rule and government of the whole or any part of the district or borough, as the case may be, and for the prevention and suppression of nuisances therein'. The Home Office has issued a number of model bylaws, including those on:

(a) noisy animals;

(b) noisy conduct at night;

(c) the playing of organs, wirelesses and gramophones;

(d) music near houses, churches and hospitals.

The breach of a bylaw is a criminal offence.

9.12 Noise Control measures under the COPA 1974

9.12.1 Construction sites

In addition to the controls contained in the EPA 1990 the other main statutory provisions controlling noise can be found in Pt III of the COPA 1974 which replaced the Noise Abatement Act 1960.

The COPA 1974 includes a number of measures which enable local authorities to control various aspects of noise. In particular, ss 59A, 60 and 61 introduced the first legislative controls over noise from construction sites.

9.12.2 Noise on construction sites

The COPA 1974 provides the means by which local authorities can control the level of noise in their areas arising from construction works. The definition of construction extends to the erection, construction, alteration, repair or maintenance of buildings, structures or roads. It also includes demolition and dredging works. Where it appears to a local authority that any of these activities are being, or are going to be, carried out on premises then the authority can serve a notice imposing requirements as to the way in which the work is to be carried out (s 60(2) of the COPA 1974). It is not necessary that a nuisance exists or could occur for the authority to resort to these powers. Sometimes local authorities will publish details of the notice in the local press.

The notice can specify the following:

(a) plant and machinery which must or must not be used;

(b) permitted hours of operation;

(c) noise levels by reference to the time of the day or to a part of the site;

(d) the time within which the notice is to be complied;

(e) the execution of works necessary for the purpose of the notice.

When the local authority issues its powers under s 60 it must take into account the matters specified in s 60(4) which are:

(a) relevant Codes of Practice issued under s 71 of the COPA 1974;

(b) the need to ensure that the BPM are employed to minimise noise;

(c) the need to protect people in the locality from the effects of noise.

It should be noted that the definition of best practicable means under s 72 of the COPA 1974 is very similar to the definition provided under the EPA 1990 (s 79(9)). The local authority is required to serve the s 60 notice on the person who appears (to the local authority) to be either carrying out or going to carry out the works. In addition, a notice can also be served on the person(s) who are responsible for or controlling the carrying out of the works. In *City of London Corp v Bovis Construction Ltd* (1989), it was held that it was sufficient that the notice was served upon the person having control of the site even if the contractor actually doing the work is not served.

It is an offence not to comply with a s 60 notice without reasonable excuse. The magistrates can fine up to £5,000 with a daily fine of £50 for continuing offences. However, it is possible to raise the defence of reasonable excuse. The phrase reasonable excuse is not defined in the Act but was considered in the case of *City of London Corp v Bovis* where Lord Bingham stated that:

> Nothing much short of an emergency, unless an event beyond a party's control, could in my view provide a reasonable excuse for contravention in a case such as this.

Where a party fails to comply with the s 60 notice the local authority also has the option to apply for an injunction. The court may grant an injunction where it appears that the criminal proceedings will not provide an adequate remedy to ensure compliance with the notice and to protect the inhabitants from noise.

A right of appeal exists against a s 60 notice providing the appeal is made within 21 days of service. The grounds for appeal are set out in the Control of Noise (Appeals) Regulations 1975 as amended (Control of Noise (Appeals) Regulations 1975 SI 1975/2116 as amended by SI 1990/2276). An appeal can suspend the notice unless the notice expressly states otherwise.

9.12.3 Prior consents for construction site noise

Given that local authorities have powers to restrict construction noise under s 60 of the COPA 1974, contractors have the right to reach some agreement with the local authority, in advance of the works taking place, about the levels and timing of noise that will take place. Section 61(3) provides that contractors can apply for consent prior to the construction work taking place. To do so the applicant must provide details of the work that is to be carried out and also the method by which it is to be carried out. In addition details must be given regarding the measures that will be taken to minimise the noise resulting from the works. If the authority considers that the application contains sufficient information that no s 60 notice would be served if the steps proposed are observed, then it must grant a consent. The authority, however, has the right to attach conditions to the consent. In setting the conditions it must take into account the relevant Codes of Practice, the best practicable means and the need to protect persons in the locality from noise.

The authority must respond to the application for prior consent within 28 days of receipt of the application. The authority can either refuse or approve the application, or alternatively it may approve the application subject to conditions. An applicant can appeal if the authority refuses to give its consent, fails to deal with the application within the 28 days, or attaches conditions to which the applicant objects. An appeal is made to the magistrates' court and must be lodged within 21 days after the expiry of the 28 days.

It is an offence to carry on the works other than in compliance with the terms of the consent. Obtaining the prior consent from the local authority can prove to be valuable since the existence of a consent can protect the contractor from any statutory nuisance proceedings brought by a local authority. However, the consent does not provide the same protection in relation to actions brought by private individuals (under s 82 of the EPA 1990). The existence and compliance with a prior consent will not provide a defence in such actions. A citizen can also seek an injunction in respect of a noise nuisance irrespective of whether there is a s 60 of the COPA 1974 prior consent. Although prior consent would appear to be a sensible step for any contractor, in practice relatively few have applied under these provisions. One of the suggested reasons for this is the view that contractors have thought that the local authorities would be too restrictive in setting conditions. Contractors have preferred to run the risk of proceedings under s 60.

9.13 Noise from loudspeakers

The noise from loudspeakers is controlled by s 62 of the COPA 1974 which provides that loudspeakers are not to be operated in streets at all for advertising any entertainment, trade or business. There is a blanket ban as far as advertising is concerned. Loudspeakers may be used for other non-advertising purposes but they may not to be operated in any event between 11 pm and 8 am the following morning. The SOSE can reduce these times but he has no power to extend the period (s 7 of the NSNA 1993).

Section 62(2) of the COPA 1974 provides exceptions for the use of loudspeakers:

(a) at any time in the street for, *inter alia*, various public service reasons, such as the police, the ambulance or fire service or the Environment Agency;

(b) in an emergency;

(c) inside vehicles for the entertainment of passengers;

(d) by ice cream vans (or vans selling perishable foods). They can play their music between noon and 7 pm;

(e) at pleasure fairs.

In relation to the last three of these exceptions there is a *caveat* that the noise must not give reasonable cause for annoyance to persons in the vicinity.

The NSNA 1993 (s 8 and Sched 2) amended s 62 of the COPA 1974 in order to allow local authorities to permit the use of loudspeakers in certain circumstances where it would otherwise be a breach of s 62.

The maximum penalty for the illegal use of a loudspeaker in a street is £5,000.

9.14 Noise from burglar alarms

There cannot be many people who have not been annoyed by the sound of burglar alarms going off for what sometimes seems like forever in the middle of the night. Burglar alarms are designed to be noisy and to arouse attention, that is their very purpose. But all to often they go off for no other reason than the operator has misused the system or a 'door has blown open'.

Section 9 of the NSNA 1993 enables local authorities to adopt a regime to deal with the problem of burglar alarms. Local authorities may impose obligations on installers of audible intruder alarms and occupiers (or any person entitled to occupy if the premises are unoccupied) to ensure that where alarms are fitted they comply with requirements to be set out in regulations by the SOSE. When a burglar alarm is installed the police must be notified of details of current key holders and the local authority must be informed of the police station where that information has been recorded. Where an alarm sounds for more than one hour and is giving persons living or working in the vicinity reasonable cause for annoyance the local authority officer has the power to enter the premises and turn it off. The officer cannot use force to do this. However, the environmental health officer, accompanied by a police officer, can enter forcibly if a warrant has been obtained.

The alarm must comply with the prescribed requirements and in particular there must be a 20 minute cut-out device. Powers of entry are provided.

9.15 Preventing neighbourhood noise

Environmental law is said to be based upon a number of principles some of which are enshrined in the European Community (EC) Treaty. One fundamental principle is the preventive principle – prevention being better than cure. In relation to noise both EC and UK legislation exists which seeks to prevent noise nuisances occurring. The consequence of successful preventative action is the reduction in noise problems.

The noise controls that have been considered so far have largely been concerned with controlling existing noise problems and resolving noise disputes, although of course the statutory nuisance provisions can be used to prevent nuisances from arising.

The remaining part of this chapter is concerned with those measures which are intended to prevent noise problems from reaching unacceptable levels in the first place.

9.15.1 Noise abatement zones

In addition to the specific powers in ss 60–61 of the COPA 1974 (described above) local authorities can also take preventative action to control noise by designating noise abatement zones. The provisions relating to noise abatement zones are found in ss 63–67 of the COPA 1974. Section 63 of the COPA 1974 makes provision for local authorities to designate all or any part of their area as a noise abatement zone. The purpose of noise abatement zones, is, according to DoE Circular 2/76, to 'prevent deterioration in environmental noise levels and achieve reductions in noise levels wherever practicable'.

If a local authority wishes to create a noise abatement zone it must issue a 'noise abatement order' specifying the types or classes of premises to which the order applies (Sched 1 to the COPA 1974 defines the procedures for establishing noise abatement zones). Originally such an order had to be confirmed by the SOSE, however this requirement was removed by the Local Government and Planning Act 1980.

Where a local authority designates an area as a noise abatement zone it must measure the level of noise emanating from those classes of premises specified by the order. It is also under a duty to maintain a noise level register of all measurements taken. In a noise abatement zone it is an offence to exceed the level of noise recorded in the noise level register without the written consent of the local authority. The local authority can consent to a noise level being exceeded by virtue of s 65 and any consent may be subject to conditions. Where such consent is denied by a local authority an applicant can appeal to the SOSE. Where the local authority consents to the registered level being exceeded then this is also recorded in the register.

If the local authority records a measurement in the register then it is obliged to serve a copy of that record on the owner or occupier of the premises from which the measurement was taken. Any person who is served with a copy of a record has the right to appeal against the record to the SOSE within 28 days by virtue of s 64. The Control of Noise (Appeals) Regulations 1975 SI 1975/2116 provide for the appeals procedure. The precise methods of measurement are determined by the Control of Noise (Measurement and Registers) Regulations 1976 SI 1976/37.

In addition, the local authority can require the reduction of noise emanating from premises covered by the noise abatement order. The local authority will issue a noise reduction notice which will state:

(a) that the level of noise must be reduced to the stated levels;

(b) the noise level allowable at different times of the day and on different days;

(c) what steps are to be taken to achieve the noise reduction; and

(d) the deadline for achieving the noise reduction.

The noise reduction stated in the notice must be practicable and achievable at a reasonable cost. It must also generate some public benefit. Parties served with a noise reduction notice have the right to appeal to the magistrates' court against the notice (the appeal must be made within three months of service of the notice). Failure to comply with the terms of a notice without reasonable excuse constitutes an offence. By virtue of s 74 of the COPA 1974 the fines may not exceed level 5 on the standard scale (£5,000) and there is provision for a daily penalty of £50. As in statutory nuisance the local authority may execute works itself and recover reasonable costs (s 69 of the COPA 1974).

Noise abatement zones have not found widespread support. This is probably because of the length of the procedures used and the resources that are needed to implement the provisions. Local authorities have largely relied on their powers under the statutory nuisance provisions in the EPA 1990 to control noise.

9.16 Emission standards and Codes of Practice

One way of reducing noise generated by certain types of transport, machines or activities is to set source emission standards. This is the approach that has been taken in a number of EC directives.

EC legislation controls noise for a variety of types of machinery including:

(a) lawnmowers;

(b) motorcycles;

(c) aircraft. Aircraft noise emission regulation is licence based. No aircraft may take off or land at a UK airport unless it has a noise certificate issued by the Civil Aviation Authority (or an equivalent licence issued by a national licensing authority) complying with the Air Navigation (Noise Certification) Ord 1990 SI 1990/1514. The 1990 order implements EC Directives (80/51/EEC), (83/206/EEC) and 89/269/EEC) which, in turn, give effect to the provisions of the 1944 Chicago Convention on Civil Aviation. Although aircraft noise controls have been 'ratcheted up' EC Directives (92/14/EC) and (98/20/EC) (implemented in the UK by the Aeroplane Noise Regulations 1999 SI 1999/1452), the noise reductions achieved have been counterbalanced by an increase in air traffic. In consequence the adverse impact of noise at some UK airports has significantly increased.

Aircraft noise is regulated by the SOSE under the Civil Aviation Act (CAA) 1982. Section 78 of the Act enables the SOSE to list specific airports (currently Heathrow, Gatwick, Stansted and Manchester) which require regulation in respect of the volume of air traffic and hours of operation. Under s 79 statutory noise insulation schemes may be set up which provide grant assistance for noise insulation works.

Noise and other environmental impacts are, by virtue of s 68(1) and s 68(3), taken into account when operating licenses are granted to airlines.

Tortious actions, such as trespass and nuisance, regarding noise disturbance caused by aircraft and airports will, in most cases, fail because of the exclusions of liability provided by s 76 and s 77, except to the extent that the airline or airport operator is acting unreasonably. In 1990 the validity of these exclusions was unsuccessfully challenged in a human rights action based on Arts 6, 8, and 13 of the European Convention on Human Rights (see *Powell and Rayner v UK* (1990) 12 EHRR 355);

(d) cars, buses and goods vehicles. Traffic related noise nuisance arises from a combination of engine noise, road noise (caused by the composition of the road surface – tarmac or concrete) and the volume of traffic using a particular stretch of road. The EC has been influential in developing product based controls, such as exhaust silencers and tyre standards, which help to combat these problems (see EC Directives (70/157/EEC), (77/212/EEC), (81/334/EEC), (84/372/EEC), (84/424/EEC) and (92/97/EC)). The main secondary legislation transposing these provisions into UK law are the Road Vehicles (Construction and Use) Regulations 1986 SI 1986/1078, the Motor Vehicles (Type Approval) (Great Britain) Regulations 1984 SI 1984/81 and 1994 SI 1994/981 and the Motor Vehicles (EC Type Approval) Regulations 1998 SI 1998/2051.

(e) tractors;

(f) construction plant and machinery.

The SOSE has the power under s 68 of the COPA 1974 to make regulations which reduce or limit the noise caused by plant or machinery both inside and outside factories and construction sites. As yet this power has not been exercised and the SOSE has preferred the use of Codes of Practice rather than legally binding standards.

9.16.1 Codes of Practice

Section 71 of the COPA 1974 enables the SOSE to prepare and approve Codes of Practice for the purpose of giving guidance on the appropriate methods of minimising noise in relation to specified types of plant and machinery.

Codes of Practice issued under s 71 include construction and open sites SI 1984/1992, 1987/1730; audible intruder alarms SI 1981/1829; ice cream van chimes SI 1981/1828; model aircraft SI 1981/1830.

Although Codes of Practice are not legally binding they may be taken into account in legal proceedings, for example, in determining whether best practicable means have been employed. The Code of Practice dealing with audible intruder alarms has now been incorporated into the NSNA 1993.

9.17 Anti-social behaviour orders

Anti-social, threatening and disruptive behaviour which causes, or is likely to cause, alarm, harassment and distress may be dealt with by means of an anti-Social behaviour order under s 51 of the Crime and Disorder Act 1998. The Act is designed to provide the police and local authorities with power to address street disturbances, as opposed to neighbour disputes. Either the local authority or the police, after consulting one another, may apply to a magistrate for an order. Breach of an order is a crime punishable by a maximum penalty of an unlimited fine or a gaol sentence of up to five years.

9.18 'Rave' parties

The Criminal Justice and Public Order Act 1994 is relevant to the control of 'rave' parties. A rave is defined as 'a gathering of one hundred or more people on land in the open air that includes the playing of amplified music'. Section 63 empowers the police to stop a rave in circumstances where the music is likely to cause serious distress to local residents.

9.19 Planning and noise

The town and country planning regime can play a large part in either causing or reducing noise problems. Bad planning can result in noisy developments being built alongside more noise sensitive operations. For this reason planning authorities are required to consider the potential for noise problems in the exercise of their planning functions. In 1994 a new Planning Policy Guidance Note (PPG 24) was introduced on planning and noise. The PPG replaces advice previously given in DoE Circular 10/73. It also takes into account the recommendations of the Noise Review Working Party which reported in October 1990.

PPG 24 provides advice to local authorities on how to use their planning powers to minimise the adverse impact of noise. In particular it outlines the considerations that should be taken into account when the authority is considering planning applications for activities which will generate noise and also for proposals in noise sensitive areas. The PPG highlights the measures that may be taken to control noise. These include:

(a) ensuring that there is adequate distance between the source of noise and noise sensitive areas;

(b) engineering solutions to reduce noise at the point of generation;

(c) controlling the times when noise generating activities can take place.

9.19.1 Noise exposure categories

In addition, PPG 24 introduces the concept of 'noise exposure' categories (NECs) for residential developments. When determining an application for a residential development near a source of noise, such as a motorway, planning authorities must first determine into which of the four noise exposure categories the proposed site falls, taking account of noise levels during the day and night. The four NECs are rated A to D. An A category means that noise need not be considered as a determining factor in granting planning permission, whereas a D category means that planning permission should normally be refused. Annex 2 of the PPG sets out detailed 'noise exposure' categories:

A – noise need not be considered as a determining factor in granting planning permission.

B – noise should be taken into account.

C – planning permission should normally be granted, but where it is granted appropriate conditions should be applied.

D – planning permission should normally be refused.

9.19.2 Planning conditions

Local planning authorities can grant planning permission for development subject to conditions which are aimed at minimising noise levels. PPG 24 is useful once again in that it describes the sorts of conditions that might be used to achieve this objective. For example, the planning authority can lay down conditions which determine that construction work cannot begin until a scheme for protecting a noise sensitive development has been approved by the authority. Other relevant conditions include:

(a) layout conditions;

(b) engineering conditions;

(c) administration conditions (such as operating times).

In *Penwith DC v SOSE* (1977) the local planning authority, in relation to an application for the extension to a factory, granted permission subject to a condition that no machinery be operated in the extension or the existing factory between the hours of 6 pm–6 am on weekdays or between 1 pm on Saturday to 8 am Monday, or on statutory holidays. The court held that the planning authority could lawfully impose such conditions.

9.19.3 The Housing Act 1996

The provisions of Pt V of the Housing Act 1996 enable public sector landlords to evict tenants who cause 'nuisance or annoyance' to neighbours.

9.19.4 Building regulations

There can be no doubt that poor sound insulation, particularly in flats is a contributing factor to neighbour noise problems. However, new buildings must comply with building regulations which can to some extent prevent noise problems occurring. The Building Regulations 1991 SI 1991/2768, enacted under the Building Act 1984, are designed to secure the health, safety, welfare and convenience of people in or about buildings. Schedule 1 to the 1991 Regulations contains the various technical requirements relating to building structures and covers various aspects relating to noise insulation. It is an offence to carry out building works in contravention of the Building Regulations.

9.20 The impact of the EC on noise pollution

Although the impact of EC upon noise regulation in the UK is not as marked as in other contexts, nevertheless, the EC has had some effect on noise controls in a national context. So far the thrust of EC noise regulation has been product based, especially in regard to motor vehicles (EC Directive (70/157/EEC) as amended in regard to engine and exhaust system noise), aircraft (EC Directive (80/51/EEC) regarding noise from sub-sonic aircraft), household appliances (EC Directive (86/594/EEC) in regard to product information on noise levels), and construction equipment.

During the mid-1990s the EC issued a Green Paper on 'Future noise policy' (COM(96)540) which highlighted the need for action in regard to railways, construction plant and other areas. Although the document makes some reference to environmental quality limit values the general thrust of EC noise policy remains focused on product based noise limits and the provision of information to consumers on product noise levels.

9.21 Alternative dispute resolution

Noise disputes are often part of a much wider neighbour dispute. Unwelcome noise is often a symptom of the disagreement between the neighbours, rather than the original cause. In which case the noise laws discussed above may be of limited use in controlling the noise and other alternative methods of resolution may be required, either in other branches of law or possibly through mediation. Equally genuine noise disputes may be dealt with outside the framework of legal control discussed so far. The following section is intended to consider the possibilities of alternative forms of dispute resolution which may lend themselves to the resolution of noise disputes.

It will often be the case that a dispute between neighbours over noise can be resolved informally. Often an environmental health officer can facilitate this informal resolution by helping the neighbours to reach some sort of compromise solution.

The DoE has shown itself keen to encourage informal resolution of problems (*Bothered by Noise?*, 1994, DoE). However, it is recognised that not all problems by be dealt with so easily. Nevertheless, the DoE has also sought to promote the use of more formal means of alternative dispute resolution and has issued a guidance note on the mechanics and benefits of alternative dispute resolution, in particular the use of mediation.

9.21.1 Mediation

Mediation is one form of alternative dispute resolution where an impartial third party seeks to help those in dispute reach a mutually acceptable agreement outside the framework of the courts. The DoE (now DEFRA) recognises that mediation will not always be the appropriate form of dispute resolution and suggests that it is more likely to work.

The advantages of mediation are clear. Mediation is normally quicker and almost certainly less expensive than legal action because its use only requires one mediator. The costs of mediation are split between the parties involved.

Mediation is also claimed to be very successful. Mediation UK, a mediation service, claims that it has an 85% success rate of reaching lasting agreements (this claim relates to all types of disputes, not just noise disputes).

Mediation was argued for most strenuously during the passage of the Noise Bill (NA 1996) before Parliament. According to the MP for Lewisham and Deptford, Joan Ruddock, 'about 60% of all mediated neighbour disputes involve noise, and estimates of their success range from 40% to 77%. Mediation is cost effective and usually costs between £200 and £300 per hour' (*Hansard*, 16 February 1996 – during the Second Reading of the Noise Bill).

NOISE POLLUTION

The problem of noise pollution

Noise 'pollution' is of growing concern both in terms of the increasing amount of noise that is generated by modern society and also because of the growing awareness of the problems it can bring. Noise, and in particular neighbourhood noise, accounts for a large share of complaints to local authorities.

The problems of legal control

Noise has traditionally been controlled at common law, principally in private nuisance actions. The courts will take into account a number of factors in determining whether noise constitutes an actionable nuisance including:

(a) the duration and time of the noise;

(b) the nature of the activity giving rise to the noise;

(c) the harm suffered by the person affected;

(d) the neighbourhood where the noise took place.

Noise as a statutory nuisance

Noise may also constitute a statutory nuisance under the provisions of s 79(1)(g) and (ga) of the EPA 1990 as amended by the Noise and Statutory Nuisance Act 1993:

(a) Section 79(1)(g) – 'noise emitted from premises so as to be prejudicial to health or a nuisance'; and

(b) Section 79(1)(ga) – 'noise that is prejudicial to health or a nuisance and is emitted from or caused by a vehicle, machinery or equipment in a street'.

Duty of local authorities

Local authorities are under a duty to serve an Abatement Notice in order to bring the noise nuisance to an end or to prevent it occurring. The provisions relating to the service of Abatement Notices and local authority powers are detailed in Chapter 8.

The NA 1996

Night time noise may be dealt with under the provisions of the NA 1996 providing the provisions have been adopted by the relevant local authority. The NA 1996 allows the Environmental Health Officer to serve an immediate Warning Notice followed by a fixed penalty notice.

COPA 1974

Noise is also controlled under the provisions of ss 60–67 of the COPA 1974. In particular:

(a) noise on construction sites is covered in ss 60 and 61. Local authorities can serve a s 60 notice to control the noise from construction (or demolition works). Alternatively, a contractor may obtain prior consent from the local authority under s 61;

(b) local authorities can take preventative action by designating noise abatement zones (s 63). It is an offence to exceed the noise levels recorded in the noise level register without the prior consent of the local authority;

(c) loudspeaker noise is controlled under s 62 of the COPA 1974;

(d) noise from burglar alarms is controlled by s 9 of the NSNA 1993.

Emission standards

In addition to these various controls, certain products, particularly motor vehicles, are governed by regulations which specify noise emission limits. The EC has also legislated extensively in this area.

Planning and noise

The adverse effects of noise can be minimised through good planning. The town and country planning regime enables local planning authorities to attach conditions to planning permissions which are aimed at reducing the impact of noise. Planning authorities are also guided by Planning Policy Guidance Note 24.

CHAPTER 10

THE COMMON LAW AND THE PRIVATE REGULATION OF ENVIRONMENTAL POLLUTION

10.1 Introduction

Most of this book is devoted to a study of the public regulation of private pollution. Command and Control regulatory regimes are employed by the Government to regulate the polluting emissions of private industry. Such legislative controls task public bodies, such as the Environment Agency and the local authorities, to regulate polluting emissions from a wide range of industries.

Command and Control legislation such as the Environmental Protection Act (EPA) 1990 and the Water Resources Act (WRA) 1991 are examples of public laws. These laws differ from criminal laws or civil laws in that each piece of legislation comprises an administrative framework designed to regulate a particular type of polluting activity, often through the use of licence based controls.

In contrast to the regulation of pollution by public regulators 'policing' compliance with the law as detailed in legislation, this chapter considers the role of the common law as a component of the patchwork of controls which currently comprise the environmental law of England and Wales. The common law, in contrast to the law in legislation, comprises various legal principles which have been developed by the judiciary in decided cases over many years. This is 'judge made' law rather than statute law. Common law actions consist of 'one on one' disputes involving an action commenced by an injured 'plaintiff' (claimant) in the civil courts against the person (defendant) who allegedly caused the injury. Thus, the common law is a mechanism to regulate the legal relations between private persons, whether individuals or companies. In the context of this book the relevant legal relations upon which we shall focus concern the resolution of disputes relating to pollution damage to property, property related interests, or personal injury. Most of these disputes require the courts to resolve competing land uses.

The most important set of common laws which have application to environmental problems in general, and pollution in particular, is the law of torts (wrongs). The primary function of the law of torts is to provide a range of remedies for any person who suffers a wrong consisting of damage to property or person (personal injury) caused by the activities of another person.

10.2 Common law actions

Where a legal person, such as an individual or a company, has suffered from environmental harm which takes the form of damage to person or property, an action in tort is usually the most appropriate remedy. The common law of torts is used to provide redress, usually in the form of compensation, for an injured person.

Although common law actions have been criticised for 'being too expensive, too long winded and too uncertain' (Bell, 1997), nevertheless it has, in recent years, proved to be a fertile ground for environmental litigation, although the judiciary have demonstrated a rather luke warm response to attempts to use the common law of torts as a mechanism to control the adverse impacts of pollution on people, property, and the wider environment. The courts have shown a preference for specific pollution legislation, such as the EPA 1990, and have shown minimal support for attempts to develop the common law as a means of resolving modern day environmental problems.

Before we consider each environmental tort in detail a few general points will be made regarding the common law and the law of torts:

(a) common law actions are largely concerned with the protection of *private rights*. These rights, such as property rights, are 'private' in the sense that they relate to humans. Currently no corresponding legal rights exist to bring an action on behalf of the environment or flora and fauna (Stone, 1972 and 1975). It is humans who resort to the common law engage in civil litigation in order to protect their own interests from actual or threatened damage arising out of the use of a neighbouring landowner's property;

(b) in contrast to the Command and Control regulatory frameworks in the EPA 1991 and WRA 1991, with their licence based pollution controls, linked to precise and monitorable licence conditions, the common law has traditionally been associated with imprecise standards. The common law attempts to balance competing private interests and looks to the reasonableness of the activities of competing landowners. It does not lay down strict numerical limits for substances contained in emissions from one person's property discharged into the environment;

(c) proving that the defendant's activities caused the damage sustained (the process of causation) is a difficult and expensive task, bearing in mind the degree of scientific uncertainty which may exist (see *Graham and Graham v ReChem International* [1996] Env LR 158). Damage caused by airborne pollutants may pose a significant evidential problem for the claimant, especially if the claimant's and defendant's properties are some distance from one another and there are other properties in the area which are generating identical or similar polluting emissions;

(d) the right to take action in most cases is strictly limited to those persons whose property or property related interests have been harmed (see *Hunter v Canary Wharf Ltd* [1997] 2 WLR 684 and *Blackburn v ARC Ltd* [1998] Env LR 469);

(e) in a common law action the court makes a largely subjective decision as to whether the defendant's activities are unreasonable, taking into account the degree of tolerance which would be expected of a reasonable neighbour;

(f) the grant of, and compliance with, a pollution discharge licence issued by a regulator under Command and Control legislation, such as the WRA 1991, does not prevent the defendant being liable in an action based on tort;

(g) the common law is mainly a reactive and compensatory mechanism. Only rarely will the courts, in such an action, grant an injunction to prevent anticipated, future damage or interference;

(h) the usual remedy, in the event that an action is successful, is an award of damages to the claimant to put him or her back in the same position that he or she would have been in had the tort not been committed. Except in the case of negligence actions, the claimant may seek an injunction to restrain the defendant's behaviour which is causing injury to the claimant's interests. The award of an injunction will almost certainly be more important to both parties than damages. Injunctions are generally only awarded to stop or restrict continuing activities;

(i) a successful claimant is not obliged to spend any damages received on restoring the environment, even if this was the basis of the complaint;

(j) injury or damage relating to some aspect of the environment valued by the public or harm to man is often a powerful factor which motivates the claimant to pursue a case in order to make a defendant accountable for the alleged wrong (Pugh and Day, 1995);

(k) the legal standard of proof in civil cases requires the claimant to prove his case 'on the balance of probabilities'. In other words, it is more likely than not that the defendant's actions caused the relevant injury to the claimant or his interests.

10.3 Remedies

The common law offers various remedies which will be sought by the claimant depending upon the particular circumstances of each case. Each remedy is discussed below.

10.3.1 Damages

The object of damages in the law of tort is to put the claimant into the position he would have been in had the harm or damage not occurred. This is particularly difficult to calculate in relation to environmental damage, because it is often the case that the cost of environmental damage can never be calculated for many years, as clean-up may take several years, or the damage can never be fully rectified.

The most common form of damages to be awarded by the courts are compensatory damages, where the claimant is compensated for any loss that has been suffered.

There are several other forms of damages which may be awarded, for example:

(a) *aggravated damages* – are awarded where the court wishes to express disapproval of the defendant's conduct and compensate the claimant who has suffered more than would normally be expected;

(b) *punitive/exemplary damages* – are awarded where it is the court's intention to punish the tortfeasor by adding an additional award onto the compensatory damages awarded, which may also have the effect of deterring others from acting in a similar fashion. The award of exemplary damages is largely governed by the rules established in *Rookes v Barnard* (1964), in which it was stated that damages of this type could only be awarded in three strict classes of cases:

- where servants of the Government act in an oppressive, arbitrary or unconstitutional way. In *Gibbons v South West Water Services Ltd* (1992), a claim in private nuisance, it was held that this could not apply to private individual's or corporations;

- where the defendant's conduct was calculated to profit from the tort. This is particularly appropriate in environmental cases, because often industrial operators feel that it would be more profitable to continue with the polluting activity and to face the consequences when paying damages, rather than to cease production or to operate with less polluting techniques;

- where the statute expressly permits the payment of exemplary damages.

10.3.2 Injunction

In addition, or as an alternative to damages, the claimant may seek an injunction.

Injunctions essentially allow the courts to require that the defendant discontinues the offending operation and/or takes action to prevent or remedy the damage or pollution that has been caused.

Injunctions can be classified as:

(a) mandatory injunctions, in which case the court will order the defendant to undo or remedy the damage, or prevent further damage from occurring;

(b) prohibitory injunctions, which order the defendant not to continue with the wrongful act. The duration of a prohibitory injunction is determined by the court with regard to the offending activity and the nature of its effects.

Injunctions provide the potential for a powerful common law weapon against polluters and their activities because they can allow the courts to adopt the exact remedy to the nature of the damage being caused. For example, it may be possible for the court to order a mandatory clean-up of a gradual chemical spillage, or prohibit the operation of a polluting activity that is affecting the defendant.

The effect of injunctions can be particularly damaging for those upon whom they are imposed, for example in the Irish case of *Bellew v Cement Ltd* (1948), an injunction closed the cement factory for three months. The effects of such an injunction are obviously detrimental to commercial interests and could therefore deter further polluting operations by the same firm or by others fearing similar results. Where an injunction requires that action is taken to prevent or minimise environmental damage, without actually closing the operation, the effects can be equally damaging because of the expense incurred. To this extent injunctions have the similar deterrent effects as legislative penalties. The financial and commercial implications of injunctions are potentially very damaging and the significance of common law injunctions should not be forgotten.

Interlocutory injunctions can also allow the court to compel the defendant to take action to cease operation or remedy the damage being caused pending the arrangement of a full hearing.

Injunctions are restricted in that they may only be granted by the court when the activity complained of is substantial, and when it would be reasonable. In order to determine this it is necessary to balance the interests of the polluting activity and significance of its impact on the environment.

The courts have the discretion to award damages and to order an injunction should it be felt necessary. This may arise where an industrial operation has caused significant environmental damage and will continue to do so unless action is taken. In a case such as this it may be appropriate to order damages, which will pay for remediation, and order an injunction to shut down the operation, or require works to minimise its environmental effects.

10.3.3 Abatement

The remedy of abatement dates back many years, although it is rarely used today since its use is not encouraged by the courts. However, it has developed under statute and is the main remedy for statutory nuisance. Under the common law, abatement is known as the 'self-help' remedy because an occupier of land affected may take action to abate the damage.

The definition of abatement was given in *Blackstone's Commentaries on the Laws of England Book III*:

> And the reason why the law allows this private and summary method of doing one's self justice, is because injuries of this kind, which obstruct or annoy or such things as are of daily convenience and use, require an immediate remedy; and cannot wait for the slow progress of the ordinary forms of law.

This point was discussed in *Burton v Winters* (1993) in which it was stated that abatement was a summary remedy which was only justified in clear and simple cases where the nuisance or trespass would not justify the expense of legal proceedings, or in an emergency where an urgent remedy is required.

A common example of abatement was given in *Smith v Giddy* (1904) in which it was held that the plaintiff was entitled to cut back the overhanging branches of his neighbour's ash and elm trees which were damaging the growth of his fruit trees.

10.4 General defences to intentional torts

An action in the law of tort may fail if the defendant can prove reliance on one of the general defences discussed below. There are also defences which are specific to particular torts, which will be discussed in relation to each text.

10.4.1 Statutory authority

If the tort has been authorised by a statute, then this will provide a complete defence, and will not allow the injured party to recover damages. The exact application of the defence of statutory authority will depend on the statute in question.

The defendant must prove that the conduct complained of has arisen as an inevitable result of the activity authorised by the statute and that the defendant has exercised reasonable care in carrying out that activity.

The authority to carry out the activity must be expressly or impliedly authorised by the statute.

An example of implied authority was given in *Allen v Gulf Oil Refining Ltd* (1979). The Gulf Oil Refining Act 1965 authorised the compulsory purchase of land, by the defendants, for the construction of a refinery. It did not explicitly authorise the operation of the refinery. The plaintiff claimed that the operation of the refinery caused a nuisance. The House of Lords held that the defence must apply because the operation of the refinery was implied by the statute and was therefore authorised.

However, this defence may not succeed where the Act specifically envisages that an action in nuisance may be brought (see *Lloyds Bank v Guardian Assurance, Trollope and Colls Ltd* (1986)).

In the case of *Budden v BP Oil Ltd and Shell Oil Ltd* (1980), the Court of Appeal accepted an argument put forward by the defence that they had complied with the relevant statutory provision, s 75(1) of the Control of Pollution Act (COPA) 1974, and accepted that the statutory standard establishes the common law standard. However, the question of whether an authorisation or consent from the Environment Agency constitutes statutory authority remains unclear.

10.4.2 *Volenti non fit injuria*

Meaning literally no injury is done to a person who consents, the defence of *volenti non fit injuria* can be pleaded by the defendant. In order for this defence to succeed, the claimant must voluntarily assume the risk. In order to do this, the claimant must be in position to make a choice as to whether or not to assume the risk and he must also know of the nature and extent of the risk.

10.4.3 Necessity

The defence of necessity is used where the defendant must choose between causing damage to the claimant's property and preventing some greater damage to the public or to a third party. This defence is effective in limited circumstances. Where the defence is raised, it can only succeed if the necessity did not arise from the defendant's negligence. It must also be proved that the defendant has acted in the public benefit, or for the protection of his own property. When determining the applicability of the defence, it is necessary for the courts to judge which of the possible outcomes would be preferred. The limitation attached to the defence of necessity is that the defendant must have acted as a reasonable man in order to avoid a greater danger.

10.4.4 Contributory negligence

Section 1 of the Law Reform (Contributory Negligence) Act 1945 provides:

> Where any person suffers damage as the result partly of his own fault and partly of the fault of any other person or persons, a claim in respect of that damage shall not be defeated by reason of the fault of the person suffering the damage, but the damages recoverable in respect thereof shall be reduced to such extent as the court thinks just and equitable having regard to the claimant's share in the responsibility for the damage.

burden of proof is placed on the defendant to establish that the claimant contributed to the damage resulting in his injuries.

This allows the amount of damages to be reduced in line with the claimant's contribution to his own loss or injury. Damages are often reduced by anything from 10% to 75%, and even a 100% reduction is not unknown.

10.5 Torts

The common law actions which are of most relevance to the private regulation of environmental pollution are the torts of nuisance, trespass, negligence, and the rule in *Rylands v Fletcher*. Of all the four torts it is nuisance which appears to be the most popular ground of action. We consider below the elements of each tort, relevant defences and available remedies.

10.6 Nuisance

Actions in nuisance may be divided into private nuisance, public nuisance and also statutory nuisance as contained in ss 79–82 of the EPA 1990, and supplemented by the Noise and Statutory Nuisance Act 1993. Statutory nuisance was dealt with in Chapter 8. A distinction must be made between the three types of nuisance because they are each significantly different from the others. The tort of private nuisance attempts to reconcile the competing interests of landowners; public nuisance is a crime which protects public rights, although an individual may bring an action where he or she has suffered damage over and above that suffered by the public generally; a statutory nuisance is one which is largely controlled by local authorities exercising their statutory powers.

Today the tort of nuisance is recognised as the area of common law which has contributed most significantly to environmental protection. It is the area of tort which is most commonly relied upon in cases concerning damage to the environment.

10.7 Private nuisance

Private nuisance attempts to achieve a balance of competing rights of neighbours to use their property as they wish. It must be stressed that not every interference with another's use or enjoyment of land can constitute a private nuisance. In order to be actionable, the conduct complained of must constitute an unreasonable interference with an occupier's interest in the beneficial use of his land.

10.7.1 Definition

Private nuisance was defined in *Read v Lyons & Co Ltd* (1947) as 'unlawful interference with a person's use or enjoyment of land or some right over, or in connection with it'.

10.7.2 The two categories of private nuisance

Traditionally private nuisance has been sub-divided into two categories:

(a) those actions involving physical damage to the claimant's land; and

(b) actions involving interference with the claimant's use or enjoyment of land (often referred to as the 'sensibility' cases).

Typically private nuisance actions, in an environmental context, relate to physical damage to property and chattels caused by the defendant's polluting emissions which come into contact with and damage the claimant's property. For example, pollutants may be blown by the wind onto the claimant's land. This is the most common type of nuisance action and it is generally the easiest to prove. Successful actions in private nuisance have been taken against defendants engaged in running various types of activity, reported in the law reports, including: an oil depot, metal foundry, brickworks, cokeworks, landfill site and coal distribution depot. The phrase 'physical damage' includes damage to premises, land, vegetation, chattels and livestock.

Private nuisance actions also relate to cases in which there is no physical damage to property but injury is caused to the claimant's use or enjoyment of land. For example, cases concerning interference with property stemming from unreasonable amounts of noise, unpleasant smells, dust, vibration and infestations emanating from the defendant's land. In order to succeed the claimant must prove that he has suffered 'inconvenience materially interfering with the ordinary physical comfort of human existence, not merely according to elegant or dainty modes and habits of living, but according to plain and sober and simple notions and habits obtaining among the English People' (see *Walter v Selfe* [1854] 4 De G & Sm 315). The focus in these cases is on what the ordinary claimant would find intolerable and not what an especially sensitive (that is, hypersensitive) person would find unreasonable and/or intolerable.

10.7.3 The characteristic features of private nuisance

The tort of nuisance is characterised by the following features:

(a) the nuisance must arise from a continuous state of affairs and not a one-off, isolated event;

(b) the defendant's actions do not have to have been the original cause of the problem. An action may be brought even though the nuisance arises as a result of pre-existing conditions on the defendant's land. For example, historic contamination;

(c) the nuisance must affect land belonging to the claimant or in which the claimant has an interest. In *Hunter and Others v Canary Wharf Ltd* [1997] 2 WLR 684, the House of Lords rejected the proposition that occupiers of property, other than owners and tenants, could sue in private nuisance. This decision has been followed in *Blackburn v ARC Ltd* [1998] Env LR 469, in which the plaintiff's common law wife, who had no proprietary interest in the plaintiff's house, had her claim in nuisance rejected;

(d) the claimant must prove that the damage sustained, whether in the form of physical damage to person, premises, or chattels, or personal discomfort, has been caused by the alleged nuisance. In many environmental pollution cases it may be difficult to prove a causal link between the nuisance and the damage sustained by the claimant;

(e) the type of damage sustained by the claimant must have been reasonably foreseeable at the time when the actions which caused the damage occurred (see *Cambridge Water Co Ltd v Eastern Counties Leather plc* [1994] 1 All ER 53). The plaintiff water company in the *Cambridge Water* case failed in its nuisance action because, at the time polluting chemicals escaped from the defendant's tannery, it was not reasonably foreseeable that solvents could migrate through sub-strata over several years and travel significant distances before contaminating the aquifer from which the water company abstracted drinking water;

(f) where the nuisance causes personal discomfort, as opposed to physical damage, the characteristics of the neighbourhood where the alleged nuisance occurs is taken into account (*St Helens Smelting v Tipping* (1865) 11 HLC 642). Residents living in an established industrial area will be expected to be more tolerant than people living in a purely residential area;

(g) nuisance, in contrast to negligence, does not allow a hypersensitive claimant redress in circumstances in which the ordinary reasonable person would not find the defendant's activities to be a nuisance;

(h) the grant of planning permission will not confer immunity upon the defendant, for liability in nuisance (*Allen v Gulf Oil Refining* [1981] AC 1001), except to the extent that planning permission, when implemented, changes the character of the area (*Wheeler v Saunders Ltd* [1996] Ch 19). Similarly the grant of, and compliance with, a licence to pollute issued by the Environment Agency will not provide the defendant with immunity from a common law action in nuisance;

(i) where a nuisance is found to exist the claimant will generally be awarded damages to place him in the position he would have been in had the nuisance not occurred. However, where the defendant is liable for a nuisance which he did not originally cause, he will only be expected to have taken reasonable steps to remedy the situation in the light of his means.

10.7.4 Reasonableness

The key issue in an action based on nuisance is that the court must judge whether the defendant is using his property reasonably. In *Saunders-Clark v Grosvenor Mansions and D'Allesandri* (1900), Buckley J stated the importance of this requirement of the tort of nuisance:

> ... the court must consider whether the defendant is using his property reasonably or not. If he is using it reasonably, there is nothing which at law can be considered a nuisance: but if he is not using it reasonably ... then the plaintiff is entitled to relief.

Whilst giving consideration to the question of whether the defendant is using his property reasonably, the court attempts to balance the competing interests of the claimant and the defendant. On the one hand, the defendant has a right to conduct activities on his land as he pleases, and on the other hand the claimant has a right to use and enjoy his property without an unreasonable amount of interference. The court must therefore determine whether, on the facts, the defendant is using his property unreasonably. In balancing the competing interests of the claimant and the defendant the courts pay particular attention to the following factors:

(a) locality;

(b) duration;

(c) sensitivity of the claimant;

(d) intention of the claimant;

(e) the defendant's use of best practicable means to minimise the nuisance;

(f) the foreseeability of the type of harm or damage complained of;

(g) the utility of the defendant's conduct.

Each of these is discussed below.

10.7.4.1 Locality

The character of the local environment is a key factor which the courts have regard to in the 'sensibility' nuisance cases. These are nuisance actions which do not involve physical damage but the claimant claims that the defendant's actions have caused injury to the use or enjoyment of the claimant's property. As a general rule a claimant who lives in a highly industrialised or urbanised neighbourhood must accept higher levels of noise and air pollution than might exist in a rural area. The classic statement of the 'locality doctrine' appears in the case of *Sturges v Bridgman* (1879) 11 Ch D 852: 'What would be a nuisance in Belgrave Square would not necessarily be so in Bermondsey.'

The locality doctrine does have limits. For example, in *Rushmer v Polsue and Alfieri Ltd* [1906] 1 Ch 234, the House of Lords upheld the grant of an injunction to the plaintiff to stop the operation of the defendant's printing press during the night. The injunction was granted despite the existence of many other printing presses in the area also operating at night. The court expressed the limits of the locality doctrine as follows: 'It does not follow that because I live, say, in the manufacturing part of Sheffield I cannot complain if a steam-hammer is introduced next door, and so worked as to render sleep at night almost impossible, although previously to its introduction my house was a reasonably comfortable abode, having regard to the local standard; and it would be no answer to say that the steam-hammer is of the most modern approved pattern and is reasonably worked. In short, if a substantial addition is found as fact in any particular case, it is no answer to say that the neighbourhood is noisy, and that the defendant's machinery is of first class character.' Also of relevance to the locality doctrine is the decision in *Gillingham BC v Medway (Chatham) Dock Co Ltd* [1993] QB 343. This case concerned the grant of planning permission to transform a former naval dockyard into a commercial port. The development generated high levels of heavy goods vehicle traffic throughout day and night which disturbed residents living adjacent to the roads giving access to the port. The local residents persuaded their local authority to take an action in public nuisance. The court held that the grant of planning permission had changed the character of the neighbourhood and therefore any allegation of nuisance was to be judged by reference to what was acceptable in a commercial, rather than a residential, area. The decision in the *Gillingham* case was subsequently clarified, by the Court of Appeal, in *Wheeler v JJ Saunders Ltd* [1996] Ch 19. Planning permission had been granted for development consisting of pig rearing units. A nuisance action was commenced in regard to smells emanating from the pig unit. The court rejected the proposition that the grant of planning permission automatically operates to create a defence to a nuisance action based on the grant of planning permission changing the character of the area. The plaintiff was awarded an injunction. The court sought to limit the application of the *Gillingham* case to developments which concerned 'strategic' planning developments (major developments). In the context of a planning decision relating to a commercial port, interference with private rights had been weighed against the public interest, and the level of interference was found to be acceptable. The decision clarified that it is the implementation of planning permission, rather than the grant of permission, which may change the character of the area.

10.7.4.2 Sensitivity of the claimant

The concept of sensitivity of the claimant has considerable potential in environmental law but has not been explored by the courts. Where the claimant is deemed to be abnormally sensitive, there can be no actionable nuisance. This was explained in *Robinson v Kilvert* (1889), in which the plaintiff claimed that heat from the defendant's property which was situated in the basement, was having an adverse effect on the brown paper stored at his premises. It was held that there was no actionable nuisance because:

> ... a man who carries on an exceptionally delicate trade cannot complain because it is injured by his neighbour doing something lawful on his property, if it is something which would not injure anything but an exceptionally delicate trade.

The rationale behind this principle is consistent with the law of nuisance, namely that each owner of property should have a right to reasonably use and enjoy his land.

A further example of abnormal sensitivity was given in the case of *Heath v Brighton* (1908). In this case the vicar of a church sought an injunction to restrain the noise from the defendant's power station. The vicar failed because the noise had neither interrupted services nor had it affected attendance at church, it merely irritated the vicar.

10.7.4.3 Duration of the nuisance

The ability to obtain redress, in a nuisance action, depends, in part, upon the claimant being able to prove that the activity alleged to constitute a nuisance is a continuing problem. In *Bolton v Stone* [1951] AC 850, the Court of Appeal rejected a nuisance action relating to the activities of the defendant cricket club because the plaintiff could only establish that cricket balls had been hit out of the ground six times in 30 years.

There are exceptions where the application of this rule could be deemed unreasonable. An example of such unreasonableness was given in *De Keyser's Royal Hotel Ltd v Spicer Bros Ltd* (1914). The case was brought on the grounds that the defendants' building operations were so loud that guests at the hotel were unable to sleep and after-dinner speakers were unable to make themselves heard. It was held that the defendants were not carrying out the operations in a reasonable and proper manner.

10.7.4.4 Intention of the defendant

The defendant's motives may also be some indication of the reasonableness of his conduct. In *Hollywood Silver Fox Farms v Emmett* (1936), the defendants' actions, which were motivated by malice, were found to be unreasonable. The courts may examine and take into account the defendant's motives which prompted the conduct complained of. In *Hollywood Silver Fox Farm v Emmett* [1936] 2 KB 468, the defendant's malicious intent to disrupt the plaintiff's fox farm by discharging a shotgun during the mating season, was held to be an actionable nuisance. Environmental malice could include the likes of noise in neighbour disputes.

10.7.4.5 Utility of the defendant's conduct

If the defendant is carrying out operations which provide a general benefit to the whole community, then the nuisance will be more reasonable or justifiable than if his motive is purely selfish or malicious. There is clearly a link between the defendant's motives and the utility of his conduct. Whilst the courts do take into account of the social utility of the defendant's activities it appears that this factor is not a key consideration (*Kennaway v Thompson* [1981] QB 88).

10.7.4.6 The defendant's use of best practicable means to minimise the nuisance

The defendant's use of best available abatement technology to minimise the impact of the alleged nuisance upon the claimant will be taken into account by the court and will be given appropriate weight. Utilisation of the best practicable means (including 'best available techniques not entailing excessive costs' and 'best available techniques'), by the defendant, does not provide an automatic defence. The courts will have regard to the severity of the impact of the defendant's activities upon the claimant and whether any further preventive action could have been taken by the defendant. Thus, a defendant who is complying with the terms of a licence to pollute may not necessarily be able to defeat a nuisance action. In *Read v J Lyons and Co Ltd* [1947] AC 156, the House of Lords, in a nuisance action in respect of an explosion at a munitions factory, held that if a man commits a nuisance it is no answer to his neighbour's complaint that he took the utmost care not to commit the nuisance. Even if a factory has been operated with reasonable care it is still open to the court to find that the defendant's activities constitute a nuisance.

10.7.4.7 The foreseeability of the type of harm or damage complained of

It is necessary for the claimant to prove that the *type* of damage caused to his or her use or enjoyment of land was *foreseeable at the time the relevant damage occurred*. The leading case on this issue is *Cambridge Water Co Ltd v Eastern Counties Leather plc* [1994] 2 AC 264. The House of Lords, in rejecting the plaintiff's private nuisance action, held that liability depended upon the foreseeability of the relevant type of damage occurring. The damage in this particular case consisted of the presence of polluting solvents in an aquifer from which the plaintiff abstracted drinking water. Although it was proved that the solvents had emanated from the defendant's property, the court held that at the time the spillages of solvents had occurred, it was not foreseeable that the escape of those solvents would result in damage to the aquifer.

10.7.5 Who can bring an action in private nuisance?

It is a long established principle that, in order to sue in nuisance, the claimant must have an interest in the land affected. This will include the occupier of the land, a tenant in possession, and it can extend to those with a variety of other legal interests in land. This has the effect of excluding public interests in private nuisance cases.

10.7.6 Against whom can a nuisance action be brought?

Action can be brought against a variety of parties, not only the 'polluter' but also those who allowed or authorised the pollution or environmental damage.

A nuisance action can be brought against the following –

(a) The creator of the nuisance: the party who creates the nuisance may always be sued. This is the case whether or not the creator of the nuisance is the occupier of the land at the time (see *Thompson v Gibson* (1841)).

(b) The occupier of the premises: the occupier will be liable in two situations:

   • if he or she creates the nuisance; or

   • if the nuisance is caused by his or her servant or agent.

   In *Leakey v National Trust* (1980), it was stated that where the nuisance is not being created by the occupier, he or she is only expected to do what is reasonable in the individual circumstances to prevent or minimise a known risk to his or her neighbour.

(c) The landlord: there is a generally recognised rule that a landlord will generally not be liable because he is not in occupation of the property, unless he has authorised the nuisance, as in *Tetley v Chitty* (1986). In this case, the local authority, as landlord, was held liable for the noise caused by go-karting activities because the authority knew, or should have known, of the nuisance before the property was let.

10.7.7 Defences

10.7.7.1 Statutory authority

This defence is only available to bodies exercising statutory powers whose activities are alleged to be causing a nuisance. To avail themselves of this defence the defendant must be able to show that it did not cause any unnecessary inconvenience in the way it carried out the activities authorised by the legislation. The court will take into account the methods and equipment used by the defendant to complete the works. It will also have regard to the scale of the development, its social utility, and the timescale within which it took the defendant to complete the development. In *Allen v Gulf Oil Refining Ltd* [1981] AC 1001, a private Act of Parliament provided the defendant oil company with statutory authority to acquire land in Milford Haven for the purpose of building an oil refinery. Once the refinery was operational local residents brought a nuisance action in regard to the smells, noise and vibration generated by the defendant's activities. The plaintiffs argued that the defence of statutory authority did not apply in this case because the relevant Act did not specifically refer to, and therefore authorise, the operation of the plant in a manner which created a nuisance. The House of Lords rejected this submission and held that the Act conferred an immunity for all acts inevitably flowing from the authority to build the refinery. The plaintiffs could only succeed if they could establish that the nuisance complained of was much greater than was necessary or where the defendant had carried out its activities negligently. In short, redress is only possible if it can be proved that the defendant failed to exercise reasonable care to minimise the nuisance. An example of a case in which the defendant failed to exercise reasonable care is *Tate & Lyle Industries Ltd v GLC* [1983] AC 509. The defendant local authority constructed a ferry terminal with the benefit of statutory authority, however, the development caused the silting up of the River Thames around the plaintiff sugar refiners' river jetties. The plaintiff sued in nuisance to recover the £50,000 it had incurred in dredging the river in order to maintain access to its jetties. The court found in favour of the plaintiff but awarded only 75% of its claim on the ground that even if the defendant had exercised reasonable care in the construction of the terminal some dredging would still have been necessary.

Whilst it is clear that special Acts of Parliament will entitle a defendant to claim the defence of statutory authority it seems that other legislative provisions, such as the grant of a pollution licence by the Environment Agency under the EPA 1990, will not, in most cases, entitle the defendant to the defence of statutory authority. In *Wheeler v JJ Saunders Ltd* [1996] Ch 19, Gibson LJ stated that 'the court should be slow to acquiesce in the extinction of private rights without compensation as a result of administrative decisions which could not be appealed and were difficult to challenge'. Gibson LJ went on to concede, however, that there might be instances where a regulatory body may legitimately override private rights.

One recent case to consider private nuisance in an environmental context is *Blackburn v ARC Ltd* [1998] Env LR 469. The case concerned a landfill site which was alleged to be causing a nuisance due to (a) litter escaping from the site, (b) odour problems relating to the failure of the defendant properly to cover over the waste and also from landfill gases, and (c) noise from lorry traffic, site machinery and gas flare.

The High Court held that the defence of statutory authority only applied if the statutory authority changed the character of the area or there was direct statutory authorisation for the development. In this case there was no change in character because the relevant permissions, planning permission and waste management licence, were of a temporary nature. The plaintiff's claim would fail if the nuisance would have inevitably resulted from the authorised activities. However, in this case, the nuisance was not inevitable and could have been avoided if the defendants had operated their site properly. The court went on to hold that where the defendant's activities did inevitably lead to the release of odours and gas in circumstances where the release could not have been avoided, then in order to establish nuisance the plaintiff must prove that the defendant's use of land was not a reasonable user. It was clear that the use of land as a waste tip which generated odours and gases was not a reasonable use of land. If the odours and gas were more than must be tolerated in modern living conditions the defendant would be liable. Additionally the court held that the principle of 'give and take', applying to the activities of neighbouring landowners (and referred to by Lord Goff in *Cambridge Water*) depended upon the defendant's use of land being a reasonable use, however, in this case the defendant's activities 'fell well outside any latitude which the law may have allowed'.

10.7.7.2 The defendant takes reasonable precautions to minimise the nuisance

The courts make a distinction between those cases in which the defendant is the original cause of the nuisance and those cases in which the defendant acquires land and continues a pre-existing nuisance. In the former case the fact that the defendant took all reasonable care to minimise the nuisance will not provide a defence because liability is strict. In *Read v Lyons* [1947] AC 156, Lord Symons stated: 'If a man commits a legal nuisance, it is no answer to his injured neighbour that he took the utmost care not to commit it. There the liability is strict.' In the later case, in which the defendant subsequently becomes aware that a nuisance is being caused and takes all reasonable precautions to minimise the nuisance then the defendant will have a defence.

10.7.7.3 The claimant came to the nuisance

It is not a defence for a defendant to argue that the claimant exposed himself to a nuisance by moving to it. This is relevant to the owners of factories which, at some point after construction, are surrounded by residential development. The law does not prevent residential property owners from taking action in regard to nuisance caused by the operation of factories, but the chances of such an action being successful are limited. The leading case on this issue is *Bliss v Hall* (1838) 4 Bing NC 183, in which the defendant established business as a tallow chandler. Three years later the plaintiff moved into the neighbouring property and commenced a nuisance action against the defendant in regard to the fumes produced by the tallow works. Tindall CJ stated: 'The plaintiff came to the house he occupies with all the rights which the common law affords, and one of them is the right to wholesome air. Unless the defendant shows a prescriptive right to carry on his business in the particular the plaintiff is entitles to judgment.' Awareness of the possibility that conflicts might arise between competing property owners will not be allowed to interfere with the operation of the town and country planning system. The High Court held in *R v Exeter CC ex p JL Thomas and Co Ltd* [1991] 1 QB 471 that a planning authority may grant planning permission for development which may give rise to complaints and legal action against the owners of existing development by owners of new developments.

10.7.7.4 One of many polluters

It is no defence to a nuisance action for the defendant to argue that the defendant's contribution to the nuisance suffered by the claimant is so insignificant that it is not actionable. The authority for this principle is *Blair v Deakin* (1887) 57 LT 522, a case in which effluent from several upstream defendants created a nuisance for a downstream factory owner. This principle should be viewed with some caution since the means to detect, measure, and identify pollutants is now very much more advanced than when this case was decided.

10.7.7.5 Prescription

The likelihood of this defence succeeding in most circumstances is remote. Whilst, in theory, it is possible to acquire an easement to pollute, in practice this defence is very difficult to establish. To succeed, the right to pollute which is claimed must be lawful (that is, not a discharge in breach of the conditions of a pollution licence), which is openly exercised, which continues for a period of at least 20 years, and which is exercised without the permission of the person against whom the right is being acquired. In *Sturges v Bridgman* (1879) 11 Ch D 852, the defendant had operated noisy machinery on his land for over 20 years. An adjoining landowner, a doctor, extended his premises by constructing a consulting room close to the boundary with the defendant's property. The doctor then commenced, and succeeded in, an action in nuisance against the defendant due to the unreasonable level of noise generated by the defendant's machines. The court rejected the defendant's argument that he had acquired an easement authorising the nuisance. The time from which the right to pollute was calculated was the time, or point, at which the nuisance began, and the time ran from the date of construction of the consulting rooms.

10.7.8 Remedies

10.7.8.1 Injunctions

To succeed in obtaining an injunction the claimant must have a strong case. The courts are reluctant to grant injunctions unless there is good evidence that the defendant's activities are having a significant and adverse impact upon the claimant which justifies restricting, totally or partially, the defendant's activities which are causing the nuisance. The following cases illustrate the circumstances in which a claim for an injunction may succeed or fail. In *Halsey v Esso Petroleum Co Ltd* [1961] WLR 683, the plaintiff successfully obtained an injunction relating to the noise from the defendant's boilers and vehicle movements to and from the plant. In *Allison v Merton, Sutton and Wandsworth AHA* [1975] CLY 2450, the plaintiff was granted an injunction to restrain the noise from the defendant's hospital boilers which interfered with the plaintiff's sleep and caused feelings of depression falling short of a clinical depressive illness. In *AG v Gastonia Coaches Ltd* [1977] RTR 219, the plaintiff successfully obtained an injunction against the defendant coach company to restrain a nuisance consisting of diesel odours and noise disturbance caused by the defendant 'revving' coach engines in a residential street. In *Blackburn v ARC Ltd* [1998] Env LR 469, the plaintiffs applied for an injunction to close down the defendant's landfill site which was alleged to be causing a nuisance due to litter, odour and vehicle movements. The landfill site only had a further three years' of 'life' left and the court declined to grant an injunction closing the site down. Whilst the court accepted that the primary remedy for continuing nuisances was an injunction, it was a discretionary remedy and in the circumstances of this case damages provided adequate compensation for the diminution in value of the plaintiff's property. The court stated that it would be open to the plaintiff to seek a further injunction at any time in the future if a repetition of the serious failures of the past were to recur.

10.7.8.2 Compensation

Compensation may be awarded to the claimant in regard to damage to property and chattels. The position regarding the recovery of compensation for personal injury caused by nuisance is unclear and therefore the claimant will include a negligence claim to cover any personal injury.

10.7.8.3 Sensibility claims

An award of damages is the norm in such cases and the sum awarded will reflect the severity and persistence of the nuisance. In *Bone v Seal* [1975] 1 All ER 787, the plaintiff was awarded £6,000, reduced to £1,000 on appeal, regarding intermittent odour problems from a neighbouring pig farm extending over a 12 year period. The Court of Appeal expressed the opinion that the original award would have been appropriate had the plaintiff experienced a serious and permanent loss of amenity.

10.7.8.4 Loss of profits

In contrast to negligence actions, in which pure economic loss is not recoverable, once damage has been proved in a nuisance action liability is strict. In appropriate cases loss of profits are recoverable. In *Blackburn v ARC Ltd* [1998] Env LR 469, the plaintiff included a claim for loss of profits relating to renovation works carried out at the plaintiff's home. The court rejected the claim on the basis that such losses were not a foreseeable consequence of the particular nuisance. Although the loss of profits claim failed the plaintiff did recover £25,000 in respect of the diminution of the value of his home.

10.7.8.5 Exemplary damages

The circumstances in which exemplary damages may be claimed are very limited. The claimant will succeed if the defendant has deliberately interfered with the claimant's property rights and has cynically calculated that his interference will produce a financial gain greater than the cost of the damage to the claimant (see *AB v South West Water Services Ltd* [1993] 1 All ER 609).

10.8 Public nuisance

The tort of public nuisance shares many of the elements of private nuisance, although there are several distinguishing factors. It is also possible for the nuisance to be actionable as both a public and private nuisance.

10.8.1 Definition

Public nuisance was defined in the case of *AG v PYA Quarries* (1957):

> A public nuisance is one which materially affects the reasonable comfort and convenience of a life of a class of Her Majesty's subjects who come within the sphere or neighbourhood of its operation; the question whether the number of persons affected is sufficient to constitute a class is one of fact in every case and it is sufficient to show that a representative cross-section of that class has been so affected for an injunction to issue.

10.8.2 The characteristic features of public nuisance

Actions in public nuisance have the advantage that no interest in land is required by a claimant in order to commence an action. The House of Lords decision in *Hunter and Others v Canary Wharf Ltd* [1997] 2 WLR 684, with its rejection of private nuisance actions by occupiers of property who have no legal rights as owners or tenants of property, is likely to increase interest in the use of public nuisance by licensees who cannot otherwise sue in nuisance.

Public nuisance must affect a wide class of the public. In contrast to private nuisance, public nuisance is a crime and this enables the Attorney General or a local authority to prosecute the defendant. An action in public nuisance may be brought by an individual or a group of citizens provided that he, she or they can establish that he, she or they have suffered special damage (damage over and above that which is suffered by the general public). Typically public nuisance actions might relate to:

(a) repeated exposure to offensive smells generated by landfill sites or incinerators;

(b) intolerable noise created by a factory which is operating 24 hours a day and disturbs many people; or

(c) widespread contamination of water supplies posing a threat to the health of a large number of people.

Public nuisance is founded on the commission of an actionable wrong which has a material effect on a large number of people. Some guidance on the numbers of people who must be affected to justify an action in public nuisance is provided by the *Docklands* case (*Hunter v Canary Wharf* [1997] 2 WLR 684). In that action approximately 600 people constituted a sufficiently wide class to mount an action relating to disturbance caused by construction dust and interference with TV reception.

The case of *R v South West Water Authority* (1991) was brought following the water pollution incident at Camelford, Cornwall, which attracted a considerable amount of press coverage at the time.

In July 1988, 20 tonnes of aluminium sulphate was put into the wrong tank at a water treatment works. Although the alarm was raised almost immediately, remedial action was not taken for several hours, during which time there were reports that the water smelt and tasted foul, that it was black, it burnt mouths and hair and stuck fingers together. It was later reported that the water had caused considerable personal injury in the form of hair loss, nail deformities, rheumatism, diarrhoea and memory loss.

The action was brought as criminal proceedings against South West Water Authority. The authority was found guilty of committing a public nuisance by supplying water contaminated with aluminium sulphate which endangered the health or comfort of the public. The authority was fined £10,000 and was ordered to pay costs of £25,000.

10.8.3 Who can bring an action in public nuisance?

Public nuisance actions may be commenced by members of the public, a local authority, or the Attorney General. Public nuisance actions will, as a general rule, only be commenced where the relevant local authority is unwilling to take action. If a member of the public commences an action he or she must have suffered substantial damage (that is greater than that suffered by the public in general). The damage must also be of a type which was reasonably foreseeable. In *Halsey v Esso Petroleum Co Ltd* [1961] 2 All ER 145, a public nuisance action was possible because oily smuts had damaged vehicles parked in the public highway, as opposed to being parked on private property. In addition, the noise of heavy vehicles travelling to and from the refinery on the public highway also justified an action in public nuisance. The special damage sustained by Halsey was damage to the paintwork of his motor car.

A public nuisance action may be commenced by a claimant where interference with a public right also violates the claimant's private rights. In *Tate & Lyle Industries Ltd v GLC* [1983] 2 AC 509, an action in public nuisance was possible because, not only did the defendant's construction work interfere with public navigation rights but it also interfered with the plaintiff's right of access to its river jetties.

Section 222 of the Local Government Act 1972 provides local authorities with a discretionary power to commence public nuisance actions. This power is used infrequently due to the preference of local authorities for their statutory nuisance powers (see Chapter 8). In contrast to private nuisance, the use of best practicable means to abate a public nuisance is a complete defence to a statutory nuisance action. This may be a factor in the decision by the public to commence a public nuisance action rather than relying upon the local authority. Also if a local authority does commence a public nuisance action aggrieved citizens will not be able to claim compensation for the damage they have suffered. Worse still, if a local authority fails to establish that a public nuisance exists, it will not be able to claim injunctive relief and aggrieved citizens may be left without a remedy.

The Attorney General is entitled to take action to redress public wrongs. In the event that an individual, who wishes to commence an action in public nuisance, cannot prove that he has suffered special damage he may request either the Attorney General, or the local authority, to take action.

10.8.4 Against whom can the action in public nuisance be brought?

As in private nuisance, an action may be brought against the following:

(a) the creator of the nuisance;

(b) the occupier of the premises;

(c) the landlord.

10.9 Defences in public nuisance and private nuisance actions

The following are defences in public and private nuisance actions:

(a) statutory authority;

(b) contributory negligence;

(c) prescription (only available in private nuisance) – the law will not allow an action in nuisance to succeed if the state of affairs which constitutes the actionable nuisance has continued for more than 20 years. For this defence to succeed, the claimant must know that the actionable nuisance has run from the beginning of this 20 year period, as was decided in *Sturges v Bridgman* (1879);

(d) consent of the claimant – in circumstances in which the claimant has consented, either expressly or impliedly, to the nuisance, the defendant cannot be liable, unless there is some negligence on his part. An example of this defence was given in *Kiddle v City Business Properties Ltd* (1942);

(e) ignorance – ignorance of the nuisance can only be classed as a defence if it is not a result of the defendant's failure to act with reasonable skill and care in order to discover the nuisance;

(f) other defences – many other defences have been raised, although few have been successful; for example, it would be no defence for the defendant to argue that the claimant had 'come to the nuisance', nor could the defendant argue that the activity is of some use to the public in general, although it may be an issue which is considered in determining whether the defendant's use of the land is reasonable.

10.10 Remedies in nuisance actions

Remedies in nuisance actions are:

(a) abatement;

(b) injunction;

(c) damages.

Damages are certainly available for physical damage to the claimant's property, although it is not clear if damages can be awarded for personal injury. Some commentators feel that an action under negligence may be the only way to claim damages for personal injury. It is also possible that damages for economic loss may be available although there is no clear judicial guidance on this point.

10.11 Negligence

Negligence actions have advantages and disadvantages. The claimant does not require an interest in land in order to sue and damages are available to compensate personal injuries. Conversely, injunctions are not available, pure economic loss and exemplary damages are not recoverable, the negligent actions of the defendant's independent contractors may shield the defendant from liability, and in contrast to other torts, fault must be proved. There are a number of situations in which negligence is probably the only cause of action available. These include situations in which the claimant has no proprietary interest, and where a public body has failed in its duty to protect the environment. For example, by failing to give a warning which results in damage (see *Scott-Whitehead v NCB* (1987) P & CR 263).

10.11.1 Definition

A definition of negligence was given by Lord Wright in *Lochgelly Iron and Coal Co v McMullen* (1954):

> Negligence means more than heedless or careless conduct ... it properly connotes the complex concepts of duty, breach and damage thereby suffered by the person to whom the duty was owing.

In order to establish negligence, the claimant must prove the following:

(a) that a duty of care is owed to the claimant by the defendant;

(b) that there is a breach of this duty;

(c) there is damage resulting from this breach of duty; and

(d) that the damage was foreseeable.

10.11.2 Duty of care

The general duty of care in negligence was established in *Donoghue v Stevenson* (1932). The general principle behind the duty of care is the 'neighbour principle' – meaning that 'you must take reasonable care to avoid acts or omissions which you can reasonably foresee would be likely to injure your neighbour'. The neighbour is defined as 'persons who are so closely and directly affected by my act that I ought reasonably to have them in contemplation as being so affected when I am directing my mind to the acts or omissions which are being called into question'.

This principle has developed over the years and it would now appear that the requirements for establishing a duty of care are:

(a) foreseeability of damage;

(b) a proximate relationship between the parties;

(c) that it is just and reasonable to impose such a duty.

10.11.3 Breach of duty of care

Once the duty of care has been established, it is necessary to go on to establish that the defendant was in breach of this duty of care and, further, that his breach resulted in damage. In order to determine whether there has been a breach of the duty of care, it is necessary to look at the conduct of the defendant and ask whether he has achieved the standard of care that is necessary if he is not to be liable. The standard used is that of the 'reasonable man'. This is an objective standard and as such no concessions are made for individual weaknesses. The courts will look at the following factors to determine whether the defendant has acted as a reasonable man:

(a) the likelihood of harm;

(b) the seriousness of the risk;

(c) the end to be achieved;

(d) the cost and practicability of avoiding the risk.

Where the duty of care relates to a specialised area, then the duty of care expected is one which would be expected from someone with those skills in the same profession, as was decided in *Bolam v Friern Hospital Management Committee* (1957). Where industrial practices are concerned, one must look to standards which are deemed reasonable by the industry concerned.

In the case of *Dominion Natural Gas Co v Collins & Perkins* (1909), it would appear that where hazardous substances are involved in the industrial practice then the standards will be judged accordingly:

> What that duty is will depend on the subject matter of the things involved. It has, however, again and again been held that in the case of articles dangerous in themselves, such as loaded firearms, poisons, explosives and other things *ejusdem generis*, there is a particular duty to take precaution imposed upon those who send forth or install such articles when it is necessarily the case that other parties will come within their proximity.

Clearly this will have important implications for those operating technical operations that involve such substances.

10.11.4 Foreseeable damage arising from the breach of the duty of care

An action in negligence can only be brought where the negligence has caused, or contributed to, personal injury or damage to property. The courts usually use the 'but for' test to determine whether the defendant's breach of duty was the cause of the damage.

Damage must also be reasonably foreseeable, as the defendant will not be liable for the unforeseen consequences of his negligent act. (See, further, *Overseas Tankship (UK) Ltd v Morts Dock & Engineering Co Ltd (The Wagon Mound)* (1961).)

Following the House of Lords decision in *Cambridge Water* [1994] 2 AC 264, foreseeability of the relevant type of harm or damage is a necessary prerequisite of liability in negligence, nuisance and the rule in *Rylands v Fletcher*. The test of foreseeability in the *Cambridge Water* case was based on what the reasonable supervisor, who was overseeing the operation of the defendant's tannery, would have foreseen as the consequence of repeated spillages of solvents over a prolonged period of time. The court held that, at the material time, the supervisor might reasonably have foreseen that repeated spillages of solvents, in relatively small quantities, might result in solvent fumes affecting the breathing of the defendant's employees, but not contamination of groundwaters. Little was known about the migration of chemicals in sub-surface strata at the relevant time the spillages were occurring and the supervisor could not reasonably have foreseen the relevant type of harm which occurred.

It should be noted that in recent years greater emphasis has been placed on the prudence of businesses employing risk assessments to identify pollution risks associated with their activities. The harmful practices which formed the basis of the *Cambridge Water* litigation occurred in the late 1970s at a time when industrial practice regarding the identification of pollution risks tended to be reactive. It was not uncommon to find that industry would do little to address pollution risks until the regulator produced guidance on specific environmental risks which it had identified.

10.11.5 Damage is a prerequisite of liability

A claimant will fail in a negligence action unless damage is proved. In some circumstances there might be difficulty in determining the precise date when the relevant damage occurred. For example, in the *Cambridge Water* case the damage to the plaintiff's proprietary right to abstract wholesome water from its borehole only occurred when the water in the borehole became unwholesome and unsaleable. This occurred when a European Community (EC) water quality Directive (80/778/EC) was implemented in UK law which set maximum permissible levels for certain chemicals, including solvents.

When tested it was found that the presence of solvents in the water exceeded the limits contained in the directive and the water could no longer be supplied for human consumption.

In the absence of statutory standards the damage occasioned to the claimant must be 'substantial' if the negligence action is to be actionable. The courts employ a 'fact and degree' test to determine when damage is substantial. In the *Docklands* case (*Hunter v Canary Wharf Ltd* [1997] 2 WLR 684), the court referred to substantial damage as 'injury impairing value or usefulness'. In determining whether damage has occurred the courts do not take into account the impact of continuing damage. This may cause problems for the claimant in deciding when to commence an action. If the action is commenced too early there may be difficulties in establishing that damage has actually occurred but if the claimant leaves it too long to commence an action he may have his claim statute barred. The court has the power to strike out an action if it is of the opinion that the damage occurred at a much earlier time than the date on which the claimant commenced the claim (s 14 of the Limitation Act 1980).

10.11.6 Proof

The doctrine of *res ipsa loquitur* (see *Scott v London & St Katherine's Docks Co* [1865] 3 H & C 596) may be invoked by a claimant to reduce the burden of proof in those cases where the claimant is alleging that the injury or damage was caused by negligence, such as the poor design or faulty operation of industrial plant. Any conviction which the defendant has and which is material to the claimant's claim, for example a public nuisance conviction, may be used in evidence to support the claimant's claim. Depending upon the degree of relevance to the claim this may be conclusive in establishing the culpability of the defendant.

10.11.7 Who can bring an action in negligence?

There is no need to prove an interest in the land which is affected, as there is in an action based on private nuisance. It is not necessary to demonstrate loss by other members of the public, which is necessary in cases brought on the grounds of public nuisance.

10.11.8 Against whom can an action in negligence be brought?

An action can be brought against any party where it can be proved that he owns a duty of care to the claimant, that there was a breach of this duty and that this resulted in foreseeable damage or injury. There are, however, policy factors which will limit actions against certain defendants, for example, judges, solicitors and barristers.

10.11.9 Defences

10.11.9.1 Compliance with regulations

The Court of Appeal decision in *Budden and Albery v BP and Shell* ([1980] JPL 586) establishes an important principle in negligence actions: compliance with regulations provides an absolute defence. In the *Budden* case, it was alleged that the defendant petrol companies had been negligent in not eliminating or reducing the lead content of their petrols by July 1978 and that this had caused personal injury to the plaintiffs. The defendants applied to have the action struck out on the basis that compliance with the relevant regulations made under s 75(1) of the COPA 1974 provided them with either a complete statutory defence or a complete answer to the allegation that the defendants had been at fault. The court accepted the second submission but not the first.

10.11.9.2 Fault

In order to avoid liability in negligence industrial defendants must be able to establish that they were, at the material time, operating in accordance with the objectively determined standards of knowledge and best practice applicable in the relevant industry. In assessing whether the defendant has attained the standard required by the duty of care the court will take a number of factors into account including:

(a) the object to be attained;

(b) the practicability of taking precautions;

(c) the existence of approved or general practice;

(d) the defendant's compliance with approved or general practice; and

(e) the risks created by the defendant's activities.

In assessing whether the defendant kept reasonably abreast of emerging risks in the relevant industry the court is likely to apply *Stokes v GKN* [1968] 1 WLR 1776, a case concerning awareness of developing knowledge of occupational health risks.

10.11.10 Remedies

Damages: it is a general principle of the tort of negligence that it is possible to claim damages for physical damage, to the person or to property and for loss consequential to this damage. It is not possible to claim for pure economic loss. (See, further, *Murphy v Brentwood DC* (1990).) Following this, it would be possible to claim damages for injuries caused by a chemical spillage which causes damage to people and property; it would be possible to claim for the clean-up costs; but it would not be possible to claim money for lost profits for the time the site was shut.

Injunction: in *Miller v Jackson* (1977), it was held that an injunction is not an available remedy in an action based in negligence.

10.12 Trespass

The tort of trespass on land has many functions. Its application for environmental purposes is a more recent development, although its use for such purposes appears to be limited as there are few reported cases.

There is some overlap between trespass to land and private nuisance, although it may be easier to bring an action on the basis of trespass because there is no requirement to prove actual damage as there is with nuisance. This is an obvious advantage and it may make an action in trespass in respect of fly-tipped waste, for example, more likely to succeed than an action in private nuisance.

10.12.1 Definition

Trespass to land is the unjustifiable physical interference with land, arising from intentional or negligent entry onto the land. A continuing trespass may be caused by continuing entry onto the land or by allowing physical matter to remain on the land.

In addition to trespass to land an action may be brought in regard to trespass to the person. Whilst it is possible to envisage a situation in which pollution generated by the defendant's activities might give rise to a claim for trespass to the person, in practice the requirement that the interference to the claimant's property or person must be direct has restricted the development of this tort.

The defendant's activities in *McDonald v Associated Fuels Ltd* [1954] DLR 775 illustrate the significance of the intentional nature of the defendant's activities which it is necessary to prove if the claimant is to succeed. The defendant delivered sawdust to the plaintiff's home by blowing it from the defendant's lorry into a storage bin at the plaintiff's home. Exhaust gases from the defendant's lorry were blown into the plaintiff's home along with the sawdust. In consequence the plaintiff was overcome by fumes, collapsed, and suffered injury. The plaintiff's claim based on the negligent actions of the defendant was successful and the court went on to confirm that an action in trespass would also have been successful on the facts. Whilst the defendant did not intend to blow exhaust fumes into the plaintiff's home it intended to do the act which directly caused the injury.

10.12.2 The characteristics of trespass

The following factors which must be present in order for an action for trespass to land to be brought are:

(a) that the trespass was direct;

(b) that the act was intentional or negligent;

(c) a causal link must be proved between the directness of the act and the inevitability of its consequences.

10.12.3 Direct

The interference must be direct rather than consequential. For example, fly-tipping tyres on to someone's property would constitute trespass whereas migration of methane from a landfill would not. The dumping of rubbish on land is a common form of trespass, even if it causes very little damage, as in *Gregory v Piper* (1820), in which the defendant disposed of his rubbish in such a way as to block a right of way. Some of the rubbish rolled against the plaintiff's wall and it was held that the defendant was liable in trespass. In this case it was stated that, in order to be direct, the injury must result from an act of the defendant. An example of this may be found in *Jones v Llanrwst UDC* (1911), in which it was held that sewage, which had been released into a river which had passed downstream and settled on the plaintiff's land, was direct and amounted to trespass.

If the trespass is indirect, then any action should be brought through the law of nuisance.

10.12.4 Intentional or negligent

In order for a trespass to be actionable, it is necessary to prove the defendant's intention or negligence. The intent requirement essentially means that the defendant, or someone under his control, must voluntarily enter the claimant's land. Involuntary entry onto, or into, the claimant's land is not sufficient to constitute trespass.

10.12.5 Causal link between the directness of the act and its effects

It is also imperative to establish a causal link between the directness of the act and the inevitability of its consequences. If the effects of the act are indirect, there can be no trespass; however, there may be a remedy for nuisance or negligence. Establishing a causal link between the defendant's act and both the directness and inevitability of the resultant damage are important restrictions on trespass actions. In *Jones v Llanrwst UDC* [1911] 1 Ch 393, sewage flowing from the defendant's drains polluted a section of river bank belonging to the plaintiff. Whilst the defendant local authority had not intended to deposit sewage onto the plaintiff's land the court held the defendant liable because it had intended the sewage to pass from its drains into the river. The court held that the trespass was sufficiently direct despite the plaintiff's property being some way downstream of the defendant's drain. By contrast, in *Esso Petroleum Co Ltd v Southport Corp* [1956] AC 218, the defendant's tanker ran aground in the Ribble Estuary. To refloat the tanker oil was emptied into the estuary where it was carried by the wind and the tide onto the plaintiff's beach. The House of Lords distinguished this case from *Jones v Llanrwst* on the ground that, unlike the inevitability of a river flowing downstream, it was not inevitable that the oil would wash up on Southport beach. The outcome of this case means that it is virtually impossible to bring a trespass action in regard to an air pollution incident due to the unpredictability of air currents which negates the necessary degree of directness. In contrast, rivers flow in defined channels.

10.12.6 Who can bring an action in trespass?

Any person who is in exclusive possession of the land can bring an action in trespass. Exclusive possession refers to the occupation or physical control of the land.

As trespass is actionable *per se*, the party bringing the action does not have to prove that the trespass has caused actual damage.

10.12.7 Against whom can a trespass action be brought?

The action can be brought against the wrongdoer who has interfered with the possession of the land. An example of this would be where someone has exceeded permission to remain on the land.

10.12.8 Defences

Defences are:

(a) necessity;

(b) licence: a licence gives the express or implied authority which will prevent the trespass from being actionable.

10.12.9 Remedies

Remedies are:

(a) *Damages* – the amount of damages awarded in actions of trespass will usually depend upon the act complained of, particularly as trespass is actionable without any evidence of damage being caused. If the trespass is deemed to be trivial, then the damages awarded will usually be nominal.

Substantial damage will, however, result in an appropriate award of compensation. However, where the trespass has physically damaged the land the level of damages awarded will reflect the reduction in the value of the land rather than the costs of remediation, as in *Lodge Holes Colliery Co Ltd v Wednesbury Corp* (1908), which does not necessarily provide a satisfactory environmental solution;

(b) *Injunction* – it will generally be easier to obtain an injunction in an action for trespass than under any other tort because there is no need to prove any damage.

The claimant may require an injunction to prevent a continuing trespass, for example, to prevent the recurrence of tipping.

10.13 The rule in *Rylands v Fletcher*

10.13.1 Definition

The classic definition of this tortious principle is found in the judgment of Blackburn J in the case of *Rylands v Fletcher* [1868] LR 3 HL 330, 'the person who for his own purposes brings on his land and collects and keeps there anything likely to do mischief if it escapes, must keep it in at his peril, and, if he does not do so, is *prima facie* answerable for all the damage which is the natural consequence of its escape'.

The case involved the construction of a reservoir on the defendant's land by independent contractors. The contractors failed to block off a number of mine shafts under the defendant's land which connected to the plaintiff's mine. When the reservoir was filled the plaintiff's mine became flooded. The defendant, although personally not at fault, was held strictly liable for the damage. He had brought onto his land and collected there something which was likely to do damage if it escaped. The defendant failed in his duty to prevent the escape and was therefore liable for all the damage which was the natural consequence of the escape.

The *Rylands v Fletcher* principle imposes strict, but not absolute, liability for damage caused by the escape of dangerous things. The principle has been applied to a wide range of escapes of substances or objects including: water, fire, gases and fumes, electricity, oil, chemicals, colliery waste, poisonous vegetation, acid smuts, explosives, vibrations, trees and animals. Because the rule imposes strict liability the claimant does not need to prove that the defendant was negligent. The claimant must establish a causal connection between the escape and the damage sustained.

An extra facet to the rule, was added by Lord Cairns, when the case reached the House of Lords. The rule was restricted to circumstances where the defendant had made a 'non-natural' use of his land. The rule applies to things not naturally (ordinarily) present on the defendant's land. The defendant incurs liability by bringing these things onto his land which subsequently escape and cause damage. This has, until the decision in *Cambridge Water*, played an important part in restricting the application of the rule. This restriction came to be associated with the idea that to fall within the rule the defendant's use of his land had to pose an increased risk of injury to others. This idea of 'non-natural' use was referred to in *Rickards v Lothian* [1913] AC 263 as 'some special use bringing with it increased danger to others and must not merely be the ordinary use of the land or such a use as is proper for the general benefit of the community'. To be able to commence an action the claimant was required to establish that the defendant's use of his land was an abnormal use involving an especially hazardous activity.

10.13.2 Which factors must be established for the rule to apply?

In *Read v Lyons* (1947), the necessary factors for establishing liability under the rule in *Rylands v Fletcher* were clarified. They are:

(a) dangerous thing likely to do mischief;

(b) brought on to land;

(c) escape;

(d) non-natural user of the land.

10.13.3 Dangerous thing likely to do mischief

The first essential factor in the application of the rule in *Rylands v Fletcher* is that it applies to 'anything likely to do mischief if it escapes'. There are numerous examples of 'dangerous things', including oil (*Smith v Great Western Railway* (1926)); noxious fumes (*West v Bristol Tramways Co* (1908)); and explosions (*Miles v Forest Rock and Granite Co (Leicestershire) Ltd* (1918)).

In determining the 'dangerous thing' the courts will use a factual test 'whether the thing is likely to do mischief if it escapes'. Following the decision in *Cambridge Water v Eastern Counties Leather plc* (1994), it would appear that there is a requirement that the damage is foreseen as a result of the escape, and possibly that the escape itself is foreseeable (see 10.13.5, below).

10.13.4 Brought on to land

It is not enough for the dangerous thing to be naturally present on the land, it must have been brought onto the land. In *Giles v Walker* (1890), there was no liability for self-sown thistledown which blew from the defendant's land onto the plaintiff's land. There may be liability in nuisance or negligence in such circumstances (see 10.6, above).

10.13.5 Escape

There must also be an escape of the 'dangerous thing' from land before there can be any liability under the rule in *Rylands v Fletcher*. It is not sufficient that there was merely the potential for escape. This was defined in the case of *Read v Lyons*, in which it was stated that escape meant an 'escape from a place when the defendant has occupation, from the place where the occupant has occupation or control over land, to a place which is outside his occupation or control'.

10.13.6 Non-natural user of the land

It is a fundamental principle of the rule that the defendant should have brought onto his land something which was not naturally there. The term 'natural' was interpreted in *Rylands v Fletcher* to mean 'that which exists in or by nature and is not artificial', although more recent cases have centred around the wider definition which covers the concept that a non-natural use is one that brings with it 'increased danger to others and must not merely be the ordinary use of land or such a use as is proper for the general benefit of the community', as was defined in *Rickards v Lothian* (1913). This was followed in *Read v Lyons* by what was essentially a policy decision, that uses which provide some public benefit would be classed as 'natural'. This point was illustrated in *British Celanese Ltd v AH Hunt (Capacitors) Ltd* (1969):

> The manufacturing of electrical and electronic components ... cannot be adjudged to be a special use ... The metal foil was there for use in the manufacture of goods of a common type which at all material times were needed for the general benefit of the community.

The decision of the House of Lords in *Cambridge Water Co v Eastern Counties Leather plc* (1994) may alter the 'non-natural user' requirement. In determining what was a non-natural user, the House of Lords took a fairly broad approach, in line with the original concept of non-natural use, which was that there should be a distinction between something naturally occurring, for example a flood, and an artificial creation such as a reservoir.

A possible reason for this view is that there is less need to restrict possible claims on the natural user ground because of the House of Lords' assertion that foreseeability would be an essential requirement which would limit unfounded claims.

10.13.7 Remoteness

The House of Lords, in *Cambridge Water Co v Eastern Counties Leather plc*, stressed the connection between nuisance and the rule in *Rylands v Fletcher* and suggested that the latter was merely an extension of the former:

> ... it would moreover lead to a more coherent body of common law principles if the rule was to be regarded as essentially an extension of the law of nuisance to isolated escapes from land.

As a result of making this connection, it was stated that the damage must be foreseeable:

> The historical connection with the law of nuisance must now be regarded as pointing towards the conclusion that foreseeability of damage is a prerequisite of the recovery of damages under the rule.

10.13.8 Who can bring an action under *Rylands v Fletcher*?

It is not clear whether it is necessary to have an interest in land to bring an action under the rule in *Rylands v Fletcher*, as there are several cases where the claimant has not had an interest, although it was suggested in *Read v Lyons* that some interest in land will be necessary.

The House of Lords' decision in *Cambridge Water Co v Easter Counties Leather plc* suggests that the rule in *Rylands v Fletcher* is merely an extension of the law of nuisance and if this is so, the ordinary principles of nuisance will apply, namely that the claimant must have an interest in land.

10.13.9 Against whom can an action in *Rylands v Fletcher* be brought?

It would appear that the defendant does not need to have any proprietary interest in the land, it is enough that he merely controls the 'dangerous thing', as was stated in *Rainham Chemical Works v Belvedere Fish Guano* (1921). This suggestion is consistent with the law of nuisance and reflects the close link between nuisance and *Rylands v Fletcher*.

10.13.10 Defences

Although it is widely acknowledged that the rule in *Rylands v Fletcher* created a regime of strict liability, liability is not absolute and the courts have developed a number of defences:

(a) Statutory authority.

(b) Necessity.

(c) Act of God:

> the act of God defence is very limited, as it can only apply to 'forces of nature which no human foresight can provide against, and of which human prudence is not bound to recognise the possibility', as defined in *Tennent v Earl of Glasgow* (1864).

(d) Common benefit:

where the 'dangerous thing' is for the benefit of both the defendant and the claimant, the defendant will not be liable for its escape. This defence is very close to the defence of consent.

(e) Independent act of a third party:

the unforeseeable act of an independent third party is a defence where the defendant has no control over the actions of the third party. The burden of proving this defence lies with the defendant.

Where the third party's act could have been foreseen or action could have been taken to prevent the consequences then the defendant will still be liable. An example of this was given in *Northwestern Utilities v London Guarantee and Accident Co Ltd* (1936).

(f) Default on the part of the claimant:

where the claimant suffers as a result of his or her own act or default the defendant cannot be liable. Where there is contributory negligence on the part of the claimant, the provisions of the Law Reform (Contributory Negligence) Act 1945 apply.

10.13.11 Remedies

Because the rule in *Rylands v Fletcher* has its origins in nuisance, the remedies available appear to be the same as those for public nuisance, namely:

(a) damages – although in *Read v Lyons* it was decided that damages would not be available for personal injury;

(b) injunction – although there is little judicial guidance on this point.

10.14 The case of *Cambridge Water Co v Eastern Counties Leather plc*

The House of Lords' decision in the case of *Cambridge Water Co v Eastern Counties Leather plc* (1994) has made a considerable impact on the interpretation and application of the common law to environmental problems.

10.14.1 The facts of the case

In September 1976, the Cambridge Water Company bought a piece of land which was formerly used as a paper mill at Sawston, Cambridgeshire, attached to which was a licence to abstract water from a borehole on the site.

Cambridge Water Company began to abstract the water for public consumption in June 1979. Unknown to the water company was the fact that the water was contaminated by a solvent which had leached into the aquifer from a nearby tannery operated by Eastern Counties Leather. The spillages of the solvent occurred regularly between 1950 and 1976, after which the tannery began to operate more efficiently. This contamination was not considered an issue until, in 1976, the EC issued Directive (80/778/EC) relating to the standards of drinking water for human consumption and contained figures relating to the maximum levels of perchloroethylene solvent which could be present in the water. The water abstracted from the borehole from Eastern Counties Leather was found to exceed these limits and use of the borehole was discontinued.

It was originally thought that the action would be brought under the WRA 1991; however this proved to be impossible as the pollution pre-dated its enactment. Cambridge Water Company began proceedings against Eastern Counties Leather on the grounds of nuisance, negligence and the rule in *Rylands v Fletcher.*

10.14.2 The High Court's decision

The action was dismissed in nuisance and negligence because it was decided that the defendants, Eastern Counties Leather, could not have foreseen the damage caused to the aquifer arising from their tannery operations.

Kennedy J also considered the application of the rule in *Rylands v Fletcher* and decided that the solvent used by Eastern Counties Leather was a 'natural use' of the land.

10.14.3 The Court of Appeal's decision

The High Court decision was reversed by the Court of Appeal and Cambridge Water Company were awarded £1 m in damages plus costs.

The decision of the Court of Appeal was based on the tort of nuisance and the case of *Ballard v Tomlinson* (1885). The Court of Appeal decided that the pollution of the aquifer by Eastern Counties Leather plc constituted an interference with Cambridge Water Company's 'natural rights' to abstract naturally occurring water which arrived beneath Cambridge Water's his land by percolation through undefined underground channels. It was decided that interference with this natural right to abstract uncontaminated groundwater constituted an actionable nuisance.

The Court of Appeal did not comment on the rule in *Rylands v Fletcher* because it was thought to be 'inapposite in the present case'.

The Court of Appeal's reversal of the High Court's decision was alarming for those who were responsible for causing pollution and provided hope for those in the same position as Cambridge Water Company who were seeking redress for environmental damage.

Appeal to the House of Lords was inevitable.

10.14.4 The House of Lords' decision

The decision of the House of Lords was awaited with a great deal of interest as it was widely anticipated that the outcome would considerably affect the future application and development of the common law and that it would clarify the principles of the common law relating to environmental damage.

The judgment contained important pronouncements on the relationship between nuisance and its effects on the rule in *Rylands v Fletcher* and the element of foreseeability. These elements are discussed below.

10.14.5 Foreseeability

The House of Lords considered the issue of foreseeability in great detail. The following passage indicates the tone of the judgment:

> ... it by no means follows that the defendant should be held liable for damage of a type which he could not reasonably foresee; and the development of the law of negligence in the past 60 years points strongly towards a requirement that such foreseeability should be a prerequisite of liability in damages for nuisance, as it is of liability in negligence.

Lord Goff went on to state that foreseeability of harm 'is a prerequisite of recovery of damages in private nuisance, as in the case of public nuisance'. Therefore there can only be liability where the interference is of a type which can be reasonably foreseen by a person in the defendant's position. In *Cambridge Water Co v Eastern Counties Leather plc* it was decided that the damage caused to the aquifer by the method of delivering the solvents was not reasonably foreseeable at the time the pollution occurred.

The element of foreseeability is an ever-changing factor in light of developments in awareness of environmental problems, and it could now be argued what was not foreseeable in 1976, would be foreseeable today. Certainly, in the light of more scientific evidence about the effects of pollutants and increasingly stringent EC controls, it will be increasingly difficult to sustain the argument that pollution is not foreseeable.

10.14.6 Nuisance and the rule in *Rylands v Fletcher*

The House of Lords considered the relationship between nuisance and the rule in *Rylands v Fletcher*, accepting the view that the rule is 'to be regarded as essentially an extension of the law of nuisance to isolated escapes from land'. In looking at the 'non-natural user' element, the House of Lords indicated that the decisions in previous cases such as *Read v Lyons*, in which a munitions works was classed as a natural user, could not stand today:

> ... the storage of substantial quantities of chemicals on industrial premises should be regarded as an almost classic case of non-natural use.

The judgment further states that the non-natural use distinction as a means of limiting the application of the rule may be unnecessary because of the introduction of the foreseeability requirement.

10.14.7 The courts and environmental protection

Also contained in the judgment was a statement referring to the development of the common law as a means of environmental protection. It was implied that it was the function of Parliament, rather than the courts, to create a statutory regime of liability for environmental damage:

> But it does not follow from these developments that a common law principle, such as the rule in *Rylands v Fletcher*, should be developed or rendered more strict to provide for liability in respect of such pollution. On the contrary, given that so much well informed and carefully structured legislation is now being put in place for this purpose, there is less need for the courts to develop a common law principle to achieve the same end, and indeed it may well be undesirable that they should do so.

10.14.8 The implications of the judgment

The judgment has been viewed by many environmentalists as being restrictive because of the affirmation of requirement of foreseeability in nuisance and the rule in *Rylands v Fletcher*. Critics of the judgment say that only very rarely will it impose liability for pollution cases such as this one. However, many commentators feel that the judgment was the only reasonable and practicable step to be taken in the circumstances, because it is unfair to penalise anyone and impose retrospective liability for operations which were considered perfectly normal and effective at the time. Neither is the judgment as restrictive as some originally interpreted, as it can provide the basis for liability where the polluter knowingly pollutes; this would cover the example of the wilful and careless polluter, or the environmental 'vandal'.

10.15 An evaluation of the common law as a means of environmental protection

It is clear that the common law does have a valid role to play in the protection of the environment. Below is a discussion of both the advantages and disadvantages of the common law in relation to actions arising out of damage to the environment.

10.15.1 Disadvantages

The first fundamental problem associated with the use of the common law to secure environmental protection is that it cannot prevent damage to the environment; its purpose instead is to compensate the owner of the land affected. The remedies can provide such compensation which may finance the remediation. This, however, is contingent upon some environmental damage being done, which is contrary to the aims of current environmental policies which are seeking to prevent the generation of pollution. The availability of compensation to remediate the environmental damage may not necessarily clean up the environmental damage satisfactorily.

Because the development of the common law control has taken place over a number of years and at a time when the environment was not highly regarded, it does not meet the specific needs of environmental protection for a number of reasons:

(a) it operates on the basis of reactive 'cure' rather than prevention;

(b) the common law creates an uncertain level of liability;

(c) it permits individuals to be guardians of the environment only on an *ad hoc* basis, given the uncertainty of establishing that the behaviour complained of was unreasonable and the evidential difficulties associated with this.

Modern environmental laws which have been developed in response to specific environmental problems are better placed to address the needs of environmental protection because they contain express standards and provisions which relate directly to many industrial operations.

Current environmental regulation is also better suited to the needs of industry as it provides standards of acceptable environmental behaviour, namely through Command and Control licence based regulatory regimes. Through these legislative frameworks industry can also seek advice and guidance as to acceptable levels and types of pollution from the Environmental Agency.

In the late 19th century it was established that the courts could not assume the place of the legislature in such cases. This was affirmed in *Cambridge Water Co v Eastern Counties Leather plc*, in which it was stated that it would not be appropriate for the courts to develop the common law principles further.

In the consultation paper issued by the Department of the Environment entitled *Framework for Contaminated Land* (1994, DoE), the Government asserts that the common law should continue to exist in its present form, and that it would be inappropriate to extend the common law through statutory provisions in order to include further defences such as a state of the art defence, or one based on environmental due diligence.

10.15.1.1 Evidence

It may be very difficult to establish the source of the pollution, and further to establish a causal link between the pollution and the damage caused. This is largely because pollution can occur in many ways, it may be an isolated incident, it may result from incidents occurring over a period of years.

Anyone wishing to use such evidence may need to employ specialist consultants to determine the source and the effects of the pollution, which often causes considerable delay and expense when bringing an action under the common law.

10.15.1.2 Costs

The cost of financing a common law action is often extremely prohibitive, especially as the availability of legal aid in such cases is very restricted. An example of a legally aided action is the *Docklands* litigation (*Hunter v Canary Wharf* (1995)).

Where legal aid is not available, it is usually only the wealthy who can take action, an example of this being the rock star Roger Daltry, who brought an action in respect of agricultural pollution which damaged his fish farm in *Beju-Bop Ltd v Home Farm (Iwerne Minster) Ltd* (1990).

The financial problems are exacerbated by the fact that an unsuccessful claimant may have to bear the defendant's legal costs as well as his own.

An action in the law of tort brought following environmental damage is often one that is hard fought by the defendant, who may be a large multinational company. They wish to avoid defeat because this may damage the image of the company, with the potential to affect trade adversely. In order to avoid defeat, the defendants will spend a considerable amount of money on legal advice, representation and presentation of alternative scientific evidence, often far more than the claimant can afford.

An example of such a case is that of *Hanrahan v Merck Sharp and Dohme* (1988), an Irish case, which had it not been for the sheer determination of the plaintiff, and the hardship suffered by him and his family to raise the finances necessary to appeal, would not have reached the Supreme Court, where the earlier decision in favour of *Merck, Sharp and Dohme* was reversed.

The introduction of contingency fees by the Law Society may have a considerable impact on environmental litigation.

10.15.1.3 Remoteness

The House of Lords' decision in *Cambridge Water Co v Eastern Counties Leather plc* introduced the element of foreseeability as a prerequisite for recovery in nuisance, and probably into the rule in *Rylands v Fletcher*.

The introduction of the foreseeability element will have the effect of limiting the claims of historic pollution. However, as foreseeability is to be determined from the state of knowledge at the time the pollution takes place, it is unlikely that a great deal of the pollution which is currently taking place will be unforeseeable.

10.15.1.4 The Limitation Act 1980

A further limitation as to the effectiveness of the common law in the protection of the environment is that the Limitation Act 1980 applies. Section 2 of the Limitation Act 1980 provides:

(a) 'an action founded on tort shall not be brought after the expiration of six years from the date on which the cause of action actually accrued';

(b) where the action is brought in respect of personal injury the basic limitation period is reduced to three years under s 11(4) of the Act, although the court has discretion to override this limitation period if it would be equitable to do so;

(c) the limitation period is calculated 'from the date on which the cause of action occurred'. The reason for the existence of the limitation period is that it would be unfair on the defendant if an action could be brought against him for an indefinite period of time.

10.15.2 Advantages

The strengthening of the statutory framework for the control of environmental pollution and environmental damage may have diminished reliance on the common law. However, it still remains an important weapon in several circumstances:

(a) for environmental pressure groups, a prolific source of litigation are Anglers' Associations which have been very successful in recent years;

(b) for individuals who are affected by environmental damage and for whom there is no relief under statutory provisions. There are many examples of this type of action;

(c) for enforcement agencies, such as the Environment Agency where a prosecution under a statutory provision cannot stand;

(d) where the pollution has taken place before the relevant legislation has come into force. This was the case in *Cambridge Water Co v Eastern Counties Leather plc* where the pollution pre-dated the WRA 1991.

10.15.2.1 Supplementary to statutory provisions

An action under the common law may also supplement the statutory provisions. For example, in the case of *National Rivers Authority* (NRA) *and Anglers Co-operative Association v Clarke* (1994), the NRA attempted to prosecute a pig-farmer, Mr Clarke, who was responsible for the release of 3 m gallons of slurry which entered the river Sapiston in Suffolk, affected 75 km of the river Sapiston, the Little Ouse and destroyed a fishery. The action against Mr Clarke was brought under ss 31(1)(a) and 32(1)(a) of the COPA 1974, and under s 4(1) of the Salmon and Freshwater Fisheries Act 1975. The Court of Appeal decided that the pig-farmer could not be liable because his knowledge of the discharge could not be proven. Had the NRA based the action on 'causing' pollution, they may have succeeded.

Following the failure of the action under the statute, the NRA, along with the Anglers Co-operative Association who were representing the interests of the local angling club, then proceeded with a civil action against Mr Clarke. This time the action succeeded and the NRA were awarded £90,000 to cover their legal costs, to investigate the extent of the damage to the fishery and pay for restocking.

The Anglers Co-operative Association were awarded £8,400 for legal expenses, and the local angling club were awarded £8,450 in damages.

10.15.2.2 Remedies

The remedies available in successful common law case actions against environmental damage are often appropriate to compensate individuals who suffer from such damage, although they may not be the most effective in remedying or deterring continuing pollution. A significant advantage of an action under common law over statutory provisions is that, under the principal torts, the claimant may recover damage for loss or personal injury. This is only rarely possible under statute. One example, however, is s 73(6) of the EPA 1990.

The remedies available in cases based on the common law are not specifically intended to meet modern environmental challenges; rather, their aim is to address affected property rights. However, they do seek to provide some sort of redress for the damage caused to the environment by virtue of the remedies of damages and an injunction.

The availability of damages is of considerable importance. Often the award of damages to the aggrieved party can provide the finances for the remediation of environmental damage. This remedy is particularly useful in cases of contaminated land because it may be possible to clean up this contamination, albeit at great cost. However, there are many areas of environmental damage which cannot be rectified, and all damages can do in such a case as this would be to compensate the owner of the land whose interests were affected.

Injunctions can be granted in a variety of situations. They may be prohibitive, in which case they will simply require that the defendant should cease operations to prevent further damage from occurring; they may be mandatory, in which case the defendant will be required to take some positive action, such as the clean-up of a contaminated site. Both types of injunction may be granted on a *quia timet* basis, which would prevent damage being done where there was a threat of it occurring.

10.15.2.3 Actions need not be restrictive

A major advantage associated with an action based on the law of tort is that the action need not be brought on one ground alone, it is not uncommon for the torts of nuisance, negligence, trespass and the rule in *Rylands v Fletcher* to be tested in one case. For example, in *Cambridge Water Co v Eastern Counties Leather plc* a judgment was originally sought on the application of nuisance, negligence and the rule in *Rylands v Fletcher*, although the House of Lords' judgment only contained reference to *Rylands v Fletcher* and nuisance.

10.16 Civil actions under statute

The general policy behind current environmental legislation is that it provides some sort of public accountability for damage to the environment. This is followed through in the EPA 1990, and also the WRA 1991.

The possibility of a common law action as a means of environmental protection has already been discussed above. However, legislation can also provide a means by which individuals can pursue civil claims against others for the breach of environmental law in order to obtain compensation, and to this extent has supplemented the common law.

Civil liability actions arising from statutes are available as follows:

(a) express statutory rights to be compensated for certain types of damage;

(b) breach of statutory duty;

(c) certain statutory provisions which extend, or sometimes restrict, rights under the common law.

Each of these will be considered in turn.

It may also be possible for an individual privately to prosecute a polluter for an offence under the statute, providing such action is not prohibited by the statute. An example under environmental legislation is s 23(1) of the EPA 1990.

10.17 Express statutory rights to damages

An example of such an express provision is s 73(6) of the EPA 1990, which states that where any damage is caused by waste which has been deposited in or on land, any person who deposited, or knowingly caused or knowingly permitted it to be deposited so as to commit an offence under ss 33(1) or 63(2) is liable for the damage caused.

Section 73(6) also provides that where the damage was wholly the fault of the person who suffered it, or the person who suffered voluntarily accepted the risk of the damage, the defences of contributory negligence and *volenti non fit injuria* will be allowed.

It is not necessary for a prosecution to be brought, it is enough that the offence has been committed.

A further example is s 60 of the WRA 1991 which provides for damages where the Environmental Agency, under s 39 of the WRA 1991, has granted water abstraction rights which impair the existing rights of third parties.

10.18 Breach of statutory duty

The general rule defining breach of statutory duty was established in *Bishop of Rochester v Bridges* (1831):

> ... where an Act creates an obligation and enforces performance in a specified manner ... that performance cannot be enforced in any other manner.

A breach of statutory duty is only actionable where it can be shown by the court that Parliament intends that the statute should grant a civil remedy, or, if the duty is owed to individuals rather than to the State as a whole, then a civil remedy will exist for the claimant to claim damages in private nuisance. Many environmental statutes which prohibit an activity or make it a criminal offence also provide for some degree of civil liability.

The question of civil liability for breach of statutory duty is addressed in both the EPA 1990 and the WRA 1991.

In order to bring an action for breach of statutory duty, the claimant must prove the following:

(a) that the statute creates an obligation;

(b) that the statute intends to allow a civil action;

(c) that the harm suffered by the claimant is within the general class of risks at which the statute is directed;

(d) that the claimant is a member of the class of persons protected by the statute;

(e) that the defendant has breached the statute; and

(f) that this breach has caused the damage complained of.

10.18.1 Defences

There are two defences available for breach of statutory duty.

(a) *Volenti non fit injuria* – the defence of *volenti non fit injuria* (that is, voluntary assumption of risk) applies to cases of breach of statutory duty.

This was decided in *ICI v Shatwell* (1965), in which the House of Lords held that it applied in cases of breach of statutory duty except where there is a statutory provision to the contrary. This defence is not available where a worker sues his employer for breach of employer's statutory duty.

(b) Contributory negligence.

10.18.2 Example of actions in breach of statutory duty

Gibbons & Others v South West Water Services (1992) was an action brought on behalf of 80 plaintiffs in respect of damage suffered by them when their drinking water supplies were contaminated with aluminium sulphate. The plaintiffs claimed for damages on the grounds of breach of statutory duty, public nuisance and breach of contract. The defendants, South West Water Services, admitted liability for breach of statutory duty and the plaintiffs were awarded compensatory damages. The plaintiffs appealed because they also claimed exemplary and/or aggravated damages; however, the original decision was upheld.

10.19 Statutory provisions which alter rights under common law

Statutory nuisance provisions in the EPA 1990 which have extended the tort of nuisance still allow an individual to bring action in a magistrates' court against a person who has created the nuisance (s 82). This section is used where the local authority has not acted to prevent or abate the statutory nuisance.

An individual aggrieved by statutory nuisance may bring an action under s 82 of the EPA 1990 (which re-enacts s 99 of the Public Health Act 1936). These proceedings will be brought against the person responsible for the nuisance. If the responsible party cannot be found, the owner of the premises may be liable, or where more than one person is responsible for the nuisance, each party may be liable under s 82, 'whether or not what any of them is responsible for would by itself amount to a nuisance'.

This action can only be brought through the magistrates' court; there is no power for an individual to serve an Abatement Notice. Notice of the individual's intention to bring proceedings must be given to the responsible parties. In the case of a noise nuisance, three days' notice must be given and, in all other cases, 21 days' notice must be given.

10.20 The EC and civil liability

Work is continuing within the European Commission on the preparation of a Draft Directive on Civil Liability for Damage to the Environment Caused by Waste, and the Green and White Papers on liability for environmental damage. The purpose of the proposed directive is to harmonise the systems of civil liability which are in place in Member States across the European Union (EU). The concept of civil liability in relation to environmental damage is already established in some Member States: it already exists in Germany, Belgium, France and Italy, and has recently been introduced in the waste management sector in Spain.

The different systems in place in the Member States may lead to unequal conditions for competition among Member States, thereby creating artificial currents of investment and wastes from those countries where less stringent standards apply for the operators.

The proposed directive has a preventative intention to encourage the polluter to take action to minimise the risks at the earliest possible stage. Its objectives are:

(a) to apply the polluter pays principle on terms conducive to completing the goal of the single market;

(b) to establish a uniform system of liability;

(c) to ensure that industry's waste related costs are reflected in the price of the product or service giving rise to the waste.

The draft directive proposes to place primary liability on the producer of the waste; this could include any person who imports waste into the EU and persons responsible for waste installations. Where the producer of the waste cannot be found, then liability will be extended to the person who has control.

It is not yet clear whether this draft directive in its current amended form will be adopted. The issue is currently being considered in a wider dialogue on environmental liability, within the Commission.

In early 2000, the Commission issued a White Paper on environmental liability which proposes a strict liability regime in regard to 'dangerous' activities (that is, a measure designed to implement the polluter pays principle) and a fault-based liability regime in regard to biodiversity damage caused by 'non-dangerous' activities. It is proposed that compensation paid by the polluter should be spent on remediation. The White Paper envisages a role for public interest groups (that is, NGOs) where public authorities fail to take appropriate action. In this case, NGOs will be entitled to take over from the defaulting public authority.

THE COMMON LAW AND THE PRIVATE REGULATION OF ENVIRONMENTAL POLLUTION

Remedies

The statutory framework of environmental control is supported by the common law torts of public and private nuisance, negligence, trespass and the rule in *Rylands v Fletcher*. Although the main purpose for such torts is essentially to protect interests in land, they have developed considerably in the field of environmental protection.

The application of these torts for environmental purposes has recently been discussed in *Cambridge Water Co v Eastern Counties Leather plc*. In particular, the case examined the torts of nuisance and the rule in *Rylands v Fletcher*. The judgment contained pronouncements on the following elements:

(a) foreseeability;

(b) the relationship between nuisance and the rule in *Rylands v Fletcher*;

(c) the role of the courts and the common law in securing environmental protection;

(d) damages;

(e) injunction;

(f) abatement.

Defences

There are several defences common to all intentional torts, and there are also those specific to individual torts.

Disadvantages associated with the common law

The disadvantages associated with the common law are:

(a) not specific to the needs of environmental protection;

(b) not suited to the needs of the polluters;

(c) evidential difficulties;

(d) costs;

(e) the limitation period.

Advantages associated with the common law

The advantages associated with the common law are:

(a) useful where there is no statutory provision;

(b) can be relied upon where the pollution pre-dates the statute;

(c) the common law is widely tested by individuals and pressure groups, who are often successful;

(d) actions may be based on more than one ground, thereby increasing chances of success.

Civil actions under statute

Individuals may also bring actions for civil liability under statute:

(a) where there is express statutory right to damages;

(b) where statutory provisions extend existing common law rights;

(c) in the tort of breach of statutory duty.

The EC is also developing a Community-wide regime of civil liability, through the Green and White Papers on environmental liability.

CHAPTER 11

PRIVATE PROSECUTION, JUDICIAL REVIEW, ACCESS TO INFORMATION AND THE PRIVATE REGULATION OF ENVIRONMENTAL POLLUTION

11.1 Introduction

In Chapter 10 we noted that legal persons, such as individuals and companies, are able to use the law of torts to obtain redress for damage to property and person caused by the polluting activities of other persons. The role of private individuals, companies and other organisations or groups is not, however, confined to litigation in the civil courts. Legal persons also have an important role to play in ensuring that the Command and Control regimes we encountered in Chapters 3–9 are properly regulated and the relevant regulators are made accountable for their decisions. Private persons have two courses of action open to them if they are unhappy with any regulatory action (or inaction) or decision. First, in the event that a regulator exercises its discretion not to prosecute a person who has breached environmental law, any person who disagrees with this decision may exercise the right (provided the right is not excluded by the relevant statute) to mount a private prosecution to bring the alleged offender to account before the criminal courts. Secondly, any person may challenge a wide range of regulatory decisions, by means of an application to the courts to have the relevant decision judicially reviewed. These two mechanisms enable the private person to 'police' the activities of public regulators. In order for private persons effectively to police the decisions of the regulators it is essential that such persons have access to regulatory records, especially those relating to breaches of environmental law and pollution licences (that is, applications for licences, the conditions attached to licences, the monitoring of polluting emissions to confirm that licences are complied with, etc). The importance of the participation of private citizens in the protection of the environment is widely recognised, especially by the European Community (EC) and the international community. The EC, in particular, has played an important part in ensuring that Member States make environmental information available to the public.

11.2 Private prosecutions

The enforcement of environmental law is not the monopoly of the pollution control authorities. Neither the Environment Agency or the local authorities exercising their respective pollution control functions, have the financial or manpower resources to ensure full enforcement of the environmental controls laid down in statute or in the permissive authorisations (licences) granted. It is for these reasons that the individuals and pressure groups can play an extremely important role in the enforcement of environmental law by bringing private criminal prosecutions. The environmental legislation considered in this book contains a number of provisions which enable citizens to bring their own prosecutions against those who commit offences under specific pollution control legislation. The Environmental Protection Act (EPA) 1990, for example, provides considerable scope for citizens to bring private prosecutions (except in the case of Pt IV of the Act, which deals with genetically modified organisms). However, it appears that these rights have not been widely recognised or taken up. There are several reasons why this might be the case and these will be considered below.

11.2.1 The right to bring a private prosecution

At common law it is a well established rule that a citizen has the right to bring a private prosecution under an Act of Parliament. This was stated in the case of *R v Stewart* (1896). The High Court allowed a private prosecution to be brought by the Royal Society for the Prevention of Cruelty to Animals under the Diseases of Animals Act 1894. The court held that a citizen has a right to prosecute under any statute unless an Act specifically precludes that right in clear words. Various statutes do specifically provide provisions which explicitly give individuals the right to enforce the statutory provisions by means of private prosecutions and clearly these rights are of particular importance in the context of pressure groups and the environment. But even in the absence of a specific statutory provision, an individual or pressure group can still bring a private prosecution under an Act of Parliament, providing that the Act does not expressly and clearly preclude such a right.

In the context of environmental protection where most businesses have statutory authority to pollute to some extent (in accordance with the conditions imposed in authorisations, etc), it is necessary to establish whether an offence has been committed. Access to information about polluting activities is essential and the public registers described below should provide the information necessary in order to assist people in identifying the firms or businesses that are committing offences. From the information on the registers, it should be possible, for example, to ascertain who is responsible for a particular discharge into a river, what the discharge consent conditions are, whether there has been any monitoring, any notices served, or previous offences. Where a person or group of persons believes that an offence has been committed, is being committed or is likely to be committed, the easiest and cheapest course of action will be to complain to the regulatory authority and ask them to take enforcement action. It has already been stated that the pollution control authorities do not have the resources to monitor every discharge or emission all of the time and they therefore rely on reports and complaints brought by people in this respect. For instance, the Anglers' Associations were often the first to draw the National River Authority's (NRA) attention to pollution incidents and fish kills. In fact, the NRA had a 24 hour hotline telephone number for people to report incidents to them and this has been continued with the transfer of functions to the Environment Agency.

However, the alternative course of action is for an individual or pressure group to bring a private prosecution (often using the information obtained from the public registers). An example of a statutory right to bring a private prosecution is s 82 of the EPA 1990 where the aggrieved citizen is given the right to prosecute statutory nuisances. This is one of the more well known 'rights' and is covered in Chapter 8 on Statutory Nuisance.

11.2.2 Problems for private prosecutors

Although private prosecutions are becoming more commonplace, there are a number of problems associated with starting such litigation which has resulted in a relatively limited number of cases. It may not always be necessary to commence a legal action; it is possible that the threat of litigation will produce the desired results. The financial cost of commencing a criminal prosecution must be taken into account. Very often, prosecutors will need to employ scientific evidence to 'prove beyond reasonable doubt' that the defendant was responsible for the offence. The legal costs will also be considerable.

Problems arise in relation to admissible evidence. Private prosecutors are not entitled, like the pollution control authorities, to enter premises and take samples, records, etc. They therefore have to rely on other evidence, such as samples taken by themselves at points of discharge and information on the public registers.

11.3 Judicial review in English law

The regulation and control of polluting activities is exercised by public regulatory authorities which have responsibility, amongst other things, for exercising their discretion and granting 'permission' to pollute in a controlled manner through the various licensing systems described in this book. This can be seen in the EPA 1990 where authorisations are required for prescribed processes, either from the Environment Agency or a local authority; consents are required for certain discharges into controlled water; and waste management licences are required for final disposals by deposit of waste on land. These 'permissions' are granted on application from the pollution control authority, subject to conditions. Alternatively, they may be refused. Rights of appeal in respect of applications lie not to the courts, but to the Secretary of State. The Secretary of State's involvement is not, however, confined to dealing with appeals concerning applications. Rights of appeal to the Secretary of State exist in a number of other circumstances, for instance in relation to refusals to vary authorisations and revocations.

Decisions taken by the pollution control authorities, and the Secretary of State using powers conferred under statute, are public law decisions and as such are amenable to judicial review. It is therefore critical that individuals and pressure groups have access to the courts in circumstances where they wish to challenge the way in which the former have, or have not, exercised their discretion properly. (Judicial review is also considered in Chapter 3.)

11.3.1 Judicial review remedies

The remedies of mandamus, certiorari and prohibition are only available in respect of the exercise of public power or public law matters. Therefore, where an applicant seeks to obtain one of these remedies they can only do so against decisions made by public bodies and not against bodies exercising private power. In most cases, it is clear which bodies are operating as public bodies in that they derive their powers from a statutory source, although in fact not all functions which arise from a statutory framework have the necessary public law element and equally bodies which derive their powers from other sources than statute (or the common law) may be involved in public law matters. This was demonstrated in *R v Panel on Take-Overs and Mergers ex p Datafin plc* (1987). However, in most cases the public law element necessary for obtaining these remedies is to be found in the statute which establishes the body in question.

11.3.2 The question of standing: do environmental pressure groups have *locus standi*?

The concept of a citizen's action is one which presumes that citizens generally should be able to bring judicial review actions in the public interest without having to show any individual harm over and above that of the general community. Although no such right of action exists in English public law, it has received some judicial support. In particular Lord Diplock in *R v Inland Revenue Comrs ex p National Federation of the Self-Employed and Small Businesses Ltd* (1982) asserted that:

> It would, in my view, be a grave lacuna in our system of public law if a pressure group, like the federation, or even a single public-spirited taxpayer, were prevented by outdated technical rules of *locus standi* from bringing the matter to the attention to the court to vindicate the rule of law and get the unlawful stopped.

However, it remains the case in English law, that in order to challenge administrative decisions, it is necessary for the person or persons seeking judicial review to demonstrate the requisite *locus standi*. The test for standing is contained in s 31(3) of the Supreme Court Act (SCA) 1981. The SCA 1981 requires a person to have 'sufficient interest' in the matter in which their application for judicial review relates. The courts have developed rules on what amounts to sufficient interest. Until recently the courts placed a restrictive interpretation and have in a number of instances ruled that environmental pressure groups could not satisfy the test. However, more recent decisions suggest that the courts are becoming more willing to accept that pressure groups have sufficient interest. Nevertheless, the reasons in these more recent cases are largely pragmatic, which it has been argued has resulted in a somewhat incoherent approach to the issue of standing.

11.3.3 *Rose Theatre Trust*: the restrictive approach

The case of *R v Secretary of State for the Environment ex p Rose Theatre Trust* (1990) illustrates the restrictive approach to judicial review actions brought by pressure groups on public interest and environmental protection matters. Developers had been granted planning permission to build an office block on the site of an Elizabethan theatre (the Rose Theatre), in London. A trust company was set up by numerous campaigners to preserve the ruins of the theatre, which was of particular historical importance because it boasted the two first performances of Shakespeare's plays. The Rose Theatre Trust sought to persuade the Secretary of State to designate the site as one of national importance and include it in the list of monuments under the Ancient Monuments and Archaeological Areas Act 1979. If the Secretary of State had done this, it would have meant that no work could begin on the site without his consent. The Secretary of State agreed that the site was of national importance but decided that it would not fall within the relevant legislation. The Theatre Trust brought the action for judicial review alleging the illegality of the Secretary of State's decision. The question was whether or not the Trust had 'sufficient interest' to bring such an action. Members of the Trust argued that since they had entered into correspondence with the Secretary of State they had the necessary interest. However, the court found that the Trust did not have *locus standi*. In reaching this decision, the court held that a challenger must show that he has 'sufficient interest in the application to which the matter relates'.

Schiemann J stated that it was necessary to consider the statute to determine whether it afforded standing to these individuals in this instance. On the facts of the case, the court held that no individual could point to anything in the statute that would serve to give them a greater right or interest than any other that the decision would be taken lawfully. The case resulted in a great deal of criticism and was a blow to the notion of public interest litigation. Among other things, in the *Rose Theatre* case, it appeared that the court was not concerned that no one could sue in such a situation, leaving the decision of the Secretary of State beyond rebuke.

The restrictive approach laid down in *Rose Theatre Trust* was, however, not followed in the judicial review action brought by the pressure group Greenpeace against Her Majesty's Inspectorate of Pollution (HMIP) in which the court was willing to grant *locus standi* to Greenpeace.

11.3.4 The *Greenpeace* case

This case (*R v Her Majesty's Inspector of Pollution ex p Greenpeace (No 2) (1994)*) involved a challenge brought by Greenpeace against the decision by HMIP to allow testing at the THORP reprocessing plant at Sellafield. British Nuclear Fuels Ltd (BNFL) argued that Greenpeace had failed to establish a sufficient interest and that their application should be set aside. However, this argument was not accepted by the court. Mr Justice Otton held Greenpeace was an eminently respectable and responsible organisation and that their genuine interest in the matter was sufficient for them to be granted *locus standi*. In reaching this welcome decision, the court took into account the following of factors:

(a) the health interests of the 2,500 Greenpeace supporters in the Cumbria region;

(b) the nature of Greenpeace as a campaigning group whose prime objective was the protection of the environment;

(c) the fact that Greenpeace had been accredited by the United Nations (UN) and several other international bodies.

Mr Justice Otton went on to say that a denial of standing would mean that the people represented by Greenpeace would not have 'an effective way to bring the issues before the court'. In saying this, Otton J declined to follow the decision in *Rose Theatre Trust* where the court was seemingly unconcerned about this particular issue. Otton J stated that a denial of standing to Greenpeace would have meant that an application for judicial review would have had to have been brought either by an individual employee of BNFL or a near neighbour. Neither would have had the resources or the expertise to bring such an action and this would have resulted in a less well informed challenge which would have stretched the court's resources.

The decision in this case is greatly welcomed. With a less restrictive view on the sufficient interest requirement, environmental pressure groups such as Greenpeace, which represent people who are directly affected by the challenged decision or action, are more likely to succeed in achieving *locus standi*. However, a note of caution: in the judgment, the court referred to the advantages of an application from Greenpeace who, with its particular experience in environmental matters and its access to experts in the realms of science, technology and law, could bring a focused relevant and well argued challenge. It seems, therefore, that the larger national or international groupings are more likely to satisfy the test than small *ad hoc* or localised groups without the benefit of a 'deep pocket' and expert back-up.

The trend towards recognising the standing of pressure groups was given further support in the case of *R v Secretary of State for Foreign Affairs ex p World Development Movement Ltd* (1995). Rose LJ held that the World Development

Movement had sufficient interest to challenge the Government's aid for the Pergau Dam scheme, on the basis that there were few other parties that could challenge the decision and also because of the prominence of the World Development Movement in the protection of aid to under-developed countries. The Worldwide Development Movement was granted standing even though its members had no direct personal interest in the issue before the court. The Court of Appeal's decision in this case is important not least because the court embarked on a detailed discussion of standing which recognised the growing willingness of the courts in recent years to grant standing to interest groups. Rose LJ stated that the real question 'is whether the applicant can show some substantial default or abuse, and not whether his personal rights or interests are involved'. Unlike the decision in *Rose Theatre Trust*, here the court made it clear that if standing were not granted then a clear illegality would not be subject to challenge.

In *R v Secretary of State for the Environment ex p Friends of the Earth and Andrew Lees* (1994), Friends of the Earth (FOE) and Andrew Lees (who was FOE's campaign director before his tragic death), challenged the decision of the Secretary of State to accept undertakings from water companies in breach of the EC Drinking Water Directive (80/778/EEC) rather than take enforcement action. In this case Andrew Lees was a resident in the area supplied by one of the water companies, Thames Water, and clearly had a direct health interest in the decision. Like the *Greenpeace* case, the fact that local people who had a local interest (in both cases the interest was in health rather than the protection of the environment *per se*) in the issue and were joined in the action with a pressure group appears to have been relevant. This was remarked upon by Otton J in the *Greenpeace* case and was also relevant in the challenge brought by Friends of the Earth. When the *FOE* case was considered by the Court of Appeal it was merely noted that the High Court had granted standing and there was no further discussion of the point.

Standing will normally be granted in cases where a pressure group or individual expects to be consulted in relation to a decision and is not. For example in *R v Poole BC ex p BEEBEE et al* (1991) the applicants represented the Worldwide Fund for Nature and the British Herpetological Society (BHS). They sought to challenge the refusal of the Secretary of State for the Environment to call in a decision of the Poole Borough Council to grant planning permission for a new housing development on land which was part of a Site for Special Scientific Interest (SSSI). The applicants had no legal interest in the land in question, however the High Court decided that they did have sufficient interest because one of the conditions of planning permission was that the developers would inform BHS in advance of any developments in order that the BHS could take steps to protect and relocate any protected species. The fact of the applicants being given the right to be informed in these circumstances was enough to give them the necessary *locus standi*. Similarly, in *R v Swale BC and Medway Ports Authority ex p the Royal Society for the Protection of Birds* (RSPB)

(1991), the RSPB were granted standing in their judicial review action. The RSPB sought to challenge a decision by the Swale Borough Council to grant planning permission to the Medway Ports Authority to reclaim 125 acres of mud flat, known as the Lappel Bank. The RSPB were granted standing on the basis that they had a legitimate expectation, based on correspondence from the borough council, that they would be consulted as an interested party before planning permission was granted and that the borough council had failed to consult them.

Of course, judicial review decisions concerning environmental law issues need not be brought by pressure groups. Individuals personally affected by decisions also have the right to seek judicial review, providing they can demonstrate sufficient interest. There are many examples in planning law of individuals seeking judicial review of planning decisions which affect them. Examples in the field of environmental law include *R v Secretary of State for Trade and Industry ex p Duddridge and Others* (1994). In this case parents were concerned about the risk of their children contracting leukemia from exposure to the electromagnetic field radiation (EMFs) from high voltage electricity cables. The Secretary of State took a decision not to limit the level of EMFs, although he had the power to do so under the provisions of the Electricity Act 1989. Standing was granted to the parents who sought to force the Secretary of State to exercise his powers. Interestingly, in this case, the applicants argued that the Secretary of State's action was in breach of the precautionary principle laid down in Art 174 (formerly 130r) of the EC Treaty. However, the Court of Appeal held that Art 174 (130r) was intended to lay down principles upon which future EC environmental policy might be based. It was not a principle that could bind the Secretary of State.

11.4 Access to information

One of the most important, if not *the* most important, requisites for individuals and pressure groups to take action is that they are equipped with the necessary information. There is a view that public access to information on the environment lends itself to improved environmental protection. Since most environmental offences involve the carrying out of unauthorised activities, the public needs to have access to information to ascertain whether the activity is authorised or not and, if it *is* authorised, whether all of the conditions attached to the authorisation are being complied with. Environmental information may also be used for less litigious purposes, for instance by consumers to identify the environmental track record of certain companies. Businesses have traditionally favoured less disclosure of information and have perceived the registers as a threat. The various provisions do allow certain information to be excluded from the public, but these provisions do not offer the opportunity for firms to exclude information simply on the grounds that it would be detrimental to their image.

11.4.1 Royal Commission on Environmental Pollution

The Royal Commission on Environmental Pollution can take much of the credit for ensuring the introduction of statutory provisions which established the creation of publicly accessible registers relating to pollution controls. The Royal Commission, in its second report, suggested that the arguments in favour of retaining environmental information on a confidential basis were not well founded:

> We doubt some of the reasons for this confidentiality and our doubts are shared by many of the witnesses from industry with whom we have spoken. It is a practice which on occasion hinders the flow of information and it leads to risks of misunderstanding on the part of the public which may be harmful to industry and government alike.

In its 10th report, the Royal Commission recommended that the public should be entitled to the fullest possible information on all forms of environmental pollution and that the onus should be placed on the polluter to substantiate a claim for exceptional treatment. It accordingly recommended that a guiding principle behind all legislative and administrative controls relating to environmental pollution should be a presumption in favour of unrestricted access for the public to information which the pollution control authorities receive by virtue of their statutory powers, with protection for secrecy only in those circumstances where a genuine case can be substantiated. It was also suggested that cases where genuine secrets are involved are, in fact, comparatively rare.

The basic premise of the Royal Commission's arguments is that the public has a right to know, that there is a need to restore public confidence in the enforcement system and, importantly, that the public has a beneficial interest in the environment.

The EPA 1990 introduced important new provisions requiring that information held by the regulatory bodies empowered by the Act be available for inspection by the public. The stated aim was that:

> Information must be freely available. Unnecessary secrecy undermines public confidence that pollution has been properly controlled. The new system of public registers which the Act introduces will increases confidence in pollution control. Furthermore it will facilitate public participation in helping to protect the environment. It will mean that every individual can become an environmental watchdog in his or her own right.

The EPA 1990, the WIA 1991 and the WRA 1991 as amended by the Environment Act 1995 and the PPCA 1999 provide for the creation of public registers, maintained by the regulatory authorities. The registers are required to be available for inspection at all reasonable times and copies of entries can be obtained for a reasonable charge. The specific statutory provisions are further supplemented by the Environmental Information Regulations 1992. In relation to all of these provisions, information may be excluded from the registers on the grounds that its disclosure would be a threat to national security or breach commercial confidentiality. The relevant registers are referred to in Chapters 3–9.

11.4.2 Other sources of environmental information

In addition to the registers of information maintained by regulators such as the EA, the local authorities and the privatised water companies, pressure groups and individuals can obtain additional information from other sources, including environmental information held by local authorities. This should be available to the general public under the Local Government (Access to Information) Act 1985. In addition, the Clean Air Act (CAA) 1993 provides that local authorities have powers to arrange for research and publicity with regard to air pollution. However, under s 34(2) of the CAA 1993, it is a criminal offence to disclose any information obtained under the CAA 1993 provisions which is a trade secret. Details of hazardous substances consents can be found in registers maintained by the Hazardous Substances Authorities who are under a duty to maintain the registers by virtue of s 28 of the Planning (Hazardous) Substances Act 1990. A number of large companies voluntarily publish information on their environmental performance, usually as an adjunct to their annual reports. In 2001, the EU Commission produced non-binding guidelines on how EU businesses should treat environmental issues in annual reports and financial accounts.

11.4.3 Environmental Information Regulations 1992

In addition to these specific provisions for the establishment of public registers, the Environmental Information Regulations 1992 make further provisions for the freedom of access to information on the environment held by public bodies. The requirements of the regulations go beyond the system of public registers, however, they are subject to a number of weaknesses. In particular, they include a long list of exceptions and provide no statutory right of appeal against a refusal to provide information.

The regulations give effect to Directive (90/313/EEC) on Freedom of Access to Information on the Environment. They place a duty on 'every relevant person' who holds any information to which the regulations apply to make the information available to every person who requests it, subject to the exceptions listed. The person supplying the information can make a charge for the supply of the information.

By reg 2(1), the regulation applies to any information which relates to the environment. Information relates to the environment if, and only if, it relates to any of the following:

(a) the state of any water or air, the state of flora or fauna, the state of any soil or the state of any natural site or other land;

(b) any activities or measures giving rise to noise or any other nuisance which adversely affect anything mentioned in sub-para (a) above or are likely adversely to affect anything so mentioned;

(c) any activities or administrative or other measures (including any environmental management programmes) which are designed to protect anything so mentioned.

11.4.3.1 Information

Information includes anything contained in records; it therefore includes information held in registers, reports and returns, as well as computer records or other records kept otherwise than in a document.

11.4.3.2 Relevant persons

The duty to furnish information is placed on 'relevant persons'. They are defined in the regulations as Ministers of the Crown, Government departments, local authorities and other persons carrying out functions of public administration at a national, regional or local level and which have responsibilities in relation to the environment. The definition has a second limb and a person or organisation may be a relevant person if they have public responsibilities for the environment which do not fall within the above description but are under the control of a person falling within that description. This second limb is capable of including the privatised water companies and sewerage undertakers which have environmental responsibilities and are in the control of Ministers of the Crown and the Environment Agency. In *Griffin v South West Water* (1995), it was held that South West Water was an emanation of the State for the purposes of an EC directive concerned with employment rights. It would therefore seem to follow that the water companies may also be subject to the regulations. However, this particular point has not yet been considered by the courts.

It is clear that the definition includes information held by the Department of the Environment and the local authorities in their various capacities as well as the Environment Agency.

11.4.3.3 The duty to make information available

The duty to make information available is owed to the person requesting the information. Those persons or organisations that are subject to the duty to make information available must ensure that:

(a) every request made for information is responded to as soon as possible;

(b) no such request is responded to more than two months after it is made;

(c) where the response to such a request contains a refusal to make information available, the refusal is in writing and specifies the reasons for the refusal.

However, the regulations make provision for the relevant person subject to the duty to:

(a) refuse a request for information in cases where a request is manifestly unreasonable or is formulated in too general a manner;

(b) impose a charge in respect of the costs reasonably attributable to the supply of the information;

(c) make the supply of any information conditional on the payment of such a charge;

(d) make the information available in such a form, and at such times and places, as may be reasonable.

11.4.3.4 Exceptions to disclosure

The regulations allow for certain categories of information to be excluded from the requirements of disclosure. A distinction is drawn between information which must be excluded and other information which may be excluded depending upon the exercise of discretion by the relevant person holding the information.

Certain information must be regarded as confidential and therefore cannot be disclosed. It will be treated as such if:

(a) the information is treated as confidential and its disclosure in response to a request for information would contravene any statutory provision or a rule of law or would involve a breach of any agreement;

(b) the information is personal information contained in records held in relation to an individual who has not given his consent to disclosure;

(c) the information is held by the relevant person in consequence of having been supplied by a person who was not under, and could not have been put under, any legal obligation to supply it to the relevant person and has not consented to its disclosure;

(d) the disclosure of the information in response to that request would, in the circumstances, increase the likelihood of damage to the environment affecting anything to which the information relates.

In addition information may be treated as confidential in the following circumstances:

(a) information relating to matters affecting international relations, national defence or public security;

(b) information relating to anything which is or has been the subject of, any legal or other proceedings (whether actual or prospective);

(c) information relating to the confidential deliberations of any relevant person or to the contents of any internal communications of a body corporate or other undertaking or organisation;

(d) information contained in a document or other record which is still in the course of completion;

(e) information affecting matters to which any commercial or industrial confidentiality attaches or any intellectual property.

11.4.3.5 Right of appeal

The regulations do not provide any specific right of appeal against a refusal to supply information. However, it is possible that a person could seek judicial review of a decision to refuse to supply information since the person from whom the information is requested is under a duty to provide it. Unfortunately, mounting a judicial review action is both difficult and expensive and it is unlikely that many individuals or pressure groups will seek this course of action. The Commission has proposed important changes to the 1990 Directive on Freedom of Access to Environmental Information, implemented in England and Wales by the Environmental Information Regulations 1992, to bring the EC into line with the 1998 UN Aarhus Convention (UN Economic Commission for Europe Convention on Access to Information, Public Participation in Decision-Making and Access to Justice in Environmental Matters). The new directive will apply to a greater range of public bodies than the 1990 directive and will include water companies and bodies holding information relevant to the transport and energy sectors. 'Environmental information' will be construed to include economic analyses (for example, cost/benefit calculations). The ability to refuse to supply environmental information will be restricted to fewer cases. The time limit within which information requested must be supplied is to be reduced to two months.

11.5 Recognition of the need for public participation

11.5.1 International recognition

At the UN conference on environment and development held in Rio de Janeiro in 1992, over 150 States and the EC agreed to Principle 10 of the Rio Declaration that 'environmental issues are best handled with participation of all concerned citizens, at the relevant level'. Non-governmental organisations (NGOs) have traditionally played an important role in the development of international law and this was particularly the case at the Rio 'Earth Summit'.

Not only were many NGOs accredited at the UN conference, many of them played a significant part in the parallel negotiations leading up to the Bio-Diversity Convention (1992) and the Convention on Climate Change (1992). The role played by NGOs was well recognised and in fact a whole Chapter of Agenda 21 was devoted to their activities.

In 1998 further progress was made internationally in regard to access to environmental information with the adoption of the Arhus Convention on Access to Information, Public Participation in Decision Making and Access to Justice in Environmental Matters. This convention mirrors the EC directive on Access to Environmental Information (90/313/EEC), save that its remit is wider, both in regard to the number of State signatories and the types of information which are to be made available (for example, the 1998 Convention covers access to health and safety information).

11.5.2 EC recognition

The EC's Fifth Environmental Action Programme also envisaged an important role for the citizens of Europe in ensuring that environmental legislation is enforced:

> Individuals and public interest groups should have practicable access to the courts in order to ensure that their legitimate interests are protected and that prescribed environmental measures are effectively enforced and illegal practices stopped.

Environmental pressure groups have been particularly active at the European level in two principal ways. First, by participating in the development of environmental law and policy and, second, by monitoring compliance with EC environmental law and complaining to the European Commission about cases where EC law has been breached or inadequately enforced. The Fourth Environmental Action Programme (1987–92) stated that one of the aims of the EC's environmental policy was to ensure that directives are not only legally implemented, but are also practically enforced. This monitoring of compliance does not rest entirely with the European Commission or the national regulatory authorities but is supported by individuals and pressure groups.

11.5.3 National recognition

The Department of the Environment has produced a publication called *Green Rights and Responsibilities: A Citizen's Guide to the Environment*, which sets out the Government's thinking on public participation in environmental protection.

In the Secretary of State's Foreword to the *Guide*, the following statement is made:

> Government provides the law and institutions within which we exercise our environmental rights and discharge our responsibilities. But unless each one of

us plays our own part, no amount of law-making will make any difference to the quality of the environment.

These environmental rights are described as:

(a) the right of access to environmental information which is held by public bodies;

(b) the right to participate in the decision making process on environmental issues; and also,

(c) the right to seek appropriate remedies in the event of a breach of environmental laws or failure to provide environmental services.

11.6 Environmental pressure groups

There is a long history of environmental pressure groups in the UK and they are considerably expert in mobilising public opinion. There are now numerous environmental pressure groups (note, they are often referred to as NGOs) some of which have very large memberships and are interested in global environmental and conservation issues. Greenpeace, FOE and the World Wide Fund for Nature are the obvious ones. In addition, there are many groups which are formed around specific issues, such as the protection of birds or particular species of animal. The RSPB enjoys a particularly large membership, is well resourced and has demonstrated its willingness to take legal action to protect specific bird habitats.

Today the large pressure groups such as Greenpeace and FOE boast large membership numbers throughout the world, in countries as diverse as Guatemala, Russia and Tunisia. These groups have developed into large organisations with significant financial and technical resources and also highly trained staff (and often volunteers) ranging from scientists to lawyers. The larger pressure groups have become skilled in organising professionally run campaigns and mobilising public support.

11.6.1 Using EC environmental law to protect the environment

Environmental pressure groups have been able to exert an influence on both the introduction and enforcement of EC environmental law and have been able to use EC environmental law rights to bring legal actions within the national courts of the Member States.

11.6.2 Lobbying at the European level

Given that so much of our current environmental legislation emanates from the EC and that the UK is obliged under Art 5 of the EC Treaty to implement and enforce such legislation, pressure groups have realised the importance of influencing the content of legislation at the European level. Indeed, the same can be said for almost all areas of EC law and Brussels now is a major centre for professional lobbyists. Environmental pressure groups representing a wide range of general and specific interests have been particularly active in bringing pressure on the EC institutions to influence the content of legislation. This has involved lobbying the European Parliament and the Commission, suggesting amendments, providing technical advice and participating in the drafting of directives. There are numerous examples of successful lobbying at EC level.

11.6.3 Environmental pressure groups and the enforcement of EC environmental law

Although it is generally only the larger and well resourced pressure groups that can exert influence on the law making process and the content of environmental legislation, almost all environmental pressure groups can play a role in the enforcement of EC environmental law. However, this is subject to at least two limitations: first, not all groups will have the financial and technical resources to bring costly legal actions, particularly where they run the risk of having to bear the other side's costs. Second, not all pressure groups will be able to challenge decisions made by planning authorities, the regulatory authorities or the Secretary of State by means of judicial review actions because of the difficulties in proving that they have *locus standi*. However, most groups can play a role in terms of monitoring compliance with EC law and they all have the right to complain directly to the European Commission when they believe that EC law is being breached.

11.6.4 Article 226 (formerly Art 169) direct actions

The European Commission receives thousands of complaints each year from pressure groups, their members and also aggrieved citizens concerning the breach of environmental law. The legal action brought by the Commission (under Art 169 of the Treaty) against the UK, *Commission v UK* (1993), concerning breaches of the Bathing Water Directive reputedly resulted from a complaint received by the Commission on a postcard from an aggrieved holidaymaker at Blackpool. However, the Commission is not under a duty to follow up every complaint and it exercises its discretion as to whether to take any action against the Member State involved. Therefore, although the Art 226 procedure offers aggrieved citizens and pressure groups an inexpensive means of attempting to secure compliance, it does not guarantee that the Commission will take any action.

11.6.5 Challenging Community environmental law before the ECJ

In addition to the possibility of complaining to the Commission, environmental pressure groups may also, where relevant, seek judicial review of EC Acts under Arts 230 (formerly 173) and 232 (formerly 175) of the Treaty. Article 230 involves the review of Acts, whereas Art 232 is concerned with omissions or the failure of the institutions to act. According to the Treaty, natural and legal persons (as opposed to the institutions and the Member States) can only seek judicial review against a decision addressed to that person or against a decision which, although in the form of a regulation, or a decision addressed to another person, which is of direct and individual concern to the former. Unlike the Member States and the community institutions, individuals and pressure groups have limited access to the European Court of Justice (ECJ) in judicial review actions. Not all 'acts' are reviewable, only decisions or regulations which are decisions in substance. The test for *locus standi* is that a person is directly and individually concerned. In a number of cases largely concerned with market regulations, the ECJ has placed a very restrictive interpretation on what is meant by the phrase 'direct and individual concern', effectively barring many applicants from bringing such actions. The test which was laid down in the leading case of *Plaumann* (1963) is that a person other than one to whom a decision is addressed will only be individually concerned:

> ... if that decision affects them by reason of certain attributes which are peculiar to them, or by reason of circumstances in which they are differentiated from all other persons, and by virtue of these factors distinguishes them individually just as in the case of the person addressed.

In terms of environmental law, two problems become immediately apparent. First, most environmental measures are in the form of directives and are therefore *prima facie* not reviewable in judicial review actions brought by individuals. It is rare for the Commission to take a formal decision concerned with environmental protection but, as the case below illustrates, they can take decisions which a bearing on the enforcement of environmental laws, albeit indirectly. Second, the *locus standi* test itself is very difficult for environmental pressure groups to satisfy. Notwithstanding that, the Court of First Instance, which has first instance jurisdiction in judicial review actions brought by natural and legal persons, has, like the English courts, recently been forced to consider the position of environmental pressure groups in the following case.

11.6.6 *Stichting Greenpeace Council and Others v EC Commission (1993)*

This case illustrates the importance of judicial review as a means of ensuring that environmental policy and law are enforced and complied with, not only by the pollution control authorities but also by the authors of the policy and law, in this instance the European Commission. The Commission, which is responsible for initiating legislation and ensuring compliance was, in this case, challenged by a number of applicants because of its decision to award financial assistance through the structural funds (regional funds to support infrastructure projects in certain regions throughout the community) for a project which had not been made subject to the Environmental Assessment Directive (85/337/EEC).

The project in question involved the construction of two power plants in the Canary Islands. The applicants included local farmers and residents, two Canary Island environmental groups and Greenpeace. They sought annulment of the Commission's decision to award a ECU 12 m grant aid towards the projects on the grounds that the grant was made for a project for which an environmental assessment should have been carried out in accordance with EC Directive (85/337/EC), and this amounted to a violation of the EC Treaty. In order for an individual or association to bring a judicial review action under Art 173 (now 230) of the EC Treaty, the complainant must show that the decision being challenged is either addressed to them, or, if addressed to another person, is of 'direct and individual concern to them'. Thus, Greenpeace had to satisfy the ECJ that it was directly and individually concerned with the Commission decision. The ECJ, following a string of previous decisions including *Plaumann* held that there was no evidence to show that the applicants were affected by virtue of features peculiar to them or that their circumstances differentiated them from all others. Therefore the applicants could not prove that they were individually concerned. It is clear from the case law on Art 173 (now 230) that the ECJ has placed a very narrow interpretation upon the phrase 'directly and individually concerned' and even in circumstances such as the case in point it will be very difficult for pressure groups to satisfy the necessary *locus standi* in such judicial review actions.

PRIVATE PROSECUTION, JUDICIAL REVIEW, ACCESS TO INFORMATION AND THE PRIVATE REGULATION OF ENVIRONMENTAL POLLUTION

Private legal persons, such as individuals, environmental groups, companies and other organisations, have a role to play in ensuring that regulators are accountable for their actions and decisions.

Recognition of the need for public participation

The participation of citizens in the protection of the environment is recognised at international, EC and national level. Inextricably linked with the desire to encourage and promote public participation is the recognition that access to information is vital.

Environmental pressure groups

Environmental pressure groups have been able to exert influence on the development of environmental law and policy particularly at the European level by lobbying.

Individuals and pressure groups can seek to ensure compliance with EC and domestic environmental law in the following ways:

(a) complaining directly to the European Commission to persuade the Commission to take direct action against a Member State under the Art 226 (formerly 169) procedure;

(b) ensuring that the EC institutions themselves comply with the Treaty and EC environmental law through an application for judicial review by the ECJ under Arts 230 (formerly 173) and 232 (formerly 175) of the EC Treaty;

(c) By means of judicial review in the national courts. This raises problems of legal standing and not all pressure groups will be able to satisfy the courts that they have the necessary sufficient interest. However, the courts have shown a greater willingness to grant *locus standi* to the more well resourced and organised pressure groups such as Greenpeace;

(d) individuals and pressure groups can bring private criminal prosecutions against persons committing environmental offences. However, in view of the burden of proof involved in criminal prosecutions and the legal costs involved, this again affords a limited opportunity;

Access to information

Access to information is vital. It is accepted that promoting better access to environmental information can improve environmental protection. Information on the state of the environment can be found in the public registers established under the relevant regulatory regime.

Environmental Information Regulations 1992

The Environmental Information Regulations 1992 make further provision for environmental information to be made available to any person requesting it.

CHAPTER 12

EUROPEAN COMMUNITY
ENVIRONMENTAL LAW AND POLICY

12.1 Introduction

In order fully to appreciate the pace of change and development of environmental law in the UK we need to consider the role played by European Community (EC) environmental law. The impact of EC environmental law and policy on national environmental law and policy is huge. Over 300 separate measures have been created by the EC which Member States have been obliged to incorporate into their own legal systems. The RCEP has established that 80% of environmental law in the UK derives from European law.

In the UK the significance of the EC is masked because most EC environmental measures take the form of directives which are transposed into UK law by means of Statutory Instruments. Without doubt the EC is the most important factor which is 'driving' the development of UK environmental law and because of its central importance the student of UK environmental law should study not only the wide range of separate EC-generated environmental laws which currently exist, but also the process by which EC environmental law is created, enforced and challenged.

This chapter examines the institutional arrangements within the EC with reference to the environment; it covers the legislative procedures, enforcement of community law, the effect of community law in the domestic legal system and EC environmental policy. These issues are clearly of importance, however, it is not appropriate in a textbook on environmental law for lengthy discussion on all of the issues involved and therefore readers are recommended to consult an EC law textbook for detailed analysis.

The later part of this chapter concerns EC environmental law and policy and deals with the following issues:

(a) the development of the EC's environmental policy and law. In particular it considers how the EC has become a key actor in the environment field, albeit in its early years it had no legal basis on which to do so. Consideration is also given to the relationship between the EC's environmental programme and other areas of EC law, in particular the aim to achieve a common market in which goods and services can move freely. The issue of whether Member States can introduce more stringent environmental laws than those laid down by the EC is also dealt with;

(b) the substantive nature of EC environmental policy and some of the principle features of the fifth and sixth Environmental Action Programmes. The chapter highlights some of the key environmental directives which are considered elsewhere in this book.

12.2 The development of the European Union (EU)

The European Economic Community (EEC) was established by the Treaty of Rome in 1957. Since that time the Community has grown from an initial membership of six (Belgium, France, Germany, The Netherlands, Luxembourg and Italy) to 15 following the accession of the UK, Denmark and Ireland in 1973, Greece in 1979, Spain and Portugal in 1986 and Austria, Finland and Sweden in January 1995. Following German reunification in 1989, East Germany was absorbed into the Community, subject to certain special transitional arrangements. It was anticipated that Norway would join at the same time as Austria, Finland and Sweden but following a 'no vote' in the Norwegian referendum, the Norwegian Government was not able to proceed to membership. In addition Cyprus, Malta and Turkey have applied to join.

12.2.1 From EEC to EC

Not only has the Community grown in size it has also considerably increased its spheres of influence by becoming very much more than an association of States pursuing economic goals. The Community can now legitimately take action in a range of areas, including environmental protection, which were never envisaged as Community interests in its formative years. The Treaty of Rome has been amended by the Single European Act (SEA) 1986, the Treaty on European Union (TEU) signed at Maastricht on 7 February 1992, and which took effect in November 1993, the Treaty of Amsterdam (ToA) in 1997 and the Treaty of Nice (ToN) in 2000. The SEA 1986 introduced a number of significant changes to the Rome Treaty designed to speed up the decision making process in Europe so that a programme of over 280 measures could be enacted in order to create the Single European Market by the self-imposed deadline of 31 December 1992. The SEA 1986 also established for the first time that the Community could legitimately take action in the field of environmental protection.

The TEU was an altogether more complex Treaty. On the one hand, it created the EU which essentially is an institutional framework for political co-operation between the Member States. However, the TEU also amended the EEC Treaty itself. Article G of the TEU introduced significant amendments to the EEC Treaty in relation to Community interests, and also procedural changes (the main one being the creation of a new legislative procedure which strengthened the power of the Parliament). A further significant change brought about by the TEU was the change in the name of the EEC to the EC. This change of name is more than symbolic and reflects the fact that the Community has developed to such an extent that it can no longer be regarded simply as an economic community pursuing economic goals.

12.3 The aims of the EC

Article 2 of the EC Treaty, which lays down the aims of the EC and as such is pivotal in determining the legal competences of the EC institutions, has been amended by the SEA 1986, the TEU 1993, the ToA 1997 and the ToN 2000. In 1957 the Treaty of Rome stated that the task of the EC was to establish a common market, progressively approximating the economic policies of the Member States to promote throughout the EC a 'harmonious development of economic activities, a continuous and balanced expansion, an increase in stability, an accelerated raising of the standard of living and closer relations between the States belonging to it'. Following the amendments to the Treaty by the SEA 1986 and the TEU 1993 the aims are more widely stated:

> The Community shall have as its task, by establishing a common market and an economic and monetary union and by implementing the common policies of activities referred to in Articles 3 and 3(a) to promote throughout the Community a harmonious, and balanced development of economic activities, sustainable development and non-inflationary growth, respecting the environment, a high degree of convergence of economic performance, a high level of employment and of social protection, the raising of the standard of living and quality of life, and economic and social cohesion and solidarity among Member States.

This expansion of EC interests has been one of the key concerns for those who fear the moves towards a federal Europe. The TEU stimulated enormous debate and, as a consequence, it did not come into effect until November 1993, following the difficulties of ratification in some Member States. In 1996 an inter-governmental conference began the process of reviewing the Treaty again.

12.4 EC competences

The institutions of the EC are entrusted with the power to enact secondary legislation in order to further the aims of the EC. It is Art 3 of the Treaty which sets out which actions can be taken in pursuit of those aims. In other words Art 3 defines what actions can be taken, or to use the jargon, it defines the EC's competences. If the EC institutions take action in an area in which the EC is not legally competent, then any such action may be annulled by the European Court of Justice (ECJ) exercising its powers of judicial review under Art 230 (formerly Art 173). Again, Art 3 has also been subject to positive amendment and now runs to a very wide ranging list of legitimate actions. Art 3 now states:

> For the purposes set out in Article 2, the activities of the Community shall include, as provided by this Treaty and in accordance with the timetable set out therein:

(a) the elimination, as between Member States, of customs duties and quantitative restrictions on the import and export of goods, and of all other measures having equivalent effect;

(b) a common commercial policy;

(c) an internal market characterised by the abolition, as between Member States, of obstacles to the free movement of goods, persons, services and capital;

(d) measures concerning the entry and movement of persons in the internal market as provided for in Article 100C;

(e) a common policy in the sphere of agriculture and fisheries;

(f) a common policy in the sphere of transport;

(g) a system ensuring that competition in the internal market is not distorted;

(h) the approximation of the laws of the Member States to the extent required for the functioning of the common market;

(i) a policy in the social sphere comprising a European Social Fund;

(j) the strengthening of economic and social cohesion;

(k) a policy in the sphere of the environment;

(l) the strengthening of the competitiveness of Community industry;

(m) the promotion of research and technological development;

(n) encouragement for the establishment and development of trans-European networks;

(o) a contribution to the attainment of a high level of health protection;

(p) a contribution to the education and training of quality and to the flowering of the cultures of the Member States;

(q) a policy in the sphere of development co-operation;

(r) the association of the overseas countries and territories in order to increase trade and promote jointly economic and social development;

(s) a contribution to the strengthening of consumer protection;

(t) measures in the spheres of energy, civil protection and tourism.

It is clear from this list that the activities of the EC are wide ranging, but on closer inspection they are not all necessarily compatible. Whilst activities aimed at protecting the environment, consumer protection and a high level of health protection may be complementary, others are not. There is a tension between the aims of securing the strengthening of the competitiveness of EC industry and environmental protection. The need to promote economic growth usually comes at an environmental cost. The creation of new businesses may make the EC more competitive in the global market and may indeed create much needed jobs and opportunities, but there will be environmental consequences and these need to be taken into account. The EC has recognised that the goal of economic growth cannot be pursued without consideration for the environment and that in promoting growth today account needs to be taken of the consequences for future generations. This view is reflected in the current desire to pursue sustainable and non-inflationary growth respecting the environment.

12.5 Sources of EC law

The EC Treaty is the primary source of EC law since it is from the Treaty that the EC institutions derive their power to enact secondary legislation. The Treaty is often described as *Traité Cadre*, which means that it is a framework treaty which sets out broad general principles and aims, but leaves the institutions to 'flesh out' and implement these aims by means of secondary legislation. The institutions of the EC are entrusted under Art 4 of the Treaty to carry out their respective functions, which include the capacity to enact secondary legislation. However, the institutions must only act within the powers conferred upon them by the Treaty and, as stated above, if they bring forward legislation in areas which the Community is not legally competent then such measures may be annulled on the ground of lack of competence (the equivalent of the *ultra vires* doctrine in English law). This is important because it prevents the EC taking action in those areas which are legitimately the domain of Member States and it prevents a transfer of power beyond that which the Member States agreed in the signing of the Treaty.

Therefore it is clear that all EC secondary legislation must derive from the Treaty and must have a legal proper basis. This is a particular point which has been of importance in environmental law and will be considered more fully below.

12.5.1 EC secondary legislation

Article 250 (formerly Art 189) of the Treaty defines the legislative powers of the institutions and the types of legal instruments available. Because these legislative Acts derive from the Treaty, they are regarded as secondary legislation and are hierarchically inferior to the Treaty which is the primary source of EC law. It is important to be familiar with the distinctions between the types of secondary legislation. However, a note of caution: the classification laid down below is not always straightforward. An Act is not always what it says it is, consequently the ECJ will look at the substance rather than the form, and has held that where a regulation fails to lay down general rules it may be a disguised decision (*Confédération Nationale des Producteurs de Fruits et Legumes v Council* (1962)).

12.5.2 Regulations

Regulations have general application, are binding in their entirety and are directly applicable in all Member States. Regulations apply equally to all Member States and can therefore be used to ensure that the law is exactly the same throughout the EC. For this reason regulations take effect within Member States either on the date specified in the Official Journal of the European Communities (all regulations and, indeed, directives must be published in the Official Journal or, in the absence of a specified date, the regulation takes effect 20 days after publication. Since regulations are binding in their entirety and directly applicable, there is no need for Member States to implement the regulation in order for it to take effect. In fact, national implementation of regulations has been held in *Leonesio v Ministero dell'Agricoltura e delle Foreste* (1971) to be incompatible with the aims of regulations.

12.5.3 Directives

Directives differ from regulations in a number of respects. Article 250 (formerly Art 189) states that:

> A Directive shall be binding as to the results to be achieved, upon each Member State to which it is addressed, but shall leave to the national authorities the choice and form of methods.

Although directives are generally addressed to all Member States, it is possible for directives to be directed to only one or more Member States, and it is equally possible for directives to be addressed to all Member States but with different conditions (such as deadlines for implementation). Directives state the 'aim to be achieved', which is binding upon the Member State, but leave the choice and means of implementation to the discretion of the Member State. Therefore directives provide that implementation should be within a certain timetable or by a certain deadline. Member States are obliged to ensure that there is effective implementation of the directive within the specified time period. Implementation by means of a Government circular will not be sufficient. Member States usually submit a copy of the implementing legislation to the Commission so that the Commission can review whether or not there has been compliance. In the UK, implementation is usually achieved by means of Statutory Instrument. The European Communities Act 1972 provides powers for Ministers to introduce delegated legislation giving effect to EC obligations in directives.

The majority of EC environmental 'Acts' take the form of directives rather than Regulations. This means that Member States play a large part in the implementation of EC environmental law and that they exercise some discretion in terms of how to achieve the aims laid down by the EC. This use of directives rather than regulations has, however, a number of consequences. At the practical level, it means that students and practitioners of environmental law should become familiar with the skills involved in 'tracking' directives and their subsequent implementation. Since this will invariably be by means of Statutory Instrument it will necessarily involve finding out whether a Statutory Instrument has been introduced or not.

However, directives are problematic in another respect in so far as there is clearly the scope for Member States to fail to implement them, either on time or indeed at all. Alternatively, there are cases where implementation takes place in form, but there may not be effective implementation in terms of adequate enforcement or remedies available. It is interesting to note that the Fourth Environmental Action Programme (1987–92) stated that one of the principal aims was to ensure that Member States apply directives fully both in terms of legal implementation and practical implementation. Given that directives are prone to such problems, it is reasonable to wonder why they are the principal means of enacting EC environmental legislation. By leaving the choice and form of implementation to the Member States, there will automatically be divergences of approach. On the other hand, directives provide a flexible means of ensuring harmonised standards whilst taking account of the differing legal and administrative systems within the Member States and, to some extent, reflect the principle of subsidiarity which is so central to the Treaty.

Directives have generated considerable case law, both within national legal systems of the Member States and also by the ECJ. The direct effect, or otherwise, of directives is considered more fully below.

12.5.4 Decisions

A decision is an individual Act 'binding in its entirety upon those to whom it is addressed'. Decisions can be addressed to Member States but can equally be addressed to individuals and companies. Because it is a binding Act, a decision has the force of law and does not require any implementation. Decisions are frequently used by the Commission in the field of competition law but are rarely used in environmental law.

12.5.5 Recommendations and opinions

In addition to regulations, directives and decisions, the Treaty also makes provision for recommendations and opinions, which are not legally binding. However, the ECJ held, in *Grimaldi v Fonds des Maladies Professionnelles* (1988), that recommendations and opinions should be of persuasive influence in the decisions of national courts.

12.5.6 Case law of the ECJ

Clearly where the ECJ gives a ruling in an individual case, that ruling is binding on the parties to the proceedings. However, that decision is also binding in all subsequent cases. National courts are bound to follow rulings of the ECJ by virtue of Art 5, which provides that Member States (which includes the national courts) are bound to ensure fulfilment of the obligations arising out of the Treaty, or resulting from actions taken by the institutions of the EC (which includes the ECJ's decisions). Moreover, s 3(2) of the European Communities Act 1972 requires national courts to take judicial notice of any decision of the ECJ. The case law of the ECJ has provided a rich source of EC law. It is the ECJ which is responsible for developing the principles of supremacy and direct effect and, as such, has been successful in securing the integration of EC law into the domestic legal systems of Member States. In its most active phases, the ECJ has been criticised for judicial law making.

12.6 The institutional framework

To understand how environmental policy and legislation is developed in the EC, it is necessary to be aware of the way in which legislation is enacted and the role of the respective EC institutions. This is particularly important when one considers the amount of environmental legislation that the EC has thus far enacted and the way in which influences can be brought to bear to affect its content (or, indeed, existence). It is also important to understand the role of the respective institutions in the enforcement of EC environmental law and the actions that they can take in the event of a breach of the community laws. The issue of enforcement is of particular importance in the light of what has already been said about the use of directives in the field of environmental law. Since the implementation of most EC environmental law rests with the Member States themselves, the EC must have the means available to ensure that such implementation is both effective and uniformly applied.

12.6.1 The institutions

Within the EC, no one institution is solely responsible for passing legislation, instead the law making process involves the Council, the Commission, the Parliament and, in some instances, the Economic and Social Affairs Committee and the Committee of the Regions. Neither is there one single law making procedure. Instead there are several, each of which involves the institutions in a number of different relationships. The Parliament cannot be regarded as the legislative body in the same way in which the UK Parliament is. Instead, the European Parliament participates, in varying degrees, in the overall process of enacting legislation, although in some instances it may play no role at all. The institution with the greatest influence is the Council of the European Union.

12.6.2 The Council of the European Union

The Council of the European Union (formerly called the Council of Ministers prior to the TEU) is made up of 15 representatives from the Member States. The representatives must be Ministers of State who are authorised to commit their respective governments. When Ministers attend Council meetings, they represent their governments and generally pursue national interests. The composition of the Council alters, depending on the subject under discussion; general Council meetings are usually attended by Foreign Affairs Ministers, environment meetings are attended by Environment Ministers and so on. Where high level policy meetings are the subject of discussion, then the Council may consist of Heads of State. However, the Heads of State are also required by the Treaty to meet at least twice a year and, when they act in this special capacity, they meet as the European Council. Each Member State takes over the presidency of the Council for a period of six months on a rotating basis.

12.6.3 The functions of the Council of Ministers

The duty of the Council is to 'ensure that the objectives set out in the Treaty are attained' and to ensure the overall co-ordination of the general economic policies of the Member States. The Council, by virtue of Art 202 (formerly Art 145), has the power to take decisions which places it in the most powerful position in terms of enacting legislation (although, as is shown below, it interacts with the other institutions in a variety of ways, depending on the specific legislative procedure that is used).

Because the Council has this power of decision making, the way in which it votes and takes decision on legislative proposals is of utmost significance. Clearly, if decisions were always taken by a simple majority (that is, 8:15) there would be scope for legislation regularly to be enacted despite the disagreement of seven Member States. Therefore, although the Treaty specifies that decisions will usually be taken by simple majority unless otherwise provided for, the Treaty does go on to provide otherwise in many instances. The provisions of the Treaty require some decisions to be taken by 'qualified majority'.

12.6.4 Qualified majority voting

In these instances each Member State has a weighted vote, the weight depending on the size of population. Therefore the larger Member States (France, Germany, Italy and the UK) each have 10 votes, Spain has eight, Belgium, Greece, The Netherlands and Portugal carry five votes, Austria and Sweden have four votes, Denmark, Ireland and Finland each have three and Luxembourg, the smallest Member State, has two votes.

Where a qualified majority is required in favour of a proposal, then 62 out of the total of 87 votes must be cast in favour of the proposal. In other words at least 25 votes are required to block a proposal. The system is complicated by a compromise agreement whereby, if the Member States achieve a total of between 23 and 25 votes against a qualified decision, then the Council is obliged, within certain limits, to try and reach a compromise solution. This system of weighting was introduced by the SEA 1986 essentially to speed up decision making in order to achieve the self-imposed deadline of achieving the single market programme by 1992. It also provides a means of decision making/voting which prevents the larger Member States effectively out-voting the smaller Member States.

Qualified majority voting is used now in relation to the majority of legislation required to complete the single market. Thus, most harmonising measures introduced under Art 95 (formerly Art 100a) will require a qualified majority vote by the Council. Qualified majority voting is also used for environmental protection measures enacted under Art 175 (formerly Art 130s).

12.6.5 Unanimous voting

In certain circumstances, the Treaty still requires that decisions are agreed unanimously. Fiscal measures, measures relating to the free movement of people or professional training are some of the areas that still require a unanimous vote. As far as environmental measures are concerned, where the proposed measures concern town and country planning, land use (with the exception of waste management and management of water resources), and energy supply, the Council is required to act unanimously. Where a unanimous vote is required, there is a much greater likelihood that the proposals will be delayed for lengthy periods until a compromise can be reached which satisfies all the Member States. It is not unknown for some proposals to have taken as long as 16 years to be agreed. The Environmental Assessment Directive (85/337/EEC) is a case in point.

12.6.6 The European Commission

The European Commission is made up of 20 Commissioners. Commissioners are appointed by common accord of the governments of the Member States. Once appointed as a commissioner, an individual must act in the interests of the EC, not taking instructions from any national government. Their independence must be beyond doubt. Each Member State appoints at least one, whilst the larger Member States and Spain put forward two. The commissioners are appointed for five years and these terms may be renewed. The Commission is headed by a President. Commissioners are each given a specific portfolio for which they are responsible.

12.6.7 The Commission Services

The Commission Services (the civil service of the EC, based largely in Brussels) is divided into a series of departments which are known as Directorate Generals. Headed up by an administrative and permanent Director General, each Director General reports to a specific commissioner. The Directorate Generals are classified by number, with Directorate General XI taking responsibility for the Environment, Nuclear Safety and Civil Protection.

12.6.8 The functions of the Commission

The functions of the European Commission are laid down in Art 211 (formerly Art 155) of the EC Treaty. The Commission acts in the capacity of executive and also plays a key role in the formation of legislation. In addition, the Commission exercises considerable powers in relation to the enforcement of EC law, having the right to bring Member States before the ECJ. In this respect the Commission is regarded as the 'watchdog' of the EC or is sometimes referred to as the 'guardian of the treaties'.

The Commission is responsible for proposing and initiating legislation. Prior to the TEU, only the Commission had this power, albeit that it was not explicitly stated in the Treaty but was implied. The Council can of course suggest proposals to the Commission, but it has no legal power to insist that legislation is brought forward, although it clearly exercises considerable political power. However, since the TEU, the Parliament now enjoys the right to require the Commission to propose any legislation that it suggests. The Council can only take legislative action on proposals that have been initiated by the Commission.

12.6.9 The European Parliament

The Parliament was originally called the European Assembly and was made up of representatives from national parliaments. However, in 1979 direct elections to the Parliament were held for the first time and the Assembly changed its name to European Parliament as required by the SEA 1986. The Parliament is now made up of 626 directly elected representatives, known as Members of the European Parliament or MEPs. At present, the electoral systems in the different Member States vary, with most States electing by means of proportional representation. The Treaty requires, however, that a uniform electoral system is eventually adopted.

12.6.10 The functions of the European Parliament

The Parliament's functions and powers have grown significantly since 1957. Prior to the SEA 1986, the Parliament acted largely in an advisory and supervisory capacity. Its involvement in the legislative procedure was limited to giving an opinion on proposed legislation, but only in relation to those areas of legislation where the Treaty specifically provided that the Parliament should be consulted. In some areas of legislation, the Council could take decisions without the need for any consultation with the Parliament.

The Parliament, as befitting the only directly elected community institution, pressed for greater powers and in particular a greater involvement in the legislative process. Its powers were increased by the SEA 1986, which gave it the right in certain circumstances to be consulted twice in relation to certain proposals and, even more significantly, by the TEU, which introduced the so called co-decision procedure, giving the Parliament, effectively, a right to veto certain legislative proposals. The way in which the Parliament votes in relation to proposals before it are specified in the Treaty. Unless otherwise provided by the Treaty, the normal voting arrangement would be by a simple majority of votes cast. However, the Treaty specifies, particularly in relation to the procedures known as Arts 251 and 252 (formerly Arts 189b and 189c), that in some instances an absolute majority is required.

The Parliament currently exercises a range of functions. Its role in the legislative process is described more fully below. It also acts in a supervisory capacity in relation to the Commission and, to a lesser extent, the Council. The Parliament has the power to dismiss the whole of the Commission with a vote of censure, provided that it can achieve a two-thirds majority in favour of such action. Although the Parliament has threatened such action on two occasions, it has never done so. The Parliament also conducts its own version of question time when it requires commissioners to answer Parliamentary questions, either verbally to the Parliament or in writing. It is in this way that the Parliament exercises a degree of control over the Commission, and this reflects the checks and balances that are built into the institutional framework. The Council of Ministers also reports to the Parliament. At the end of each presidency period, the outgoing President of the Council reports to the Parliament on the achievements during the presidency period.

Since the TEU 1993, the Parliament has been given the power to set up a Committee of Inquiry to investigate alleged contraventions or maladministration in the implementation of EC law and has also been required to appoint an Ombudsman for maladministration.

12.6.11 The Parliament and the environment

The political composition of the Parliament is wide ranging, with large representations from both the left and right of the political spectrum. The Parliament also has its own select Committee on Environment, Public Health and Consumer Protection which has about 50 members. The Parliament receives a number of petitions from environmental pressure groups and these are usually passed on to the Commission to deal with under the Art 226 (formerly Art 169) proceedings (see below). The value of petitioning Parliament is that it can lend a political impetus to the process which may be persuasive when the Commission decides upon enforcement proceedings.

12.6.12 The ECJ

Article 220 (formerly Art 164) of the Treaty provides that the role of the ECJ is to 'ensure that in the interpretation and application of this Treaty the law is observed'. Various other Treaty Articles deal with its jurisdiction in relation to cases brought by Member States, against Member States, against the institutions themselves and also its relationship with the national courts of the Member States. These will be discussed more fully below in relation to the enforcement of EC law. The ECJ itself is made up of 15 judges chosen from people whose independence is beyond doubt. The ECJ is assisted by nine Advocate Generals who help it by presenting an analysis of the cases before it and also, importantly, their recommendations in the form of an opinion. The ECJ reaches its decisions in private and presents a single judgment known as a collegiate judgment. This means, in fact, that there is no record of any dissenting judgment. It is often very useful when reading judgments of the ECJ to read also the opinion of the Advocate General. Whilst the judges are not bound to follow the Advocate General's recommendations, where they do, the opinion provides a very useful indication of the ECJ's reasoning.

In addition to the ECJ, there is also the European Court of First Instance, which was created in 1988 to alleviate some of the workload of the ECJ. The Court of First Instance, has limited jurisdiction and cannot give preliminary rulings under Art 234 (formerly Art 177), or deal with cases brought by or against the Member States. The Court can act as a Court of First Instance in EC competition law cases and judicial review cases brought by 'natural and legal persons'.

12.6.13 The balance of power between the Member States

The following diagram provides a detailed breakdown of the number of MEPs' votes in Council and Commissioners for each of the 15 Member States.

Member State	MEPs	Votes at Council	Commissioners
Austria	21	4	1
Belgium	25	5	1
Denmark	16	3	1
Finland	16	3	1
France	87	10	2
Germany	99	10	2
Greece	25	5	1
Ireland	15	3	1
Italy	87	10	2
Luxembourg	6	2	1
Netherlands	31	5	1
Portugal	25	5	1
Spain	64	8	2
Sweden	22	4	1
United Kingdom	87	10	2
TOTAL	626	87	20

12.7 The legislative procedure

The process of enacting EC secondary legislation is complex; however, there are two underlying fundamental principles which govern it. The first is that, in order to enact EC secondary legislation, the Treaty must provide a legal base for such action. The EC institutions have no power to enact legislation that does not serve the aims of the EC. To do so would mean that they were acting unlawfully. However, it should be noted that Art 308 (formerly Art 235) of the Treaty provides a residual power to enable the institutions to take action to achieve community objectives, notwithstanding the absence of an explicit legal basis.

The second point of importance is that the Treaty defines how the relevant legislation will be enacted. The legislative procedure that will be employed to enact the secondary legislation depends entirely upon the Treaty article under which the legislation is based. This point is of particular importance in the field of environmental law, where it is possible to enact environmental legislation either under Art 95 (formerly Art 100a) or under Art 173 (formerly Art 130). Article 95 requires measures to be adopted under the co-decision procedure, whereas Art 173 requires the co-operation procedure.

12.7.1 Initiation of legislation and the legislative processes

Legislative proposals are initiated by the Commission. In practice, the Commission consults with a variety of groups as to the content of the legislation and it is in this way that environmental pressure groups can influence the content of environmental legislation. Once the proposal has been drafted and agreed by the Commission, it is sent to the Council.

There are a number of ways in which the proposal will be dealt with from this point, however the main procedures are as follows:

(a) Council legislation without consultation of the European Parliament: where the Council takes a final decision on the Commission proposal without the involvement of the Parliament;

(b) the Consultation Procedure: in this procedure the Parliament must be consulted before the Council reaches its final decision. The Council must take account of the Parliament's opinion, although the opinion is not binding on the Council;

(c) the Co-operation Procedure: introduced by the SEA 1986. This procedure is strictly called the Art 252 (formerly Art 189c) procedure. The procedure enables the Parliament to have two opportunities to consider the proposal (rather like adding a second reading to the process). The Parliament can suggest amendments to the draft proposal. If the Council does not accept the Parliamentary amendments, then it is forced to act unanimously in order to enact the legislative proposal. It is in this way that the Parliament exerts some influence on the content of legislation;

(d) the Co-decision Procedure or Art 251 (formerly Art 189b) procedure was introduced by the TEU 1993. The procedure is complicated but greatly enhances the role of the Parliament. The effect of the co-decision procedure is to provide for the possibility of a third reading. The procedure follows that of the co-operation procedure until the final stage. Where the Council does not approve Parliamentary amendments, a conciliation committee of equal numbers of the Council and the Parliament attempt to agree a joint text. If the joint text cannot be agreed, then the proposed measure fails.

In addition to these main procedures, there are others – such as the Assent Procedure and the Conciliation procedure.

Since there are clearly differences between the procedures, in terms of the powers of the Parliament and the voting in the Council of Ministers, the question of which Treaty Article should be used has significant implications in relation to environmental legislation.

12.8 Enforcement of EC law

Member States are obliged to fulfil their EC law obligations and not to do anything which would jeopardise the attainment of the Treaty.

12.8.1 Member States' obligation to comply with EC law

Member States are required by Art 5 to fulfil their obligations as members of the EC. They are specifically required to take all appropriate measures, whether general or particular, to ensure fulfilment of the obligations arising out of the Treaty, or resulting from action take by the institutions. Such action embraces both EC policy, secondary legislation and decisions of the ECJ and Court of First Instance. In addition, Member States must not take any measures which could jeopardise the attainment of the Treaty objectives.

Failure to fulfil obligations can take many forms:

(a) introducing legislation in contravention to the Treaty: this happened in relation to the Merchant Shipping Act 1988 which contravened the basic principle of non-discrimination on the grounds of nationality and resulted in the *Factortame* litigation and the case *Commission v UK* (1989);

(b) failure to implement directives either at all, or on time: the Commission has brought numerous actions against Member States on these grounds. For example, the case of *Commission v UK* (1993);

(c) partial or incorrect implementation of a directive;

(d) inadequate enforcement of a directive.

It can be seen therefore that Member States are under a duty to implement directives effectively and on time. Since EC environmental legislation is largely in the form of directives rather than regulations the opportunities for Member States avoiding or delaying their obligations under environmental directives are considerable. The non-implementation of environmental Directives has given rise to a number of direct actions before the ECJ (see below), for example in *Commission v UK* (1993) (Case C-337/89) concerning non-implementation by the UK of Directive (80/778/EC) concerned with drinking water intended for human consumption. This was the first case in which the UK was found to be in breach of an EC environmental Directive. Another example of a direct action against the UK can be found in *Commission v UK* (1993) (Case 56/90) where the UK was found to be in breach of its obligation under EC law in respect of the Bathing Water Directive (76/160/EC). In addition to a direct action against a Member State for non-implementation it is also possible that the failure to implement may be challenged indirectly in the national courts. This happened in the judicial review proceedings brought by FOE in *R v Secretary of State for the Environment ex p FOE and Another* (1995).

12.8.2 Direct actions against Member States

The main direct sanction against Member States is provided for by Art 226 (formerly Art 169) of the Treaty, which enables the European Commission to commence legal proceedings against Member States before the ECJ. Article 226 provides for two pre-litigation stages before court proceedings are taken. If the Commission believes that a Member State is in breach of its community obligations, it can inform the Member State in question by means of a letter of formal notice, known as an 'Article 226' letter, which sets out the nature of the infringement and the course of action to be taken. This only usually happens after informal negotiations have been exhausted. The letter must state all the grounds for complaint. Member States must then be given an adequate time period to make their observations on the alleged breach. If the Commission is still not satisfied that the Member State is complying with its obligations, then it can take the next step of issuing a 'reasoned opinion'. This formally records the infringement and requires the Member State to take the necessary action to bring the infringement to an end. Normally the Member State will be given a deadline by which it must take appropriate action.

Following these two pre-litigation steps, the Commission can, if it chooses, commence legal proceedings against the Member State before the ECJ (such cases appear as the *Commission v UK* or *Commission v Italy* and so on). The number of cases brought before the ECJ under Art 226 are increasing each year. A number of points need to be made in relation to Art 226 proceedings:

(a) the Commission often acts on the basis of complaints made by aggrieved citizens or pressure groups. The number of complaints received in 1993 was 1,040. In addition, the Commission also receives numerous petitions from pressure groups, trade unions and so on. It is in this respect that individuals and pressure groups can exert pressure on the Commission to deal with breaches of environmental law. Complainants do not have to satisfy any legal or sufficient interest in the matter complained of. Therefore Art 226 provides an inexpensive means by which interested parties can seek to enforce EC law;

(b) the Commission is not bound to investigate or follow through all complaints nor is it bound to commence Art 226 proceedings. In fact the Commission exercises discretion at all stages. This was confirmed by the ECJ in *Star Fruit Co v Commission* (1989);

(c) Member States have raised various mitigating factors and defences but these have rarely succeeded. In *Commission v Ireland* (1981), concerning Ireland's failure to implement Directive (77/91/EEC), the ECJ held that a Member State may not plead provisions, practices or circumstances existing in its internal legal system in order to justify a failure to comply with obligations resulting from EC directives.

In addition to Art 226 (formerly Art 169), Art 227 (formerly Art 170) provides for a similar procedure enabling one Member State to bring an action against another Member State. It is very rare for Member States to resort to Art 227. Member States are, in fact, required to ask the Commission to commence proceedings, and only when the Commission has failed to issue a reasoned opinion does this option become available. However, it is more likely that Member States will resolve their differences at the political level through the Council of Ministers rather than resorting to legal action before the ECJ.

12.8.3 Fines

Where a Member State is found to be in breach of its EC obligations, the ECJ will issue a declaration to that effect. Failure to comply with the declaration and remedy the situation will result in the Member State being in breach of both Art 228 (formerly Art 171) and Art 5. Prior to the TEU, the ECJ's powers were limited to issuing a declaration. However, its powers have been enhanced by the TEU and the ECJ now has the power to impose a fine where a Member State continues to breach its obligations after a ECJ declaration. The fine is not automatic; the Commission is required to recommence proceedings against the defaulting Member State before a fine can be imposed.

12.8.4 Judicial review of EC law

The Treaty also gives the ECJ the jurisdiction to review the acts of the EC institutions and to annul them on specific grounds. The power of the ECJ in this respect is important, because it acts as check on the other EC institutions which have been given significant powers under the Treaty. Article 230 (formerly Art 173) specifies which 'acts' are reviewable, who may bring judicial review proceedings, the grounds on which review proceedings may be brought and the time limits for bringing such actions.

Judicial review in EC law is complex particularly in relation to actions brought by aggrieved individuals.

12.8.5 Reviewable acts

The ECJ can review the legality of acts adopted jointly by the European Parliament and the Council, of acts of the Council, of the Commission and of the European Central Bank other than recommendations and opinions and of acts of the European Parliament intended to have legal effect vis à vis third parties. 'Acts' are not defined other than in the negative sense, in that they do not include recommendations or opinions, which, of course, are not legally binding. It is clear therefore that regulations, directives and decisions are 'acts' in this sense and therefore 'reviewable acts'. However, the ECJ has not confined the interpretation of 'acts' to secondary legislation and, in various cases, has held that they include all measures taken by the institutions which are designed to have legal effect irrespective of their nature or form.

12.8.6 Who can bring an action?

Article 230 (formerly Art 173) draws a distinction between the Member States and the institutions on the one hand, and natural and legal persons on the other. The Member States and the Council and the Commission are so called privileged applicants. They can commence judicial review proceedings in relation to any reviewable act, they do not have to demonstrate or prove a legal interest. In other words, they automatically have standing. The Parliament does not have the same general right, but can bring an action to protect its prerogative powers. The position with regard to individuals or 'natural or legal persons', a classification which encompasses environmental pressure groups, is unfortunately much more complex and restrictive.

Article 230 states that any natural or legal person may institute proceedings against 'a Decision addressed to that person, or a Decision which, although in the form of a Regulation or a Decision addressed to another person, is of direct and individual concern to himself'.

In essence there are three situations where a non-privileged person can bring actions for judicial review:

(a) where the applicant is directly addressed by the decision;

(b) where a regulation is really a disguised decision;

(c) where the decision is addressed to another person, which can include a Member State (*Plaumann & Co v Commission* (1963)).

In the cases of (b) and (c) the applicant also has to prove that the reviewable act is also of direct and individual concern. The tests laid down by the ECJ in relation to direct and individual concern have been very restrictive, making it extremely difficult for individuals to overcome this hurdle of standing. There is as yet no automatic right for pressure groups to bring judicial review actions.

12.8.7 Grounds for review

Once an applicant has established that he or she has standing then they must then go on to establish the grounds for review. These are laid down in Art 230(2) and can often overlap in individual cases. They are:

(a) lack of competence;

(b) infringement of an essential procedural requirement;

(c) infringement of the Treaty or of any rule of law relating to the application of the Treaty; and

(d) misuse of power.

12.8.8 Time limits

Article 230 (formerly Art 173) contains strict time limits regarding the commencement of judicial review actions. Proceedings must be instituted within two months of the publication of the challenged measure, or of its notification to the claimant, or in the absence of either of these, two months from the date on which it came to the knowledge of the claimant.

12.9 Indirect enforcement through the national courts

Given that Art 226 (formerly Art 169) proceedings can only be brought by the Commission and that individuals have in practice so little access to the ECJ under Art 230 (formerly Art 173), it is vital to understand how EC law can be enforced within the national legal system by domestic courts. The ECJ has established through its rulings, that individuals can raise issues of EC law in the context of legal proceedings in order to secure rights under EC law. So, for example, it is possible to use EC law to establish legal rights (*Marshall v Southampton AHA* (1986)), or as a defence in criminal prosecutions (*Publico Ministero v Ratti* (1979)).

In order to ensure that EC law is applied by national courts in a uniform manner, Art 234 (formerly Art 177) provides that the domestic courts can refer matters of interpretation and validity of EC law provisions to the ECJ in order to obtain a ruling. This is known as the preliminary rulings procedure.

12.9.1 The preliminary rulings procedure

The ECJ has jurisdiction to give preliminary rulings concerning the interpretation of the Treaty, the validity and interpretation of acts of the institutions of the EC and the interpretation of the statutes of bodies established by an act of the Council. It is worth emphasising that the ECJ can only interpret the Treaty; it cannot, as is the case with secondary legislation, question its validity.

If a question arises in the context of national court proceedings about an issue of EC law then that court or tribunal may, if it considers that decision is necessary to enable it to give judgment, request the ECJ to give a ruling. This is known as the Art 234 procedure. It enables national courts to refer questions on interpretation of EC law to the ECJ. Once the ECJ gives its preliminary ruling, the national court is bound by it and must apply it to the facts of the case. The ECJ is not deciding on the facts or the outcome of the national court case, neither is it acting as an appeal court. Instead it is essentially co-operating with the national court in order that the EC law provisions may be interpreted correctly. The ECJ is well placed to give this authoritative interpretation of EC law given its 'panoramic view' of the community and of its institutions (*per* Lord Bingham in *Customs and Excise Comrs v Aps Samex* (1983)). When the national court seeks a preliminary ruling from the ECJ, the court proceedings are suspended until the ECJ has given its ruling.

The ECJ cannot pass judgment on the compatibility of domestic law with EC law. In circumstances where the ECJ has been asked to do this (since it is often in cases involving a conflict between domestic and EC law that questions of interpretation are raised) the ECJ frequently rephrases the question from the national court in order to provide the interpretation of the relevant community law provision.

12.9.2 When should a national court refer a question to the ECJ?

The Treaty draws a distinction between courts which may refer a question and courts which shall refer a question to the ECJ. Article 234(3) (formerly Art 177(3)) states that courts from which there is no judicial remedy (no right of appeal) shall refer, whereas other (lower) courts exercise a discretion (that is, may refer). Despite this distinction a court need only refer if it considers that a decision from the ECJ is necessary in order to enable it to give judgment. Therefore all courts exercise a discretion in determining whether a referral is necessary. In *Customs and Excise v Aps Samex* (1983) Lord Bingham gave the following guidance:

> ... if the facts have been found and the Community law issue is critical to the court's final decision, the appropriate course is ordinarily to refer the issue to

the European Court of Justice unless the national court can with complete confidence resolve the issue itself.

In considering whether it can with complete confidence resolve the issue itself, the national court must be mindful of the difference between national and Community legislation; of the pitfalls which face a national court when venturing into an unfamiliar field; of the need for uniform interpretation throughout the Community and of the great advantages enjoyed by the Court of Justice in construing Community instruments.

12.9.3 A court must refer on questions of validity

The exercise of discretion is qualified in relation to questions concerning the validity of EC law raised in the context of national litigation. In *Firma Foto-Frost v Hauptzollamt Lübeck Ost* (1988), the ECJ explicitly stated that national courts do not have the power to declare acts of the EC institutions invalid. Therefore, where a question about the validity of EC law is raised, then the national court must seek a preliminary ruling from the ECJ.

12.9.4 Importance of Art 234 procedure

The Art 234 (formerly Art 177) procedure has provided the main vehicle for the ECJ to develop the principles of direct effect and supremacy, dealt with in the following section. Many individuals have benefited from the Art 234 procedure as a result of the ECJ interpreting various EC provisions in such a way as to deem them directly effective and thus enforceable in national courts. There have been relatively few Art 234 rulings concerning environmental law. In the UK the first reference on an environmental law matter was made by the House of Lords in the case of *R v Secretary of State for the Environment ex p RSPB* (1995).

12.10 The EC as a new legal order

Commentators have described EC law as 'unique' in international law terms, largely because of the extent to which EC law penetrates the domestic legal systems of the Member States and confers enforceable legal rights upon individuals. The ECJ has itself stated that the EC:

> ... constitutes a new legal order of international law for the benefit of which the states have limited their sovereign rights, albeit within limited fields and the subjects of which comprise not only Member States but also their nationals.

This statement was made by the ECJ in the leading case of *Van Gend en Loos v Nederlandse Administratie der Belastingen* (1962). At the time when the ECJ made this statement, the role of the EC was limited. However, since that time the EC has extended its competences and the transfer of sovereign rights referred to in the judgment extends to less limited fields. The issue of the transfer of power away from Member States has caused major problems for a number of the Member States, particularly when those States sought to ratify and incorporate the new TEU into their domestic legal systems. An expression of this concern came with the Danish 'no' vote in the referendum held on whether the Danish Government should ratify the new Treaty. Therefore, a principal amendment to the TEU was the introduction in Art 5 (formerly Art 3B) of the principle of subsidiarity.

12.10.1 Subsidiarity

This provides that in areas which do not fall within the EC's exclusive competence, the EC shall only take action if and so far as the objectives of the proposed action cannot be sufficiently achieved by the Member States and can therefore, by reason of the scale or effects of the proposed action, be better achieved by the EC. Furthermore, any action by the EC shall not go beyond what is necessary to achieve the objectives of the Treaty, recognition of another fundamental principle of EC law – the principle of proportionality.

12.10.2 The relationship between EC law and UK law

The relationship between EC law and national law is one which has dominated many articles and textbooks and which is usually covered within the context of most constitutional or public law courses. Therefore, it is not the intention of this section to cover this subject in great detail. However, in view of the volume of EC environmental law that has been introduced, it is necessary to reflect on the way in which EC law is incorporated into the English legal system and, in particular, on the issues arising when there has not been adequate implementation of directives. EC law is incorporated into English law by the European Communities Act 1972 (as amended).

12.11 Supremacy of EC law

The EC Treaty does not specifically make reference to the issue of supremacy or the relationship between EC law and national law. However, this relationship is of the utmost importance. The ECJ has in a number of famous decisions made it clear that priority is to be accorded to EC law and that EC law should prevail over conflicting national provisions. To allow otherwise would undermine the very being of the EC and its principal aim of establishing a common market.

As early as 1962, in the case of *Van Gend en Loos* (1962), it was established by the ECJ that the Member States had limited their sovereign rights and that the EC constituted a new legal order. The ECJ went further in *Costa v ENEL* (1964) when it stated that:

> ... the transfer by the States ... to the Community legal system of the rights and obligations arising under the Treaty carries with it a permanent limitation of their sovereign rights against which a subsequent unilateral act incompatible with the concept of the Community cannot prevail.

National courts are required to apply provisions of EC law and to give full effect to those provisions and, if necessary, to set aside any conflicting provisions of national legislation, even if adopted after the relevant community law provision (*Amministrazione delle Finanze dello Stato v Simmenthal* (1978)).

12.12 Effect of EC law

In addition to the principle of supremacy, the ECJ has also addressed the problem of the effect of EC law throughout the Member States. The aim of the EC is to achieve a common market where goods, people, services and capital can move freely. It is therefore necessary to achieve uniformity throughout the EC of the standards and provisions established at EC level. This need to secure uniformity of EC law is evidenced by the nature of regulations and also by the presence of the Art 234 procedure. However, a large amount of EC law, particularly environmental law, takes the form of directives, and directives do not guarantee immediate uniformity in the same way that regulations do. The failure by a Member State to implement a directive can distort the standards laid down at Community level and can potentially leave people in one Member State with fewer rights than those in another where there has been full implementation. However, the ECJ has asserted that Member States should not benefit from their failure to implement a directive and has developed a number of principles which enable Community law to take effect even where there has not been formal implementation by the State.

These are:

(a) *direct effect* – the concept of direct effect allows litigants in national courts to rely directly on the terms of EC measures, notwithstanding that those terms have not been fully implemented into the domestic legal system. However, certain conditions must be satisfied before a measure can be directly effective;

(b) *indirect effect or the duty of interpretation* – the concept of indirect effect stems from the obligations placed on national courts to interpret national law in accordance with EC law;

(c) *damages against the State* – in certain circumstances damages may be awarded in favour of individuals who have suffered loss as a result of the failure of a Member State to implement EC law properly.

12.12.1 Direct effect of EC law

The concept or principle of direct effect has been developed by the ECJ in a number of cases dealing with Treaty articles, regulations, directives and decisions. It was first established in the *Van Gend en Loos* case in relation to Art 12 of the Treaty. In the course of an Art 234 (formerly Art 177) reference the ECJ ruled that Art 12 was capable of direct effect and could be relied upon by individuals before national court and tribunals. The ECJ stated that:

> The objective of the EEC Treaty, which is to establish a common market, the functioning of which is of direct concern to interested parties in the Community, implies that this Treaty is more than an agreement which merely creates mutual obligations between the contracting states.

As a consequence, *Van Gend en Loos* was able to rely on the Treaty article to secure enforceable rights in the Dutch courts.

12.12.2 Conditions for direct effect

The ECJ laid down three conditions which must be satisfied in order for a provision to be directly effective:

(a) the content of the relevant provision must be both clear and precise;

(b) the relevant provision must be unconditional; and

(c) the provision must leave no room for the exercise of discretion by the Member State.

Following the *Van Gend en Loos* case, the ECJ has held a large number of Treaty articles to be directly effective. The criteria laid down have been applied generously and, as a result, even measures which are not particularly clear or precise have been deemed to be capable of direct effect. In addition to Treaty articles, the ECJ has established that EC secondary legislation is also capable of direct effect. Regulations which are described in Art 249 (formerly Art 189) as 'directly applicable' may also be directly effective if they can satisfy the test laid down by the Court.

12.12.3 Direct effect of directives

It was thought that directives, by their nature, could not be capable of direct effect because they could not satisfy the requirement that they leave no room for the exercise of discretion by the Member State. However, the existence of discretion concerning the means of implementation of directives has not prevented them from being directly effective. The ECJ in *Van Duyn v Home Office* (1971) established conclusively that directives were capable of direct effect and therefore could be enforceable at the suit of individuals in the national courts, providing the provisions of the directive could satisfy the requirements laid down in *Van Gend en Loos*. (It should be noted that these tests are applied not to a directive as a whole but to the relevant provision that is being considered, such as an article of a directive or a particular paragraph.) It follows that directives are only capable of direct effect after the period for implementation by the Member State has expired (*Publico Ministero v Tullio Ratti* (1979)). Until expiry of the implementation period, Member States are free to rely on existing national law, even if it conflicts with the requirements of a directive which is not yet due for implementation.

12.12.4 Direct effect of environmental measures?

It is clearly not possible to state that all EC environmental measures are capable of being directly effective, since many are couched in very vague and uncertain terms and others are dependent on certain criteria being satisfied and will not satisfy the requirement that the provisions are unconditional. However, Ludwig Kramer, a leading author on EC environmental law, suggests that certain types of provision may be capable of direct effect, in particular directives which lay down specific maximum values for permissible discharges, or provisions which prohibit the use or discharge of certain specified substances. He asserts that certain directives such as the Drinking Water Directive (80/778/EEC), and also the Environmental Impact Assessment Directive (85/337/EEC), are capable of direct effect.

The question of the direct effect of both these directives has been considered in a number of cases. In *Commission v UK* (1993) (Case C-337/89) the Commission brought an action against the UK in respect of the Drinking Water Directive (80/778/EEC). The Directive required Member States to set drinking water quality standards not exceeding 'maximum admissible concentrations' (MACs). The directive required formal implementation by 18 July 1982 and required the standards to be met by 18 July 1985. The UK had taken no steps to formally implement the directive by 1987 and so the Commission commenced proceedings under Art 226 (formerly Art 169) of the EC Treaty. In 1989 the UK implemented the Water Supply (Water Quality) Regulations 1989 SI 1989/1147; however, the Commission continued with the proceedings arguing that the UK had not fully met the standards set in the directive in all parts of the UK. (Specifically that 28 supply zones in England and 17 supply zones in Scotland did not comply with MACs relating to nitrates and lead, and that there had been no formal implementation of the directive in Northern Ireland.) The ECJ found that the UK was in breach of its obligations under the directive. By way of defence the UK had argued that it had taken all practical steps to secure compliance with the directive but the ECJ held that this argument could not justify the UK's failure to implement the directive. The ECJ held that the UK had formally breached the directive by failing to pass legislation to implement the directive and had also substantively breached the directive by failing to achieve the MACs specified in the directive with regard to nitrates. The ECJ held that the MACs were enforceable obligations and implied as such that they were capable of direct effect. The consequence of direct effect being that the provisions may create legally enforceable rights in the national courts (see *Van Duyn* above). The decision in *Commission v UK* gave rise to further litigation in *R v Secretary of State for the Environment ex p FOE and Another* (1995) in which the English Court of Appeal accepted that the MACs laid down in the directive were capable of direct effect.

The direct effect of the Environmental Assessment Directive (85/337/EEC) has been considered in a number of cases. In *Twyford Parish Council v Secretary of State for Transport* (1992) it was held that the requirement to carry out an Environmental Assessment was directly effective in relation to those projects listed in Annex 1 of the directive (Annex 1 lists projects where an environmental assessment is mandatory whereas Annex 2 lists projects where an environmental assessment is discretionary).

12.12.5 No horizontal direct effect of directives

As far as directives are concerned, it is well established that litigants in national proceedings can only benefit from the direct effect of a directive in actions against the State or an emanation of the State (*Marshall v Southampton AHA* (1986)). Therefore, one of the particular problems in relation to directives is that they will not be directly enforceable against individuals (to use the jargon, they are said not to be horizontally directly effective). The ECJ has been consistent in the line that it has taken in relation to directives, maintaining that they can only be directly enforceable against the State or an emanation of the State and that they are not capable of being directly effective against individuals. The consequence of this is that individuals and environmental pressure groups cannot rely on the direct effect of an unimplemented directive against private companies.

12.12.6 An emanation of the State?

Because of this limitation in relation to the direct effect of directives, it becomes necessary to define what is meant by the State or an emanation of the State. The ECJ has interpreted the phrase widely. In *Foster v British Gas* (1991), it was held that bodies responsible for the provision of public services and which have greater powers than are normally accorded to individuals or corporations are to be construed as emanations of the State. The issue was raised in the case of *Griffin v South West Water* (1995).

This case is of particular importance in environmental law because it involved the question of whether South West Water could be construed as an emanation of the State. The action concerned a directive relating to employment issues but the decision of the court is of wider significance. Blackburn J held that South West Water was an emanation of the State because the privatised water company was 'a State authority'. He asserted that the relevant question was not whether the body in question is under the control of the State, but rather whether the public service in question is in control of the State. The fact that the overall control of water services is exercised by the State was the relevant factor, not the legal form of the body, nor the fact that the body was a commercial concern. Blackburn J went on to say:

> It is also irrelevant that the body does not carry out any of the traditional functions of the state. It is irrelevant too that the state does not possess day-to-day control over the activities of the body.

The judgment is of particular significance since it paves the way for other directives, in the field of environmental law in particular, to be directly effective against the water companies, as emanations of the State.

12.13 The duty of interpretation approach

Whilst the direct effect doctrine may assist individuals to obtain enforceable legal rights in the national courts in actions against the State or emanations of the State, it will not assist individuals bringing actions against other individuals. This is a clear anomaly but has been justified by the ECJ on the grounds that because directives are addressed to Member States they may not of themselves impose obligations on an individual. However, the ECJ has put forward other ways in which individuals can seek to rely on directives, even where the directives are not capable of direct effect (because they cannot satisfy the relevant conditions) or where the action is a horizontal one against another individual. The first of these approaches is sometimes called 'indirect effect', but a more appropriate way of describing it is the 'duty of interpretation'. The approach was first put forward in the case of *Von Colson v Land Nordrhein-Westfalen* (1983) and later extended in impact in the case of *Marleasing SA v La Commercial Internacional de Alimentacion SA* (1989).

In *Von Colson*, the ECJ held that national courts (as emanations of the State and therefore equally bound by Art 5 of the Treaty) are under a duty to interpret national law, as far as possible, in the light of the directive which generated the national legislation. In other words, the national legislation should be construed to give effect to the purpose of the directive.

The judgment in *Marleasing*, which affirmed the position in *Von Colson*, was really quite remarkable in that the ECJ came to the view that the duty of interpretation also extended to national provisions whether they were introduced before or after a directive. The ECJ stated that in applying national law:

> ... whether the provisions in question [ie, the national provisions] were adopted before or after the Directive, the national court called upon to interpret

it is required to do so, as far as possible, in the light of the wording and the purpose of the Directive in order to achieve the result pursued by the latter ...

The response of the English courts has been mixed. In *Webb v EMO Air Cargo (UK) Ltd* (1993), Lord Keith stated that the ECJ had, in the *Marleasing* decision, only required national courts to construe national legislation to give effect to a directive only if it was possible to do so. He went on to say that it would only be possible to do so where a domestic law was 'open to an interpretation consistent with the directive whether or not it is also open to an interpretation inconsistent with it'. However, in the case of *Wychavon DC v Secretary of State and Others* (1994), the High Court showed itself to be very unwilling to apply this principle.

12.14 Damages against the State

In *Francovich and Bonifaci v Italian State* (1991), the ECJ extended yet further the impact of directives. The case is important in that lays down the principle that Member States may be sued for damages as a result of their failure to implement a directive. The ECJ in its previous judgments had been clear that Member States should not be able to benefit from their failure to implement directives in actions brought against the State by individuals and that Member States could not plead their failure to implement by way of defence. The *Francovich* judgment was a further extension of this and may well prove to be important in the enforcement of environmental directives.

The facts are as follows: Mr Francovich was owed 6 m lire by his insolvent employers. However, because he was unable to enforce a judgment against them, he brought an action against the Italian Government for compensation. Under a Council Directive (80/987/EEC) aimed at protecting employees in the event of the insolvency of their employers, Member States were required to ensure that a system was set up to meet outstanding pay arrears for employees in the event of their employers' insolvency. The Italian Government had not implemented the directive and had not set up any system to act as guarantor in these circumstances. Francovich, however, could not rely on the direct effect of the Directive since it was not sufficiently clear and precise. However, the ECJ held that, subject to three conditions, damages are available against the State for failure to implement the directive.

12.14.1 The conditions for State liability

The conditions for State liability laid down in *Francovich* were:

(a) the result prescribed by the directive should be the grant of rights to individuals;

(b) it must be possible to identify those rights on the basis of the provisions of the directive; and

(c) there must be a causal link between the breach of the State's obligation and the loss and damage suffered by the injured parties.

Following *Francovich*, therefore, it is possible to bring an action for damages against a State which has failed to implement a directive, providing the conditions listed above are satisfied. If these conditions are satisfied, there is a right on the part of individuals to obtain reparation from the State. The *Francovich* decision is extremely important. It opens the way for individuals who can prove explicit legal rights under directives to sue the State for damages, providing they can prove the causal link referred to. As far as environmental law is concerned it may prove difficult to identify the grant of rights to individuals in directives which are enacted for environmental protection purposes. It will also be difficult (as is the case in much environmental litigation) to prove causation.

The decision in *Francovich* referred expressly to damages arising from failure to implement a directive, however the issue of State liability has been further considered in the joined cases of *Brasserie du Pêcheur SA v Germany and R v Secretary of State for Transport ex p Factortame Ltd and Others* (1996). This case concerned the application of the *Francovich* decision to breaches of primary Treaty provisions rather than directives. In *Brasserie du Pêcheur SA* a French company claimed it had suffered loss as a result of German legislation on Beer purity which was shown later in *Commission v Germany* (1987) (Case 178/84) to be in breach of Art 28 (formerly Art 30). In *Factortame* a Spanish fishing company was claiming for the losses it incurred as a consequence of the UK's breach of Art 52. The ECJ held that where a Member State has a wide discretion in implementing EC policies (unlike the situation where a Member State has no discretion as to whether it implements a directive) the conditions under which it may incur liability must be the same as those under which the EC institutions incur liability under a comparable situation, which are laid down in Art 215 of the Treaty which deals with the non-contractual liability of the EC. In such circumstances EC law confers a right to reparation where three conditions are met: the rule of law infringed must be intended to confer rights on individuals; the breach must be *sufficiently serious*; and there must be a direct causal link between the breach of the obligation resting on the State and the damage sustained by the injured parties. The decisive test for finding that a breach of EC law is sufficiently serious is whether the Member State manifestly and gravely disregarded the limits of its discretion. Thus the conditions for State liability in relation to primary Treaty obligations are more stringent than in relation to obligations under a directive. It should also be noted that in *Brasserie du Pêcheur* and *Factortame* the relevant Treaty provisions were 28 (formerly 30) and 52 respectively, both of which are directly effective. Articles 174–76 (formerly Arts 130r–t) which is concerned with environmental protection contains a number of generalised principles, such as the precautionary principle and the polluter pays principle, and it is difficult to see how its provisions are intended to confer rights on individuals or to be capable of direct effect. However, it clearly remains open for the ECJ to rule to the contrary.

12.15 The development of a Community environmental policy

12.15.1 Introduction

When the EEC was formed in 1958 by the Treaty of Rome, the major concern of the founding members was the creation of a common market throughout the six Member States. The Treaty of Rome concentrated primarily on economic issues and there was no specific reference to the environment. It was not until the SEA 1986 that Title VII 'Environment' was incorporated into the Treaty, giving the Community a legal competence in the field of environmental protection for the first time. However, despite the lack of an explicit legal basis the Community had in the intervening years taken numerous measures to protect the environment. It had also managed to develop its own interventionist environmental policy using other powers under the Treaty, namely Articles 94 and 308 (formerly Arts 100 and 235).

The position today is that the EC has a well developed environmental policy, enjoys specific powers to enact legislation in the environmental field and has enacted over 300 environmentally related measures largely in the form of directives. In fact, it could be argued that environmental policy has equal standing with economic and social policy. Environmental policy now enjoys a unique status in EC law by virtue of Art 174 (formerly Art 130r) that requires environmental protection requirements to be integrated into the definition and implementation of other EC policies.

12.15.2 Environmental policy and law before the SEA 1986 (1957–86)

As stated above, the Treaty of Rome made no reference to the environment. The authors of the Treaty and founding members were principally concerned to establish a common market for goods. Article 2 of the Treaty stated the aims of the Community as 'establishing a common market and progressively approximating the economic policies of Member States, to promote throughout the Community a harmonious development of economic activities, a continuous and balanced expansion, an increase in stability, an accelerated raising of the standard of living and closer relations between the States belonging to it'.

Since the institutions of the EC can only legally act within the limits of the powers conferred upon them by the EC Treaty, legislation in the early days of the Community was largely concerned with economic issues and market regulation. However, despite the absence of any specific powers, the Community did in fact introduce a large number of directives which impacted either directly or indirectly upon the environment. As early as 1967, the Community had introduced a directive on the classification, packaging and labelling of dangerous substances. The introduction of the legislation was aimed not specifically at protecting the environment, but rather at harmonising standards in relation to the packaging and labelling of dangerous substances, but it nevertheless had indirect implications for the environment. This early environmental legislation was introduced either under Art 94 (formerly Art 100) or Art 308 (formerly Art 235).

12.15.2.1 Articles 94 and 308 (formerly Arts 100 and 235)

Article 94 provided for measures to be introduced to secure the approximation of laws affecting the functioning of the common market. Environmental measures enacted on the basis of Art 94 were justified on the basis that different levels and standards of environmental protection in the different Member States would interfere with the creation of a common market by distorting competition. In other words, if the standards of environmental protection are low in one Member State compared to another with more rigorous standards, then industrialists in the former State spend less on meeting environmental protection standards than industrialists in the latter Member State. This disparity may give the industrialist in the Member State with the lower standards a competitive edge (in a sense they will be benefiting from a hidden subsidy) and this may distort the patterns of trade. An example of a directive enacted under Art 94 is Directive (78/659/EEC) on the quality of freshwater needing protection or improvement in order to support fish life. Although it is clear that this is an environmental protection measure in its own right, the preamble to the directive states that 'differences between the provisions ... in the various Member States as regards the quality of waters capable of supporting the life of freshwater fish may create unequal conditions of competition and thus directly affect the functioning of the common market'.

Article 308, on the other hand, is a residual power which enables action to be taken by the institutions even where the Treaty has not provided the necessary powers, but where it is 'necessary to attain, in the course of the operation of the common market, one of the objectives of the Community'. Measures such as Council Directive (79/409/EEC) on the Conservation of Wild Birds were adopted under Art 308 exclusively. The justification for the Wild Birds Directive in particular was that the conservation of wild birds was necessary to attain the Community's objective of improving living conditions throughout the common market. Therefore, the measure was justified rather tentatively by reference to Art 2 of the Treaty of Rome. In a similar way Art 308 has been used to justify other policy areas such as regional policy, which were not explicitly stated within the Treaty, but which were construed as being Community interests.

12.15.2.2 The Stockholm Conference and the emergence of a Community environmental policy

These early environmental measures were not introduced as part of a coherent strategy on the environment which, at this stage, the Community did not have. However, the early 1970s saw a ground swell in public opinion about the environment and also marked the beginning of the Community's environmental policy. In 1972 a United Nations conference was held in Stockholm to consider the human environment. The Conference was significant because it marked the beginnings of international co-operation in the field of the environment, and it is from this date that environmental law has become a legitimate and important area of international law. It is also important in Community law terms because it was followed by the Paris Summit in October 1972, when the Heads of State and governments of the Member States of the Community declared:

> Economic expansion is not an end in itself. Its firm aim should be to enable disparities in living conditions to be reduced. It must take place with the participation of all the social partners. It should result in an improvement in the quality of life as well as in standards of living. As befits the genius of Europe, particular attention will be given to intangible values and to protecting the environment, so that progress may really be put at the service of mankind.

12.15.2.3 Environmental Action Programmes

Following this recognition of the importance of protecting the environment, the Commission was requested to draw up an Action Programme on the environment. This first Action Programme for the period 1973–76 was adopted in 1973. Since that time the Community has produced four more Action Programmes:

Action Programmes	Period	Citation
First	1973–76	C112, 20.12.73
Second	1977–81	C139, 13.6.77
Third	1982–86	C46, 17.2.83
Fourth	1987–92	C328, 7.12.87
Fifth	1993–2000	C138,17.5.93
Sixth	2001–10	

The Action Programmes are essentially political statements, which outline the Community's intentions for legislation and other activities in the years ahead. The First Action Programme started with a general statement of the objectives and principles of a Community environmental policy and then went on to list the actions that the Commission would bring forward. It also listed 11 principles which are still largely applicable today.

Although the Community had begun to develop an environmental policy as early as 1973, it still faced the problem that there was no real constitutional basis for that policy. Legislation was still largely enacted on the basis that different standards of environmental protection throughout the Community would distort competition, would hamper the establishment of a common market and had to be justified accordingly. However, the SEA 1986 provided for the first time a specific legal basis upon which the Community could legislate in the field of environmental protection.

12.15.3 The SEA 1986

The SEA 1986 marked a key stage in the development of the EC's environmental protection policy. It resulted in the incorporation of a new Title, specifically on the environment, into the EEC Treaty and in doing so introduced Arts 174–76 (formerly Arts 130r–t) into the Treaty.

In addition, Art 94 (formerly Art 100) was also amended by the SEA 1986 and a new Art 100a was introduced, which provided that qualified majority voting in the Council of Ministers would be the normal voting procedure in relation to the harmonising measures pursued under this article. This change was introduced essentially to speed up the decision making process in relation to harmonising measures needed to complete the Single Market by 1992. A further amendment in relation to the new Art 95 (formerly Art 100a) was the requirement that the Commission would, when making proposals which concerned environmental protection, take as a base a high level of protection. This was significant because it was recognition in the Treaty itself that approximation measures enacted under Art 95 (formerly Art 100a) could legitimately be concerned with environmental protection and was also important in so far as it meant that environmental measures were not exclusively in the domain of Art 173 (formerly Art 130).

12.15.4 The TEU 1992

The TEU, signed in Maastricht in 1992, gave effect to a number of significant amendments relating to environmental law. These can be briefly stated as follows:

(a) the EEC became the EC, in recognition that it is more than just an economic community;

(b) Art 2 refers to sustainable and non-inflationary growth respecting the environment;

(c) Art 3 established that there should be a policy in the sphere of the environment;

(d) Art 95 (formerly Art 100a) was amended so that the procedure used for harmonising legislation is the co-decision procedure, thus allowing the Parliament the right of veto in relation to such legislation;

(e) Art 173 (formerly Art 130) was amended and, in particular, changed the legislative procedure so that, with certain exceptions, environmental legislation could now be enacted using the co-operation procedure, thus giving the Parliament a greater degree of control than it had previously. The amended article also built in the requirement that Community environmental policy should aim at a high level of protection.

12.15.5 The ECJ and the development of environmental law

Even before the SEA 1986 was amended to incorporate a Community competence in the field of the environment, the ECJ had recognised that the environment and environmental protection was an 'essential' component of Community policy, even to the extent that protection of the environment could hinder the free movement of goods within the Community, one of the fundamental principles of Community law.

In *Procureur de la République v ADBHU* (1983), the ECJ stated that there could be no doubt that the protection of the environment constitutes an objective of general interest which the Community could legitimately pursue. The case involved an action in the French courts to dissolve the Association de défense de bruleurs d'huiles usagées, an association established in 1980 to defend the interests of manufacturers, dealers and users of heating appliances designed to burn fuel oil and waste oils. In their defence, the Association contested the validity of Directive (75/439/EEC) which aims to protect the environment against the risks from waste oils. The Association contested that the directive was contrary to the principles of freedom of trade, free movement of goods and freedom of competition. The French court sought a ruling from the ECJ on the interpretation and validity of the directive, using the Art 234 (formerly Art 177) preliminary rulings procedure. In reaching its decision that the directive was valid, the ECJ held that:

> The Directive must be seen in the perspective of environmental protection, which is one of the Community's essential objectives.

One of the significant features about the ECJ's judgment in this case is that it came to this conclusion at a time when the Treaty did not provide any specific explicit legal basis for environmental action. The case predated the introduction of Arts 174–76 (formerly Arts 130r–t). The view that environmental protection could constitute one of the Community's essential objectives was reinforced and developed in *Commission v Denmark* (1988), often known as the *Danish Bottles* case.

12.15.5.1 The Danish Bottles case

The *Danish Bottles* case is important because it raises two very important issues. First, it considered the question of whether Member States could introduce more stringent environmental laws than the rest of the Community; and, second, because it also concerned the related issue of the relationship between environmental protection and the free movement of goods as required by Art 28 (formerly Art 30) of the Treaty. It therefore merits detailed attention.

In 1981 the Danish Government, concerned about the environmental consequences of litter and waste from discarded metal cans, instituted a system requiring beer and soft drinks to be marketed only in containers that could be reused. The use of metal cans was forbidden. Containers needed to meet the requirements laid down and be approved by the Danish National Agency for the Protection of the Environment. In 1984 the legislation was amended so that non-approved containers were permitted subject to very strict limits and also to a deposit and return system. Although the object of the system was to reduce the numbers of discarded metal tins, it had as an effect a potential restriction on competition. Manufacturers of beers and soft drinks outside Denmark could sell their products throughout the Community but not in Denmark unless they could comply with the Danish deposit and return system. Therefore the Danish manufacturers were in effect protected from external competition.

The European Commission commenced proceedings against the Danish Government under Art 226 (formerly Art 169) of the EC Treaty. The Commission alleged that the introduction of a system, under which all containers for beers and soft drinks must be returnable, was contrary to Art 28 of the Treaty. Article 28 which is concerned with the free movement of goods, provides that quantitative measures on imports and all measures having equivalent effect to quantitative restrictions shall be prohibited. Member States are prohibited from introducing quantitative measures such as bans or quotas, or any measure which has equivalent effect. The definition of measures having equivalent effect was provided by the ECJ in *Procureur du Roi v Dassonville* (1974) as 'all trading rules enacted by Member States which are capable of hindering, directly or indirectly, actually or potentially, intra-Community trade'. The Commission argued that the introduction of the Danish rules were capable of hindering trade of beer and soft drinks into Denmark and as such were contrary to Art 28.

The ECJ based its decision in this case on an earlier and landmark decision in the case commonly known as the *Cassis de Dijon* case, *Rewe-Zentral AG Bundesmonopolver-wältung für Branntwein* (1979). In *Cassis* it was held that in the absence of Community rules, Member States could introduce certain measures relating to the marketing of products if the measures were necessary to satisfy certain mandatory requirements (known as the *rule of reason*). The Danish

Government argued in the *Danish Bottles* case that the mandatory deposit and return system was justified by a mandatory requirement, namely the protection of the environment. The ECJ accepted that the protection of the environment could constitute a mandatory requirement, given the ECJ's previous decision in *Procureur de la République* that the protection of the environment is one of the Community's essential objectives and also given the provisions of the SEA 1986. The question which remained for the ECJ to decide was whether the Danish rules were necessary in order to satisfy the mandatory requirement, or whether the environment could be protected in ways which were less restrictive to trade. In other words the ECJ had to apply a test of proportionality. The ECJ accepted that the deposit and return system for empty containers was an 'indispensable element of a system intended to ensure the re-use of containers and therefore appears necessary to achieve the aims pursued by the contested rules'. Turning to the system for non-approved containers and the strict limit on the amount of containers that could be imported in non-approved containers (non-approved containers could be used where the quantity of marketed drinks did not exceed 3,000 hecti-litres per year per producer), the ECJ held that the Danish rules were disproportionate. The reasoning was that the system for non-approved containers was also capable of protecting the environment (non-approved containers were subject to a deposit and return system), and since the quantity of imports was limited, the limitation to 3,000 hecti-litres was excessive.

12.15.6 Environmental legislation after the SEA 1986

It has been established thus far that both the Treaty and the ECJ in its case law have recognised the importance of Community environmental policy. One would be forgiven for thinking that, after the SEA 1986 and the provisions of Arts 174–76 (formerly Arts 130r–t), the development of Community environmental law from that point in time was simply a matter of developing new environmental initiatives and laws under that Treaty article. However, the introduction of Arts 174–76 brought with it a number of particular problems. As stated above, prior to its introduction the Commission had to rely on Arts 94 and 308 (formerly Arts 100 and 235) to justify environmental measures, and sometimes measures were challenged by Member States. The introduction of this new explicit legal base, however, did not mean that from 1987 onwards all environmental legislation would be enacted under Arts 174–76. It is still clearly the case that some legislation is intended to protect the environment *per se*, whereas other legislative acts are intended to approximate standards. The question therefore became, 'which was the correct legal basis for environmental action – Art 95 (formerly Art 100a) or Art 174?'

12.15.6.1 The correct legal basis?

The issue of which is the correct legal basis is not simply one of academic importance. The choice of Treaty article upon which EC secondary legislation is based has very real legal (and political) consequences. It is important for the following reasons:

(a) The ECJ has the jurisdiction to review and annul secondary legislation on the basis that the legislation is either *ultra vires* (that is, there is no legal basis for the relevant legislation) or on the grounds that there has been an infringement of an essential procedural requirement, which would include cases of legislation being enacted using the 'incorrect' legal basis.

(b) The Treaty stipulates which of the legislative procedures is to be used in relation to specific types of legislation. Therefore, legislation enacted under Art 95 (formerly Art 100a) is to be adopted using the co-decision procedure, whereas legislation enacted under Arts 174–76 (formerly Arts 130r–t) requires the co-operation procedure (with certain exceptions in Art 130(s)(2)). This in turn determines the voting arrangements in the Council of Ministers and the amount of control that can be exerted upon the legislation by the European Parliament. From the Parliament's perspective it exercises more control over Art 95 (formerly Art 100a) legislation than it does over legislation under Arts 174–76 (formerly Arts 130r–t). The Council on the other hand exercises more control over legislation under Arts 174–76 (formerly Arts 130r–t). Hence the question of which Treaty article is used becomes one of political significance and may have a bearing on the final content of the legislation.

(c) The purpose of legislation enacted under Arts 95 (formerly Art 100a) and 173 (formerly Art 130) is intrinsically different and has consequences in terms of whether Member States can introduce more stringent environmental controls. The purpose of Art 95 (formerly Art 100a) is to secure a uniform standard throughout the Community and Member States are not able to introduce different standards and thus distort the functioning of the common market (albeit there is a limited exception to this under Art 95(4) (formerly Art 100a(4)) which is dealt with later). Articles 174–76 (formerly Arts 130r–t) on the other hand are concerned with environmental protection in its own right and Art 176 (formerly Art 130t) specifically enables Member States to maintain or introduce more stringent protective measures, although such measures must be compatible with the Treaty and they must be notified to the Commission.

The use of the correct Treaty article is, therefore, of real practical and legal importance and has been particularly so in relation to EC environmental law. The issue of whether the correct legal basis has been used, therefore, can give rise to legal challenge before the ECJ exercising its powers of judicial review under Art 230 (formerly Art 173) and has in fact caused problems in terms of the smooth implementation of environmental policy. In particular, the institutions themselves have disagreed over the proper legal basis for environmental action. The EC Council has favoured Arts 174–76 (formerly Arts 130r–t), because of its desire to retain the greatest degree of control over such legislation, whereas the Commission and the Parliament have preferred the use of Art 95 (formerly Art 100a). A number of occasions have arisen where there has been dispute over which is the correct article to use and, in fact, the issue is still not fully resolved. The issue fell to be considered by the ECJ in *EC Commission v EC Council* (1989), known as the *Titanium Dioxide* case.

12.15.6.2 *The* Titanium Dioxide *decision*

In 1989, the European Commission brought an action against the Council of Ministers, arguing that it had incorrectly used Art 175 (formerly Art 130s) for the adoption of the Titanium Dioxide Directive (Council Directive (78/176/EEC) on waste from the titanium dioxide industry). When the Commission had originally proposed the directive, it had put it forward as an internal market harmonisation measure under Art 95 (formerly Art 100a). However, the Council of Ministers subsequently decided (unanimously) to alter the legal basis and adopt the directive under Art 175 (formerly Art 130s).

The ECJ decided in favour of the Commission. It noted that the Titanium Dioxide Directive had two aims; the first was to protect the environment from titanium dioxide pollution and the second was to harmonise the conditions relating to the titanium dioxide industry in the Community. The ECJ held that, where there are two aims and, therefore, two possible legal bases, then normally both should be used. However, in this instance it was not possible to use both Arts 95 (100a) and 173 (130) since the legislative procedures required under both were different. Therefore one single legal basis had to be used. The ECJ came to the conclusion that the correct basis was Art 95 (formerly Art 100a). In reaching this decision the ECJ referred to the second paragraph of Art 130r which states that 'environmental protection requirements shall be a component of the Community's other policies'. They took this to mean that Arts 174–76 (formerly Arts 130r–t) were not the only provisions of the Treaty concerned with environmental protection.

Environmental measures could therefore legitimately be enacted under other Treaty articles. In relation to Art 95 (formerly Art 100a), the ECJ noted that the Commission, when initiating proposals in the health, safety, consumer and environment spheres must take as a base a 'high level of environment protection'. According to the ECJ, this meant that the objective of protecting the environment contained in Art 174 (formerly Art 130r) could also be achieved through harmonisation measures based under Art 95 (formerly Art 100a). The ECJ therefore effectively came to the decision that measures enacted under Arts 174–76 (formerly Arts 130r–t) were concerned solely with the protection of the environment, whereas Article 95 (formerly Art 100a) covered initiatives designed to protect the environment and promote the single market.

12.15.6.3 The correct legal basis reviewed again

The judgment of the ECJ in the *Titanium Dioxide* case was welcomed by the Commission. Not only did it uphold the Commission's argument, it also effectively gave the go-ahead for environmental protection measures to be incorporated as part of the single market programme. However, the ECJ was asked to consider the issue once again in *Commission v Council (Waste Disposal)* (1991). Like the *Titanium Dioxide* case, this case involved a judicial review action brought by the European Commission against the Council of Ministers for its use of Art 175 (130s) in the adoption of Directive (91/156/EEC) on waste disposal. The Commission contested that the directive had been incorrectly adopted under Art 175 (formerly Art 130s) and that it should have been adopted as an Art 95 (formerly Art 100a) measure. However, the ECJ came to a different conclusion in this case.

The ECJ held that, whilst it was true that waste had to be regarded as a product which should be able to move freely around the Community, mandatory environmental protection requirements justified exceptions to the free movement of waste. In these circumstances, the directive could not be intended to promote the free movement of waste within the Community. There was not sufficient justification for recourse to Art 95 (formerly Art 100a) where harmonisation of conditions of the market was only an ancillary effect of the measure adopted. The judgment in this case may have an effect upon the Commission's programme of legislation in so far as that, unless the Commission can clearly justify measures as harmonisation measures, they must proceed under Art 175 (formerly Art 130s).

12.15.7 Stricter environmental rules in Member States and the freedom of movement of goods

Another very important difference between the use of the two Treaty articles is the extent to which Member States can introduce stricter environmental protection rules than the Community-wide rules or standards. This is an issue of twofold importance.

On the one hand, it is a matter of concern to those Member States that place a particularly strong emphasis upon environmental protection and wish to secure the highest levels of protection. For some Member States, harmonisation suggests harmonising down rather than up, and this is unsatisfactory to them. This is likely to be an important issue to Sweden and Austria, in particular, which have in place certain environmental protection measures which are stricter than prevailing Community-wide measures.

On the other hand, the second and inextricably related issue is the extent to which stricter environmental protection rules can be permitted where they hamper or restrict the freedom of movement of goods required by Art 28 (formerly Art 30).

*12.15.7.1 The relationship between environmental protection and the free
movement of goods*

The free movement of goods throughout the Community is regarded as one of
the fundamental cornerstones of EC law. Article 28 (formerly Art 30) of the EC
Treaty prohibits quantitative restrictions and measures of equivalent effect
which restrict the free circulation of goods. Measures which are introduced by
Member States which have the effect of hindering the free circulation of goods
across borders, therefore, are prohibited. Even where measures apply equally
to domestic and imported goods (known as indistinctly applicable measures)
the measures may still breach Art 28 (30) where they affect interstate trade. The
types of measure which have been held to breach Art 28 (30) range from more
obvious measures such as bans and import quotas to 'buy national' campaigns
which have the effect of discriminating against imports. Article 28 (30) has
been used widely in litigation and its scope has been widely defined by the
ECJ (see *Procureur du Roi v Dassonville* (1974)).

Article 30 (formerly Art 36) provides a list of six exceptions to Art 28 (30)
whereby Member States may attempt to justify any measures which breach
Art 28 (30). The list is exhaustive. Breaches of Art 28 (30) may be justified on
the grounds of public morality; public policy or public security; the protection
of health and life of humans, animals or plants; the protection of national
treasures possessing artistic, historic or archaeological value; or the protection
of industrial or commercial property. However, Art 30 (formerly Art 36)
stipulates that measures can not be justified if they constitute a means of
arbitrary discrimination or a disguised restriction on trade between Member
States. The terms of Art 30 (36) have been subject to a narrow interpretation by
the ECJ, which has been keen to preserve the fundamental freedom of goods,
and the ECJ has not been willing to extend the list of exceptions provided by
Art 30 (36). In terms of environmental protection measures, it may be possible
to justify them on the basis that they are necessary to protect the health and life
of humans, animals or plants. However, the ECJ has been very reluctant to
permit measures under this particular head. The burden of proof falls squarely
on Member States to demonstrate that a measure is necessary to achieve the
protection claimed and, importantly, that the measure is proportionate to the
aims. In the main, the cases have been concerned with measures aimed at
protecting the health of humans rather than plants or animals. Article 30 (36),
therefore, provides little support for national environmental protection
measures which effect interstate trade.

Measures which have the effect of discriminating against imported goods
may, however, be permitted if they apply equally to domestic and imported
goods and they satisfy the requirements laid down by the ECJ in the case
known as *Cassis de Dijon (Rewe-Zentrale v Bundesmonopolver-wältung für
Branntwein* (1979)). The ECJ stated that in the absence of Community measures
or standards Member States were free to regulate the production and
marketing of goods and that:

> Obstacles to movement in the Community resulting from disparities between the national laws relating to the marketing of the products in question must be accepted in so far as those provisions may be recognised as being necessary in order to satisfy mandatory requirements relating in particular to the effectiveness of fiscal supervision, the protection of public health, the fairness of commercial transaction and the defence of the consumer.

Therefore, in relation to indistinctly applicable measures (those which apply to all goods irrespective of whether they are produced nationally or imported) Member States can, in the absence of EC measures, introduce national measures which are necessary to satisfy certain mandatory requirements. Unlike the terms of Art 30 (36) which is exhaustive, the list of matters which constitute 'mandatory requirements' has been extended to include environmental protection. The *Danish Bottles* case (*Commission v Denmark*), referred to above at 12.15.5.1, above, resulted in environmental protection being added to the list of issues that could constitute a mandatory requirement. Thus, in the absence of relevant EC environmental protection measures, Member States may be able to introduce national rules which have the effect of restricting the free movement of goods, but are necessary to secure the mandatory requirement of environmental protection. It should be noted that the rule in *Cassis de Dijon* only applies in the absence of EC standards. The programme of harmonisation pursued by the Commission will reduce the effectiveness of this ruling.

12.15.7.2 Stricter environmental protection measures: Art 176 (formerly Art 130t)

Article 176 (130t) provides that the protective measures adopted under Art 175 (formerly Art 130s) shall not prevent any Member State from maintaining or introducing more stringent protective measures providing that these measures are compatible with the Treaty. In other words, a Member State may introduce environmental protection measures which go beyond those adopted by the EC under Art 173 (formerly Art 130), but they must not infringe other Treaty provisions, particularly Art 30 (formerly Art 36). Therefore, Art 176 (130t) provides a balance between the Member States right to adopt measures, against the right of the Community to legislate in this area. Measures introduced under Art 95 (formerly Art 100a) are introduced with the intention of approximating laws and, therefore, Member States ought not to apply national measures which differ from EC measures adopted under this article. However, there is one specific exception provided for in Art 95(4) (formerly Art 100a(4)) whereby Member States may, in certain circumstances, apply stricter rules. The provision only operates when the Community harmonisation measure is adopted by the Council acting by a qualified majority. Where a Member State (which presumably has voted against the harmonising measure in question) wishes to apply different national measures relating to the protection of the environment, they must obtain the consent of the Commission to do so. The Member State in question must notify the

Commission of its intentions and the Commission must then confirm (or otherwise reject) the national provisions. In reaching its decision, the Commission must verify that the national measures in question are not a means of arbitrary discrimination or a disguised restriction of trade between the Member States. Further provision exists for the Commission or any Member State to bring the matter before the ECJ if they believe that a Member State is improperly using the powers provided for in Art 95(4) (100a(4)). Such a challenge was mounted by France in the so called *PCP* case.

12.15.7.3 The PCP case

France v the Commission of the EC (1994) concerned the use of Art 95(4) (100a(4)). Following the adoption of Directive (91/173/EEC) (which was amending Directive (76/769/EEC)) Germany applied for a derogation under Art 95(4) (100a(4)). Directive (91/173/EEC) was adopted under Art 95 (100a) and concerned the marketing and use of substances and preparations containing pesticide and preservative pentachlorophenol (PCP). At the time of its adoption, Germany had in place much stricter standards, setting lower concentration limits on PCP. The Council of Ministers had reached a decision on the directive by qualified majority vote, with Germany voting against the measure. Germany sought to maintain its own stricter standards and therefore asked the Commission for confirmation under Art 95(4) (100a(4)). The Commission granted Germany the derogation, despite strong opposition from France, Italy and Greece who were concerned about the impact of the German measure on imports of their leather goods into Germany. The case involved an action for judicial review under Art 230 (173) of the Treaty brought by France against the Commission's decision. The ECJ, accepting that the Commission's decision was a reviewable act, held that Art 95(4) (100a(4)) should be interpreted restrictively and that it is up to the Member State seeking the derogation to prove that the measure is both necessary and proportionate, and that there are no other suitable means of achieving the aim pursued in a manner which is less restrictive of the free movement of goods. In the case in hand the ECJ annulled the Commission's decision but only on procedural grounds, the Commission had failed to adequately justify their position. The Commission subsequently took a second decision, reaffirming its original position but this time ensuring there was sufficient justification.

12.15.8 The Community's Environmental Action Programmes

The European Community's First Action Programme for the Environment was adopted by the Council of Ministers on 22 December 1973. It set Community-wide objectives to resolve urgent pollution problems concerning water, air and soil. More importantly, it also established 11 principles upon which the Community's environmental policy is based. The Second, Third and Fourth Action Programmes continued in much the same vein as the first, only providing refinements to the Community's objectives. They concentrated upon specific environmental media: air, water, waste. In particular, many of the policy aims, subsequently translated into directives, were concerned with setting emission limits. They were seen largely as 'end of pipe' solutions or 'fire fighting' measures. However, they were not entirely reactive in nature and over the subsequent programmes there was a growing emphasis on prevention rather than cure. The Fifth Action Programme represented a departure and change in thinking. On 26 June 1990, the Heads of State of the Member States called for the Fifth Action Programme to be drawn up on the principles of sustainable development, preventative and precautionary action and shared responsibility.

12.15.8.1 The Fifth Environmental Action Programme – Towards Sustainability

The Fifth Environmental Action Programme covers the period 1993 to 2000 and, to that extent, differs from the previous programmes in that it covers a seven year period rather than five. The programme also marks a more important departure from previous programmes in its approach. Entitled *Towards Sustainability* the latest programme does not concern itself with the protection of specific environmental media, such as air, water or land. Instead, the programme concentrates on five key sectors of activity which have significant impacts on the state of the environment. The five sectors are: industry, energy, transport, agriculture and tourism. In the field of transport, for example, the Commission has produced a Green Paper on transport entitled *Sustainable Mobility*. This recommends the transfer from private transport use to more public transport and considers using fiscal measures such as road pricing and higher fuel prices to reduce demand. Agriculture, as another key sector is responsible for a significant amount of environmental damage and there is recognition that the Common Agricultural Policy has been responsible for a negative impact on the environment. The aims of the Fifth Action Programme in this regard are to reduce the impact of agriculture on the environment by encouraging farmers to see themselves as 'guardians of the countryside' and to reduce in particular the pollution from nitrates and phosphates.

12.15.8.2 Sustainability

The emphasis in the Fifth Action Programme is sustainable development. One of the best definitions of sustainable development is the one provided in the Bruntland Report *Our Common Future* which set the agenda for discussions about the relationship between economic growth and protection of the environment. The report states that sustainable development is:

> ... economic development which meets the needs of the present generation without compromising the ability of future generations to meet their own needs.

The TEU 1993 introduced the principle of sustainability explicitly into the EC Treaty for the first time in Art 2.

12.15.8.3 Shared responsibility

Another feature of the Fifth Environmental Action Programme is the emphasis that is placed on 'shared responsibility'. Inherent in the Fifth Action Programme is the belief that everyone shares a responsibility towards the environment and that there must be an 'optimum involvement of all sectors of society'. To this end, it will be necessary to change patterns of behaviour of producers, consumers, government and citizens, and there is a greater need for information campaigns to raise public awareness. Access to environmental information is seen as a key element in enabling citizens to assist with the monitoring of pollution throughout the community and also as a means of exercising consumer preferences for 'green' products and producers.

12.15.8.4 Types of environmental measures

The Action Programmes provide the broad policy framework from which the Commission can initiate legislative proposals. However, the Fifth Action Programme recognises that environmental protection cannot be secured entirely by legal and regulatory measures. In a review of the measures available to improve the environment, the Commission states that future environmental policy will be based on four types of measure:

(a) regulatory instruments;

(b) market based measures;

(c) support measures such as education, information and research; and

(d) financial support mechanisms.

12.15.8.5 Review of Fifth Action Programme

In 1995, the Commission carried out a detailed review of the Fifth Action Programme, as required by the Action Programme itself, given the time period in which the programme spans. The review involved wide consultation with various governmental and non-governmental organisations, and concentrated on the latest scientific data and also the results of the Conference on Environment (the Earth Summit) held in Rio in June 1992. Several issues were prominent in the review, a number of which are highlighted below.

(a) *Public awareness, information and education* – the Commission reaffirmed its commitment to extending awareness of environmental issues and has introduced a Community Action Programme specifically aimed at promoting non-governmental organisations active in the field of environmental protection.

(b) *Economic, fiscal and legal instruments* – one of the aims of the Fifth Action Programme was to diversify the range of instruments used beyond legislative measures. One of the principal measures proposed has been the introduction of tax on carbon dioxide emissions and energy.

(c) *Financial instruments* – the LIFE Programme has been extended to cover the period 1996–99.

(d) *International co-operation* – in 1995 the EU participated in a number of International initiatives including the third Pan-European Conference of Environment Ministers, which brought together Ministerial representatives from United Nations and OECD countries, together with several environmental pressure groups.

12.15.8.6 *The Sixth Environmental Action Programme*

The Sixth Environmental Action Programme proposals are set out in 'Environment 2010: Our Future, Our Choice'. The new programme focuses on the following priority areas: climate change; nature and bio-diversity; environment and health; and sustainable use of natural resources and sustainable management of wastes.

Objectives have been set for each priority area. In line with Kyoto Protocol commitments, there is a target of an 8% reduction in greenhouse gases, based on 1990 levels of the six main gases, during 2008–12. The programme also sets a target for noise reduction: 10% less people suffering from long term high levels of noise by 2010, rising to 20% by 2020. Efforts are to be made to 'protect and restore the functioning of natural systems and halt the loss of biodiversity' and to protect soils against erosion and pollution. Also of note are the following objectives: 12% of total energy use to be derived from renewable sources by 2010; loss of biodiversity to be halted by 2010; only chemicals which do not have significant adverse impacts on man and the environment to be produced and used by 2020; fossil fuel subsidies to be phased out; and economic growth de-coupled from resource usage.

As well as the priority areas, the new action programme details five 'approaches' to be taken in regard to environmental issues. These approaches relate to: (i) improving implementation of current directives; (ii) integrating environmental concerns into other policy areas; (iii) working with the market to improve environmental performance. This will involve a drive to encourage improved take-up of EMAS and voluntary agreements; (iv) ensuring that better quality information is more accessible to the public; and (v) improving land use planning and management decisions. It is anticipated that this will necessitate the introduction of legislation on strategic environmental assessment of policies and plans.

12.15.9 Objectives and principles of EC environmental policy

The environmental policy and programme of the EC is based upon a number of fundamental principles which underpin the legislative framework These principles, like the policy that stems from them, have evolved over time. The First Action Programme listed 11 key principles, which although they have developed since, still form the basis of EC policy. These 11 principles are:

1   pollution should be prevented at source rather than dealt with after the event;

2   environmental issues must be taken into account at the earliest possible stage in planning and other technical decision making processes;

3   abusive exploitation of natural resources should be avoided;

4   the standard of knowledge in the EU should be improved to promote effective action for environmental conservation and improvement;

5   the polluter should pay for preventing and eliminating 'nuisances', subject to limited exceptions and transitional arrangements;

6   activities in one country should not degrade the environment of another;

7   the EU and the Member States must in their environmental policies have regard to the interests of developing countries and should aim to prevent, or minimise, any adverse effects on their economic development;

8   there should be a clearly defined long term European environmental policy that includes participation in international organisations and co-operation at both regional and international levels;

9   environmental protection is a matter for everyone in the EU at all levels; their co-operation, and the harnessing of social forces, is necessary for success. Education should ensure the whole Community accepts its responsibilities for future generations;

10 appropriate action levels must be established – local, regional, national, Community and international – for each type of pollution area to be protected;

11 major aspects of national environmental protection policies should be harmonised. Economic growth should not be view from purely quantitative aspects.

A number of these principles are of significant importance and have now been incorporated formally into the Treaty by Art 173 (formerly Art 130) and are consequently enforceable by the ECJ. The principles discussed below have also shaped UK environmental policy and underpin the framework not only for EC legislation but also UK legislation. Article 174 (formerly Art 130r) sets out the basic principles of environmental policy.

12.15.9.1 Current environmental policy and principles

Article 173 (130) identifies the aims of EC environmental policy and the fundamental principles upon which legislative action should be taken.

The objectives of the EC's environmental policy are that it should contribute to:

(a) preserving, protecting and improving the quality of the environment;

(b) protecting human health;

(c) the prudent and rational utilisation of natural resources; and

(d) promoting measures at international level to deal with regional or worldwide environmental problems.

Community policy is based on the following principles:

(a) the precautionary principle;

(b) the preventive principle; and

(c) the polluter pays principle.

12.15.9.2 Environmental policy and other EC interests

One of the most unique features about the EC's environmental policy is its status in relation to other policy areas. Article 174(2) (130r(2)) requires that environmental considerations are a mandatory component of decisions in all policy areas. 'Environmental protection requirements must be integrated into the definition and implementation of other Community policies.' This special status was confirmed by the ECJ in *Commission v Belgium* (1992).

12.15.9.3 International involvement

Community policy on the environment is required to contribute to promoting measures at the international level to deal with both regional and worldwide environmental problems. In the early days of its environmental policy, the EC was mainly concerned with controlling pollution within the Community. However, it was soon recognised that pollution has no frontiers and that there is a need to co-operate with non-EC countries. Article 174(4) (130r(4)) requires that both the EC and the Member States, within their respective spheres of competence, co-operate with third world countries and with the competent international organisations such as the United Nations.

12.15.10 Environmental legislation

The EC has enacted over 300 legislative Acts which are either directly or indirectly concerned with environmental protection. It is clearly not possible within the scope of this book to cover all of this legislation, the majority of which has been incorporated into UK law and is rightly regarded now as domestic law. However, it is possible to identify certain types of legislation and it is clear that the EC has adopted various approaches aimed at combating pollution and protecting various environmental media. The approaches taken may be categorised as follows.

12.15.10.1 Quality standards approach

A number of directives set quality objectives and limit values for different media. With regard to water, for example, five directives have been adopted which establish water quality objectives for different uses of water. The most important is Directive (75/440/EEC) which establishes the quality required for surface water which is intended for drinking. Directive (80/778/EEC) sets standards for water intended for human consumption, (78/659/EEC) for fish and (79/923/EEC) for shellfish, and also Directive (76/160/EEC) which sets standards for water used for bathing purposes. Directives setting air quality objectives and limit values include (82/884/EEC) – lead and (85/203/EEC) – nitrogen dioxide.

12.15.10.2 Control of dangerous substances

Another approach that the EC has adopted is to control the use, discharge or emission of dangerous substances. Framework Directive (76/464/EEC) is particularly important in this regard since it is concerned with the control of certain dangerous substances discharged into the aquatic environment. This directive provides a list of dangerous substances which are either to be eliminated (List I substances) or to be progressively reduced (List II substances). Subsequent daughter directives have since been adopted relating to specific discharges of dangerous substances from industrial discharges. These include Council Directives (82/176/EEC) and (84/156/EEC) – mercury; Directive (83/513/EEC) – cadmium; and (84/491/EEC) – lindane. Additionally, Directive (86/280/EEC) (as amended) deals with certain other dangerous substances.

12.15.10.3 Vehicle emission standards

Directive (70/220/EEC) was introduced to minimise air pollution from car exhaust fumes, and did this by prescribing limit values for certain gaseous emissions. This was followed by a similar Directive (72/306/EEC), in relation to diesel engines. These have been amended by subsequent legislation, increasing the stringency of the controls. Now all new petrol engine cars must be fitted with a three-way catalytic converter by virtue of Directive (91/441/EEC).

12.15.10.4 Product quality standards

Certain directives aim to restrict the level of polluting substances in products. For example, Directive (78/611/EEC) set the maximum content of lead in petrol.

12.15.11 Enforcement of environmental legislation

The 1995 Annual Report of the European Commission states that, in 1995, the Commission sent 90 Art 226 (formerly Art 169) letters concerning breaches of EC environmental law and issued 26 reasoned opinions. In 1993, there were seven cases before the ECJ involving environmental law. However, the report does more than simply provide statistics; it deals with certain problem areas. Certain directives have caused more problems than others, notably the Environmental Assessment Directive (85/337/EEC), the Wild Birds Directive (79/409/EEC) and directives relating to waste and discharges into the aquatic environment. There have also been complaints about the implementation of the Environmental Access to Information Directive in the UK. However the report states that 'the lion's share of infringements of Community environment Directives relate to Environmental Assessment Directive 85/337/EEC'.

The report indicates that the incorrect application of environmental law is most commonly detected through complaints from EC citizens and through questions put to MEPs. It is certainly the case that Directorate General XI does not have the resources to police and monitor compliance with the legislation and is dependent upon receiving these complaints. The EC has been criticised for being quicker to make environmental laws rather than introducing procedures to ensure that they are implemented properly. Unlike Directorate General IV which is concerned with competition policy, Directorate General XI does not benefit from specific powers of investigation. In the field of competition law, the Commission has the power under Council Regulation (EEC) 17/62 to carry out investigations (including the so called dawn raids of companies) and to conduct hearings to enforce Arts 85 and 86 of the Treaty.

12.15.12 The European Environment Agency

In May 1990 the Council of Ministers adopted Council Regulation (EEC) 1210/90 setting up the European Environmental Agency (EEA). After much debate the agency was eventually set up in Copenhagen and became fully operational in 1995. The EEA's main area of activity is data collection, analysis and dissemination. It is supported in this role by an Environmental Information and Observation Network.

The EEA published its first report in 2000. 'Environmental Signals 2000' identifies a number of areas of concern including the adverse effects of increases in: transport volume, waste streams; energy usage; greenhouse gas emissions; and intensive agricultural production.

EUROPEAN COMMUNITY
ENVIRONMENTAL LAW AND POLICY

The development of the EU

The EEC was established in 1957 by the Treaty of Rome. The EEC had an initial membership of six. Since that time the Treaty has been amended by the SEA 1986, the TEU 1992 which established the EC, the Treaty of Amsterdam 1997 and the Treaty of Nice 2000. The EEC is now called the European Community (EC). The membership has grown from six to 15. The aims and competences of the EC have also expanded and the EC can no longer be regarded simply as a community pursuing economic goals.

Sources of EC law

The EC Treaty is the primary source of EC law which lays down the overall aims of the EC (Art 2) and Community competences (Art 3). As a framework Treaty it requires fleshing out by means of 'secondary legislation' comprising:

(a) regulations;

(b) directives;

(c) decisions;

(d) recommendations and opinions (which have no binding legal force).

The institutional framework

The institutions of the EC are entrusted to achieve the tasks laid down in the Treaty and to this end they have the power to enact the secondary legislation.

Enforcement of EC law

Member States are obliged (Art 5) to fulfil their EC law obligations and not to do anything which would jeopardise the attainment of the Treaty. As such they must not introduce laws which conflict with EC law and they must take all the appropriate steps to implement directives effectively and by the time specified in the directive.

The ECJ is charged with ensuring that EC law is observed (Art 164). Its jurisdiction is laid down in further Treaty articles.

(a) Articles 226–28 (formerly Arts 169–71) – the ECJ can make a declaration that a Member State has failed to fulfil its EC law obligations and it can also fine a Member State that fails to comply with such a declaration. Actions against Member States are brought by the Commission.

(b) Article 230 (formerly Art 173) – the ECJ can judicially review 'acts' of the community institutions on the grounds laid down in that article. 'Acts' have been construed in the widest sense. Member States and the institutions are 'privileged applicants' whereas natural and legal persons have to satisfy the test of 'direct and individual concern'.

(c) Article 234 (formerly Art 177) – the preliminary rulings procedure enables national courts to ask the ECJ to interpret relevant provisions of EC law. The interpretation given by the ECJ is binding on all Member States and must be followed by the national courts.

The EC as a new legal order

EC law has been described as a 'new legal order'. It provides for legal rights which may be directly enforceable within the national courts. The ECJ has developed various ways in which individuals can benefit from EC law provisions, even where Member States have failed to implement those provisions:

(a) *direct effect* – Treaty articles, regulations, directives and decisions may be directly effective providing they can satisfy the tests laid down in *Van Gend en Loos*;

(b) *national courts* – are under a duty (by virtue of Art 5) to interpret national legislation in the relevant area in order to give effect to a directive (*Marleasing*);

(c) *Member States* – may be liable in an action for damages if it can be established that there is a direct relationship between the losses suffered by a person as a consequence of the State's failure to implement a directive (*Francovich*).

The development of a community environmental policy

Environmental policy and law before the SEA 1986

Since the creation of the EEC, almost 40 years ago, the Community has greatly extended its spheres of influences (competences). Originally an economic community, the Treaty of Rome did not provide a legal basis for the Community to take any action in the field of environmental protection.

The Community's activities in relation to the environment can be dated back to the UN Conference on the Environment held in Stockholm in 1972 and which led to the Community's first Environmental Action Programme.

Before the SEA 1986, the Community had no specific legal basis to adopt environmental protection measures, but nevertheless adopted many measures under Arts 94 (formerly Art 100) or 308 (formerly Art 235).

The ECJ in *Procureur de la République v ADBHU* (1983) affirmed that environmental protection was an essential component of Community policy notwithstanding the absence of an explicit legal basis.

The SEA 1986

The SEA 1986 introduced Arts 174–76 (formerly Arts 130r–t) which provided for the first time a legal basis on which the Community institutions could introduce measures aimed at protecting the environment in its own right, rather than having to justify them as harmonisation measures under Art 95 (100a).

Environmental legislation after the SEA 1986

Despite the introduction of Arts 174–76 (130r–t), certain measures were still adopted under Art 95 (formerly Art 100a). This led to challenges before the ECJ (*EC Commission v EC Council* (1989), known as the *Titanium Dioxide* case).

The Community's Environmental Action Programmes

Community environmental policy is based on fundamental principles which underpin the legislative measures:

(a) precautionary principle;

(b) preventative principle;

(c) polluter pays principle.

The Community's Environmental Action programmes set out the EC's policy agenda, usually in five yearly programmes.

CHAPTER 13

FACTORS 'DRIVING' THE DEVELOPMENT OF ENVIRONMENTAL LAW

Apart from the major developmental influence of the European Community (EC) on UK environmental law and policy which we considered in Chapter 12 the following factors are also helping to drive the rapid development of environmental law in the UK.

13.1 International environmental law

The significance of international environmental law has grown rapidly with the emergence of global environmental threats the most important of which is undoubtedly climate change. International environmental legal measures have a 'trickle down', indirect impact on national legal systems and legal persons (such as individuals and companies). This is so because international environmental law relates to actions between States (that is, negotiating and concluding treaties). Before international treaties are able to affect the national legal systems of States who have signed the relevant treaty they must be incorporated into the national law by legislation. Prior to the incorporation into national law the terms of international agreements cannot be used by private persons as the basis of an action against the State, public bodies, or other private persons.

International environmental law is important in the following respects:

(a) it focuses attention on the existence of global problems and the need for international solutions to those problems; and

(b) it has pioneered and developed important legal and policy principles (for example, sustainable development and the precautionary principle) which are so influential that they have been incorporated into the national environmental law and policy of individual nation States and regional communities of States, such as the EC. By way of example, the UK`s participation in the 1992 Rio 'Earth Summit' (the UN Conference on Environment and Development), and the conclusion of 'Agenda 21', led to the emergence of 'sustainable development' as a key component of UK national environmental policy. Several policy important documents were subsequently prepared including: the 1990 White Paper, *This Common Inheritance* (Cm 1200); *Sustainable Development: The UK Strategy* (Cm 2426) in 1994; and *A Better Quality of Life: A Strategy for Sustainable Development for the United Kingdom* (Cm 4345) in 1999. In turn, national policy has led to the incorporation of sustainable development policies at the local level, for example, the appearance of sustainable development policies in local authority town and country planning development plans.

The most commonly cited expression of the Sustainable Development Principle is to be found in a 1987 United Nations conference on 'Our Common Future' (The *Bruntland Report*): 'Development that meets the needs of the present without compromising the ability of future generations to meet their own needs.' The principle is clearly anthropocentric – viewing the environment from a human centred, human needs perspective. It also exhibits elements of equality and fairness in its concern for the rights of present day societies, both rich and poor, and for the right of future generations to be able to develop the earth's available resources. The principle has, to a certain extent, moved beyond the status of a pure policy tool and has become incorporated into a number of documents as an important legal principle. It forms part of 'Agenda 21' requirements and more importantly is incorporated into Art 2 of the EC Treaty (see 1997 Treaty of Amsterdam) as a fundamental principle. Thus the EC now has the task 'to promote throughout the Community harmonious, balanced and sustainable development of economic activities'. The principle has also made an appearance in a UK context, for example, in s 1 of the Natural Heritage (Scotland) Act 1991 and s 4 of the Environment Act 1995. References to sustainable development in UK legislation generally require regard to be had to the principle but do not go so far as to impose any legal obligation to ensure that sustainable development is achieved. The Environment Agency's statutory duties are worded in such a way that the principle is merely a guide to the way in which the agency should exercise its functions. The importance of sustainable development concerns its impact upon government and regulatory policy by providing targets and tools to monitor progress. These developments, in turn, affect the Command and Control regulatory regimes we encountered in earlier chapters. Pollution licence conditions may be tightened to give effect to international agreements.

13.2 Public concern

13.2.1 What is public concern and why is it important?

Public concern, in an environmental pollution context, is the fear of actual or threatened adverse impacts of emissions from industrial, commercial, and agricultural activity upon an individual's core interests. Therefore anything which threatens the security of an individual, especially in regard to health, family, property, money, or employment will trigger a strong defensive reaction. Quite simply the public will vehemently oppose those pollution related risks which it considers to be unacceptable. Furedi captures the essence of such concerns when he observes:

> Safety has become the fundamental value of the 1990s. Passions that were once devoted to struggle to save the world (or keep it the same) are now invested in trying to ensure that we are safe. (Furedi, 1997).

In order to fully appreciate the significance of public concern and its potential impact on government, regulatory agencies, and regulated businesses we must take note of the role of the media. The media report on what it believes to be the chief concerns of its principal client: the public. The media, through its editorial control of the items it deems newsworthy, sensitises the public to selected risks. Currently pollution related concerns are high on the media's agenda and, over time, pollution related issues become a pressing concern for most people. This shift in the public perception is borne out by one leading law firm which specialises in pollution related claims, which has noted the 'enormous increase in public concern regarding environmental pollution' (Pugh and Day, 1995).

The public is assailed on all sides by both local and global threats including: climate change, acid rain, destruction of habitat, resource depletion, industrial pollution, and nuclear waste disposal. At the same time public confidence in science and scientific experts has been severely dented by a string of environmental controversies which have been linked with adverse health impacts: BSE, genetically modified crops, ozone depletion and traffic related asthma.

What the public values and what the public fears are two related issues which are capable of forming important inputs into environmental policy and environmental decision making. The public values a healthy environment and any development, such as the construction of a waste incinerator, which appears to threaten such deeply held values, beliefs or convictions is likely to generate controversy. Currently the planning system seems to be the main forum in which development decisions, relating to permission to build 'risky' developments, come head to head with public concerns relating to health, safety and the environmental issues. Almost without exception any development proposal which is believed to impact adversely upon humans will stimulate vociferous opposition. Controversies over the siting of waste incinerators, electricity power lines, low level nuclear waste storage facilities, and similar unwanted developments are reported daily in the media.

The issues which concern the public undoubtedly have an influence upon what the media deem newsworthy. The more the media reports on an issue of public concern, such as environmental pollution, the more the public are sensitised to that issue and its attendant risks. In turn, public concern impacts upon Government pre-occupations and may generate policy proposals, at both central and local levels. In some instances public concern may force the Government to propose new legislation, as in the case of dangerous dogs, or firearms. Public concerns permeate society and impact upon the activities of the regulators (as can be seen in the Environment Agency's enforcement and prosecution policy, and in its agreement to trial an extended public consultation process in regard to licensing applications which generate high levels of public concern), and the regulated (as is evident in the decision of Shell to reverse its plan to decommission the Brent Spar oil rig at sea).

Public concern is not only instrumental in influencing Government policy and proposals for new legislation but it can have a powerful, localised, impact on regulators and regulated businesses. Media coverage of pollution incidents may alert the public to the pollution risks associated with the operation of specific company plants. In turn, this may result in public pressure on the regulator to prosecute the offending polluter. Regulators, such as the Environment Agency, operate in a political environment and are acutely aware that it needs to be seen to be doing its job, as this is understood by the public. In such circumstances the regulator may exercise its discretion to prosecute to placate the public rather than employing its administrative enforcement powers. Regulated businesses are also increasingly aware of the power of public concern and opposition. Unpopular development proposals, such as the proposed construction of a new factory or extension to an existing facility, may be blocked by widespread opposition to the relevant proposal. Usually public concern is expressed at the planning stage but increasingly the public will seek participation in the decision making of environmental regulators, especially in regard to the issue and variation of licenses.

13.2.2 Public concern and the legitimacy of environmental decision making

Tapping into public concerns and values is problematic for both central and local government. It is not easy to discern, or measure, the extent of public concern in regard to a specific risk. The public is not an homogeneous group whose opinions are easily sounded out. Experience at local government level in the drafting and consultation upon development plans (which comprise a collection of policies guiding development control decisions in the planning process) is illustrative of the problem. Only major landholders and businesses tend to make inputs into the development plan process. They do so primarily to protect their own interests. In contrast, few individuals bother to master the background detail to the consultation process (which requires a major investment of time and effort) prior to making any input into the process. In an effort to address this problem both central and local government have experimented with focus groups, citizen juries, and citizen advisory forums, in an effort to ascertain reliable indications of public values and concerns. These initiatives recognise, to a greater or lesser extent, the need to bring the public 'up to speed' before reliable information on public concerns and values may be elicited. Obtaining accurate information is vital because only then will the Government be reasonably certain that its policies will be perceived as legitimate by the public. Values and concerns thus form an essential element of policymaking. Policies which do not reflect the true concerns and values of the public will be unreliable guides for decision makers. Failing to consult properly can wrongfoot the Government and lead to a public outcry which may force the Government to rethink its proposals. An example of the consequences of failing to obtain reliable information on public concerns can be seen in the public outcry and subsequent rejection, by Hampshire County Council, of a proposal to build a large waste incinerator on the outskirts of Portsmouth (Stanley, 2000).

Until the late 1990s the principal Command and Control decision making process in which the public vented their concerns about the tolerability of risks created by development proposals was the town and country planning system. There are signs that the demand for public participation in the licensing decisions of the Environment Agency and the local authorities is growing. The Environment Agency has recently announced that it is trialing a system of improved and extended consultation with the public in regard to a selected number of sites which raise matters of significant public concern. The Environment Agency has announced that its objective in engaging in extended consultation is to 'provide an opportunity for fully informing the public and engaging them in debate during the decision making process. In this way, decisions will be better informed, and because they have greater public involvement, more widely accepted'. So far the extended consultation process has been piloted at several facilities, including a power station, a waste treatment plant, a cement works, and a nuclear plant. The Environment Agency anticipates that 20–50 licence applications each year will utilise the extended consultation process.

In the past the Government has responded to important shifts in public concern by adopting reactive, legislative 'fixes', as demonstrated by the passage of the Deposit of Poisonous Wastes Act 1972 and Clean Air Acts of the 1950s. These laws were passed in response to environmental problems (fly-tipping dangerous waste and the health effects of smogs) which captured the attention of the public and media and led to demands for decisive action. Legislation which goes with the grain of society's perceptions of acceptable environmental behaviour will have widespread support because it is perceived as necessary. The Government must learn the lesson that it cannot afford to wait until a situation becomes intolerable before it acts. There are encouraging signs that the Government is beginning to adopt a less reactive approach to environmental pollution problems as demonstrated by its pro-active policy development of the national air, waste, and water strategies.

13.2.3 The causes of high levels of public concern

Since public concern often arises from actual or threatened exposure to levels of pollution which the public perceives as too risky and therefore unacceptable we need to consider the following linked issues: what is risk, and what factors help to generate public perception of unacceptable risk exposure?

13.2.3.1 What is risk?

Every one of us, of necessity, is a risk taker. In the act of a crossing a public highway, overtaking another vehicle in our own motor car, or smoking cigarettes, we are all involved in a continual process of risk taking. Our own experiences of risk taking, be they rewards or losses, influence our own risk taking behaviour and the opinion each of us holds of what constitutes a 'risky' activity. Why then are some risks surrounded by controversy and are considered to be less acceptable than other activities which involve the taking of risks? Why is environmental pollution, such as the airborne emissions from waste incinerators, associated with unacceptable risk taking and the creation of high levels of public concern?

These questions can only be effectively answered if we develop a better understanding of the concept of risk. John Adams, a leading author on risk, has divided risk into three categories in an effort to explain why the public is more fearful of some risks rather than others (Adams, 1995). Risks may be directly perceptible to each of us through our own, unaided senses; risks may be perceptible with the aid of science and technology; or risks may be 'virtual risks'. In crossing a busy road we are using our own unaided senses to perceive the direct risk that oncoming vehicles may injure us. We do not need to carry out a formal risk assessment to convince us that we should exercise a high degree of care in such circumstances. Similarly the risks and rewards of driving fast are directly apparent to us. Each individual has an 'in-built' risk thermostat which guides his or her risk taking behaviour. Some people are risk seeking whilst others are risk averse and the setting of each individual's risk thermostat will vary with that person's life experiences. Occasionally an individual's risk thermostat will conflict with attempts by regulators and safety experts to manage risks for him or her. We may choose to ignore speed limit warning signs in the pursuit of speed. Despite the efforts of government many of us will continue to insist on taking more risks than the safety authorities believe we should take.

Risks perceived through science require us to use scientific apparatus to perceive the relevant risk. We cannot see a virus with the naked eye but we can observe it under the microscope, however, without training we cannot understand what we are seeing or form any impression on the risk of infection. Science helps us to assess risk in those cases in which the mechanism between exposure to infection and the onset of the disease is well known. Science helps us assess the relevant risk and its acceptability or tolerability. In those cases where the science is uncertain we may resort to the use of objective risk assessments to provide us with statistical information to guide our risk taking behaviour. In the world of risk assessments activities which have less than a 'one in a million' risk of resulting in death are generally considered to be safe. Risk assessments are frequently used in assessing the risk of workplace accidents and they have also been used to demonstrate the relatively remote risk of chemical spillages occurring at a waste transfer station (see *Envirocor*

Waste Holdings Ltd v Secretary of State for the Environment (1996)). Whilst these assessments are helpful aids in environmental decision making nevertheless they represent an experts best 'guestimate' of the likelihood of an adverse outcome actually materialising. Whilst risk experts may be familiar with the statistical risk ratings of various activities, the ordinary individual may have rather more difficulty in coming to a satisfactory conclusion on whether a one in a million risk of dying of cancer caused by polluting emissions from a new factory is an acceptable risk.

Virtual risks are those risks, such as the risk to health associated with the consumption of meat potentially infected with BSE, which are surrounded by great uncertainty and in regard to which scientists themselves cannot agree whether the relevant activity is safe. An environmental pollution example is the public concern, generated by the emission of carcinogenic dioxins from waste incinerators. When faced with scientists who profoundly disagree with one another the public is forced to impose meaning on uncertainty. In such circumstances the public make an assessment of the relevant risk based upon the subjective criteria discussed below.

Public concern is increasingly relevant to environmental decision making. Public concern is now a consideration which, when relevant, must be taken into account by local planning authorities when determining the outcome of planning applications. The pollution risks associated with the granting of licences to industry to discharge substances into the environment may generate public concern. Increasingly the affected members of the public wish to participate in regulatory decisions which affect their well being. Public concern is also instrumental in the commencement of some common law actions in which residents living in the vicinity of polluting industry choose to take on big business in the courts because of the fear of the ill effects of pollution in their neighbourhood.

13.2.3.2 The factors generating public perception of unacceptable risk exposure

Research has demonstrated that the public use 'rules of thumb' to reduce the burden involved in processing the mass of information available to them in regard to the assessment of risks. The public largely rely upon what they are able to recall about a particular risk when calculating the likelihood of an event occurring or recurring. This may lead to significant differences of opinion between what activities the risk experts tell us is safe and what the public perceive as safe. For example, the public tend to overestimate the risk of death and injury from infrequent causes, such as hurricanes, but underestimate the loss of life from asthma.

The nature and extent of media coverage of a risk is a key factor influencing public perception and public concern. A specialist law firm, which has considerable experience of environmental pollution claims, believes that media interest in environmental pollution will ensure that health problems associated with these activities are well reported. The same firm reported that it had received a total of 1,500 telephone calls from potential plaintiffs, concerned about the risks of breast implants, following two television appearances by a representative of the firm on the ITN news.

The types of event which the media deem newsworthy, the graphic imagery employed, and the timescale within which an issue remains newsworthy, all influence public recollection. The media report on what it believes to be of most concern to most of the public for most of the time. Reporting is biased in favour of stories relating to health, money, crime, education, and the environment. Media reporting of industrial accidents causing death, injury, and environmental damage, create a climate in which the public will voice its objections to both existing and proposed developments which threaten the fundamental concerns of the public: the ability to live in a healthy, pollution free, and safe local environment. It is not surprising to discover that the public are concerned with threats to their health. Where industrial activities threaten these fundamental concerns the following expressions of concern are to be expected: is this waste incinerator poisoning the neighbourhood with toxic atmospheric emissions?; will the construction of this chemical plant close to residential properties blight property values? These are typical and rational reactions to what the public perceives as threats to its core concerns.

The degree of public trust in the organisation which will be managing a risk influences the opinion of the public as to the acceptability of the activity creating the risk. If the organisation which will be managing the risk has a poor track record in risk management it can expect public opposition. For example, would the public in the immediate years after the Bhopal disaster be behaving irrationally if it steadfastly resisted a proposal by Union Carbide to build a chemical plant in the heart of the British countryside, even though the chemical company could demonstrate, using objectively calculated risk assessments, that the proposed plant would be safe?

If a hazard is perceived by the public as being imposed on it, the risks created by the relevant activity will be less acceptable than if the risks were assumed voluntarily. The case of *R v Secretary of State for Trade and Industry ex p Duddridge* (1996) illustrates the heightened public opposition to development which the public perceives as being unjustly imposed upon it against its will. If the public believe that they have no personal control over a risk then the level of public concern experienced will be higher than those circumstances in which the public retain some degree of control over risk exposure. For example, public concern relating to polluting emissions from a new factory may be defused if the site operator provides equipment and training to enable the public to monitor plant emissions independently of data collected by the factory itself.

The number of people potentially at risk from, for example, the risk of explosion at a petro-chemical plant, is a further factor which the public take into account when assessing the tolerability of a hazard. Also of significance is the way in which the hazard manifests itself. Contrast the graphic media depiction of how the victims of the Piper Alpha oil rig inferno met their deaths and the minimal media interest in the plight of shipworkers whose hearing has been severely damaged by constant exposure to loud noises. In the former incident the injuries caused were immediate, graphic and horrific, whilst in the case of widespread deafness in shipyards the injuries were neither observable or immediately apparent.

New risks are problematic because the public is unfamiliar with the extent and nature of the risks generated by the relevant activity. Genetic engineering, biotechnology, and the risks of exposure to electro-magnetic field radiation are three examples of the uncertainty created by newly emergent risks which are not yet fully understood by experts and the public. Any accident involving new technologies, such as biotechnology, may be perceived by the public as confirmation that the activity is inherently dangerous and therefore any risks associated with such risky technology is not acceptable.

Man-made risks, such as those associated with the nuclear power industry, cause the public to fear far more than hazards which are 'natural', such as the risk of property damage caused by living on a flood plain.

The perception that risks are inequitably distributed in society also affects their acceptability. The waste industry is currently grappling with this issue in regard to finding sites to 'host' new landfills or waste incinerators. The perception of the local community that it is to be the dumping ground for other people's waste generated by the entire county often galvanises the affected public to take action to resist the proposal.

Research has demonstrated that a combination of the factors outlined above may combine to evoke a powerful negative public reaction. Hazards may cause 'dread' or 'unknown' risk reactions amongst the public. Dread risks are those which are characterised by a lack of personal control, inequitable distribution of risks and benefits, the existence of a threat to future generations, the risk increases over time, and the risk has catastrophic potential to injure man or the environment. The issues raised by objectors to the construction of a waste incinerator in Gateshead illustrate the dread risk caused by public concern over exposure to dioxins emitted from the incinerator. 'Unknown' reactions relate to hazards which are unobservable, which are not fully understood by science, and their impacts on man and the environment are difficult to assess. Hazards generated by nuclear power plants may prompt this type of extreme reaction. Occasionally the combination of public concern criteria produces a public outcry compelling the Government and the regulators to take swift and decisive action to address such concerns. The post-Dunblane disaster 'Snowdrop' campaign subjected the Government to intense and sustained pressure to ban certain firearms.

13.3 Emerging regulatory mechanisms

Recognition of the fact that Command and Control licence based pollution controls are never going to be the complete answer to environmental pollution regulation has led to greater interest in using the market to provide incentive based pollution controls. Market mechanisms (otherwise referred to as economic instruments) are not generally as expensive to set up and run as a standard Command and Control regulatory regime. A 'market mechanism' is any tool which uses fiscal incentives or deterrents in order to achieve environmental objectives. These mechanisms do not involve the use of the law to compel companies or individuals to act in a particular way. They are persuasive rather than coercive.

The Government, in restoring market mechanisms, aims to send a 'signal' to consumers and industrialists encouraging them to behave in ways which will reduce the environmental damage they cause. Thus, a motorist may be faced with progressive rises in petrol prices designed to encourage him or her to use public transport. Similarly a manufacturing company may be faced with increased waste disposal costs, due to the landfill tax, designed to encourage waste minimisation through recycling. Annex A to the 1990 White Paper, *This Common Inheritance* (Cm 1200) lists the Government's preferred tools: charging schemes, subsidies, deposit/refund schemes, enforcement incentives and markets in pollution credits.

13.3.1 Tradeable pollution permits (emissions trading)

This regulatory mechanism is designed to create a market in pollution credits. Such schemes are operational in the USA, Canada, and in some European States, but not in the UK. Currently emissions trading is focused on creating markets in 'greenhouse' gas emissions from power generating plants burning fossil fuels. Such schemes fix an upper ceiling for emissions of specified chemical substances (for example, carbon dioxide) and firms operating in the industries emitting these substances bid for pollution credits. Over time the regulator reduces the number of credits in circulation and this results in an increase in the price of the pollution credits. This provides a financial incentive for participating firms to reduce their need for credits by developing less polluting methods of production.

Section 3(5) of the EPA 1990 enables the Secretary of State for the Environment to establish tradable pollution permit schemes in the UK. The concept could be applied to water pollution discharges to controlled waters from point sources, such as discharge pipes. It is difficult to see how the concept could apply to power generation in the UK where there are very few generators and therefore no opportunity to create a viable market. One of the key texts in this area is Pearce and Barbier's, *Blueprint for a Sustainable Economy'* (2000, Earthscan).

Just as this book was going to press, the Government was finalising the details of an emissions trading scheme. The voluntary scheme forms part of the Government's strategy ('Climate Change: the UK Programme' November 2000) to meet its Kyoto Protocol target of a 12.5% percentile) reduction on 1990 emission levels of the six main greenhouse gases (see p 267 regarding the Kyoto Protocol) by 2010. It is estimated that the emissions trading scheme will deliver an annual reduction of 2 m tonnes of carbon by 2010.

The scheme is open to virtually all private and public sector organisations whose activities result in the emission of the six greenhouse gases either directly into the environment or indirectly (via the use of electricity). There are two main participants in the scheme: (i) Agreement Participants. These are organisations covered by a climate change levy agreement negotiated between the Government and the relevant industry; and (ii) Direct Entry Participants. These organisations are not covered by a climate change levy agreement. These organisations must meet reduction targets set as a condition of entry to the trading scheme.

Details of the proposed emissions trading scheme are to be found on the DEFRA website.

13.3.2 Charging schemes

This approach to pollution regulation involves the recovery of the costs of operating a Command and Control regulatory regime. Licence fees charged by the regulator may be designed to recover all or part of the regulator's operational costs, such as the administrative costs involved in processing licence applications, pollution monitoring, and enforcement action. Higher fees may be charged on polluters whose emissions cost more to process, treat, and monitor. The fees currently charged for waste, water, and Integrated Pollution Control (IPC)/Integrated Pollution Prevention and Control (IPPC) licences are examples of this approach. The Environment Agency is currently testing an 'enforced self-regulation' scheme in the waste management industry called 'OPRA' (operator pollution risk appraisal). Licence holders who score consistently well in Environment Agency risk assessment visits will be visited less frequently and the savings in monitoring costs made by the Environment Agency will be reflected in reduced annual licence fees. Licence holders who have an accredited environmental management scheme in place, such as ISO 14001, will find that their environmental risk 'score' is reduced. The lower the score the less often the Environment Agency will visit the licence holders premises.

13.3.3 Enforcement incentives

Regulators, such as the Environment Agency, may use their enforcement powers in ways which encourage licence holders to comply with the terms of their licences. The threat of prosecution offers a dual incentive: not only the financial penalties and legal costs which a court may impose upon conviction of an environmental offence but also the damage to a licence holder's reputation as an environmentally responsible business as the progress of a court case is reported in the media. Large companies are more likely to comply with the law, not in consequence of the financial impact of a fine, but as a result of the damage which adverse media coverage may have on sales and company image. The EA publishes details of companies it wishes to 'name and shame' on its website. The regulator may also use its powers of remediation, for example, s 161 of the Water Resources Act 1991 and s 59 of the Environmental Protection Act 1990, to recover the cost of clean-up from the polluter. The use of these powers is not dependent upon a linked criminal prosecution and the costs of remediation may far exceed any fine imposed by a court for breach of environmental law. In addition, the regulator has administrative powers, for example, Enforcement Notices and Anti-Pollution Works Notices, to compel licence holders to install costly pollution abatement equipment and pollution prevention devices.

Polluters also must have regard to the risk of civil actions commenced by individuals whose property or health has been damaged by the polluters' activities. Victims of pollution incidents may use the torts of negligence, nuisance, trespass, and the rule in *Rylands v Fletcher* to recover compensation for their losses. For example, the *Cambridge Water Co* case involved a claim of £1 m.

13.3.4 Subsidies and grants

Grants may be made available by Government departments as an incentive towards the cost of installation of pollution prevention devices. For example, grants are available for the construction of plant to treat silage effluent and management agreements provide for payments to farmers who agree, by contract, to certain restrictions on their farming methods in environmentally sensitive areas such as Sites of Special Scientific Interest and nitrate sensitive areas.

13.3.5 Deposit and refund schemes

Perhaps the most famous of these schemes was established by the Danish law (the full details of which are examined in Case 302/86 *Commission v Denmark* [1988] ECR 4607), requiring beer and soft drinks containers to be returnable (see 12.15.5.1 above). The European Court of Justice upheld the relevant law, even though it interfered with the operation of the common market, because the scheme was justifiable on environmental protection grounds.

13.3.6 Environmental contracts (environmental covenants)

Governments, whether national, regional or local, and industry associations may enter into contracts with one another to regulate pollution. Several countries, but not as yet the UK, have made use of this tool. For example, the Rotterdam municipality (local authority) in Holland has concluded an environmental contract with the German chemical industry relating to the pollution of the mouth of the River Rhine. The mouth of the Rhine has been contaminated with heavy metals. These contaminants form part of the silt lying on the river bed of the estuary. When the Rotterdam municipality dredges the navigation channels in the river the silt it collects is too contaminated to dump at sea. A special containment facility (the schlufter) has therefore been built to store the contaminated silt. The environmental contract provides that the German chemical industry will reduce heavy metal discharges to agreed limits by 2005. If the terms of the agreement are breached the Rotterdam municipality will sue the German chemical industry for the costs involved in constructing the schlufter and any future extension of that facility (see ENDS 1992 (205 and 211) and 1993 (224)).

13.4 Human rights

Human rights represents an emerging area in which individuals and environmental groups may use rights based arguments to challenge the decisions of public authorities. The courts, as well as regulatory agencies, are public bodies for the purposes of the Human Rights Act (HRA) 1998 and are therefore constrained to act in a way which is compatible with the rights enshrined in the European Convention on Human Rights. The HRA 1998 requires the courts to take into account, in their decisions, not only the rights granted to citizens by the Convention, but also the judgments, and opinions of the European Court and the Commission. National legislation must, as far as possible, be read so as to give effect to the Convention rights, even if this means that the court will depart from a previous decision which would otherwise have been binding on it. It will be unlawful for the courts, and other public bodies, to act in ways which are incompatible with Convention rights (unless the public authority could not have acted differently because of the existence of incompatible legislation).

National courts are empowered to grant such remedies which they consider 'just and appropriate'. This power will enable the courts both to award damages for breach of human rights, and in appropriate cases, quash incompatible subordinate legislation.

Debate as to the potential impact of the Convention and 1998 Act currently centre upon two issues: (i) to what extent the Convention and the HRA 1998 guarantee substantive environmental human rights; and (ii) to what extent the Convention and the HRA 1998 guarantee procedural environmental human rights.

13.4.1 Substantive environmental human rights

The Convention does not directly address the question of whether an individual has a right to a decent environment nevertheless the Convention has been used by litigants as the basis of a number of claims the objective of which was to secure an acceptable level of environmental quality.

13.4.1.1 The right to life

Article 2 of the Convention provides that 'Everyone's right to life shall be protected by law'. At first sight it seems unlikely that such a right could serve the interests of environmental protection, however, it would appear that breaches of Art 2 are not restricted to the protection of physical life. Both significant interference with the quality of life and a threat to life caused by the activities of a public authority could form the basis of an Art 2 action. For example, in *Guerra v Italy* (1998) ECHR Series A, two members of the European Court of Human Rights were of the opinion that a government which withheld information about circumstances which created a foreseeable and substantial risk of damage to physical health and physical integrity could amount to a breach of Art 2. In the *Guerra* case the applicants lived only 1 km from a chemical plant which was discharging large quantities of inflammable gases into the environment. It was argued that the gases could cause chemical reactions leading to the release of highly toxic substances. The chemical plant had a 'checkered' operational history. Various accidents had occurred including an incident in 1976 when 150 people had been hospitalised with serious arsenic poisoning. The applicants complained that the 'Seveso' Directive on the Control of Major Accident Hazards had not been complied with. The directive required the local authorities to advise the local population in regard to the relevant hazards from the plant and the procedures and plans in place to safeguard the local population, but this had not been done. Although the court ruled that the claim under Art 2 was inadmissible, since it had already decided the case on the basis of Art 8, the comments of the two concurring members of the court are significant for they indicate that public authorities have a positive obligation to safeguard a citizen's right to life.

Whilst decision makers in public authorities must be mindful of the need to protect the health and well being of the authority's citizens, Art 2 does not oblige a public authority to provide a healthy environment for its population. Article 2 actions are therefore only likely to stand a reasonable prospect of success when the relevant claim relates to allegations of unreasonable exposure to pollution risks. Even then the court will be wary of imposing unreasonable burdens upon public authorities. Thus, in *Osman v UK* (1999) 5 BHRC 293 an Art 2 claim based on negligent policing, the court stated that the right to life 'must be interpreted in a way that does not impose an impossible or disproportionate burden on the authorities. Accordingly not every risk to life can entail for the authorities a Convention requirement to take operational measures to prevent the risk from arising'. In view of this decision it remains to be seen whether the suggested link between traffic pollution and asthma will form the basis of a successful Art 2 action.

13.4.1.2 The right to privacy and family life

Article 8 provides that:

(1) Everyone has the right to respect for his private life and family life, his home and his correspondence.

(2) There shall be no interference by a public authority with the exercise of this right except such as in accordance with the law and is necessary in a democratic society in the interest of national security, public safety or the economic well-being of the country, for the prevention of disorder or crime, for the protection of health or morals, or for the protection of the rights and freedoms of others.

Article 8 imposes a positive obligation on States to take reasonable and appropriate measures to secure the rights of applicants and a negative obligation not to interfere with Art 8 rights unless these are justified by Art 8(2). In the case of *Powell and Rayner v UK* (1990) 12 EHRR 355 applicants who lived close to Heathrow airport based their action on Art 8. The applicants alleged that the noise from the airport adversely affected the quality of their private lives and the scope for enjoying the amenities of their homes and so breached their Art 8 rights. Both applicants, along with approximately 6,500 other residents, lived in an area considered to be one of high noise annoyance. The court rejected the applicant's action because of the qualification, in Art 8(2), to strike a balance between the competing interests of the applicants and the wider community. In balancing the relevant interests the court had regard to (i) the fact that residents had received compensation for noise disturbance, (ii) the noise abatement measures which had been taken by the airport, (iii) the economic importance of Heathrow airport to the country (for example, in 1998 Heathrow handled cargo to the value of £26.3 bn, contributed £16 m in local rents and rates, generated £200 m to the UK's balance of payments, and provided over 48,000 jobs), and (iv) the use, by the UK Government, of a regulatory regime to control noise pollution rather than favouring the use of civil actions to resolve noise disputes.

In *Lopez Ostra v Spain* (1995) 20 EHRR 277 waste treatment plants were constructed on municipal land just 12 metres from the applicant's home. The operators omitted to acquire a licence authorising their 'nuisance causing' activities. The applicant alleged that odour and noise emissions from the waste treatment plants were causing health problems and were disrupting home life. The court found that as the emissions exceeded permitted limits they could endanger the health of citizens living nearby. The court stated, 'severe environmental pollution may affect individual's well being and prevent them from enjoying their private and family life adversely, without however, seriously endangering their health'. The court found in favour of the applicant and awarded 4 m pesetas compensation. There had been an interference with the applicant's Art 8 rights and the interference was not justified by the Art 8(2) qualification. The court noted that whilst the key objective of Art 8 was to protect citizens against arbitrary interference by public authorities, a public body's duty under Art 8 included a positive obligation to ensure effective respect for private and family life. The court concluded that the economic benefit of the treatment plants to the local community did not outweigh the applicant's right to respect for her home and home life. Article 8 could therefore be a fertile source of human rights litigation in circumstances where inaction by a public body exposes citizens to the adverse impacts of environmental pollution. For example, a judicial review action against a regulator is possible in circumstances where the regulator refuses to take enforcement action against a person, such as an IPPC licensed facility, whose emissions are interfering with the Article 8 rights of citizens living close to the polluter.

There is an interesting contrast between the decisions in *Lopez Ostra* and *Powell and Rayner*. In the successful *Lopez Ostra* case, the economic interests were relatively narrow economic interests comprising the private tanneries who used the waste treatment plants. In *Powell and Rayner*, the relevant economic interests at Heathrow airport were of a different order of magnitude altogether and were not confined to a narrow range of private interests.

In *Khatun and Others v UK* (unreported, 1 July 1998) a complaint was made to the European Court of Human Rights arising out of the disturbance caused by the Canary Wharf development. Residents living close to the development were affected by construction dust, could not use their gardens, and were forced to close their windows in the height of summer resulting in excessive heat levels in their homes. The court rejected the claims and accepted the developers submissions relating to the public benefit arising from the regeneration of Docklands. The court recognised the 'pressing social need' of the project and concluded that a fair balance had been struck between the interference with the applicant's home and private life and the wider public benefit. The *Khatun* case provides an example of the private interests of a developer winning out, as a result of a public decision, over the adverse impacts of the development on the applicants. In this case the court was able to identify a public economic benefit which justified the interference complained of.

The significance of the HRA 1998 in the context of Art 8 rights is illustrated by the recent planning case involving the *Kings Hill Collective*. The Kings Hill Collective is a group of people who believe in pursuing a sustainable lifestyle. The collective constructed a number of low impact dwellings known as 'benders' (wooden and canvass shelters) near Shepton Mallet without the benefit of planning permission. An Enforcement Notice was served on the collective requiring the removal of the benders. The collective appealed unsuccessfully to the Secretary of State for the Environment against the Enforcement Notice. Subsequently the collective made an application to have the Secretary of State's decision judicially reviewed. The Court of Appeal confirmed the decision of the High Court that the Secretary of State had erred in not considering whether or not a decision adverse to the collective would breach Art 8. The decision was remitted to the Secretary of State for reconsideration and the original decision was reversed. Although the erection of the benders was a development which was contrary to the planning policies in the relevant development plan (and therefore the presumption was that the outcome of the appeal would be in accordance with the development plan – see s 54(A) of the Town and Country Planning Act 1990) the appellant's human rights were material considerations of significant weight. Upholding the Enforcement Notice was a serious interference with the appellant's Art 8 rights. Breach of the right to a private and home life had to be balanced against the wider public interest issues comprising the effect of the benders on the surrounding landscape, traffic generation, and the potential precedent effect of the bender development. The Secretary of State concluded that the development would not have a significant adverse impact on the public interests, and after taking Art 8 into account, he concluded that these factors outweighed the planning presumption in favour of development which accords with the development plan. Accordingly the enforcement notice appeal was upheld and retrospective planning permission was granted.

13.4.1.3 The right to property

Article 1 of Protocol 1 states that:

> Every natural or legal person is entitled to the peaceful enjoyment of his possessions. No one shall be deprived of his possessions except in the general public interest and subject to the conditions provided for by law and by the general principles of international law.

> The preceding provisions shall not, however, in any way impair the right of a state to enforce such laws as it deems necessary to control the use of property in accordance with the general interest or to secure the payment of other taxes or contributions or penalties.

In *Powell and Rayner v UK*, it was stated that Art 1 does not, in principle, guarantee a right to the peaceful enjoyment of possessions in a pleasant environment. It is unlikely that the article will be capable of forming the basis of an action relating to loss of amenity, such as a pleasant view. Industry may be able to rely on the Art 1 right to challenge the decisions of public bodies which, although taken with the object of protecting the natural environment for the general benefit of society (the general public interest), interfere with industry's right to peaceful enjoyment. In *Fredin v Sweden* (1991) ECHR Series A No 192, the applicant's licence to extract gravel from his land was revoked (by a public body) following changes in Swedish nature conservation law. In rejecting the applicant's claim the European Court of Human Rights took note of the following factors: (i) the revocation decision was a property related control; (ii) the Swedish authorities had a legitimate objective in revoking the permission – environmental protection, and (iii) the applicant had no legitimate expectation that the permission would not be revoked. It seems that interference with the right to property will be justified where the interference is in conformity with planning laws and is designed to protect the environment (see *Pine Valley Developments v Ireland* (1991) ECHR Series A No 222).

13.4.2 Procedural rights

13.4.2.1 The right to a fair trial

Article 6(1) states:

> In the determination of his civil rights and obligations or of any criminal charge against him everyone is entitled to a fair and public hearing within a reasonable time by an independent and impartial tribunal established by law.

Whilst there is no civil right which guarantees a decent environment for the purposes of Art 6 the right to property is a civil right and therefore any State action which affects that right is subject to the provisions of Art 6. For example, the grant or refusal of planning permission are subject to Art 6. In addition, third parties whose properties are affected by the grant of planning permission to adjacent property owners are also subject to Art 6.

The *Alconbury* case concerned a planning application to develop a redundant Ministry of Defence airfield as a distribution centre. Planning permission had been refused by the planning committee of the local planning authority and an appeal against the refusal followed. The Secretary of State used his/her 'call in' power to recover jurisdiction in the case at the appeal stage. This was a case in which the Government stood to gain from a decision to allow the development to proceed. A legal challenge was launched against the Secretary of State's action based on Art 6 (the right to a hearing before an 'independent and impartial tribunal').

The High Court ruled in favour of the applicants and held that the Secretary of State's role as both policy maker and decision-maker on the 'called in' planning application was incompatible with the Human Rights Act. In effect the Secretary of State was judge in his/her own cause. The court went on to state that in its opinion, the inquiry system provided an adequate safeguard for the public where a planning inspector took a decision in regard to a planning appeal but not where the Secretary of State took the decision. An appeal to the House of Lords followed swiftly. The House of Lords reversed the High Court's ruling and held that the Secretary of State's powers are not incompatible with the Human Rights Act 1998. The court held that the whilst the Secretary of State's consideration of the case, using his/her 'call in' power, was not an impartial hearing, nevertheless, this was not the decisive factor. It was enough that the Secretary of State's decision was subject to a judicial body which did provide the Art 6 guarantees. (In such cases, a right exists enabling the applicant to apply to the higher courts against the decision of the Secretary of State on a point of law.) Importantly the judicial control over the Secretary of

State's hearing of the matter did not require a rehearing of the merits of the case in order for the current process to amount to a sufficient review of the legality of the decision and the procedures which were followed in reaching that decision. The courts' judicial review powers and the accountability of the Secretary of State to Parliament were adequate safeguards under the Human Rights Act 1998.

The right to a fair hearing may also be the subject of legal challenge relating to the use of enforcement powers by regulatory bodies. Regulators, such as the Environment Agency, often have legal powers which may be used to force defendants to incriminate themselves. In *Hertfordshire CC ex p Green Environmental Industries Ltd and John Moynihan* [1998] Env LR 153, the county council conducted an investigation into allegations of illegal fly-tipping of waste by Mr Moynihan. The council used its powers to require Mr Moynihan to assist the council with its inquiries. Mr Moynihan challenged the use of the council's powers on the grounds that their use infringed the rule against self-incrimination and the right to remain silent. The Court of Appeal rejected these arguments and dismissed the case. The council was entitled to select the power under which it obtained evidence in regard to alleged breaches of the law. This case contrasts with the decision of the European Court of Human Rights in *Saunders v UK* (1997) 23 EHRR 313, in which the court found that the use of similar powers by the Department of Trade and Industry was in breach of Art 6.

13.4.2.2 The right to freedom of expression

Article 10 provides:

1 Everyone has the right to freedom of expression. This right shall include freedom to hold opinions and to receive and impart information and ideas without interference by public authority and regardless of frontiers.

2 The exercise of these freedoms, since it carries with it duties and responsibilities, may be subject to such formalities, conditions, restrictions, or penalties as are prescribed by law and are necessary in a democratic society.

In *Guerra v Italy* (see above), the application of Art 10 to the facts of the case were considered. Both the Commission and Court had interesting remarks to make concerning the relevance of Art 10 rights in circumstances in which State inaction exposes citizens to environmental risks. The failure of the Italian authorities to inform the applicant about the pollution risks generated by the waste treatment plants and the failure to provide information, as required by the Control of Major Accident Hazards Directive, infringed Art 10. The Commission was of the opinion that the provision of information to the public was an essential means to protect the health and well being of the population. Article 10 conferred on the local population who had been affected, or who might be affected, by the activity representing a threat to the environment, a right to receive such information. The Court agreed with the Commission but found, in the circumstances of the *Guerra* case, that there was no positive obligation on the State to collect and disseminate such information.

FACTORS 'DRIVING' THE DEVELOPMENT OF ENVIRONMENTAL LAW

International environmental law

The significance of international environmental law has grown rapidly with the recognition of global environmental problems, for example, the 'greenhouse effect', global warming and climate change.

International environmental law is important for two reasons:

(i) it focuses attention on the existence of global problems and the need for international solutions to those problems; and

(ii) it has pioneered and developed important legal and policy principles, for example, sustainability and the precautionary principle.

Private persons (such as companies and individuals) enjoy no rights under international treaties and conventions entitling them to take action against the State, public bodies or other private persons unless the relevant treaty provisions have been incorporated into national law by legislation.

Public concern

Public fears relating to the adverse impacts of polluting discharges may have a significant impact on national and local government environmental decision making and policy processes.

Public concern is a material consideration in planning decisions although the pollution regulators are not, as yet, legally obliged to take public concern into account in their licence decisions.

Environmental decision makers will increasingly be required to factor into their decisions an improved understanding of the factors which generate public concern.

Emerging regulatory tools

Command and Control licence-based regimes are not the complete answer to the regulation of polluting discharges into the environment. The Government is now actively pursuing the introduction of various 'market mechanisms' into the UK. Some of these regulatory devices, such as eco-taxes (for example, the landfill tax), are already in use and others, such as emission trading schemes, are pending.

Human rights

The implementation of the Human Rights Act 1998 may lead to a significant increase in challenges to regulatory decisions based on the following human rights (included in the European Convention on Human Rights and replicated in the Human Rights Act 1998):

Article 2 – the right to life;

Article 8 – the right to privacy and family life;

Article 1 of Protocol 1 – the right to property;

Article 6 – the right to a fair trial; and

Article 10 – the right to freedom of expression.

FURTHER READING

Information available on the Internet

(Please note that some of the following sites may require a subscription charge to access the relevant website. Readers who are university students should check whether their own university library has taken out the relevant subscriptions.)

UK websites

Butterworths website: www.butterworths.co.uk

Casetrack: www.casetrack.com

CCH New Law: www.cchnewlaw.co.uk

Current Legal Information: http://193.118.187.160

Delia Venables environmental law website: www.venables.co.uk

DEFRA (Department of Environment, Food, and Rural Affairs): www.defra.gov.uk

DETR website: www.detr.gov.uk

DTLR (Department of Transport, Land and the Regions): www.dtlr.gov.uk

ENDS: www.ends.co.uk/envdaily/ – see also www.ends.co.uk/report/index.htm

Environment Agency website: www.environment.gov.uk

Friends of the Earth: www.foe.org.uk

General Government website: www.open.gov.uk

Greenchannel: www.greenchannel.com

Greenpeace: www.greenpeace.org.uk

Kent University Law Dept website: http://library.ukc.ac.uk/library/lawlinks

Lawtel: www.lawtel.co.uk

Sweet & Maxwell website: www.sweetandmaxwell.co.uk

EC websites

DG XI website: www.europa.eu.int/comm/environment/policy_en.htm

EC main website: www.europa.eu.int/eur-lex/en/index.html

Homepage of the EU Environment Directorate: www.europa.eu.int/ comm/dgs/environment/index_en.htm

Policy index on the EU homepage: www.europa.eu.int/pol/env/index _en.htm

University of Maastricht: www.asser.nl/EEL.index.htm

Fifth Action Programme: www.europa.eu.int/comm/environment/newprg/global.htm

International environmental law websites

Pace University USA: www.law.pace.edu/env

World Trade Organisation: www.wto.org

Encyclopaedias

Commercial Environmental Law and Liability (published by Longmans)

Encyclopaedia of Environmental Law (published by Sweet & Maxwell)

Garner's Environmental Law (published by Butterworths)

Detailed texts

Burnett-Hall, *Environmental Law*, 1995, London: Sweet & Maxwell

Woolley, J *et al*, *Environmental Law*, 2000, Oxford: OUP

Environmental law collections of supplementary materials

Elworthy, S and Holder, J, *Environmental Protection: Text and Materials*, 1997, London: Butterworths

Sunkin, M, Ong, D and Wight, R, *Sourcebook on Environmental Law*, 2nd edn, 2001, London: Cavendish Publishing

Waite, A, *Butterworths Environmental Law Handbook*, 2001, London: Butterworths (a collection of statutes, statutory instruments, statutory guidance, EC and international instruments)

Journals

ENDS (published by Environmental Data Services)

Environment Action (published by the Environment Agency and available via the EA's website))

Environmental Law and Liability (published by Lawtext)

Environmental Law and Management (published by Lawtext)

Environmental Law Review (published by Blackstone)

Journal of Environmental Law (published by OUP)

Journal of Environmental Law and Planning (published by Sweet & Maxwell)

Water Law (published by Lawtext)

Law Reports

Environmental Law Reports (published by Sweet & Maxwell)

Environmental regulation

The Environment Agency publishes (i) its own journal entitled Environment Action which is available free on request from the agency's Bristol headquarters and (ii) Annual Reports

Ayres, I and Braithwaite, J, *Responsive Regulation: Transcending the Deregulation Debate*, 1992, New York: OUP

Baldwin, R and Cave, M, *Understanding Regulation*, 1999, Oxford: OUP

Baldwin, R, Scott and Hood (eds), *A Reader on Regulation*, 1999, Oxford: OUP

Bardach, E and Kagan, RA, *Going by the Book: The Problem of Regulatory Unreasonableness*, 1982, Philadelphia: Temple UP

Braithwaite, J, *To Punish or Persuade: Enforcement of Coal Mine Safety*, 1985, Albany, New York: State University of New York Press

De Prez, P, 'Excuses, excuses: the ritual trivialisation of environmental prosecutions' (2000) JEL 65

Gunningham and Grabosky, *Smart Regulation: Designing Environmental Policy*, 1998, Oxford: Clarendon

Hawkins, K, *Environment and Enforcement: Regulation and the Social Definition of Pollution*, 1984, Oxford: Clarendon

Hilson, C, *Regulating Pollution: A UK and EC Perspective*, 2000, Oxford: Hart

Howarth, W, 'Self-monitoring, self-policing, self-incrimination and pollution law' (1997) MLR 200

Hutter, BM, *A Reader in Environmental Law*, 1997, Oxford: OUP

McLoughlin and Bellinger, *Environmental Pollution Control: An Introduction to the Principles and Practice of Administration*, 1993, Graham and Trotman

Richardson, G, Ogus, A and Burrows, P, *Policing Pollution – A Study of Regulation and Enforcement*, 1982, Oxford: Clarendon

Rowan-Robinson, J and Ross, A, 'The enforcement of environmental regulation in Britain' (1994) JPL 200

Royal Commission on Environmental Pollution, 21st Report, *Setting Environmental Standards*, Cm 4053, 1998, London: HMSO

Vogel, D, *National Styles of Regulation*, 1986, Cornell, USA: Cornell UP

Wilson, *Making Environmental Laws Work*, 1999, Oxford: Hart

Water pollution

Ball, S, '*Cambridge Water*: what does it decide?' (1994) Water Law 61

Bates, J, *Water and Drainage Law* (looseleaf updated regularly for subscribers) London: Sweet & Maxwell

Birch, *Poison in the System*, 1988, Greenpeace

Environment Agency (annual report on water pollution incidents), eg, *Water Pollution Incidents in England and Wales* , 1998, Environment Agency

Friends of the Earth, *Slippery Customers*, 1997

Hilson, C, '*Cambridge Water* revisited' (1996) Water Law 126

Howarth, W, 'Poisonous, noxious or polluting' (1993) MLR 171

Howarth, W, *Water Pollution Law*, 1988, Shaw and Sons

Kinnersley, *Coming Clean: The Politics of Water and the Environment*, 1994, Harmondsworth: Penguin

McFarlane, S, 'The *Empress* decision: a plea for common sense' [1998] 9 WLAW 104

Maloney and Richardson, *Managing Policy Change in Britain: The Politics of Water*, 1995, Edinburgh: Edinburgh UP

Ryan, 'Unforeseeable but not unusual; the validity of the *Empress* test' (1998) JEL 345

Shelbourn, C, 'Historic pollution – does the polluter pay?' (1994) JPL 703

Stanley, N, 'The *Empress* decision and causing water pollution: a new approach to Section 85(1) Water Resources Act 1991 strict liability' (1999) Water Law 37

Water Law Journal (published by Law Text)

Wilkinson, D, 'Diluting liability for continuing escapes' (1994) MLR 799

Waste management

Bates, J, *UK Waste Law*, 1997, London: Sweet & Maxwell

DETR, *Waste Strategy for England and Wales 2000*, Cm 4693, 2000, London: HMSO

Lawrence, *Waste Regulation Law*, 2000, London: Butterworths

Royal Commission on Environmental Pollution, *Tackling Waste: The Duty of Care*, Cm 2675, 1985, London: HMSO

IPC and IPPC

Allot, *IPC – The First Three Years*, 1994, Environmental Data Services

Backes and Betlem (eds), *Integrated Pollution Prevention and Control; The EEC Directive from a Comparative Legal and Economic Perspective*, 1999 Dordrecht: Kluwer

DoE, *Integrated Pollution Control: A Practical Guide*, 1993, London: HMSO

Emmott and Haigh, 'Integrated Pollution Prevention and Control: UK and EC approaches and possible next steps' (1996) JEL 301

Mehta, A and Hawkins, K, 'IPC and its impact: perspectives from industry' (1998) JEL 61

Purdue, M, 'Integrated Pollution Control and the Environmental Protection Act 1990: a coming of age for environmental law?' (1991) 54 MLR 534

Air pollution

DETR, *Air Quality Strategy*, Cm 4548, 2000, London: HMSO

DoE, *National Air Quality Strategy for England, Scotland, Wales and Northern Ireland*, Cm 4548, 2000, London: HMSO

Hughes, Parpworth, and Upson, *Air Pollution Law and Regulation*, 1998, Bristol: Jordans

National Society for Clean Air, *Pollution Handbook* (published annually): NSCA

Contaminated land

DETR, Circular 2/2000, *Contaminated Land: Implementation of Part IIA of the Environmental Protection Act 1990*, 2000, London: HMSO

Steele, J, 'Remedies and remediation: issues in environmental liability' (1995) 58 MLR 615

Tromans and Turrell-Clarke, *Contaminated Land*, 1994, London: Sweet & Maxwell

Statutory nuisance

Malcolm, R, 'Statutory nuisance: enforcement issues and the meaning of "prejudicial to health"' (1999) 1 Env LR 210

Moran, 'Statutory nuisance and environmental protection' (1994) Environmental Policy and Practice 129

Waite, A, 'Neighbourhood noise in the UK' (1994) Environmental Law and Management 130

Noise

Adams and McManus, *Noise and Noise Law: A Practical Approach*, 1994, Wiley Chancery

McManus, F, 'The EC Green Paper on future noise policy and its impact on the United Kingdom' (1999) European Public Law 125

Penn, *Noise Control: The Law and its Enforcement*, 1995, Shaw and Sons

Common law

Bell, S, *Environmental Law*, 4th edn, 1997, London: Blackstone

Brenner, 'Nuisance law and the industrial revolution' (1974) J Legal Studies 403

Buckley, RA *The Modern Law of Negligence*, 1993, London: Butterworths

Buckley, RA, *The Law of Nuisance*, 1981, London: Butterworths

Cane, P (ed), *Accidents, Compensation and the Law*, 1993, London: Weidenfeld & Nicolson

Charlesworth, J and Perry, RA, *Charlesworth and Perry on Negligence*, 1997, London: Sweet & Maxwell

Furedi, F, *Culture of Fear*, 1997, London: Cassells

Gearty, C, 'The place of nuisance in a modern law of torts' (1989) CLJ 214

Harpwood, V, *Principles of Tort Law*, 2000, London: Cavendish Publishing

Law Commission, *Civil Liability for Dangerous Things and Activities*, Law Com 13, 1967, London: HMSO

McClaren, 'Nuisance law and the industrial revolution – some lessons from social history' (1983) OJLS 155

Ogus and Richardson, 'Economics and the environment: a study of private nuisance' [1977] CLJ 284

Pugh, C and Day, M, *Pollution and Personal Injury: Toxic Torts II*, 1995, London: Cameron May

Spencer, J, 'Public nuisance – a critical examination' (1989) CLJ 55

Stanley, N, 'Contentious planning disputes: an insoluable problem' [2000] JPL 1226, pp 1226–39

Steele, J, 'Private law and the environment: nuisance in context' (1995) 15 LS 236

EC environmental law

Collier (ed), *Deregulation in the European Union: Environmental Perspectives*, 1998, London: Routledge

Gillies, D, *A Guide to EC Environmental Law*, 1999, Earthscan

Haigh, N, *Manual of Environmental Policy: The EC and Britain* (looseleaf text updated regularly), Longmans

Holder, J (ed), *The Implementation of EC Environmental Law in the UK*, 1997, Wiley

Kramer, L, *EC Environmental Law*, 1999, London: Sweet & Maxwell

Lowe and Ward, *British Environmental Policy and Europe*, 1998, London: Routledge

Scott, J, *EC Environmental Law*, 1998, Longmans

Somsen, H (ed), *Protecting the European Environment: the Enforcement of EC Environmental Law*, 1997, London: Blackstone

International environmental law

Birnie, P and Boyle, A, *International Law and the Environment*, 1992 Oxford: OUP

Sands, P, *Principles of International Environmental Law*, 1995, Manchester: Manchester UP

Risk and public concern

Beck, U, *Risk Society*, 1992, London: Sage

Stanley, N, 'Public concern: the decision-maker's dilemma' (1998) JPL 919

Tromans, S, 'Environmental risk and the planning system' (1996) JEL 354

Human rights and environmental rights

Boyle, A and Anderson, M, *Human Rights Approaches to Environmental Protection*, 1996, Oxford: OUP

Hardin, G, 'The tragedy of the commons', in Markandya, A and Richardson, J (eds), *The Earthscan Reader in Environmental Economics*, 1992, London: Earthscan

Miller, C, *Environmental Rights: Critical Perspectives*, 1998, London: Routledge

Vogler, J, *The Global Commons: A Regime Analysis*, 1995, Wiley

INDEX